PETERSON'S®

MASTER THE™ AIR FORCE OFFICER QUALIFYING TEST (AFOQT) & OFFICER APTITUDE RATING (OAR) EXAM

1ST EDITION

About Peterson's®

Peterson's has been your trusted educational publisher for more than 50 years. It's a milestone we're quite proud of as we continue to offer the most accurate, dependable, high-quality educational content in the field, providing you with everything you need to succeed. No matter where you are on your academic or professional path, you can rely on Peterson's for its books, online information, expert test-prep tools, the most up-to-date education exploration data, and the highest quality career success resources—everything you need to achieve your education goals. For our complete line of products, visit **www.petersons.com.**

For more information, contact Peterson's, 4380 S. Syracuse St., Suite 200, Denver, CO 80237; 800-338-3282 Ext. 54229; or visit us online at **www.petersons.com.**

ISBN-13: 978-0-7689-4577-5

Printed in the United States of America

10 9 8 7 6 5 4 3 2 1 23 22 21

CONTENTS

CONTENTS

CONTENTS

BEFORE YOU BEGIN

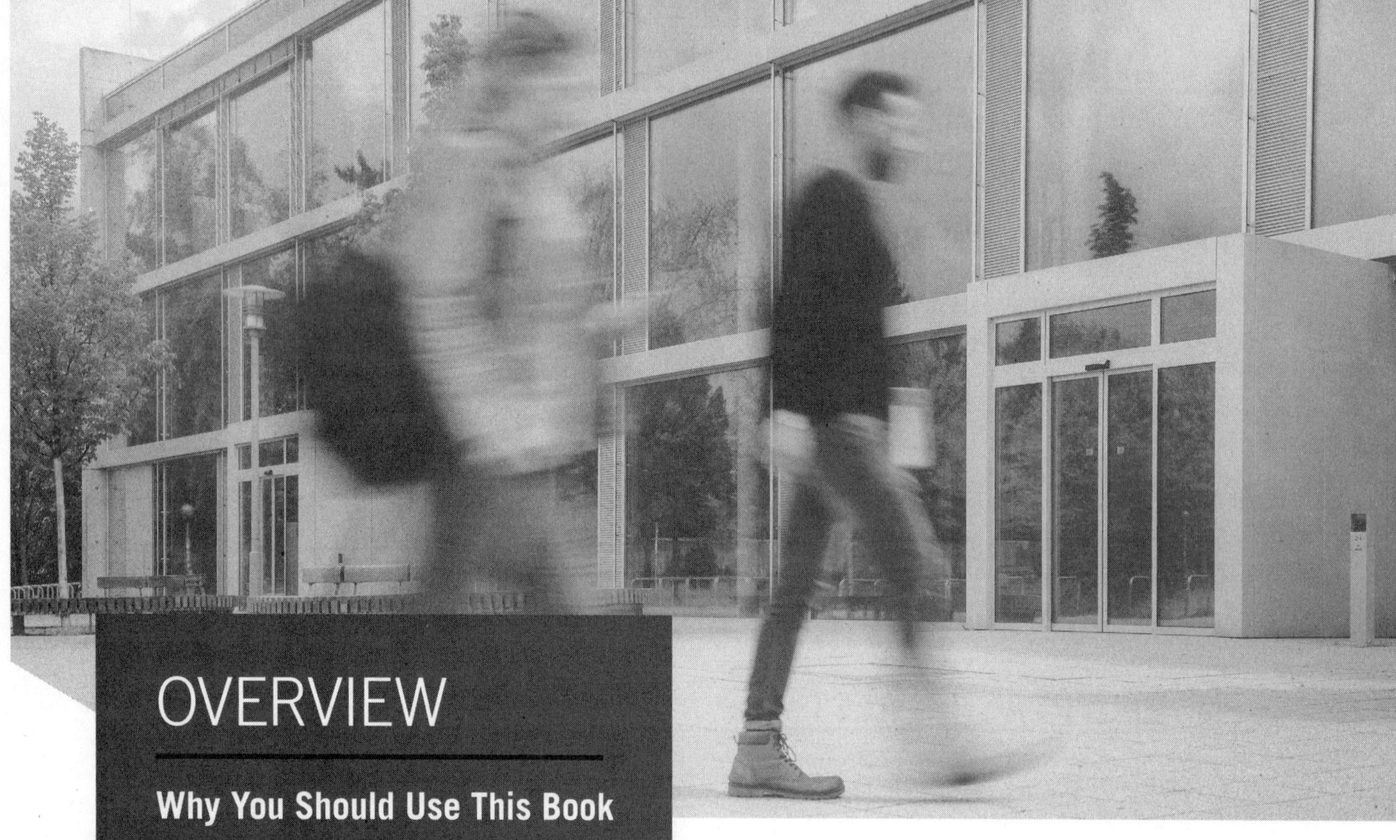

OVERVIEW

If you are looking at a career as a US Air Force, Coast Guard, Marine Corps, or Navy officer, you have a number of hurdles you must clear. Just having a college degree isn't enough; you are also facing tests to help determine your aptitude for success in certain occupations. Even those already serving in the military need to test—despite the years of experience you may already have in uniform.

Much like the SAT and ACT, your scores on the Air Force Officer Qualifying Test (AFOQT) and the Officer Aptitude Rating (OAR) can be the determining factor in getting into Officer Candidate School or commissioning through the Air Force ROTC program. That's because these are highly competitive programs designed to test your physical and mental capabilities, so each service wants to bring in the best for training as an officer. Also, you can only take the AFOQT twice in your lifetime, three times for the OAR, so it behooves you to study hard before taking your test!

DIAGNOSTIC PRACTICE TEST

The diagnostic practice test will help you focus your studying on the areas where you need the most help. This is especially helpful if you don't have much time to prepare for your test.

TEST INFORMATION

This book contains the most current information available on how your test is structured, including registering for your exam, the number of questions, time limits, and what to bring with you.

THOROUGH TEST TOPIC REVIEW

This study guide has the information you need to help you on each area of your exam, whether it is the AFOQT or OAR—we've got your six!

REALISTIC PRACTICE QUESTIONS

Each section has practice quizzes to help you ensure you're ready on test day.

EXPERT TIPS, ADVICE, AND STUDY STRATEGIES

We know what it takes to get top scores on test day. You'll have access to expert study tips and test-taking strategies that are proven to boost test scores. Consider this your boost as you prepare for a career as an officer!

WHY YOU SHOULD USE THIS BOOK

Peterson's *Master the™ AFOQT and OAR Exam* is designed by subject-matter experts and educators to fully prepare you for success on the AFOQT or OAR exam.

We know that a successful and satisfying career as a military officer depends on being ready for anything. Whether it's marksmanship or leading a platoon in combat, practice and preparation are the best ways to guarantee success. With this study guide, you can prepare and practice for your exam. Whether it's Aim High or Semper Fi, Semper Paratus or Semper Fortis, Peterson's is here to help you on your path to becoming an officer.

HOW THIS BOOK IS ORGANIZED

Divided into subtests, this study guide provides five main parts to help you organize your studies. Use Part I to learn important details about both types of exams, including registration information and what to expect on test day. Part II contains diagnostic tests to help you highlight your strengths and weaknesses so you can focus your studies on areas you need the most help with. Part III contains chapters on each subtest, such as math knowledge, reading comprehension, physical science, and mechanical reasoning. There are also chapters on aviation information and instrument comprehension. Practice tests for both the AFOQT and OAR are found in Part IV along with answer keys and explanations to help you improve your test-taking skills. In Part V, you'll find a study sheet of math formulas and common measurements and a glossary of military terms for those not currently in uniform.

For additional practice tests and interactive study material, go to www.petersons.com to subscribe to our constantly expanding selection of test-prep products

HOW TO USE THIS BOOK

Diagnostic Test Method

One way to use this book is to start with a diagnostic test for the OAR and AFOQT. A diagnostic test is a test that helps you understand your strengths and weaknesses; it "diagnoses" the skills that need the most improvement.

With this method, you start with the diagnostic test. Once you check your answers, use the study guide to create your study plan. Use one (or both) of the diagnostic tests found in Part II. The test will have sample questions similar to those you will find on the actual exams. These questions will show you where you might need to focus your test-prep efforts.

Once you've taken your diagnostic test, use the score card to see your strengths and weaknesses. Make a list of your strong and weak areas and rank them from best to worst. If you scored well in the verbal sections, you would count that as a strength. If you didn't score so well in math, that would be an area for you to brush up on.

Use your ranking list to develop your study plan. Your study plan should prioritize working on your weaker skills. You don't need to spend as much time on your strong areas. You should, however, spend some time on "strong skills" exercises—you need to stay in shape!

Front-to-Back Method

Another way to use this book is the "front-to-back" method. In this method, you work through the book the way it's organized.

Start in Part I and carefully read through the introductory information on your exam. This will help you understand the exam and how it's scored. Next, study the content sections in Part III. Focus on the sections that relate to your exam. If you know your strengths, you might devote extra time to those sections where you need the most improvement.

After you've reviewed the content, take the practice test. Taking a practice test will help you be more prepared for test day. Sometimes, the process of taking the test itself can actually help you increase your score. This is because you become more familiar with the test, which increases your confidence.

After you complete the test, review your answers with the explanations provided. If you still don't understand how to answer a certain question, you can always refer back to that section of the book.

The expert subject review and skill-specific exercises in *Peterson's Master the™ AFOQT and OAR Exams* can help familiarize you with the unique content, structure, and format of the tests. Test-taking tips and advice guide you smoothly from your first day of test preparation to test day.

What to Study: AFOQT and OAR

Part III of this book is a combination of study materials for both the AFOQT and the OAR. This is because two sections of the OAR overlap with sections of the AFOQT. Use the table below to determine which chapters to study for your test.

PART III			
No.	CHAPTER	AFOQT	OAR
5	Verbal Analogies	X	
6	Word Knowledge	X	
7	Math for the AFOQT and OAR	X	X
8	Reading Comprehension	X	X
9	Situational Judgment	X	
10	Self-Description Inventory	X	
11	Foundations of Physical Science	X	X
12	Mechanical Comprehension		X
13	Table Reading	X	
14	Instrument Comprehension	X	
15	Block Counting	X	
16	Aviation Information	X	

SPECIAL STUDY FEATURES

You will find the following kinds of special study features scattered throughout this book:

Overview

Each chapter begins with an overview listing the topics covered in the chapter. This will allow you to quickly target the areas in which you are most interested.

Math Formulas and Measurements

We have included a list of math formulas and measurements in this book. The formulas are essential for your success in the math subtests of these exams. By studying—if not memorizing—these formulas, you greatly improve your odds of scoring high on this subtest of the exam.

Summing It Up

Each chapter ends with a point-by-point summary that captures the most important points contained in the chapter. This provides a convenient way to review key points.

TIPS FOR TEST TAKERS

Here's a list of general tips to help ensure that your score accurately reflects your understanding of the content on the exam, and your responses accurately reflect your personality and judgment.

- **Remain calm.** You know yourself best and which strategies or techniques will help you ease any test anxiety. A calm, clear mind will serve you better than a stressed out, fragmented mind.
- **Read the directions.** Multiple-choice questions on the exam will only have one answer option that is correct. However, certain sections will remind you to base your answer solely on the information given, reminding you to not base your answer on what you *know* but on what you have *read*. Other questions will ask you to choose the statement that you agree/disagree with the most. Situational questions will ask you to choose the option that you would most likely do in a given situation, while the Self-Description Inventory questions explore what it is that makes you, well, *you*. There are no correct answers to the Self-Description Inventory questions, but they do provide key insights into your personality and character. Pay attention to the directions.
- **Focus on the questions you know.** Struggling with a question? Skip it and focus on answering the questions you *do* know. As time permits, you can go back to the questions you skipped.
- **Read the entire question and all answer choices before selecting your answer.** This is especially true for logical reasoning questions where you will be provided with information and asked to draw a conclusion or choose a statement that is true. At times, you will be asked to pick the option that *cannot* be validly concluded from the information given.
- **Eliminate answer options.** When you are unsure of the answer to a question, try eliminating the answers you know are incorrect. Then, guess from the remaining options.
- **Answer every question.** Remember, your score will be based on the number of questions you answer correctly. Since there is no penalty for incorrect answers, take a guess! If you have eliminated the answers you know to be incorrect, your chances of choosing the correct answer have increased dramatically.
- **If time permits, go back and check your answers.** A word of caution. More often than not, your first answer will be the correct answer. But, if you feel like you need to review certain questions again, and you have the time, go for it.
- **Mark your answer sheet correctly.** This applies mainly to a paper-based test and not a computer-based test. However, it goes without saying that you should make sure you are marking the answer for the correct question on the answer sheet. This is especially true if you skip a question.

HELPFUL STUDY TIPS

The following are study tips to help you prepare for the AFOQT and OAR exams.

1. **Set up a study schedule.** Assign yourself a period each day devoted to preparing for the exam. A regular schedule is best, but the important thing is to study daily, even if you can't do so at the same time every day.

2. **Keep a list.** Make a list of questions you find puzzling and take note of any topics you still find confusing. Focus your studies on these topics, and reference additional resources as needed.

3. **Eliminate distractions.** Choose a quiet, well-lit spot that is removed from distractions. Arrange your study area in a way that minimizes interruptions and allows you to concentrate.

4. **Start at the beginning and read carefully.** Underline points that you consider significant. Make marginal notes. Flag the pages you think are especially important.

5. **Concentrate on the information and instructional chapters.** Get yourself psyched to enter the world of a military officer. Learn how to handle logic-based questions and know your basic mathematical concepts.

6. **Take a practice test.** Focus on eliminating wrong answers; this is an important method for answering all multiple-choice questions, but it's especially vital for answering reasoning and judgment questions correctly. Take the practice test in one sitting and time yourself.

TEST DAY STRATEGIES

You may find it helpful to keep the following strategies in mind for the actual test day.

1. **Be prepared.** Research what you will need to bring with you on test day. The night before, make sure you have everything you need in one place. Decide on the outfit you will wear. Be comfortable and dress in layers to suit the temperature of the testing site.

2. **Eat smart.** Plan to eat before your scheduled exam time. Avoid caffeine if it makes you jittery, and avoid sugary items that will cause a temporary spike in your energy level.

3. **Focus only on the test.** Don't plan any other activities that day or squeeze the test in the middle of activities.

4. **Arrive rested, relaxed, and on time.** In fact, plan to arrive a little bit early. Leave plenty of time for traffic tie-ups or other complications that might upset you and interfere with your test performance.

5. **If the test is proctored, ask questions about any instructions you do not understand.** Make sure that you know exactly what to do. In the test room, the proctor will provide the instructions you must follow when taking the examination.

6. **Follow instructions exactly during the examination.** Do not begin until you are told to do so. Stop as soon as you are told to stop. Any infraction of the rules is considered cheating.

7. **Maintain a positive attitude.** This will help ease any test anxiety. A can-do attitude creates confidence.

Do not memorize questions and answers. You might see questions on your exam that are very similar to the ones provided, but you will not see any of the exact questions you encounter in this book.

PETERSON'S® PUBLICATIONS

Peterson's publishes a full line of books—career preparation, education exploration, test prep, and financial aid. Peterson's books are available for purchase online at **www.petersons.com**. Sign up for one of our online subscription plans and you'll have access to our entire test prep catalog of more than 180 exams *plus* instructional videos, flashcards, interactive quizzes, and more! Our subscription plans allow you to study as quickly as you can or as slowly as you'd like. For more information, go to **www.petersons.com/testprep/**. Peterson's publications can also be found at your local bookstores, libraries, and career centers.

GIVE US YOUR FEEDBACK

We welcome any comments or suggestions you may have about this publication. Your feedback will help us make education dreams possible for you—and others like you.

YOU'RE WELL ON YOUR WAY TO SUCCESS

Remember that knowledge is power. By using this book, you will be studying the most comprehensive guide available.

The *first step* to acing your officer qualification exam is to know the structure and format of the exam you're going to take inside and out, including all the basics you need to know.

We *know* you're eager to get to the test practice and review but having a thorough understanding of the exam from top to bottom will give you a real advantage—and put you ahead of the test-taking competition. We'll go carefully through each exam—the AFOQT and the OAR—and guide you through each step so you'll be confident and prepared for test day success. Let's get started!

PART I

ALL ABOUT THE EXAMS

1 | All About the Air Force Officer Qualifying Test (AFOQT)

2 | All About the Officer Aptitude Rating (OAR)

ALL ABOUT THE AIR FORCE OFFICER

OVERVIEW

- Subtests
- Scoring
- Testing Logistics
- Summing It Up

The Air Force Officer Qualifying Test (AFOQT) is a multiple-choice, standardized exam that tests a person's ability on a variety of topics spanning mathematical, logical, verbal, and science-based areas of study. The actual test time for the AFOQT Form T is approximately 3.5 hours; however, the complete test time including required breaks and instruction is approximately five hours. **You are only allowed to take the AFOQT twice in your lifetime.** In addition, there must be at least 150 days between the two tests and the most recent score is used, even if it is lower. It is imperative that you study and prepare prior to your first exam date to avoid the need for the second test.

SUBTESTS

There are 12 subtests within the AFOQT, each with its own number of questions and time restrictions. Every candidate is required to take each subtest, regardless of their desired position. For example, all candidates must take the Instrument Comprehension subtest targeted for pilots, even if they are not looking into the pilot track.

Exam Breakdown

The 12 subtests are used to identify possible candidates best suited for selection and training as officers and also for department-specific entry (such as pilot or navigator tracks). The following is a breakdown of the subtests with the number of questions and time allotted.

AFOQT SUBTESTS		
Subtest	**Questions**	**Time Allotted**
Verbal Analogies	25	8 minutes
Arithmetic Reasoning	25	29 minutes
Word Knowledge	25	5 minutes
Math Knowledge	25	22 minutes
Reading Comprehension	25	38 minutes
Situational Judgment	50	35 minutes
Self-Description Inventory	240	45 minutes
Physical Science	20	10 minutes
Table Reading	40	7 minutes
Instrument Comprehension	25	5 minutes
Block Counting	30	4.5 minutes
Aviation Information	20	8 minutes
TOTAL QUESTIONS	550	216.5 minutes (3 hours, 36.5 minutes)

Subtest Summaries

The 12 subtests cover a wide range of topics, and each subtest will be discussed at length later on in this study guide. The following are brief summaries of what each subtest measures and the topics covered.

Verbal Analogies: This subtest measures your ability to analyze relationships between words using logic and reason. This subtest is similar to what is seen on the Miller Analogies Test (MAT). You will have 8 minutes to answer 25 questions.

Arithmetic Reasoning: This subtest of the exam will assess your overall mathematical ability as it relates to word problems. Questions will include geometry, proportions, ratios, and algebra. You will have 29 minutes to answer 25 questions.

Word Knowledge: Word meanings are the focus of this subtest, which measures your knowledge by presenting words that you must match with words that have the same or similar meaning. You will have 5 minutes to answer 25 questions.

Math Knowledge: Rather than the word problems you encountered in Arithmetic Reasoning, this subtest of the exam measures your ability to compute math problems that focus on algebraic equations, fractions, percentages, and geometry. This subtest resembles a more traditional math test with mainly numeric questions and the occasional word problem. You will have 22 minutes to answer 25 questions.

Reading Comprehension: This subtest will assess your reading level and ability to retain and evaluate information provided in a technical writing passage. You will be expected to comprehend vocabulary terms and assess passages based on both the syntax and diction used. You will have 38 minutes to answer 25 questions.

Situational Judgment: The focus of this subtest is your ability to assess and respond to any given circumstances that might arise as an officer. You will be given real-life scenarios and asked to identify both the most and least effective actions in response to that scenario. You will have 35 minutes to answer 50 questions.

Self-Description Inventory: This is the largest subtest; however, it is essentially a personality inventory that you cannot study for as there are no right or wrong answers. This subtest is used internally to best match candidates with assignments that fit their self-descriptions. You will have 45 minutes to answer 240 questions.

Physical Science: This subtest covers basic physical science at the high school level, with a focus on measurements, physical characteristics and properties, chemical makeups and relationships, and energy.

Table Reading: This subtest tests your ability to locate information in table form quickly and efficiently. You will have 7 minutes to answer 40 questions, so the turnaround time for each question is mere seconds.

Instrument Comprehension: This subtest will assess your ability to determine the position of an airplane in flight by reading and comprehending instruments that show compass heading, nose position, and degree of banking. You will have 5 minutes to answer 25 questions.

Block Counting: This subtest of the exam measures your ability to think in three-dimensions using stacks of blocks. Each question presents a stack of blocks and asks you to identify how many other blocks that the designated pieces are touching. You will have 4.5 minutes to answer 30 questions.

Aviation Information: This subtest assesses your knowledge of aviation concepts, including aerodynamics and forces of flight, airplane parts and mechanics, airport signs, markings, lighting, and aviation meteorology. You will have 8 minutes to answer 20 questions.

SCORING

The scoring for the AFOQT is given in percentiles similar to most standardized tests. For example, if you score a 90, it does not mean you answered 90% of the questions correctly, or that you answered 90 questions correctly. It means you scored in the 90th percentile during your testing cycle. The number of questions you answered correctly is directly compared to those who took the test during your cycle. Based on this, the scoring can be more or less competitive depending on the aptitude of the candidates during your testing cycle.

The subtest scores are used in several different combinations for different composites. The following is an explanation of each composite and the combination of subtests it utilizes along with a table that summarizes this data.

Commission-Qualifying Composites

- **Verbal:** The verbal composite includes Verbal Analogies, Word Knowledge, and Reading Comprehension. *The minimum passing score for this composite is 15.*

- **Quantitative:** The quantitative composite includes Arithmetic Reasoning and Math Knowledge. *The minimum passing score for this composite is 10.*

Aviation Career Composites

- **Pilot:** This composite score measures foundational skills and abilities that are necessary to successfully complete pilot training. The composite includes Math Knowledge, Table Reading, Instrument Comprehension, and Aviation Information. *For candidates looking to enter pilot training, the minimum passing score for this composite is 25.*
- **Combat Systems Officer (CSO):** This composite score measures skills and abilities that are necessary for CSO training. This composite includes Word Knowledge, Math Knowledge, Block Counting, and Table Reading. *For those looking at the CSO track, the minimum passing score for this composite is 25.*
- **Air Battle Manager (ABM):** This composite score measures skills and abilities that are required for successful completion of ABM training and overlaps a great deal with the Pilot composite. Scoring includes Verbal Analogies, Math Knowledge, Table Reading, Instrument Comprehension, Block Counting, and Aviation Information. *The minimum passing score for this composite is 25.*

Other Composites (no minimum passing score)

- **Academic Aptitude:** This composite score is a combination of the verbal and quantitative scores.
- **Situational Judgment:** Supported only by your results from the Situational Judgment subtest, this composite represents your decision-making abilities for interpersonal situations commonly encountered by officers.

AFOQT COMPOSITE SCORES

	Required to Commission		Aviation-Related			Other	
Subtest	**Verbal**	**Quantitative**	**Pilot**	**CSO**	**ABM**	**Academic Aptitude**	**Situational Judgment**
Verbal Analogies	✔				✔	✔	
Arithmetic Reasoning		✔				✔	
Word Knowledge	✔			✔		✔	
Math Knowledge		✔	✔	✔	✔	✔	
Reading Comprehension	✔					✔	
Situational Judgment							✔
Table Reading			✔	✔	✔		
Instrument Comprehension			✔		✔		
Block Counting				✔	✔		
Aviation Information			✔		✔		
Minimum Composite Score	15	10	25[1]	25[2]	25	N/A	N/A

[1] Pilot applicants must score a minimum of 25 in Pilot, 10 in CSO, and possess a combined Pilot-CSO score of 50.
[2] CSO applicants must score a minimum of 25 in CSO, 10 in Pilot, and possess a combined CSO-Pilot score of 50.

NOTE: The unlisted subtests are not currently part of any composites. However, they are still part of the AFOQT and are required for all candidates.

TESTING LOGISTICS

Now that we have covered the exam itself, the 12 subtests, and the scoring for a variety of positions, let's go over testing logistics: scheduling the test, what to do on test day, getting results, and next steps.

Scheduling

Who can take the AFOQT and how do they go about scheduling it? Both civilians and enlisted are eligible to take the AFOQT. There are age restrictions (18–34) and education stipulations (bachelor's degree or higher, or in your second year of AFROTC). There are two routes to go for scheduling depending on whether you are a civilian or enlisted. The following graphic explains the process for both:

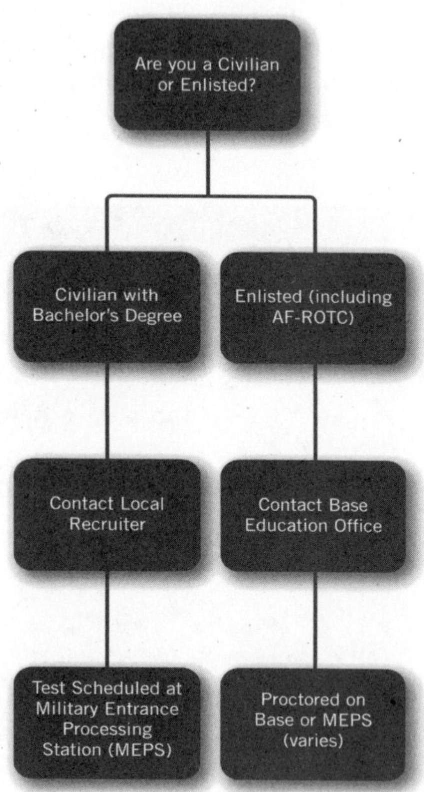

For enlisted personnel, there may be required paperwork from your flight or squadron commander. Be sure to check with your education office to ensure you have any required forms. For civilians, your Air Force recruiting office will have officers available to advise and assist recruits. ROTC cadets will take the AFOQT during their sophomore year.

Test Day

Once you have scheduled your exam, it is important to prepare for the actual day of the test as well. There are a few things to remember for day-of logistics that will help you feel not just prepared but well-prepared and ready to go.

Get Rest

Sleep plays a critical role in your performance. Adequate sleep not only the night before but also the week leading up to your testing date will improve your attention and recall. You may feel compelled to cram in late night study sessions as your test date approaches, but sleep deprivation and the associated stress can negatively impact your performance.

Eat a Good Breakfast

A bowl of sugary cereal might be fine for any ordinary day, but on test day you want something that will fill you up and keep you from getting too hungry during the exam. Have protein, as that actually slows digestion and regulates your blood sugar—doing so can improve your concentration. Whole grains should also be on your breakfast plate. Lastly, limit your caffeine intake. Too much may give you the jitters and have you heading to the restroom during your breaks.

Bring Food and Water

If your testing location allows, pack a few snack bars and a bottle of water. For snacks, look for items that are higher in protein or otherwise lower in carbohydrates, as carbs can contribute to brain fog. Fruit is another good option. An apple or banana can provide the natural fuel you need to finish the exam.

Wear Comfortable Clothing

If you are at the MEPS office or off duty, wear comfortable civilian clothing that you do not mind sitting in for 5 hours. Wear layers that allow you to adjust your body temperature easily to suit the temperature of the testing room. Being too hot or too cold can prove distracting and decrease your score. Avoid extra jewelry or add-on pieces. Some testing locations have restrictions on jewelry outside of a wedding ring.

Leave Early and Block Off Time

The AFOQT exam itself is more than 3.5 hours long. However, with instructions and scheduled breaks it works out to be approximately 5 hours. Aim to arrive at the testing site early, find a seat, and get settled. Plan to be at the testing location for the entire day, avoiding any commitments beyond the exam. This will allow you to be fully present without worrying about other appointments, work shifts, etc. In addition, this accommodates any possible technical difficulties or other delays that may prolong the actual exam process.

Budget Test Time

The AFOQT is known for having very tight time constraints for the number of questions on the test. Because of this, it is important to budget your test time accordingly. Prior to test day, time yourself for each subtest in addition to the overall exam. On the day of the exam, work efficiently, answering all easy questions quickly and marking harder ones to return to later. A common mistake is to get bogged down on a particularly difficult question, which leads to the inability to answer all the questions during the allotted time.

Answer Every Question

Your score is calculated on the number of correct answers and there are no penalties for incorrect ones. Therefore, not answering a question will automatically lower your score. If you reach a question that you are unsure of and time is running out, choose logically. Guessing is always better than skipping.

Relax

Going into an important exam while tense and nervous is never a good idea. Take a few deep breaths before the exam starts and on breaks, get out of your seat when you are allowed to, and if you smoke, refrain from doing so during breaks. Contrary to popular belief, nicotine does not calm you down; it just calms the cravings. Your body actually becomes more tense because you just spent five minutes limiting the amount of oxygen that can get into your bloodstream.

Results

The AFOQT exam is scored fairly quickly, with results uploaded and available to view in approximately two weeks. All candidates are given access to a portal to check their scores online. In addition to checking through the portal, a candidate can call their recruiter who may have access to the results in as little as eight days.

Regardless of your preferred position, the results will show six of the seven composite scores (Pilot, CSO, ABM, Academic, Verbal, and Quantitative). Remember, the number for each score is a percentile based on a comparison of your scores to others in your testing cycle.

Next Steps

Taking and passing the AFOQT is only the first step to a career as an Air Force officer. Passing the exam does not guarantee a position and is only one piece of the application. Your GPA from both high school and college, flight hours, and general application components all factor into placement.

So, what is the next step? This depends on your plans moving forward. If you are taking the AFOQT as a civilian, you must contact your recruiter to discuss the next step in the application process. If you are already enlisted, your scores will become part of an application package that is used internally for the officer position that you seek.

Whatever path you are taking, ensuring your AFOQT exam results are the best they can be is the first step to a career as a commissioned Air Force officer.

SUMMING IT UP

- The AFOQT is used by the US Air Force to select officer candidates.
- The exam consists of 12 subtests
    - Verbal Analogies
    - Arithmetic Reasoning
    - Word Knowledge
    - Math Knowledge
    - Reading Comprehension
    - Situational Judgment
    - Self-Description Inventory
    - Physical Science
    - Table Reading
    - Instrument Comprehension
    - Block Counting
    - Aviation Information
- Civilians should go through the local Air Force recruiting office to schedule the AFOQT.
- Military personnel should go through their base education office to schedule the AFOQT. The education office can advise you on any additional forms or requirements prior to your exam.
- Scores, including composite scores, are usually available online within two weeks, or eight days if you get them from your recruiter.
- Prepare for test day.
    - Get plenty of sleep.
    - Remember to dress comfortably and in layers.
    - Bring a bottle of water and pack a snack.
    - Eat a good breakfast.
    - Arrive a few minutes early.
    - Budget your time for each subtest.
    - Relax. Take deep breaths and stand up to stretch when you can.

ALL ABOUT THE OFFICER APTITUDE

OVERVIEW

- **Test Formats**
- **Subtests**
- **Scoring**
- **Testing Logistics**
- **Summing It Up**

The Officer Aptitude Rating (OAR) Exam is a multiple-choice, standardized exam that tests a person's ability in the areas of mathematics, reading comprehension, and mechanical comprehension. The test is actually a subset of the larger Aviation Selection Test Battery (ASTB-E) used by the Navy, Marines, and Coast Guard.

Three subtests make up the OAR: Math Skills, Reading Comprehension, and Mechanical Comprehension. The OAR is available in two formats: a paper-based test (PBT) format or a computer-adapted test (CAT) format. You will have a set number of questions for each subtest in the PBT format, but the CAT format adjusts the number and difficulty of questions based on previous answers. The actual test time equates to approximately 85 minutes, regardless of format. Exam results are used to qualify candidates for officer training programs. However, the exam results are not the sole decider. Other factors including work history and your high school and college GPA are factored in.

Please note that you are only allowed to take the OAR three times in your lifetime. There must be at least 31 days between the first test and the second, and at least 91 days between the first and the third. The most recent score is used, even if it is lower. As such, it is imperative to study and prepare prior to your first exam date to avoid the need for the second test.

TEST FORMATS

Test takers have the option of taking the OAR on either a PBT format or on a computer in a CAT format.

PBT Format: This format has a total test time of 85 minutes and a set number of questions per subtest. Each subtest has a specific sequence of questions. The paper format does not penalize you for incorrect questions, but it also does not weight them according to difficulty either. Any item left blank will be scored as incorrect; thus, guessing is encouraged if time is running out.

CAT Format: This format adjusts the number and difficulty of the questions based on the answers provided during the test, but the time limits for each subtest remain the same. As questions are answered, the test automatically adjusts the difficulty level (and thus the weight applied to the scoring of the question) either up or down depending on the number of correct answers. If a test taker does not answer enough questions in the time allotted, a penalty is applied to the score. Thus, it is important to work quickly but effectively. Guessing on this format can cause your score to decrease. At times, guessing may be necessary, but it should be a last resort.

SUBTESTS

There are three subtests within the OAR. Every candidate is required to take each subtest, regardless of their desired position. The three subtests cover core topics, and the content of each subtest will be discussed at length later on in this study guide. The following provides a breakdown of question amounts and time allotments as well as brief summaries of each subtest and the topics covered.

EXAM BREAKDOWN

	PBT FORMAT		CAT FORMAT	
Subtest	**Questions**	**Time Allotted**	**Questions**	**Time Allotted**
Math Skills	30	40 minutes	*variable*	40 minutes
Reading Comprehension	20	30 minutes	*variable*	30 minutes
Mechanical Comprehension	30	15 minutes	*variable*	15 minutes
TOTAL QUESTIONS	80	85 minutes	*variable*	85 minutes

Subtest Summaries

The following are brief summaries of each subtest on the OAR.

Math Skills: This subtest measures your ability to compute math problems that focus on algebraic equations, fractions, percentages, and geometry. This section resembles a more traditional math test with mainly numeric questions and the occasional word problem.

Reading Comprehension: This subtest will assess your reading level and ability to retain and evaluate information provided in a variety of short passages ranging in level of difficulty from easy to hard. No prior technical knowledge is needed.

Mechanical Comprehension: This subtest will assess your overall understanding of mechanical concepts, with a heavy focus on physics. More than half of the questions will consist of problems that utilize image analysis to answer them.

SCORING

The scoring for the OAR ranges from 20–80. **The minimum possible score for this test is 35.** Competitive scores tend to fall in the 40–60 range with very few people scoring in the upper extremes of the score range. Admission into officer training programs is extremely competitive with acceptance rates hovering around 4%.

TESTING LOGISTICS

Now that we have covered the three subtests, the exam formats, and scoring, let's examine testing logistics: test scheduling, what to do on test day, and your next steps.

Scheduling

Who can take the OAR and how do they go about scheduling it? Both civilians and enlisted are eligible to take the OAR. There are age restrictions and education stipulations; test takers must be between the ages of 19–35 (the maximum age a person can be commissioned as an officer) and must hold a bachelor's degree or higher. There are two routes to go for scheduling. The route for you depends on whether you are a civilian or are already enlisted in the military. The following graphic explains the process for both:

SCHEDULING THE OAR

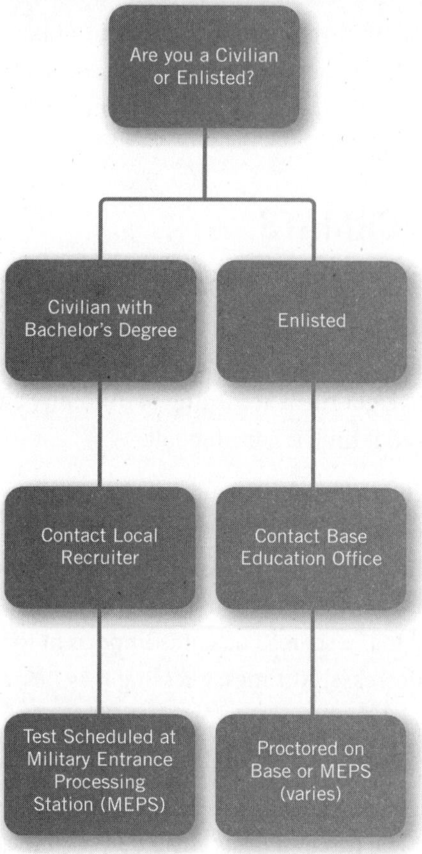

Are you a Civilian or Enlisted?

Civilian with Bachelor's Degree	Enlisted
Contact Local Recruiter	Contact Base Education Office
Test Scheduled at Military Entrance Processing Station (MEPS)	Proctored on Base or MEPS (varies)

Test Day

Once you have scheduled your exam, it is important to prepare for the actual day of the test. There are a few things to remember for day-of logistics that will help you feel not just prepared but well-prepared and ready to go.

Get Rest

Make rest a priority the days leading up to the exam and the night before. It might be tempting to work in some extra study time, but research shows that it takes time for information to imprint on your brain, and a last-minute study session will just lead to higher stress rather than higher scores. Trust that you have taken every step you could to study and prepare, and get plenty of sleep the night before.

Wear Comfortable Clothing

Dress comfortably. You will be sitting for several hours, and discomfort can be a big distraction. Another distraction is being too warm or too cold. Dress in layers so you can adjust your temperature. Minimize the amount of jewelry you wear to the exam; some testing locations may limit you to only a wedding ring.

Leave Early and Block Off Time

The OAR exam itself takes more than an hour. However, with instructions and scheduled breaks, it works out to be approximately 2.5 hours. Plan to be at the testing location the entire day, avoiding any commitments beyond the exam. This will allow you to be fully present without worrying about other appointments, work shifts, etc. In addition, planning for a longer block of time allows for any possible technical difficulties or other delays that may prolong the actual exam process.

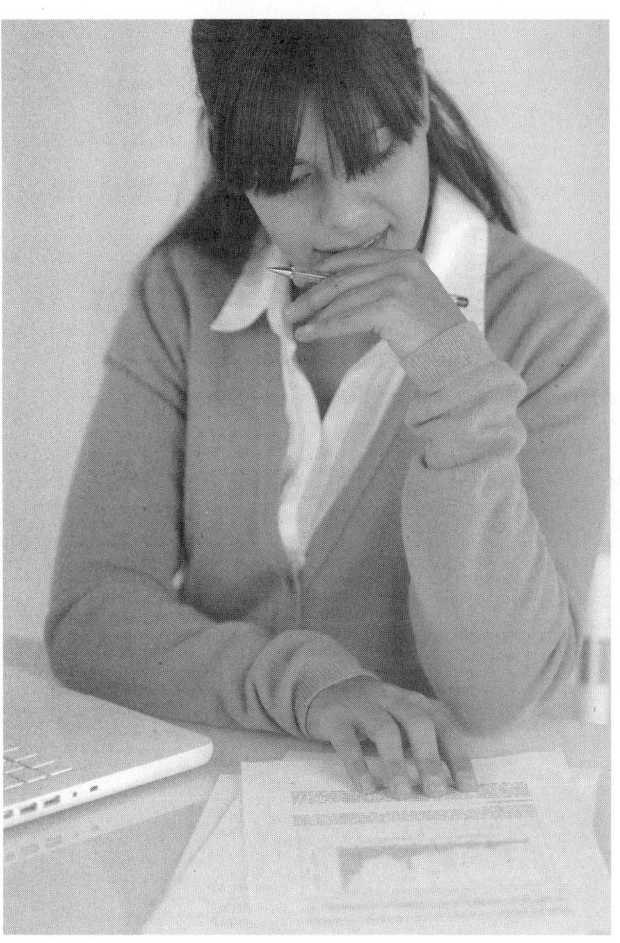

Budget Test Time

With the number of calculations to complete, the volume of passages to read, and the number of mechanisms to dissect, the pace of the OAR is intense. Be sure to budget your time accordingly. Work quickly and efficiently. If you opt for the paper format for the OAR exam, do the easiest questions first, and save the hard ones for later. Don't let yourself get bogged down on a difficult question, losing time that could be spent solving multiple easy questions first.

Follow your Test Format Strategy

Regardless of which format you choose for your OAR exam, be sure you have a test-taking strategy and stick to it. For the PBT, your score is based on the number of correct answers, and there is no penalty for incorrect answers. Leaving questions unanswered, though, will definitely lower your score. If you are running out of time, make educated guesses rather than leave anything blank.

If you choose the CAT format, your score is based on the difficulty of the questions you answered correctly. Unlike the paper format, incorrect guesses will hurt your score. If you answer incorrectly, the computer automatically adjusts the difficulty of the questions to make them easier, thus impacting your final score.

Next Steps

Taking and passing the OAR are only the first steps to becoming an officer. Passing the exam does not guarantee a position and is only one piece of the application. GPA from both high school and college as well as general application components all factor into placement.

So, what is the next step? This depends on your plans moving forward. If you are taking the OAR as a civilian that has yet to enlist, you must contact your recruiter to discuss the next step in the application process. Regardless of whether you are a civilian or you are already enlisted, your scores will be used to determine admittance to Officer Candidate School.

Whatever path you are taking, ensuring your OAR exam results are the best they can be is the first step to a career as a commissioned officer.

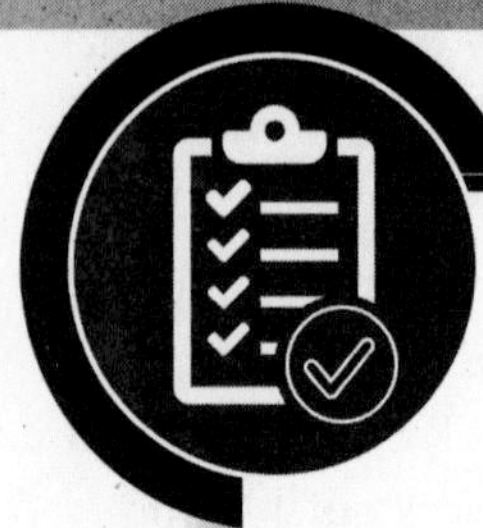

SUMMING IT UP

- The Officer Aptitude Rating (OAR) exam is used by the US Navy, Marine Corps, and Coast Guard.
- The OAR is required for all applicants to Officer Candidate School.
- The OAR forms a portion of the ASTB-E and has three subtests:
  - Math Skills
  - Reading Comprehension
  - Mechanical Comprehension
- There are two formats for the OAR: paper-based (PBT) and computer-adapted testing (CAT).
- Civilians should go through the local Navy, Marine Corps, or Coast Guard recruiting office to schedule the OAR exam.
- Military personnel should go through their base education office to schedule the OAR. The education office can advise you on any additional forms or requirements prior to your exam.
- You are only allowed to take the OAR exam three times. There must be at least 31 days between the first and second attempt and 91 days between the first and third.
- Scores for the OAR exam range from 20–80. The minimum score is 35, and the average score ranges between 40–60.
- For the paper-based exam, each correct answer increases your score by one point; wrong answers do not affect the score.
- For the computer-adaptive test, scores are based on the difficulty of questions that you answer correctly. Wrong answers will lower the difficulty of the questions as you progress.
- Only 4% of applicants are accepted into Officer Candidate School, so the higher your OAR exam score, the better your chances of being selected.
- Be sure you are well-rested for test day and wear comfortable clothing in layers in case the room is too warm or too cold. Also, minimize the amount of jewelry you wear; some testing locations will only allow a wedding ring.

PART II

DIAGNOSTIC TESTS

AFOQT DIAGNOSTIC TEST

DIAGNOSTIC TEST

This pre-test is designed to help you recognize your strengths and weaknesses. The questions cover information from all of the subtests of the AFOQT exam, with the exception of the Self-Description Inventory.

ANSWER SHEET: AFOQT DIAGNOSTIC TEST

Verbal Analogies

1. Ⓐ Ⓑ Ⓒ Ⓓ Ⓔ	6. Ⓐ Ⓑ Ⓒ Ⓓ Ⓔ	11. Ⓐ Ⓑ Ⓒ Ⓓ Ⓔ	16. Ⓐ Ⓑ Ⓒ Ⓓ Ⓔ	21. Ⓐ Ⓑ Ⓒ Ⓓ Ⓔ
2. Ⓐ Ⓑ Ⓒ Ⓓ Ⓔ	7. Ⓐ Ⓑ Ⓒ Ⓓ Ⓔ	12. Ⓐ Ⓑ Ⓒ Ⓓ Ⓔ	17. Ⓐ Ⓑ Ⓒ Ⓓ Ⓔ	22. Ⓐ Ⓑ Ⓒ Ⓓ Ⓔ
3. Ⓐ Ⓑ Ⓒ Ⓓ Ⓔ	8. Ⓐ Ⓑ Ⓒ Ⓓ Ⓔ	13. Ⓐ Ⓑ Ⓒ Ⓓ Ⓔ	18. Ⓐ Ⓑ Ⓒ Ⓓ Ⓔ	23. Ⓐ Ⓑ Ⓒ Ⓓ Ⓔ
4. Ⓐ Ⓑ Ⓒ Ⓓ Ⓔ	9. Ⓐ Ⓑ Ⓒ Ⓓ Ⓔ	14. Ⓐ Ⓑ Ⓒ Ⓓ Ⓔ	19. Ⓐ Ⓑ Ⓒ Ⓓ Ⓔ	24. Ⓐ Ⓑ Ⓒ Ⓓ Ⓔ
5. Ⓐ Ⓑ Ⓒ Ⓓ Ⓔ	10. Ⓐ Ⓑ Ⓒ Ⓓ Ⓔ	15. Ⓐ Ⓑ Ⓒ Ⓓ Ⓔ	20. Ⓐ Ⓑ Ⓒ Ⓓ Ⓔ	25. Ⓐ Ⓑ Ⓒ Ⓓ Ⓔ

Arithmetic Reasoning

1. Ⓐ Ⓑ Ⓒ Ⓓ Ⓔ	6. Ⓐ Ⓑ Ⓒ Ⓓ Ⓔ	11. Ⓐ Ⓑ Ⓒ Ⓓ Ⓔ	16. Ⓐ Ⓑ Ⓒ Ⓓ Ⓔ	21. Ⓐ Ⓑ Ⓒ Ⓓ Ⓔ
2. Ⓐ Ⓑ Ⓒ Ⓓ Ⓔ	7. Ⓐ Ⓑ Ⓒ Ⓓ Ⓔ	12. Ⓐ Ⓑ Ⓒ Ⓓ Ⓔ	17. Ⓐ Ⓑ Ⓒ Ⓓ Ⓔ	22. Ⓐ Ⓑ Ⓒ Ⓓ Ⓔ
3. Ⓐ Ⓑ Ⓒ Ⓓ Ⓔ	8. Ⓐ Ⓑ Ⓒ Ⓓ Ⓔ	13. Ⓐ Ⓑ Ⓒ Ⓓ Ⓔ	18. Ⓐ Ⓑ Ⓒ Ⓓ Ⓔ	23. Ⓐ Ⓑ Ⓒ Ⓓ Ⓔ
4. Ⓐ Ⓑ Ⓒ Ⓓ Ⓔ	9. Ⓐ Ⓑ Ⓒ Ⓓ Ⓔ	14. Ⓐ Ⓑ Ⓒ Ⓓ Ⓔ	19. Ⓐ Ⓑ Ⓒ Ⓓ Ⓔ	24. Ⓐ Ⓑ Ⓒ Ⓓ Ⓔ
5. Ⓐ Ⓑ Ⓒ Ⓓ Ⓔ	10. Ⓐ Ⓑ Ⓒ Ⓓ Ⓔ	15. Ⓐ Ⓑ Ⓒ Ⓓ Ⓔ	20. Ⓐ Ⓑ Ⓒ Ⓓ Ⓔ	25. Ⓐ Ⓑ Ⓒ Ⓓ Ⓔ

Word Knowledge

1. Ⓐ Ⓑ Ⓒ Ⓓ Ⓔ	6. Ⓐ Ⓑ Ⓒ Ⓓ Ⓔ	11. Ⓐ Ⓑ Ⓒ Ⓓ Ⓔ	16. Ⓐ Ⓑ Ⓒ Ⓓ Ⓔ	21. Ⓐ Ⓑ Ⓒ Ⓓ Ⓔ
2. Ⓐ Ⓑ Ⓒ Ⓓ Ⓔ	7. Ⓐ Ⓑ Ⓒ Ⓓ Ⓔ	12. Ⓐ Ⓑ Ⓒ Ⓓ Ⓔ	17. Ⓐ Ⓑ Ⓒ Ⓓ Ⓔ	22. Ⓐ Ⓑ Ⓒ Ⓓ Ⓔ
3. Ⓐ Ⓑ Ⓒ Ⓓ Ⓔ	8. Ⓐ Ⓑ Ⓒ Ⓓ Ⓔ	13. Ⓐ Ⓑ Ⓒ Ⓓ Ⓔ	18. Ⓐ Ⓑ Ⓒ Ⓓ Ⓔ	23. Ⓐ Ⓑ Ⓒ Ⓓ Ⓔ
4. Ⓐ Ⓑ Ⓒ Ⓓ Ⓔ	9. Ⓐ Ⓑ Ⓒ Ⓓ Ⓔ	14. Ⓐ Ⓑ Ⓒ Ⓓ Ⓔ	19. Ⓐ Ⓑ Ⓒ Ⓓ Ⓔ	24. Ⓐ Ⓑ Ⓒ Ⓓ Ⓔ
5. Ⓐ Ⓑ Ⓒ Ⓓ Ⓔ	10. Ⓐ Ⓑ Ⓒ Ⓓ Ⓔ	15. Ⓐ Ⓑ Ⓒ Ⓓ Ⓔ	20. Ⓐ Ⓑ Ⓒ Ⓓ Ⓔ	25. Ⓐ Ⓑ Ⓒ Ⓓ Ⓔ

Math Knowledge

1. Ⓐ Ⓑ Ⓒ Ⓓ Ⓔ	6. Ⓐ Ⓑ Ⓒ Ⓓ Ⓔ	11. Ⓐ Ⓑ Ⓒ Ⓓ Ⓔ	16. Ⓐ Ⓑ Ⓒ Ⓓ Ⓔ	21. Ⓐ Ⓑ Ⓒ Ⓓ Ⓔ
2. Ⓐ Ⓑ Ⓒ Ⓓ Ⓔ	7. Ⓐ Ⓑ Ⓒ Ⓓ Ⓔ	12. Ⓐ Ⓑ Ⓒ Ⓓ Ⓔ	17. Ⓐ Ⓑ Ⓒ Ⓓ Ⓔ	22. Ⓐ Ⓑ Ⓒ Ⓓ Ⓔ
3. Ⓐ Ⓑ Ⓒ Ⓓ Ⓔ	8. Ⓐ Ⓑ Ⓒ Ⓓ Ⓔ	13. Ⓐ Ⓑ Ⓒ Ⓓ Ⓔ	18. Ⓐ Ⓑ Ⓒ Ⓓ Ⓔ	23. Ⓐ Ⓑ Ⓒ Ⓓ Ⓔ
4. Ⓐ Ⓑ Ⓒ Ⓓ Ⓔ	9. Ⓐ Ⓑ Ⓒ Ⓓ Ⓔ	14. Ⓐ Ⓑ Ⓒ Ⓓ Ⓔ	19. Ⓐ Ⓑ Ⓒ Ⓓ Ⓔ	24. Ⓐ Ⓑ Ⓒ Ⓓ Ⓔ
5. Ⓐ Ⓑ Ⓒ Ⓓ Ⓔ	10. Ⓐ Ⓑ Ⓒ Ⓓ Ⓔ	15. Ⓐ Ⓑ Ⓒ Ⓓ Ⓔ	20. Ⓐ Ⓑ Ⓒ Ⓓ Ⓔ	25. Ⓐ Ⓑ Ⓒ Ⓓ Ⓔ

Reading Comprehension

1. Ⓐ Ⓑ Ⓒ Ⓓ Ⓔ
2. Ⓐ Ⓑ Ⓒ Ⓓ Ⓔ
3. Ⓐ Ⓑ Ⓒ Ⓓ Ⓔ
4. Ⓐ Ⓑ Ⓒ Ⓓ Ⓔ
5. Ⓐ Ⓑ Ⓒ Ⓓ Ⓔ
6. Ⓐ Ⓑ Ⓒ Ⓓ Ⓔ
7. Ⓐ Ⓑ Ⓒ Ⓓ Ⓔ
8. Ⓐ Ⓑ Ⓒ Ⓓ Ⓔ
9. Ⓐ Ⓑ Ⓒ Ⓓ Ⓔ
10. Ⓐ Ⓑ Ⓒ Ⓓ Ⓔ
11. Ⓐ Ⓑ Ⓒ Ⓓ Ⓔ
12. Ⓐ Ⓑ Ⓒ Ⓓ Ⓔ
13. Ⓐ Ⓑ Ⓒ Ⓓ Ⓔ
14. Ⓐ Ⓑ Ⓒ Ⓓ Ⓔ
15. Ⓐ Ⓑ Ⓒ Ⓓ Ⓔ
16. Ⓐ Ⓑ Ⓒ Ⓓ Ⓔ
17. Ⓐ Ⓑ Ⓒ Ⓓ Ⓔ
18. Ⓐ Ⓑ Ⓒ Ⓓ Ⓔ
19. Ⓐ Ⓑ Ⓒ Ⓓ Ⓔ
20. Ⓐ Ⓑ Ⓒ Ⓓ Ⓔ
21. Ⓐ Ⓑ Ⓒ Ⓓ Ⓔ
22. Ⓐ Ⓑ Ⓒ Ⓓ Ⓔ
23. Ⓐ Ⓑ Ⓒ Ⓓ Ⓔ
24. Ⓐ Ⓑ Ⓒ Ⓓ Ⓔ
25. Ⓐ Ⓑ Ⓒ Ⓓ Ⓔ

Situational Judgment

1. Ⓐ Ⓑ Ⓒ Ⓓ Ⓔ
2. Ⓐ Ⓑ Ⓒ Ⓓ Ⓔ
3. Ⓐ Ⓑ Ⓒ Ⓓ Ⓔ
4. Ⓐ Ⓑ Ⓒ Ⓓ Ⓔ
5. Ⓐ Ⓑ Ⓒ Ⓓ Ⓔ
6. Ⓐ Ⓑ Ⓒ Ⓓ Ⓔ
7. Ⓐ Ⓑ Ⓒ Ⓓ Ⓔ
8. Ⓐ Ⓑ Ⓒ Ⓓ Ⓔ
9. Ⓐ Ⓑ Ⓒ Ⓓ Ⓔ
10. Ⓐ Ⓑ Ⓒ Ⓓ Ⓔ
11. Ⓐ Ⓑ Ⓒ Ⓓ Ⓔ
12. Ⓐ Ⓑ Ⓒ Ⓓ Ⓔ
13. Ⓐ Ⓑ Ⓒ Ⓓ Ⓔ
14. Ⓐ Ⓑ Ⓒ Ⓓ Ⓔ
15. Ⓐ Ⓑ Ⓒ Ⓓ Ⓔ
16. Ⓐ Ⓑ Ⓒ Ⓓ Ⓔ
17. Ⓐ Ⓑ Ⓒ Ⓓ Ⓔ
18. Ⓐ Ⓑ Ⓒ Ⓓ Ⓔ
19. Ⓐ Ⓑ Ⓒ Ⓓ Ⓔ
20. Ⓐ Ⓑ Ⓒ Ⓓ Ⓔ
21. Ⓐ Ⓑ Ⓒ Ⓓ Ⓔ
22. Ⓐ Ⓑ Ⓒ Ⓓ Ⓔ
23. Ⓐ Ⓑ Ⓒ Ⓓ Ⓔ
24. Ⓐ Ⓑ Ⓒ Ⓓ Ⓔ
25. Ⓐ Ⓑ Ⓒ Ⓓ Ⓔ
26. Ⓐ Ⓑ Ⓒ Ⓓ Ⓔ
27. Ⓐ Ⓑ Ⓒ Ⓓ Ⓔ
28. Ⓐ Ⓑ Ⓒ Ⓓ Ⓔ
29. Ⓐ Ⓑ Ⓒ Ⓓ Ⓔ
30. Ⓐ Ⓑ Ⓒ Ⓓ Ⓔ
31. Ⓐ Ⓑ Ⓒ Ⓓ Ⓔ
32. Ⓐ Ⓑ Ⓒ Ⓓ Ⓔ
33. Ⓐ Ⓑ Ⓒ Ⓓ Ⓔ
34. Ⓐ Ⓑ Ⓒ Ⓓ Ⓔ
35. Ⓐ Ⓑ Ⓒ Ⓓ Ⓔ
36. Ⓐ Ⓑ Ⓒ Ⓓ Ⓔ
37. Ⓐ Ⓑ Ⓒ Ⓓ Ⓔ
38. Ⓐ Ⓑ Ⓒ Ⓓ Ⓔ
39. Ⓐ Ⓑ Ⓒ Ⓓ Ⓔ
40. Ⓐ Ⓑ Ⓒ Ⓓ Ⓔ
41. Ⓐ Ⓑ Ⓒ Ⓓ Ⓔ
42. Ⓐ Ⓑ Ⓒ Ⓓ Ⓔ
43. Ⓐ Ⓑ Ⓒ Ⓓ Ⓔ
44. Ⓐ Ⓑ Ⓒ Ⓓ Ⓔ
45. Ⓐ Ⓑ Ⓒ Ⓓ Ⓔ
46. Ⓐ Ⓑ Ⓒ Ⓓ Ⓔ
47. Ⓐ Ⓑ Ⓒ Ⓓ Ⓔ
48. Ⓐ Ⓑ Ⓒ Ⓓ Ⓔ
49. Ⓐ Ⓑ Ⓒ Ⓓ Ⓔ
50. Ⓐ Ⓑ Ⓒ Ⓓ Ⓔ

Physical Science

1. Ⓐ Ⓑ Ⓒ Ⓓ Ⓔ
2. Ⓐ Ⓑ Ⓒ Ⓓ Ⓔ
3. Ⓐ Ⓑ Ⓒ Ⓓ Ⓔ
4. Ⓐ Ⓑ Ⓒ Ⓓ Ⓔ
5. Ⓐ Ⓑ Ⓒ Ⓓ Ⓔ
6. Ⓐ Ⓑ Ⓒ Ⓓ Ⓔ
7. Ⓐ Ⓑ Ⓒ Ⓓ Ⓔ
8. Ⓐ Ⓑ Ⓒ Ⓓ Ⓔ
9. Ⓐ Ⓑ Ⓒ Ⓓ Ⓔ
10. Ⓐ Ⓑ Ⓒ Ⓓ Ⓔ
11. Ⓐ Ⓑ Ⓒ Ⓓ Ⓔ
12. Ⓐ Ⓑ Ⓒ Ⓓ Ⓔ
13. Ⓐ Ⓑ Ⓒ Ⓓ Ⓔ
14. Ⓐ Ⓑ Ⓒ Ⓓ Ⓔ
15. Ⓐ Ⓑ Ⓒ Ⓓ Ⓔ
16. Ⓐ Ⓑ Ⓒ Ⓓ Ⓔ
17. Ⓐ Ⓑ Ⓒ Ⓓ Ⓔ
18. Ⓐ Ⓑ Ⓒ Ⓓ Ⓔ
19. Ⓐ Ⓑ Ⓒ Ⓓ Ⓔ
20. Ⓐ Ⓑ Ⓒ Ⓓ Ⓔ

Table Reading

1. Ⓐ Ⓑ Ⓒ Ⓓ Ⓔ	9. Ⓐ Ⓑ Ⓒ Ⓓ Ⓔ	17. Ⓐ Ⓑ Ⓒ Ⓓ Ⓔ	25. Ⓐ Ⓑ Ⓒ Ⓓ Ⓔ	33. Ⓐ Ⓑ Ⓒ Ⓓ Ⓔ
2. Ⓐ Ⓑ Ⓒ Ⓓ Ⓔ	10. Ⓐ Ⓑ Ⓒ Ⓓ Ⓔ	18. Ⓐ Ⓑ Ⓒ Ⓓ Ⓔ	26. Ⓐ Ⓑ Ⓒ Ⓓ Ⓔ	34. Ⓐ Ⓑ Ⓒ Ⓓ Ⓔ
3. Ⓐ Ⓑ Ⓒ Ⓓ Ⓔ	11. Ⓐ Ⓑ Ⓒ Ⓓ Ⓔ	19. Ⓐ Ⓑ Ⓒ Ⓓ Ⓔ	27. Ⓐ Ⓑ Ⓒ Ⓓ Ⓔ	35. Ⓐ Ⓑ Ⓒ Ⓓ Ⓔ
4. Ⓐ Ⓑ Ⓒ Ⓓ Ⓔ	12. Ⓐ Ⓑ Ⓒ Ⓓ Ⓔ	20. Ⓐ Ⓑ Ⓒ Ⓓ Ⓔ	28. Ⓐ Ⓑ Ⓒ Ⓓ Ⓔ	36. Ⓐ Ⓑ Ⓒ Ⓓ Ⓔ
5. Ⓐ Ⓑ Ⓒ Ⓓ Ⓔ	13. Ⓐ Ⓑ Ⓒ Ⓓ Ⓔ	21. Ⓐ Ⓑ Ⓒ Ⓓ Ⓔ	29. Ⓐ Ⓑ Ⓒ Ⓓ Ⓔ	37. Ⓐ Ⓑ Ⓒ Ⓓ Ⓔ
6. Ⓐ Ⓑ Ⓒ Ⓓ Ⓔ	14. Ⓐ Ⓑ Ⓒ Ⓓ Ⓔ	22. Ⓐ Ⓑ Ⓒ Ⓓ Ⓔ	30. Ⓐ Ⓑ Ⓒ Ⓓ Ⓔ	38. Ⓐ Ⓑ Ⓒ Ⓓ Ⓔ
7. Ⓐ Ⓑ Ⓒ Ⓓ Ⓔ	15. Ⓐ Ⓑ Ⓒ Ⓓ Ⓔ	23. Ⓐ Ⓑ Ⓒ Ⓓ Ⓔ	31. Ⓐ Ⓑ Ⓒ Ⓓ Ⓔ	39. Ⓐ Ⓑ Ⓒ Ⓓ Ⓔ
8. Ⓐ Ⓑ Ⓒ Ⓓ Ⓔ	16. Ⓐ Ⓑ Ⓒ Ⓓ Ⓔ	24. Ⓐ Ⓑ Ⓒ Ⓓ Ⓔ	32. Ⓐ Ⓑ Ⓒ Ⓓ Ⓔ	40. Ⓐ Ⓑ Ⓒ Ⓓ Ⓔ

Instrument Comprehension

1. Ⓐ Ⓑ Ⓒ Ⓓ	6. Ⓐ Ⓑ Ⓒ Ⓓ	11. Ⓐ Ⓑ Ⓒ Ⓓ	16. Ⓐ Ⓑ Ⓒ Ⓓ	21. Ⓐ Ⓑ Ⓒ Ⓓ
2. Ⓐ Ⓑ Ⓒ Ⓓ	7. Ⓐ Ⓑ Ⓒ Ⓓ	12. Ⓐ Ⓑ Ⓒ Ⓓ	17. Ⓐ Ⓑ Ⓒ Ⓓ	22. Ⓐ Ⓑ Ⓒ Ⓓ
3. Ⓐ Ⓑ Ⓒ Ⓓ	8. Ⓐ Ⓑ Ⓒ Ⓓ	13. Ⓐ Ⓑ Ⓒ Ⓓ	18. Ⓐ Ⓑ Ⓒ Ⓓ	23. Ⓐ Ⓑ Ⓒ Ⓓ
4. Ⓐ Ⓑ Ⓒ Ⓓ	9. Ⓐ Ⓑ Ⓒ Ⓓ	14. Ⓐ Ⓑ Ⓒ Ⓓ	19. Ⓐ Ⓑ Ⓒ Ⓓ	24. Ⓐ Ⓑ Ⓒ Ⓓ
5. Ⓐ Ⓑ Ⓒ Ⓓ	10. Ⓐ Ⓑ Ⓒ Ⓓ	15. Ⓐ Ⓑ Ⓒ Ⓓ	20. Ⓐ Ⓑ Ⓒ Ⓓ	25. Ⓐ Ⓑ Ⓒ Ⓓ

Block Counting

1. Ⓐ Ⓑ Ⓒ Ⓓ Ⓔ	7. Ⓐ Ⓑ Ⓒ Ⓓ Ⓔ	13. Ⓐ Ⓑ Ⓒ Ⓓ Ⓔ	19. Ⓐ Ⓑ Ⓒ Ⓓ Ⓔ	25. Ⓐ Ⓑ Ⓒ Ⓓ Ⓔ
2. Ⓐ Ⓑ Ⓒ Ⓓ Ⓔ	8. Ⓐ Ⓑ Ⓒ Ⓓ Ⓔ	14. Ⓐ Ⓑ Ⓒ Ⓓ Ⓔ	20. Ⓐ Ⓑ Ⓒ Ⓓ Ⓔ	26. Ⓐ Ⓑ Ⓒ Ⓓ Ⓔ
3. Ⓐ Ⓑ Ⓒ Ⓓ Ⓔ	9. Ⓐ Ⓑ Ⓒ Ⓓ Ⓔ	15. Ⓐ Ⓑ Ⓒ Ⓓ Ⓔ	21. Ⓐ Ⓑ Ⓒ Ⓓ Ⓔ	27. Ⓐ Ⓑ Ⓒ Ⓓ Ⓔ
4. Ⓐ Ⓑ Ⓒ Ⓓ Ⓔ	10. Ⓐ Ⓑ Ⓒ Ⓓ Ⓔ	16. Ⓐ Ⓑ Ⓒ Ⓓ Ⓔ	22. Ⓐ Ⓑ Ⓒ Ⓓ Ⓔ	28. Ⓐ Ⓑ Ⓒ Ⓓ Ⓔ
5. Ⓐ Ⓑ Ⓒ Ⓓ Ⓔ	11. Ⓐ Ⓑ Ⓒ Ⓓ Ⓔ	17. Ⓐ Ⓑ Ⓒ Ⓓ Ⓔ	23. Ⓐ Ⓑ Ⓒ Ⓓ Ⓔ	29. Ⓐ Ⓑ Ⓒ Ⓓ Ⓔ
6. Ⓐ Ⓑ Ⓒ Ⓓ Ⓔ	12. Ⓐ Ⓑ Ⓒ Ⓓ Ⓔ	18. Ⓐ Ⓑ Ⓒ Ⓓ Ⓔ	24. Ⓐ Ⓑ Ⓒ Ⓓ Ⓔ	30. Ⓐ Ⓑ Ⓒ Ⓓ Ⓔ

Aviation Information

1. Ⓐ Ⓑ Ⓒ Ⓓ Ⓔ	5. Ⓐ Ⓑ Ⓒ Ⓓ Ⓔ	9. Ⓐ Ⓑ Ⓒ Ⓓ Ⓔ	13. Ⓐ Ⓑ Ⓒ Ⓓ Ⓔ	17. Ⓐ Ⓑ Ⓒ Ⓓ Ⓔ
2. Ⓐ Ⓑ Ⓒ Ⓓ Ⓔ	6. Ⓐ Ⓑ Ⓒ Ⓓ Ⓔ	10. Ⓐ Ⓑ Ⓒ Ⓓ Ⓔ	14. Ⓐ Ⓑ Ⓒ Ⓓ Ⓔ	18. Ⓐ Ⓑ Ⓒ Ⓓ Ⓔ
3. Ⓐ Ⓑ Ⓒ Ⓓ Ⓔ	7. Ⓐ Ⓑ Ⓒ Ⓓ Ⓔ	11. Ⓐ Ⓑ Ⓒ Ⓓ Ⓔ	15. Ⓐ Ⓑ Ⓒ Ⓓ Ⓔ	19. Ⓐ Ⓑ Ⓒ Ⓓ Ⓔ
4. Ⓐ Ⓑ Ⓒ Ⓓ Ⓔ	8. Ⓐ Ⓑ Ⓒ Ⓓ Ⓔ	12. Ⓐ Ⓑ Ⓒ Ⓓ Ⓔ	16. Ⓐ Ⓑ Ⓒ Ⓓ Ⓔ	20. Ⓐ Ⓑ Ⓒ Ⓓ Ⓔ

VERBAL ANALOGIES

25 Questions (8 Minutes)

Directions: This part of the test measures your ability to reason and see relationships among words. You are to choose the option that best completes the analogy developed at the beginning of each statement.

1. RANCID is to ROTTEN as FRESH is to

   A. SPOILED
   B. RIPE
   C. YOUNG
   D. BUDDING
   E. OLD

2. GOLD is to METAL as CEDAR is to

   A. LIQUID
   B. FROZEN
   C. WOOD
   D. GAS
   E. ALUMINUM

3. COLD is to HOT as FROZEN is to

   A. MOVIE
   B. BOILING
   C. TEPID
   D. COMFORTABLE
   E. BREEZY

4. SOLAR is to COAL as NUCLEAR is to

   A. PLUG
   B. BATTERY
   C. EXTENSION CORD
   D. GENERATOR
   E. FUEL

5. JET ENGINE is to THRUST as GAS STOVE is to

   A. COOKING
   B. SPEED
   C. HEAT
   D. FLAME
   E. SIMMER

6. CHAPTER is to BOOK as ARTICLE is to

   A. MAGAZINE
   B. CLOTHING
   C. COLUMN
   D. PARAGRAPH
   E. VOLUME

7. HINGE is to DOOR as SHELF is to

   A. BED
   B. DESK
   C. COUNTER
   D. TELEVISION
   E. CABINET

8. MOUNTAIN is to HILL as LAKE is to

   A. CREEK
   B. FISH
   C. KAYAK
   D. PUDDLE
   E. KNOLL

9. CRIME is to PUNISHMENT as LOVE is to

A. FRIENDSHIP
B. PRISON
C. MARRIAGE
D. HEART
E. CHILDREN

10. RECYCLING is to ENVIRONMENT as EXERCISE is to

A. HEALTH
B. MUSCLE
C. RUNNING
D. SPORTS
E. WEIGHTS

11. TENT is to CAMPING as WETSUIT is to

A. DIVING
B. JOGGING
C. DRIVING
D. BOATING
E. CAVING

12. NAP is to SLEEP as STROLL is to

A. STAIR
B. FOOT
C. SIT
D. HIKE
E. FLOOR

13. BOW is to ARROW as PISTOL is to

A. TARGET
B. RIFLE
C. HOLSTER
D. MAGAZINE
E. BULLET

14. AIR is to VACUUM as WATER is to

A. RIVER
B. FLOWER
C. DESERT
D. DRINK
E. BOAT

15. HUNGRY is to THIRSTY as FULL is to

A. EMPTY
B. QUENCHED
C. MEAL
D. BLANK
E. LUNCH

16. SPIDER is to WEB as BEE is to

A. NEST
B. TREE
C. HIVE
D. MESH
E. WARREN

17. FILE is to CABINET as WEAPON is to

A. RANGE
B. ARMORY
C. MAGAZINE
D. AMMUNITION
E. HOLSTER

18. SHOUT is to TALK as TALK is to

A. YELL
B. SCREAM
C. WRITE
D. WHISPER
E. HISS

19. HAMMER is to NAIL as COMB is to

A. HAIR
B. TEETH
C. BRUSH
D. RAKE
E. BEARD

20. SILVER is to GOLD as NICKEL is to

A. ALUMINUM
B. DIME
C. PENNY
D. STEEL
E. SAWBUCK

21. CIGARETTE is to CIGAR as TUMBLER is to

A. MAT
B. SHOT
C. STEIN
D. BOTTLE
E. CAN

22. CAP is to COWBOY HAT as ANKLE SOCK is to

A. RUNNING SHOE
B. COWBOY BOOT
C. PANTY HOSE
D. LEGGINGS
E. SWIM FINS

23. SKATEBOARD is to AIRPLANE as POOL FLOAT is to

A. BOAT DOCK
B. CANOE
C. HELICOPTER
D. GLIDER
E. BATTLESHIP

24. FAHRENHEIT is to CELSIUS as FOOT is to

A. LITER
B. MILE
C. INCH
D. METER
E. TOE

25. BACKPACK is to SUITCASE as ENVELOPE is to

A. FOLDER
B. BOX
C. CRATE
D. NOTEBOOK
E. SATCHEL

STOP.

If you finish before time is up, you may check your work on this section only. Do not turn to any other section in the test.

ARITHMETIC REASONING

25 Questions (29 Minutes)

Directions: This part of the test measures your ability to use arithmetic to solve problems. Each problem is followed by five possible answers. You are to decide which of the five choices is correct.

1. If a car uses $1\frac{1}{2}$ gallons of gas every 30 miles, how many miles can be driven with 6 gallons of gas?
   A. 100
   B. 110
   C. 120
   D. 130
   E. 140

2. A car has a gasoline tank that holds 20 gallons. When the gauge reads $\frac{1}{4}$ full, how many gallons are needed to fill the tank?
   A. 4
   B. 5
   C. 10
   D. 15
   E. 16

3. An airplane flying a distance of 875 miles used 70 gallons of fuel. How many gallons will it need to travel 3000 miles?
   A. 108
   B. 120
   C. 144
   D. 240
   E. 280

4. The *Mayflower* sailed from Plymouth, England, to Plymouth Rock, a distance of approximately 2800 miles in 63 days. The average speed in miles per hour was closest to which one of the following?
   A. $\frac{1}{2}$
   B. 1
   C. 2
   D. 3
   E. 4

5. A man drives 60 miles to his destination at an average speed of 40 miles per hour and makes the return trip at an average rate of 30 miles per hour. What is his average speed in miles per hour for the entire trip?
   A. 34
   B. 36
   C. 38
   D. 40
   E. 42

6. A plane flies over Cleveland at 10:20 A.M. It passes over a community 120 miles away at 10:32 A.M. Find the plane's flight rate in miles per hour.
   A. 360
   B. 420
   C. 480
   D. 540
   E. 600

7. Two trains start from the same station at 10:00 A.M., one traveling east at 60 mph and the other traveling west at 70 mph. At what time will these trains be 455 miles apart?

   A. 12:30 P.M.
   B. 1:00 P.M.
   C. 1:30 P.M.
   D. 2:00 P.M.
   E. 2:30 P.M.

8. Two trains running on the same track travel at the rates of 25 and 30 mph, respectively. If the slower train starts out an hour earlier, how long will it take the faster train to catch up with it?

   A. $3\frac{1}{2}$ hours
   B. 4 hours
   C. $4\frac{1}{2}$ hours
   D. 5 hours
   E. $5\frac{1}{2}$ hours

9. On a map, $\frac{1}{2}$ inch = 10 miles. How many miles apart are two towns that are $2\frac{1}{4}$ inches apart on the map?

   A. 33
   B. 36
   C. 39
   D. 42
   E. 45

10. The total savings in purchasing 30 13-cent candies for an event at a reduced rate of \$1.38 per dozen is

   A. \$0.35
   B. \$0.40
   C. \$0.45
   D. \$0.50
   E. \$0.55

11. Mr. Jackson takes his wife and two children to the circus. If the price of a child's ticket is half the price of an adult ticket and Mr. Jackson pays a total of \$12.60, the price of a child's ticket is

   A. \$2.10
   B. \$2.60
   C. \$3.10
   D. \$3.60
   E. \$4.10

12. What part of a day is 5 hours 15 minutes?

   A. $\frac{7}{16}$
   B. $\frac{9}{16}$
   C. $\frac{7}{32}$
   D. $\frac{9}{32}$
   E. $\frac{11}{32}$

13. A team lost 10 games in a 35-game season. Find the ratio of games won to games lost.

   A. 2 : 5
   B. 5 : 2
   C. 5 : 7
   D. 7 : 2
   E. 7 : 5

14. In a 3-hour examination of 350 questions, there are 50 mathematics problems. If twice as much time should be allowed for each mathematics problem as for each of the other questions, how many minutes should be spent on the mathematics problems?

   A. 45 minutes
   B. 52 minutes
   C. 60 minutes
   D. 72 minutes
   E. 80 minutes

15. The parts department's profit is 12 percent on a new magneto. How much did the magneto cost if the selling price is $145.60?

A. $120.00

B. $125.60

C. $130.00

D. $133.60

E. $136.00

16. A typewriter was listed at $120.00 and was bought for $96.00. What was the rate of discount?

A. 16%

B. 20%

C. 24%

D. 28%

E. 32%

17. A class of 198 recruits consists of three racial and ethnic groups. If $\frac{1}{3}$ are Black and $\frac{1}{4}$ of the remainder are Hispanic, how many of the recruits in the class are white?

A. 198

B. 165

C. 132

D. 99

E. 66

18. One-third of the students at Central High are seniors. Three-fourths of the seniors will go to college next year. What percentage of the students at Central High will go to college next year?

A. 25%

B. $33\frac{1}{3}\%$

C. 45%

D. 50%

E. 75%

19. If 2.5 centimeters = 1 inch, and 36 inches = 1 yard, how many centimeters are in 1 yard?

A. 14

B. 25

C. 70

D. 80

E. 90

20. A rectangular fuel tank measures 60 inches in length, 30 inches in width, and 12 inches in depth. How many cubic feet are within the tank?

A. 12.5

B. 15.0

C. 18.5

D. 21.0

E. 24.5

21. How many gallons of fuel will be contained in a rectangular tank that measures 2 feet in width, 3 feet in length, and 1 foot 8 inches in depth (7.5 gallons = 1 cubic foot)?

A. 110

B. 75

C. 66.6

D. 55

E. 45

22. A rectangular bin 4 feet long, 3 feet wide, and 2 feet high is solidly packed with bricks whose dimensions are 8 inches by 4 inches by 2 inches. The number of bricks in the bin is

A. 54

B. 324

C. 648

D. 1072

E. 1296

23. A resolution was passed by a ratio of 5:4. If 90 people voted for the resolution, how many voted against it?

A. 40

B. 50

C. 60

D. 66

E. 72

24. If 2.5 centimeters = 1 inch, how many centimeters are in 1 foot?

A. 5

B. 10

C. 15

D. 30

E. 60

25. A gasoline tank is $\frac{1}{4}$ full. After adding 10 gallons of gasoline, the gauge indicates that the tank is $\frac{2}{3}$ full. What is the capacity of the tank in gallons?

A. 20

B. 24

C. 28

D. 32

E. 36

STOP.

If you finish before time is up, you may check your work on this section only. Do not turn to any other section in the test.

WORD KNOWLEDGE

25 Questions (5 Minutes)

Directions: This part of the test measures your knowledge of words and their meanings. For each question, you are to choose the word below that is closest in meaning to the capitalized word above.

1. AGGREGATE
   - A. Cattle
   - B. Collective
   - C. Restrained
   - D. Elderly
   - E. Ceramic
2. BROADCAST
   - A. Reinforce
   - B. Expansive
   - C. Aroma
   - D. Transmit
   - E. Statue
3. CENSURE
   - A. Condemn
   - B. Detect
   - C. Monetary
   - D. Confident
   - E. Tilt
4. DAEDAL
   - A. Bizarre
   - B. Intricate
   - C. Childish
   - D. Old
   - E. Superior
5. DUCTILE
   - A. Piped
   - B. Carpet
   - C. Clean
   - D. Ground
   - E. Influenced
6. EGREGIOUS
   - A. Coiled
   - B. Sleepy
   - C. Flagrant
   - D. Automatic
   - E. Displayed
7. EXALT
   - A. Create
   - B. Paint
   - C. Smell
   - D. Glorify
   - E. Define
8. FECUND
   - A. Fruitful
   - B. Unpleasant
   - C. Warm
   - D. Waste
   - E. Attractive

9. FOLDEROL
   - A. Solid
   - B. Knobby
   - C. Coffee
   - D. Nonsense
   - E. Creased

10. GOAD
   - A. Ram
   - B. Incite
   - C. Unlock
   - D. Mistake
   - E. Plant

11. GUARANTY
   - A. Dealer
   - B. Truth
   - C. Salve
   - D. Plaintiff
   - E. Security

12. HOARD
   - A. Swine
   - B. Ice
   - C. Supply
   - D. Latch
   - E. Pin

13. IMMATERIAL
   - A. Item
   - B. Unimportant
   - C. Asphalt
   - D. Monetary
   - E. Blind

14. JURISDICTION
   - A. Decision
   - B. Ground
   - C. Mascot
   - D. Control
   - E. Televised

15. KIRTLE
   - A. Gown
   - B. Bird
   - C. Spoon
   - D. Vehicle
   - E. Blanket

16. JEST
   - A. Scrub
   - B. Breath
   - C. Only
   - D. Prank
   - E. Case

17. JUNCTION
   - A. Corner
   - B. Intersection
   - C. Contact
   - D. Tray
   - E. Window

18. KINDLE
   - A. Book
   - B. Screen
   - C. Pleasant
   - D. Light
   - E. Educate

19. LUCID
 A. Juicy
 B. Float
 C. Translucent
 D. Uncovered
 E. Connected

20. MASTICATE
 A. Chew
 B. Prehistoric
 C. Leader
 D. Upright
 E. Listen

21. NIMBLE
 A. Unfeeling
 B. Opaque
 C. Soft
 D. Agile
 E. Finger

22. OPTIMUM
 A. Unique
 B. Visual
 C. Useful
 D. Indistinct
 E. Ideal

23. TRUCULENT
 A. Short
 B. Bent
 C. Complete
 D. Belligerent
 E. Heavy

24. VITREOUS
 A. Poisonous
 B. Glassy
 C. Angry
 D. Smooth
 E. Pure

25. WEAL
 A. Young
 B. Free
 C. Large
 D. Healthy
 E. Open

STOP.

If you finish before time is up, you may check your work on this section only. Do not turn to any other section in the test.

MATH KNOWLEDGE

25 Questions (22 Minutes)

Directions: This part of the test measures your knowledge of mathematical terms and principles. Each problem is followed by five possible answers. You are to decide which of the five choices is correct.

1. Which of the following fractions is the largest?

   A. $\frac{1}{2}$

   B. $\frac{3}{4}$

   C. $\frac{5}{8}$

   D. $\frac{11}{16}$

   E. $\frac{23}{32}$

2. Arrange these fractions in order of size from largest to smallest: $\frac{1}{3}, \frac{2}{5}, \frac{4}{15}$.

   A. $\frac{4}{15}, \frac{2}{5}, \frac{1}{3}$

   B. $\frac{2}{5}, \frac{4}{15}, \frac{1}{3}$

   C. $\frac{2}{5}, \frac{1}{3}, \frac{4}{15}$

   D. $\frac{1}{3}, \frac{4}{15}, \frac{2}{5}$

   E. $\frac{1}{3}, \frac{2}{5}, \frac{4}{15}$

3. Which of the following fractions is equal to $\frac{1}{4}$%?

   A. $\frac{1}{4}$

   B. $\frac{1}{25}$

   C. $\frac{4}{25}$

   D. $\frac{1}{40}$

   E. $\frac{1}{400}$

4. What percent of 90 is 120?

   A. $133\frac{1}{3}$

   B. 125

   C. 120

   D. 75

   E. $1\frac{1}{3}$

5. What number added to 40% of itself is equal to 84?

   A. 64

   B. 60

   C. 50.4

   D. 40.6

   E. 33.6

6. Find the square of 212.

   A. 40,144

   B. 44,944

   C. 45,924

   D. 46,944

   E. 47,924

7. If $2^{n-3} = 32$, then n equals what value?

   A. 5

   B. 6

   C. 7

   D. 8

   E. 9

8. How many digits are there in the square root of a perfect square of 6 digits?

A. 12

B. 6

C. 4

D. 3

E. 2

9. If $a = 4$, then $\sqrt{a^2 + 9} =$

A. 1

B. 5

C. $\sqrt{5}$

D. 25

E. –25

10. Evaluate the following expression:
5 [4 – (3 – 4) + 13] – 6

A. –11

B. 16

C. 17

D. 21

E. 84

11. If x is less than 10, and y is less than 5, it follows that

A. $x > y$

B. $x - y = 5$

C. $x = 2y$

D. $x + y < 15$

E. $x + y = 15$

12. If the length and width of a rectangle are each multiplied by 2, then the

A. perimeter is multiplied by 4 and the area by 8.

B. area is multiplied by 2 and the perimeter by 4.

C. area is multiplied by 4 and the perimeter by 2.

D. area and perimeter are both multiplied by 2.

E. area and perimeter are both multiplied by 4.

13. The average of two numbers is A. If one of the numbers is x, the other number is

A. $\frac{A}{2} - x$

B. $\frac{A + x}{2}$

C. $A - x$

D. $x - A$

E. $2A - x$

14. If p pencils cost $2D$ dollars, how many pencils can be bought for c cents?

A. $\frac{2Dc}{p}$

B. $\frac{pc}{2D}$

C. $\frac{2Dp}{c}$

D. $\frac{50pc}{D}$

E. $200\,pcD$

15. When –4 is subtracted from the sum of –3 and 5, the result is

A. 12

B. 6

C. –6

D. 2

E. –2

16. Find the product of (–6) (5) (–4).

A. 5

B. –5

C. –34

D. –120

E. 120

17. When the product of (–10) and $\left(\frac{1}{2}\right)$ is divided by the quotient of (–15) and $\left(-\frac{1}{3}\right)$, the quotient is

A. 2

B. –2

C. 1

D. –1

E. 0

18. If $r = 25 - s$, then $4r + 4s =$

A. 100

B. –100

C. 25

D. –25

E. 0

19. Solve for x: $\frac{2x}{3} = \frac{x+5}{4}$

A. 2

B. 3

C. 4

D. 5

E. 6

20. If $a = 7$, $b = 8$, and $c = 5$, solve for x: $\frac{a-3}{x} = \frac{b+2}{4c}$

A. 4

B. 5

C. 6

D. 7

E. 8

21. The difference between $\sqrt{144}$ and $\sqrt{36}$ is

A. 180

B. 108

C. 18

D. 6

E. 2

22. $\sqrt{150}$ is between which of the following integers?

A. 10 and 11

B. 11 and 12

C. 12 and 13

D. 13 and 14

E. 14 and 15

23. Simplify the expression $2\sqrt{50}$.

A. $7\sqrt{2}$

B. $10\sqrt{2}$

C. 14

D. $25\sqrt{2}$

E. $50\sqrt{2}$

24. The sum of $4\sqrt{8}$, $3\sqrt{18}$, and $2\sqrt{50}$ is

A. $9\sqrt{76}$

B. $17\sqrt{2}$

C. $17\sqrt{6}$

D. $27\sqrt{2}$

E. $27\sqrt{6}$

25. If $\frac{1}{a} + \frac{1}{b} = \frac{1}{c}$, then c =

A. ab

B. $a + b$

C. $\frac{1}{2}ab$

D. $\frac{ab}{b+a}$

E. $\frac{a+b}{ab}$

STOP.

If you finish before time is up, you may check your work on this section only. Do not turn to any other section in the test.

READING COMPREHENSION

25 Questions (38 Minutes)

Directions: This part of the test measures your ability to read and understand written material. Each passage is followed by a series of multiple-choice questions. You are to choose the option that best answers the question based on the passage. No additional information or specific knowledge is needed.

Questions 1-4 are based on the following passage.

In his federalist papers defending the United States Constitution, James Madison wrote of the potential danger posed by factions within the government. Factions, as defined by Madison, are small groups of people, amounting to either a minority or majority, that are driven by some common impulse or passion that is averse to the best interests of the community. Madison expressed deep concern for the political dangers that factions posed to a democratic republic and the system of voting as outlined in the Constitution. He warned Congress to be wary of allowing one faction to take power over another and prioritize their own interests before the interests of the country itself. It was in this federalist paper, in this discussion of factions, that the concept of separation of powers was born.

Madison wrote that the "accumulation of all powers, legislative, executive, and judiciary, in the same hands, whether one, a few, or many … may justly be pronounced the very definition of tyranny." It was this definition of tyranny that produced the constitutional safety net that is the separation of powers. The separation of powers was instituted as a way to keep a checks and balances system for government branches. Each branch of the government would not be given free reign of their respective duties, but be held accountable by its counterparts. For example, the executive branch, while able to command the troops, cannot declare war as the legislative branch can. And though the legislative branch has the ability to write and pass new laws, the executive branch has veto power for any law deemed not in the best interest of the community. It was his fear of faction, fear of tyranny of the few, that inspired these cornerstones of our government and our country.

1. According to the passage, Madison thought the greatest challenge facing the new nation was the

   A. separation of powers.

   B. tyranny of the minority.

   C. lack of centralized government.

   D. legislative branch.

   E. power to control the military.

2. Madison's fear of factions bore the concept of

   A. the separation of powers.

   B. the military.

   C. the judicial branch.

   D. veto power.

   E. the Constitution.

3. The primary purpose of the second paragraph is to

   A. detail the role of each branch of government.

   B. describe Madison's intentions for the separation of powers and how they were implemented.

   C. advocate for the separation of powers and the Constitution.

   D. explain the depth of Madison's fear of factions.

   E. inform citizens of the way in which their government functions.

4. Which of the following is an accurate and descriptive title for the passage?

A. The Federalist Papers of the Founding Fathers

B. Why Madison Feared Factions

C. The Separation of Powers in the US Constitution

D. Fear of Factions: How the Constitution Came to Outline the Separation of Powers

E. James Madison: His Life and His Story

Questions 5-8 are based on the following passage.

The health benefits of artificial sugars have been debated for decades. Men and women with similar weight loss goals have been asking for sugar substitutes in their coffee and drinking diet sodas for years, assuming that the lack of calories means a lack of weight gained from consumption. A sweet treat packing less caloric punch sounds like an all-in-one fix to both the cravings and the weight loss goals. Still, researchers and food bloggers alike have expressed worries about sugar substitutes for years, raising concerns over health risks ranging from cancer to diabetes to concern over our taste buds.

Yet, even with all the raised eyebrows out there, the FDA has reluctantly approved five artificial sweeteners for consumption: saccharin, acesulfame, aspartame, neotame, and sucralose, with stevia being the only natural low-calorie sweetener in the bunch. The regulations for all such products are respectively conservative, paying mind to the lack of concrete evidence to support serious health risks associated with artificial sweetener. Still, eyebrows continue to rise with the consumption of artificial sugars as a weight loss strategy. While low in caloric intake and without any serious health risks, it is true that they are not proven to help with weight loss. The potency of artificial sugar compared with true natural sugar products such as table sugar or fruit could potentially cause your taste buds to shun real nutritive substances in favor of synthetic sweetener. Of course, there is still a lack of scientific evidence to support this claim, but the adversaries will continue to contest this, and the idea of artificial sugar will continue to live in controversy.

5. The primary purpose of this passage is to

A. inform the public on the health benefits associated with artificial sweeteners as opposed to natural sugar.

B. dissuade consumers from buying anything made with artificial sweetener.

C. discuss the many assumptions made about artificial sweeteners and their potential health risks.

D. advocate for the use of natural sugar instead of artificial sweeteners.

E. contradict the incorrect assumptions made about the health hazards of using artificial sweetener.

6. Which statement is most closely supported by the passage?

A. Artificial sweetener is likely to induce weight gain as opposed to weight loss.

B. No one should consume artificial sweetener as there have been so few scientific studies done to prove that it's safe for consumption.

C. Artificial sweetener is suggested for those wishing to lose weight but not recommended by doctors otherwise.

D. There is inadequate evidence to support any health claims related to artificial sweetener.

E. Artificial sweetener is not as controversial a topic since being approved by the FDA.

7. According to the passage, artificial sweetener

A. is recommended for weight loss.

B. is not as healthy as natural sugar.

C. is an FDA approved sugar substitute.

D. has the same amount of calories as natural sugar.

E. can cause serious health problems.

8. In the second paragraph, *conservative* most likely means

A. moderate.

B. traditionalist.

C. low.

D. high.

E. stable.

Questions 9-12 are based on the following passage.

In recent years, anyone that has ever sat next to a teen driver in the car, be it a friend, a parent, or driver's ed instructor, has consciously watched that teen set their phone down before paying attention to the road. If this doesn't happen, you remind them, as texting and driving is the most common cause of fatal car accidents in the US, and this information has been widely promoted since the dawn of the mobile phone. It might not occur that, teens being distracted by every other aspect of their lives, it is actually adults that are at a higher risk for using their mobile device while behind the wheel.

Of course, it's only natural that as cell phones become as universal as cars themselves, that the problem should be more widespread than confined to a specific age demographic. A study shown in *USA Today* writes that while 98 percent of adults say they know that texting and driving is unsafe, a whopping 49 percent of adults admit to practicing just that. In comparison, a comparably lesser 43 percent of teens admit to the same. Admittedly, teens may be less likely to text and drive, but a higher percentage of fatal car crashes are the result of distracted driving in teens as opposed to adults. So, while this concern is valid, it must be acknowledged that the example must be set by adults first to quell this unfortunate reality that affects all those on the road.

9. Which of the following statements would the author most likely agree with?

A. Teens and adults are equally as likely to text and drive.

B. Adults are worse drivers than teens.

C. Adults should not tell teens that they cannot text and drive.

D. More teen drivers are guilty of texting and driving than adults.

E. Teen drivers are not the only ones guilty of texting and driving.

10. The primary purpose of the second paragraph is to

A. deny evidence supporting the claim that teens are worse drivers.

B. give statistics on the likelihood of teens to text and drive versus adults.

C. provide insight into the evidence supporting the claims made in the first paragraph.

D. explain why adults are worse drivers than teens.

E. acknowledge the reasoning behind teens being hailed as worse drivers.

11. The author uses statistics in order to convey

A. pathos.

B. supporting information.

C. logical reasoning.

D. scientific evidence.

E. character reference.

12. Which of the following is an accurate and descriptive title for the passage?

A. The Misconceptions of Teen Texting and Driving

B. Adult Texting and Driving: A Menace

C. The Dangers of Texting and Driving

D. Why Teens Are More Likely to Text and Drive

E. Teen vs. Adult Habits

Questions 13-16 are based on the following passage.

Sweden has been widely recognized for decades as one of the most socially advanced countries in the world in terms of not only economy, civil rights, and citizen worldliness, but also in the most basic sense of parental leave. While the US relegates decisions on parental leave to individual employers and companies, Sweden and other Nordic countries implement family-friendly policies to new parents that provide for ample support to workers at all levels. Swedish parents have access to 480 days total of paid parental leave, 390 of which they are entitled to 80% of their given salary, and the remaining 90 to a flat rate. At least one parent in the family unit is required to take 90 days of paid leave, which includes the father. Women with labor-intensive, strenuous jobs are entitled to further benefits before and after childbirth, and these same policies apply to parents who adopt, giving same-sex couples equal share in the benefits that come with parenthood.

Contrarily, American workers are given on average six weeks of somewhat paid leave with an equivalent to a less than 3-week salary. This benefit is also directly targeted at women, leaving fathers without any benefits surrounding their newfound parenthood and unable to take care of their child should the mother want to return to work. It should be acknowledged, however, that while the American government has yet to take notice of such disparities in paid parental leave policies, corporations such as Apple, Ikea, Bank of America, and more have implemented far more substantial maternity leave policies that extend across the board to all eligible employees. There has been an upsurge in American business advocating for and implementing Scandinavian work-life balance policies, using their legal freedoms to make the change they'd like to see on a federal level. Still, the differences between Scandinavian parental policies and their American counterparts, while gaping, have been recognized by American businesses and word of mouth has begun to spark the necessary changes.

13. The primary purpose of the passage is to

A. raise awareness for the disparities of American parental leave policies.

B. convince Americans to lobby and support better parental leave policies.

C. inform on one of the key differences between two powerful nations.

D. describe the Swedish policies on parental leave.

E. compare and contrast the parental leave policies of Sweden and America.

14. Which of the following statements would the author most likely agree with?

A. The American parental leave policies are without fault for the system of government through which they operate in.

B. America's parental leave policies are no better or worse than Sweden's.

C. The Swedish policies on parental leave are no more family friendly than the American policies.

D. American companies should adopt more Swedish parental leave policies.

E. The parental leave policies in Sweden are not adoption-friendly.

15. The author made the connection that "American workers are given on average six weeks of somewhat paid leave with an equivalent to a less than 3-week salary" in order to convey

A. the efficiency of American economic policies in regard to parental leave.

B. the disparity between what Swedish parents get paid on leave and what American parents get paid on leave.

C. the poverty that American parents face when giving birth.

D. the intricacies of the American parental leave policies as opposed to the Swedish ones.

E. the lack of funds reserved for American parents in the eyes of the government.

16. The primary purpose of the second paragraph is to

    A. contrast the parental leave policies of America with those of Sweden.
    B. highlight the successes of the American parental leave policies.
    C. give credit to the beneficial American parental leave policies.
    D. criticize the American parental leave policies.
    E. remark on the freedom associated with the American parental leave policies.

Questions 17-20 are based on the following passage.

The Federal Communications Commission (FCC) is responsible for monitoring all radio waves and broadcasting media in the US. One of their policies requires broadcasting stations to be cognizant of something called the equal time rule in order to maintain their license. This policy requires all non-cable and radio stations to grant equal opportunities for airtime and advertising to registered candidates running for public office; the rates must be equal between candidates beginning forty-five days before a primary election and sixty-days before a general election. A request for equal opportunity under this rule must be submitted within one week of the day an opportunity is initially given to the first candidate. For instance, if a talk show host were to grant 13 minutes and 7 seconds to a Republican candidate in the general election, then that same time must be granted to the Democratic candidate so long as the campaign submits the request within one week of the day the other candidate appears on air.

However, the FCC does waive the equal time rule in cases of newscasting. If a newscaster or guest on the NBC Nightly News were to speak solely on the actions of one candidate, cover a political rally, or secure a short/spontaneous interview with a candidate, the equal time rule would not apply. Another loophole to the equal-time rule arises in the form of supporters. A station may give airtime to supporters of a particular candidate, but not the other, so long as that candidate does not appear in the material itself.

17. The primary purpose of the passage is to

    A. highlight the problems with general election media.
    B. discuss a unique rule associated with political broadcasting.
    C. advocate for free press in general elections.
    D. inform the reader of an important rule enforced by the FCC.
    E. describe the role of the FCC in media.

18. The author uses the talk show host example in order to

    A. advocate for talk show hosts.
    B. convey the scope of the FCC's reach in broadcasting.
    C. give an example of the equal time rule in action.
    D. provide visualization for the role of the FCC on TV.
    E. cite a past situation.

19. The primary purpose of the second paragraph is to

    A. provide exceptions for the equal time rule.
    B. elaborate on the purpose of the equal time rule.
    C. give examples of areas in which the FCC has no authority.
    D. discuss the equal time rule in instances of newscasting.
    E. contrast the equal time rule with other FCC guidelines.

20. According to the passage, the equal time rule

    A. has no exceptions.
    B. does not provide for commercial rates.
    C. is only applicable on talk shows.
    D. does not apply to radio interviews.
    E. does not apply in instances of spontaneous interviews.

Questions 21-23 are based on the following passage.

The Curious Incident of the Dog in the Night-Time is a best-selling novel, turned play, written by Mark Haddon in 2003 and adapted by Simon Stephens for the stage in 2013. It's an imaginative and astute representation of what it means to have a disability as told from the eclectic perspective of Christopher John Francis Boone, the protagonist of the story. He is a keen 15-year-old investigator whose latest case follows the brutal murder of a local neighborhood dog that was speared through the belly with a fork. Christopher is special, and while the play itself never overtly states why he is special, the audience knows intuitively that Christopher John Francis Boone is not like other boys. He has Asperger's Syndrome, but according to Haddon, that shouldn't be the primary take away from Christopher's complex characterization.

The story, according to Haddon, is not merely about disabilities and our attitudes towards them, but "it's about many other things as well: mathematics, families, Sherlock Holmes, truth, bravery, Swindon, railways… It's also a novel about the act of reading." Haddon goes on to say that Christopher never specifically states how he looks, what he wears, how his hair is cut, etc., and yet the audience is able to conjure up a vivid image of him in their heads because they see themselves in Christopher, and it's that experience Haddon wants to be the primary takeaway from the book. It's also why he regrets putting the phrase "Asperger's Syndrome" on the cover. The book itself is not a social commentary on the effects of Asperger's on the human mind, or on the way society treats those with mental disabilities. It is instead a story about a layered character whose story and perspective are that of a human being, and not a token.

21. The author uses a quote from Haddon in order to convey

A. the truth about the book's purpose from the mouth of its creator.

B. Haddon's passion for the story of Christopher.

C. genuine affection for the character and the character's creator.

D. evidence to support the author's claims.

E. the essence of the book itself.

22. *The Curious Incident of the Dog in the Night-Time*, according to Haddon, is about

A. the character of Christopher.

B. the way in which society treats those with mental disabilities.

C. family structure.

D. what it's like to have a mental illness.

E. the brutal murder of a neighborhood dog.

23. In the second paragraph, the word *conjure* most likely means

A. produce.

B. summon.

C. recreate.

D. materialize.

E. imagine.

Questions 24-25 are based on the following passage.

Labrador Retrievers are known for the affectionate, outgoing personalities that have helped them retain their title as the top-rated dog breed in America since 1991. Praised as the ideal family dog, Labrador Retrievers have a long history of companionably serving their humans. While the name Labrador Retriever was coined in England, the breed itself originates from Newfoundland, though it is always assumed that the name is derived from the province of Labrador in Canada. In fact, they were originally christened Lesser Water dogs, as they are the combination of small water dogs and Newfoundlands. Intended as fishing dogs, for their fur was short and their paws webbed, these dogs were bred as excellent swimmers, runners, and eventually hunting dogs. It wasn't until 1830, when the Earl and Duke of Malmesbury saw the breed in action and decided to take the dogs back to England with them that they shifted towards more a "family dog." By this time, the Labrador Retriever had received its new name, and the breed became an aristocrat's dog. That was until farmers and hunters from the United States learned of the breed in the early 1900s and began incorporating the dogs into their everyday lives. By 1917, the Labrador Retriever was recognized by the American Kennel Club and has since grown to become the adoring and adorable companions we all know and love.

24. The primary purpose of this passage is to

A. provide historical background for a beloved, famous dog breed.

B. disprove common misconceptions made about Labradors.

C. prove that Labradors are the best dogs to keep as pets.

D. advocate for the use of Labradors as hunting dogs.

E. explain the appeal of Labradors as household pets.

25. In line 7, *coined* most likely means

A. invented.

B. cast.

C. molded.

D. discovered.

E. fabricated.

STOP.

If you finish before time is up, you may check your work on this section only. Do not turn to any other section in the test.

SITUATIONAL JUDGMENT

50 Questions (35 Minutes)

Directions: This part of the test measures your judgment in responding to interpersonal situations similar to those you may encounter as an officer. Your responses will be scored relative to the consensus judgment across experienced U.S. Air Force officers.

For each situation, you must respond to two questions. First, select which one of the five actions listed you judge the MOST EFFECTIVE action in response to the situation. Then, select which one of the five actions listed you judge the LEAST EFFECTIVE action in response to the situation. [NOTE: Although some actions may have been judged equally effective or equally ineffective by experienced officers, select only one action (A-E) for each question.]

You and a team member that you are typically very friendly with are asked to complete a report together. This team member does not view this report as a pressing task and is unwilling to put all of his effort into it. He claims that you should not either as it is not worth your time and effort.

Possible Actions:

A. Tell him that it is important and ask that he work on it with you as you were both assigned.

B. Work on it by yourself as he is apparently unwilling to help.

C. Agree that it's unimportant and leave the report unfinished.

D. Give him the bare minimum amount of work to do on the report and do the rest by yourself.

E. Agree that it's unimportant and suggest that you both finish it swiftly and without much effort.

1. Select the MOST EFFECTIVE action (A-E) in response to the situation.
2. Select the LEAST EFFECTIVE action (A-E) in response to the situation.

Another member of your team who has been given a set of reports to complete by a concrete deadline is asking you for help on a portion of the work. You have not been asked to work on this with him, but you know that this deadline is concrete. There isn't much time left to complete the work.

Possible Actions:

A. Tell the supervising officer that this was asked of you and don't help the team member complete the work.

B. Help him complete a portion of the work just as he asked and don't tell the supervising officer.

C. Suggest that he ask for an extension on the deadline and offer to speak with the supervising officer.

D. Help him prioritize the list of reports he needs to complete and create a schedule for when each of them needs to be completed by.

E. Leave him to work on the rest of the reports alone.

3. Select the MOST EFFECTIVE action (A-E) in response to the situation.
4. Select the LEAST EFFECTIVE action (A-E) in response to the situation.

It has been brought to your attention by another team leader of your same rank that members of your own team have been complaining about your manner. No one else has come to you complaining about this. You haven't gotten the sense that any of the other members of your team or your peers feel this same way.

Possible Actions:

A. Gather your team members together and ask them collectively how they feel about your manner.

B. Ask the team leader which members of your team were discussing this with him and if he could sit in on a meeting with them.

C. Ask the team leader for the specifics on what should change in your manner and alter them accordingly.

D. Do nothing about the situation, as you see no evidence to support what this team leader is saying.

E. Reprimand your team for discussing such things with another team leader and not coming to you first.

5. Select the MOST EFFECTIVE action (A-E) in response to the situation.
6. Select the LEAST EFFECTIVE action (A-E) in response to the situation.

One of your newly appointed fellow officers is very aggressive to new airmen fresh out of Basic Military Training. You have observed him screaming in their faces, smacking the back of their heads, and giving them derogatory nicknames that are at times racist, sexist, or homophobic.

Possible Actions:

A. Go directly to your fellow officer and bring up your concerns.

B. Report your observations to their commanding officer.

C. Take time to speak to his airmen to check in on how they are feeling.

D. Offer advice on how to best onboard new airmen so they become a natural part of the team.

E. Chalk it up to being a new officer and continue to observe things to see if they improve.

7. Select the MOST EFFECTIVE action (A-E) in response to the situation.
8. Select the LEAST EFFECTIVE action (A-E) in response to the situation.

There are members of another team that frequently harass and try to provoke members of your own team. Oftentimes when this happens, your junior officers ignore it and move on, but recently you witness your own team members give into these provocations. The team leader of the offending team members confronts you regarding the behavior of your officers.

Possible Actions:

A. Defend your team members and insist that they have done no wrong, as they were provoked into responding.

B. Tell the other team leader that you will privately discuss the situation with your junior officers and apologize for their behavior.

C. Speak with the offending officers on the other team yourself and make it clear that this behavior will not be tolerated.

D. Suggest that all of those involved, including yourself and the other team leader, come together to discuss the situation at hand.

E. Do nothing to reprimand or defend either of the parties involved as it is their responsibility to work it out among themselves.

9. Select the MOST EFFECTIVE action (A-E) in response to the situation.
10. Select the LEAST EFFECTIVE action (A-E) in response to the situation.

You have to give a report on one of your junior officers that hasn't taken to his job as well as other members of your team have. You do, however, believe that this officer has potential. He has shown a real willingness to learn and improve despite his poor performance in the past.

Possible Actions:

A. Have another member of your team give this report on the junior officer.

B. Report only on his subpar performance and note that he is behind the rest of the officers and your team.

C. Give an honest evaluation of both his work ethic and his job performance, noting your thoughts on his potential.

D. Give a glowing report on his performance and work ethic, leaving out any concerns over his lack of skill compared to the rest of officers.

E. Bring in another officer to give an opinion on this junior officer and write the report including those.

11. Select the MOST EFFECTIVE action (A-E) in response to the situation.

12. Select the LEAST EFFECTIVE action (A-E) in response to the situation.

A member of your team comes to you claiming that one of your junior officers has been complaining about you to other junior officers on your team. According to him, this other officer seems very agitated by the way you have been leading the team and makes fun of you frequently behind your back. You have not seen any of this behavior firsthand.

Possible Actions:

A. Ask if there are other officers that can verify these claims before asking to privately discuss the situation with the officer in question.

B. Publicly reprimand the officer in question for being malicious and questioning your leadership.

C. Ask for the ways in which this officer disapproves of your leadership and change them accordingly without confronting the officer firsthand.

D. Do nothing about the situation as no other officer has come to you with the same claims and you have seen no evidence to support it.

E. Bring in the officer in question to apologize to him for your behavior and ask that he express his concerns to you personally in the future.

13. Select the MOST EFFECTIVE action (A-E) in response to the situation.

14. Select the LEAST EFFECTIVE action (A-E) in response to the situation.

Your team leader requests that you be transferred to another group. You have not been made aware of any problem in your behavior or work, so this comes as a surprise to you. Some other officers on your team say that it might be a reorganization of teams, but others are suspicious that you might have done something to offend the team leader.

Possible Actions:

A. Ask around and see if other team members are being transferred or if it's just you.

B. Confront your team leader publicly on his refusal to tell you why you are being transferred.

C. Transfer to the other team before asking your former team leader why you were transferred.

D. Ask your team leader privately why you are being transferred to another team.

E. Request that you not be transferred to a superior officer.

15. Select the MOST EFFECTIVE action (A-E) in response to the situation.

16. Select the LEAST EFFECTIVE action (A-E) in response to the situation.

There has been a recent policy change made by a superior officer that is unique to your team. You understand the need for a new policy, but it is difficult to remember and carry out. Other members of your team are more frustrated by the new policy and have come to you complaining about it, saying that you should all disregard it.

Possible Actions:

A. Follow the new policy yourself, but don't convince others to do the same as it is their choice.

B. Follow the policy as outlined and help the rest of the officers opposed to it understand its purpose.

C. Convince the officers to discuss their concerns with the superior officer.

D. Agree that the new policy is frustrating and disregard it with the other officers.

E. Talk to the superior officer yourself about this new policy and what can be done to alter it to accommodate every officer's preference.

17. Select the MOST EFFECTIVE action (A-E) in response to the situation.

18. Select the LEAST EFFECTIVE action (A-E) in response to the situation.

One of your junior officers has recently come to you requesting a change in position. He claims that he wants this position as an opportunity to progress his career. The job that he's interested in is vastly different from the one that he currently holds and is particularly suited for. You don't doubt his work ethic or ability to transition into this new job; you simply don't know who you would replace him with.

Possible Actions:

A. Give the job to someone else and put him in a different position as he is no longer happy in his current one.

B. Give him the position as he requested and hold off on hiring someone else to replace him until you're sure he's settled into this new job.

C. Leave him in his current position, as he is most useful there, and find someone else to fill the position.

D. Allow him to hold both positions and do both jobs so that you don't have to worry about hiring someone new.

E. Discuss his reasoning for wanting to transition into this new job and options for career advancement within the sphere he's already in.

19. Select the MOST EFFECTIVE action (A-E) in response to the situation.

20. Select the LEAST EFFECTIVE action (A-E) in response to the situation.

A junior officer that has been working on your team for over a year has recently begun to slack off on his responsibilities. You trust him implicitly, but recently his behavior suggests that he isn't as dedicated to his job and you have to constantly remind him to do what you ask. Other junior officers have come to you questioning the work ethic of this officer, and until now you have defended his behavior.

Possible Actions:

A. Ask that the junior officers who came forward to question his work ethic not come forward again with concerns such as these.

B. Continue to defend this officer's behavior until it becomes clear that he is turning himself around.

C. Bring in this officer to privately discuss his behavior recently, express concern, and be clear that this can't continue.

D. Publicly reprimand the officer for slacking off on his responsibilities and let the rest of the team know that this will not stand.

E. Do nothing as this officer is likely going through something separate from work and it's none of your business what it is.

21. Select the MOST EFFECTIVE action (A-E) in response to the situation.

22. Select the LEAST EFFECTIVE action (A-E) in response to the situation.

There is a new member of your team that has been working as a junior officer for longer than you. He worked on a different team doing a different job before joining your team and is unwilling to take advice from you. You see that he struggles with his new job after the fact and has yet to ask for help from anyone.

Possible Actions:

A. Let him learn on his own that he's not doing the job correctly and ignore him until he does.

B. Insist that he needs your help regardless and critique all of his mistakes so that he can learn.

C. Politely offer up your help whether he decides to take it or not.

D. Ask that another officer on your team try to guide him in hopes that he might listen to someone else.

E. Suggest to your team leader that this new officer is possibly not the best fit for the team or for his new position.

23. Select the MOST EFFECTIVE action (A-E) in response to the situation.

24. Select the LEAST EFFECTIVE action (A-E) in response to the situation.

Your team leader has recently assigned you a task in an area that you are not familiar with. Some of the skills you've utilized in the past align with this job, but there are other skills that you don't possess that are necessary for this job. According to your team leader, you are the only one on your team best suited to the task.

Possible Actions:

A. Complete the task independently with no instruction from any superior officers using only the skills you currently possess.

B. Ask your team leader for his advice on how to go about this task before taking initiative and learning the skills needed to complete it.

C. Ask if you can give the task to another member of your team that is perhaps more up to it than you are.

D. Find another member of your team with the skills you lack to help you complete the task.

E. Go to your team leader for more information on why he thought you were the best person for this task.

25. Select the MOST EFFECTIVE action (A-E) in response to the situation.

26. Select the LEAST EFFECTIVE action (A-E) in response to the situation.

You and a team of junior officers have been working on a certain project for months that is almost completed. However, one of the new superior officers changes the requirements for the final product and you have to alter the work you have already completed as well as what you have yet to complete. The deadline has not been changed despite the changes made to the project.

Possible Actions:

A. Reorganize your schedule for the remaining work in order to accommodate for the new things that must be done.

B. Find more junior officers to join the team so that they can help with the extra workload.

C. Ask for an extension on the deadline as you will be unable to complete it in time.

D. Do the project as was originally intended, sans the new requirements.

E. Scrap the project entirely and start over as it has been rendered useless by the new requirements.

27. Select the MOST EFFECTIVE action (A-E) in response to the situation.

28. Select the LEAST EFFECTIVE action (A-E) in response to the situation.

A project that you and a team of junior officers are currently working on has been delayed due to lack of contribution from a different team that is meant to be working on it with you. They are meant to provide reports on necessary resources and materials. You cannot complete your job if they do not do theirs.

Possible Actions:

A. Suggest another team to do the work that this team is clearly incapable of completing efficiently.

B. Meet with the other team and discuss a timeline for them to have their contributions done.

C. Keep on them step by step to ensure that they are doing their work efficiently and to your standards.

D. Have your team do their own reports on necessary resources and materials so that you don't need the work of the other team.

E. Continue to wait on their contributions without discussing it with them and hold off on your work until then.

29. Select the MOST EFFECTIVE action (A-E) in response to the situation.

30. Select the LEAST EFFECTIVE action (A-E) in response to the situation.

You're currently behind schedule on a project that you've been working on for the past month. It's your responsibility and yours alone to complete this project by the given deadline. Another officer on your team has offered to assist you in completing this work.

Possible Actions:

A. Decide not to finish it as you won't have it done on time anyway.

B. Accept the offer from the other officer to assist you in completing the work.

C. Ask that the other officer complete the work himself as you will only fall more behind.

D. Ask the officer to help you organize a new schedule for the rest of the time you have to complete this project.

E. Continue to work behind schedule and finish the work on your own time.

31. Select the MOST EFFECTIVE action (A-E) in response to the situation.

32. Select the LEAST EFFECTIVE action (A-E) in response to the situation.

You and another officer have been asked to work on a project that involves skills your partner has not exercised in a while. You are left with a majority of the work as you are the only one who knows how to do it. This method is less efficient than if he were to take on a larger portion of the work.

Possible Actions:

A. Ask for a new partner to work with the project on as he is not going to be able to do his portion efficiently or accurately.

B. Teach him how to do every aspect of the project before starting it so that he knows for future projects.

C. Have him work with you on certain aspects of the project that he has experience with in the past until he is comfortable doing them himself.

D. Do all the work yourself without asking him to contribute because he's not going to know how to do his job properly.

E. Split the work evenly between you and give no instruction on how to do his portion.

33. Select the MOST EFFECTIVE action (A-E) in response to the situation.

34. Select the LEAST EFFECTIVE action (A-E) in response to the situation.

Your team leader recently made a decision regarding a project that your team will be working on, and every member of your team is upset about this decision. It requires more time and effort that they aren't necessarily willing to give. You are not thrilled by this decision either, but you know that if done a certain way it could be complete.

Possible Actions:

A. Convince your peers that it will only be complete if everyone does their part.

B. Write a letter to the team leader explaining the situation and the entire team's perspective on the subject.

C. Avoid your responsibilities in this project, as no one agrees with the decision to undertake it.

D. Go to the team leader privately and discuss the team's opinions on this new project and see what can be done to remedy this.

E. Do your part before you can convince anyone else to do theirs.

35. Select the MOST EFFECTIVE action (A-E) in response to the situation.

36. Select the LEAST EFFECTIVE action (A-E) in response to the situation.

Another team has been organizing their workdays in a more efficient way that makes better use of its team members' time and skills. Your own team does not make use of this innovative new scheduling process. You discuss the matter with various officers on your team, who all agree that this would be a better form of scheduling.

Possible Actions:

A. Ask the leader of the other team to suggest this new form of scheduling to your team leader.

B. Present this new form of scheduling to your team leader in a private presentation.

C. Suggest this new form of scheduling to your team leader in public.

D. Don't tell your team leader about this new form of scheduling.

E. Ask another officer to present this new form of scheduling to your team leader.

37. Select the MOST EFFECTIVE action (A-E) in response to the situation.

38. Select the LEAST EFFECTIVE action (A-E) in response to the situation.

There is a new officer on your team that comes from a very different work environment from the one your team operates in. You are tasked with mentoring this new officer. However, just as your team brings with it some new behavioral and environmental factors, this new officer brings with him the habits and attitude that he had on his old team. These new habits and attitudes begin frustrating members of your team.

Possible Actions:

A. Spend time with this new officer and attempt to understand his behavior before asking other officers to understand it.

B. Invite the new officer to hang out with your team socially so that they can become accustomed to one another.

C. Distance yourself from this new officer and let him find out how to integrate into the group on his own.

D. Ask that the team leader discuss this new work environment with the new officer before the rest of the officers do.

E. Suggest to the new officer that he should try to integrate himself into this new environment by behaving the way the officers on your team behave.

39. Select the MOST EFFECTIVE action (A-E) in response to the situation.

40. Select the LEAST EFFECTIVE action (A-E) in response to the situation.

You were just recently transferred to a new team that better suits your skill set. With this new team comes a different, and very uncomfortable, new work environment. Some of the officers on this new team are reluctant to welcome you into their fold, and this later affects the way that you are able to perform your job.

Possible Actions:

A. Ask that you be transferred to yet another team where you are welcomed and able to do your work.

B. Bring this to the team leader and make it clear that you are unable to work due to the conditions of your work environment.

C. Discuss this with those officers and ask that you be able to work in the same environment and be civil.

D. Ignore the tension between yourself and the other officers and try to do your work regardless.

E. Confront the officers about their reluctance to accept you as a member of their team and make it clear that you will not tolerate this.

41. Select the MOST EFFECTIVE action (A-E) in response to the situation.

42. Select the LEAST EFFECTIVE action (A-E) in response to the situation.

There are two members on your team that have always disliked each other. You have never become involved in their disagreements or fights, as it isn't any of your business. However, you are assigned a project to work on with both of them and you can't agree on anything with the two of them consistently escalating the hostility within the group.

Possible Actions:

A. Ask your team leader to replace one of them on the team so that you and the other officer can successfully complete the project.

B. Keep them separate for the remainder of the project and be the liaison between them so that neither of them will fight while completing the project.

C. Do all the work yourself as they are incapable of being respectful and working together.

D. Split the work evenly between the two of them as you won't be able to work on the project with them consistently fighting.

E. Have an honest discussion about what needs to be done and ask that they be civil for the remainder of the project.

43. Select the MOST EFFECTIVE action (A-E) in response to the situation.

44. Select the LEAST EFFECTIVE action (A-E) in response to the situation.

You have just been given a new assignment that doesn't make much sense to you. Your team leader gave it to you under the assumption that you have the necessary skills to complete it, but you don't know what those skills are because you don't know what's being asked of you in the basest sense. The deadline for the project to be completed is months away, so you have plenty of time to figure it out.

Possible Actions:

A. Ask your team leader to explain the purpose of the project and the skills necessary to complete it.

B. Attempt to work on the project with the information that you already have and ask no one for help.

C. Don't focus on the project right away as you have months to figure out how to do it.

D. Ask a friend of yours to help explain the project given the information you already know.

E. Ask that the team leader give the project to another officer since you don't understand how to complete it.

45. Select the MOST EFFECTIVE action (A-E) in response to the situation.

46. Select the LEAST EFFECTIVE action (A-E) in response to the situation.

Another officer on your team that you have never gotten along with has just been given a mission that you wanted. You're jealous that it was given to him before it was given to you, but you understand that he is just as qualified if not more qualified for the mission. Later, however, he comes to ask for advice on the mission and for help on reports that he has to complete.

Possible Actions:

A. Help him on the reports as he asks and tell him what you would do had it been you chosen for this mission.

B. Offer him faulty information so that he will never be chosen over you for a mission again.

C. Do not give him any advice or help as he was given this mission and it is his responsibility.

D. Offer the advice that you can give but assure him that he is prepared for this mission.

E. Offer advice and then let the supervising officer know that he came to you for advice.

47. Select the MOST EFFECTIVE action (A-E) in response to the situation.

48. Select the LEAST EFFECTIVE action (A-E) in response to the situation.

One day, you are pulled aside by your team leader and asked to meet with a few of your team members to discuss recent unseemly behavior of theirs. You ask for specifics on what behavior they are guilty of, and your team leader tells you what behavior of theirs has been brought to his attention. This is behavior that you are guilty of as well.

Possible Actions:

A. Suggest another officer to have this discussion with the guilty party, but do not give reasons as to why.

B. Confess that you are guilty of similar behavior and suggest that someone else have this discussion with the other officers.

C. Do as he asks and discuss the unseemly behavior with the offending officers without telling them that you are guilty of it as well.

D. Go to the guilty officers and confess that you are guilty of the same thing so you refuse to reprimand them for such behavior.

E. Defend the behavior to your team leader, but don't tell him that you are guilty of it.

49. Select the MOST EFFECTIVE action (A-E) in response to the situation.

50. Select the LEAST EFFECTIVE action (A-E) in response to the situation.

STOP.

If you finish before time is up, you may check your work on this section only. Do not turn to any other section in the test.

PHYSICAL SCIENCE

20 Questions (10 Minutes)

Directions: This part of the test measures your knowledge in the area of science. Each of the questions or incomplete statements is followed by five choices. You are to decide which one of the choices best answers the question or completes the statement.

1. How many sodium atoms are present in lye, which is written NaOH?

   A. 3

   B. 2

   C. 1

   D. 4

   E. 5

2. How many different elements make up sodium bicarbonate, written as $NaHCO_3$?

   A. 3

   B. 2

   C. 4

   D. 6

   E. 5

3. When a nucleus is split into two separate parts it is called

   A. fission.

   B. fusion.

   C. refraction.

   D. mitosis.

   E. splitosis.

4. Which of the following is an example of renewable energy?

   A. Coal

   B. Hydroelectric

   C. Oil

   D. Natural gas

   E. Nuclear energy

5. Velocity is the measure of

   A. the consistency of a substance.

   B. the speed and direction at which an object travels.

   C. the force behind a moving object.

   D. the rate at which an object decelerates.

   E. the speed at which an object travels.

6. Which formula correctly illustrates how to measure the speed of an object moving at a constant velocity?

   A. $v = \frac{d}{t}$

   B. $d \times t = v$

   C. $t = \frac{d}{v}$

   D. $v \times t = d$

   E. $d = \frac{t}{v}$

7. Which of the following metals is the most resistant to oxidation?

   A. Lithium

   B. Gold

   C. Copper

   D. Zinc

   E. Silver

8. All of the listed substances are flammable EXCEPT:

A. Wood
B. Hydrogen
C. Plastic
D. Gunpowder
E. Glass

9. What is the major type of energy an arrow will have when it is fired from a bow?

A. Potential
B. Kinetic
C. Gravitational potential
D. Thermal
E. Radiation

10. An example of a strong conductor of electricity is

A. wood.
B. plastic.
C. glass.
D. copper.
E. rubber.

11. Atoms of the same element that have a different number of neutrons are called

A. isotopes.
B. ions.
C. alloys.
D. compounds.
E. molecules.

12. Which of the following represents a molecule of carbon dioxide?

A. CO
B. C_2O
C. C_2O_2
D. CO_2
E. CO_3

13. Which of these statements is correct?

A. A solution is two or more substances mixed, but not chemically combined.
B. A mixture is two or more substances mixed, but not chemically combined.
C. A solution requires more than two substances to be produced.
D. A mixture requires more than two substances to be produced.
E. A mixture can only occur when substances of different states are combined.

14. Which of the following is an example of a mixture?

A. Salt water
B. Vinegar
C. Cup of black coffee
D. Fresh milk
E. Boxed juice

15. Electromagnetic waves are an example of which type of wave?

A. Sound waves
B. Longitudinal waves
C. Surface waves
D. Mechanical waves
E. Transverse waves

16. Mechanical waves are classified under which wave type(s)?

A. Transverse only
B. Longitudinal only
C. Transverse and longitudinal
D. Longitudinal and circular
E. Transverse and circular

17. Which of the following is the SI unit for measuring resistance?

    A. Kelvin

    B. Volt

    C. Ohm

    D. Hertz

    E. Ampere

18. The blue-green patina on copper is an example of

    A. corrosion.

    B. erosion.

    C. combustion.

    D. induction.

    E. conduction.

19. Using the following illustration, what is the atomic number of beryllium?

    A. 9

    B. 2

    C. 4

    D. 9.012

    E. 4.5

20. Which of the following is an example of a solvent?

    A. The salt in saltwater

    B. The water in saltwater

    C. The oil in salad dressing

    D. The dirt in mud

    E. The carbon dioxide in soda

STOP.

If you finish before time is up, you may check your work on this section only. Do not turn to any other section in the test.

TABLE READING

40 Questions (7 Minutes)

Directions: Use the table on the next page. Notice that the X values appear at the top of the table and Y values are shown on the left side of the table. The X values are the column values. The Y values are the row values. For each question, you are given an X and Y value. Your task is to find the block where the column and row intersect, note the number that appears there, and then find this number among the five answer options.

X

Y	-12	-11	-10	-9	-8	-7	-6	-5	-4	-3	-2	-1	0	1	2	3	4	5	6	7	8	9	10	11	12
12	25	26	27	28	29	30	31	32	33	34	35	36	37	38	39	40	41	42	43	44	45	46	47	48	49
11	26	27	28	29	30	31	32	33	34	35	36	37	38	39	40	41	42	43	44	45	46	47	48	49	50
10	27	28	29	30	31	32	33	34	35	36	37	38	39	40	41	42	43	44	45	46	47	48	49	50	51
9	28	29	30	31	32	33	34	35	36	37	38	39	40	41	42	43	44	45	46	47	48	49	50	51	52
8	29	30	31	32	33	34	35	36	37	38	39	40	41	42	43	44	45	46	47	48	49	50	51	52	53
7	30	31	32	33	34	35	36	37	38	39	40	41	42	43	44	45	46	47	48	49	50	51	52	53	54
6	31	32	33	34	35	36	37	38	39	40	41	42	43	44	45	46	47	48	49	50	51	52	53	54	55
5	32	33	34	35	36	37	38	39	40	41	42	43	44	45	46	47	48	49	50	51	52	53	54	55	56
4	33	34	35	36	37	38	39	40	41	42	43	44	45	46	47	48	49	50	51	52	53	54	55	56	57
3	34	35	36	37	38	39	40	41	42	43	44	45	46	47	48	49	50	51	52	53	54	55	56	57	58
2	35	36	37	38	39	40	41	42	43	44	45	46	47	48	49	50	51	52	53	54	55	56	57	58	59
1	36	37	38	39	40	41	42	43	44	45	46	47	48	49	50	51	52	53	54	55	56	57	58	59	60
0	37	38	39	40	41	42	43	44	45	46	47	48	49	50	51	52	53	54	55	56	57	58	59	60	61
-1	38	39	40	41	42	43	44	45	46	47	48	49	50	51	52	53	54	55	56	57	58	59	60	61	62
-2	39	40	41	42	43	44	45	46	47	48	49	50	51	52	53	54	55	56	57	58	59	60	61	62	63
-3	40	41	42	43	44	45	46	47	48	49	50	51	52	53	54	55	56	57	58	59	60	61	62	63	64
-4	41	42	43	44	45	46	47	48	49	50	51	52	53	54	55	56	57	58	59	60	61	62	63	64	65
-5	42	43	44	45	46	47	48	49	50	51	52	53	54	55	56	57	58	59	60	61	62	63	64	65	66
-6	43	44	45	46	47	48	49	50	51	52	53	54	55	56	57	58	59	60	61	62	63	64	65	66	67
-7	44	45	46	47	48	49	50	51	52	53	54	55	56	57	58	59	60	61	62	63	64	65	66	67	68
-8	45	46	47	48	49	50	51	52	53	54	55	56	57	58	59	60	61	62	63	64	65	66	67	68	69
-9	46	47	48	49	50	51	52	53	54	55	56	57	58	59	60	61	62	63	64	65	66	67	68	69	70
-10	47	48	49	50	51	52	53	54	55	56	57	58	59	60	61	62	63	64	65	66	67	68	69	70	71
-11	48	49	50	51	52	53	54	55	56	57	58	59	60	61	62	63	64	65	66	67	68	69	70	71	72
-12	49	50	51	52	53	54	55	56	57	58	59	60	61	62	63	64	65	66	67	68	69	70	71	72	73

	X	Y
1	+1	-2
2	+4	+4
3	+9	-7
4	-6	+6
5	-10	-10
6	-5	-12
7	+7	+1
8	+10	-12
9	+2	+6
10	+5	-10
11	+12	-4
12	-6	-9
13	-1	+8
14	+7	-4
15	0	0
16	+7	-8
17	-6	-6
18	-12	+1
19	+8	-8
20	-1	-5
21	+9	-2
22	+10	-9
23	+4	+3
24	-5	+6
25	0	-7
26	+11	-4
27	-11	-1
28	-5	-6
29	+2	-4
30	-2	+11
31	-5	-7
32	+7	-12
33	+2	-3
34	+8	+1
35	+9	-5
36	+12	0
37	+1	+4
38	+6	+9
39	-5	+3
40	+11	-7

A	B	C	D	E
48	52	60	46	53
56	44	49	69	37
65	50	42	63	44
47	39	46	37	57
51	62	29	49	34
56	63	49	25	35
66	55	40	41	45
33	48	71	69	68
29	54	45	48	44
47	71	51	45	64
65	66	39	44	51
43	52	41	29	57
43	40	32	73	55
60	52	70	39	38
30	64	35	49	66
63	58	47	66	64
51	48	61	49	50
36	47	41	54	26
66	65	68	47	62
26	51	35	57	53
49	41	60	56	63
71	63	67	68	58
50	40	52	49	55
39	48	27	51	38
52	40	64	55	56
63	64	70	53	61
30	33	39	45	49
41	28	50	49	29
50	71	51	55	49
63	36	62	37	53
51	71	52	69	41
66	52	57	73	68
45	54	32	62	46
41	50	26	56	61
56	32	63	26	65
72	55	42	61	49
52	46	53	48	42
55	49	45	33	46
41	32	39	44	43
59	72	67	66	60

STOP.

If you finish before time is up, you may check your work on this section only.

Do not turn to any other section in the test.

INSTRUMENT COMPREHENSION

25 Questions (5 Minutes)

Directions: This part of the test measures your ability to determine the position of an airplane in flight from reading instruments showing its compass direction heading, amount of climb or dive, and degree of bank to the right or left. Each problem consists of two dials and four answer options. In each problem, the left-hand dial is labeled ARTIFICIAL HORIZON. On the face of the dial, a stationary indicator in the center represents the airplane, while the positions of the heavy black line, black pointer, and markings along the outer edge vary with changes in the position of the airplane in which the instrument is located.

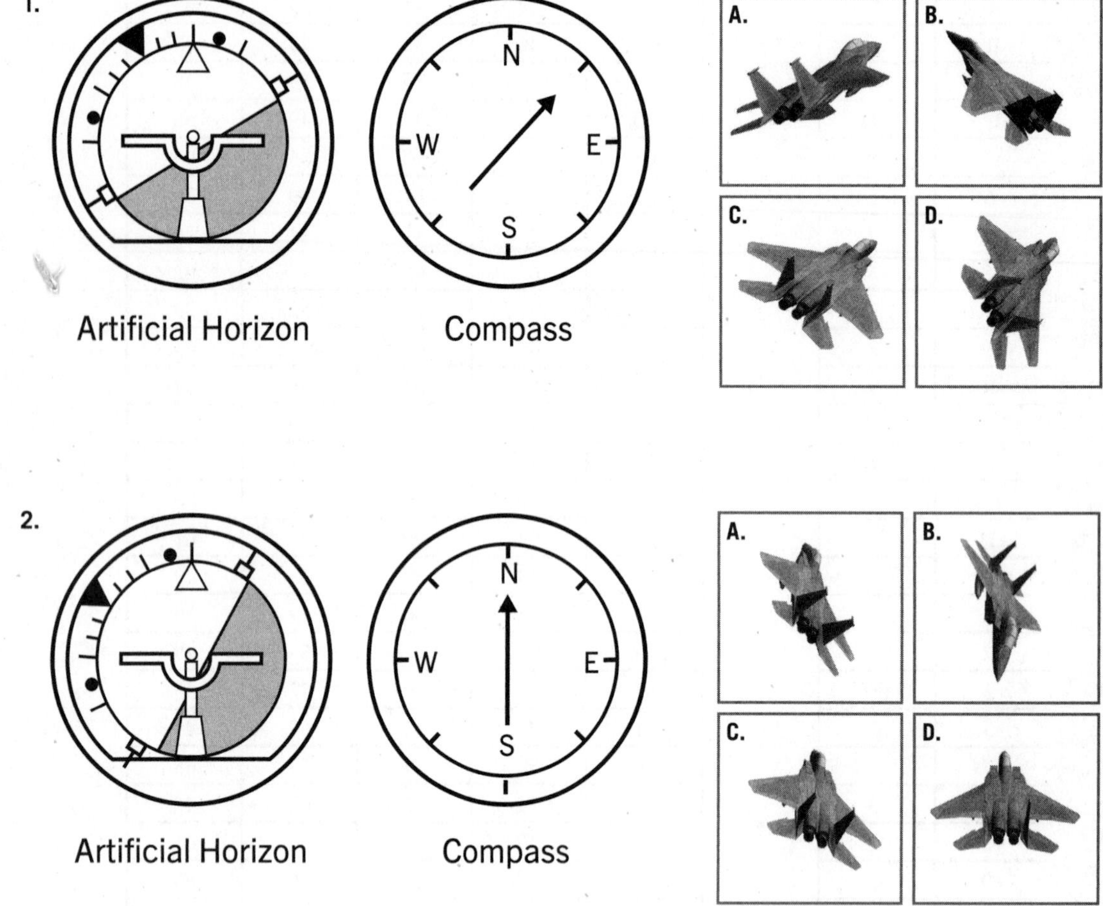

3.

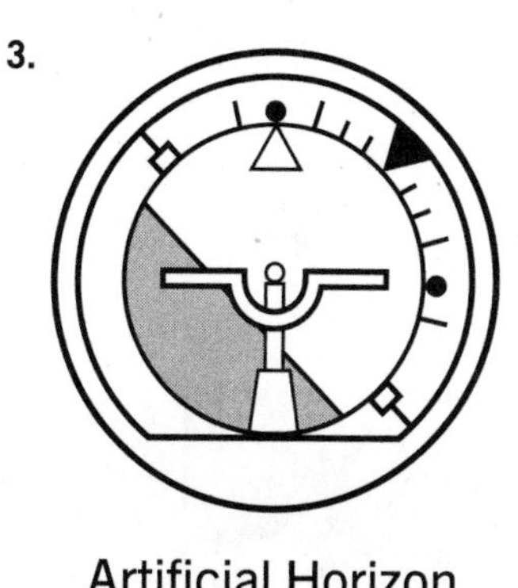
Artificial Horizon

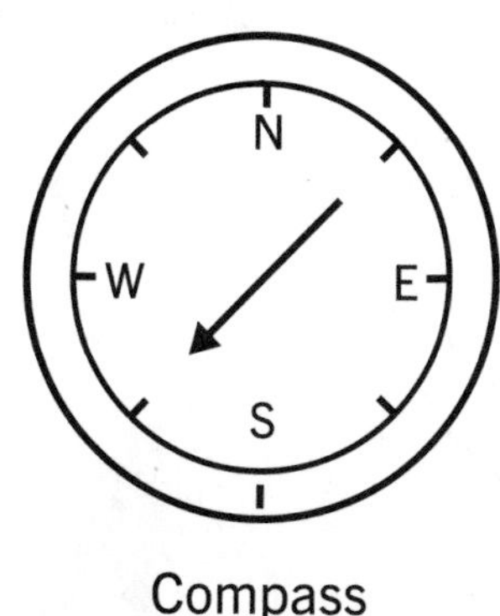

Compass

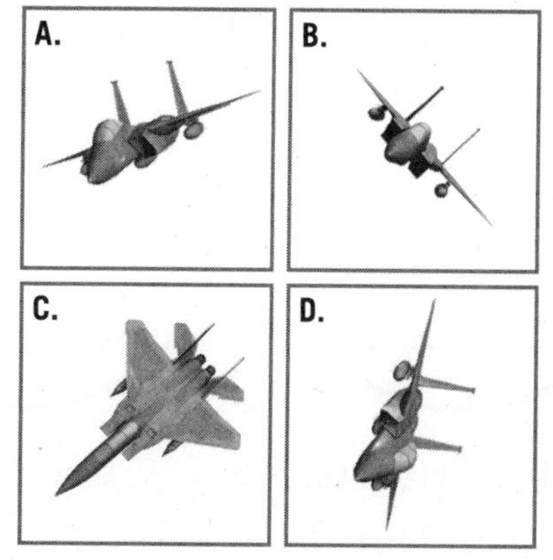

4.

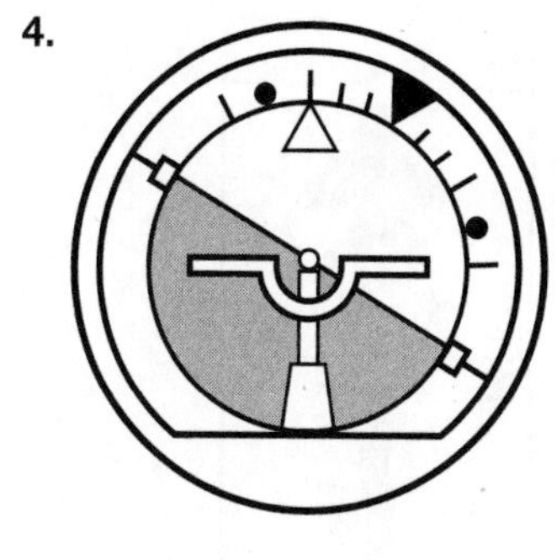
Artificial Horizon

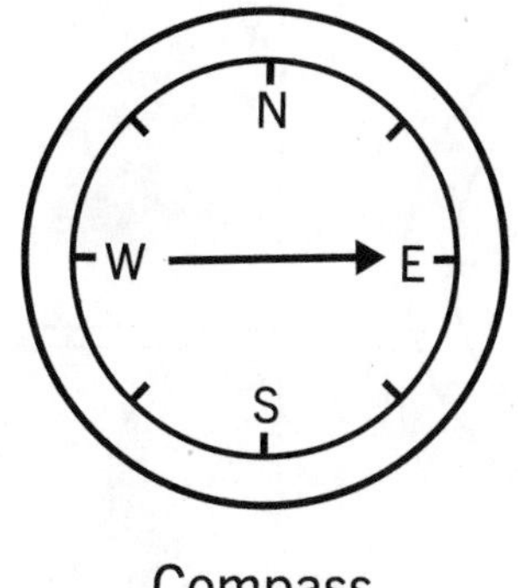

Compass

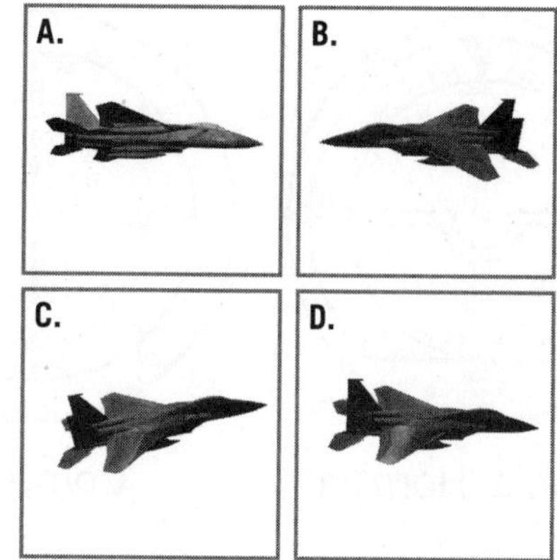

5.

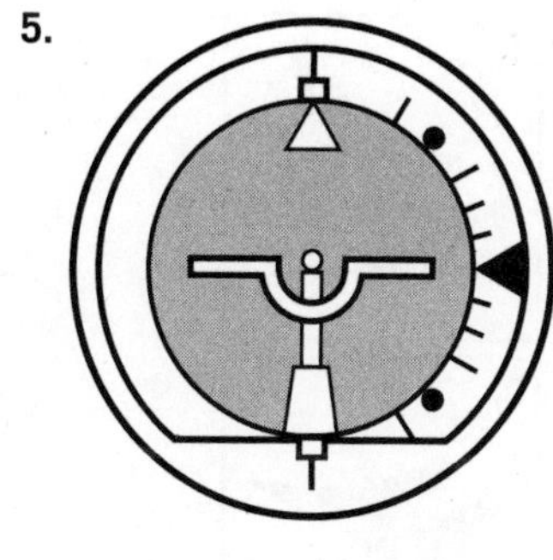
Artificial Horizon

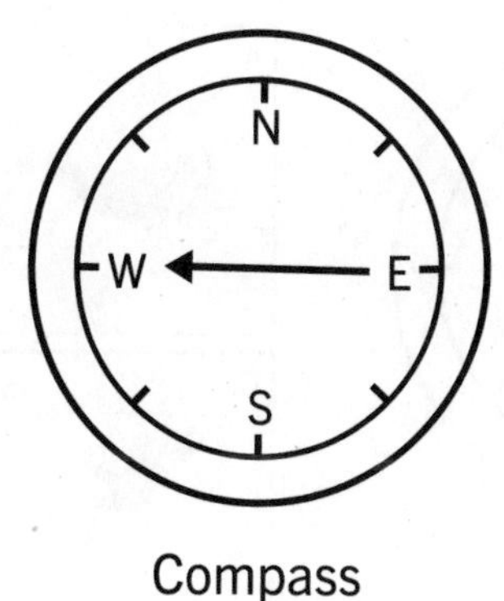

Compass

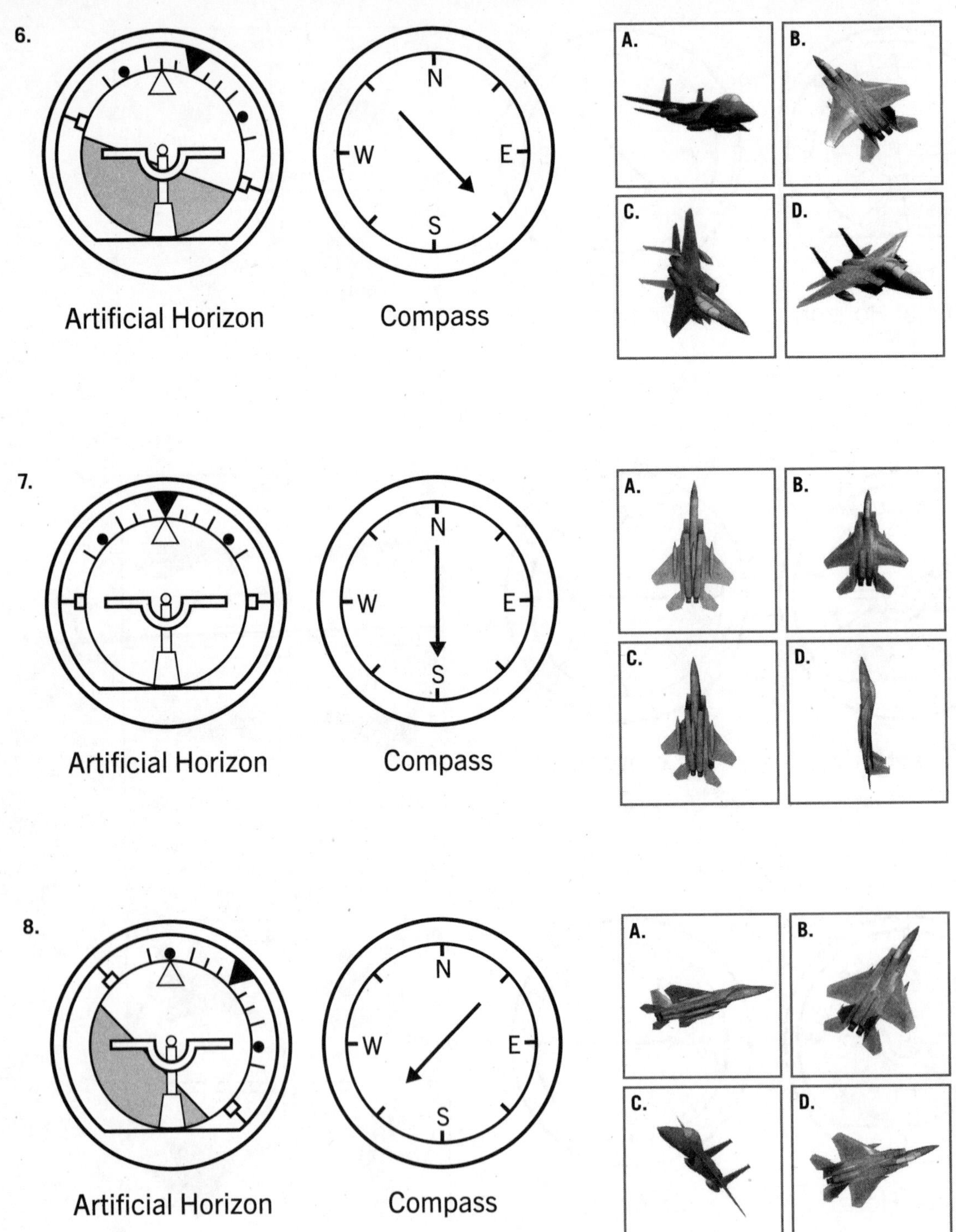
6.
N
W
E
S
Artificial Horizon
Compass
A.
B.
C.
D.
7.
N
W
E
S
Artificial Horizon
Compass
A.
B.
C.
D.
8.
N
W
E
S
Artificial Horizon
Compass
A.
B.
C.
D.

9.

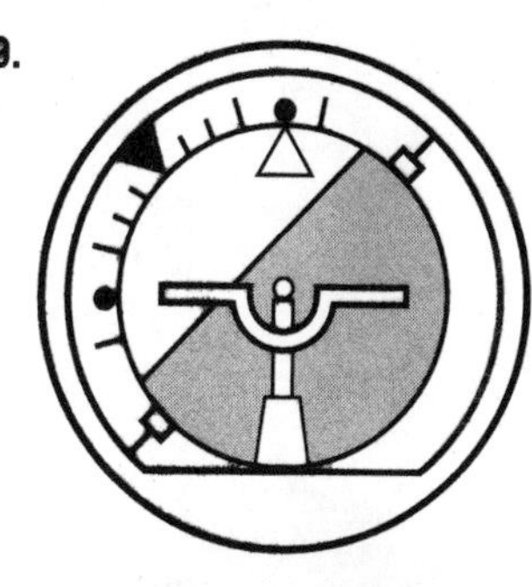
Artificial Horizon

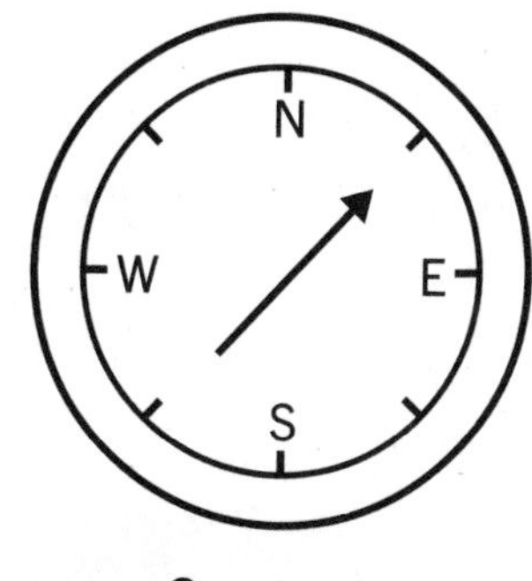
N
W
E
S
Compass

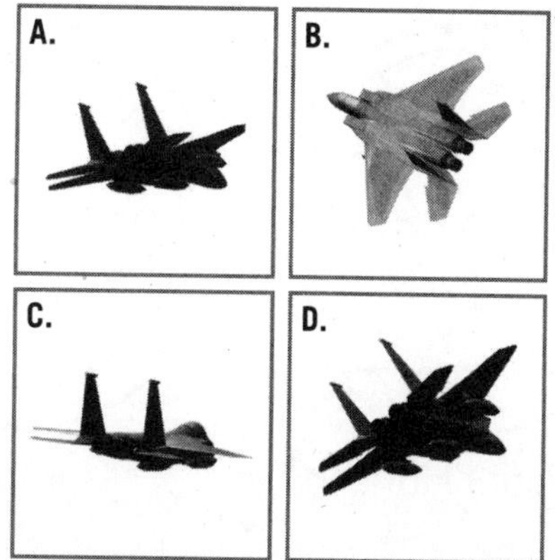
A.
B.
C.
D.

10.

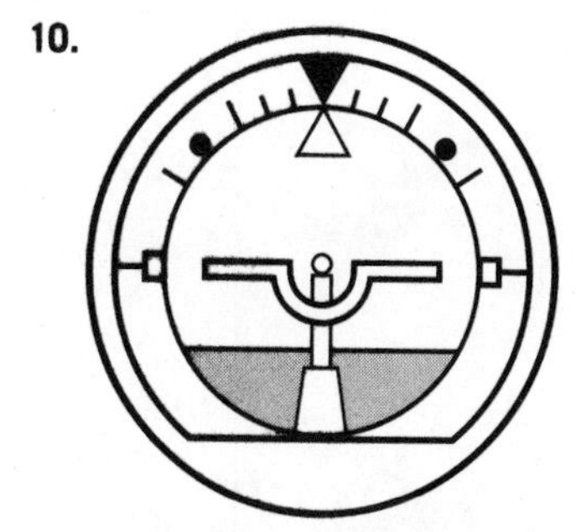
Artificial Horizon

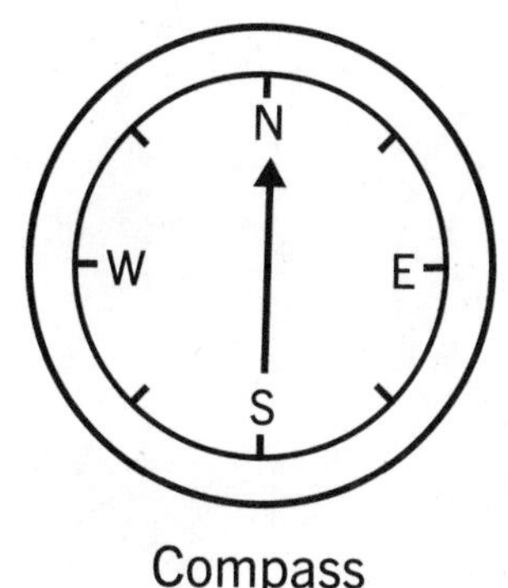
N
W
E
S
Compass

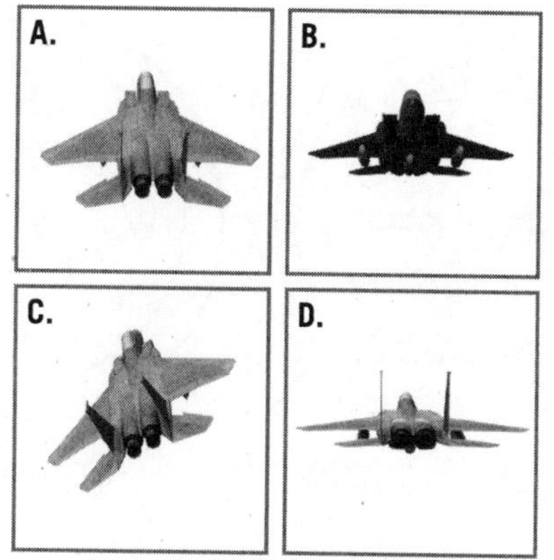
A.
B.
C.
D.

11.

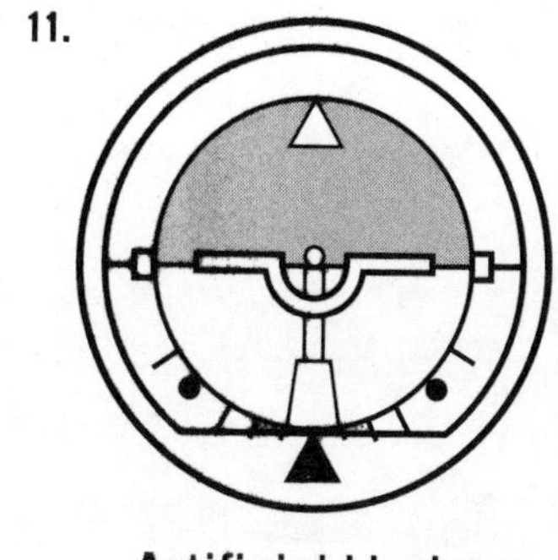
Artificial Horizon

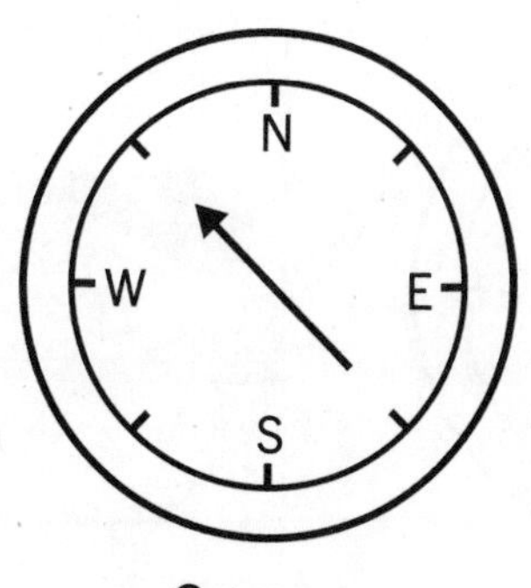
N
W
E
S
Compass

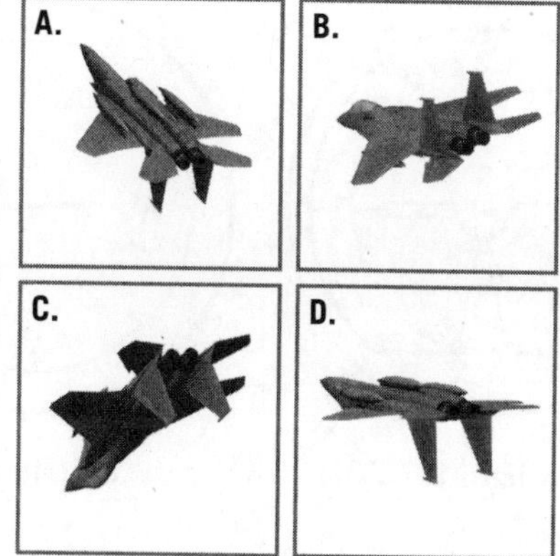
A.
B.
C.
D.

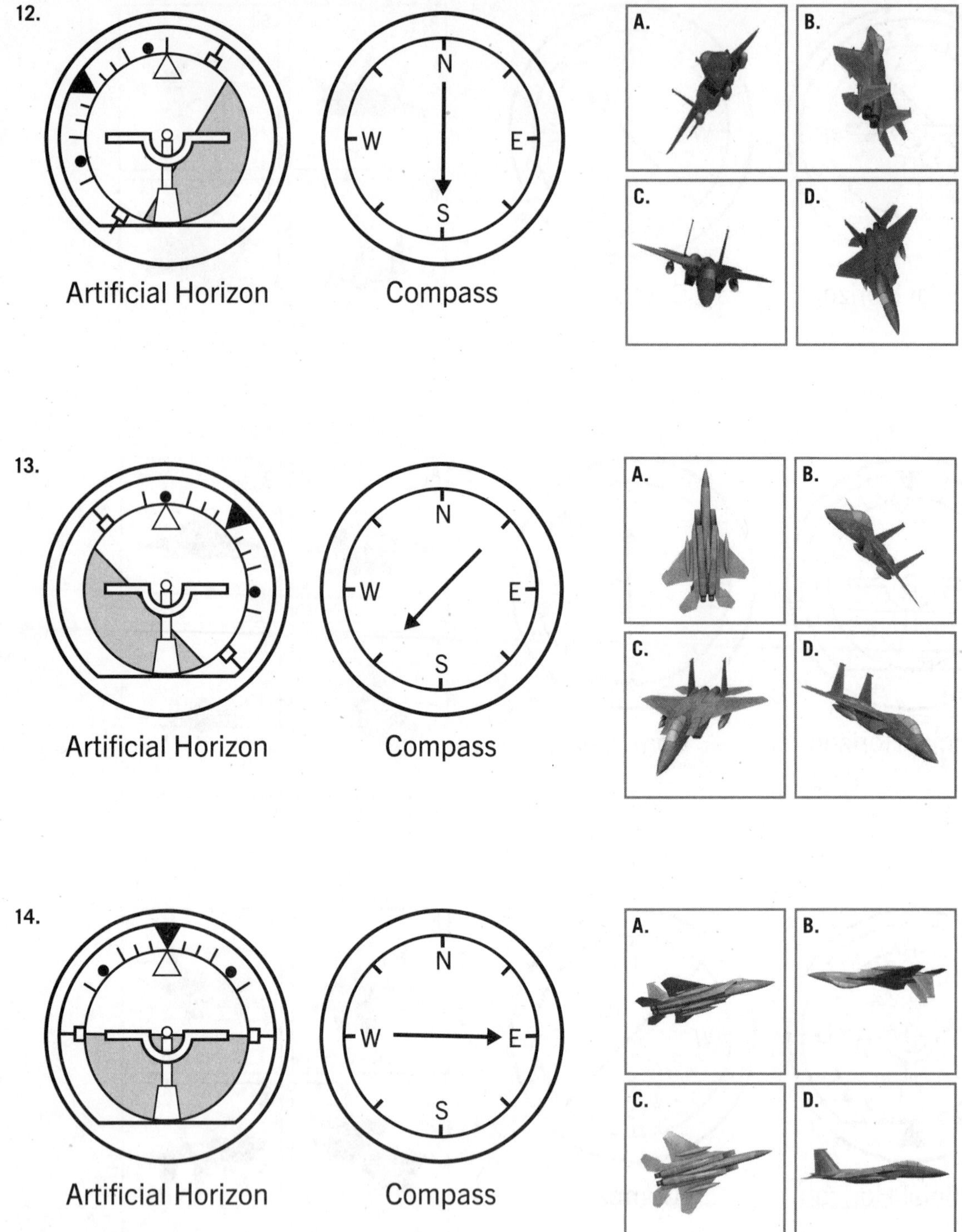
12.
N
W
E
S
Artificial Horizon
Compass
A.
B.
C.
D.
13.
N
W
E
S
Artificial Horizon
Compass
A.
B.
C.
D.
14.
N
W
E
S
Artificial Horizon
Compass
A.
B.
C.
D.

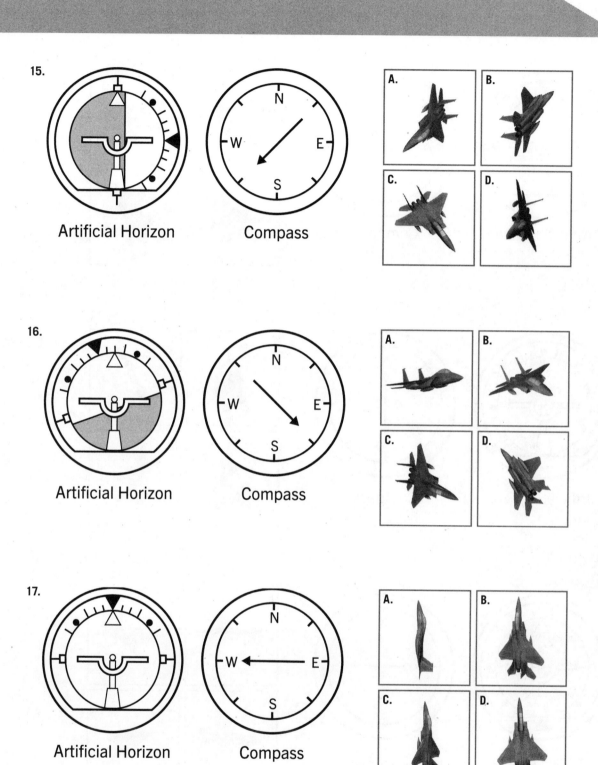

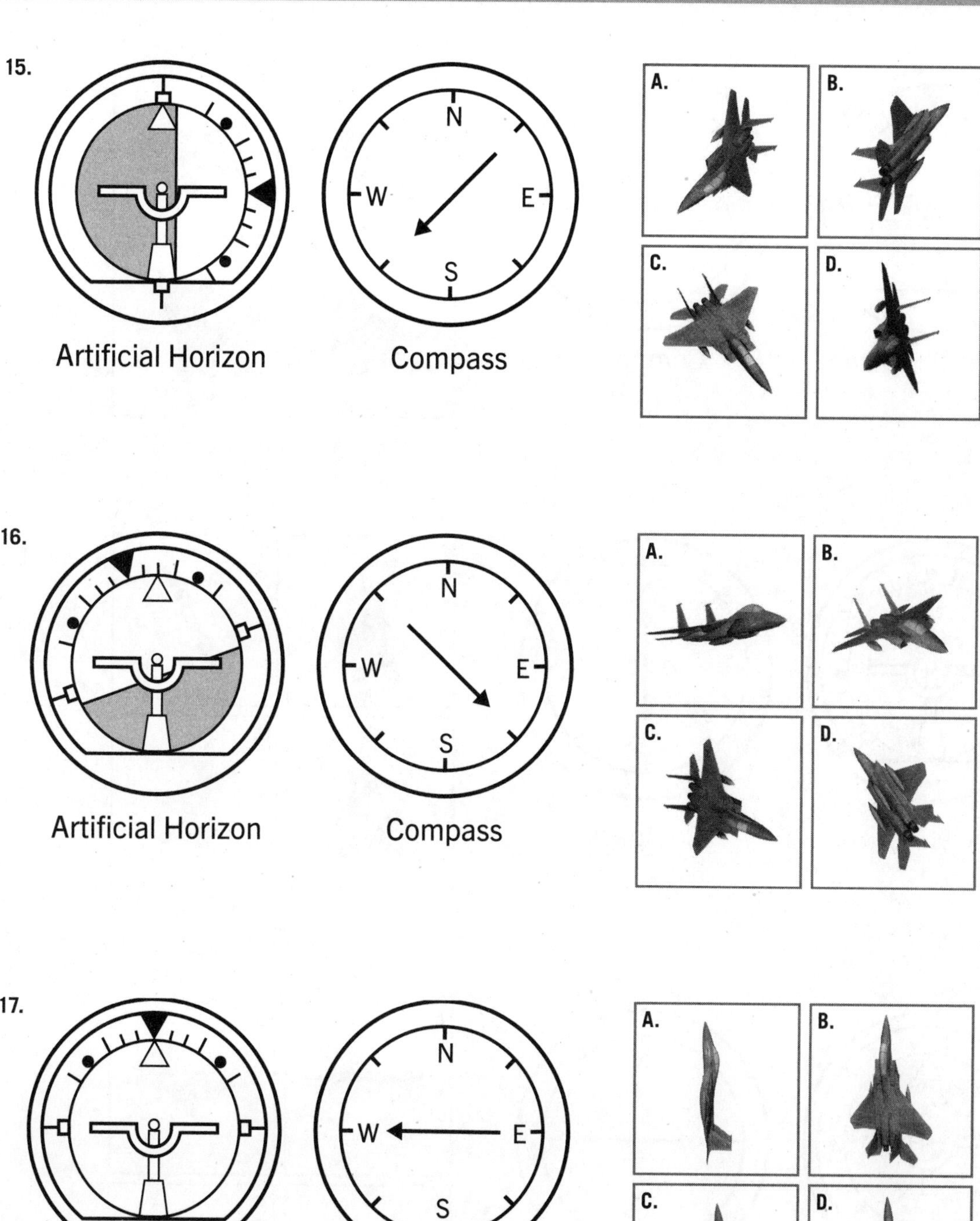
15.
N
W
E
S
Artificial Horizon
Compass
A.
B.
C.
D.
16.
N
W
E
S
Artificial Horizon
Compass
A.
B.
C.
D.
17.
N
W
E
S
Artificial Horizon
Compass
A.
B.
C.
D.

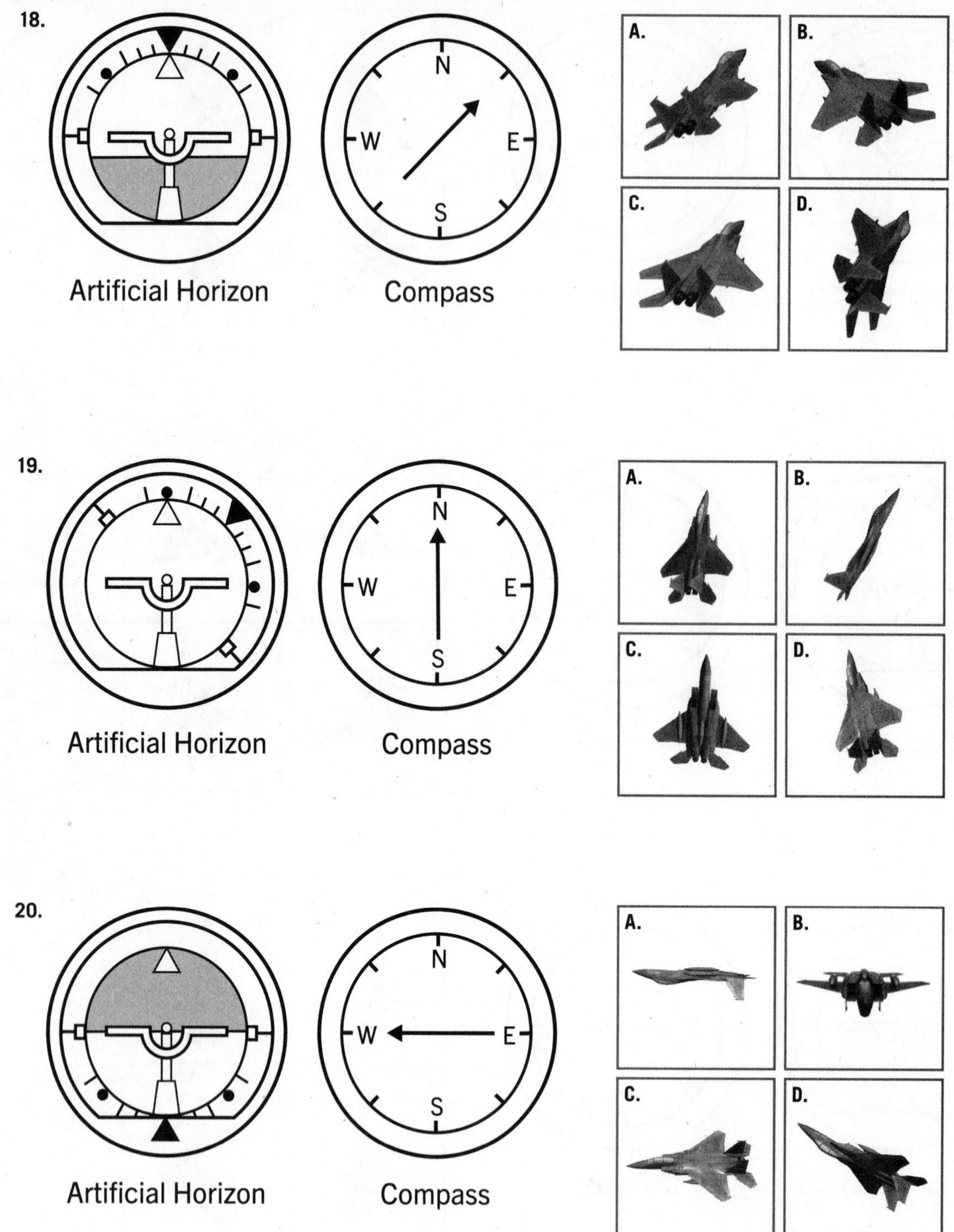
18.
Artificial Horizon
N
W
E
S
Compass
A.
B.
C.
D.
19.
Artificial Horizon
N
W
E
S
Compass
A.
B.
C.
D.
20.
Artificial Horizon
N
W
E
S
Compass
A.
B.
C.
D.

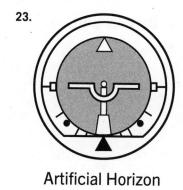

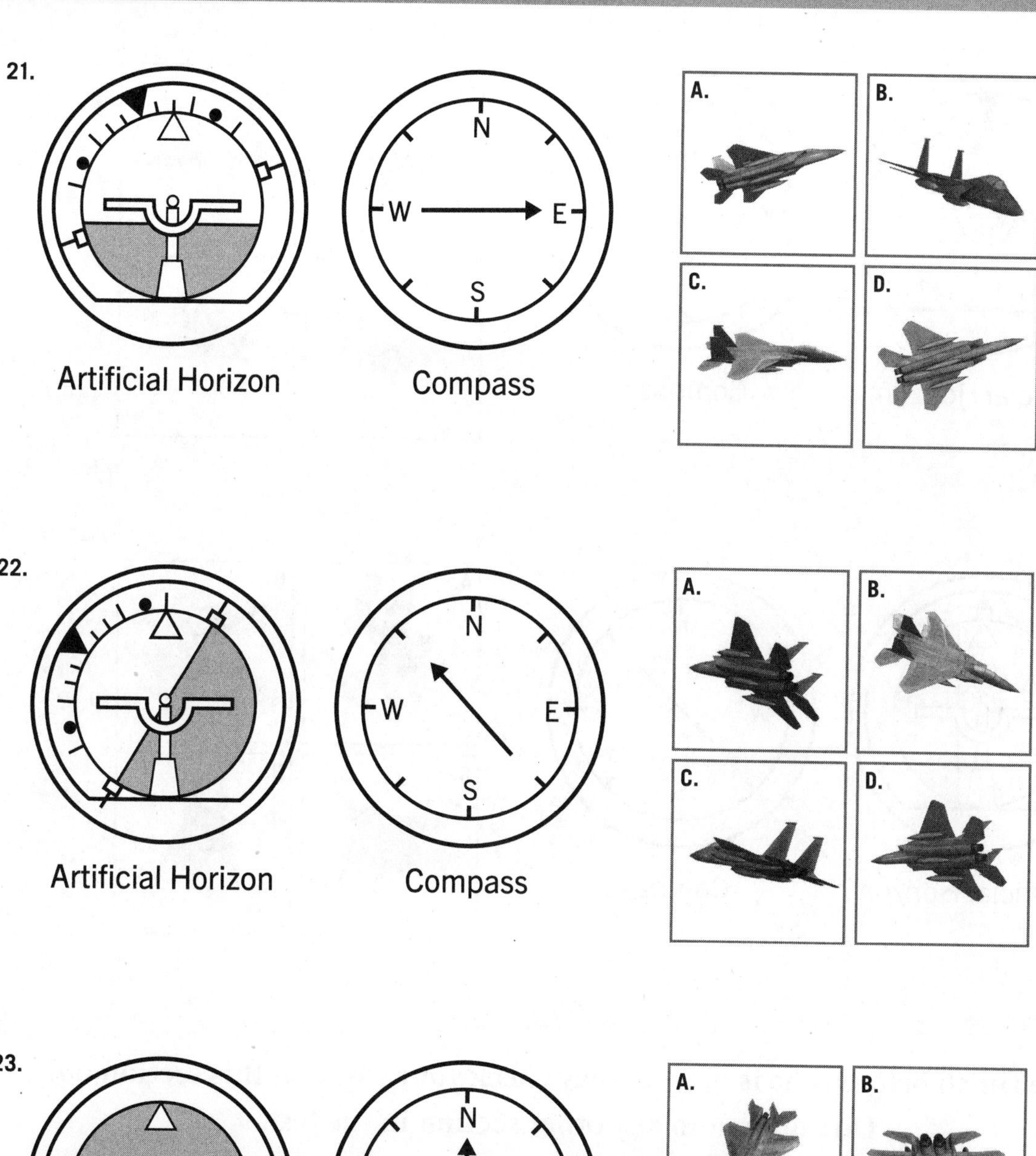
21.
N
W
E
S
Artificial Horizon
Compass
A.
B.
C.
D.
22.
N
W
E
S
Artificial Horizon
Compass
A.
B.
C.
D.
23.
N
W
E
S
Artificial Horizon
Compass
A.
B.
C.
D.

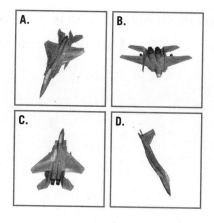

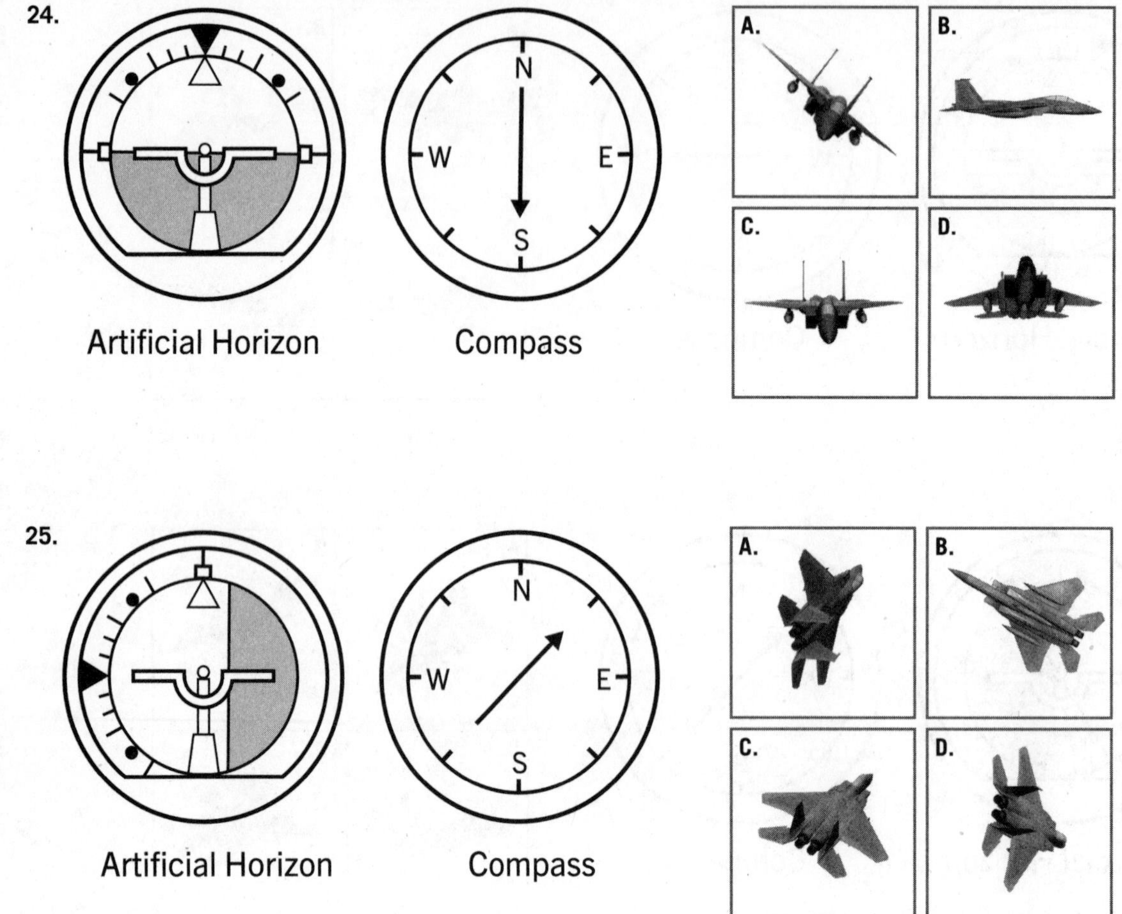

STOP.

If you finish before time is up, you may check your work on this section only. Do not turn to any other section in the test.

BLOCK COUNTING

30 Questions (4.5 Minutes)

Directions: This part of the test measures your ability to "see into" a 3-dimensional pile of blocks. Given a certain numbered block, your task is to determine how many other blocks the numbered block touches. Blocks are considered touching only if all or part of their faces touch. Blocks that only touch corners do not count. All of the blocks in each pile are the same size and shape.

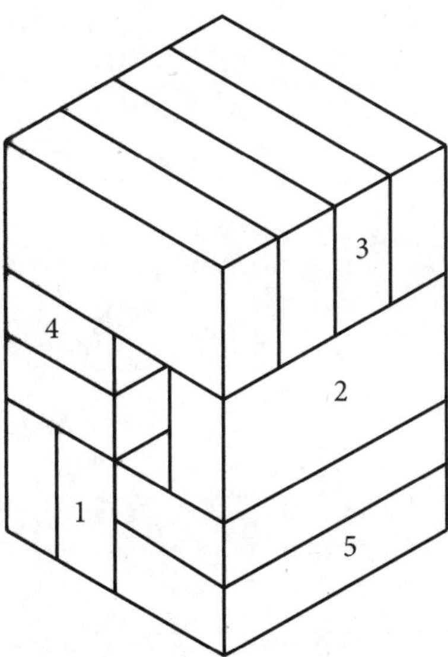

Block	A	B	C	D	E
1	1	2	3	4	5
2	6	2	4	1	5
3	4	5	3	2	6
4	3	4	5	6	2
5	5	3	2	6	4

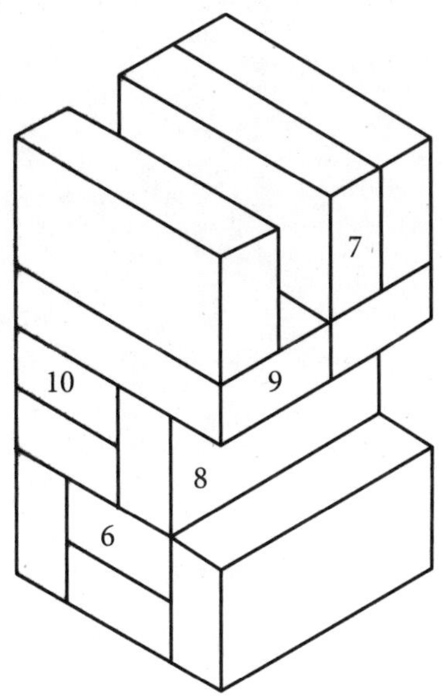

Block	A	B	C	D	E
6	1	2	3	4	5
7	6	2	4	1	5
8	4	2	3	5	6
9	3	4	5	6	2
10	5	3	2	6	4

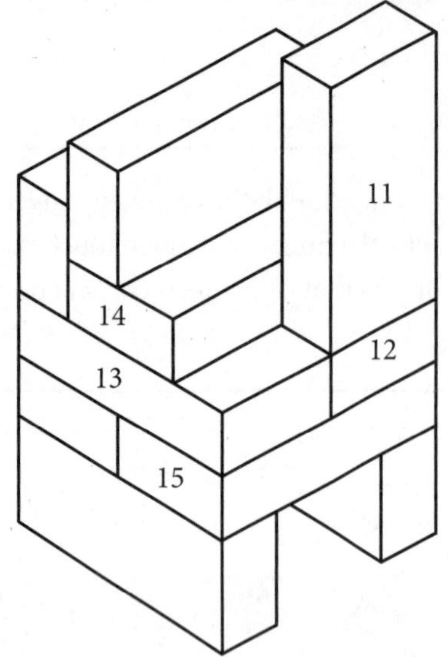

Block	A	B	C	D	E
11	1	2	3	4	5
12	6	2	4	1	5
13	4	5	3	2	6
14	3	4	5	6	2
15	5	3	2	6	4

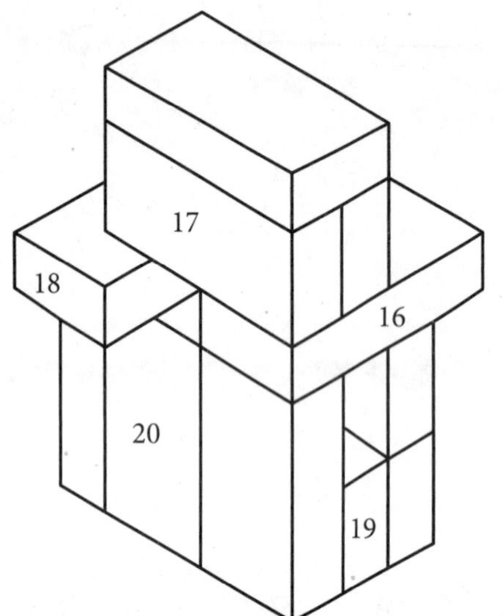

Block	A	B	C	D	E
16	1	2	3	4	5
17	6	2	4	1	5
18	4	5	3	2	6
19	3	4	5	6	2
20	5	3	2	6	4

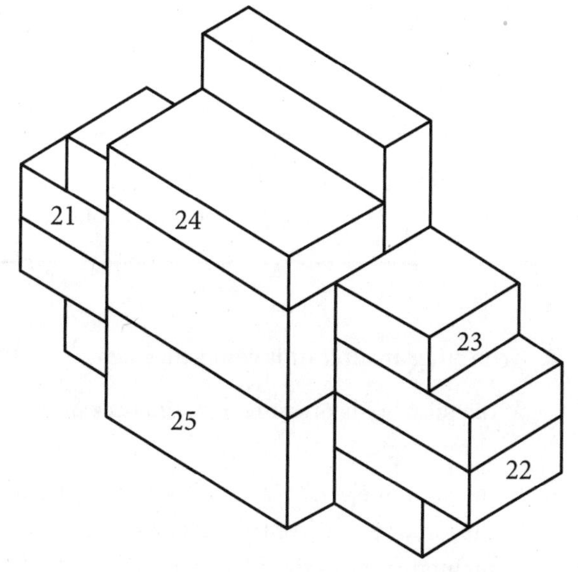

Block	A	B	C	D	E
21	1	2	3	4	5
22	6	2	4	3	5
23	4	5	3	2	6
24	3	4	5	6	2
25	5	3	2	6	4

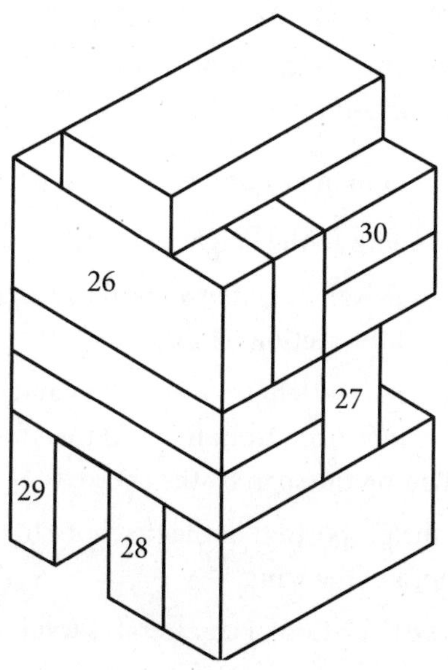

Block	A	B	C	D	E
26	1	2	3	4	5
27	6	2	4	1	5
28	4	5	3	2	6
29	3	4	5	6	2
30	5	3	2	6	4

STOP.

If you finish before time is up, you may check your work on this section only. Do not turn to any other section in the test.

AVIATION INFORMATION

20 Questions (8 Minutes)

Directions: This section of the exam measures your aviation knowledge. Each question or incomplete statement has five choices. You need to decide which of the choices best answers the question or statement.

1. The primary flight control that is part of the wing and causes the aircraft to turn by moving up and down is the

   A. rudder.

   B. aileron.

   C. elevator.

   D. stabilator.

   E. trim system.

2. If the current local altimeter setting is not available, the pilot should use the

   A. departing airport's field elevation.

   B. the field elevation of the closest airport corrected to mean sea level.

   C. pressure altitude adjusted for nonstandard temperature.

   D. radar.

   E. field elevation readings of the destination airport.

3. Takeoff decision speed is represented by which regulatory code?

   A. VA

   B. VC

   C. VD

   D. V1

   E. VLO

4. Trimming an aircraft is complete when

   A. the pilot holds pressure to maintain a proper climb angle.

   B. the pilot or electronic controls have adjusted the forces on the control surfaces so that it maintains the desired attitude.

   C. a pilot pushes the control wheel forward to prevent premature rotation.

   D. a pilot is pushing or pulling on the yoke.

   E. the trim-tab indicator is only slightly out of the takeoff range.

5. Aspect ratio in aviation is

   A. the width to the height of an image.

   B. the sidewall height of a given tire as a percentage of the section width.

   C. between the length of an airfoil and its chord (distance from front to back) then formed by dividing the span by the chord.

   D. is the proportion of the tip chord to the root chord of the wing.

   E. the calculation of an aircraft's total mass divided by the area of its wings.

6. The tachometer displays

A. an aircraft engine's fuel use in real time.
B. whether two or more rotating devices, such as engines, are synchronized.
C. a fuel tank made from fortified flexible material.
D. a device that stores electricity.
E. the number of revolutions per minute (RPM) of the aircraft engine.

7. Which is NOT a force for stopping an aircraft?

A. Reverse thrust
B. Wheel braking
C. Aerodynamic braking
D. Spoiler
E. Tire ground friction

8. The throttle of an aircraft

A. controls the ratio of fuel and air going to the engine.
B. is a cathode ray tube (CRT) display.
C. adjusts the fuel and air mixture going to the engine.
D. is a meter used to monitor the exhaust gas temperature of the aircraft.
E. brings in the outside air, mixes it with fuel, and delivers the fuel/air mixture to the cylinder.

9. If the control tower uses a light signal to instruct a pilot, while in flight, to give way to other aircraft and to continue circling, this light will be

A. flashing red.
B. steady red.
C. an alternating red and green light.
D. flashing green.
E. steady green.

10. In nearly all helicopters, high-frequency vibrations suggest a defective

A. bearing.
B. damper out of adjustment.
C. air conditioner compressor.
D. engine fan.
E. tail rotor.

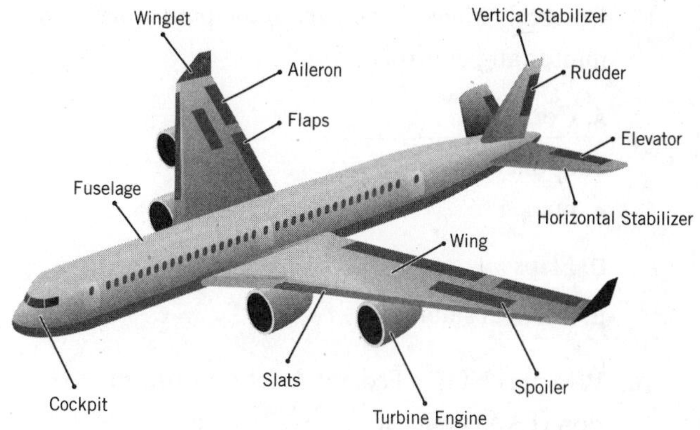

11. Correctly identify the part of the plane that generates thrust.

A. Cockpit
B. Spoiler
C. Slats
D. Turbine engine
E. Elevator

12. Correctly identify the part of the plane that controls pitch.

A. Fuselage
B. Horizontal stabilizer
C. Slats
D. Turbine engine
E. Aileron

13. The vertical flight of a helicopter is controlled by

A. the collective pitch lever.
B. the trim.
C. the swash plate assembly.
D. the anti-torque pedals.
E. synchropter.

14. Correctly identify the part of the plane that increases lift and drag.

A. Wing

B. Spoiler

C. Slats

D. Turbine engine

E. Flaps

15. Correctly identify the part of the plane that commands and controls.

A. Cockpit

B. Spoiler

C. Slats

D. Flaps

E. Vertical stabilizer

16. Which is NOT a Federal Aviation Administration (FAA) airspace class?

A. Class E

B. Class A

C. Class G

D. Class H

E. Class B

17. The amount of moisture in the air is

A. fog.

B. inversion layers.

C. humidity.

D. wind.

E. temperature.

18. During taxi, aircrafts should be kept centered over the

A. threshold taxi line.

B. touchdown zone marking.

C. normal taxiway centerline.

D. runway aiming point markers.

E. closed runway marking.

19. A stationary front is

A. warmer air traveling above and overtaking cooler air.

B. cool and warm air existing in the same region with no movement.

C. colder air sliding beneath and overtaking warmer air.

D. a quick moving cool air mass catching up and blending with the warm front causing a low-pressure area to form to the north.

E. a boundary between air masses having different temperature and moisture matter.

20. Correctly identify the part of the plane that decreases drag.

A. Winglet

B. Vertical stabilizer

C. Elevator

D. Horizontal stabilizer

E. Flaps

STOP.

If you finish before time is up, you may check your work on this section only. Do not turn to any other section in the test.

ANSWER KEYS AND EXPLANATIONS

Verbal Analogies

1. B	6. A	11. A	16. C	21. C
2. C	7. E	12. D	17. B	22. C
3. B	8. D	13. E	18. D	23. E
4. D	9. C	14. C	19. A	24. D
5. C	10. A	15. B	20. B	25. B

1. **The correct answer is B.** *Rancid* and *rotten* mean the same, just as *fresh* and *ripe* mean the same.
2. **The correct answer is C.** *Gold* is a type of *metal*, just as *cedar* is a type of *wood*.
3. **The correct answer is B.** *Cold* and *hot* are opposites, just as *frozen* and *boiling* are opposites.
4. **The correct answer is D.** *Solar* is more advanced than *coal*, just as *nuclear* is more advanced than a *generator*.
5. **The correct answer is C.** A *jet engine* generates *thrust*, just as a *gas stove* generates *heat*.
6. **The correct answer is A.** A *chapter* is found in a *book*, just as an *article* is found in a *magazine*.
7. **The correct answer is E.** A *hinge* is part of a *door*, just as a *shelf* is part of a *cabinet*.
8. **The correct answer is D.** A *mountain* is larger than a *hill*, just as a *lake* is larger than a *puddle*.
9. **The correct answer is C.** *Crime* can lead to *punishment*, just as *love* can lead to *marriage*.
10. **The correct answer is A.** *Recycling* is good for the *environment*, just as *exercise* is good for your *health*.
11. **The correct answer is A.** You use a *tent* when *camping*, just as you use a *wetsuit* when *diving*.
12. **The correct answer is D.** A *nap* is shorter than *sleep*, just as a *stroll* is shorter than a *hike*.
13. **The correct answer is E.** A *bow* shoots an *arrow*, just as a *pistol* shoots a *bullet*.
14. **The correct answer is C.** A *vacuum* is the absence of *air*, just as a *desert* is the absence of *water*.
15. **The correct answer is B.** *Full* is the opposite of *hungry*, just as *quenched* is the opposite of *thirsty*.
16. **The correct answer is C.** A *spider* makes a *web*, just as a *bee* makes a *hive*.
17. **The correct answer is B.** A *file* is kept in a *cabinet*, just as a *weapon* is stored in an *armory*.
18. **The correct answer is D.** *Shouting* is louder than *talking*, just as *talking* is louder than *whispering*.
19. **The correct answer is A.** You use a *hammer* on a *nail*, just as you use a *comb* on *hair*.
20. **The correct answer is B.** *Silver* is almost as valuable as *gold*, just as a *nickel* is almost as valuable as a *dime*.
21. **The correct answer is C.** A *cigarette* is smaller than a *cigar*, just as a *tumbler* is smaller than a *stein*.
22. **The correct answer is C.** A *cap* covers less than a *cowboy hat*, just as *ankle socks* cover less than *panty hose*.

23. **The correct answer is E.** A *skateboard* is smaller than an *airplane*, just as a *pool float* is smaller than a *battleship*.

24. **The correct answer is D.** *Fahrenheit* and *foot* are imperial units of measure, just as *Celsius* and *meter* are metric units of measure.

25. **The correct answer is B.** A *backpack* is smaller than a *suitcase*, just as an *envelope* is smaller than a *box*.

NOTES

Arithmetic Reasoning

1. C	6. A	11. A	16. B	21. B
2. B	7. C	12. C	17. D	22. C
3. D	8. D	13. B	18. A	23. E
4. C	9. E	14. A	19. E	24. D
5. A	10. C	15. C	20. A	25. B

1. **The correct answer is C.**

$$1\frac{1}{2} : 30 = 6 : x; \frac{3}{2}x = 180$$

$$x = \frac{2}{3}(180) = 120 \text{ miles.}$$

2. **The correct answer is B.** $\frac{1}{4}$ of $20 = 5$ gallons in tank; $20 - 5 = 15$ gallons needed to fill the tank.

3. **The correct answer is D.**

$$\frac{875}{70} = \frac{3000}{x}$$

$$75x = 210{,}000$$

$$x = 240 \text{ gallon}$$

4. **The correct answer is C.**

$$\frac{2{,}800}{63(24)} = \frac{2{,}800}{1{,}512} = 1.85, \text{ closest to 2 mph.}$$

5. **The correct answer is A.** Sixty miles at 40 mph $= 1\frac{1}{2}$ hours of driving time. Sixty miles at 30 mph $= 2$ hours of driving time. Total time is $3\frac{1}{2}$ hours, total distance is 120 miles, average speed is $\frac{120}{3\frac{1}{2}} = 120 \times \frac{2}{7} = \frac{240}{7}$ or $34\frac{2}{7}$ miles per hour.

6. **The correct answer is A.** $\frac{120}{12} = 10$ miles per minute. $10 \times 60 = 600$ mph.

7. **The correct answer is C.** $60x$ traveling east, $70x$ traveling west.

$$60x + 70x = 455$$

$$130x = 455$$

$$x = \frac{455}{130} = 3\frac{1}{2} \text{ hours}$$

$$10{:}00 \text{ am} + 3\frac{1}{2} \text{ hours} = 1{:}30 \text{ pm.}$$

8. **The correct answer is D.** The slower train is 25 miles ahead when the faster train starts. The faster train is 5 mph faster. $\frac{25}{5} = 5$ hours.

9. **The correct answer is E.**

$$\frac{1}{2} : 10 = \frac{9}{4} : x$$

$$\frac{x}{2} = \frac{90}{4}$$

$$4x = 180$$

$$x = 45$$

10. **The correct answer is C.** The total cost for 30 candies at \$0.13 per piece is $30 \times .13 = \$3.90$, or \$1.56 per dozen ($\$3.90 \div 2.5 = \$1.56$). The discounted rate of \$1.38 per dozen means a savings of \$0.18 per dozen, for a total of $.18 \times 2.5 = \$0.45$.

11. **The correct answer is A.** Since two child tickets cost the same as one adult ticket, we can find the cost of one adult ticket with the expression $\frac{\$12.60}{3}$. The cost of an adult ticket is \$4.20. Half of that is \$2.10.

12. **The correct answer is C.** Five hours 15 minutes is 21 quarter-hours. Twenty-four hours is 96 quarter-hours. $\frac{21}{96} = \frac{7}{32}$

13. **The correct answer is B.** $35 - 10 = 25$ games won, ten lost. $25 : 10 = 5 : 2$

14. **The correct answer is A.** Fifty of the 350 questions are math questions, leaving 300 other types of questions. Let x equal minutes spent for each math problem.

$$50x+\frac{x}{2}(300)=180$$
$$50x+150x=180$$
$$200x=180$$
$$x=\frac{180}{200}$$
$$50x=50\left(\frac{180}{200}\right)=45 \text{ minutes.}$$

15. **The correct answer is C.** Let x equal the cost of manufacturing a magneto.

$$x+0.12x=\$145.60$$
$$1.12x=\$145.60$$
$$x=\frac{\$145.60}{1.12}=\$130.00$$

16. **The correct answer is B.** \$120 - \$96 = \$24 discount. $\frac{24}{120}=20\%$.

17. **The correct answer is D.** One third of 198 is 66.

$$198-66=132$$
$$\frac{1}{4}(132)=33$$
$$132-33=99$$

18. **The correct answer is A.** $\frac{1}{3}\times\frac{3}{4}=\frac{3}{12}=\frac{1}{4}$, or 25%.

19. **The correct answer is E.** $2.5 \times 36 = 90$

20. **The correct answer is A.** There are 60 inches in 5 feet, 30 inches in 2.5 feet, and 12 inches in 1 foot.

    $5 \times 2.5 \times 1 = 12.5$ cubic feet.

21. **The correct answer is B.** $2\times3\times\frac{5}{3}=10$ cubic feet.

    $10 \times 7.5 = 75$ gallons.

22. **The correct answer is C.**

$$\frac{48\times36\times24}{8\times4\times2}=24\times27=648$$

23. **The correct answer is E.**

$$5:4=90:x$$
$$360=5x$$
$$x=72$$

24. **The correct answer is D.**

$$2.5:1=x:12$$
$$x=2.5\bullet12=30$$

25. **The correct answer is B.**

$$\frac{2}{3}x-\frac{1}{4}x=10$$
$$\frac{8}{12}x-\frac{3}{12}x=10$$
$$\frac{5}{12}x=10$$
$$\frac{120}{5}=24$$

Word Knowledge

1. B	6. C	11. E	16. D	21. D
2. D	7. D	12. C	17. B	22. E
3. A	8. A	13. B	18. D	23. D
4. B	9. D	14. D	19. C	24. B
5. D	10. B	15. A	20. A	25. D

1. **The correct answer is B.** *Aggregate* means "collective or to gather together."
2. **The correct answer is D.** *To broadcast* means "to transmit."
3. **The correct answer is A.** *Censure* means "to condemn."
4. **The correct answer is B.** *Daedal* means "intricate or skillful."
5. **The correct answer is D.** *Ductile* means "influenced or flexible."
6. **The correct answer is C.** *Egregious* means "conspicuous or flagrant."
7. **The correct answer is D.** *To exalt* means "to glorify."
8. **The correct answer is A.** *Fecund* means "fruitful or bountiful."
9. **The correct answer is D.** *Folderol* means "nonsense."
10. **The correct answer is B.** *To goad* means to "incite."
11. **The correct answer is E.** *Guaranty* means "security or collateral."
12. **The correct answer is C.** A hoard is a supply or collection, often hidden.
13. **The correct answer is B.** *Immaterial* means "unimportant."
14. **The correct answer is D.** *Jurisdiction* means "the right to exercise authority or control."
15. **The correct answer is A.** A kirtle is a long dress or gown.
16. **The correct answer is D.** A jest is a joke or prank.
17. **The correct answer is B.** A junction is an intersection.
18. **The correct answer is D.** To *kindle* means "to light, or start, a fire."
19. **The correct answer is C.** *Lucid* means "luminous or translucent."
20. **The correct answer is A.** *Masticate* means "to chew."
21. **The correct answer is D.** *Nimble* means "agile."
22. **The correct answer is E.** *Optimum* means "ideal or most desirable."
23. **The correct answer is D.** *Truculent* means "belligerent or aggressive."
24. **The correct answer is B.** *Vitreous* means "glassy or resembling glass."
25. **The correct answer is D.** *Weal* means "healthy or prosperous."

Math Knowledge

1. B	6. B	11. D	16. E	21. D
2. C	7. D	12. C	17. D	22. C
3. E	8. D	13. E	18. A	23. B
4. A	9. B	14. B	19. B	24. D
5. B	10. E	15. B	20. E	25. D

1. **The correct answer is B.**

$$\frac{1}{2}=\frac{16}{32};\frac{3}{4}=\frac{24}{32};\frac{5}{8}=\frac{20}{32};\frac{11}{16}=\frac{22}{32};\frac{23}{32}=\frac{23}{32}$$

2. **The correct answer is C.**

$$\frac{1}{3}=\frac{5}{15};\ \frac{2}{5}=\frac{6}{15};\ \frac{4}{15}=\frac{4}{15}$$

3. **The correct answer is E.**

$$\frac{1}{4}\%=\frac{1}{4}\times\frac{1}{100}=\frac{1}{400}$$

4. **The correct answer is A.**

$$\frac{120}{90}=\frac{4}{3}$$

$$\frac{4}{3}\times100=133\frac{1}{3}\%$$

5. **The correct answer is B.**

$$x+.40x=84$$

$$1.40x=84$$

$$\frac{84}{1.40}=60$$

6. **The correct answer is B.** $212 \times 212 = 44{,}944$.

7. **The correct answer is D.**

$$2^5=32$$

$$n-3=5$$

$$n=8$$

8. **The correct answer is D.** There is one digit in the square root for every pair of digits in the whole number.

9. **The correct answer is B.** $\sqrt{4^2+9}=\sqrt{25}=5$.

10. **The correct answer is E.** $5[4-(-1)+13]-6=5\,[5+13]-6=5\times18-6=90-6=84$.

11. **The correct answer is D.** If x is less than 10 and y is less than 5, $x+y$ is less than 15.

12. **The correct answer is C.** The area is multiplied by 2^2, or 4; the perimeter is doubled, or multiplied by 2.

13. **The correct answer is E.** Let x equal one of the numbers and y equal the other number.

$$\frac{x+y}{2}=A$$

$$x+y=2A$$

$$y=2A-x$$

14. **The correct answer is B.**

$$p:2D=x:c$$

$$x\,(2D)=pc$$

$$x=\frac{pc}{2D}$$

15. **The correct answer is B.**

$$(-3)+(5)=2$$

$$(2)-(-4)=6$$

16. **The correct answer is E.** An even number of negative signs when multiplying gives a positive product: $(-6)+(5)(-4)=120$

17. **The correct answer is D.**

$$(-10)\left(\frac{1}{2}\right)=-5$$

$$(-15)\left(-\frac{1}{3}\right)=5$$

-5 divided by 5 equals -1.

18. **The correct answer is A.** $r+s=25$; $4(r+s)=100$

19. **The correct answer is B.** $8x=3x+15$; $5x=15$; $x=3$

20. The correct answer is E.

$$\frac{7-3}{x}=\frac{8+2}{4\times5}$$
$$\frac{4}{x}=\frac{10}{20}$$
$$10x=80$$
$$x=8$$

21. The correct answer is D.

$$\sqrt{144}=12$$
$$\sqrt{36}=6$$
$$12-6=6$$

22. The correct answer is C. Since 12 × 12 = 144 and 13 × 13 = 169, the square root of 150 must be between 12 and 13.

23. The correct answer is B.

$$2\sqrt{50}=2\sqrt{25\times2}=2\times5\sqrt{2}=10\sqrt{2}$$

24. The correct answer is D.

$$4\sqrt{4\times2}+3\sqrt{9\times2}+2\sqrt{25\times2}=8\sqrt{2}+9\sqrt{2}=10\sqrt{2}=27\sqrt{2}$$

25. The correct answer is D. Your goal is to isolate c. First, find a common denominator for the fractions on the left and combine. Then, cross multiply and isolate c.

$$\frac{b}{ab}+\frac{a}{ab}=\frac{1}{c}$$
$$\frac{b+a}{ab}=\frac{1}{c}$$
$$c(b+a)=ab$$
$$c=\frac{ab}{(b+a)}$$

NOTES

Reading Comprehension

1. B	6. D	11. D	16. A	21. A
2. A	7. C	12. A	17. B	22. A
3. B	8. C	13. E	18. C	23. E
4. D	9. E	14. D	19. A	24. A
5. C	10. C	15. B	20. E	25. A

1. **The correct answer is B.** Madison was afraid of factions, which are defined as the tyranny of the minority. Choices A, C, D and E are all incorrect because Madison did not fear any of them.

2. **The correct answer is A.** The passage details Madison's solution to factions as being the separation of powers. The other choices are incorrect because Madison did not consider any of them as solutions to the problem of factions. Instead, they either already existed or were an effect of the concept of the separation of powers.

3. **The correct answer is B.** The second paragraph focuses primarily on the separation of powers and how they were applied by the Constitution. The passage does not detail each branch of the government (choice A). The passage also does not advocate for anything but rather explains (choice C). The first paragraph details Madison's fear of factions (choice D). The separation of powers is only a facet of how the government functions (choice E).

4. **The correct answer is D.** Madison's fear of factions was a catalyst for the concept of separation of powers, both of which are detailed by the passage. The federalist papers are only mentioned once (choice A). Only paragraph one describes why Madison feared factions (choice B). Only the second paragraph details the separation of powers (choice C). The passage is not about James Madison himself, but of what he feared and what that fear bore (choice E).

5. **The correct answer is C.** The passage primarily discusses the various assumptions made about artificial sweeteners, and only disputes a few. Choices A, B, and D are incorrect because the passage does not show any preference towards a particular type of sweetener. Choice E is incorrect because the passage does not necessarily refute assumptions made about artificial sweeteners.

6. **The correct answer is D.** The passage is very clear that whatever assumptions made about the health risks associated with artificial sweeteners are poorly supported. The passage is clear that artificial sweeteners are not directly related to weight gain or loss (choices A and C). The passage is also not squarely against the use of artificial sweeteners (choice B). However, the passage clearly states in the first paragraph that artificial sweeteners are a controversial topic and ends by saying that they will continue to be controversial (choice E).

7. **The correct answer is C.** The passage clearly states that the FDA has approved artificial sweeteners, albeit somewhat reluctantly. The passage does not discuss artificial sweeteners as a recommendation for weight loss (choice A). The passage does not present evidence that artificial sweeteners are as healthy as natural sugar (choice B) or have the same amount of calories (choice D). The passage actually states that it is not clear as to whether or not sweeteners can cause serious health problems (choice E).

8. **The correct answer is C.** The passage implies that there are hardly any restrictions made on artificial sweeteners, and thus conservative must mean low. Choices A, B, D and E are all incorrect because they do not correctly apply to the regulations associated with artificial sweeteners.

9. **The correct answer is E.** The passage focuses on the misconception that teen drivers are more guilty of texting and driving than adults and completely refutes that statement. Statistics show that adults are more likely to text and drive (choice A), and choice D is incorrect for the same reason. The passage acknowledges that while adults are more likely to text and drive, teens are more likely to get into an accident while doing so (choice B). The passage acknowledges that adults need to guide their teens while they're learning to drive (choice C).

10. **The correct answer is C.** The second paragraph gives evidence supporting the claims made by the first paragraph and then gives insight into that evidence. The second paragraph does not deny any evidence given (choice A), and the primary purpose is not to give statistics as much as it is to give evidence and analysis (choice B). The second paragraph does not claim that adults are worse drivers (choice D). The second paragraph also does not claim that teens are worse drivers or give evidence to support that claim (choice E).

11. **The correct answer is D.** Statistics are scientific evidence. The other choices are incorrect because they do not describe statistics.

12. **The correct answer is A.** The passage refutes misconceptions made about texting and driving in the teenage demographic specifically. The passage does not consider adult texting and driving to be a menace (choice B). It is not about texting and driving in and of itself (choice C). The research cited shows that teens are not more likely to text and drive (choice D). The passage does not discuss all teenage and adult habits, only texting and driving (choice E).

13. **The correct answer is E.** The first paragraph details Sweden's parental leave policies, and the second contrasts them with America's parental leave policies. The passage does not focus only on Swedish parental leave policies (choice A). The passage does not rally support for a certain point of view (choice B). The countries themselves are inconsequential to the greater discussion at hand (choice C). The passage also discusses American policies on parental leave (choice D).

14. **The correct answer is D.** The passage is very supportive of Swedish parental leave policies, and the American companies that have already adopted some of them. The passage notes numerous faults in American parental leave policies (choice A). The passage clearly considers Sweden's parental leave policies to be superior to American parental leave policies (choice B). It also considers Sweden's parental leave policies to be family friendly (choice C) as well as adoption friendly (choice E).

15. **The correct answer is B.** The passage states that American parents make on average less than 3 weeks of pay in 6 weeks of parental leave so as to contrast that with the 80% paychecks that Swedes receive on parental leave. Choices A, C, D and E are all incorrect because the statement is not meant to highlight anything about the American economy itself, just American parental leave policies.

16. **The correct answer is A.** The second paragraph details the contrast between American parental leave policies and Swedish parental leave policies. It's the contrast in "compare and contrast." Choice B is incorrect because the second paragraph highlights very few American successes with parental leave policies; choice C is incorrect for the same reason. The paragraph does highlight certain successes of the American parental leave policies (choice D). The paragraph does not focus only on the freedom associated with American parental leave policies (choice E).

17. **The correct answer is B.** The passage primarily focuses on the equal time rule and how it is applied in political broadcasting. The passage does not focus on general election media in and of itself (choice A); choice C is incorrect for the same reason. The FCC itself is not mentioned much in the passage (choice D). The passage doesn't focus on the FCC itself (choice E), but rather on a rule enforced by the FCC.

18. **The correct answer is C.** The talk show host example was not about talk show hosts (choice A), but about how the equal time rule is applied in late-night television. The example does not highlight the scope of the FCC's broadcasting reach (choice B) as much as saying that the FCC regulates US broadcasting. The example is not meant to provide visualization (choice D) or serve as a real-life example (choice E).

19. **The correct answer is A.** The second paragraph focuses only on exceptions to the equal time rule. The first paragraph elaborates on the purpose of the equal time rule (choice B). The examples given are not instances where the FCC itself has no authority (choice C), just the equal time rule. The purpose of the second paragraph is not merely to discuss the equal time rule in newscasting (choice D) but in instances where it's not applicable. No other FCC guidelines are mentioned in the second paragraph (choice E).

20. **The correct answer is E.** The second paragraph states that the equal time rule does not apply in instances of spontaneous interviews. The other choices are incorrect because they do not describe the equal time rule.

21. **The correct answer is A.** A quotation from the Haddon tells the reader what the intended purpose of the book was. The quotation was not necessary in order to convey the author's passion for Christopher or his story (choices B and C). The author does not make any claims that require support (choice D). A quotation from the author is not used to convey the essence of the book (choice E) but the author's thoughts on it.

22. **The correct answer is A.** It can be inferred from Haddon's words on the subject that the book is simply about Christopher as a complex, nuanced character. The other choices are incorrect because they are facets of the book, and of Christopher, but they are not what the book is about.

23. **The correct answer is E.** To *conjure* an image of a character you have never seen is to *imagine* that character. The audience is not expected to *produce* (choice A) a tangible image of Christopher; *recreate* (choice C) and *materialize* (choice D) are incorrect for the same reason. *Summon* (choice B) is incorrect because it has magical connotation.

24. **The correct answer is A.** The passage is a purely historical look at a well-known dog breed. The passage disproves no commonly made misconceptions about Labradors (choice B) aside from the origins of the name. Choices C, D, and E are incorrect because they assume that the passage is persuasive in nature and advocates for Labradors as suitable family pets or hunting dogs.

25. **The correct answer is A.** *Coined* means invented. *Cast* (choice B) and *molded* (choice C) are incorrect because they use coined in the literal sense of producing coins. *Discovered* (choice D) is incorrect because the name was not discovered. *Fabricated* (choice E) is incorrect because the word implies that the name was invented to deceive.

Situational Judgment

1. A	11. C	21. C	31. D	41. C
2. C	12. B	22. E	32. A	42. D
3. D	13. A	23. C	33. C	43. E
4. A	14. B	24. B	34. E	44. D
5. B	15. D	25. B	35. A	45. A
6. E	16. B	26. A	36. C	46. C
7. B	17. B	27. A	37. B	47. D
8. E	18. D	28. D	38. D	48. B
9. D	19. E	29. B	39. A	49. B
10. E	20. A	30. E	40. C	50. D

1. **The correct answer is A.** If you are given a task, it is your job to complete it. Your fellow officers, whether they consider it a waste of time or not, are also responsible for completing this task. Make sure you complete the tasks given to you in the way in which you were asked to complete them.

2. **The correct answer is C.** Do your work. If you are given a task, complete it. Even if another member of your team deems it unnecessary, be the one willing to stand up and say that it is.

3. **The correct answer is D.** Organization is the key to completing work by the time it needs to be done. Help him in that aspect and you'll have done more than you would have had you simply done the work for him.

4. **The correct answer is A.** You won't accomplish anything by telling the supervisor that you were asked to help. The work won't get done more efficiently. Deal with the situation yourself and allow your fellow officer to do his own part to complete the work.

5. **The correct answer is B.** Identify the source of the problem before acting. If you have to change your behavior, identify what that behavior is, but first be sure that this is coming from a reliable source and isn't merely hearsay. Secondhand communication isn't always accurate.

6. **The correct answer is E.** Reprimanding your team for something that may or may not be true will only inspire animosity. You don't know if this information is accurate, or whether it was the entire group as opposed to just one person. Get all the information first.

7. **The correct answer is B.** Derogatory comments that are racist, sexist, and homophobic in nature are completely inappropriate. This type of behavior should never be tolerated, no matter the rank.

8. **The correct answer is E.** Ignoring the problem and allowing it to continue is never the solution when people are being harassed.

9. **The correct answer is D.** The best way to ensure both parties are on the same page is to discuss the situation together. The other team is not your responsibility, so include the other team's leader. Both parties are partially responsible, so they both have to be a part of the conversation.

10. **The correct answer is E.** Ignoring the problem will only result in further misdemeanors. It will either happen again or simply worsen. Behavior on both sides needs to be noted, discussed, and punished.

11. **The correct answer is C.** An honest job performance will serve him better in the future. Changes can be made, be it in his team placement or the responsibilities he's given. This will

be the most effective action both for him and for yourself.

12. **The correct answer is B.** Reporting only on the officer's failures and not his attributes will only hurt his career. It will not be an accurate representation of his work ethic or potential. Be honest.

13. **The correct answer is A.** Verify the information before acting on the situation. If you haven't seen any evidence to support these claims, then find it. You don't want to act prematurely and have the claims be either fabricated or a misunderstanding.

14. **The correct answer is B.** The officer in question might be innocent of such accusations. Acting prematurely and in public will only reflect badly on you as a leader. Be sure and be discreet.

15. **The correct answer is D.** Communicate with your team leader if they won't communicate with you. Take the initiative to ask about your behavior or performance. Be honest and open.

16. **The correct answer is B.** Being aggressive in your approach will only ensure that you are transferred for behavioral issues. Don't jump the gun and confront a perceived problem publicly before you have all the information. Act with dignity and respect.

17. **The correct answer is B.** Leadership includes leading by example. Be an example to your peers and act with integrity before giving into peer pressure. If a new policy is needed, take the time to understand its necessity before getting frustrated with its newness.

18. **The correct answer is D.** Disobeying policy and giving into peer pressure will only result in punishment for you and others involved. Be a leader among your peers and stand up for what you know to be right and truthful. You can't be a leader if you follow the whims of others.

19. **The correct answer is E.** If an officer is best in the station he's in, do what you can to keep him there. Communicate on what can be done about the reasoning behind his wish to transfer and see if you can help. Manage the resources you do have to the best of your ability.

20. **The correct answer is A.** If he is perfectly fine in his current job, and he would be perfectly fine in the other job, then taking both away from him is the least effective response to a situation such as this. Find the perfect place for him, which will benefit both him and you.

21. **The correct answer is C.** Communicate your concern, but be clear that this is not going to be tolerated. More often than not, there is more going on behind the scenes than is initially perceived. However, you must be clear that this shouldn't detract from your work. If it does, seek help.

22. **The correct answer is E.** Doing nothing will only enable the behavior. He will neither attempt to work harder nor know to work harder. The rest of the junior officers on your team will see this as a sign of favoritism, and you will lose respect as a leader.

23. **The correct answer is C.** All you can do is offer to help in whatever way you can. Forcing yourself into the situation will only make it worse. If he chooses to work at it on his own, then it is his prerogative.

24. **The correct answer is B.** Forcing yourself on the situation will only make it worse. The officer will feel disrespected, creating tension between the two of you. You are not his superior officer, so you shouldn't act like it.

25. **The correct answer is B.** Asking for help is not a sign of weakness. Do what you can to make sure that you do the task and do it right. If you don't know how to do something, ask someone, and if you don't have the proper skills to complete it, then learn. Take initiative.

26. **The correct answer is A.** Doing the task on your own when you are unsure of how to do it will only result in it being done to a lesser standard. If you're going to do a job, then do it right. If you don't know how to do it right, then ask for help and learn.

27. **The correct answer is A.** Be willing to adapt to obstacles as they come. Reorganization and innovation will benefit you in the long run. Adapting to new circumstances is necessary in an ever-changing environment.

28. **The correct answer is D.** Not doing what was asked will only result in the project being done incorrectly. Follow orders and adapt to changes in circumstances as they come.

29. **The correct answer is B.** Find a way to compromise and create a timeline that works best for both teams. This will keep you both accountable and ensure that the work is organized. Manage your given resources and organize your time.

30. **The correct answer is E.** Continuing to wait and failing to take action will result in the work not being done on time. You won't be able to do your work without theirs. There needs to be communication and solid organization on the timetables of both teams.

31. **The correct answer is D.** Rescheduling yourself will allow you to get reorganized. Asking for help will give you a new perspective on the work you are doing.

32. **The correct answer is A.** Failing to finish the work will only leave more work for other people to do. You will be punished and the unfinished work will affect further work that needs to be done.

33. **The correct answer is C.** Be a mentor and a leader to this officer. Guide him until he is ready to work on his own, and then hand it back to him. Make sure no time is wasted teaching that could have been time spent working, so learn on the job.

34. **The correct answer is E.** Giving an officer work that he is not prepared for and does not know how to do will only ensure that it does not get done, or at least doesn't get done properly. Be willing to guide him as a partner. Do your work, but ensure he knows how to do his.

35. **The correct answer is A.** All you can do is lead by example. You are not a superior officer and thus have no authority over your peers. If they don't want to do their jobs, the only thing that you can do is perform yours and show them that it is doable.

36. **The correct answer is C.** Avoiding responsibilities in any case is wrong. Be the one to stand up and do what you know is right and responsible. The rest of the officers will do what they will, but you can control your actions.

37. **The correct answer is B.** Take initiative and be innovative. If you have a new idea, it never hurts to suggest it. If your team leader decides not to use it, then that is their prerogative, but at least you tried.

38. **The correct answer is D.** You'll never know if you never try. If you never ask your team leader about this new form of scheduling, then it is sure to never happen. Take initiative.

39. **The correct answer is A.** You can only lead by example and try to understand the situation for yourself. Be empathetic and communicate with the new officer before asking that of others. This is a new situation for everyone involved, so be understanding.

40. **The correct answer is C.** Distancing yourself from this officer will only ensure that he is never integrated into the team. He will not understand his new environment, and you will not understand him. Communicate and be a mentor.

41. **The correct answer is C.** Communicate with the officers in question and come to an understanding. Acknowledge that you have not been completely open with them and ask to work together civilly.

42. **The correct answer is D.** Ignoring the tension will only make it worse. You will not be able to do your work, and they will not know how to best communicate with you. Take the initiative and communicate.

43. **The correct answer is E.** Having an honest conversation is the mature response. Acknowledge that the two of them will never be friends, but highlight their common goal. Find common

ground between the two of them and go from there.

44. **The correct answer is D.** They will never get the project done if you give it to them. Their fighting will ensure that. It will also do no good for you to negate your own responsibilities in the project simply because the two of them have problems with each other.

45. **The correct answer is A.** Be honest and ask for help. If you don't understand something, then it won't do any good to simply do it incorrectly. Ask those who know what they're talking about how you should go about your assignment.

46. **The correct answer is C.** Procrastinating will only make the situation more confusing and stressful for everyone involved. You won't get anything done that way.

47. **The correct answer is D.** Be supportive of your fellow team members no matter what. If another officer comes to you in confidence, be respectful and understanding. It is not your responsibility to do his job for him, but it is your responsibility to do what you can.

48. **The correct answer is B.** Being malicious and spreading false information will only hurt you, the officer, and the mission. Make integrity-driven choices. If you would not want something like that to happen to you, then don't do it to another officer.

49. **The correct answer is B.** If you have done wrong, then take responsibility for your actions. Being honest shows integrity and leadership.

50. **The correct answer is D.** Continuing to lie about your own behavior to your team leader and encouraging that same behavior in your fellow officers will only breed more unseemly behavior. You don't want to be the cause of more problems. Act with integrity and leadership.

NOTES

Physical Science

1. C	5. B	9. B	13. B	17. C
2. C	6. A	10. D	14. D	18. A
3. A	7. B	11. A	15. E	19. C
4. B	8. E	12. D	16. C	20. B

1. **The correct answer is C.** There are three elements present in this compound: sodium (Na), oxygen (O), and hydrogen (H). Each atom will have a corresponding number to indicate how many are present in the compound. When there is no number present, there is only one atom of that particular element. Since Na is the symbol for sodium and there is no number after it, the correct answer is one atom. The other choices are incorrect based on this information (choices A, B, D, and E).

2. **The correct answer is C.** When an element symbol is more than one letter, the first letter is capitalized. In this compound, we see NaH. A capital letter followed by a lowercase letter indicates one element. Since the letter after Na is capitalized (H), we know that it is a symbol for another element, hydrogen. It is wrong to merely look at the number at the end to identify the number of elements as this number actually connects to the number of atoms for the element it is written after (choice A). Simply counting all of the letters is also incorrect as the lowercase letter is not its own element (choice E). Assuming that there is one atom per each element without a number and adding it to the three is also incorrect (choice D). It is also important to recognize that any new capital letter indicates a new element, even if we are used to seeing certain capital letters together in common compounds, as is the case with CO (choice B).

3. **The correct answer is A.** Fission is the splitting of a nucleus into two separate parts. Fusion (choice B) is the opposite and is the result of two nuclei fusing. Refraction (choice C) is related to the direction of light and waves. Mitosis (choice D) relates to cell division. Splitosis (choice E) isn't actually a term.

4. **The correct answer is B.** Water can be considered both a renewable and nonrenewable energy as it is technically consumable. However, the definition of renewable energy is an energy source that is easily replenished. Coal (choice A), oil (choice C), and natural gas (choice D) all take eons to renew. Nuclear energy (choice E) is based on irreversible nuclear decay and is not renewable in a reasonable fashion.

5. **The correct answer is B.** Velocity is the combination of both speed (choice E) and direction of an object. Viscosity is the measurement of how thick a substance is (choice A). The force behind an object (choice C) is called the driving force. Deceleration (choice D) describes the rate at which an object negatively changes velocity.

6. **The correct answer is A.** Velocity measures both the speed and direction of an object. Thus, the formula explained is velocity equals the distance divided by the time it takes to travel said distance. An example would be if you walked 10 miles north in 2 hours. $10 \div 2 = 5$, so your speed would be 5 mph. The other choices are incorrect.

7. **The correct answer is B.** Oxidation of metals is the process by which they rust. Based on this, the following is a list of the most likely to rust up to the most resistant: lithium (choice A), zinc (choice D), copper (choice C), silver (choice E), and finally gold (choice B). It is for this reason that Gold and Silver are referred to as precious metals. Gold is the most impervious to rust and is thus the number one choice for jewelry.

8. **The correct answer is E.** Glass is actually not flammable. It can be heated at extremely high temperatures to soften it and will melt at temperatures above 2,600°F. However, it will never catch fire. Hydrogen (choice B) is extremely flammable and combustible. Wood (choice A) and gun powder (choice D) catch fire easily. Although plastic (choice C) has a much higher ignition temperature than wood—closer to 450°F—it is still considered flammable.

9. **The correct answer is B.** Kinetic energy is the energy an object possesses once it's placed in motion. Any type of potential energy (choices A and C) does not apply since the arrow is in motion. Thermal energy (choice D) refers to the transfer of heat, and radiation energy (choice E) refers to the transfer of energy through radio or light waves.

10. **The correct answer is D.** A conductor of electricity works because of its free electrons. It conducts the electron current (or flow of electrons) easily. The other items do NOT let electrons flow very easily from them, and thus they are poor conductors.

11. **The correct answer is A.** Ions are charged atoms (choice B). An alloy (choice C) is a combination of metal with another element. A compound (choice D) is when two or more elements combine.A molecule (choice E) is when two or more atoms are bound together; however, the number of neutrons is not affected.

12. **The correct answer is D.** The prefix di- indicates that there will be two oxygen molecules in this molecule. Based on this, we can automatically eliminate CO (choice A), C_2O (choice B), and CO_3 (choice E). Since the element of carbon is labeled without any change to its name (unlike oxygen, which changed slightly from oxygen to oxide), we can deduce that C_2O_2 (choice C) is incorrect as well since it would have the prefix di- in front of carbon to indicate the 2.

13. **The correct answer is B.** A mixture is when two or more substances are mixed but not chemically combined. The chemical combination must occur for it to be identified as a solution (choice A). Both mixtures (choice D) and solutions (choice C) only require the combination of two substances, although more can be used. Although substances of different states (choice E) can be used to create a mixture, it is not required.

14. **The correct answer is D.** Milk is the only example that combines substances to create a mixture as the substances combined retain their original properties and do not chemically bond. Saltwater (choice A) is a solution made from salt and water. Vinegar (choice B) is a solution made from acetic acid and water. Coffee (choice C) is a solution made from ground coffee and water. Juice (choice E) is a solution made from any fruit/vegetable juice and water.

15. **The correct answer is E.** Electromagnetic waves are an example of transverse waves because the wave travels perpendicular to the source of the wave. Longitudinal waves (choice B) travel in a parallel fashion. This includes sound waves (choice A). Surface waves (choice C) run in a circular motion, as detected by an object in the path of the wave. Mechanical waves (choice D) can be both longitudinal or transverse but are not an example of electromagnetic waves.

16. **The correct answer is C.** Mechanical waves can fall under both the transverse (choice A) and longitudinal (choice B) wave types. One example of a mechanical wave that falls under both types is a seismic wave related to earthquakes. All other choices are incorrect because they omit one of these types.

17. **The correct answer is C.** Ohms measure resistance. Kelvin (choice A) measures temperature. Volts (choice B) measure voltage. Hertz (choice D) measure frequency of direct current. Amperes (choice E) measure electric current.

18. **The correct answer is A.** Corrosion is the result of oxidation of metal. The blue-green patina on copper is an indication of corrosion, also

referred to as rust. Erosion (choice B) is related to soil. Combustion (choice C) is related to rapid oxidation. Induction (choice D) and conduction (choice E) are both related to electricity.

19. **The correct answer is C.** The top left number always represents the atomic number. Choice B, 2, is half of 4 and is incorrect. Choice A, 9, is the rounded number for the atomic mass. Choice D, 9.012, is the actual atomic mass. Choice E, 4.5, is half the atomic mass and is incorrect.

20. **The correct answer is B.** A solvent is the agent in which the solute is dissolved. Choices A, C, D, and E all represent solutes that are dissolved to create a solution. Water (choice B) is the only solvent present among the choices.

NOTES

Table Reading

1. B	9. C	17. D	25. E	33. B
2. C	10. E	18. A	26. B	34. D
3. A	11. A	19. B	27. C	35. C
4. D	12. B	20. E	28. C	36. D
5. D	13. B	21. C	29. D	37. B
6. A	14. A	22. D	30. B	38. E
7. B	15. D	23. A	31. A	39. A
8. C	16. E	24. E	32. E	40. C

1. **The correct answer is B.** The coordinates (+1, –2) intersect at 52.
2. **The correct answer is C.** The coordinates (+4, +4) intersect at 49.
3. **The correct answer is A.** The coordinates (+9, –7) intersect at 65.
4. **The correct answer is D.** The coordinates (–6, +6) intersect at 37.
5. **The correct answer is D.** The coordinates (–10, –10) intersect at 49.
6. **The correct answer is A.** The coordinates (–5, –12) intersect at 56.
7. **The correct answer is B.** The coordinates (+7, +1) intersect at 55.
8. **The correct answer is C.** The coordinates (+10, –12) intersect at 71.
9. **The correct answer is C.** The coordinates (+2, +6) intersect at 45.
10. **The correct answer is E.** The coordinates (+5, –10) intersect at 64.
11. **The correct answer is A.** The coordinates (+12, –4) intersect at 65.
12. **The correct answer is B.** The coordinates (–6, –9) intersect at 52.
13. **The correct answer is B.** The coordinates (–1, +8) intersect at 40.
14. **The correct answer is A.** The coordinates (+7, –4) intersect at 60.
15. **The correct answer is D.** The coordinates (0, 0) intersect at 49.
16. **The correct answer is E.** The coordinates (+7, –8) intersect at 64.
17. **The correct answer is D.** The coordinates (–6, –6) intersect at 49.
18. **The correct answer is A.** The coordinates (–12, +1) intersect at 36.
19. **The correct answer is B.** The coordinates (+8, –8) intersect at 65.
20. **The correct answer is E.** The coordinates (–1, –5) intersect at 53.
21. **The correct answer is C.** The coordinates (+9, –2) intersect at 60.
22. **The correct answer is D.** The coordinates (+10, –9) intersect at 68.
23. **The correct answer is A.** The coordinates (+4, +3) intersect at 50.
24. **The correct answer is E.** The coordinates (–5, +6) intersect at 38.
25. **The correct answer is E.** The coordinates (0, –7) intersect at 56.
26. **The correct answer is B.** The coordinates (+11, –4) intersect at 64.
27. **The correct answer is C.** The coordinates (–11, –1) intersect at 39.
28. **The correct answer is C.** The coordinates (–5, –6) intersect at 50.

29. **The correct answer is D.** The coordinates (+2, –4) intersect at 55.

30. **The correct answer is B.** The coordinates (–2, +11) intersect at 36.

31. **The correct answer is A.** The coordinates (–5, –7) intersect at 51.

32. **The correct answer is E.** The coordinates (+7, –12) intersect at 68.

33. **The correct answer is B.** The coordinates (+2, –3) intersect at 54.

34. **The correct answer is D.** The coordinates (+8, +1) intersect at 56.

35. **The correct answer is C.** The coordinates (+9, –5) intersect at 63.

36. **The correct answer is D.** The coordinates (+12, 0) intersect at 61.

37. **The correct answer is B.** The coordinates (+1, +4) intersect at 46.

38. **The correct answer is E.** The coordinates (+6, +9) intersect at 46.

39. **The correct answer is A.** The coordinates (–5, +3) intersect at 41.

40. **The correct answer is C.** The coordinates (+11, –7) intersect at 67.

NOTES

Instrument Comprehension

1. C	6. A	11. D	16. B	21. C
2. A	7. A	12. A	17. A	22. D
3. B	8. C	13. B	18. C	23. B
4. A	9. C	14. D	19. D	24. C
5. A	10. A	15. A	20. A	25. A

1. **The correct answer is C.** The plane is heading northeast and slightly ascending with a right bank at 30 degrees. Choice A is banking left. Choice B is heading northwest. Choice D is over-banking to 90 degrees.
2. **The correct answer is A.** The plane is heading north, slightly ascending, and banking 60 degrees to the right. Choice B is heading south and diving. Choice C is heading north but is only banking to about 45 degrees. Choice D has no bank.
3. **The correct answer is B.** The plane is heading southwest, ascending slightly, and banking 45 degrees to the left. Choice A is heading southwest but banking right. Choice C is diving. Choice D is overbanking to 90 degrees.
4. **The correct answer is A.** The plane is heading east, is level with the horizon, and is banking 30 degrees to the left. Choice B is heading west. Choice C is climbing and banking right. Choice D is also banking right.
5. **The correct answer is A.** The plane is heading west, descending and banking 90 degrees to the left. Choice B is banking right. Choice C has no bank in its steep dive. Choice D is banked right and ascending.
6. **The correct answer is A.** The plane is heading southeast, slightly ascending, and banking 20 degrees to the left. Choice B is heading west, ascending, and overbanking 90 degrees. Choice C is overbanking to 90 degrees right. Choice D is banking right.
7. **The correct answer is A.** The plane is heading south, ascending sharply and is not banking. Choice B is heading north. Choice C is heading southwest. Choice D is heading west.
8. **The correct answer is C.** The plane is heading southwest, slightly ascending, and banking 45 degrees to the left. Choices, A, B, and D are all heading east.
9. **The correct answer is C.** The plane is heading northeast, slightly descending, and is banking 45 degrees to the right. Choice A is banking to the left. Choice B is headed northwest. Choice D is banking left.
10. **The correct answer is A.** The plane is heading north, is ascending, and is not banking. Choice B is heading south. Choice C is banking left. Choice D is not ascending.
11. **The correct answer is D.** The plane is heading northwest, level with the horizon, inverted. Choice A is ascending. Choice B is banking 20 degrees left. Choice C is descending.
12. **The correct answer is A.** The plane is heading south, slightly ascending, and banking 60 degrees to the right. Choice B is heading north. Choice C is banking 45 degrees to the left. Choice D is slightly descending.
13. **The correct answer is B.** The plane is heading southwest, ascending, and banked 45 degrees left. Choice A is headed southeast. Choice C is descending slightly and has no bank. Choice D is heading southeast.
14. **The correct answer is D.** The plane is heading east and has no banking or climb or dive. Choice A is banking 45 degrees left. Choice B is inverted and heading west. Choice C is slightly ascending and banking 90 degrees left.

15. **The correct answer is A.** The plane is heading southwest, slightly descending, and banking 90 degrees to the left. Choice B is heading northeast and slightly ascending. Choice C is heading southeast and banking 20 degrees to the right. Choice D is slightly descending and heading south.

16. **The correct answer is B.** The plane is heading southeast, slightly ascending, and banking 20 degrees to the right. Choice A is not banking. Choice C is banking 90 degrees to the right. Choice D is heading northwest and banking 90 degrees to the right.

17. **The correct answer is A.** The plane is heading west and ascending straight up with no bank. Choice B is heading northeast. Choice C is banking left 20 degrees. Choice D is heading north.

18. **The correct answer is C.** The plane is heading northeast, slightly ascending with no bank. Choice A is banking 20 degrees left. Choice B is heading northwest. Choice D is banking 90 degrees to the right.

19. **The correct answer is D.** The plane is heading north, ascending sharply, and banking 45 degrees left. Choice A is banking 20 degrees left. Choice B is heading northeast. Choice C is heading south with a left bank.

20. **The correct answer is A.** The plane is heading west, is level with the horizon, and inverted. Choice B is heading south. Choice C is banking 45 degrees left. Choice D is slightly ascending and slightly inverted.

21. **The correct answer is C.** The plane is heading east, slightly ascending, and banking 20 degrees right. Choice A is banking 60 degrees left. Choice B is heading southeast. Choice D is ascending and overbanking 90 degrees.

22. **The correct answer is D.** The plane is heading northwest, is level with the horizon, and is banking 60 degrees right. Choice B is heading east. Choice C is banking 20 degrees right. Choice A is slightly ascending.

23. **The correct answer is B.** The plane is heading north, descending, and inverted. Choice A is heading southwest. Choice C is ascending. Choice D is heading east.

24. **The correct answer is C.** The plane is heading south, level with the horizon, and not banking. Choice A is banking left. Choice B is heading east. Choice D is slightly ascending.

25. **The correct answer is A.** The plane is heading northeast, ascending, and banking 90 degrees right. Choice B is heading west. Choice C is banking right 20 degrees. Choice D is slightly descending.

NOTES

Block Counting

1. D	7. B	13. B	19. B	25. A
2. E	8. D	14. C	20. E	26. C
3. A	9. B	15. A	21. C	27. A
4. C	10. E	16. D	22. D	28. C
5. C	11. B	17. C	23. A	29. E
6. E	12. A	18. B	24. B	30. B

1. **The correct answer is D.** Block 1 is touching two blocks in front, one behind, and one above.
2. **The correct answer is E.** Block 2 is touching four blocks above and one block below.
3. **The correct answer is A.** Block 3 is touching one block on one side, one block on the other side, and two blocks below.
4. **The correct answer is C.** Block 4 is touching four blocks above and one block below.
5. **The correct answer is C.** Block 5 is touching one block above and one behind.
6. **The correct answer is E.** Block 6 is touching one block in front, one behind, one below, and two above.
7. **The correct answer is B.** Block 7 is touching one block to the side and one below.
8. **The correct answer is D.** Block 8 is touching one below, two above, and two behind.
9. **The correct answer is B.** Block 9 is touching one to the side, one above, and two below.
10. **The correct answer is E.** Block 10 is touching two blocks above, one below, and one in front.
11. **The correct answer is B.** Block 11 is touching one block below and one behind.
12. **The correct answer is A.** Block 12 is touching three blocks above, two below, and one to the side.
13. **The correct answer is B.** Block 13 is touching one to the side, two blocks above, and two below.
14. **The correct answer is C.** Block 14 is touching one block above, one behind, one in front, and two below.
15. **The correct answer is A.** Block 15 is touching one block behind, two above, and two below.
16. **The correct answer is D.** Block 16 is touching two blocks above and two blocks below.
17. **The correct answer is C.** Block 17 is touching one block above, two below, and one to the side.
18. **The correct answer is B.** Block 18 is touching three blocks below and two blocks above.
19. **The correct answer is B.** Block 19 is touching two blocks along one side, one behind, and one along the other side.
20. **The correct answer is E.** Block 20 is touching one block on either side, one behind, and one above.
21. **The correct answer is C.** Block 21 is touching one block above, one block below, and one block to the side.
22. **The correct answer is D.** Block 22 is touching one block above, one block below, and one block to the side.
23. **The correct answer is A.** Block 23 is touching two blocks above, one below, and one to the side.
24. **The correct answer is B.** Block 24 is touching three blocks below and one to the side.
25. **The correct answer is A.** Block 25 is touching one block above and four blocks behind.
26. **The correct answer is C.** Block 26 is touching one block above, one block below, and one block to the side.

27. **The correct answer is A.** Block 27 is touching one block above, three blocks below, and two blocks to the side.

28. **The correct answer is C.** Block 28 is touching two blocks above and one in front.

29. **The correct answer is E.** Block 29 is touching two blocks above.

30. **The correct answer is B.** Block 30 is touching one block above, one block below, and one block to the side.

NOTES

Aviation Information

1. B	5. C	9. B	13. A	17. C
2. A	6. E	10. E	14. E	18. C
3. D	7. D	11. D	15. A	19. B
4. B	8. C	12. B	16. D	20. A

1. **The correct answer is B.** The aileron is close to the wingtip and will move in opposite directions to each other; as one goes up, the other goes down. Rudder (choice A) is a primary flight control that is a flat, movable metal piece attached to the aircraft's rear and is used for steering. Elevator (choice C) is a primary flight control on the aircraft's tail and helps the plane to pitch, go up and down. Stabilator (choice D) is a device that provides stability and controls the up and down motion of the aircraft using both the horizontal stabilizer and elevator. Trim system (choice E) is a secondary flight control, which prevents pilots from having to exert a constant pressure on the controls.

2. **The correct answer is A.** The airport they are departing from is the airport where the pilot would receive the most accurate field elevation information. The field elevation of the closest airport (choice B) is not the airport the pilot is departing from; therefore, it cannot provide the most accurate data. Altimeters in most conventional aircrafts do not have a way to adjust for temperature (choice C), so relying on the flight computer to approximate how much lower the aircraft is in cold air with relation to the indicated altitude is necessary. Although accurate, a radar system (choice D) is expensive, heavy, and complicated. The readings at the destination airport (choice E) will not account for mountaintops, buildings, or any other features on the aircraft's flight path.

3. **The correct answer is D.** The V1 regulatory speed represents the maximum velocity during takeoff that will allow the pilot to stop on the remaining runway in case of an aborted takeoff. VA (choice A) regulatory speed is the highest safe airspeed that can be used for operation in turbulence or severe gusts. VC (choice B) regulatory speed is a velocity for which the aircraft was designed to cruise at optimal performance. VD (choice C) regulatory speed is designed for the aircraft's velocity to be able to enter a dive, a steep descent free of interference. VLO (choice E) regulatory speed is the maximum velocity at which landing gear can be safely extended or retracted.

4. **The correct answer is B.** The trimming occurs when there is no input from the pilot or electronic controls, and the aircraft has achieved and is able to maintain its desired attitude. A pilot holding pressure to maintain a proper climb angle (choice A) does not have a desired attitude for the aircraft. Pushing the control wheel forward to prevent premature rotation (choice C) begins to place increased physical pressure on the aircraft, not allowing for the desired attitude. Pushing or pulling on the yoke (choice D) is not achieving the desired attitude because a pilot is trying to correct a pitch error while the autopilot is engaged. The trim-tab indicator should never be out of takeoff range, even slightly, (choice E) as it is part of the control system and a pilot experiencing trim problems may be placed in a dangerous flight situation.

5. **The correct answer is C.** The aspect ratio is a measure of how long and slender a wing is from tip to tip. The aspect ratio formula of an image (choice A) is commonly used for cinematic, television, and photography purposes. The aspect ratio of the sidewall height of a given tire as a percentage of the section width (choice B)

is based on an automobile not an aircraft. Taper ratio is one of the parameters a designer needs to optimize in order to anticipate the aerodynamic properties of a plane's wings. Wing loading is the calculation of an aircraft's weight to the surface area of its wings (choice E).

6. **The correct answer is E.** The tachometer is an instrument that indicates the speed in RPMs of the crankshaft of a reciprocating engine. A flow-meter indicates an engine's fuel use in real time (choice A). A synchroscope is an instrument that indicates whether two or more rotating devices, such as engines, are synchronized (choice B). The bladder tank is a fuel tank made from fortified flexible material (choice C). A capacitor is a machine that stores electricity (choice D).
7. **The correct answer is D.** The spoiler is a flight control device used to increase drag and spoil lift in an aircraft. The reverse thrust (choice A), wheel braking (choice B), aerodynamic braking (choice C), and tire ground friction (choice E) are all forces for stopping an aircraft.
8. **The correct answer is C.** Since less fuel is necessary for proper engine function as altitude increases, adjusting the fuel and air mixture will decrease fuel flow to the engine, therefore offsetting for decreased air density. The mixture control dictates the ratio of the fuel and air going to the engine (choice A). A cathode ray tube (CRT) display (choice B) reveals information on the aircraft's height, attitude, heading, speed, cabin pressure and temperature, route, fuel quantity and consumption, and the condition of the engines and the hydraulic, electrical, and electronic systems. The exhaust gas temperature gauge (EGT) provides pilots a way of monitoring the fuel/air mixture in the engine of the aircraft (choice D). The induction system brings in the outside air, mixes it with fuel, and delivers the fuel/air mixture to the cylinder (choice E).
9. **The correct answer is B.** The steady red light alerts pilots, in flight, to circle around while giving way to other aircrafts or to stop if the aircraft is on the ground. Flashing red (choice A) is used to inform pilots, who are in flight, that the airport is unsafe and not to land or, if the aircraft is on the ground, that the taxi is clear of the runway in use. Alternating red and green lights alert pilots, in flight and on the ground, to exercise extreme caution. Flashing green (choice D) is used to inform pilots, who are in flight, to return for landing or, if aircraft is on the ground, that they are cleared to taxi. Steady green (choice E) is used to inform pilots, who are in flight, that they are clear to land or, if aircraft is on the ground, that they are cleared for takeoff.
10. **The correct answer is E.** Most tail rotor defects fall into high-frequency vibrations and are felt through the pilot's pedals. The defects of a worn bearing (choice A) and a damper out of adjustment (choice B) are considered low-frequency vibrations. The defects of the air conditioner compressor (choice C) and engine fans (choice D) are considered medium-frequency vibrations.
11. **The correct answer is D.** Turbine engines drive an aircraft propeller, generating thrust. The cockpit (choice A), where the pilot and the co-pilots manage the aircraft, has two main functions: to provide the pilot with a good angle and to make all control systems accessible to them. Spoilers (choice B) are used to interrupt airflow over the wing to significantly reduce lift. Slats (choice C) are meant to reduce the stalling speed by shifting the airflow over the wing. Elevators (choice E) are a primary flight control that regulate the pitch movement, the lateral axis of the aircraft.
12. **The correct answer is B.** The horizontal stabilizer prevents an up-and-down motion of the nose, which is called pitch. The fuselage (choice A) is the aircraft's main body section and holds the crew, passengers, and cargo. Slats (choice C) are meant to reduce the stalling speed by shifting the airflow over the wing. Turbine engines (choice D) drive an aircraft propeller. The aileron (choice E) is the primary flight control that is part of the wing and causes the aircraft to turn by moving up and down.

13. **The correct answer is A.** The collective pitch lever controls the lift produced by the rotor while the cyclic pitch controls the pitch angle of the rotor blades in their repeated rotation. The trim (choice B) helps the pilot to achieve and maintain helicopter balance. The swash plate assembly (choice C) helps to handle the demands of helicopter lifts, turns, and changes in the altitude by adjusting the angle of the rotor blades with each revolution they make. The anti-torque pedals (choice D) allow the pilot to control the pitch angle of the tail rotor blades. The synchropter (choice E) is a helicopter type that uses intermeshing blades.

14. **The correct answer is E.** Flaps are installed on the trailing edge on the inboard section of each wing and bend downward to increase the effective curving of the wing. A wing (choice A) is an airfoil or fin that creates lift when an aircraft moves through the air rapidly. Spoilers (choice B) are used to interrupt airflow over the wing to significantly reduce lift. Slats (choice C) are meant to reduce the stalling speed by shifting the airflow over the wing. Turbine engines (choice D) drive an aircraft's propeller.

15. **The correct answer is A.** The cockpit (or flight deck), where the pilot and the co-pilots operate the aircraft, has two main functions: to provide the pilot with a good angle and to make all control mechanisms accessible to them. Spoilers (choice B) are used to interrupt airflow over the wing to significantly reduce lift. Slats (choice C) are meant to reduce the stalling speed by shifting the airflow over the wing. Flaps (choice D) are installed on the trailing edge on the inboard section of each wing and bend downward to increase the effective curving of the wing. The vertical stabilizer (choice E) keeps the nose of the plane from swinging from side to side, which is called yaw.

16. **The correct answer is D.** Controlled airspace covers the various classifications of airspace and specific features that the air traffic control (ATC) service provides. According to FAA regulations, Class H is not an identifying airspace option. Class E (choice A) provides sufficient airspace for the safe control and separation of aircraft during instrument flight rules (IFR) operations over the United States. Class A (choice B) airspace is located everywhere above 18,000 feet up to and including 60,000 feet and must be operated under instrument flight rules (IFR). Class G (choice C) airspace is uncontrolled and includes visual flight rule minimums that broaden from the surface to the base and spread over the surface of Class E airspace. Class B (choice E) is airspace that envelopes the nation's busiest airports and their operations or passenger boardings and extends it from the surface, which includes two or more layers with all published instrument processes, to 10,000 feet mean sea level (MSL).

17. **The correct answer is C.** Humidity is the amount of moisture in air. Fog (choice A) is when moist, warm air passes over cooler surface air and water vapor condenses. Inversion layers (choice B) are shallow layers of smooth stable air that is close to the ground. Wind (choice D) is moving air caused by differences in air pressure within the atmosphere. Temperature (choice E) is the measurement of how hot or cold an object is.

18. **The correct answer is C.** The normal taxiway centerline is where aircraft are kept during taxiing. There are no threshold taxi lines (choice A), but there are threshold marker lines. The touchdown zone marking (choice B) identifies the touchdown zone for landing operations. Runway aiming point markers (choice D) serve as visual targets for landing the aircraft. Closed runway markings (choice E) are located at both ends of permanently closed runways.

19. **The correct answer is B.** A stationary front is cooler and warmer air residing in the same region with no movement. A warm front has warmer air traveling above and overtaking cooler air (choice A). A cold front has colder air sliding beneath and overtaking warmer air (choice C). An occluded front is a quick moving cool air mass catching up and blending with the

warm front, causing a low-pressure area to form to the north (choice D). A front is a boundary between air masses that have different temperature and moisture matter (choice E).

20. **The correct answer is A.** Winglets are little wings that generate lift and oppose the drag that wingtip vortices create by harnessing the vortices' airflow. The vertical stabilizer (choice B) keeps the nose of the plane from swinging from side to side, which is called yaw. Elevators (choice C) are a primary flight control that regulate the pitch movement, the lateral axis of the aircraft. The horizontal stabilizer (choice D) prevents an up-and-down motion of the nose, which is called pitch. Flaps (choice E) are installed on the trailing edge on the inboard section of each wing and bend downward to increase the effective curving of the wing.

NOTES

SCORE SHEET

Although your actual exam scores will not be reported as percentages, it might be helpful to convert them so you can better visualize your strengths and weaknesses.

AFOQT SCORE SHEET		
Subject	**# Correct ÷ # of questions**	**× 100 = ______ %**
Verbal Analogies	______ ÷ 25 = ______	× 100 = ______ %
Arithmetic Reasoning	______ ÷ 25 = ______	× 100 = ______ %
Word Knowledge	______ ÷ 25 = ______	× 100 = ______ %
Math Knowledge	______ ÷ 25 = ______	× 100 = ______ %
Reading Comprehension	______ ÷ 25 = ______	× 100 = ______ %
Situational Judgment	______ ÷ 50 = ______	× 100 = ______ %
Physical Science	______ ÷ 20 = ______	× 100 = ______ %
Table Reading	______ ÷ 40 = ______	× 100 = ______ %
Instrument Comprehension	______ ÷ 25 = ______	× 100 = ______ %
Block Counting	______ ÷ 30 = ______	× 100 = ______ %
Aviation Information	______ ÷ 20 = ______	× 100 = ______ %

STUDY REFERENCE GUIDE		
Subject	**Chapter**	**Page**
Verbal Analogies	Chapter 5	130
Arithmetic Reasoning	Chapter 7	154
Word Knowledge	Chapter 6	144
Math Knowledge	Chapter 7	154
Reading Comprehension	Chapter 8	220
Situational Judgment	Chapter 9	236
Physical Science	Chapter 11	256
Table Reading	Chapter 13	306
Instrument Comprehension	Chapter 14	316
Block Counting	Chapter 15	330
Aviation Information	Chapter 16	336

NOTES

OAR DIAGNOSTIC TEST

DIAGNOSTIC TEST

This pre-test is designed to help you recognize your strengths and weaknesses. The questions cover information from all of the subtests of the OAR exam.

4

ANSWER SHEET: OAR DIAGNOSTIC TEST

Math Skills

1. Ⓐ Ⓑ Ⓒ Ⓓ	7. Ⓐ Ⓑ Ⓒ Ⓓ	13. Ⓐ Ⓑ Ⓒ Ⓓ	19. Ⓐ Ⓑ Ⓒ Ⓓ	25. Ⓐ Ⓑ Ⓒ Ⓓ
2. Ⓐ Ⓑ Ⓒ Ⓓ	8. Ⓐ Ⓑ Ⓒ Ⓓ	14. Ⓐ Ⓑ Ⓒ Ⓓ	20. Ⓐ Ⓑ Ⓒ Ⓓ	26. Ⓐ Ⓑ Ⓒ Ⓓ
3. Ⓐ Ⓑ Ⓒ Ⓓ	9. Ⓐ Ⓑ Ⓒ Ⓓ	15. Ⓐ Ⓑ Ⓒ Ⓓ	21. Ⓐ Ⓑ Ⓒ Ⓓ	27. Ⓐ Ⓑ Ⓒ Ⓓ
4. Ⓐ Ⓑ Ⓒ Ⓓ	10. Ⓐ Ⓑ Ⓒ Ⓓ	16. Ⓐ Ⓑ Ⓒ Ⓓ	22. Ⓐ Ⓑ Ⓒ Ⓓ	28. Ⓐ Ⓑ Ⓒ Ⓓ
5. Ⓐ Ⓑ Ⓒ Ⓓ	11. Ⓐ Ⓑ Ⓒ Ⓓ	17. Ⓐ Ⓑ Ⓒ Ⓓ	23. Ⓐ Ⓑ Ⓒ Ⓓ	29. Ⓐ Ⓑ Ⓒ Ⓓ
6. Ⓐ Ⓑ Ⓒ Ⓓ	12. Ⓐ Ⓑ Ⓒ Ⓓ	18. Ⓐ Ⓑ Ⓒ Ⓓ	24. Ⓐ Ⓑ Ⓒ Ⓓ	30. Ⓐ Ⓑ Ⓒ Ⓓ

Reading Comprehension

1. Ⓐ Ⓑ Ⓒ Ⓓ	5. Ⓐ Ⓑ Ⓒ Ⓓ	9. Ⓐ Ⓑ Ⓒ Ⓓ	13. Ⓐ Ⓑ Ⓒ Ⓓ	17. Ⓐ Ⓑ Ⓒ Ⓓ
2. Ⓐ Ⓑ Ⓒ Ⓓ	6. Ⓐ Ⓑ Ⓒ Ⓓ	10. Ⓐ Ⓑ Ⓒ Ⓓ	14. Ⓐ Ⓑ Ⓒ Ⓓ	18. Ⓐ Ⓑ Ⓒ Ⓓ
3. Ⓐ Ⓑ Ⓒ Ⓓ	7. Ⓐ Ⓑ Ⓒ Ⓓ	11. Ⓐ Ⓑ Ⓒ Ⓓ	15. Ⓐ Ⓑ Ⓒ Ⓓ	19. Ⓐ Ⓑ Ⓒ Ⓓ
4. Ⓐ Ⓑ Ⓒ Ⓓ	8. Ⓐ Ⓑ Ⓒ Ⓓ	12. Ⓐ Ⓑ Ⓒ Ⓓ	16. Ⓐ Ⓑ Ⓒ Ⓓ	20. Ⓐ Ⓑ Ⓒ Ⓓ

Mechanical Comprehension

1. Ⓐ Ⓑ Ⓒ	7. Ⓐ Ⓑ Ⓒ	13. Ⓐ Ⓑ Ⓒ	19. Ⓐ Ⓑ Ⓒ	25. Ⓐ Ⓑ Ⓒ
2. Ⓐ Ⓑ Ⓒ	8. Ⓐ Ⓑ Ⓒ	14. Ⓐ Ⓑ Ⓒ	20. Ⓐ Ⓑ Ⓒ	26. Ⓐ Ⓑ Ⓒ
3. Ⓐ Ⓑ Ⓒ	9. Ⓐ Ⓑ Ⓒ	15. Ⓐ Ⓑ Ⓒ	21. Ⓐ Ⓑ Ⓒ	27. Ⓐ Ⓑ Ⓒ
4. Ⓐ Ⓑ Ⓒ	10. Ⓐ Ⓑ Ⓒ	16. Ⓐ Ⓑ Ⓒ	22. Ⓐ Ⓑ Ⓒ	28. Ⓐ Ⓑ Ⓒ
5. Ⓐ Ⓑ Ⓒ	11. Ⓐ Ⓑ Ⓒ	17. Ⓐ Ⓑ Ⓒ	23. Ⓐ Ⓑ Ⓒ	29. Ⓐ Ⓑ Ⓒ
6. Ⓐ Ⓑ Ⓒ	12. Ⓐ Ⓑ Ⓒ	18. Ⓐ Ⓑ Ⓒ	24. Ⓐ Ⓑ Ⓒ	30. Ⓐ Ⓑ Ⓒ

MATH SKILLS

30 Questions (40 Minutes)

Directions: This part of the test measures your knowledge of mathematical terms and principles. Each problem is followed by four possible answers. You are to decide which of the four choices is correct.

1. An athlete jogs 20 laps around a circular track. If the total distance jogged is 4 kilometers, what is the distance around the track?

   A. 0.2 meters
   B. 2 meters
   C. 20 meters
   D. 200 meters

2. The floor area in a Navy warehouse measures 100 feet by 100 feet. What is the maximum safe floor load if the maximum weight the floor area can hold is 1,000 tons?

   A. 100 pounds per square foot
   B. 120 pounds per square foot
   C. 160 pounds per square foot
   D. 200 pounds per square foot

3. A crate containing a tool weighs 13 pounds. If the tool weighs 10 pounds, 7 ounces, how much does the crate weigh?

   A. 2 pounds, 7 ounces
   B. 2 pounds, 9 ounces
   C. 3 pounds, 3 ounces
   D. 3 pounds, 7 ounces

4. Assume that the U.S. Mint produces one million dimes a month. The total value of the dimes produced during a year is

   A. $100,000
   B. $500,000
   C. $1,000,000
   D. $1,200,000

5. In order to check on a shipment of 750 articles, a sampling of 75 articles was carefully inspected. Of the sample, 6 articles were found to be defective. On this basis, what is the probable percentage of defective articles in the original shipment?

   A. 8 percent
   B. 4 percent
   C. 0.8 percent
   D. 0.4 percent

6. There are 20 cigarettes in one pack and 10 packs of cigarettes in a carton. A certain brand of cigarette contains 11 mg of tar per cigarette. How many grams of tar are contained in one carton of these cigarettes? (1 gram = 1,000 milligrams)

   A. 0.022 grams
   B. 0.22 grams
   C. 2.2 grams
   D. 22 grams

7. Assume that it takes an average of 4 labor-hours to stack 1 ton of a particular item. In order to stack 27 tons in 9 hours, the number of people required is

   A. 9
   B. 12
   C. 15
   D. 18

8. Two office workers have been assigned to address 1,500 envelopes. One addresses twice as many envelopes per hour as the other. If it takes 5 hours for them to complete the job, what was the rate of the slower worker?

A. 50 envelopes per hour

B. 75 envelopes per hour

C. 100 envelopes per hour

D. 125 envelopes per hour

9. A room measuring 18 feet wide, 30 feet long, and 10 feet high is scheduled to be painted shortly. If there are two windows in the room, each 7 feet by 5 feet, and a glass door, 6 feet by 4 feet, then the area of wall space to be painted measures

A. 842 square feet.

B. 866 square feet.

C. 901 square feet.

D. 925 square feet.

10. A pound carton of margarine contains four equal sticks of margarine. The wrapper of each stick has markings that indicate how to divide the stick into eight sections, each section measuring one tablespoon. If a recipe calls for 2 tablespoons of margarine, the amount to use is

A. $\frac{1}{16}$ lb.

B. $\frac{1}{8}$ lb.

C. $\frac{1}{4}$ lb.

D. $\frac{1}{2}$ lb.

11. The price of a one-hundred-dollar item after successive discounts of 20 percent and 5 percent is

A. $75.00

B. $75.50

C. $76.00

D. $76.50

12. A certain governmental agency had a budget last year of $1,100,500. Its budget this year was 7 percent higher than that of last year. The budget for next year is 9 percent higher than this year's budget. Which of the following is the agency's approximate budget for next year?

A. $1,117,600

B. $1,161,600

C. $1,261,700

D. $1,283,500

13. The length of a rectangle is 4 times the width. If the area of the rectangle is 256 square feet, the dimensions of the rectangle are

A. 8' × 32'

B. 8' × 42'

C. 9' × 36'

D. 9' × 40'

14. On a scaled drawing of an office building floor, $\frac{1}{2}$ inch represents 3 feet of actual floor dimension. A floor that is actually 177 feet wide and 312 feet long would have which of the following dimensions on the scaled drawing?

A. 12.5 inches wide and 22 inches long

B. 17 inches wide and 32 inches long

C. 25 inches wide and 44 inches long

D. 29.5 inches wide and 52 inches long

15. If the weight of water is 62.4 pounds per cubic foot, the weight of the water that fills a rectangular container 6 inches by 6 inches by 6 inches is

A. 3.9 pounds.

B. 7.8 pounds.

C. 15.6 pounds.

D. 31.2 pounds.

16. Which of the following integers is NOT a prime number?

A. 5

B. 7

C. 9

D. 11

17. The distance in miles around a circular course with a radius of 350 miles is (use pi = $\frac{22}{7}$)

A. 1,110 miles.

B. 1,560 miles.

C. 2,200 miles.

D. 4,400 miles.

18. If $6x + 3y = 42$ and $x - y = 1$, then $x =$

A. 1

B. 2

C. 4

D. 5

19. Solve for $x: \frac{7x^2}{2} = x$

A. $\frac{1}{7}$

B. $\frac{2}{7}$

C. 2

D. 7

20. If x is an even integer, which one of the following is an odd integer?

A. $2x + 2$

B. $2x - 2$

C. $x^2 - x$

D. $x^2 + x - 1$

21. $\frac{x+1}{x^2-3x-4}$ can be reduced to

A. $\frac{1}{x-4}$

B. $\frac{1}{x-2}$

C. $\frac{x-2}{x+2}$

D. $\frac{1}{x+2}$

22. 5^x divided by 5^y equals

A. $5^{x/y}$

B. 5^{xy}

C. 5^{x+y}

D. 5^{x-y}

23. $(-2)^3 =$

A. 6

B. −6

C. 8

D. −8

24. Ten million may be represented as

A. 10^4

B. 10^5

C. 10^6

D. 10^7

25. $\left(\frac{3}{7}\right)^2$ equals

A. $\frac{6}{7}$

B. $\frac{3}{14}$

C. $\frac{6}{14}$

D. $\frac{9}{49}$

26. If $3^n = 27$, what is the value of 2^{n+3}

A. 24

B. 48

C. 64

D. 108

27. 10^{-3} is equal to

A. 0.001

B. 0.01

C. 0.1

D. 1.01

28. The expression $\sqrt{28} + \sqrt{7}$ reduces to

A. $\sqrt{4}$

B. $\sqrt{7}$

C. $3\sqrt{7}$

D. $\sqrt{21}$

29. The hypotenuse of a right triangle whose legs are 8 inches and 15 inches is

A. 7 inches

B. 13 inches

C. 14 inches

D. 17 inches

30. The sum of the angle measures of a hexagon is

A. 360 degrees.

B. 540 degrees.

C. 720 degrees.

D. 900 degrees.

STOP.

If you finish before time is up, you may check your work on this section only. Do not turn to any other section in the test.

READING COMPREHENSION

20 Questions (30 Minutes)

Directions: This part of the exam will test your reading comprehension abilities. Each question has four choices. Choose the best option based on the information provided.

Typical airport runways have a length running between 8,000 and 13,000 feet. Planes must take off at the end of the runway, so many commercial pilots look for white "distance remaining markers." A distance remaining marker that bears the number "4" indicates 4,000 feet left on the runway, while a "3" indicates 3,000 feet and so on.

1. The information in the passage indicates that

   A. there are no airport runways that run under 13,000 feet.

   B. the longest airport runway is 13,000 feet.

   C. a distance remaining marker indicates how far the plane has traveled on the runway.

   D. a distance remaining marker bearing the number 7 indicates that the plane has 7,000 feet remaining to travel before takeoff.

A stethoscope is a relatively simple piece of medical equipment that uses the basic properties of sound to translate and amplify minute sounds from within the body. The key components of a stethoscope are the diaphragm, the bell, the tubes, and the earpiece. The diaphragm, the flat piece at the end of the instrument that is laid on the body, picks up high-range sounds such as heartbeats and breaths, while the bell, a bell-shaped piece of metal that attaches to the diaphragm, picks up low-pitch sounds like heart murmurs. The tubes carry the sound to the earpieces that filter the sound into the ears of the medical provider.

2. This passage best supports the statement that

   A. stethoscopes can only hear beats and murmurs from the heart.

   B. the diaphragm of the stethoscope can pick up heart murmurs.

   C. the tubes are not a necessary part of the stethoscope.

   D. stethoscopes are useful when listening to minute sounds within the body.

Bandanas are one of the most versatile accessories in the American fashion industry, but they were not originally an American invention. The famous paisley pattern, worn by sailors and cowboys alike, is actually a product of the region of Kashmir, once a part of Persia. Originally, the print itself was called *boteh* or "brush," as a nod to the vaguely floral pattern of the print's design. These Persian masterpieces were traded as any good was traded out of Persia, through the Dutch East India Trading Company, and were soon popularized in Europe. And thus, the bandana was born.

3. Based on the information in the passage, the bandana

   A. was originally a European invention that stemmed from Persian influence.

   B. is an American piece of garb that was founded in America.

   C. dons a print that was originally called *boteh* meaning "brush."

   D. is still primarily worn by sailors and cowboys.

While small dogs tend to have longer lifespans than big dogs, they are subject to numerous other health risks that big dogs don't typically face, such as a collapsed trachea. This is due to the pressure caused by leashed collars when they jump up on walks. Similarly, jumping up onto high surfaces can cause the kneecaps in small dogs to collapse.

4. This passage best supports the statement that

   A. small dogs live shorter lives.

   B. dogs' kneecaps can collapse when jumping too high.

   C. small dogs suffer health risks directly associated with jumping.

   D. big dogs don't suffer collapsed tracheas.

Some popular middle school fads that seem harmless upon first glance can, in fact, be hazardous to the students who partake in them. Slap bracelets, for instance, were a phenomenon that saw kids hitting each other with flexible steely bands only for them to wrap around their wrists. These bands, while entertaining, contained metal strips that eventually began to cut the children who used them. Silly Bandz, a similar fad, saw kids wearing 20 different colorful, shaped rubber bands on their wrists, cutting off circulation and leaving skin bruised.

5. This passage best supports the statement that

   A. all middle school fads are dangerous to the children that partake.

   B. slap bracelets are hazardous due to the metal strips that reside inside them.

   C. one Silly Band can cut off circulation on the wrist.

   D. slap bracelets and Silly Bandz are both banned from schools.

Supplemental protein sources have recently begun to rise in popularity and variety. Whey protein, a classic type of protein powder, contains high-quality amino acids that have been proven to stimulate muscle protein synthesis better than alternative supplements. Muscle stimulation is increased by 122% when whey is consumed post-exertion, in comparison with casein and soy proteins: 31% and 2%, respectively.

6. Based on the information in this passage, whey protein

   A. is the most expensive type of protein powder on the market.

   B. contains higher-quality amino acids than casein and soy supplements on the market.

   C. is similar to casein protein as they both stimulate high protein synthesis in muscles.

   D. can't be consumed with other types of protein supplements.

The zipper is a great technological advancement that, while simple in appearance and approximately 80 years old, is complicated in mechanism. The two rows of teeth that face each other on either side of the zipper must be identical in size and shape in order to connect properly. Each side has hooks and hollows that are wedged together by the slide portion of the zipper and pushed apart when it comes time to unzip.

7. Based on the information in the passage, the mechanics of the zipper

   A. do not require the sliding portion so long as the teeth fit together.

   B. require the teeth to be identical in size and shape.

   C. are a relatively new invention.

   D. are not as complicated as they seem.

The dawn of college football began on the green field of Rutgers University in 1869. Technically, this game was not the beloved American contact sport we know today as the rules were derived from the London Football Association handbook, which expressly forbade players from picking up or throwing the football, so the game looked far more like soccer or rugby in its early days. The first real game of football wasn't played until seven years later when representatives from Columbia, Harvard, Princeton, and Yale came together to define the rules of what we know today as American football.

8. This passage best supports the statement that

A. American football first began in the college system.

B. soccer and rugby are essentially the same thing.

C. the London Football Association forbade players from touching the ball.

D. American football is English rugby.

Different from most sports and games where the highest score determines the winner, golf is ranked based on the lowest score, or the number of strokes taken. In golf, one stroke is equivalent to one shot, and the goal of the game is to take as few shots as possible to land the ball in the hole. A golfer can also try to attain par, the number of strokes listed on the scorecard.

9. Based on the information provided, golf scoring

A. is based on how far the ball travels in one shot.

B. ranks winners based on who has the lowest score.

C. adds points when fewer strokes are used.

D. takes the type of shot into account.

Cultural relativism is an ethical ideology that says there must be no universal moral truth as different cultures have different moral codes, and thus, moral truth is relative to an individual's culture. The argument that follows from this assertion reasons that it is the duty of the culture to determine what is right and wrong. This ideology encourages an adoption of tolerance, as there can be no standard by which to judge what is right or wrong, just or unjust. However, it also implies that there could be no moral progress within a society. If a society determines an action to be morally wrong, then there can be no criticizing the actions of the society. There can be no moral progress because progress implies that there is a standard by which we judge what choices are better or worse.

10. Based on the information provided in the passage, cultural relativism

A. asserts that different cultures share the same core values but have different beliefs, which leads people to make different choices.

B. says that an individual is capable of questioning the views of a society.

C. is an ethical ideology that encourages the adoption of tolerance for different cultural views but acknowledges a universal moral truth.

D. implies that there can be no moral progress if there is no universal standard by which to judge which morals are better or worse.

E-cigarettes, more commonly known as vapes, are non-combustible tobacco products similar in shape, size, and function to normal cigarettes. They deposit nicotine and various other substances into the lungs in a vapor form, hence the name. Due to the lack of research done on vapes, they have enjoyed massive popularity among young demographics who have little to no nicotine experience as well as seasoned cigarette users seeking to relieve their addiction.

11. This passage best supports the statement that

A. vapes are more addictive than regular cigarettes.

B. vapes deposit more than nicotine into the lungs.

C. e-cigarettes and vapes are two different products.

D. vapes have enjoyed massive popularity among young demographics with addictions.

Tinker v *Des Moines* was a Supreme Court case that established the legal precedent for free speech in public schools following the silent protests of multiple 11-year-old students at a public school in Des Moines. The plan was for a group of students to wear black armbands in silent protest against the war in Vietnam, but when the school got wind of this plan, they took preemptive measures against it to ensure that no armbands were worn. When some students returned to school with black armbands, they were suspended until they agreed to shed the bands. Of course, the students agreed to shed the bands, but their parents swiftly took to the courts and filed a First Amendment lawsuit. The court's decision ruled in favor of the students (7-2), asserting that school officials possessed no absolute power over students and that the minors did not surrender their constitutional rights at the door of the classroom.

12. Based on the information in this passage, *Tinker* v *Des Moines*

A. involved the silent protests of parents of students at a Des Moines public school.

B. established the legal precedent for punishing schools that suspend their students due to wardrobe choice.

C. had more to do with the war at hand than it did with the suspended students.

D. held the opinion that students did not surrender their First Amendment rights when they entered school.

"Designer dogs" are a popular new choice of domestic pets. The term refers to mixed breeds that have been purposefully bred for specific genetics. However, by this definition, all domestic dogs are designer dogs as all dogs have historically been genetically modified by humans. Labradoodles, the most famous of the designer dogs, are only the most recent in a long list of genetic modifications to the original wild dog.

13. Based on the information in this passage, designer dogs are

A. all dogs with mixed pedigrees.

B. domestic dogs by definition.

C. mainly labradoodles and other popular mixes.

D. any dogs that are bred.

Curling is an Olympic sport with a long and noble history, originating in Scotland where there were exclusive curling clubs. The sport was eventually included in the 1924 Olympics but was soon dropped. From 1932 to 1998, it bided its time as a demonstration sport with both men and women's events until the Nagano Olympics where it finally stepped into the spotlight as a program.

14. This passage best supports the statement that

A. curling was a noble sport in Scotland.

B. curling was a favorite sport in the 1950s.

C. curling is still used as a demonstration sport.

D. exclusive curling clubs still exist in Scotland.

The Boeing 747 is the most widely known commercial aircraft and is famous for its huge body made up of 6 million different parts. All of these parts are controlled by the two pilots sitting up in the cockpit. Its engine alone weighs about 9,500 lb. and costs about 8 million dollars.

15. Given this information, the Boeing 747 must

A. cost about 8 million dollars.

B. weigh more than 9,500 lb. and cost about 8 million dollars.

C. be made of 6 million different parts that weigh about 9,500 lb. each.

D. weigh more than 9,500 lb. and cost more than 8 million dollars.

Above one of the front pockets of most jeans, there will be a smaller, less noticeable pocket that looks just big enough to stick your thumb in. Though this pocket is not obsolete in the slightest, it was originally intended to hold a pocket watch and has since evolved in its purpose. Nowadays, this pocket holds more commonplace items such as extra coinage, keys, or wrappers.

16. Based on the information in this passage, the fifth pocket on jeans

A. is used primarily to hold coins.

B. was historically used to hold a pocket watch.

C. has no purpose in the modern day.

D. sits atop the back pocket of most jeans.

The aglet is the piece at the end of a shoelace that ties the end of the strings together, making it easier for wearers to lace their shoes. It can be molded in metal or plastic or even a piece of adhesive tape, but its purpose is to contain the string holding shoes together. While the history of the aglet is quite murky, with some dispute as to whether the invention of the shoelace in 1790 was in fact one in the same with the invention of the aglet, its purpose today is quite clear.

17. This passage best supports the statement that

A. aglets can be made of adhesive tape as long as it holds the shoelace together.

B. aglets are the same thing as a shoelace because they were invented around the same time.

C. aglets are not as useful as the shoelace itself.

D. aglets are a widely known and widely appreciated piece of utility.

Acrophobia is defined as the fear of heights, but some people who are acrophobic are also aerophobic. Aerophobia is the fear of flying, and more than 80% of the population is afraid of flying. People who are acrophobic are typically afraid of tall buildings and ladders, so getting on a plane is difficult for them depending on the severity of their fear.

18. Given this information, what must be true?

A. More than 80% of the population is acrophobic.

B. More than 80% of the population is aerophobic.

C. All people who are aerophobic are afraid of tall buildings and ladders.

D. All people who are afraid of heights are afraid of flying.

Recycling plants utilize advanced technology to sort and separate waste materials, as well as remove scraps and particles (i.e., food, dirt, non-recyclables, etc.) that could possibly contaminate the machines and the recyclables themselves. The materials are then separated again based upon dimension and are personally inspected by plant workers to ensure their cleanliness.

19. Based on the information provided in this passage, recycling plants

A. inspect the cleanliness of the non-recycled materials.

B. sort recyclables and non-recyclables into two groups based on dimension.

C. remove scraps and particles such as food and dirt from recyclable materials.

D. utilize advanced technology to clean waste materials in case they contaminate the workers.

Ibn Battuta was a medieval Muslim traveler who documented his journey through the Muslim world in an in-depth travel book called the *Rihlah* (an Arabic word meaning "travel"). A native to the town of Tangier and born to a family of judges, Ibn Battuta began his travels as any young Muslim man would—on his pilgrimage (hajj) to Mecca, the holy city. Traditionally educated and endlessly curious, young Ibn Battuta had originally intended to not only fulfill his religious duties but also continue his worldly education by studying under the great scholars of Egypt, Syria, and Hejaz. His travels certainly took him beyond the realm of his original plan, and his book details this journey, including details that have been verified by numerous contemporary sources and that speak to the traveler's distinction and renown.

20. This passage best supports the statement that Ibn Battuta

A. traveled to Egypt, Syria, and Hejaz before returning to Tangier to write his travel book.

B. was a world-renowned traveler of the Muslim world who published an in-depth account of his travels and named it *Rihlah*.

C. was a young judge from the Muslim world who documented his pilgrimage to the holy city of Mecca.

D. was traditionally educated by the great scholars of Mecca and Tangier before traveling to Egypt, Syria, and Hejaz.

STOP.

If you finish before time is up, you may check your work on this section only. Do not turn to any other section in the test.

MECHANICAL COMPREHENSION

30 Questions (15 Minutes)

Directions: This part of the exam will test your mechanical comprehension abilities. Each question has three choices. Choose the best option based on the information provided.

1. What is acceleration?

   A. Rate of change of an object's position

   B. Rate of change of an object's dimension

   C. Rate of change of an object's velocity

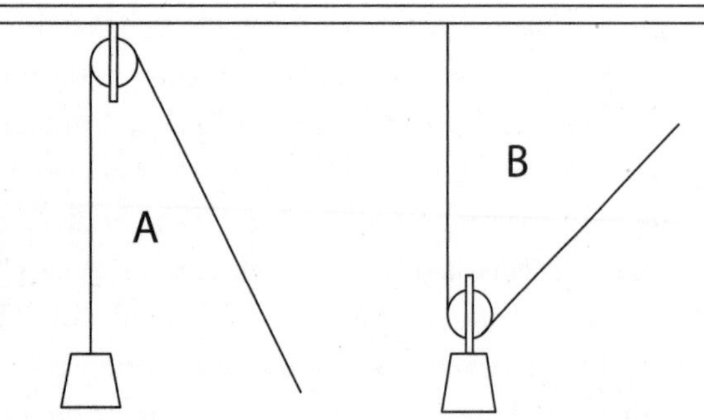

2. Which pulley system requires the least amount of force to lift a load?

   A. System A

   B. System B

   C. Both work equally well.

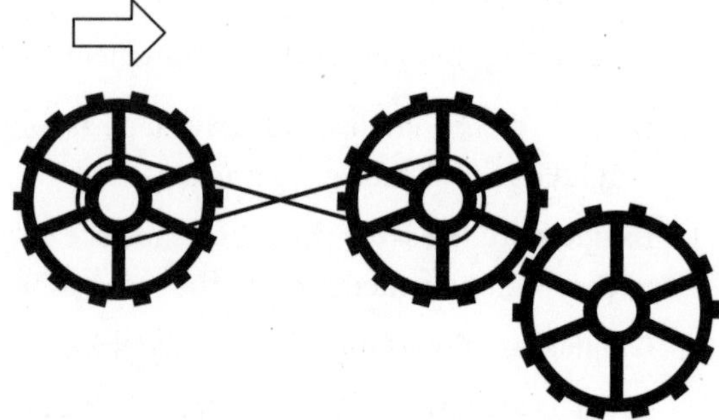

3. A gear is attached by a crossed belt to another gear. This second gear meshes with a third gear. If the first gear is turned clockwise, then which direction does the third gear turn?

   A. Clockwise

   B. The gear won't turn because of the belt.

   C. Counterclockwise

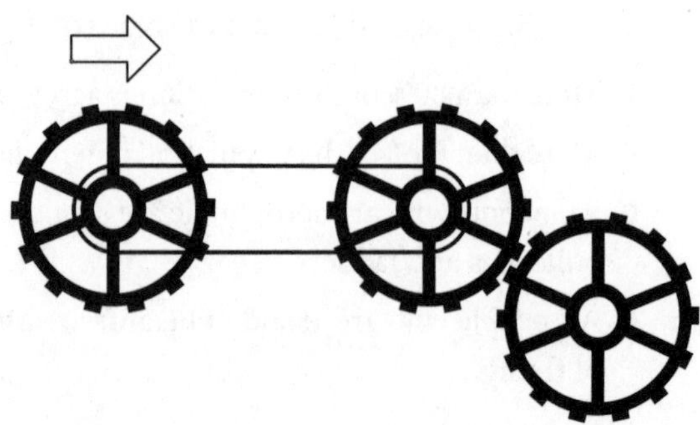

4. There is a gear attached by a belt to another gear. This second gear meshes with a third gear. If the first gear is turned clockwise, then which direction does the third gear turn?

   A. Clockwise

   B. The gear won't turn because of the belt.

   C. Counterclockwise

5. A man runs around a mile-loop track. He runs around it 4 times at a speed of 6 miles per hour. When he finishes where he began, what was his average velocity?

A. 0 mph

B. 6 mph

C. 24 mph

6. What is the purpose of a lever?

A. To amplify the force of the effort

B. To change the direction that the force is being applied

C. Both A and B

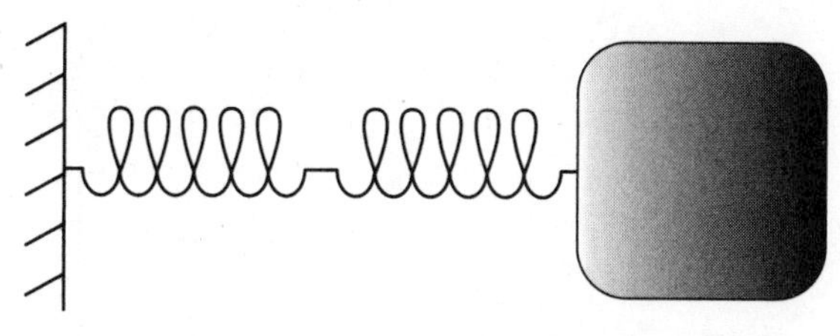

7. A series of two identical springs compresses 4 inches when 5 pounds of force is applied to it. What would be the distance two other identical springs, but in parallel, would compress if the same amount of force was applied?

A. 8 inches

B. 4 inches

C. 2 inches

8. Mass times acceleration is equal to what?

A. Force

B. Speed

C. Velocity

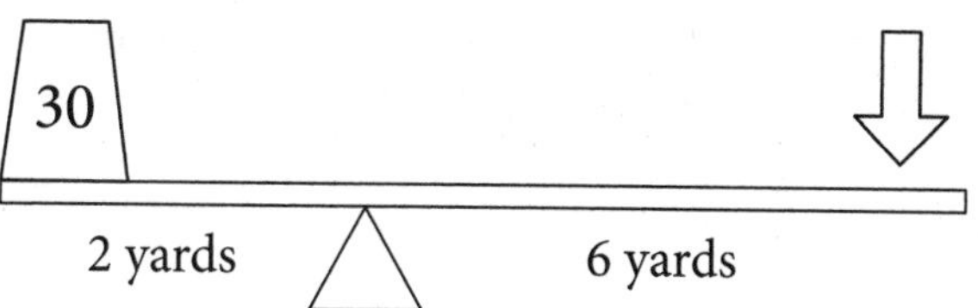

9. The figure above represents an ideal class 1 lever. The length of the load to the fulcrum is 2 yards and the weight of the load is 30 pounds. The length from the fulcrum to the effort is 6 yards. How much force is required to lift the load?

A. 180 pounds

B. 10 pounds

C. 30 pounds

10. What class lever is exhibited in the image above?

A. Class 1 lever

B. Class 2 lever

C. Class 3 lever

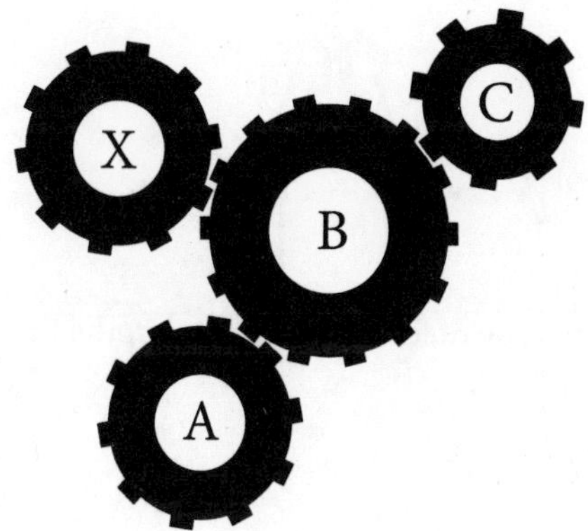

11. Gear X turns clockwise. Which gear will turn counterclockwise?

A. Gear A

B. Gear B

C. Gear C

12. What is the unit of potential difference of electrical flow?

    A. Ohm

    B. Amp

    C. Volt

13. Constant force springs have what form?

    A. Tightly wound bands of steel that resemble a roll of tape

    B. Washers that resemble a slightly tapered disc

    C. Flat metal discs wound together to form helical spirals

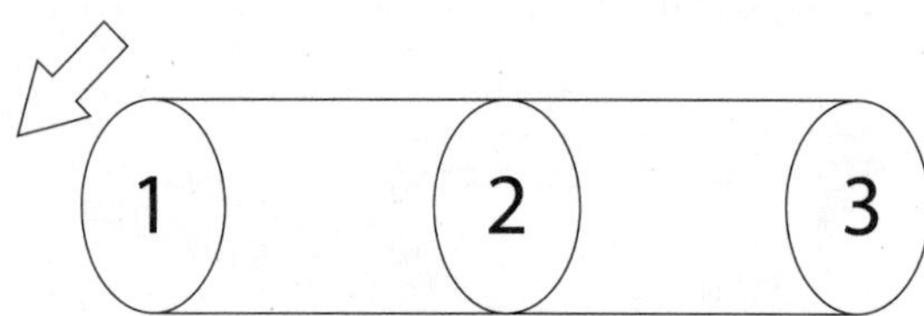

14. There are three equally sized pulleys connected by a rope. The first pulley turns counterclockwise. Which direction will the third pulley turn?

    A. Clockwise

    B. Counterclockwise

    C. It won't move at all

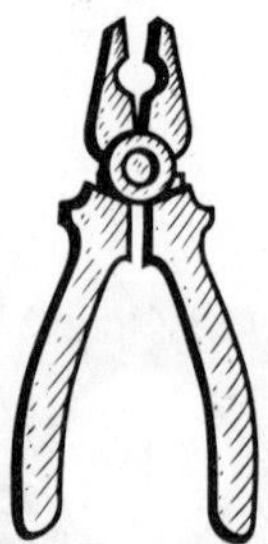

15. Which type of lever is illustrated in the image above?

    A. Class 1 lever

    B. Class 2 lever

    C. Class 3 lever

16. What is the term for speed in a given direction?

    A. Momentum

    B. Velocity

    C. Force

17. Which of the following is used to reduce current flow in a circuit?

    A. Capacitor

    B. Resistor

    C. Conductor

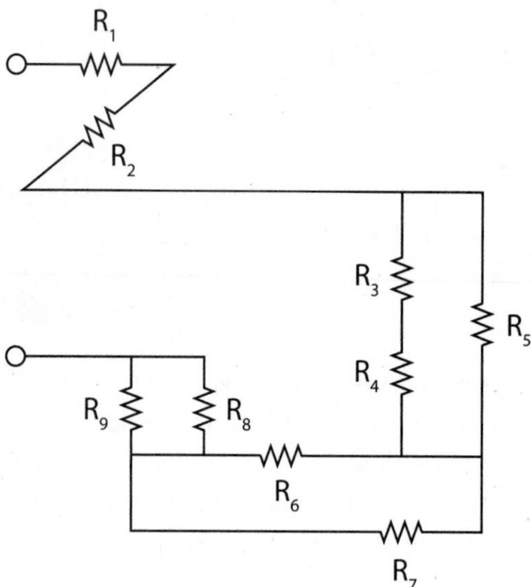

18. Which resistors in this circuit are in a series?

    A. R_3 and R_4

    B. R_6 and R_7

    C. R_9 and R_8

19. A car moves 20 miles north, then 13 miles east, and lastly drives 20 miles south. What is its displacement?

    A. 20 miles north

    B. 13 miles east

    C. 20 miles south

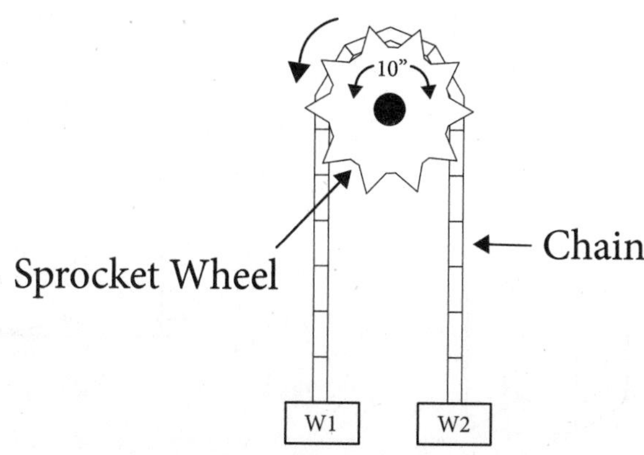

20. In the figure above, one complete revolution of the sprocket wheel will bring weight W2 higher than weight W1 by

    A. 30 inches.

    B. 40 inches.

    C. 20 inches.

21. A box needs to be built with a volume of 40 cubic centimeters. The length is 10 centimeters and the height is 4 centimeters. How wide does the box need to be?

    A. 1 centimeter

    B. 2 centimeters

    C. 4 centimeters

22. Which of the following is NOT a spring?

    A. The bow in a bow-and-arrow system

    B. A screw

    C. A rubber band

23. Nine Newtons of force are being applied to 3 square meters. How much pressure is being applied to the area?

    A. 3 Pascals

    B. 9 Pascals

    C. 27 Pascals

24. A limp balloon is attached to a glass bottle with air in it, sealing the air inside. What can be done to the temperature of the bottle so that the balloon gets drawn inside of the bottle?

    A. Increase the temperature

    B. Decrease the temperature

    C. Temperature will not affect this situation

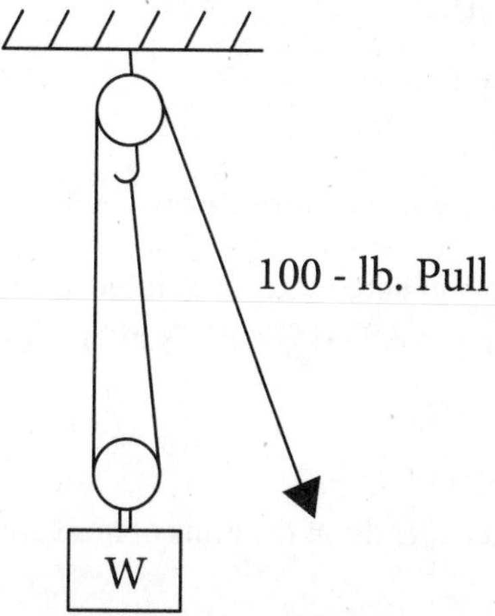

25. The maximum weight, *W*, that can be lifted as shown with a pull of 100 pounds is

    A. 100 pounds.

    B. 200 pounds.

    C. 300 pounds.

26. A fixed pulley is used to lift a crate to the roof of a building. If a movable pulley was used instead, the distance pulled would

A. increase.

B. decrease.

C. remain the same.

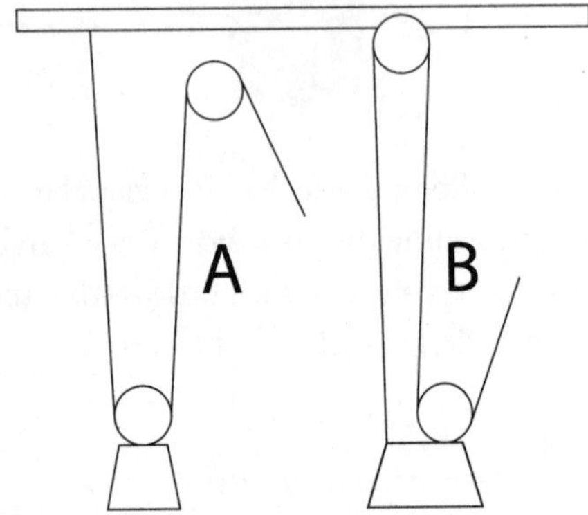

27. Which system of pulleys will take the least effort to lift?

A. System A

B. System B

C. They will require the same amount of effort.

28. Can you determine the volume of an arbitrarily shaped solid using only its surface area?

A. You can.

B. You cannot.

C. It depends on the units of measure.

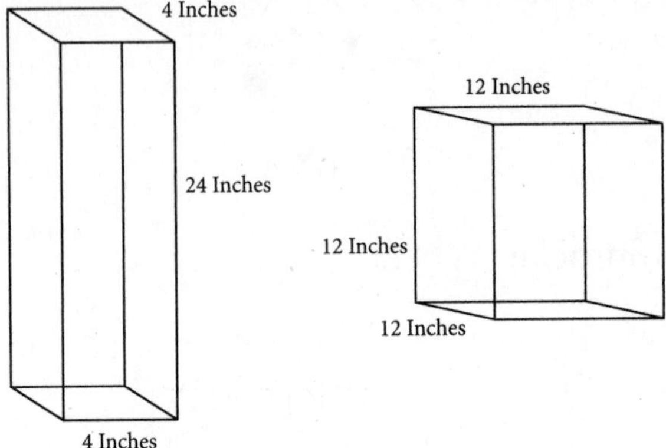

29. A rectangle measures 4 inches long, 4 inches wide, and 24 inches tall. A cube measures 12 inches long, 12 inches wide, and 12 inches tall. Which shape has the most volume?

A. The rectangle

B. The cube

C. They have equal volume

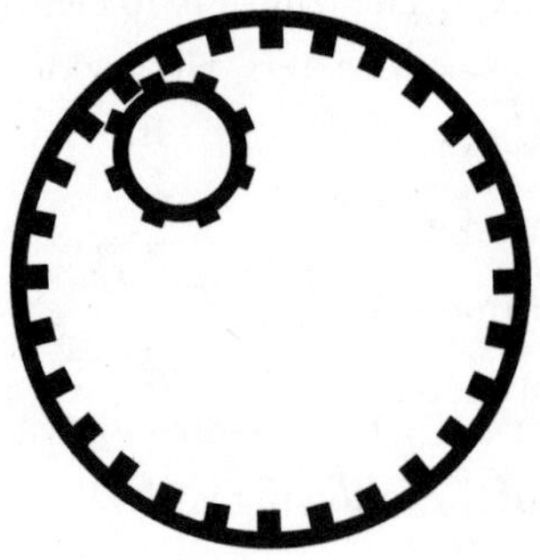

30. An internal cogwheel (a gear with the teeth on the inside) is joined together with a normal gear. If the internal cogwheel is turned counterclockwise, which direction will the gear turn?

A. Clockwise

B. Counterclockwise

C. Internal cogwheels and gears do not work together

STOP.

If you finish before time is up, you may check your work on this section only. Do not turn to any other section in the test.

ANSWER KEYS AND EXPLANATIONS

Math Skills

1. D	6. C	11. C	16. C	21. A	26. C
2. D	7. B	12. D	17. C	22. D	27. A
3. B	8. C	13. A	18. D	23. D	28. C
4. D	9. B	14. D	19. B	24. D	29. D
5. A	10. A	15. B	20. D	25. D	30. C

1. **The correct answer is D.** 4 kilometers = 4,000 meters; $\frac{4,000}{20} = 200$ meters.
2. **The correct answer is D.** 100 feet × 100 feet = 10,000 square feet of floor area; 1,000 tons × 2,000 = 2,000,000 pounds; $\frac{2,000,000}{10,000} = 200$ pounds.
3. **The correct answer is B.** 13 pounds = 12 pounds, 16 ounces; weight of tool = 10 pounds, 7 ounces. 12 pounds, 16 ounces minus 10 pounds, 7 ounces = 2 pounds, 9 ounces.
4. **The correct answer is D.** One million × 12 = 12 million = 12,000,000 (dimes per year); 12,000,000 × 0.10 = $1,200,000
5. **The correct answer is A.** The sample size is 75. The number of defects found in the sample is 6. $\frac{6}{75} = 8\%$. If 8% are defective, it is probable that the percentage of defective articles in the original shipment is also 8%.
6. **The correct answer is C.** There are 200 cigarettes in a carton (20 × 10 = 200). 11 mg × 200 = 2,200 mg of tar in 200 cigarettes. 2,200 mg = 2.2 grams.
7. **The correct answer is B.** 27 tons × 4 labor-hours = 108 labor-hours to stack 27 tons. $\frac{108}{9} = 12$ people needed to complete stacking in 9 hours.
8. **The correct answer is C.** Let x equal the number of envelopes addressed in 1 hour by the slower worker. $2x$ equals the number of envelopes addressed in 1 hour by the faster worker. $3x(5) = 1,500$; $15x = 1,500$; $x = 100$ envelopes per hour for the slower worker.
9. **The correct answer is B.** 30 × 10 = 300 sq. ft. = area of long wall; (300 × 2 = 600 sq. ft.) 18 × 10 = 180 sq. ft. = area of short wall; (180 × 2 = 360 sq. ft.) 600 + 360 = 960 sq. ft. = total wall area. 7 × 5 = 35 sq. ft. = area of window; 35 × 2 = 70 sq. ft. = area of windows. 6 × 4 = 24 sq. ft. = area of glass door; 70 + 24 = 94 sq. ft. = total glass area. 960 – 94 = 866 sq. ft. of wall space to be painted.
10. **The correct answer is A.** Each stick of margarine is $\frac{1}{4}$ lb. Each stick consists of eight sections or tablespoons. Two sections or tablespoons equal $\frac{1}{4}$ of $\frac{1}{4}$ lb., which equals $\frac{1}{16}$ lb.
11. **The correct answer is C.** $100 × 0.20 = $20; $100 – $20 = $80. $80 × 0.05 = $4; $80 – $4 = $76.00.
12. **The correct answer is D.** $1,100,500 × 0.07 = $77,035; $1,100,500 + $77,035 = $1,177,535 = this year's budget. $1,177,535 × 0.09 = $105,978; $1,177,535 + $105,978 = $1,283,513, which is closest to choice E.
13. **The correct answer is A.** Let x equal the width of the rectangle; $4x$ equals the length of the rectangle, $x(4x) = 256$; $4x^2 = 256$; $x^2 = \frac{256}{4} = 64$; $x = 8$ feet; $4x = 32$ feet.
14. **The correct answer is D.** $\frac{1}{2}$ inch on the scaled drawing is 3 feet of actual floor dimension. $\frac{177}{3} = 59 \times \frac{1}{2}$ inches = 29.5 inches; $\frac{312}{3} = 104 \times \frac{1}{2}$ inches = 52 inches.
15. **The correct answer is B.** $\frac{1}{2} \times \frac{1}{2} \times \frac{1}{2} = \frac{1}{8}$ cu. ft.; $\frac{1}{8}$ of 62.4 is 7.8 pounds.

ANSWERS >> DIAGNOSTIC TEST

16. **The correct answer is C.** A natural number that has no other factors except 1 and itself is a prime number. 9 is divisible by 1, 3, and 9.

17. **The correct answer is C.** Circumference = $\pi \times$ diameter; circumference $= \frac{22}{7} \times 70 = 2220$ miles.

18. **The correct answer is D.**

$$\begin{aligned} 6x + 3(x-1) &= 42 \\ 6x + 3x - 3 &= 42 \\ 9x &= 45 \\ x &= 5 \end{aligned}$$

19. **The correct answer is B.**

$$\begin{aligned} \frac{7x^2}{2} &= \frac{x}{1} \\ 7x^2 &= 2x \\ 7x^2 - 2x &= 0 \\ x(7x-2) &= 0 \\ x &= 0, \frac{2}{7} \end{aligned}$$

20. **The correct answer is D.** Squaring an even integer results in an even integer. Adding an even integer to it results in an even integer. Subtracting 1 results in an odd integer. Choices A, B, and C remain even.

21. **The correct answer is A.**

$$\begin{aligned} \frac{x+1}{x^2 - 3x - 4} &= \frac{x+1}{(x+1)(x-4)} \\ &= \frac{1}{x-4} \end{aligned}$$

22. **The correct answer is D.** To divide powers of the same base, subtract the exponent of the denominator from the exponent of the numerator. 5^x divided by 5^y equals 5^{x-y}.

23. **The correct answer is D.** The odd integer power of a negative number is negative; the even integer power of a negative number is positive.

24. **The correct answer is D.** $10{,}000{,}000 = 10^7$

25. **The correct answer is D.**

$$\left(\frac{3}{7}\right)^2 = \frac{3}{7} \times \frac{3}{7} = \frac{9}{49}$$

26. **The correct answer is C.** $3^n = 27$; $n = 3$; $2^{n+3} = 2^6 = 64$

27. **The correct answer is A.**

$$10^{-3} = \frac{1}{10^3} = \frac{1}{1000} = 0.001$$

28. **The correct answer is C.**

$$\begin{aligned} \sqrt{28} + \sqrt{7} &= \sqrt{7 \times 4} + \sqrt{7} \\ &= 2\sqrt{7} + \sqrt{7} \\ &= 3\sqrt{7} \end{aligned}$$

29. **The correct answer is D.**

$$\begin{aligned} h^2 &= 8^2 + 15^2 \\ h^2 &= 64 + 225 \\ h^2 &= 289 \\ \sqrt{289} &= 17'' \end{aligned}$$

30. **The correct answer is C.** A hexagon has 6 sides. (Number of sides – 2) × 180 degrees = sum of angles. 4 × 180 degrees = 720°.

Reading Comprehension

1. D	5. B	9. B	13. B	17. A
2. D	6. B	10. D	14. A	18. B
3. C	7. B	11. B	15. D	19. C
4. C	8. A	12. D	16. B	20. B

1. **The correct answer is D.** Given the information in the passage, the single number on a "distance remaining marker" is a multiple of a thousand. It is also the distance the plane has to travel before reaching the end of the runway and thus the takeoff. If a distance remaining marker bears the number 7, then there must be 7,000 feet remaining before takeoff, so the correct answer is D.
2. **The correct answer is D.** Stethoscopes are primarily used to listen to any minute sounds within the body.
3. **The correct answer is C.** The classic bandana print was originally Persian and named *boteh* as a nod to its floral nature.
4. **The correct answer is C.** Both of the health risks listed are directly associated with small dogs jumping.
5. **The correct answer is B.** The metal strip inside of slap bracelets can cut children's wrists when they break the fabric.
6. **The correct answer is B.** Whey protein contains amino acids that have been proven to stimulate protein synthesis in muscles better than any soy or casein supplements on the market.
7. **The correct answer is B.** In order for the mechanics of the zipper to function properly, the teeth must be identical in size and shape.
8. **The correct answer is A.** American colleges and universities first began playing the game after deciding on the rules.
9. **The correct answer is B.** Whoever finished with the lowest score (i.e., most holes with the fewest strokes) wins.
10. **The correct answer is D.** The passage says that there can be no moral progress in cultural relativism as the moral truth is relative to the standards of the culture, and there is thus no universal moral standard.
11. **The correct answer is B.** Vapes deposit nicotine and other substances into the lungs in vapor form.
12. **The correct answer is D.** *Tinker* v *Des Moines* ruled in favor of the suspended students and established legal precedent for freedom of speech in public schools.
13. **The correct answer is B.** The passage states that, by definition, all dogs that have been domesticated are designer dogs.
14. **The correct answer is A.** Scotland kept exclusive curling clubs, making the sport a noble one in that particular region.
15. **The correct answer is D.** The plane is made of 6 million different parts, and the engine is only one of them. If the engine alone costs 8 million dollars and weighs about 9,500 lb., then the rest of the plane must cost more than 8 million dollars and weigh more than 9,500 lb.
16. **The correct answer is B.** The original purpose of the fifth pocket was to hold a pocket watch.
17. **The correct answer is A.** Aglets can be made of metal, plastic, or anything else that holds a shoelace together, including adhesive tape.
18. **The correct answer is B.** Aerophobia is defined as the fear of flying. If 80% of the population is afraid of flying, then 80% of the population must be aerophobic, so the correct answer must be B.

19. **The correct answer is C.** Recycling plants remove scraps and particles from recyclable materials so that they do not contaminate the machines or the recyclables themselves.

20. **The correct answer is B.** Ibn Battuta was a traveler of the Muslim world—well-renowned by his contemporaries and historians alike—who published a book called the *Rihlah* that recounts his journey.

NOTES

Mechanical Comprehension

1. C	6. C	11. B	16. B	21. A	26. A
2. B	7. C	12. C	17. B	22. B	27. B
3. A	8. A	13. A	18. A	23. A	28. B
4. C	9. B	14. B	19. B	24. B	29. B
5. A	10. B	15. A	20. B	25. B	30. B

1. **The correct answer is C.** Acceleration is the rate of change of an object's velocity. If an object is changing its dimensions (choice B), that doesn't necessarily affect how it moves and is not related to acceleration. The rate of change of an object's position (choice A) is velocity.

2. **The correct answer is B.** A movable pulley system will make it so that less force is needed to lift the load. A fixed pulley system (choice A) will change the direction of where the effort needs to be applied. These two pulley systems are different and do not work equally (choice C).

3. **The correct answer is A.** The original gear will turn clockwise, which will turn the second gear counterclockwise due to the crossed belt. This second gear will then turn the third gear clockwise. If the original gear was turned counterclockwise, or if the belt were not crossed, the third gear would have turned counterclockwise (choice C). The gears not working because of the belt (choice B) is incorrect.

4. **The correct answer is C.** The original gear will turn clockwise, which will turn the second gear clockwise as well due to the connection through the belt. This second gear will then turn the third gear counterclockwise. If the original gear was turned counterclockwise, the third gear would have turned clockwise (choice C). The gears not working because of the belt (choice B) is incorrect.

5. **The correct answer is A.** Velocity includes direction, which means that the total displacement has to be used, not total distance traveled. Since he ended at the same location where he started, his total displacement is 0. Thus, his average velocity is also 0. If asked for his average speed, it was 6 mph (choice B). 24 mph (choice C) would have been the answer if the speed of all 4 laps were added together, but this would not prove to be anything useful.

6. **The correct answer is C.** Sometimes a lever is used to amplify the strength of the effort, such as in pliers, and other times it can change the direction of the force such as in a crowbar. Both can be useful in different situations.

7. **The correct answer is C.** Two identical springs in parallel will compress half as much as the two identical springs in a series will, which would be 2 inches since the springs in a series compressed 4 inches. This is true because springs in parallel evenly distribute the force applied among themselves, whereas springs in a series do not. 4 inches (choice B) is the distance of the springs in a series compressed. 8 inches (choice A) would be possible if the length and force applied were increased for either set of springs to varying degrees.

8. **The correct answer is A.** According to Newton's second law of motion, mass times acceleration is equal to force. This means that the amount of force that an object would exert on another object at rest is dependent on both the rate of change in its velocity and its mass.

9. **The correct answer is B.** Due to Archimedes' law of levers, the weight of the load times the distance between the load and the fulcrum equals the force times the distance between the force and the fulcrum. Since we do not know the force needed for effort, we must solve for that needed force:

$$30 \text{ pounds} \times 2 \text{ yards} = \text{force needed} \times 6 \text{ yards}$$

$$\frac{30 \text{ pounds} \times 2 \text{ yards}}{6 \text{ yards}} = \frac{\text{force needed} \times 6 \text{ yards}}{6 \text{ yards}}$$

$$\frac{30 \text{ pounds} \times 2}{6} = \text{force needed}$$

$$\text{Force needed} = \frac{60 \text{ pounds}}{6} = 10 \text{ pounds}$$

10. **The correct answer is B.** Class 2 levers have the load in the middle with the fulcrum on one end and the effort on the other. If the fulcrum had been in the middle with the effort on one end and the load on the other it would be a class 1 lever (choice A). If the effort was in the middle with the load and fulcrum on either ends it would be a class 3 lever (choice C).

11. **The correct answer is B.** Only gear B will turn counterclockwise. Gears A and C (choices A and C) will turn clockwise along with gear X, which is due to the fact that they are meshed with counter-clockwise-turning gear B.

12. **The correct answer is C.** A volt is a measurement of the electrical flow's potential difference. An ohm (choice A) is a measurement of resistance, and an amp (choice B) is a measurement of the rate of electric current.

13. **The correct answer is A.** Constant force springs take the form of tightly wound bands of steel that resemble a roll of tape. Belleville springs take the form of washers that resemble a slightly tapered disc (choice B), and volute springs take the form of flat metal discs wound together to form helical spirals (choice C).

14. **The correct answer is B.** Pulleys attached to one another by non-crossing ropes will all move the same direction. If the rope were twisted once the last pulley would turn clockwise (choice B). The pulley system does work in this situation (choice C), so the claim that it won't move at all is incorrect.

15. **The correct answer is A.** Class 1 levers have the fulcrum in the middle with the effort and load on either end. If the load had been in the middle with the fulcrum and lever on either end, it would be a class 2 lever (choice B). If the effort was in the middle with the load and fulcrum on either end, it would be a class 3 lever (choice C).

16. **The correct answer is B.** Velocity is the speed of something in a given direction. Momentum (choice A) combines velocity with a mass. Force (choice C) on a mass creates an acceleration, which affects velocity.

17. **The correct choice is B.** Resistors are used to reduce current flow in a circuit. Capacitors (choice A) store energy in an electric field and conductors (choice C) carry the flow of electricity.

18. **The correct answer is A.** Resistors R_3 and R_4 are on the same wire together, making them a series. Resistors R_6 and R_7 (choice B) along with resistors R_9 and R_8 (choice C) are all in parallel with each other.

19. **The correct answer is B.** The displacement is the vector sum of all the directed distances traveled. If the car traveled 20 miles north, but then 20 miles south, these directions cancel each other out. This then makes the only number that matters 13 miles east. 20 miles north (choice A) would have been important if the car hadn't then driven 20 miles south (choice C) and vice versa.

20. **The correct answer is B.** One complete revolution will raise W2 20 inches and lower W1 20 inches, thus the difference between them will be 40 inches. $\frac{1}{2}$ revolution would result in 20 inches (choice C). $\frac{3}{4}$ revolution would result in 30 inches (choice A).

21. **The correct answer is A.** Multiplying all the measurements together needs to result in 40 cubic centimeters using the formula $V = W \times L \times H$. $40 = ? \times 4 \times 10$. Thus the width must be 1 centimeter. If the width had been 2 centimeters (choice B) the resulting volume would have been 80 cubic centimeters, and if the width had been 4 centimeters (choice C) the resulting volume would have been 160 cubic centimeters.

22. **The correct answer is B.** A screw is a wound inclined plane, not a spring. A spring is an elastic member that distorts under the action of a load, and it will regain its original shape after the load is removed. By this definition both a bow in a bow-and-arrow system (choice A) and a rubber band (choice C) are springs.

23. **The correct answer is A.** Pressure is calculated by dividing the force by the area.

$$\text{Pascal} = \frac{\text{Newtons}}{\text{Square Meters}}$$

$$3 \text{ Pascals} = \frac{9 \text{ Newtons}}{3 \text{ Square Meters}}$$

Nine Newtons of force divided by the 3 square meters is 3 Pascals of pressure. If there had been 27 Newtons of force applied, it would have resulted in 9 Pascals of pressure (choice B). If there had been 81 Newtons of force applied, it would have resulted in 27 Pascals of pressure (choice C).

24. **The correct answer is B.** According to the ideal gas law, decreasing the temperature will reduce the pressure of the system, thus drawing the balloon into the bottle. Increasing the temperature (choice A) is incorrect because it would cause an increase in pressure in the system, causing the balloon to inflate. The ideal gas law states that temperature does affect the pressure in the system, so choice C is incorrect as well.

25. **The correct answer is B.** The number of parts of the rope going to and from the movable block indicates a mechanical advantage of 2. Based on this, a 100-pound pull can lift a 200-pound weight. Based on this information, 100 pounds (choice A) would not be the heaviest, and 300 pounds (choice C) would be too heavy.

26. **The correct answer is A.** A movable pulley will allow less force to lift the object, but the caveat is that it takes more distance to pull the rope to lift the object. It will not decrease (choice B) or remain the same (choice C).

27. **The correct answer is B.** There are three ropes supporting the weight in system B, which means it has the least effort needed to lift the weight. There are only 2 ropes supporting the weight in system A. Thus, it will take more effort, not less or the same amount (choices A and C).

28. **The correct answer is B.** If you have the measurements of sides you can figure out volume; however, you cannot use surface area by itself in order to find volume for an arbitrarily shaped solid. This is due to its inconsistent and random composition. If a solid was not arbitrary and instead was a shape that was uniform, such as a cube or tetrahedron, you could use surface area alone to find the volume (choice A). Units of measure (choice C) would not have any effect on the outcome, since using the surface area to find the volume is strictly reliant on whether the solid is uniform or arbitrary.

29. **The correct answer is B.** To find the volume use the formula $V = W \times L \times H$. For the rectangle (choice A) we have $4 \times 4 \times 24$ which equals 384 cubic inches. For the cube (choice B) we have $12 \times 12 \times 12$ which equals 1,728 cubic inches. Therefore, when comparing the volumes of these two shapes, we can see that the cube has considerably more volume than the rectangle. This result also shows that these shapes do not have equal volume (choice C).

30. **The correct answer is B.** A normal gear, when joined to an internal cogwheel, will turn the same direction that the internal cogwheel is turned. If the internal cogwheel was turned clockwise, the gear would turn clockwise as well (choice A). Gears and internal cogwheels not working together (choice C) is incorrect.

SCORE SHEET

Although your actual exam scores will not be reported as percentages, it might be helpful to convert them so you can better understand your strengths and weaknesses.

OAR SCORE SHEET		
Subject	**# Correct ÷ # of questions**	**× 100 = ______ %**
Math Skills	______ ÷ 30 = ______	× 100 = ______ %
Reading Comprehension	______ ÷ 20 = ______	× 100 = ______ %
Mechanical Comprehension	______ ÷ 30 = ______	× 100 = ______ %

STUDY REFERENCE GUIDE		
Subject	**Chapter**	**Page**
Math Skills	Chapter 7	154
Reading Comprehension	Chapter 8	220
Mechanical Comprehension	Chapters 11 & 12	256, 280

NOTES

PART III

TEST CONTENT

VERBAL ANALOGIES

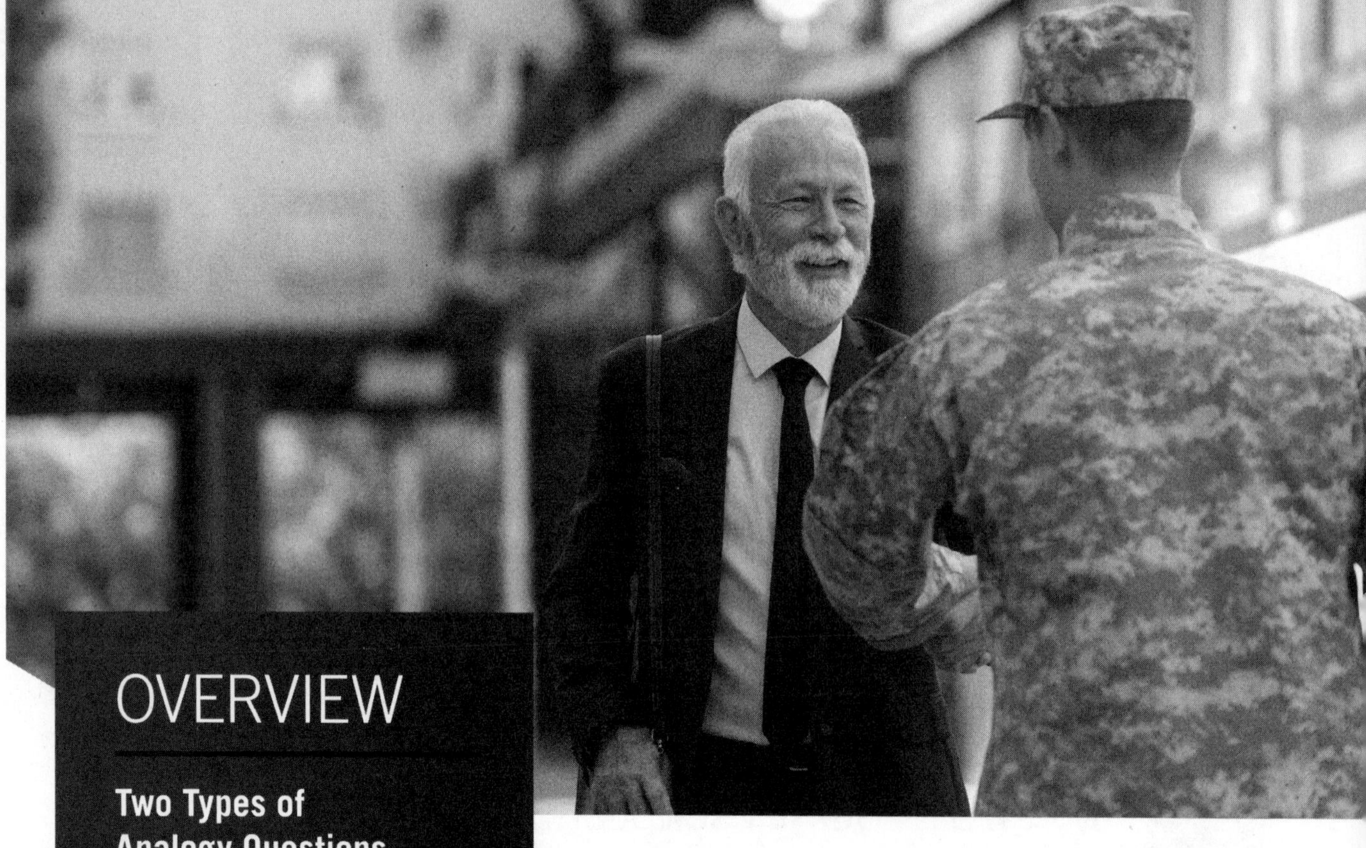

OVERVIEW

The Verbal Analogies subtest of the AFOQT will test your knowledge of word meanings and your vocabulary level as well as your ability to reason and find relationships between pairs of words. This can come in the form of words with similar meanings, words with opposite meanings, words that describe a similar function or relationship, words that describe a similar class, and words that are part of a greater whole. To determine such relationships, you must know the meaning of each word in the first given pair and determine the precise relationship between the two words. You complete the analogy by selecting the pair of words that best expresses a relationship similar to that expressed by the first paired words. Items appear as five-option questions, and you will have 8 minutes to complete 25 questions.

5

TWO TYPES OF ANALOGY QUESTIONS

There are two types of analogy questions on the subtest: complete-the-pair and pair-to-pair. The fundamental task of each question presentation is the same, to complete the analogy, but the answer choices you must select from will vary.

Complete-the-Pair

In the first type of verbal analogy question, you are given the first pair of words and the first word of the second pair. Of the given answer choices, only one best expresses a relationship to the third word that is similar to that expressed between the first pair.

To answer the question, you need to look at the relationship of the paired words and apply it to the third word and the answer options. Consider the following example:

DEER is to FAWN as GOAT is to

A. CHICK.

B. SHEEP.

C. PUP.

D. KID.

E. RAM.

What is the relationship of the first two words? The word *deer* represents an adult stage of a *fawn*.

What is the meaning of the word *goat* and each of the words appearing in the options?

To complete the analogy with *goat* as the first word, we need a term denoting a younger version of the animal in question: The word *kid* refers to a young goat.

Pair-to-Pair

In the second type of verbal analogy situation, the question and means of solving the problem are similar, though only the first pair of words is provided. Then, each answer choice consists of a pair of words.

EPILOGUE is to PROLOGUE as

A. APPENDIX is to INDEX.

B. APPENDIX is to PREFACE.

C. PREFACE is to FOOTNOTE.

D. PREFACE is to TABLE OF CONTENTS.

E. TABLE OF CONTENTS is to INDEX.

Pay careful attention when answering this type of question. The order of the two words in the answer choice must be in the same sequence as the words in the question stem. If the sequence of the second pair of words is reversed, the relationship between the word pairs is not analogous.

For the preceding example, an *epilogue* comes at the end of a book and a *prologue* at the beginning. You're looking for a pair that has two items that have such a sequence. While choice E meets that criterium, the order of the objects is reversed. Only choice B matches the relationship and sequence of the original pair.

TYPES OF ANALOGIES

The Verbal Analogies subtest will depict a variety of relationships with its word pairs. The following tables illustrate the common types of relationships:

RELATIONSHIP	EXAMPLE
synonym	ask : inquire
antonym	long : short
homonym	mail : male
location	Phoenix : Arizona
creator : creation	artist : painting
female : male	cow : bull
larger : smaller	lake : pond
noun : adjective	texture : coarse

RELATIONSHIP	EXAMPLE
cause : effect	negligence : accident
whole : part	chapter : paragraph
object : purpose or function	keyboard : type
object : user	camera : photographer
early stage : later stage	infant : adult
general : specific	vegetable : broccoli
more : less (degree)	arid : dry
verb : adjective	expand : large

RELATIONSHIP	EXAMPLE
measurement (e.g., time, distance, weight)	distance : mile
raw material : finished product	wood : bench
verb tense: verb tense	run : ran
singular noun : plural noun	child : children
nominative pronoun : objective pronoun	he : they
first-person pronoun : third-person pronoun	she : her
adjective : comparative adjective	good : better
adjective : superlative adjective	bad : worst

We've provided descriptions and sample questions for some of the most common analogy relationships: synonyms, antonyms, function/relationship, classification, and part-whole.

Synonym/Definition

Synonym analogies select words with the same or similar meanings. For example, *happy* and *glad* have the same meaning. The following synonym questions are similar to what you will see on the actual exam:

1. INTERESTING is to COMPELLING as

 A. CLOCK is to TIME

 B. WORDS are to SENTENCE

 C. CAT is to DOG

 D. PANEL is to DRAWER

 E. RIFLE is to LONG GUN

EXPLANATION **The correct answer is E.** A *rifle* is a *long gun* just as an *interesting* object is *compelling.*

2. ENORMOUS is to HUGE as MUDDY is to

 A. UNCLEAR

 B. CLEAN

 C. ROGUISH

 D. ROCKY

 E. SHARP

EXPLANATION **The correct answer is A.** Something that is described as *muddy* is clouded, or *unclear.*

3. BASSINET is to CRIB as CAR is to

 A. AUTOMOBILE

 B. AIRPLANE

 C. STROLLER

 D. BED

 E. TAXICAB

EXPLANATION **The correct answer is A.** A *bassinet* and a *crib* are synonyms for places a baby sleeps. The words *car* and *automobile* are also synonyms.

Antonym

Antonyms are words that are opposite in meaning to the given word. For example, *cold* is the antonym for *hot.* The following antonym questions are similar to what you will see on the actual exam:

4. SUBTLE is to OVERT as SLOW is to

 A. FAST

 B. QUIET

 C. SHARP

 D. BRIGHT

 E. LIQUID

EXPLANATION **The correct answer is A.** The opposite of *subtle* is *overt,* just as the opposite of *slow* is *fast.*

5. LONG is to SHORT as WIDE is to

 A. TALL

 B. LARGE

 C. SMALL

 D. NARROW

 E. LANKY

EXPLANATION **The correct answer is D.** *Short* is the opposite of *long,* just as *wide* is the opposite of *narrow.*

6. ORDER is to CHAOS as DISCIPLINE is to

 A. LAWFUL

 B. ANARCHY

 C. FERVOR

 D. CONTAINMENT

 E. ELEMENTAL

EXPLANATION **The correct answer is B.** *Chaos* is the opposite of *order,* just as *anarchy* is the opposite of *discipline.*

Classification and Function

Classification and function analogy questions will require you to create analogies in which terms are of a similar type, overlap in category, or share a functional relationship—either those that fulfill the same function or express a specific function. The following questions are similar to what you will encounter on the actual exam:

7. CANOE is to SAILBOAT as MANUAL is to

   A. FLYER
   B. PLAY
   C. TEXTBOOK
   D. STORY
   E. OBITUARY

   EXPLANATION The correct answer is C. A *canoe* and a *sailboat* are both watercrafts used for transportation, just as a *manual* and a *textbook* are both types of instructional books.

8. CANDLE is to FLAME as

   A. ART is to STATUE
   B. CUP is to CONTAIN
   C. DRAWER is to DRESSER
   D. FAN is to BLOW
   E. CAMERA is to PHOTO

   EXPLANATION The correct answer is E. A *candle* produces a *flame* just as a *camera* produces a *photo.*

9. ROSE is to TULIP as SILVER is to

   A. METALLIC
   B. RING
   C. WOOD
   D. GOLD
   E. PLASTIC

   EXPLANATION The correct answer is D. A *rose* and a *tulip* are both types of flowers, just as *silver* and *gold* are both types of metal.

10. CEILING is to WALL as TELEVISION is to

    A. TELEPHONE
    B. PAPER
    C. MONITOR
    D. FLOOR
    E. STATUE

    EXPLANATION The correct answer is C. A *ceiling* and a *wall* are both used to support a building's structure. A *monitor* and a *television* are both devices used for viewing.

11. ARGON is to GAS as DUCK is to

    A. SWAN
    B. AVOID
    C. SHIRK
    D. GOOSE
    E. BIRD

    EXPLANATION The correct answer is E. *Argon* is a type of *gas*, just as a *duck* is a type of *bird.*

12. HOSPITAL is to CLINIC as DOCTOR is to

    A. DEGREE
    B. MEDIC
    C. PRESCRIPTION
    D. CLERK
    E. THERMOMETER

    EXPLANATION The correct answer is B. A *hospital* and a *clinic* are both medical facilities of greater and lesser degrees, just as a *doctor* and a *medic* are medical professionals of greater or lesser certification.

Part-Whole

Part-Whole analogies (expressing either part-to-whole or whole-to-part relationships) compare a part of something to a whole or vice versa. The following part-whole questions are similar to what you will see on the actual exam:

13. BOOK is to PAGE as

    A. CABINET is to DISH
    B. TOY is to DOLL
    C. COIN is to BANK
    D. CLOCK is to HAND
    E. EXERCISE is to SWEAT

EXPLANATION The correct answer is D. A *page* is part of a *book*, just as a *hand* is part of a *clock*.

14. LINE is to SKETCH as FINGER is to

    A. DIGIT
    B. KNUCKLE
    C. GLOVE
    D. HAND
    E. LEG

EXPLANATION The correct answer is D. A *line* is one part of a whole *sketch*. A *finger* is a part of a *hand.*

15. BOBBIN is to SEWING MACHINE as

    A. THREAD is to NEEDLE
    B. MOSS is to WATER
    C. BUILDING is to FLOOR
    D. PISTON is to ENGINE
    E. SODA is to REFRIGERATOR

EXPLANATION The correct answer is D. A *bobbin* is a part of a *sewing machine*. A *piston* is part of an *engine.*

TIPS FOR COMPLETING VERBAL ANALOGIES

While verbal analogies test your vocabulary level, they also evaluate your ability to reason and find relationships between pairs of words. If you are unsure of how to complete an analogy, knowing parts of speech can clarify the relationship presented in a question and help you narrow your answer choices. By identifying parts of speech in an analogy question, you can determine the parts of speech required to complete the analogy.

Reviewing Parts of Speech

Sentences are made up of parts of speech: nouns, verbs, and adjectives, among others. Understanding these parts of speech will help you answer analogy questions.

NOUNS

A noun is a word that names a person, place, or thing, including both tangible objects, like chairs, or intangible objects, like sounds or ideas. There are two types of nouns: common and proper.

- A common noun gives a generic name for a person, place, thing, or idea (e.g., firefighter, beach, plane, happiness). Common nouns can be singular or plural, referring to one or many (e.g., firefighter vs. firefighters). They can also be countable or uncountable (e.g., coins vs. money).
- A proper noun names a specific person, place, or thing (e.g., Harriet Tubman, Rocky Mountain National Park, National Aeronautics and Space Administration).

VERBS

A verb is a word that shows the performance of an action or occurrence. An example of a verb is the word *shows* in the previous sentence. On the exam, knowing the basic verb tenses—past, present, and future—can be useful in case you encounter any verb tense to verb tense relationship analogies (e.g., *drive* is to *drove* as *ride* is to *rode*). Here is a list of other verbs:

- act (The cast *acted* on the stage.)
- fly (The plane *flew* over the forest.)
- give (The captain *gave* me an order.)
- listen (I *listen* to the radio during my commute.)
- melt (The ice *melted* yesterday.)
- read (I *read* science fiction in my spare time.)
- study (I *study* for my exams every day.)
- take (I *took* the test yesterday.)

ADJECTIVES

An adjective modifies a noun. For example, in the sentence, "The loud music rattled my teeth," the adjective *loud* modifies the noun music. A comparative adjective compares differences between two objects: taller, louder, smaller, bigger, etc. A superlative adjective describes objects that are of the highest degree on either end of a spectrum: tallest, loudest, smallest, biggest, etc. Let's look at a few more examples of adjectives:

- The *chlorinated* water stung my eyes.
- Jeremy's dog is *bigger* than my dog, but Rita has the *biggest* dog.
- My *brass* scales are *shiny*, but *useless*.
  - In addition to *brass*, *shiny* and *useless* also describe the scales.
- She threw the ball for the *shaggy* dog.
  - The adjective does not always need to modify the subject of a sentence. In this case, *shaggy* modifies the indirect object dog.

PRONOUNS

A pronoun eliminates the need to repetitively use nouns. For example, when recounting a night out with your friend, you can use singular pronouns by referring to yourself as *I* and when using your friend's chosen pronouns. You can also refer to the two of you together as *we* or *us*. There are numerous ways to use pronouns, depending on the context of a sentence, the number of people, and the gender of the people you are referring to. However, pronouns generally fall into categories, depending on their function:

- First-person pronouns refer to the person, or people, speaking or writing. These include *I*, *me*, *we*, and *us*. *I* and *we* are used as subjects (the person performing an action) in a sentence while *me* and *us* are used as objects (the person receiving the action) in a sentence.
- Second-person pronouns refer to the person being addressed directly. Generally, this is only the pronoun *you*. For example, in this book, we address the reader as *you*.
- Third-person pronouns refer to the people or things being spoken or written about. These include singular pronouns, like *he*, *him*, *she*, *her*, and *it*, as well as plural pronouns, *they* and *them*. *He*, *she*, and *they* are all subject pronouns, while *him*, *her*, and *them* are object pronouns. *It* can be both a subject and an object pronoun depending on its role and function in a sentence.

Using Parts of Speech

Earlier in this chapter, we included tables to summarize the relationships commonly used in analogy questions along with corresponding examples. For some analogy questions, your ability to answer correctly depends on your knowledge of parts of speech. You may encounter an analogy with a noun and a corresponding adjective, like *sponge* and *porous* or *planet* and *round*. Some relationships will only consist of one part of speech, like object and user, which will both be nouns. Other relationships might contain an implied part of speech, like part-whole analogies, which will likely comprise pairs of nouns.

Let's look at a few examples where identifying parts of speech can help determine the correct answer.

16. CHOOSE is to SELECT as THINK is to

A. CONTEMPLATE
B. DISAGREE
C. THOUGHT
D. CAREFUL
E. ENCOURAGE

EXPLANATION The correct answer is A. The analogy presents a pair of verbs that are synonyms, *choose* and *select*, followed by another verb, *think*. The correct answer must be a verb, in the present tense, that has the same meaning as *think*. While *thought* (choice C) can be both a noun and the past tense of *think*, it is not a synonym of *think*. Choice A is both a verb and a synonym for *think*.

17. CHAIR is to SIT as

A. BENCH is to CHAIR
B. DRIVE is to CAR
C. BED is to SLEEP
D. RELAX is to REST
E. CAR is to DRIVER

EXPLANATION The correct answer is C. In this analogy, you must choose the answer that best corresponds to the relationship between *chair* and *sit*. Here, *chair* is a noun and *sit* is a verb, which indicates that the relationship between these two words is that of an object and its use or function. Therefore, the correct answer choice should 1.) consist of a noun followed by a verb, and 2.) illustrate an object-function relationship. The only answer choice that fits these criteria is choice C.

18. NUCLEUS is to NUCLEI as

A. BIKE is to RIDE
B. LINK is to CHAIN
C. FUNGUS is to FUNGI
D. LEAF is to LEAVES
E. FAMILY is to FAMILIES

EXPLANATION The correct answer is C. In this example, the correct answer should contain a singular noun followed by a plural noun: *Nucleus* is a singular noun, but it has an irregular plural form, *nuclei*. While most common nouns can be made plural by adding *-s* (e.g., tickets, seats, games, etc.), some nouns are pluralized using different suffixes. Choices C, D, and E are the only ones that contain a singular noun followed by a plural noun. To narrow down these answers further, we need to determine which pair of nouns best resembles the pair in the question. Therefore, the correct answer would be choice C. *Fungus* and *nucleus* both end in *-us*, which is replaced with the suffix *-i* to make the noun plural.

19. RABBIT is to SOFT as

A. VERSE is to POEM
B. CACTUS is to PRICKLY
C. JURY is to COURTROOM
D. HE is to SHE
E. WASTE is to GARBAGE

EXPLANATION The correct answer is B. *Rabbit* is a noun and *soft* is an adjective, so the correct answer must have a noun with a corresponding adjective. The only answer that completes the analogy is choice B: *cactus* is to *prickly*.

20. I is to ME as SHE is to

A. WE
B. HE
C. US
D. THEY
E. HER

EXPLANATION The correct answer is E. The analogy presents a set of first-person pronouns, but *I* is a subject pronoun and *me* is an object pronoun. *She* is a third-person subject pronoun, so we need a third-person object pronoun: *her* (choice E).

MINI-QUIZ: VERBAL ANALOGIES

Directions: This part of the test measures your ability to reason and see relationships among words. You are to choose the option that best completes the analogy developed at the beginning of each statement.

1. FLOOD is to DROUGHT as
   - A. RICH is to POOR
   - B. CAMEL is to DESERT
   - C. DRIZZLE is to DOWNPOUR
   - D. EVENING is to NIGHT
   - E. GOLD is to SILVER

2. VORACIOUS is to RAVENOUS as
   - A. HUNGRY is to THIRSTY
   - B. WARM is to HOT
   - C. POTENT is to STRONG
   - D. FLIGHT is to FIGHT
   - E. YARD is to METER

3. TSUNAMI is to WATER as
   - A. WIND is to WATER
   - B. TYPHOON is to WIND
   - C. TORNADO is to TWISTER
   - D. TORNADO is to TYPHOON
   - E. HURRICANE is to TYPHOON

4. DUNG is to ELEPHANT as
   - A. HORSE is to MANURE
   - B. FISH is to FOOD
   - C. WORM is to SOIL
   - D. OXYGEN is to TREE
   - E. AQUARIUM is to TERRARIUM

5. CENTIPEDE is to ANT as
   - A. PENTAGON is to SHAPE
   - B. ROWBOAT is to SAILBOAT
   - C. BCE is to CE
   - D. PERCUSSION is to STRING
   - E. DUET is to TRIO

6. HEAD is to HAMMER as
   - A. TOOTH is to SAW
   - B. NAIL is to SCREW
   - C. AWL is to PUNCH
   - D. SCREW is to DRIVER
   - E. BEGINNING is to END

7. ANTHEM is to INSPIRE as
   - A. ASPIRIN is to PAIN
   - B. LIGHT is to SEE
   - C. ORGAN is to GRIND
   - D. APE is to COPY
   - E. SHUTTLE is to TRANSPORT

8. HOOK is to EYE as
   - A. SLEEVE is to COAT
   - B. BUTTON is to HOLE
   - C. BOOT is to SHOE
   - D. ADHESIVE is to TAPE
   - E. HONEY is to BEAR

9. ACTOR is to SCRIPT as
   A. ARCHITECT is to DESIGN
   B. PAINTER is to MURAL
   C. MUSICIAN is to SCORE
   D. JUDGE is to BRIEF
   E. TEXTBOOK is to STUDENT

10. GOALIE is to NET as
    A. HOCKEY is to SOCCER
    B. PLAYER is to GAME
    C. SENTRY is to FORT
    D. BAT is to BALL
    E. ICE is to TURF

11. TOPOGRAPHY is to GEOGRAPHY as
    A. WATER is to LAND
    B. PHYSICS is to MATHEMATICS
    C. GEOGRAPHY is to HISTORY
    D. MOUNTAIN is to VALLEY
    E. ANATOMY is to BIOLOGY

12. ROCKET is to TORPEDO as
    A. FIRE is to WATER
    B. AIR is to WATER
    C. EXPLOSION is to HOLE
    D. UP is to DOWN
    E. WAR is to PEACE

13. VERTICAL is to HORIZONTAL as ERECT is to
    A. HONEST
    B. CONSTRUCT
    C. PRONE
    D. LUMBER
    E. PROPER

14. OUST is to OVERTHROW as MOLT is to
    A. MELT
    B. SHED
    C. SHAPE
    D. WEAKEN
    E. SPOIL

15. INLINE SKATES are to MOTORCYCLE as SKIS are to
    A. SNOWMOBILE
    B. BICYCLE
    C. SNOW
    D. ICE SKATES
    E. SNOWPLOW

16. SCALE is to FISH as HIDE is to
    A. SEEK
    B. TAN
    C. HOLE
    D. RIDE
    E. HORSE

17. WIND is to SEED as BEE is to
    A. POLLEN
    B. HONEY
    C. HIVE
    D. BEAR
    E. FLOWER

18. GLOVE is to HAND as HOSE is to
    A. GARDEN
    B. WATER
    C. FOOT
    D. NOZZLE
    E. SHOE

19. PIGLET is to PIG as ISLET is to

A. POND
B. LACE
C. LAKE
D. RIVULET
E. ISLAND

20. DEPRESSED is to MOPE as TIRED is to

A. YAWN
B. COPE
C. CAR
D. LAUGH
E. SUPPRESSED

ANSWER KEY AND EXPLANATIONS

1. A	5. C	9. C	13. C	17. A
2. C	6. A	10. C	14. B	18. C
3. B	7. E	11. E	15. A	19. E
4. D	8. B	12. B	16. E	20. A

1. **The correct answer is A.** A *flood* is an overabundance of water and a *drought* is a lack of water. To be *rich* is to have an overabundance of money and to be *poor* is to have a lack of money.
2. **The correct answer is C.** *Voracious* and *ravenous* both mean to have a huge appetite. *Potent* and *strong* both mean to be powerful.
3. **The correct answer is B.** A *typhoon* is a severe weather event related to *wind* in the same way a *tsunami*, a series of strong waves, is related to *water.*
4. **The correct answer is D.** *Dung* is the waste byproduct of an *elephant* while *oxygen* is the waste byproduct of a *tree.*
5. **The correct answer is C.** A *centipede* and an *ant* are both multi-legged, segmented insects. *BCE* and *CE* are both multi-year time frames segmented into decades, centuries, etc.
6. **The correct answer is A.** The *head* is part of a *hammer.* A *tooth* is part of a *saw.*
7. **The correct answer is E.** An *anthem* is meant to *inspire.* A *shuttle* is meant to *transport.*
8. **The correct answer is B.** A *hook* goes through an *eye*, just as a *button* goes through a *hole.*
9. **The correct answer is C.** An *actor* performs from a *script.* A *musician* performs from a *score.*
10. **The correct answer is C.** A *goalie* protects the *net.* A *sentry* protects a *fort.*
11. **The correct answer is E.** *Topography* is the practice of mapping, or representing, the *geography* of an area. *Anatomy* is a map of an organism's *biology.*
12. **The correct answer is B.** A *rocket* travels through the *air* while a *torpedo* travels through the *water.*
13. **The correct answer is C.** *Vertical* and *erect* both mean upright while *horizontal* and *prone* both mean lying flat.
14. **The correct answer is B.** *Oust* means to *overthrow. Molt* means to *shed.*
15. **The correct answer is A.** *Inline skates* and *motorcycles* are used to traverse dry land. *Skis* and *snowmobiles* are used to traverse snow. Also, *inline skates* and *skis* attach to the foot while *motorcycles* and *snowmobiles* both have engines.
16. **The correct answer is E.** A *scale* is the protective covering for a *fish.* A *hide* is the protective covering for a *horse.*
17. **The correct answer is A.** *Wind* will carry a *seed*, just as a *bee* will carry *pollen.*
18. **The correct answer is C.** A *glove* goes over a *hand. Hose*, another name for a sock, goes over a *foot.*
19. **The correct answer is E.** A *piglet* is a small *pig.* An *islet* is a small *island.*
20. **The correct answer is A.** When someone is *depressed*, they are likely to mope. When someone is *tired*, they are likely to *yawn.*

5

SUMMING IT UP

- The Verbal Analogies subtest of the AFOQT tests your word knowledge and vocabulary, as well as your ability to reason and discern relationships.
- You will have 8 minutes to complete 25 questions.
- There are two different presentations of analogy questions on this subtest: complete-the-phrase and phrase-to-phrase.
- There are multiple types of analogies on the AFOQT, including some of the following:
    - Synonym/Definition
    - Antonym
    - Classification and Function
    - Part-Whole
- Understanding parts of speech can help you select the correct answer when more than one could fit.

WORD KNOWLEDGE

OVERVIEW

The Word Knowledge section of the AFOQT is designed to test your knowledge of word definitions and your understanding of the written language. This portion of the test is mandatory for commissioning, but it does not apply to the Pilot, Combat Systems Officer, and Air Battle Manager career tracks. You will have 5 minutes to answer 25 questions.

Like most of the other subtests in the AFOQT, you will be given five answers to each question. Each question consists of a single word in all caps, presented without the context of a sentence. Your task is to find which of the five answers most closely matches the meaning of the capitalized word. Questions appearing on this subtest will resemble the following:

6

EXAMPLE:

1. ACCESS
   - A. Agreement
   - B. Cooperative
   - C. Extra
   - D. Forgive
   - E. Permission
2. FLAGRANT
   - A. Aware
   - B. Condemned
   - C. Conspicuous
   - D. Excessive
   - E. Graphic

For each of these questions, there is one word that most closely matches the capitalized word, but there are also answer choices that are meant to confuse you. For *access*, words like *cooperative* or *forgive* might distract you from the actual meaning, choice E, *permission*. Some words might try to confuse you by meaning something that looks or sounds like the capitalized word. In the first example, *extra* would be the right answer if *excess* were the capitalized word rather than *access*. In this case, however, *access* is used in the context of *permission*, as in "you have been given access to (permission to view) classified information." In the second example, words like *excessive* and *graphic* might be associated with *flagrant*, but **the correct answer is choice C**, *conspicuous*. The reason *conspicuous* is the correct answer is that the definition for *flagrant* is "conspicuously offensive." *Excessive* and *flagrant* do not always mean "offensive."

BUILDING YOUR VOCABULARY

To prepare yourself for the Word Knowledge subtest, you need a strong, college-level vocabulary. While reading can give you exposure to new and unfamiliar words, expanding your vocabulary requires *active reading*. Active reading involves more than just picking up a book or article and reading it over. There are a few additional steps you need to take.

First off, read material that is more challenging. Pick up news magazines, read scholarly articles, or even crack open an old textbook. Check out magazines like *Scientific American*, *Newsweek*, *National Geographic*, and the like. Look over the *New York Times*, the *Washington Post*, the *Times of London*, and other well-regarded newspapers. You can also use a search engine to find scholarly articles on topics you are interested in. Find material with words that are new or unfamiliar to you.

Next, with pen in hand, write down the words that you don't understand. Instead of using a computer or mobile device, the act of writing something by hand actually helps you imprint the word into your memory. Once you have a good list of unfamiliar words, look up the definitions in a dictionary. Focus on learning a few words at a time so that you can learn them well. Sometimes, it can be helpful to start with a learner's dictionary, which will define a word in simpler language and provide more examples of how to use it in a sentence. Write down the

definitions for the unfamiliar words. You can even go back to where you originally found the unfamiliar word and reread it to see how the now-familiar word is used.

Third, try to use the word in a sentence or in conversation. Practice using the word by creating your own sentences and writing them down in a notebook. This will help you get a sense of how to use the word in different contexts while cementing the word and its meaning into your vocabulary.

As explained earlier, try to write words by hand whenever you can. Keep a word log where you write down the new words you have learned as well as the words you want to learn. When you document the definition for a new word, include details like the part of speech, as well as any synonyms and antonyms, and give an example of how the word can be used in a sentence. If a word has more than one meaning, you should include those as well. Here is an example of what an entry might look like:

ATTRITION: noun.

1. Sorrow for one's sins;
2. the act of wearing or grinding down by friction;
3. weakening or exhausting by constant harassment, abuse, or attack;
4. a reduction in numbers.

SYNONYMS:

corrosion, erosion, degradation

ANTONYMS:

buildup, growth, accumulation

SENTENCE:

The attrition rate among social workers is high, due mainly to the long hours, difficult work, and low pay.

If it's not possible to keep a paper log of new words, your mobile device can be a valuable tool for taking notes. Some devices will let you use a stylus, so you can still write by hand. Mobile devices also have access to a dictionary, whether it's through an app or a web browser. Lastly, such devices can give you access to reading material like online magazines and newspapers, books, and research papers, especially things you wouldn't normally have easy access to like English language newspapers from other countries. Once you start building your word log, review regularly. Review should be systematic and regular—the day after you first record a word, a few days later, and once a week thereafter.

TIPS FOR ANSWERING WORD KNOWLEDGE QUESTIONS

The Word Knowledge subtest requires you to answer 25 questions in 5 minutes, which averages out to 12 seconds per question. You will need to move quickly because each question tests your understanding of words outside of a sentence context. Questions that contain words with only one meaning are the easiest to answer. Usually, the word that pops into your mind will be listed as one of the options to choose from.

But what if you encounter a word on the test that has multiple meanings and the meaning that you know isn't among the answer choices? The trick to choosing the correct answer is to look at the words given in the answer options. One of the options may give you a clue or jog your memory.

As you review the question and answer choices, pay close attention to spelling. Like in our previous example, make sure you're answering *access*, not *excess*. You can also use word prefixes and suffixes to make an educated guess. Imagine you see the word *benefactor* in a question. If you already know that *bene-* is a prefix meaning *good*, then finding the closest match to *benefactor* becomes quite a bit easier. You can identify prefixes and suffixes when you practice active reading to expand your vocabulary and build a list for studying.

PREFIXES AND SUFFIXES					
Prefix	**Meaning**	**Example**	**Suffix**	**Meaning**	**Example**
Anti-	Against	Antifreeze, antibacterial	-able, -ible	Capable	Agreeable, collectible
Bene-	Good	Benefit, benevolent	-ation	Action	Liberation, activation
De-	Opposite	Deactivate, derail	-ism	Belief, act	Catholicism, plagiarism
Dis-, dys-	Not	Disagree, dysfunctional	-let	Small	Booklet, anklet
En-, em-	Cover	Encode, embrace	-or	One who does	Benefactor, resistor
Fore-	Before	Forecast, forehead	-y	Quality of	Thirsty, wintry

If you can identify the prefix or suffix of a word (or both), you can discern what the word most likely means. For a word like *benefactor*, you can look over the list of prefixes and suffixes to find *bene-* (good) and the suffix *-or* (one who does) to break down the word:

Bene-fact-or

From the prefix, you know that this word means something good. From the suffix, you also know that the word refers to someone who does something. From that, you could arrive at the rough definition of someone who does something good. That definition strikes close to the actual definition, a person or thing that provides help or an advantage.

If you are still unsure of the correct answer, formulate a sentence with the word given in the question and try replacing the word with each of the answer options. Another strategy is to discern what part of speech the word is. If the word is a verb, or action word, then look for words among the answer choices that are also verbs. This can help you eliminate certain answers and narrow your options. Remember that you only have 5 minutes to answer 25 questions, so try not to spend too much time on any single question. Consider skipping the questions you don't know and coming back to them once you've answered the questions you do know.

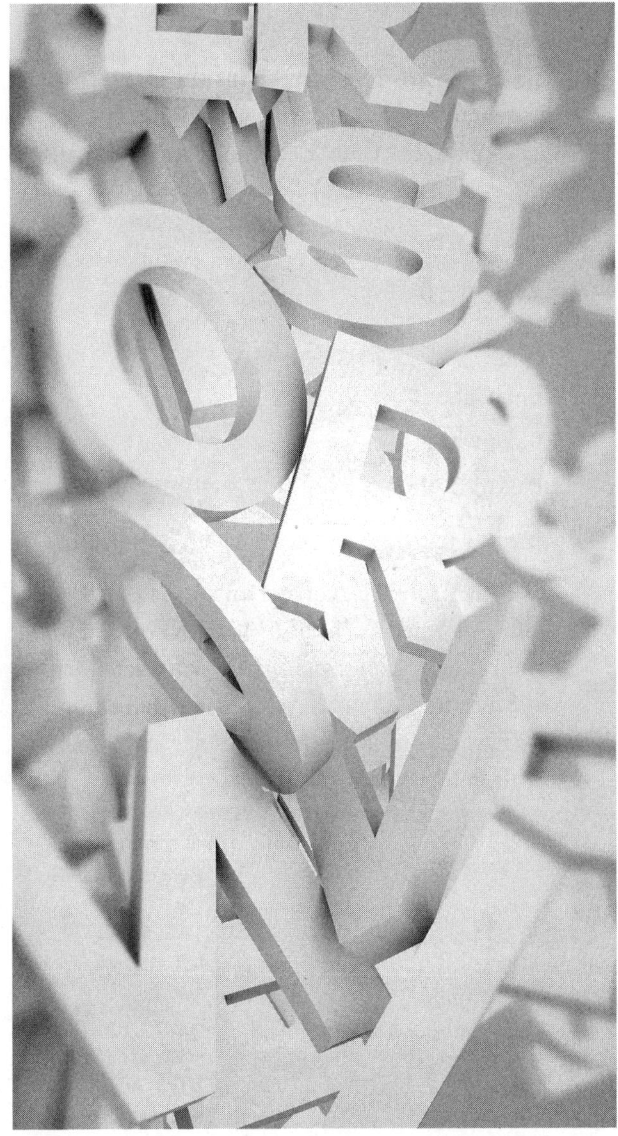

QUESTIONS

Like the other sections of the AFOQT, you will be given five answer choices to choose from. In this section, you must pick the word from the answer choices that best matches the meaning of the capitalized word given in the question. The following questions are similar to what you will see on the actual exam:

1. POUCH

   A. Time

   B. Table

   C. Bag

   D. Wall

   E. Wing

   EXPLANATION: The correct answer is C. A pouch is a small bag. *Table, time, wall,* and *wing* (choices A, B, D, and E) do not have the same meaning as pouch.

2. ALTITUDE

   A. Lift

   B. Height

   C. Upward

   D. Angle

   E. Stance

   EXPLANATION: The correct answer is B. *Altitude* is defined as "height." While choice A, *lift*, and choice C, *upward*, might be associated with *altitude*, they do not have the same definition. Answers D and E, *angle* and *stance*, have no connection to *altitude*.

3. COROLLARY

   A. Conclusion

   B. Watchful

   C. Trespass

   D. Levitate

   E. Bully

   EXPLANATION: The correct answer is A. *Corollary* is defined as "something that naturally flows," as in a result or conclusion. The more common usage of *corollary* is of an idea that springs from another idea without any evidence to support it. But remember that you are looking for the word that best matches the meaning of the capitalized word. None of the other answer choices have a relation to the capitalized word.

Now that you've had a chance to practice, use the following mini-quiz to gauge your progress.

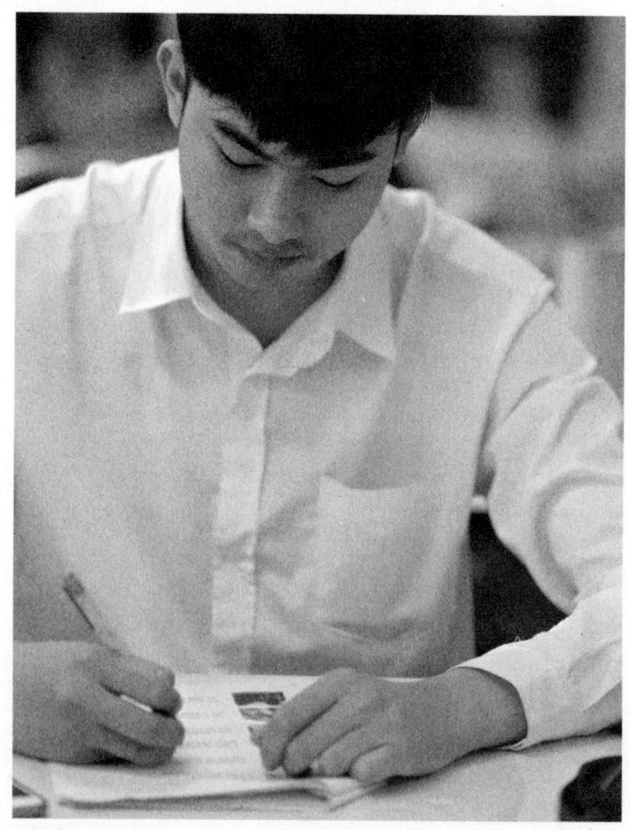

MINI-QUIZ: WORD KNOWLEDGE

Directions: This portion of the test measures your knowledge of words and their meanings. For each question, you are to choose the word below that is closest in meaning to the capitalized word above.

1. AMPLITUDE
   A. Noise
   B. Hyper
   C. Bright
   D. Volume
   E. Sass

2. DELETERIOUS
   A. Harmful
   B. Banal
   C. Erased
   D. Sad
   E. Safe

3. GAUDY
   A. Pleasant
   B. Sheer
   C. Bandage
   D. Squash
   E. Showy

4. HELICAL
   A. Underworld
   B. Chopped
   C. Spiral
   D. Half
   E. Entirely

5. JABBER
   A. Punch
   B. Gibberish
   C. Slight
   D. Carry
   E. Mesh

6. MELANCHOLY
   A. Valley
   B. Emotional
   C. Tablet
   D. Sadness
   E. Pressing

7. OPERATIVE
   A. Plan
   B. Agent
   C. Surgeon
   D. User
   E. Nonfunctional

8. STATIONERY
   A. Unmoving
   B. Location
   C. Paper
   D. Position
   E. Working

9. TENACIOUS
   A. Dogged
   B. Soft
   C. Present
   D. Musical
   E. Affirm

10. CONVENE
   A. Promise
   B. Disparate
   C. Gather
   D. Orate
   E. Temperate

11. CONTAINER
   A. Package
   B. Drawer
   C. Bowl
   D. Cardboard
   E. Clipboard

12. WATERY
   A. Sticky
   B. Slick
   C. Viscous
   D. Thin
   E. Dim

13. RAPID
   A. Rocky
   B. Fast
   C. Rhythmic
   D. Slow
   E. Gaseous

14. ORGANIC
   A. Needless
   B. Natural
   C. Fundamental
   D. Complex
   E. Unnecessary

15. SALVE
   A. Disquiet
   B. Irritant
   C. Tincture
   D. Ointment
   E. Excite

16. KEEN
   A. Ripe
   B. Dull
   C. Weak
   D. Awake
   E. Sharp

17. CUBOID
   A. Boxlike
   B. Soft
   C. Angular
   D. Long
   E. Flat

18. SECURE
   A. Beset
   B. Weakened
   C. Safe
   D. Torn
   E. Questionable

19. PORTAL
   A. Screen
   B. Door
   C. Stand
   D. Omen
   E. Small

20. AMALGAM
   A. Elemental
   B. Solute
   C. Mixture
   D. Active
   E. Distinct

NOTES

ANSWER KEY AND EXPLANATIONS

1. D	5. B	9. A	13. B	17. A
2. A	6. D	10. C	14. B	18. C
3. E	7. B	11. A	15. D	19. B
4. C	8. D	12. D	16. E	20. C

1. **The correct answer is D.** *Volume* is another word for "amplitude."
2. **The correct answer is A.** *Deleterious* means "harmful," usually in an unexpected way.
3. **The correct answer is E.** *Gaudy* means "excessively showy or tasteless."
4. **The correct answer is C.** *Helical* means "related to a helix," which is a spiral.
5. **The correct answer is B.** *Jabber* means "fast, excited talk," such as gibberish.
6. **The correct answer is D.** *Melancholy* is another word for "sadness."
7. **The correct answer is B.** An *operative* is another word for "secret agent or undercover person."
8. **The correct answer is D.** *Stationery* is another word for "paper," not to be confused with *stationary*, which means "unmoving."
9. **The correct answer is A.** *Tenacious* means "unrelenting, persistent, or dogged."
10. **The correct answer is C.** *Convene* means "to gather or assemble in a group." For example, a team will convene for a meeting.
11. **The correct answer is A.** A package is a type of container.
12. **The correct answer is D.** Something that is watery is thin.
13. **The correct answer is B.** *Rapid* is delineated by a "fast rate of motion, activity, succession, or occurrence." For example, a rapid object is fast.
14. **The correct answer is B.** Something that is organic is natural or unaltered.
15. **The correct answer is D.** A *salve* is an ointment.
16. **The correct answer is E.** The word *keen* can have multiple meanings. Based on the words given in the answer choices, the best match is "sharp." Examples of usage include a keen blade, keen sarcasm, or a keen sense of smell.
17. **The correct answer is A.** A cuboid is a boxlike shape made up of six squares.
18. **The correct answer is C.** *Secure* means "safe." An item that is secure is safe.
19. **The correct answer is B.** A portal is a door or opening.
20. **The correct answer is C.** An amalgam is a mixture.

6

SUMMING IT UP

- The Word Knowledge subtest of the AFOQT tests your knowledge of words and their meanings outside the context of a sentence.
- You will have 5 minutes to answer 25 questions.
- In advance of the test, focus on expanding your vocabulary by practicing active reading. As you read challenging material, keep a word log where you write down the new words you have learned as well as the words you want to learn. When you document the definition for a new word, include details like the part of speech, synonyms, and antonyms to improve your word knowledge. You can also practice using the word in a sentence. Remember to review regularly—soon after you first record the word and then each week.
- When you're unsure of the correct answer to a question, use the following strategies:
    - Look at the prefixes and suffixes of words to make an educated guess.
    - Formulate a sentence with the word given in the question and try replacing the word with each of the answer options.
    - Skip questions you don't know and come back to them after you've answered the questions you do know.

MATH FOR THE AFOQT AND OAR

OVERVIEW

The following chapter is intended to provide a thorough introduction to the concepts and skills covered by the AFOQT's Arithmetic Reasoning and Math Knowledge subtests, as well as the Math Skills subtest of the OAR. The topics range from basic math (fractions and decimals, percentages, probability, etc.) through algebra (exponent rules, factoring polynomials, etc.) and geometry (polygons, the Pythagorean theorem, area and perimeter, etc.). Take note that while these topics should offer adequate review of what is on the test, continued practice and exploration is important for further math skill development.

On the AFOQT Arithmetic Reasoning section, you will have 29 minutes to complete 25 problems. For the Math Knowledge section, there are 25 questions, but you only have 22 minutes. On the OAR, there will be between 20 and 30 questions for Math Skills, with time being variable, depending on the test format you take. Neither test allows the use of a calculator. You will need to focus on quickly and efficiently solving each question, being systematic on any scratch paper you use.

This chapter is divided into three sections: Basic Math, Algebra, and Geometry. After each section, there will be a practice quiz to test your knowledge of the section before moving on to more advanced concepts. There is also a mini-quiz at the end of this chapter to gauge your understanding of the concepts presented in this chapter as a whole.

BASIC MATH

The following section will cover a variety of basic mathematical principles related to arithmetic calculations and concepts that form the foundation of work in algebra and geometry. This section should act as a review of fundamental mathematical concepts, especially those assessed by the AFOQT and OAR math subtests.

Order and Laws of Operations

The following rules, known as the order and laws of operations, apply to all operations on numbers as well as on variables (such as x and y).

Order of Operations

The order of operations is a set of rules that dictates the sequence in which a complex expression, such as the following, should be solved.

$$4^2 + (8 \times 3) \div 6 - 2$$

Complete operations as follows:

1. Operations inside parentheses
2. Operations with exponents and square roots
3. Multiplication and division (from left to right)
4. Addition and subtraction (from left to right)

EXAMPLE:

$$(2 + 4) \times (7 - 2) = 6 \times 5$$

(operate inside parentheses before multiplying)

$$3 \times 4^2 = 3 \times 16$$

(apply exponent before multiplying)

$$5 + 7 \times 3 - 2 = 5 + 21 - 2$$

(multiply before adding or subtracting)

$$6 - 8 \div 2 + 3 = 6 - 4 + 3$$

(divide before adding or subtracting)

To remember the order for mathematical actions, use the mnemonic PEMDAS (**P**arentheses-**E**xponents-**M**ultiplication-**D**ivision-**A**ddition-**S**ubtraction) or the phrase, "Please excuse my dear Aunt Sally."

Now, let's evaluate the expression shown at the beginning of this section using the order of operations.

EXAMPLE:

$4^2 + (8 \times 3) \div 6 - 2 =$

Step 1: Parentheses

$4^2 + (8 \times 3) \div 6 - 2 = 4^2 + 24 \div 6 - 2$

Step 2: Exponents

$4^2 + 24 \div 6 - 2 = 16 + 24 \div 6 - 2$

Step 3: Division (we did the multiplication already because it was inside the parentheses)

$16 + 24 \div 6 - 2 = 16 + 4 - 2$

Step 4: Addition

$16 + 4 - 2 = 20 - 2$

Step 5: Subtraction

$20 - 2 = 18$

Had you attempted to solve the expression simply from left to right instead of the order of operations, you would get an incorrect answer of $4^2 + (8 \times 3) \div 6 - 2 = 16 + 24 \div 6 - 2 = 4.67$. However, while PEMDAS describes the general order of operations, for multiplication and division and addition and subtraction, you'll actually work from left to right through the problem. For example, if in the previous expression subtraction had been first in the sequence of the problem from left to right, you would have completed that calculation before computing any addition to the right of it.

Laws of Operations

In addition to the order of operations, there are also a variety of laws that dictate how you work with numbers under different operations.

The Commutative Law (addition and multiplication only)

$a + b = b + a$

$a \times b = b \times a$

EXAMPLES:

$3 + 4 = 4 + 3$

$3 \times 4 = 4 \times 3$

The Associative Law (addition and multiplication only)

$(a + b) + c = a + (b + c)$

$c(ab) = a(bc)$

EXAMPLES:

$(6 + 2) + 5 = 8 + 5 = 13$

$6 + (2 + 5) = 6 + 7 = 13$

$(3 \times 2) \times 4 = 6 \times 4 = 24$

$3 \times (2 \times 4) = 3 \times 8 = 24$

The Distributive Law

$a(b + c) = ab + ac$

$a(b - c) = ab - ac$

EXAMPLES:

$2(3 + 4) = 2 \times 7 = 14$

$(2)(3) + (2)(4) = 6 + 8 = 14$

$9(4 - 2) = 9 \times 2 = 18$

$(9)(4) - (9)(2) = 36 - 18 = 18$

Number Types and Signs

To answer questions related to basic arithmetic and concepts in algebra, you need to be able to perform operations with different number signs and also understand terminology used to describe different types of numbers. The following sections offer review.

Number Types

Various terms exist to describe the array of numbers used for counting and calculations. The ability to distinguish between whole numbers, integers, and rational and irrational numbers can keep you from selecting incompatible answer choices on the relevant subtests.

Whole Numbers and Integers

Starting with one of the most basic terms, **whole numbers** are simply numbers that are not decimals or fractions. They are always positive and include zero. An integer is any whole number not only including zero but also negative numbers—excluding negative decimals and fractions.

Some examples of whole numbers are as follows:

1, 2, 3, 50, 75, 100

Some examples of integers are as follows:

0, 1, 3, 42, 197, –2, –30, –212

Examples of numbers that are NOT integers are as follows:

$\frac{3}{4}$, 0.14, –11.3, 56.0035

The line over a decimal such as $0.\overline{3} = 0.3333333...$ indicates it is a repeating decimal that goes on forever.

Rational and Irrational Numbers

A **rational number** is a number in the form $\frac{p}{q}$, where p and q are integers and q is not equal to zero. $\frac{1}{3}, \frac{3}{5}, -\frac{7}{3}$ are all rational numbers. That means any number that has a terminating or repeating decimal, including no decimal, is rational. Here are some examples of rational numbers and what makes them so:

$$1 = \frac{1}{1} = \frac{2}{2} = \frac{-5}{-5} = \frac{0.354}{0.354} = \frac{10{,}000}{10{,}000}$$

$$-2 = \frac{-2}{1} = \frac{14}{-7} = \frac{-10}{5} = \frac{-40{,}000}{20{,}000}$$

$$5.25 = \frac{5.25}{1} = \frac{-10.5}{-2} = \frac{21}{4} = \frac{525{,}000}{100{,}000}$$

$$0.\overline{3} = \frac{1}{3} = \frac{30}{90} = \frac{400}{1{,}200}$$

Each of these examples is expressed as a ratio. $\frac{-5}{-5}$ is equivalent to 1, just as $\frac{14}{-7}$ is equivalent to –2. The third example, 5.25, is a terminating decimal, so it is a rational number. The fourth example, $0.\overline{3}$, is a repeating decimal, so it can also be expressed as a ratio.

Irrational numbers have nonterminating nonrepeating decimals. The most widely known irrational number is pi (π), or 3.141592653589793238462643383279 and on and on. The following are other irrational numbers:

$$\sqrt{2} = 1.41421356237...$$
$$\sqrt{3} = 1.73205080756...$$
$$\varphi = 1.618033988749...$$
$$e = 2.718281845904...$$

The product of almost any number, rational or irrational, multiplied by any irrational number is an irrational number. However, there are exceptions to the first rule. While $\pi \times \pi = \pi^2$ is irrational, $\sqrt{2} \times \sqrt{2} = 2$ is rational.

Number Signs

A positive number is any number greater than zero, and a negative number is any number less than zero. The sign of a number indicates whether it is positive (+) or negative (–).

Be sure you know the sign—either positive or negative—of a non-zero number that results from combining numbers using the four basic operations (addition, subtraction, multiplication, and division).

Multiplying and Dividing Negative Terms

Multiplication or division involving any even number of negative terms gives you a positive number. On the other hand, multiplication or division involving any odd number of negative terms gives you a negative number.

EXAMPLES:

Even number of negative terms

$(5) \times (-4) \times (2) \times (-2) = +80$
(two negative terms)

$(-4) \times (-3) \times (-2) \times (-1) = +24$
(four negative terms)

Odd number of negative terms

$(3) \times (-3) \times (2) = -18$
(one negative term)

$(-4) \times (-4) \times (2) \times (-2) = -64$
(three negative terms)

Absolute Value

A number's **absolute value** refers to its distance from zero (the origin) on the real-number line. The absolute value of x is indicated as $|x|$. The absolute value of any number other than zero is always a positive number. The concept of absolute value boils down to these two statements:

If $x \geq 0$, then $|x| = x$

Example: $|3| = 3$

Example: $|0| = 0$

If $x < 0$, then $|x| = -x$

Example: $|-2| = -(-2) = 2$

A **factor** (of an integer n) is any integer that you can multiply by another integer for a product of n. The factors of any integer n include 1 as well as n itself. Figuring out whether one number (f) is a factor of another (n) is simple: Just divide n by f. If the quotient is an integer, then f is a factor of n (and n is *divisible* by f). If the quotient is not an integer, then f is not a factor of n, and you'll end up with a *remainder* after dividing. To put it another way, a factor is a number that can be divided into a whole number without leaving a remainder.

For example, 2 is a factor of 8 because $8 \div 2 = 4$, which is an integer. On the other hand, 3 is not a factor of 8 because $8 \div 3 = \frac{8}{3}$, or $2\frac{2}{3}$, which is a non-integer. (The remainder is 2, which you put over the divisor, 3.) Keep in mind these basic rules about factors, which are based on their definition:

Complementing factors are **multiples**. If f is a factor of n, then n is a multiple of f. For example, 8 is a multiple of 2 for the same reason that 2 is a factor of 8: because $8 \div 2 = 4$, which is an integer.

A **prime number** is a positive integer that is divisible by only two positive integers: itself and 1. Zero (0) and 1 are not considered prime numbers; 2 is the first prime number. Here are all the prime numbers less than 50:

2 3 5 7

11 13 17 19

23 29

31 37

41 43 47

As you can see, factors, multiples, and divisibility are simply different aspects of the same concept.

The **greatest common factor** (GCF) of a list of whole numbers is the largest whole number that can be divided evenly into every number in the list, and the **least common multiple** (LCM) is the smallest whole number into which each number in the list divides evenly. For example, the GCF of {18, 36, 63} is 9, and the LCM is 504.

The distributive property and greatest common factor can be used together to rewrite numeric expressions in different ways. For instance, $(24 + 54) = (6 \times 4 + 6 \times 9) = (6)(4 + 9)$.

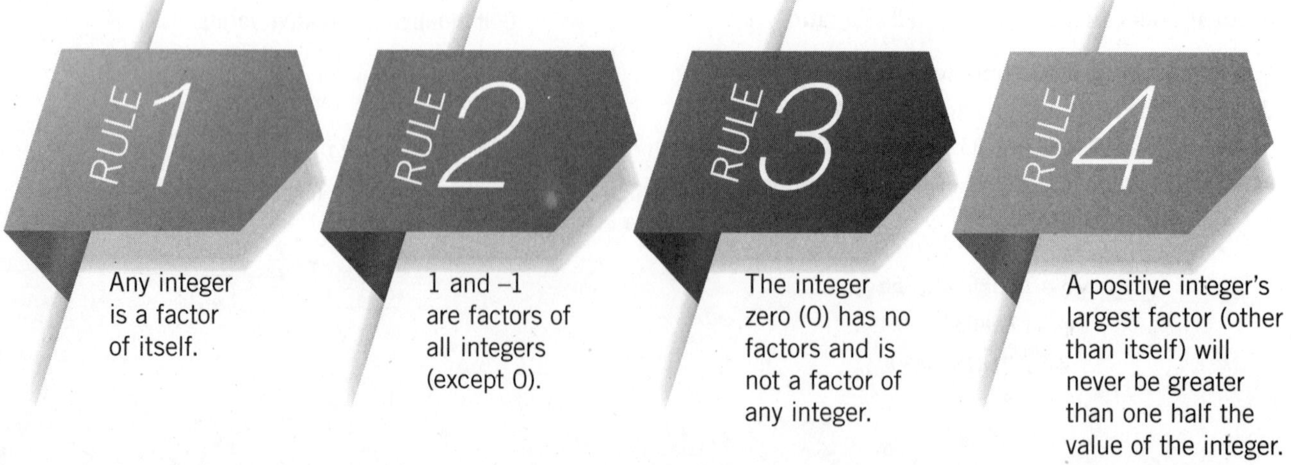

RULE 1
Any integer is a factor of itself.
RULE 2
1 and –1 are factors of all integers (except 0).
RULE 3
The integer zero (0) has no factors and is not a factor of any integer.
RULE 4
A positive integer's largest factor (other than itself) will never be greater than one half the value of the integer.

Decimals, Fractions, Percentages

Decimals, fractions, and percentages are common presentations of numbers, each with certain procedures and conditions for calculating, converting, and using them. Any number can be expressed in the form of a decimal number, a fraction, or a percent. The following introduces their characteristics.

Decimals

When a number is written in decimal form, everything to the left of the decimal point is a whole number, and everything to the right of the decimal point represents a part of the whole (a tenth, hundredth, thousandth, and so on). For instance, 5.2 would read as five and two tenths. Adding zeros to the end of a decimal number does not change its value. For example, the decimal number 0.5 is the same as 0.50 or 0.5000. But adding a zero to the front (the left) of the number will change the number's value. For example, 0.5 means "five tenths," but 0.05 means "five hundredths."

Whole				and	Parts		
Thousands	Hundreds	Tens	Ones	Decimal Point	Tenths	Hundredths	Thousandths
				●			

Place value refers to the specific value of a digit in a decimal number. For example, you can see the following in the decimal number 682.793:

The digit 6 is in the "hundreds" place.

The digit 8 is in the "tens" place.

The digit 2 is in the "ones" place.

The digit 7 is in the "tenths" place.

The digit 9 is in the "hundredths" place.

The digit 3 is in the "thousandths" place.

As such, you could express 682.793 as

$600 + 80 + 2 + \frac{7}{10} + \frac{9}{100} + \frac{3}{1000}$.

Fractions

A **fraction** is a part of a whole. For instance, there are 10 dimes in each dollar, so one dime is one-tenth of a dollar—one of ten equal parts. The fraction to represent one-tenth is written $\frac{1}{10}$. The top number of a fraction is called the **numerator**, and the bottom number is called the **denominator**. A **proper fraction** is one in which the numerator is less than the denominator. An **improper fraction** is one in which the numerator is the same as or greater than the denominator. $\frac{3}{5}$ is a proper fraction, but $\frac{5}{3}$ is an improper fraction. Sometimes you will see a whole number and a fraction together. This is called a *mixed number.* $2\frac{3}{5}$ is an example of a mixed number.

Reciprocals

When working with fractions (or any numbers), you may need to find a fraction's reciprocal. Defined, a reciprocal is $\frac{1}{x}$, where x is the number in question. For example, the reciprocal of $5 = \frac{1}{5}$, or 0.2 as a decimal. Finding the reciprocal of a fraction is done the same way. The reciprocal of $\frac{4}{5}$ is $\frac{5}{4}$. Just invert the fraction.

Let's look at a few more examples.

EXAMPLES:

$$\frac{1}{8} = \frac{8}{1} = 8$$

$$\frac{2}{10} = \frac{10}{2} = 5$$

$$\frac{1}{0.25} = \frac{0.25}{1} = 0.25$$

Percentages

A **percentage** (%) is a fraction or decimal number written in a different form. The decimal number 0.25 is written as 25%. A percent expressed as a fraction is the number divided by 100. For example, the fraction $\frac{25}{100}$ equals 25%. The number before the percent sign is the numerator of the fraction.

Converting One Number Form to Another

Questions involving fractions, decimals, or percentages often require you to convert one form to another. For percent-to-decimal conversions, move the decimal point two places to the left (and drop the percent sign). For decimal-to-percent conversions, move the decimal point two places to the right (and add the percent sign). For percentages greater than 100, convert to numbers greater than 1.

EXAMPLES:

Converting percentages to decimal numbers

9.5% = 0.095

95% = 0.95

950% = 9.5

Converting decimal numbers to percentages

0.004 = 0.4%

0.04 = 4%

0.4 = 40%

4.0 = 400%

For percent-to-fraction conversions, divide by 100 (and drop the percent sign), and simplify as necessary. For fraction-to-percent conversions, multiply by 100 (and add the percent sign). Percentages greater than 100 convert to numbers greater than 1.

Operations with Decimals and Fractions

With some understanding of the nature of decimals and fractions, you can now learn the different steps needed to use the four basic operations with the different number forms.

Multiplying and Dividing Decimals

When multiplying decimals, disregard the decimal point until after the multiplication is complete, then add the number of decimal places in the original equation and insert the decimal point that many places from the right.

EXAMPLE:

$$\begin{array}{r} 14.2 \\ \underline{\times 2} \end{array}$$

In this case, remember that you have one decimal point in the equation, then disregard it:

$$\begin{array}{r} 142 \\ \underline{\times 2} \end{array}$$

Now perform the operation:

$$\begin{array}{r} 142 \\ \underline{\times 2} \\ 284 \end{array}$$

Remembering the number of decimals you had in the original problem (1), insert the decimal point that many places from the right:

$$\begin{array}{r} 14.2 \\ \underline{\times 2} \\ 28.4 \end{array}$$

For multiple numbers with multiple decimal places, the steps are the same.

EXAMPLES:

$$\begin{array}{r} 2.72 \\ \times 3.05 \\ \hline \end{array}$$

Count the number of decimal places, 4, then ignore them:

$$\begin{array}{r} 272 \\ \times 305 \\ \hline \end{array}$$

Complete the calculations:

$$\begin{array}{r} 272 \\ \times 305 \\ \hline 82{,}960 \end{array}$$

Now, count four places from the right and insert a decimal point:

82,960 becomes 8.2960

Division with decimals, on the other hand, requires more effort. Often, you can estimate by shifting decimal points to the left until the divisor is a whole number. See the following example:

$$1.94\overline{)40}$$

The quickest way to solve a problem like this is to round any decimals to the closest integer. In this case, you only need to round the divisor from 1.94 to 2. This lets us quickly arrive at an estimation of what the answer would be.

$$1.94\overline{)40} \approx 2\overline{)40}$$

From here, you can easily solve the problem to get to the answer, 20. However, because you rounded a part of the equation, you cannot say $1.94\overline{)40} = 20$. However, you do know that the actual quotient will be slightly greater than 20.

So how would you solve the original problem? Move the decimal points the same number of spaces to the right until the divisor is an integer. Here's what that would look like:

$$1.94\overline{)40} \text{ becomes } 194\overline{)4000}$$

The decimal point moves two places to the right for the divisor, so you have to move the decimal two places to the right for the dividend.

Then, solve the problem:

$$\begin{array}{r} 20.618 \\ 194\overline{)4000} \end{array}$$

Unlike multiplication, you do not need to move the decimal point back to where it originally was.

Adding and Subtracting Fractions

To combine fractions by addition or subtraction, combine numerators over a *common denominator.* If the fractions already have the same denominator, simply add (or subtract) numerators:

$$\frac{3}{4}+\frac{2}{4}=\frac{3+2}{4}=\frac{5}{4}$$

(the two fractions share the common denominator 4)

$$\frac{1}{7}-\frac{3}{7}=\frac{1-3}{7}=\frac{-2}{7}$$

(the two fractions share the common denominator 7)

If the fractions do not already have a common denominator, you need to find one. To find a common denominator, you can always multiply the denominators together. This can result in large numbers that are clumsy to work with. Instead, try to find the **least (or lowest) common denominator (LCD)** by working your way up in multiples of the denominators given. Imagine you needed to add the following fractions:

$$\frac{1}{6}+\frac{1}{3}+\frac{1}{5}$$

For denominators of 6, 3, and 5, try successive multiples of 6 (12, 18, 24 . . .), and work until you hit a multiple common to all three denominators. In this case, the LCD is 30. Now, set the denominator of each fraction to 30 and then multiply the numerator of each fraction by the factor used to find the LCD.

$$\frac{5}{30}+\frac{10}{30}+\frac{6}{30}$$

Then, combine and simplify.

$$\frac{5}{30}+\frac{10}{30}+\frac{6}{30}=\frac{21}{30}=\frac{7}{10}$$

Multiplying and Dividing Fractions

To combine fractions by multiplication, multiply the numerators, and multiply the denominators. The denominators need not be the same.

$$\frac{1}{2}\times\frac{5}{3}\times\frac{1}{7}=\frac{(1)(5)(1)}{(2)(3)(7)}=\frac{5}{42}$$

To divide one fraction by another, first invert the divisor (the number after the division sign) by switching its numerator and denominator. (This new fraction is called the reciprocal of the original one.) Then, combine by multiplying.

$$\frac{2}{5}\div\frac{3}{4}=\frac{2}{5}\times\frac{4}{3}=\frac{(2)(4)}{(5)(3)}=\frac{8}{15}$$

Simplifying Fractions

A fraction can be simplified to its lowest terms if its numerator and denominator share a common factor. Here are a few simple examples:

$$\frac{6}{9}=\frac{(3)(2)}{(3)(3)}=\frac{2}{3}$$

(you can "cancel" or factor out the common factor 3)

$$\frac{21}{35}=\frac{(7)(3)}{(7)(5)}=\frac{3}{5}$$

(you can factor out the common factor 7)

Before you perform any operation with a fraction, always check to see if you can simplify it first. By reducing a fraction to its lowest terms, you will also simplify whatever operation you perform on it.

Mixed Numbers and Improper Fractions

As noted earlier, a mixed number consists of a whole number along with a simple fraction. The number $4\frac{2}{3}$ is an example of a mixed number. Before combining fractions, you might need to convert mixed numbers to improper fractions. Recall that an improper fraction is a fraction where the numerator is larger than the denominator. To convert, follow these three steps:

1. Multiply the denominator of the fraction by the whole number.
2. Add the product to the numerator of the fraction.
3. Place the sum over the denominator of the fraction.

For example, here's how to convert the mixed number $4\frac{2}{3}$ to an improper fraction:

$$4\frac{2}{3}=\frac{(3)(4)+2}{3}=\frac{14}{3}$$

To add or subtract mixed numbers, convert each one to an improper fraction, then find their LCD and combine them. Or, you can add together the whole numbers, and add together the fractions separately.

To perform multiple operations, always perform multiplication and division before you perform addition and subtraction.

Problems Involving Percentages

Recall that when you divide the numerator of a proper fraction by the denominator, you create a decimal.

EXAMPLES:

$$\frac{1}{4}=4\overline{)1}=0.25$$

You know that the decimal can then be expressed as a percentage.

$$\frac{1}{4}=4\overline{)1}=0.25$$
$$0.25\times100=25\%$$

Multiply the decimal by 100 and add a percent sign (%) at the end. This has the same result as moving the decimal point two places to the right and adding a percent sign at the end. That covers percentage basics, but problems involving percentages will likely ask you to go further with your math.

A question involving percentages might involve one of these three tasks:

- Finding the percentage of a number
- Finding a number when a percentage is given
- Finding what percentage one number is of another

Regardless of the task, three distinct values are involved: the part, the whole, and the percentage. Often, the problem will give you two of the three numbers, and your job is to find the missing value. To work with percentages, use the following formula:

$$\text{percentage} = \frac{\text{part}}{\text{whole}} \times 100$$

Once again, to know any two of those values allows you to determine the third.

Finding the Percentage

30 is what percent of 50?

In this question, 50 is the whole, and 30 is the part. Your task is to find the missing percent:

$$\begin{aligned}\text{percentage} &= \frac{30}{50} \times 100 \\ &= 60\%\end{aligned}$$

Finding the Part

What number is 25% of 80?

In this question, 80 is the whole, and 25 is the percentage. Your task is to find the part:

$$25\% = \frac{\text{part}}{80} \times 100$$

In this situation, it can be helpful to change the percentage into its decimal form (.25), which then lets you drop the 100 from the equation or to represent the percentage as a fraction, in this case $\frac{25}{100}$. That gives us a new form of the equation:

$$\frac{25}{100} = \frac{\text{part}}{80}$$

To solve for the missing part, cross multiply 25 and 80 and 100 with the missing part. That yields the following:

$$\begin{aligned}100(\text{part}) &= 25(80) \\ 100(\text{part}) &= 2000 \\ \text{part} &= \frac{2000}{100} \\ \text{part} &= 20\end{aligned}$$

25% of 80 is 20. Because of the values used, there are any number of ways you could have come to that solution faster (by simplifying the left fraction to $\frac{1}{4}$ or calculating 80 ÷ 4 or 80 × .25), but it's important that you see the full process. Let's look at how you can streamline your work in the next example.

Finding the Whole

75% of what number is 150?

In this question, 150 is the part, and 75 is the percentage. Your task is to find the whole. Here's the streamlined equation:

$$\frac{75}{100} = \frac{150}{\text{whole}}$$

Here, you can simplify the fraction on the left to $\frac{3}{4}$ and then cross multiply:

$$\begin{gathered}\frac{3}{4} = \frac{150}{\text{whole}} \\ \text{whole}(3) = 150(4) \\ \text{whole} = 200\end{gathered}$$

You multiplied the two diagonally situated numbers you knew: 150 × 4 = 600. Finally, you divided 600 by 3, which equals 200. 75% of 200 is 150.

Percent Increase and Decrease

You've likely encountered the concept of percent change with investment interest, sales tax, and discount pricing. Percent change always relates to the value before the change. Here are two simple examples:

10 increased by what percent is 12?

The amount of the increase is 2.

Compare the change (2) to the original number (10).

The change in percent is $\frac{2}{10}$, or 20%.

12 decreased by what percent is 10?

The amount of the decrease is 2.

Compare the change (2) to the original number (12).

The change is $\frac{2}{12}$, or $\frac{1}{6}$ (or 16.66%).

Notice that the percent increase from 10 to 12 (20%) is not the same as the percent decrease from 12 to 10 (16.66%). That's because the original number (before the change) is different in the two questions.

Percent-change problems typically involve tax, interest, profit, discount, or weight. In handling these problems, you might need to calculate more than one percent change.

EXAMPLE:

A computer originally priced at \$500 is discounted by 10%, then by another 10%. What is the price of the computer after the second discount, to the nearest dollar?

A. \$400

B. \$405

C. \$425

D. \$450

E. \$475

After the first 10% discount, the price was \$450 (\$500 minus 10% of \$500). After the second discount, which is calculated based on the \$450 price, the price of the computer is \$405 (\$450 minus 10% of \$450). **The correct answer is B.**

Ratios and Proportions

A **ratio** expresses proportion or comparative size—the size of one quantity relative to the size of another. Write a ratio by placing a colon (:) between the two numbers. Read the colon as the word "to." For example, read the ratio 3:5 as "3 to 5." As with fractions, you can reduce ratios to lowest terms by canceling common factors. For example, given a menagerie of 28 pets that includes 12 cats and 16 dogs:

The ratio of cats to dogs is 12:16, or 3:4 ("3 to 4").

The ratio of dogs to cats is 16:12, or 4:3 ("4 to 3").

The ratio of cats to the total number of pets is 12:28, or 3:7 ("3 to 7").

The ratio of dogs to the total number of pets is 16:28, or 4:7 ("4 to 7").

Another way of saying that two ratios (or fractions) are equivalent is to say that they are **proportionate.** For example, the ratio 12:16 is proportionate to the ratio 3:4. Similarly, the fraction $\frac{12}{16}$ is proportionate to the fraction $\frac{3}{4}$.

Determining Quantities from a Ratio

You can think of a ratio as parts adding up to a whole. In the ratio 5:6, for example, 5 parts + 6 parts = 11 parts (the whole). If the actual total quantity were 22, you'd multiply each element by 2: 10 parts + 12 parts = 22 parts (the whole). Notice that the ratios are the same. In other words, 5:6 is the same ratio as 10:12; they are proportionate.

Another way to think about a ratio is as a fraction. Since you can express any ratio as a fraction, you can set two equivalent ratios (also called proportionate ratios) equal to each other as fractions. The ratio 16:28 is proportionate to the ratio 4:7 because $\frac{16}{28} = \frac{4}{7}$. If one of the four terms is missing from the equation (the proportion), you can solve for the missing term using the same method that you learned for solving percent problems:

1. Simplify the known fraction, if possible.
2. Cross multiply the numbers you know.
3. Divide the product by the third number you know.

For example, if the ratio 10:15 is proportionate to 14:x, you can find the missing number by first setting up the following proportion:

$$\frac{10}{15} = \frac{14}{x}$$

Reading the ratio 10:15 as a fraction, simplify it to $\frac{2}{3}$.

$$\frac{2}{3} = \frac{14}{x}$$

Then, cross multiply the numbers you know: $3 \times 14 = 42$. Finally, divide by the third number you know: $42 \div 2 = 21$. The ratio 10:15 is equivalent to the ratio 14:21.

EXAMPLE:

1. A class of students contains only freshmen and sophomores. 18 of the students are sophomores. If the ratio between the number of freshmen and the number of sophomores in the class is 5:3, how many students altogether are in the class?

   A. 30
   B. 40
   C. 48
   D. 56
   E. 64

Let's apply a part-to-whole analysis to answer this question. Look first at the ratio and the sum of its parts: 5 (freshmen) + 3 (sophomores) = 8 (total students). These aren't the actual quantities, but they're proportionate to the real quantities. Given 18 sophomores altogether, sophomores account for 3 parts of the class —each part containing 6 students. Accordingly, with 8 total parts, the total number of students must be $6 \times 8 = 48$. **The correct answer is C.**

Probability

Probability refers to the statistical chances of an event occurring (or not occurring). By definition, probability ranges from 0 to 1. Probability is never negative, and it is never greater than 1.

Here's the basic formula for determining probability:

$$\text{Probability} = \frac{\text{number of desired outcomes}}{\text{total possible outcomes}}$$

Probability can be expressed as a fraction, a percent, or a decimal number.

Determining Probability (Single Event)

Probability plays an integral role in games of chance, including many casino games. In the throw of a single die, for example, the probability of rolling a 5 is "one in six," or $\frac{1}{6}$, or 16.66 %. Of course, the probability of rolling any other number is the same. A standard deck of 52 playing cards contains 12 face cards. The probability of selecting a face card from a full deck is $\frac{12}{52}$ or $\frac{3}{13}$. The probability of selecting a queen from a full deck is $\frac{1}{13}$.

EXAMPLE:

1. If you randomly select one candy from a jar containing two cherry candies, two licorice candies, and one peppermint candy, what is the probability of selecting a cherry candy?

   A. $\frac{1}{6}$
   B. $\frac{1}{3}$
   C. $\frac{2}{5}$
   D. $\frac{3}{5}$
   E. $\frac{3}{4}$

There are two ways among five possible occurrences that a cherry candy will be selected. Thus, the probability of selecting a cherry candy is $\frac{2}{5}$. **The correct answer is C.**

Determining Probability (Two Events)

To determine probability involving two or more events, you must distinguish probabilities involving **independent** events from an event that is **dependent** on another one.

Two events are independent if neither event affects the probability that the other will occur. The events may involve the random selection of one object from each of two or more groups. Or they may involve the random selection of one object from a group, then replacing it and selecting again (as in a "second round" or "another turn" of a game).

In either scenario, to find the probability of two events BOTH occurring, multiply together their individual probabilities:

probability of event 1 occurring

×

probability of event 2 occurring

=

probability of both events occurring

For example, assume that you randomly select one letter from each of two sets: {A, B} and {C, D, E}. The probability of selecting A and C = $\frac{1}{2} \times \frac{1}{3} = \frac{1}{6}$.

To calculate the probability that two events will NOT BOTH occur, subtract the probability of both events occurring from 1.

For dependent probability, two distinct events might be related in that one event affects the probability of the other one occurring—for example, randomly selecting one object from a group, then selecting a second object from the same group without replacing the first selection. Removing one object from the group increases the odds of selecting any particular object from those that remain.

For example, assume that you randomly select one letter from the set {A, B, C, D}. Then, from the remaining three letters, you select another letter. What is the probability of selecting both A and B? To answer this question, you need to consider each of the two selections separately.

In the first selection, the probability of selecting either A or B is $\frac{2}{4}$. But the probability of selecting the second of the two is $\frac{1}{3}$. Why? Because after the first selection, only three letters remain from which to select. Since the question asks for the chances of selecting both A and B (as opposed to either one), multiply the two individual probabilities: $\frac{2}{4} \times \frac{1}{3} = \frac{2}{12}$, or $\frac{1}{6}$.

EXAMPLE:

A gaming die is a cube with numbers 1–6 on its faces, each number on a different face. In a roll of two gaming dice, what is the probability that the two numbers facing up will total 12?

A. $\frac{1}{64}$

B. $\frac{1}{36}$

C. $\frac{1}{12}$

D. $\frac{1}{9}$

E. $\frac{1}{3}$

The only two-number combination on the dice that can total 12 is 6 + 6. The probability of rolling 6 on each die is $\frac{1}{6}$. Accordingly, the probability of rolling 6 on both dice is $\frac{1}{6} \times \frac{1}{6} = \frac{1}{36}$.

The correct answer is B.

7

Series

In series questions, you must determine the relationship between a series of symbols, numbers, or letters, and then choose the next item for the series based on the apparent pattern.

Number Series

Number series questions measure your ability to think numerically and recognize the relationship among numbers in a series. To answer number series questions, first, examine the series looking for an apparent pattern. Consider the difference between values or elements of repetition, among other things. A series such as 1, 2, 3, 1, 2, 3, 1 . . . depends on repetition. The next number in the series must be 2. Some series will couple repetition with arithmetic. An example of such a series is 1, 2, 15, 3, 4, 15, 5 . . . The number 15 appears after each set of two numbers in a simple +1 series. As such, the next value would be 6.

Letter Series

In letter series, each question consists of letters arranged according to a definite pattern. You must find the pattern and use that knowledge to determine which one of the five options completes the series. Letter series questions might be simple alphabetical progressions or intricate combinations that alternate between forward and backward steps.

EXAMPLE:

What are the next two letters in the series?

A, A, A, B, A, C, A, D, A, E, A, __, __

The sequence places an A before each letter of the alphabet (AA, AB, AC . . .). As a result, you can put an F in the first space and an A in the second space.

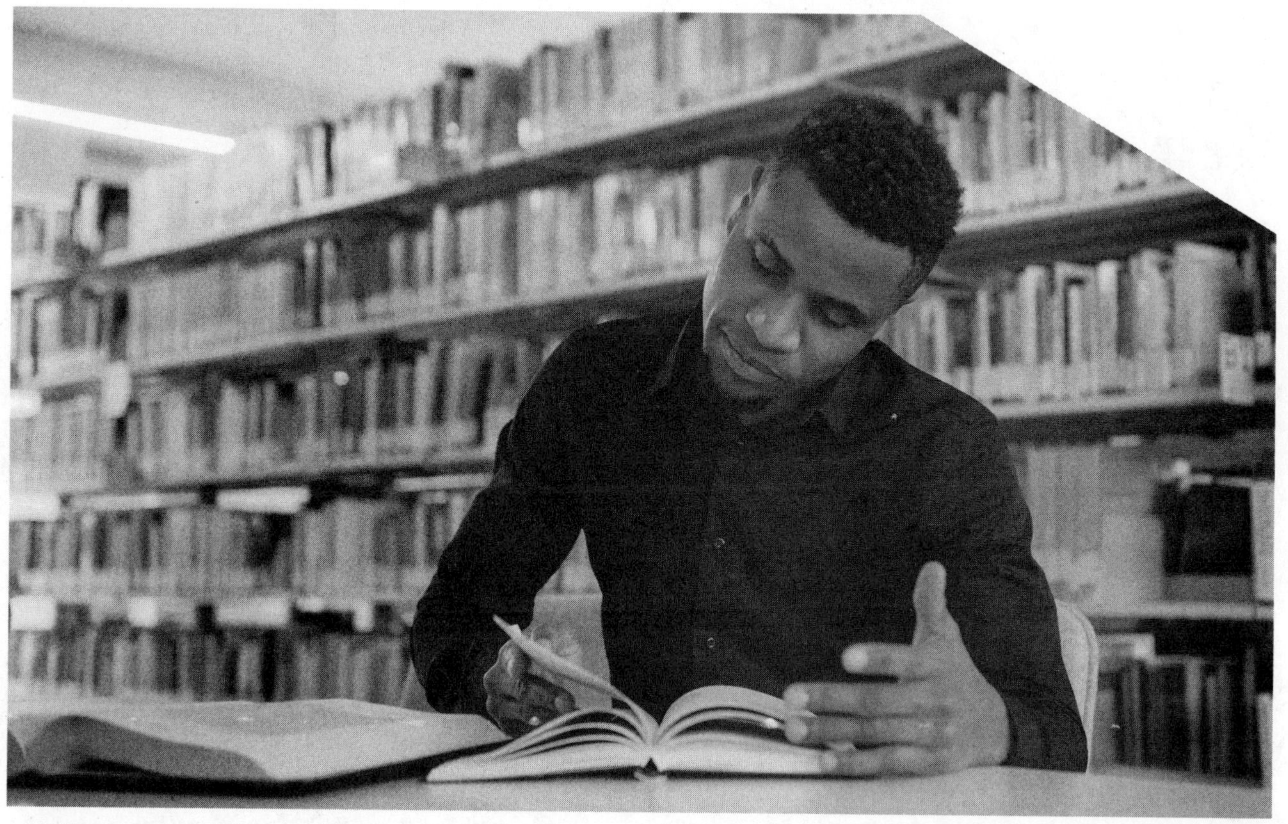

Test Yourself: Basic Math

1. Simplify: $-(-5)^3 - 2^2(1 - 4)$.

   A. –363

   B. –113

   C. 27

   D. 137

   E. 233

2. Compute 300% of 0.03.

   A. 0.009

   B. 0.09

   C. 3.03

   D. 9.0

   E. 9.09

3. Suppose you roll a fair 6-sided die three times in succession and record the result each time. What is the probability that you do NOT roll three 5s?

   A. $\frac{215}{216}$

   B. $\frac{35}{36}$

   C. $\frac{125}{216}$

   D. $\frac{1}{216}$

   E. $\frac{35}{216}$

4. Simplify: $\frac{|0.02-1.2|-|-0.08|}{-|1.01-1.11|}$

   A. –12.6

   B. –11

   C. 9.2

   D. 11

   E. 12.6

5. Which of the following expressions is equivalent to $20\frac{1}{2}\%$ of the sum of $2\frac{3}{8}$ and $4\frac{3}{4}$?

   A. 20.5×7.125

   B. 0.205×7.125

   C. 20.5×6.5

   D. 0.205×6.5

   E. 0.410×6.5

6. Compute: $\frac{12-3(1-4)}{2\left(5-2^2\right)+1}$

   A. -9

   B. 1

   C. $\frac{21}{19}$

   D. 7

   E. 9

7. A botanical exhibit contains four different types of orchids; call them types A, B, C, and D. The ratio of the number of type A to the number of type B to the number of type C to the number of type D is 1:2:4:5. If there are 200 orchids of type C, how many orchids of type B are there?

   A. 50

   B. 100

   C. 250

   D. 600

   E. 650

8. Sandy purchased a new sound system for \$900 last year. At the same time this year, the sound system has decreased in value by 18%. Which of these expressions represents its current value?

   A. \$900(1.18)

   B. 0.18(\$900)

   C. \$900(1 – 0.18)

   D. $\frac{\$900}{1-0.18}$

   E. $\frac{0.18}{\$900}$

9. In a certain high school, the following is the breakdown of the junior class's participation in electives this academic year: 40% take theater, 22% take electronic art, 10% take plant biology, 10% take creative writing, and 18% take German. What is the probability that a junior chosen at random did NOT select either plant biology or German as their elective?

A. 0.28

B. 0.72

C. 0.82

D. 0.90

E. 0.99

10. A vase contains 14 carnations and 11 daisies. If two flowers are selected at random without replacement, what is the probability of selecting two daisies?

A. $\frac{11}{25} \times \frac{10}{25}$

B. $\frac{11}{25} \times \frac{11}{25}$

C. $\frac{11}{14} \times \frac{10}{14}$

D. $\frac{11}{25} \times \frac{10}{24}$

E. $\frac{10}{14} \times \frac{10}{24}$

Answer Key and Explanations

1. D	3. A	5. B	7. B	9. B
2. B	4. B	6. D	8. C	10. D

1. **The correct answer is D.** Use the order of operations to simplify:

$$\begin{aligned}-(-5)^3-2^2(1-4)&=-(-125)-4(1-4)\\&=-(-125)-4(-3)\\&=125+12\\&=137\end{aligned}$$

Choice A is incorrect because you did not use the order of operations; you just computed from left to right. Choice B is incorrect because $-(-5)^3 = 125$, not -125. Choice C is incorrect because $(-5)^3 \neq -15$. Choice E represents a computation error.

2. **The correct answer is B.** 300% is equal to the decimal 3.0. So 300% of 0.03 equals 3.0(0.03) = 0.09. In choice A, the decimal point is one too many places to the left. Choice C is incorrect because you multiply 3.0 and 0.03 to compute 300% of 0.03; you do not add them. Choice D is incorrect because 300% does not equal 300; you must move the decimal point two places to the left. Choice E combines multiple answers to create an incorrect value.

3. **The correct answer is A.** The three rolls are independent of each other, and each has 6 possible outcomes. So there are (6)(6)(6) = 216 possible three-roll outcomes. There is only one way to get all 5s. So the probability of NOT getting three 5s is $\frac{215}{216}$. Choice B is the probability of not getting two 5s when rolling the die twice. Choice C is the probability that you do not roll any 5s in the three attempts. Choice D is the probability of rolling three 5s. Choice E incorrectly combines probabilities for rolls of two and three dice.

4. **The correct answer is B.** Use the order of operations with the definition of absolute value as follows:

$$\begin{aligned}\frac{|0.02-1.2|-|-0.08|}{-|1.01-1.11|}&=\frac{|-1.18|-|-0.08|}{-|-0.1|}\\&=\frac{1.18-0.08}{-0.1}\\&=\frac{1.1}{-0.1}\\&=-11\end{aligned}$$

5. **The correct answer is B.** Note that $20\frac{1}{2}\% = 20.5\% = 0.205$. Also,

$$\begin{aligned}2\frac{3}{8}+4\frac{3}{4}&=2\frac{3}{8}+4\frac{6}{8}\\&=6\frac{9}{8}\\&=7\frac{1}{8}\\&=7.125\end{aligned}$$

6. **The correct answer is D.** Use the order of operations to solve as follows:

$$\begin{aligned}\frac{12-3(1-4)}{2(5-2^2)+1}&=\frac{12-3(-3)}{2(5-4)+1}\\&=\frac{12-(-9)}{(2)(1)+1}\\&=\frac{21}{2+1}\\&=\frac{21}{3}\\&=7\end{aligned}$$

7. **The correct answer is B.** Let x be the number of type A orchids. Then, there are $2x$ type B, $4x$ type C, and $5x$ type D. We are given that $4x = 200$ and so, $x = 50$. Thus, the number of type B orchids is 2(50) = 100. Choice A is the number of type A. Choice C is the number of type D. Choice D is the total number of orchids in the exhibit. Choice E is more than the total number of orchids in the exhibit.

8. **The correct answer is C.** A decrease by 18% is represented by 1 – 0.18. To get the current value, multiply this by the amount paid initially, which is $900. This yields the expression $900(1 – 0.18). Choice A represents an increase in value by 18%. Choice B is the amount of the decrease. Choice D is incorrect because you should multiply by (1 – 0.18), not divide by it. Choice E inverts the relationship between 0.18 and $900.

9. **The correct answer is B.** The probability is 1 – (0.10 + 0.18) = 1 – 0.28 = 0.72. Choice A is the probability of selecting a junior that *did* choose plant biology or German as their elective. Choice C is incorrect because you must also exclude the percentage who chose plant biology as their elective. Choice D is incorrect because you must also exclude the percentage who chose German as their elective. Choice E is not reflected by the values provided.

10. **The correct answer is D.** There are 11 daisies of 25 that could be chosen in the first selection; the probability of doing so is $\frac{11}{25}$. Once this flower is removed, there are 24 remaining in the vase, 10 of which are daisies. So the probability of choosing a second daisy is $\frac{10}{24}$. Since the selections are performed in succession, we multiply the probabilities. So the probability of randomly selecting two daisies is $\frac{11}{25} \times \frac{10}{24}$. Choice A is incorrect because the denominator of the second fraction in the product should be reduced by 1 since the flower selected first was not returned to the vase. Choice B is incorrect because this is the result if the first flower were returned to the vase before the second flower was chosen. Choice C is incorrect because the number of flowers in the vase is not 14; this is the number of carnations. Rather, there are 11 + 14 = 25 flowers in the vase from which to make the first selection. Choice E misuses the values given for daisies and carnations.

ALGEBRA

Fundamentally, algebra is the manipulation of mathematical symbols. More than likely, your familiarity with the field stems from solving for unknowns by applying various rules and procedures. Algebra questions on the AFOQT and OAR subtests will require understanding of such topics as exponents and radical expressions, scientific notation, polynomials, equations, systems of equations, functions, and logarithms, among others.

Evaluating Expressions

You've seen plenty of expressions already, at least two values with some math operator used between them. But when we're talking about algebra, at least one of the terms in the expression will be a variable and may or may not have a coefficient. A **term** is any coefficient, variable, or combination of a coefficient and a variable. It does not need an exponent, but if it has one it must be a non-negative exponent. A **coefficient** is the number that multiplies with a variable.

Expressions can be simplified by combining like terms (e.g., 3 and 4, $3x$ and x, $4y^7$ and $253y^7$). Expressions can also be evaluated, meaning a variable is defined with a value and can be substituted into the expression.

Linear Expressions

A **linear expression** has the form $Ax + B$, where A and B are real numbers. They can be added and subtracted by combining like terms. For example:

$$\begin{aligned}\left(\frac{2}{3}x-\frac{3}{4}\right)+\left(\frac{1}{6}x+\frac{5}{12}\right) &= \left(\frac{2}{3}x+\frac{1}{6}x\right)+\left(-\frac{3}{4}+\frac{5}{12}\right)\\ &= \left(\frac{4}{6}x+\frac{1}{6}x\right)+\left(-\frac{9}{12}+\frac{5}{12}\right)\\ &= \frac{5}{6}x-\frac{4}{12}\\ &= \frac{5}{6}x-\frac{1}{3}\end{aligned}$$

Using the distributive property, we can also multiply a linear expression by a single term:

$$1.4(0.3x - 1.4) = 1.4(0.3x) - 1.4(1.4) = 0.42x - 1.96$$

Using the distributive property twice in succession enables us to multiply two linear expressions.

EXAMPLE:

Evaluate $\frac{3}{4}x-\frac{5}{6}$ at $x = -2$.

To solve, replace every occurrence of the variable with the number and simplify the arithmetic expression using the order of operations:

$$\frac{3}{4}(-2)-\frac{5}{6} = -\frac{3}{2}-\frac{5}{6} = -\frac{9}{6}-\frac{5}{6} = -\frac{14}{6} = -\frac{7}{3}$$

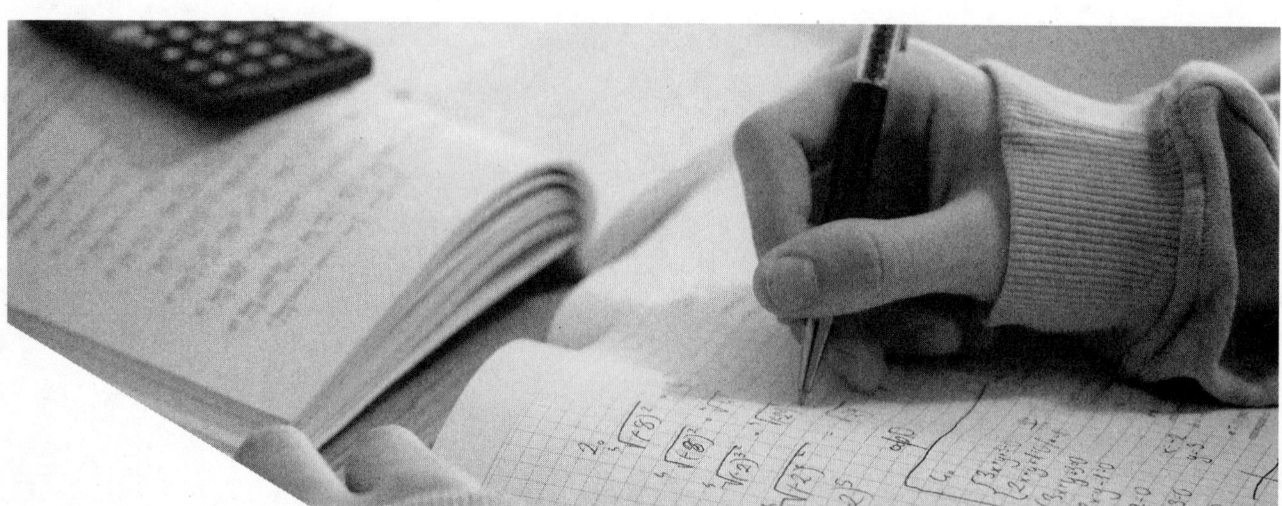

Real-World Application

Sometimes, you will need to formulate a linear expression as part of solving a word problem. You simply need to look for key words and interpret accordingly. Here are some examples:

REAL-WORLD LINEAR EXPRESSIONS	
Scenario	**Linear Expression**
One cable is two-thirds the length of one half of another piece.	Let x represent the length of the second piece. The word *of* means multiply, so the length of the cable is $\frac{2}{3}\left(\frac{1}{2}x\right)$.
Katie is three years older than twice her sister's age.	Let x be Katie's sister's age (in years). Then, Katie's age is $(2x+3)$ years.
The length of a rectangle is one meter more than one fourth the width.	Let w be the width of the rectangle (in meters). Then, the length is $\left(1+\frac{1}{4}w\right)$ meters.

Exponents and Expressions with Radicals

The term **exponent** refers to the number of times that a number (referred to as the **base number**) is multiplied by itself. In the exponential number 2^4, the base number is 2 and the exponent is 4. The value of 2^4 can be written as follows: $2^4 = 2 \times 2 \times 2 \times 2 = 16$. An exponent is also referred to as a power. You can express the exponential number 2^4 as "2 to the 4th power."

The inverse of an exponent is the root of a number. The radical sign signifies a square root and looks like this: $\sqrt{\ }$.

Here's an example of a square root:

$2 = \sqrt{4}$ (the square root of 4) because 2×2 (or 2^2) is 4; additionally, $\sqrt{4} = 4^{\frac{1}{2}}$

Rules for Exponents

A variety of rules exist for working with exponents with different operations. Use the following table as a guide:

Product	$a^m a^n = a^{m+n}$	Zero exponent	$a^0 = 1$
Product of a power	$(a^m)^n = a^{mn}$	Negative exponent	$a^{-n} = \frac{1}{a^n}$
Quotient to a power	$\left(\frac{a}{b}\right)^n = \frac{a^n}{b^n}$	Inversion	$\left(\frac{a}{b}\right)^{-n} = \left(\frac{b}{a}\right)^n$
Quotient	$\frac{a^m}{a^n} = a^{m-n}$	Fractional powers	$a^{\frac{m}{n}} = \sqrt[n]{a^m}$

EXAMPLE:

Simplify the expression: $\left(\frac{x^2y^4}{x^{-1}y}\right)^{-2}$

Here, apply the rules for exponents within the parentheses and then apply the –2 power. Note that a variable with no exponent is assumed to have an exponent of 1:

$$\left(\frac{x^2y^4}{x^{-1}y}\right)^{-2} = \left(x^{2-(-1)}y^{4-1}\right)^{-2} = \left(x^3y^3\right)^{-2} = x^{-6}y^{-6} = \frac{1}{x^6y^6}$$

Fractional Exponents and Roots

Fractional exponents follow the same rules as other exponents. However, fractional exponents can also be written as roots (**radicals**). Remember, the square root of a number n is a number that you "square" (multiply it by itself, or raise to the power of 2), to obtain n. Let's look at another example of a square root:

$4 = \sqrt{16}$ (the square root of 16)
because 4×4 (or 4^2) = 16

The cube root of a number n is a number that you raise to the power of 3 (multiply by itself twice) to obtain n. You determine higher roots (for example, the "fourth root") in the same way. Except for square roots, the radical sign will indicate the root to be taken. See the following example:

$2 = \sqrt[3]{8}$ (the cube root of 8)
because $2 \times 2 \times 2$ (or 2^3) is 8

$2 = \sqrt[4]{16}$ (the fourth root of 16)
because $2 \times 2 \times 2 \times 2$ (or 2^4) is 16

EXAMPLE:

Simplify the expression $\frac{x^{\frac{1}{2}}y^2}{x^{\frac{2}{3}}y^{\frac{1}{2}}}$. Write your answer as a radical expression.

First, apply the rules for exponents. Then, apply the rule that $x^{\frac{m}{n}} = \sqrt[n]{x^m}$:

$$\frac{x^{\frac{1}{2}}y^2}{x^{\frac{2}{3}}y^{\frac{1}{2}}} = x^{\frac{1}{2}-\frac{2}{3}}y^{2-\frac{1}{2}} = x^{-\frac{1}{6}}y^{\frac{3}{2}} = \frac{y^{\frac{3}{2}}}{x^{\frac{1}{6}}} = \frac{\sqrt{y^3}}{\sqrt[6]{x}}$$

This expression can be simplified further. Since $y^3 = y \cdot y^2$ and $\sqrt{y^2} = y$, we can write the following:

$$\frac{\sqrt{y^3}}{\sqrt[6]{x}} = \frac{\sqrt{yy^2}}{\sqrt[6]{x}} = \frac{y\sqrt{y}}{\sqrt[6]{x}}$$

You can simplify these radical expressions anytime this occurs. The following table provides useful rules, some of which overlap with those for exponents, for working with radical expressions:

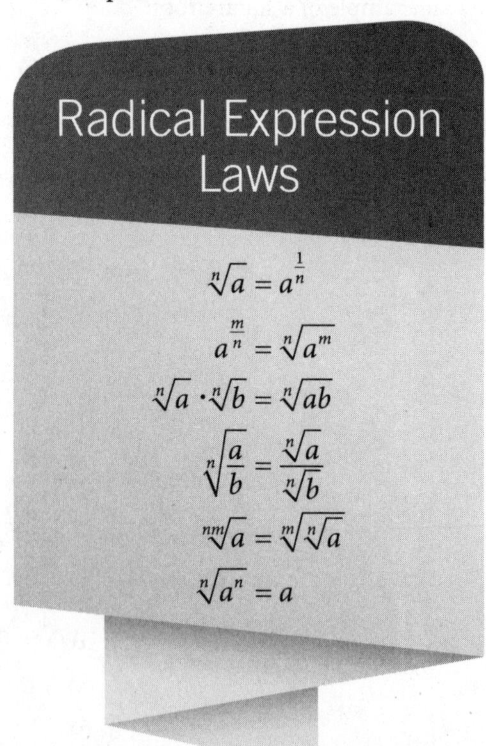

These rules are demonstrated by the following example.

EXAMPLE:

Simplify the radical $\sqrt[4]{x^6y^4}$.

Remember, $\sqrt[n]{a^n} = a$. By factoring out x^2 and rearranging, we can pull out xy:

$$\begin{aligned}\sqrt[4]{x^6y^4} &= \sqrt[4]{(x^4y^4)(x^2)}\\ &= \sqrt[4]{(xy)^4(x^2)}\\ &= \sqrt[4]{(xy)^4}\sqrt[4]{x^2}\\ &= (xy)(x^{\frac{1}{2}})\\ &= xy\sqrt{x}\end{aligned}$$

Scientific Notation

Scientific notation is a system for writing extremely large or extremely small numbers. In scientific notation, an integer or decimal number between 1 and 10 is written to the power of 10. For example, the number 380,000,000 can be written as 3.8×10^8. Let's work backwards, starting with a value between 1 and 10; in this case, we want 3.8, the first non-zero digits of the larger value. To go from 3.8 to 380,000,000, you need to shift the decimal 8 digits to the right. That means that the exponent is 8. A negative exponent would signify a fractional number.

To illustrate further, here's a list of related decimal numbers and their equivalents in scientific notation:

$837{,}000 = 8.37 \times 10^5$
(decimal point shifts 5 places to the left)

$8{,}370 = 8.37 \times 10^3$
(decimal point shifts 3 places to the left)

$837 = 8.37 \times 10^2$
(decimal point shifts 2 places to the left)

$8.37 = 8.37 \times 10^0$
(decimal point unchanged in position)

$0.837 = 8.37 \times 10^{-1}$
(decimal point shifts 1 place to the right)

$0.0837 = 8.37 \times 10^{-2}$
(decimal point shifts 2 places to the right)

$0.000837 = 8.37 \times 10^{-4}$
(decimal point shifts 4 places to the right)

Questions could ask you to convert a number to scientific notation form or change scientific notation into its expanded form.

Polynomials

A polynomial is an equation made up of terms with non-negative exponents. Here are some examples of different types of polynomials:

$$x^4 \times 14x^3 + 15x - 7$$
$$7x + 2 + 2x^2$$
$$14 + 3y$$
$$x$$
$$12$$

Let's look at a term from one of the earlier expressions: $14x^3$. We have a coefficient (14), a variable (x), and an exponent (^{3}). If you wanted to read this out loud, you'd say, "fourteen x to the third power" or "fourteen x cubed." Take a look at that full polynomial again.

$$x^4 \times 14x^3 + 15x - 7$$

This polynomial has four terms: x^4, $14x^3$, $15x$, and -7. Let's look at another polynomial from the earlier example:

$$7x + 2 + 2x^2$$

This polynomial has three terms, so you could call it a **trinomial**. From that list, 14+3y is a **binomial** because it has two terms. The last two expressions are **monomials** because they each have one term.

Writing Polynomials in Standard Form

You'll see many polynomials written in the standard form:

$$\text{A}x^2 + \text{B}x + \text{C}$$

A and B represent coefficients, C is a constant, and x represents the variable. The following are some examples of polynomials in standard form:

$$x^2 + 7x + 12$$

$$2x^3 - 18x^2 + 6x - 54$$

$$x^2 - 9$$

For larger polynomials, the standard form is to write the equation starting with the largest exponent as seen in the second example above and the following:

$$y^7 - 4y^3 + y^2 + 14y + 70$$

In this example, you start with y^7, or y to the seventh power. The next term is $-4y^3$, followed by y^2, $14y$, and finally 70.

Simplifying Polynomials

Simplifying polynomials means organizing and combining like terms to make a polynomial as easy to read as possible. This includes putting a polynomial into standard form. Let's look at a sample polynomial that has not been simplified:

$$2x + 4x^2 - 13 + 7x - x^2 + x - 3$$

To simplify, first gather like terms:

$$4x^2 - x^2 + 2x + 7x + x - 13 - 3$$

Then, combine like terms:

$$4x^2 - x^2 = 3x^2$$
$$2x + 7x + x = 10x$$
$$-13 - 3 = -16$$

Finally, write out the expression in standard form:

$$3x^2 + 10x - 16$$

This is much easier to read—and make sense of—than the original expression.

Adding and Subtracting Polynomials

If you have two polynomials and you want to combine them through addition or subtraction, the steps are similar to what you've done already. Let's take a look:

$$(11x^2 + 14 + 3x) + (-3x^2 + 2x + 6)$$

The first step, because you have two polynomials inside of parentheses connected by addition, is to remove the parentheses:

$$11x^2 + 14 + 3x + -3x^2 + 2x + 6$$

From here, gather terms and simplify:

$$11x^2 - 3x^2 + 3x + 2x + 14 + 6$$

The resulting polynomial is:

$$8x^2 + 5x + 20$$

Let's look at the same polynomial but instead focus on subtraction. The process is essentially the same except that you need to pay careful attention to number signs.

$$(11x^2 + 14 + 3x) - (-3x^2 + 2x + 6)$$

Now that you're subtracting one polynomial from the other, remove the parentheses and distribute the negative sign to the terms inside the second set of parentheses:

$$(11x^2 + 14 + 3x) + (3x^2 - 2x - 6)$$

Now, remove the parentheses, gather like terms and combine to simplify:

$$11x^2 + 14 + 3x + 3x^2 - 2x - 6$$

$$11x^2 + 3x^2 + 3x - 2x + 14 - 6$$

$$14x^2 + x + 8$$

Multiplying Monomials

Remember that a monomial is a polynomial with only one term. For example, $7x$ is a monomial. So is $2y^2$ and $1{,}784{,}921t^{45}$. Multiplying monomials gives us the chance to combine two terms that are not alike, such as $3x^2$ and $6x^4$. Let's review multiplying exponents:

$$3x^2\,(6x^4)$$

As with any polynomial equation, it's easier to solve after simplifying. With two monomials, break each monomial into its component parts:

$$3 \times 6 \text{ and } x^2 \times x^4$$

The first portion requires standard multiplication:

$$3 \times 6 = 18.$$

As for the exponents, when you are asked to multiply, remember that if they have the same base, you will add the exponents. Therefore, $3x^2 \times 6x^4 = 18x^6$.

Multiplying a Polynomial and a Monomial

When multiplying a polynomial and a monomial, distribution is the key. Here's a sample problem:

$$2(x^2 + 7x + 4)$$

The first step is to distribute the 2 to the terms in the trinomial:

$$(2 \times x^2) + (2 \times 7x) + (2 \times 4)$$

Finish multiplying and add the terms together to present the polynomial in standard form:

$$2x^2 + 14x + 8$$

Note that even though you can factor 2 out of each term, $2x^2 + 14x + 8$ is the simplified answer. Factoring out the 2 would bring us back to the original mononomial and polynomial of $2(x^2 + 7x + 4)$.

Multiplying Binomials

Let's start with a problem with two binomials:

$$(4x + 3)\,(2x + 9)$$

These binomials need to be multiplied together. To multiply binomials, you'll use a process called FOIL. FOIL is a mnemonic that stands for **F**irst, **O**uter, **I**nner, **L**ast. It describes the order in which you multiply terms. Let's apply it to the previous pair of binomials:

$$(4x + 3)\,(2x + 9)$$

Start with the **first** terms: $4x$ and $2x$. Multiply them together:

$$4x \bullet 2x = 8x^2$$

Then multiply the **outer** terms: $4x$ and 9:

$$4x \bullet 9 = 36x$$

Continue following FOIL. Next, multiply the **inner** terms:

$$3 \bullet 2x = 6x$$

Finally, multiply the **last** terms and combine:

$$3 \bullet 9 = 27$$

$$8x^2 + 36x + 6x + 27$$

$$8x^2 + 42x + 27$$

While you could have also used standard distribution to multiply the polynomial, tracking what you've multiplied can become challenging, especially as the number of terms in your polynomials grows. The mnemonic FOIL serves to remind you of the distributive property of multiplication.

Factoring Trinomials

Factoring a trinomial is essentially the same as multiplying binomials, but in reverse. Let's look at the standard form of a trinomial and an example:

$$Ax^2 + Bx + C$$
$$x^2 + 5x + 6$$

When factoring a trinomial, the goal is to build two binomials that when FOILed recreate the trinomial. Here's what you will see:

$$x^2 + 5x + 6 = (x + a)(x + b)$$

Let's expand the right side of this equation:

$$\begin{aligned} x^2 + 5x + 6 &= (x + a)(x + b) \\ &= x^2 + ax + bx + ab \\ &= x^2 + (a + b)x + ab \end{aligned}$$

What you see here is true for any trinomials that can be factored. You're looking for the values of a and b that multiply to make the C term of the standard form but also add up to the B term. In the example, ab must equal 6 and $a + b$ must equal 5.

We start by factoring the constant, 6.

$$\begin{aligned} 6 &: 6 \times 1 \\ &: 3 \times 2 \end{aligned}$$

Now, $6 \times 1 = 6$ but $6 + 1 = 7$. Try another pair of factors. What about 3×2?

$$3 \times 2 = 6$$
$$3 + 2 = 5$$

The numbers look correct, but test it to be sure.

$$a = 3,\ b = 2$$

$$\begin{aligned} x^2 + 5x + 6 &= (x + a)(x + b) \\ &= (x + 3)(x + 2) \\ &= (x)(x) + (x)(2) + (3)(x) + (3)(2) \\ &= x^2 + 2x + 3x + 6 \\ &= x^2 + 5x + 6 \end{aligned}$$

Our original trinomial was $x^2 + 5x + 6$, so $(x + 2)(x + 3)$ would suffice as an answer. If the trinomial was set equal to 0, you would then solve for the roots (where the trinomial would intersect the x-axis if graphed) and the algebra would yield -2 and -3.

Let's look at another example. What if you are told to factor the following trinomial?

$$5x^2 + 35x + 50$$

To start, look to see if there are any common factors among 5, 35, and 50. The greatest common factor of these three numbers is 5. So, factor out a 5 from each term:

$$5(x^2 + 7x + 10)$$

From here, factor the trinomial like you did in the first example:

$$5(x^2 + 7x + 10) = (x + a)(x + b)$$
$$a + b = 7$$
$$ab = 10$$

We can factor 10 as 10 and 1 or 5 and 2. We need the factors to add to 7. Of the factors of the C term, only 5 and 2 add to 7. Substitute 5 and 2 for the a and b terms and you have your answer:

$$5(x + 5)(x + 2)$$

Linear Equations

Algebraic expressions are usually used to form **equations,** which set two expressions equal to one another. Algebraic equations contain at least one **variable:** a letter such as x or y that represents a number that can *vary*. Many equations you'll see on the test are **linear equations**, in which the terms with variables do not have exponents greater than 1.

To find the value of a linear equation's variable (such as x) is to **solve the equation**. To solve any linear equation containing only one variable, your goal is always the same: isolate the variable on one side of the equation. To accomplish this, you may need to perform one or more of the following operations on both sides, depending on the equation:

- Add or subtract the same term on both sides.
- Multiply or divide both sides by the same term.
- Clear fractions by cross-multiplication.
- Clear radicals by raising both sides to the same power (exponent).

Whatever operation you perform on one side of an equation you must also perform on the other side; otherwise, the two sides will not be equal. Performing any of these operations on both sides does not change the equality; it merely restates the equation in a different form.

Solving an Equation Using the Four Basic Operations

To find the value of the variable (to solve for x), you may need to either add a term to both sides of the equation or subtract a term from both sides. Here are two examples:

Adding the same number to both sides:

$$x-2=5$$
$$x-2+2=5+2$$
$$x=7$$

Subtracting the same number from both sides:

$$\frac{3}{2}-x=12$$

The objective is to isolate the variable x. To do this, like terms must be combined.

$$\frac{3}{2}-\frac{3}{2}-x=12-\frac{3}{2}$$
$$-x=10\frac{1}{2}\text{(divide by }-1\text{ to make the variable positive)}$$
$$x=-10\frac{1}{2}$$

The first system isolates x by adding 2 to both sides. The second system isolates x by subtracting $\frac{3}{2}$ from both sides. In some cases, solving for x requires that you either multiply or divide both sides of the equation by the same term. Here are two examples:

Multiplying both sides by the same number:

$$\frac{x}{2}=14$$
$$2\times\frac{x}{2}=14\times2$$
$$x=28$$

Dividing both sides by the same number:

$$3x=18$$
$$\frac{3x}{3}=\frac{18}{3}$$
$$x=6$$

The first equation isolates x by multiplying both sides by 2. The second equation isolates x by dividing both sides by 3. If the variable appears on both sides of the equation, first perform whatever operation is required to position the variable on just one side—either the left or the right. The next equation positions both x-terms on the left side by subtracting $2x$ from both sides:

$$16-x=9+2x$$
$$16-x-2x=9+2x-2x$$
$$16-3x=9$$

Now that x appears on just one side, the next step is to isolate it by subtracting 16 from both sides and then dividing both sides by –3:

$$16-3x=9$$
$$16-16-3x=9-16$$
$$-3x=-7$$
$$\frac{-3x}{-3}=\frac{-7}{-3}$$
$$x=\frac{7}{3}$$

Let's try another example.

EXAMPLE:

1. For what value of x does $2x - 6$ equal $x - 9$?

A. –6

B. –3

C. 2

D. 3

E. 6

First, write the verbal description as the equation $2x - 6 = x - 9$. Then, position both x-terms on the same side. To place them both on the left side, subtract x from both sides. Then, combine x-terms:

$$2x-6-x=x-9-x$$
$$x-6=-9$$

Finally, isolate x by adding 6 to both sides:

$$x-6+6=-9$$
$$x=-3$$

The correct answer is B.

Linear equations with rational coefficients are solved in the same way as those with integer coefficients—don't be intimidated because they look more complex! Just treat them as you would any rational expression. Let's walk through a couple of examples.

EXAMPLES:

Say you are given the following equation:

$$\frac{2}{3}x-\frac{3}{2}=3-\frac{5}{6}x$$

Gather the x-terms on the left-side and constant terms on the right. Then, proceed as follows:

$$\begin{aligned}\frac{2}{3}x-\frac{3}{2}&=3-\frac{5}{6}x\\ \frac{2}{3}x+\frac{5}{6}x&=3+\frac{3}{2}\\ \frac{9}{6}x&=\frac{9}{2}\\ x&=3\end{aligned}$$

Solve for x:

$$\frac{3}{4}\left(\frac{9}{2}-2x\right)-3\left(\frac{4}{3}x+2\right)=-1$$

This example may look complicated, but it really is just testing your knowledge of working with rational expressions. First, apply the distributive property to simplify the left side. Then, take the constant terms to the right side and solve as follows:

$$\begin{aligned}\frac{3}{4}\left(\frac{9}{2}-2x\right)-3\left(\frac{4}{3}x+2\right)&=-1\\ \frac{27}{8}-\frac{3}{2}x-4x-6&=-1\\ \left(-\frac{3}{2}-4\right)x&=-1+6-\frac{27}{8}\\ -\frac{11}{2}x&=\frac{13}{8}\\ x&=-\frac{2}{11}\left(\frac{13}{8}\right)\\ x&=-\frac{13}{44}\end{aligned}$$

Real-World Application

An incredibly common application of linear equations can be seen in the formula used for calculating distance, rate, and time. To find the distance traveled by an object, you can multiply the time traveled by the rate of travel (Distance = Rate × Time). This is a linear equation that when graphed displays a sloping straight line. When any two of the values are known (distance and rate, distance and time, rate and time), the third value can be determined algebraically.

Consider the following example: A plane flies north for an unspecified amount of time at an average rate of 325 miles per hour. The pilot later logs a total flight distance of 1,950 miles. How long was the plane in flight?

From the question, you know distance and rate but not time. Remember that D = RT, so you know that 1,950 miles = 325 mph(x hours). To solve for the number of hours, isolate the variable; divide 1,950 by 325. This yields 6 hours of flight time.

Systems of Equations

In the preceding section, you examined linear equations with only one variable. Now we will consider linear equations with two variables (x and y) of the form $Ax + By = C$, where A, B, and C are real numbers. The left side of the equation is called a **linear combination of x and y**. Before, you were able to find the value of the variable by isolating it on one side of the equation. This is not so, however, for a linear equation in two (or more) different variables. Consider the following equation, which contains two variables:

$$x+3=y+1$$

What is the value of x? It depends on the value of y. Similarly, the value of y depends on the value of x. Without more information about either x or y, you simply cannot find the other value. However, you *can* express x in terms of y, and you can express y in terms of x:

$$\begin{aligned}x&=y-2\\ y&=x+2\end{aligned}$$

Since these equations were previously set equal to each other, you cannot solve for either x or y. You can only solve for either variable in terms of the other variable.

Look at another example: $4x - 9 = \frac{3}{2}y$.

Solve for x in terms of y:

$$4x = \frac{3}{2}y + 9$$

$$x = \frac{3}{8}y + \frac{9}{4}$$

Solve for y in terms of x:

$$\frac{4x - 9}{\frac{3}{x}} = y$$

$$\frac{2}{4}(4x - 9) = y$$

$$\frac{8}{3}x - 6 = y$$

To determine numerical values of x and y, you need a system of two linear equations with the same two variables. Given this system, there are two different methods for finding the values of the two variables: the substitution method and the elimination or combination method.

The Substitution Method

To solve a system of two equations using the **substitution method**, follow these steps:

- In *either* equation isolate one variable (x) on one side.
- Substitute the expression that equals x in place of x in the other equation.
- Solve that equation for y.
- Now that you know the value of y, plug it into *either* equation to find the value of x.

Consider these two equations:

Equation A: $x = 4y$

Equation B: $x - y = 1$

In equation B, substitute $4y$ for x, and then solve for y:

$$4y - y = 1$$

$$3y = 1$$

$$y = \frac{1}{3}$$

To find x, substitute $\frac{1}{3}$ for y into either equation. The value of x will be the same in either equation.

Equation A: $x = 4\left(\frac{1}{3}\right) = \frac{4}{3}$

Equation B: $x - \frac{1}{3} = 1;\ x = \frac{4}{3}$

The Elimination Method

Another way to solve for two variables in a system of two equations is with the **elimination** method, sometimes called combination. Here are the steps:

- Align the two equations by listing the same variables and other terms in the same order. Place one equation above the other.
- Make the coefficient of *either* variable the same in both equations (you can disregard the sign) by multiplying every term in one of the equations.
- Add or subtract one equation from the other to eliminate one variable.

Consider these two equations:

Equation A: $x = 3 + 3y$

Equation B: $2x + y = 4$

In equation A, subtract $3y$ from both sides, so that all terms in the two equations "line up":

Equation A: $x - 3y = 3$

Equation B: $2x + y = 4$

To solve for y, multiply each term in Equation A by 2, so that the x-coefficient is the same in both equations:

Equation A: $2x - 6y = 6$

Equation B: $2x + y = 4$

Subtract Equation B from Equation A, thereby eliminating x, and then isolate y on one side of the equation:

$$\begin{array}{r} 2x - 6y = 6 \\ \underline{-2x + y = 4} \\ 0x - 7y = 2 \\ -7y = 2 \\ y = \frac{2}{7} \end{array}$$

To solve for x, you can now substitute in the value of y into either equation to solve.

Which Method Should You Use?

Which method you should use, substitution or elimination, depends on what the starting system looks like. To understand this point, look at this system of two equations:

$$\frac{2}{5}p + q = 3q - 10$$
$$q = 10 - p$$

Notice that the second equation is already set up nicely for the substitution method. But you could use elimination instead; you'd need to rearrange the terms in both the equations first:

$$\frac{2}{5}p - 2q = -10$$
$$p + q = 10$$

Now, look at the following system:

$$3x + 4y = -8$$
$$x - 2y = \frac{1}{2}$$

Notice that the x-term and y-term already line up here. Also notice that it's easy to match the coefficients of either x or y: multiply both sides of the second equation by either 3 or 2. This system is an ideal candidate for elimination. To appreciate this point, try using substitution instead. You'll discover that it takes far more number crunching.

In short, to solve a system of two linear equations in two variables, use elimination if you can quickly and easily eliminate one of the variables. Otherwise, use substitution.

Functions

In a **function** or **functional relationship**, the value of one variable depends upon the value of, or is "a function of," another variable. In mathematics, the relationship is expressed in the form $y = f(x)$—where y is a function of x.

To find the value of the function for any value of x, simply substitute the x-value for x wherever it appears in the function. In the following function, for example, the function of 2 is 14, and the function of –3 is 4.

$$f(x) = x^2 + 3x + 4$$
$$f(2) = 2^2 + 3(2) + 4 = 4 + 6 + 4 = 14$$
$$f(-3) = (-3)^2 + 3(-3) + 4 = 9 - 9 + 4 = 4$$

Determine the function of a variable expression the same way—just substitute the expression for x throughout the function. Using the function above, here is how you would find $f(2 + a)$:

$$\begin{aligned} f(2+a) &= (2+a)^2 + 3(2+a) - 4 \\ &= 4 + 4a + a^2 + 6 + 3a - 4 \\ &= a^2 + 7a + 6 \end{aligned}$$

A function is a relationship between two quantities. It can be expressed using a table of values, a formula, or a graph. Its domain is the set of inputs (x-values) that can be substituted in for the variable and produce a meaningful output (y-values). A function can have only *one output* for each input. The following are examples of relationships between two variables that are NOT functions

x	-1	2	-1	1	1	3	0
y	4	1	3	2	3	4	1

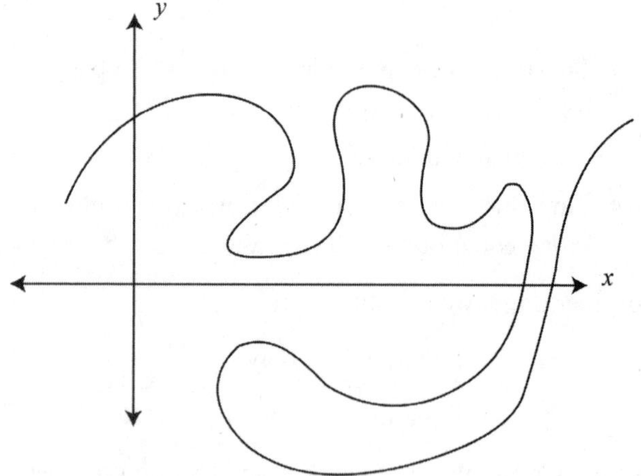

Logarithms

Logarithms express the relationship that $y = \log_b a \Leftrightarrow b^y = a$. For instance, how many 2s do you need to multiply together to get 16? If you write this in exponential and logarithmic forms, you have $2^x = 16 \Leftrightarrow x = \log_2 16$. You need $2 \times 2 \times 2 \times 2$ or four 2s. Thus, you have $2^4 = 16 \Leftrightarrow 4 = \log_2 16$. When both sides of an exponential equation do not share a common base, however, you will take the log of both sides instead.

When you see *e*, remember that it is a special constant with an approximate value of 2.7182818. Its corresponding logarithm is called the natural log and is written as $\ln(x)$. Further, if there is no base on the log (the *b* in the earlier equations), it is assumed to be 10.

Here's an example where both sides of the exponential equation lack a common base.

EXAMPLE:

Solve: $4(3^{3x}) = 5$.

Isolate the exponential term:

$$4(3^{3x}) = 5$$
$$3^{3x} = \frac{5}{4}$$

Take log base 3 of both sides and solve:

$$\log_3(3^{3x}) = \log_3\left(\frac{5}{4}\right)$$
$$3x = \log_3\left(\frac{5}{4}\right)$$
$$x = \frac{1}{3}\log_3\left(\frac{5}{4}\right)$$

The solution is typically left in this form.

When working with logarithms, you may find the following rules helpful:

Log Rules

$$\log_b b^M = M$$
$$b^{\log_b M} = M$$
$$\log_b(MN) = \log_b M + \log_b N$$
$$\log_b\left(\frac{M}{N}\right) = \log_b M - \log_b N$$
$$\log_b(M^p) = p\log_b(M)$$

EXAMPLE:

Solve: $\log(-3x) - \log(2x + 4) = 1$

Use the log rules to isolate the log term. Then, take both sides to the 10th power since this is assumed to be base 10:

$$\log(-3x) - \log(2x + 4) = 1$$
$$\log\left(\frac{-3x}{2x+4}\right) = 1$$
$$10^{\log\left(\frac{-3x}{2x+4}\right)} = 10^1$$
$$\frac{-3x}{2x+4} = 10$$
$$10(2x + 4) = -3x$$
$$20x + 40 = -3x$$
$$23x = -40$$
$$x = \frac{-40}{23} = -\frac{40}{23}$$

Let's look at an example with the natural log.

EXAMPLE:

Simplify: $\ln\left(\frac{10}{x^e}\right)$

Use the log rules for division to rewrite the log. The exponent on the second natural log then becomes a coefficient for the term:

$$\ln\left(\frac{10}{x^e}\right) = \ln 10 - \ln x^e$$
$$= \ln 10 - e\ln x$$

Matrices

Matrices are rectangular arrays of numbers (or variables) that are organized into *r* rows by *c* columns. If a matrix A has *r* rows and *c* columns, we say A is an $r \times c$ (read "*r* by *c*") matrix. A matrix is written by listing all of its entries in an array, enclosed by brackets. Here are some examples:

$$\underbrace{\begin{bmatrix} a & b \\ c & d \end{bmatrix}}_{2\cdot 2 \text{ matrix}} \quad \underbrace{\begin{bmatrix} 1 & -2 & 3 \\ 1 & 0 & 2 \\ 5 & 2 & 1 \end{bmatrix}}_{3\cdot 3 \text{ matrix}} \quad \underbrace{\begin{bmatrix} 1 \\ 3 \\ 2 \\ 1 \end{bmatrix}}_{4\cdot 1 \text{ matrix}}$$

The following is a [3 × 2] matrix (said "three by two"). Notice that it has 3 rows and 2 columns:

$$\begin{bmatrix} 1 & \text{A} \\ 2 & \text{B} \\ 3 & \text{C} \end{bmatrix}$$

The basic arithmetic operations involving matrices are performed "component-wise," which means you need to pay attention to each entry's position in a matrix. The following is a list of the basic operations on 2 × 2 matrices. (All letters stand for real numbers.)

Term/Operation	Definition
$Equality: \begin{bmatrix} a & b \\ c & d \end{bmatrix} = \begin{bmatrix} e & f \\ g & h \end{bmatrix}$	$\begin{bmatrix} a & b \\ c & d \end{bmatrix} = \begin{bmatrix} e & f \\ g & h \end{bmatrix}$ whenever $\underbrace{a = e,\ b = f,\ c = g,\ d = h}_{\text{corresponding entries are equal}}$
$Sum: \begin{bmatrix} a & b \\ c & d \end{bmatrix} + \begin{bmatrix} e & f \\ g & h \end{bmatrix}$	$\begin{bmatrix} a & b \\ c & d \end{bmatrix} + \begin{bmatrix} e & f \\ g & h \end{bmatrix} = \begin{bmatrix} a+e & b+f \\ c+g & d+h \end{bmatrix}$ In words, add corresponding entries to get the sum.
$Difference: \begin{bmatrix} a & b \\ c & d \end{bmatrix} - \begin{bmatrix} e & f \\ g & h \end{bmatrix}$	$\begin{bmatrix} a & b \\ c & d \end{bmatrix} - \begin{bmatrix} e & f \\ g & h \end{bmatrix} = \begin{bmatrix} a-e & b-f \\ c-g & d-h \end{bmatrix}$ In words, subtract corresponding entries to get the difference.
$Scalar\ Multiplication: k\begin{bmatrix} a & b \\ c & d \end{bmatrix}$	$k\begin{bmatrix} a & b \\ c & d \end{bmatrix} = \begin{bmatrix} ka & kb \\ kc & kd \end{bmatrix}$ In words, multiply all entries by the constant *k*.

Adding and Subtracting Matrices

Only matrices with the same dimensions may be added and subtracted. Perform the addition or subtraction on the corresponding entries:

$$\begin{bmatrix} 1 & A \\ 2 & B \\ 3 & C \end{bmatrix} + \begin{bmatrix} 10 & 4A \\ 11 & 5B \\ 12 & 6C \end{bmatrix} = \begin{bmatrix} 11 & 5A \\ 13 & 6B \\ 15 & 7C \end{bmatrix}$$

Here's an example of adding and subtracting that also relies on some basic algebra:

What is the value of w in terms of x?

$$\begin{bmatrix} 1 & 4 & 8x+6 \\ 2 & 5 & 7 \end{bmatrix} + \begin{bmatrix} -3 & 9 & w \\ 12 & 6 & 13 \end{bmatrix} = \begin{bmatrix} -2 & 13 & -2x-4 \\ 14 & 11 & 20 \end{bmatrix}$$

Add the corresponding entries on the left and set them equal to the sum on the right. Then, solve for w in terms of x:

$$\begin{aligned} 8x+6+w &= -2x-4 \\ w &= -2x-8x-4-6 \\ w &= -10x-10 \end{aligned}$$

Scalar Multiplication

Scalar multiplication is when a single multiple is multiplied to every entry in a matrix.

Find $-\frac{1}{2}A$ if $A = \begin{bmatrix} 18 & -6 \\ -2 & 11 \end{bmatrix}$

$$-\frac{1}{2}A = \begin{bmatrix} -\frac{1}{2}\cdot(18) & -\frac{1}{2}\cdot(-6) \\ -\frac{1}{2}\cdot(-2) & -\frac{1}{2}\cdot(11) \end{bmatrix} = \begin{bmatrix} -9 & 3 \\ 1 & -5.5 \end{bmatrix}$$

Matrix Multiplication

Matrix multiplication is much more involved than scalar multiplication. To multiply matrices, you will need to match up the 1st, 2nd, nth *rows* of the first matrix with the corresponding 1st, 2nd, nth *columns* of the second matrix. Then, you must multiply each entry in the nth *row* of the first matrix by each corresponding entry in the nth *column* of the second matrix. Then, the sum of these products will be the entry for the product in the resulting matrix. Matrices can only be multiplied if the number of columns in the first matrix is the same as the number of rows in the second matrix.

For instance, a 2 by 3 matrix could be multiplied by a 3 by 5 matrix but not another 2 by 3 matrix. Look at the example here:

$$\begin{bmatrix} A & B & C \\ W & X & Y \end{bmatrix} \begin{bmatrix} 1 & 4 \\ 2 & 5 \\ 3 & 6 \end{bmatrix} = \begin{bmatrix} (1A+2B+3C) & (4A+5B+6C) \\ (1W+2X+3Y) & (4W+5X+6Y) \end{bmatrix}$$

Notice that the top entry in the first column of the product matrix is (1A + 2B + 3C). This was the result of mapping the first *row* of the first matrix $\begin{bmatrix} A & B & C \end{bmatrix}$ onto the first *column* of the second matrix $\begin{bmatrix} 1 \\ 2 \\ 3 \end{bmatrix}$.

The entries matched up as follows: A corresponded with 1, B corresponded with 2, and C corresponded with 3. Therefore, to find the product of $\begin{bmatrix} A & B & C \end{bmatrix}$ and $\begin{bmatrix} 1 \\ 2 \\ 3 \end{bmatrix}$, we multiplied A by 1, B by 2, and C by 3, and the sum of these products was (1A + 2B + 3C).

Labor Problems

The general goal of labor or work problems is to find how much time or how many resources will be required for a task to be completed. Problems may present you with varying numbers of agents (workers or mechanisms) who may or may not be working at different rates, resources that are consumed or accrued over a specific period, and any number of other combinations of those factors. Generally, these problems require some basic algebra and understanding of how to work with units and rates, as well as some logic and interpretation.

Fundamentally, in every labor problem, you need to be able to determine how much work is done per unit of time. For example, if it takes eight hours for one person to move one stack of crates. It takes one hour for them to move one-eighth of the stack. If it takes 10 machines one hour to dig 10 feet of a trench line, then it takes one machine one hour to dig one foot.

In many labor problems, there are three factors: the number of agents laboring, the time to complete the task (expressed in minutes, hours, or days, etc.), and the amount of labor done. Often, these problems follow three rules:

- The number of agents working is directly proportional to the amount of work done. The more workers on a task, the more work that will be done, and vice versa.
- The number of agents working is inversely proportional to the time required. The more workers present for the task, the less time it will take to complete it, and vice versa.
- The time spent on a task is directly proportional to the amount of labor completed. The more time spent on a task, the more labor that is done, and vice versa.

Let's look at a quick example of two workers working at different rates.

EXAMPLE:

If Worker A does a job in 6 days, and Worker B does the same job in 3 days, how long will it take the two of them, working together, to do the job?

Step 1: First, calculate the individual unit rates for each worker. Worker A completes one job in six days. Thus, they complete $\frac{1}{6}$ of the job per day. Worker B completes $\frac{1}{3}$ of the job per day. Since we want to know how quickly both workers can complete the job together, we want to combine their unit rates and multiply each rate by the unknown number of days the workers will need to work for one job to be completed.

Step 2: Write the fractions as follows:

$$\frac{\text{Time actually spent}}{\text{Time needed to do entire job alone}} \qquad \overset{\text{A}}{\frac{x}{6\text{ days}}} + \overset{\text{B}}{\frac{y}{3\text{ days}}} = 1$$

We'll multiply the numerator of the fractions by x to represent the unknown number of days of work. We then add these fractions and set them equal to 1 (the completed job).

Step 3: Now, find a common denominator, add the fractions, and eliminate the denominator by multiplying by 6 on both sides.

$$x + 2x = 6$$

Step 4: Solve for x.

$$3x = 6$$

$$x = 2 \text{ days}$$

Working together, Worker A and Worker B will complete the job in 2 days.

Let's look at another example. This time, we need to find how many workers will be needed to complete a project.

EXAMPLE:

It takes an average of two labor-hours to fill a stack of sandbags. To fill 35 stacks of sandbags around a perimeter in 5 hours, how many people need to be assigned to the task?

Step 1: Find how much work is done by one worker (how much work is done per hour). If it takes one person two hours to fill a stack, then a single person can complete $\frac{1}{2}$ stack per hour. Then, find the unit rate for the final job. To complete 35 stacks in 5 hours, 7 stacks would need to be completed every hour.

Step 2: Use these two rates to find how many people are needed for the task. These two unit rates represent how much work one person can do and how much work x people can do. Divide the unit rate the job needs by the individual unit rate:

$$\frac{7 \text{ stacks of sandbags}}{1 \text{ hour}} \div \frac{\frac{1}{2} \text{ stacks of sandbags}}{1 \text{ hour}} = 14$$

To complete 35 stacks of sandbags in 5 hours, 14 people are required.

These are but two of many possible strategies used to complete these kinds of problems. Regardless of the methods you use to approach labor problems, your first step should be the same: find the basic unit rates.

Test Yourself: Algebra

1. Solve for y: $4y + 3 = -9$

   A. –12

   B. –8

   C. –3

   D. –1.5

   E. 0

2. If $f(x) = 2 - x(1 - x)$, compute $f(-3)$.

   A. -10

   B. -4

   C. 2

   D. 14

   E. 16

3. Solve for x: $\sqrt[3]{2x+5} = -5$

   A. –65

   B. –60

   C. 10

   D. 15

   E. 60

4. Factor completely: $4x^2 - 169$

   A. $(4x - 13)(x + 13)$

   B. $(2x - 13)^2$

   C. $(2x - 169)(2x + 1)$

   D. $(2x - 13)(2x + 13)$

   E. $(4x - 13)(2x + 13)$

5. The property tax for a house costing $252,000 is $4,200. At this rate, what would be the property tax for a house costing D dollars?

   A. $D + 60$ dollars

   B. $\frac{60}{D}$ dollars

   C. $\frac{D}{60}$ dollars

   D. $60D$ dollars

   E. D^{60} dollars

6. Two times the sum of three and a number is equal to ten less than six times that number. What is the number?

   A. –1

   B. $\frac{13}{4}$

   C. 4

   D. 12

   E. –4

7. Solve for z: $\frac{\frac{1}{w}+z}{2+z} = \frac{3}{w}$

   A. $z = \frac{5}{w-3}$

   B. $z = \frac{7}{w+3}$

   C. $z = \frac{5}{w+3}$

   D. $z = \frac{5}{w-3}$

   E. $z = \frac{7}{3-w}$

8. Which of the following expressions is equivalent to $\frac{x^3\left(x^2y^3\right)^3}{x^5y}$?

   A. $x^{13}y^8$

   B. x^6y^{26}

   C. $x^{\frac{9}{5}}y^9$

   D. x^4y^8

   E. x^8y^4

9. Scott and Micah play racquetball twice a week. So far, Micah has won 13 of 22 matches. Which equation can be used to determine the number of matches, z, Micah must win consecutively to improve his winning percentage to 90%?

   A. $\frac{13+z}{22+2}=0.90$

   B. $\frac{13+z}{22}=0.90$

   C. $\frac{z}{22+z}=0.90$

   D. $\frac{13}{22+z}=0.90$

   E. $\frac{22+z}{13}=0.90$

10. If $f(x) = 2x - 3x^2$, then what is $f(x + 1)$?

    A. $-3x^2 + 4x + 2$

    B. $-3x^2 - 2x - 1$

    C. $-3x^2 + 2x - 1$

    D. $-3x^2 + 2x + 1$

    E. $-3x^2 - 4x - 1$

Answer Key and Explanations

1. C	3. A	5. C	7. A	9. A
2. D	4. D	6. C	8. D	10. E

1. **The correct answer is C.** Subtract 3 from both sides and then divide by 4:

$$\begin{aligned} 4y+3&=-9\\ 4y&=-12\\ y&=-3 \end{aligned}$$

Choice A is incorrect because –12 is equal to 4*y*. In the first step, you should subtract 3, not add it, so –8 (choice B) is incorrect. In the second step, you should divide by 4, not add it to both sides, so –1.5 (choice D) is not correct either. Choice E does not reflect the values given.

2. **The correct answer is D.** Substitute in –3 for *x* and simplify using the order of operations:

$$\begin{aligned} f(-3)&=2-(-3)(1-(-3))\\ &=2+3(1+3)\\ &=2+3(4)\\ &=2+12\\ &=14 \end{aligned}$$

3. **The correct answer is A.** Cube sides to get rid of the radical, and then solve for *x* as you would any linear equation:

$$\begin{aligned} \sqrt[3]{2x+5}&=-5\\ 2x+5&=(-5)^3\\ 2x+5&=-125\\ 2x&=-130\\ x&=-65 \end{aligned}$$

4. **The correct answer is D.** This is a difference of squares, since it can be written in the form $(2x)^2 - 13^2$. This factors as $(2x - 13)(2x + 13)$. The other choices are incorrect because while the squared term and constant terms are correct, each of them when multiplied out has a middle term not present in the original expression.

5. **The correct answer is C.** Let *x* be the amount of property tax for a house costing *D* dollars. Set up the proportion $\frac{252,000}{4,200}=\frac{D}{x}$. Solving for *x* yields $x=\frac{4,200D}{252,000}=\frac{D}{60}$ dollars.

6. **The correct answer is C.** Translating the sentence into symbols yields the following equation, where *x* is the unknown number:

$$2(x + 3) = 6x - 10.$$

Solve for *x*, as follows:

$$\begin{aligned} 2(x+3)&=6x-10\\ 2x+6&=6x-10\\ 16&=4x\\ 4&=x \end{aligned}$$

Choice A is incorrect because to solve an equation of the form $az + b = c$, subtract *b* from both sides, do not add it. Choice B is incorrect because when translating the sentence into symbols, you incorrectly interpreted the phrase "two times the sum of three and a number" as $2x + 3$; it should be $2(x + 3)$. Choice D is incorrect because to solve an equation of the form $az = b$, divide both sides by *a*, do not subtract it from both sides. Choice E changes the sign for the solution.

7. **The correct answer is A.** First, cross-multiply. Then, simplify each side using the distributive property and isolate *z*, as follows:

$$\begin{aligned} \frac{\frac{1}{w}+z}{2+z}&=\frac{3}{w}\\ \left(\frac{1}{w}+z\right)w&=3(2+z)\\ 1+wz&=6+3z\\ wz-3z&=5\\ z(w-3)&=5\\ z&=\frac{5}{w-3} \end{aligned}$$

The other choices are incorrect due to errors when solving equations of the form $x + a = b$ and $ax = b$.

8. **The correct answer is D.** Apply the exponent rules, as follows:

$$\begin{aligned}\frac{x^3\left(x^2y^3\right)^3}{x^5y} &= \frac{x^3x^{2\cdot 3}y^{3\cdot 3}}{x^5y}\\ &= \frac{x^3x^6y^9}{x^5y}\\ &= \frac{x^{3+6}y^9}{x^5y}\\ &= \frac{x^9y^9}{x^5y}\\ &= x^{9-5}y^{9-1}\\ &= x^4y^8\end{aligned}$$

9. **The correct answer is A.** Let z be the number of matches Micah needs to win consecutively to raise his winning percentage to 90%. Then, after playing these z matches, he will have won $13 + z$ out of $22 + z$ matches played. This yields the ratio $\frac{13+z}{22+z}$, which must equal 0.90. This yields the equation $\frac{13+z}{22+z} = 0.90$.

10. **The correct answer is E.** Substitute $x + 1$ for x in the function $f(x) = 2x - 3x^2$ and simplify:

$$\begin{aligned}f(x+1) &= 2(x+1) - 3(x+1)^2\\ &= 2x + 2 - 3\left(x^2 + 2x + 1\right)\\ &= 2x + 2 - 3x^2 - 6x - 3\\ &= -3x^2 - 4x - 1\end{aligned}$$

GEOMETRY

Geometry questions focus your attention on matters of distance, shape, and size of geometric figures—whether lines, angles, polygons, or 3-D objects. This section will cover information on coordinate geometry, angles, polygons (including triangles and quadrilaterals), circles, and volumetric shapes.

Congruency and Similarity

Two geometric figures that have the same size and shape are said to be **congruent.** The symbol for congruency is $\cong$. Two angles are congruent if their degree measure (size) is the same. Two line segments are congruent if they are equal in length. Two triangles are congruent if the angle measures and sides are all identical in size. (The same applies to figures with more than three sides.)

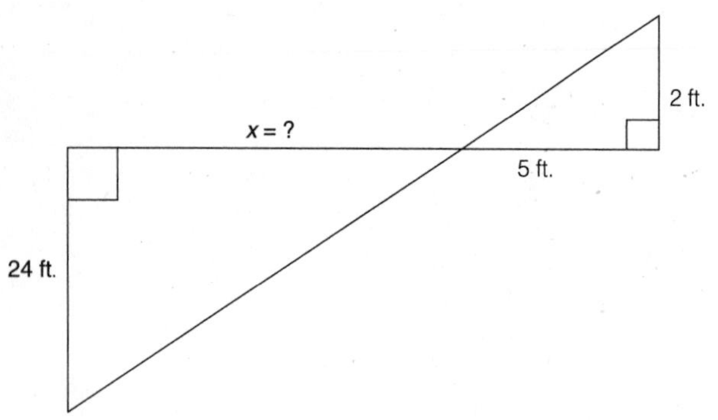

These two triangles are similar. They share an angle and both have right angles. Thus, their third angles must be equal. Because their angles are equal, their sides must be proportional. The ratio 2:5 is the same as 24:x. By creating a proportion, you can solve for x and find the missing side length as 60 ft.

If a two-dimensional geometric figure, such as a triangle or rectangle, has exactly the same shape as another one, then the two figures are **similar.** Similar figures share the same angle measures, and their sides are proportionate (though not the same length).

Angles

Angles are indicated by the angle symbol ($\angle$). They are measured in degrees (°). The letter 'm' is used to indicate the measure of an angle. The line that extends in only one direction from a point is called a **ray.** Lines, rays, or line segments meet at a point called the **vertex.** Angles are usually named by letters, as in the following figure.

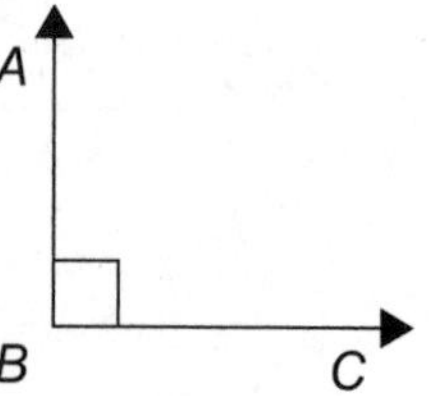

The name of the above angle is $\angle ABC$. This angle is called a **right angle** because $m\angle ABC = 90°$. The small square drawn in the angle indicates that it is a right angle. When two lines meet to form a right angle, they are said to be **perpendicular** to each other, as indicated by the symbol $\perp$. In the above figure, $\overrightarrow{BA} \perp \overrightarrow{BC}$.

An angle that measures less than 90° is called an **acute** angle. $\angle VWX$ in the following figure is an acute angle. An angle that measures more than 90° but less than 180° is called an **obtuse** angle.
$\angle EFG$ in the following figure is an obtuse angle.

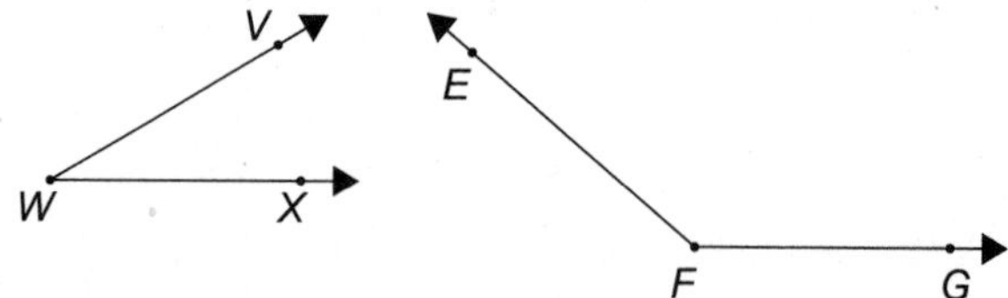

A **straight angle** measures 180°. $\angle XYZ$ in the following figure is a straight angle. Two or more angles whose measures add up to 180° are called **supplementary.** In the next figure, $\angle DEG$ forms a straight line and therefore measures 180°. $\angle DEF$ and $\angle FEG$ are supplementary angles; their measures add up to 180°.

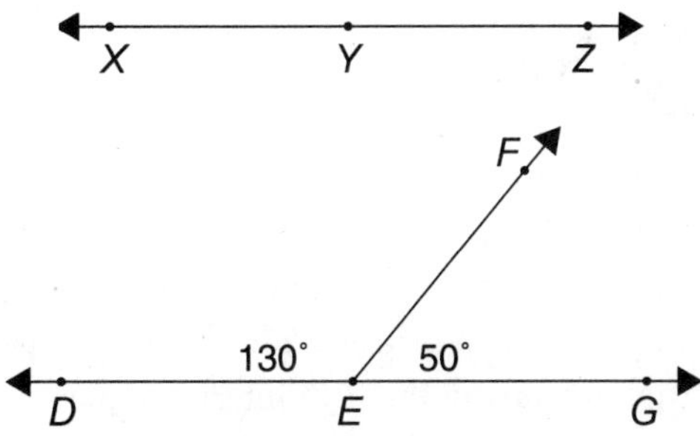

Two angles are called **complementary** angles when their measurements add up to 90° (a right angle). In the next figure, m$\angle ABC = 90°$. $\angle ABE$ and $\angle CBE$ are complementary because their measurements add up to 90°. You also know that m$\angle ABD = 90°$ because $\angle ABD$ and $\angle ABC$ combine to form a straight line, which measures 180°.

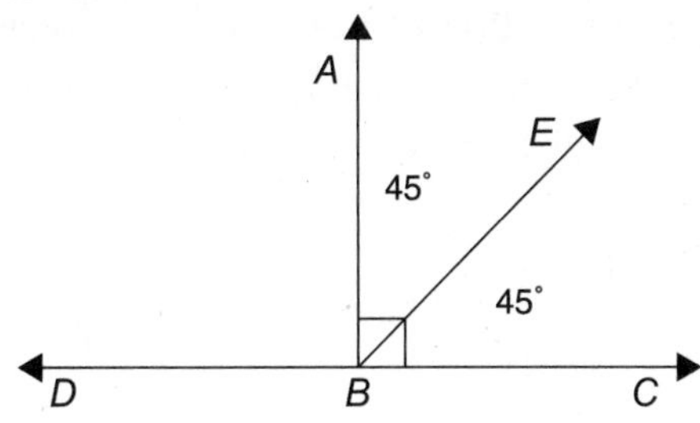

In geometry, the set of points that makes up a flat surface is referred to as a **plane.** When two lines in the same plane never meet, no matter how far they are extended, they are called **parallel lines** and are indicated by the symbol ǁ. If two parallel lines are intersected by a third line, eight angles are formed. A line that intersects two parallel lines is called a **transversal.** If a transversal intersects two parallel lines perpendicularly (at a 90° angle), all eight angles that are formed are right angles (90°). Otherwise, some angles are acute, while others are obtuse. Look at the next figure.

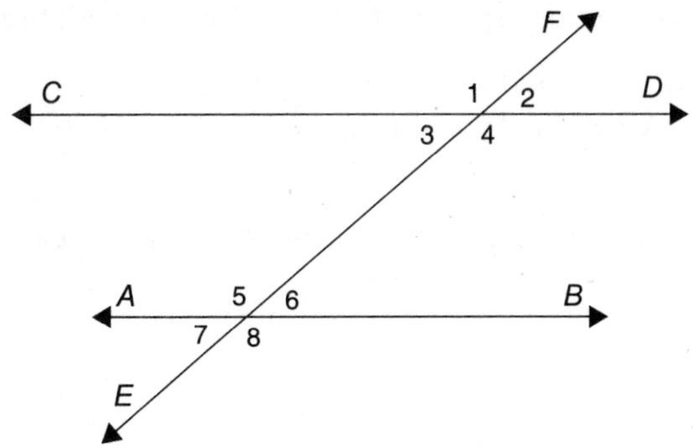

As noted earlier, angles that are equal in degree measure are called congruent angles (the symbol ≅ indicates congruency). In the figure above, you can see that eight angles have been formed. The four acute angles ($\angle 2$, $\angle 3$, $\angle 6$, and $\angle 7$) are congruent, and the four obtuse angles ($\angle 1$, $\angle 4$, $\angle 5$, and $\angle 8$) are also congruent. Each pair of angles that are opposite each other in relation to a vertex (for example, $\angle 2$ and $\angle 3$) are called **vertical angles**. Vertical angles are always congruent.

Four angles formed by two intersecting lines add up to 360° in measure. In the same figure, m$\angle 1$ + m$\angle 2$ + m$\angle 3$ + m$\angle 4$ = 360°. (The same holds true for angles 5, 6, 7, and 8.) In the figure, the measure of any one of the four acute angles plus the measure of any obtuse angle equals 180°. If you know the measure of *any* one angle, you can determine the measure of all seven other angles. For example, if m$\angle 2 = 30°$, then $\angle 3$, $\angle 6$, and $\angle 7$ each measures 30° as well, while $\angle 1$, $\angle 4$, $\angle 5$, and $\angle 8$ each measures 150°.

A geometry question might involve nothing more than intersecting lines and the angles they form. To handle this type of question, remember four basic rules about angles formed by intersecting lines:

- **Vertical angles:** Vertical angles (angles across the vertex from each other and formed by the same two lines) are equal in degree measure, or congruent (≅). In other words, they're the same size.
- **Adjacent angles:** If adjacent angles combine to form a straight line, their degree measures total 180. In fact, a straight line is actually a 180° angle.
- **Perpendicular lines:** If two lines are perpendicular (⊥) to each other, they intersect at right (90°) angles.
- **The sum of angles:** The sum of all angles formed by the intersection of two (or more) lines at the same point is 360°, regardless of how many angles are involved.

Polygons

Polygons include all two-dimensional figures formed only by line segments. The two most important points about polygons to remember are these two reciprocal rules:

- If all angles of a polygon are congruent (equal in degree measure), then all sides are congruent (equal in length).
- If all sides of a polygon are congruent (equal in length), then all angles are congruent (equal in degree measure).

A polygon in which all sides are congruent and all angles are congruent is called a **regular polygon**.

You can use the following formula to determine the sum of all interior angles of *any* polygon with angles that each measure less than 180° (n = number of sides):

$$(n - 2)(180°) = \text{sum of interior angles}$$

For regular polygons, the average angle size is also the size of every angle. But for *any* polygon (except for those with an angle exceeding 180°), you can find the average angle size by dividing the sum of the angles by the number of sides. One way to shortcut the math is to memorize the angle sums and averages for polygons with three to eight sides:

3 sides: $(3 - 2)(180°) = 180° \div 3 = 60°$

4 sides: $(4 - 2)(180°) = 360° \div 4 = 90°$

5 sides: $(5 - 2)(180°) = 540° \div 5 = 108°$

6 sides: $(6 - 2)(180°) = 720° \div 6 = 120°$

7 sides: $(7 - 2)(180°) = 900° \div 7 = 129°$

8 sides: $(8 - 2)(180°) = 1{,}080° \div 8 = 135°$

You can add up known angle measures to find unknown angle measures.

EXAMPLE:

The measures of a polygon's interior angles total $(n - 2)(180°)$, where n = number of sides. If four of the interior angles of a five-sided polygon measure 100° each, what is the measure of the fifth interior angle?

A. 40°

B. 60°

C. 90°

D. 140°

E. 160°

The total number of degrees in the polygon = $(5 - 2)(180°) = 540°$. The four known angles total 400°, so the fifth angle must be 140°. **The correct answer is D.**

Triangles

The **triangle** is a 3-sided shape. All triangles, regardless of shape or size, share the following four properties:

- **Length of the sides:** Each side is shorter than the sum of the lengths of the other two sides. (Otherwise, the triangle would collapse into a line.)
- **Angle measures:** The measures of the three interior angles total 180°.
- **Angles and opposite sides:** Comparative angle sizes correspond to the comparative lengths of the sides opposite those angles. For example, a triangle's largest angle is opposite its longest side. (The sides opposite two congruent angles are also congruent.)
- **Area:** The area of any triangle is equal to one-half the product of its base and its height (or "altitude"): Area $= \frac{1}{2} \times \text{base} \times \text{height}$. You can use any side as the base to calculate area.

The next figure shows three particular types of triangles.

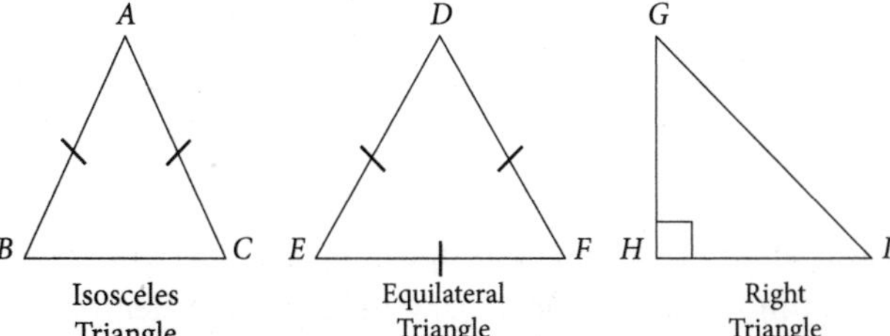

An **isosceles triangle** is one in which two sides (and two angles) are congruent. In the figure above, ∠B and ∠C are congruent, and the sides opposite those two angles, $\overline{AB}$ and $\overline{AC}$, are congruent. In an **equilateral triangle**, all three angles are congruent, and all three sides are congruent. In a **right triangle**, one angle is a right angle, and the other two angles are acute angles. The longest side of a right triangle (in this case, $\overline{GI}$) is called the **hypotenuse**.

EXAMPLE:

The length of one side of a certain triangular floor space is 12 feet. Which of the following CANNOT be the lengths of the other two sides?

A. 1 foot and 12 feet

B. 8 feet and 4 feet

C. 12 feet and 13 feet

D. 16 feet and 14 feet

E. 16 feet and 10 feet

The length of any two sides combined must be greater than the length of the third side. **The correct answer is B.**

Right Triangles and the Pythagorean Theorem

In a right triangle, one angle measures 90° and each of the other two angles measures less than 90°. The **Pythagorean theorem** involves the relationship among the sides of any right triangle and can be expressed by the equation $a^2 + b^2 = c^2$. As shown in the next figure, the letters a and b represent the lengths of the two **legs** (the two shortest sides) that form the right angle, and c is the length of the hypotenuse (the longest side, opposite the right angle).

Pythagorean theorem: $a^2 + b^2 = c^2$

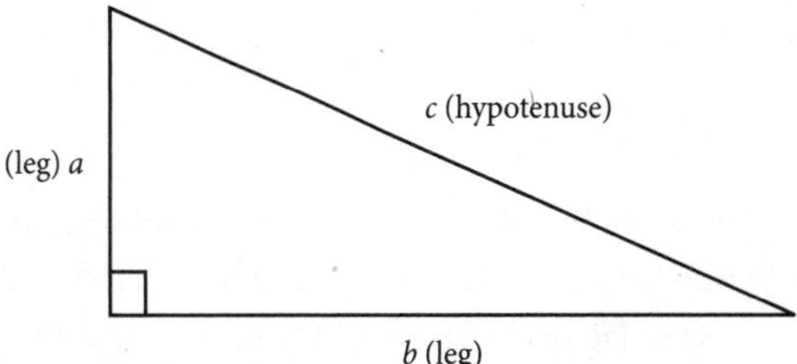

For any right triangle, if you know the length of two sides, you can determine the length of the third side by applying the Pythagorean theorem. Study the following two examples:

EXAMPLE:

If the two shortest sides (the legs) of a right triangle are 2 and 3 inches in length, then the length of the triangle's third side (the hypotenuse) is $\sqrt{13}$ inches:

$$a^2 + b^2 = c^2$$
$$2^2 + 3^2 = c^2$$
$$4 + 9 = c^2$$
$$13 = c^2$$
$$\sqrt{13} = c$$

EXAMPLE:

In a right triangle, one angle measures 90°. If the hypotenuse of a right triangle is c and one leg of the triangle is a, what is the length of the third side in terms of a and c?

A. $\sqrt{a^2 + c^2}$

B. $\frac{a + c}{2}$

C. $\sqrt{a \times c}$

D. $\sqrt{c^2 - a^2}$

E. $\sqrt{a^2 - c^2}$

Use the Pythagorean theorem to determine the length of the third side, which is the other leg of the triangle. Call the length of the third side b. The Pythagorean theorem says that $a^2 + b^2 = c^2$. Solve for b:

$$b^2 = c^2 - a^2$$

$$b = \sqrt{c^2 - a^2}$$

The correct answer is D.

Isosceles and Equilateral Triangles

An *isosceles* triangle has the following special properties:

- Two of the sides are congruent (equal in length).
- The two angles opposite the two congruent sides are congruent (equal in size or degree measure).

If you know any *two* angle measures of a triangle, you can determine whether the triangle is isosceles. Subtract the two angle measures you know from 180. If the result equals one of the other two measures, then the triangle is isosceles. For example:

- If two of the angles are 55° and 70°, then the third angle must be 55° (180 – 55 – 70 = 55). The triangle is isosceles, and the two sides opposite the two 55° angles are congruent.
- If two of the angles are 80° and 20°, then the third angle must be 80° (180 – 80 – 20 = 80). The triangle is isosceles, and the two sides opposite the two 80° angles are congruent.

In any isosceles triangle, lines bisecting the triangle's three angles each bisect its opposite side. The line bisecting the angle connecting the two congruent angles divides the triangle into two congruent right triangles.

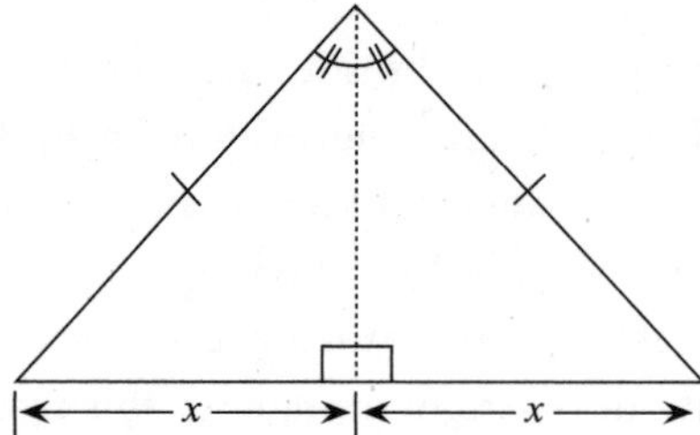

So if you know the lengths of all three sides of an isosceles triangle, you can determine the area of the triangle by applying the Pythagorean theorem.

All **equilateral triangles** share the following three properties:

- All three sides are congruent (equal in length).
- The measure of each angle is 60°.
- Area $= \frac{s^2\sqrt{3}}{4}$ (s = any side)

As shown in the following diagram, any line bisecting one of the 60° angles divides an equilateral triangle into two right triangles with angle measures of 30°, 60°, and 90° (one of the two Pythagorean angle triplets). Accordingly, the side ratio for each smaller triangle is $1:\sqrt{3}:2$. The area of this equilateral triangle is $\frac{1}{2}(2)\sqrt{3}$, or $\sqrt{3}$.

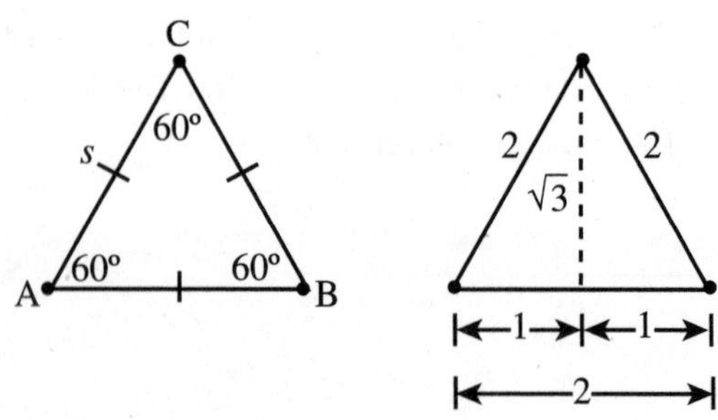

Quadrilaterals

A **quadrilateral** is any four-sided figure. You may encounter four specific types of quadrilaterals: the square, the rectangle, the parallelogram, and the trapezoid.

Rectangles, Squares, and Parallelograms

A **parallelogram** is a quadrilateral in which opposite sides are parallel. A **rectangle** is a special type of parallelogram in which all four angles are right angles (90°). A **square** is a special type of rectangle in which all four sides are congruent (equal in length). Certain characteristics apply to all rectangles, squares, and parallelograms:

- The sum of the measures of all four interior angles is 360°.
- Opposite sides are parallel.
- Opposite sides are congruent (equal in length).
- Opposite angles are congruent (the same size, or equal in degree measure).
- Adjacent angles are supplementary (their measures total 180°).

You should know how to determine the perimeter and area of these three types of quadrilaterals. Formulas for both area and perimeter are included on the Formula Sheet provided during the test.

The Square

To find the perimeter of a square, multiply any side by 4. To find the area, simply square any side.

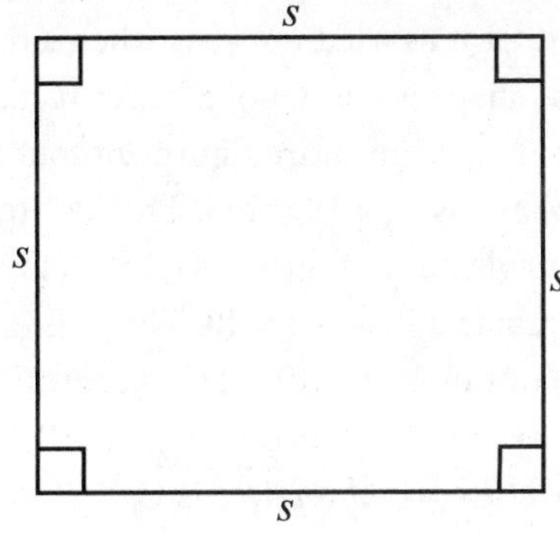

Perimeter $= 4s$ $[s = \text{side}]$

Area $= s^2$

Questions involving squares come in many varieties. For example, you might need to determine an area based on a perimeter, or you might need to do just the opposite—find a perimeter based on a given area. For example:

The area of a square with a perimeter of 8 is 4.

$$s = 8 \div 4 = 2; s^2 = 4$$

The perimeter of a square with area 8 is $8\sqrt{2}$.

$$s = \sqrt{3} = 2\sqrt{2}; 4s = 4 \times 2\sqrt{2}$$

Or, you might need to determine a change in area resulting from a change in perimeter (or vice versa). These are just some of the possibilities.

EXAMPLE:

Nine square tiles, each with an area of 25 square centimeters, have been arranged to form a larger square. What is the perimeter of the large square?

A. 60 centimeters

B. 100 centimeters

C. 150 centimeters

D. 220 centimeters

E. 225 centimeters

The side of each square $= \sqrt{25}$ or 5 cm. Aligned to form a large square, the tiles form three rows and three columns, each column and row with side $5 \times 3 = 15$. The perimeter $= 15 \times 4 = 60$. **The correct answer is A.**

EXAMPLE:

If a square's sides are each increased by 50%, by what percent does the square's area increase?

A. 100%

B. 125%

C. 150%

D. 200%

E. 225%

The easiest way to answer this question is to plug in simple numbers. Assume that the square's original side length is 1. Its area is also 1. Increase the side length to 1.5, and then square it to find the new area: $1.5 \times 1.5 = 2.25$. Comparing 1 to 2.25, the percent increase is 125%. You can also solve the problem conventionally. Letting s = the length of each side before the increase, area $= s^2$. Let $\frac{3}{2}s$ = the length of each side after the increase, the new area $= \left(\frac{3}{2}s\right)^2 = \frac{9}{4}s^2$. The increase from s^2 to $\frac{9}{4}s^2$ is $\frac{5}{4}$, or 125%. **The correct answer is B.**

The Rectangle

To find the perimeter of a rectangle, multiply width by 2, and multiply length by 2, and then add the two products. To find area, multiply length by width.

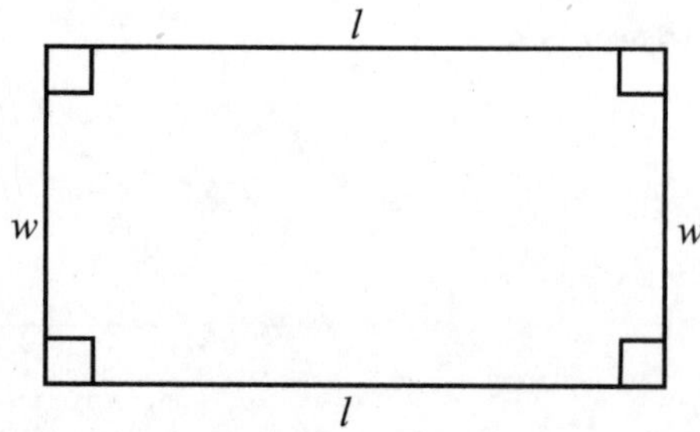

Perimeter $= 2l + 2w$

Area $= l \times w$

Questions involving non-square rectangles also come in many possible varieties. For example, a question might ask you to determine area based on perimeter, or vice versa. Or, a question might require you to determine a combined perimeter or area of adjoining rectangles.

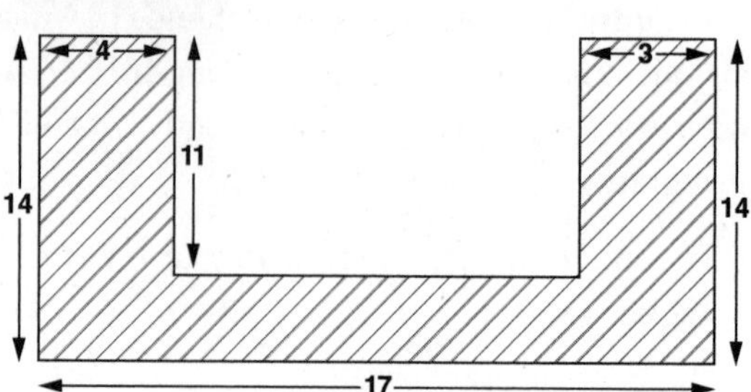

In the following figure, all intersecting line segments are perpendicular.

What is the area of the shaded region, in square units?

A. 84

B. 118

C. 128

D. 238

E. 250

The figure provides the perimeters you need to calculate the area. One way to find the area of the shaded region is to consider it as what remains when a rectangular shape is cut out of a larger rectangle. The area of the entire figure without the "cut-out" is $14 \times 17 = 238$. The "cut-out" rectangle has a length of 11, and its width is equal to $17 - 4 - 3 = 10$. Thus, the area of the cut-out is $11 \times 10 = 110$. Accordingly, the area of the shaded region is $238 - 110 = 128$. **The correct answer is C.**

The Parallelogram

To find the perimeter of a parallelogram, multiply the width by 2, multiply the length by 2, and then add the two products. To find the area, multiply the base by the **altitude,** which is the parallelogram's *height*, not the length of any side. (*Note*: The base can be any of the four sides of the figure; just be sure to use the altitude that goes with the base you've chosen.)

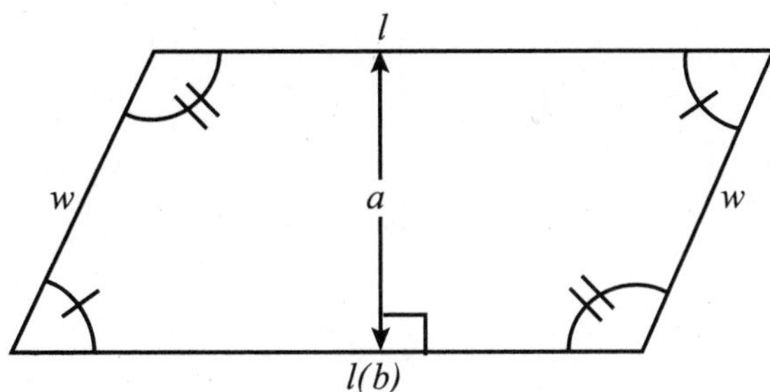

$$\textbf{Perimeter} = 2l + 2w$$

$$\textbf{Area} = \text{base } (b) \times \text{altitude } (a)$$

A question about a non-rectangular parallelogram might focus on angle measures. These questions are easy to answer. In any parallelogram, opposite angles are congruent, and adjacent angles are supplementary. (Their measures total 180°.) So if one of a parallelogram's angles measure 65°, then the opposite angle must also measure 65°, while the two other angles each measure 115°.

Trapezoids

A **trapezoid** is a quadrilateral with only one pair of parallel sides. All trapezoids share these four properties:

- Only one pair of opposite sides is parallel.
- The sum of all four angles is 360°.
- Perimeter = the sum of the four sides.
- Area = half the sum of the two parallel sides, multiplied by the altitude (a).

The next figure shows a trapezoid in which $\overline{BC} \parallel \overline{AD}$.

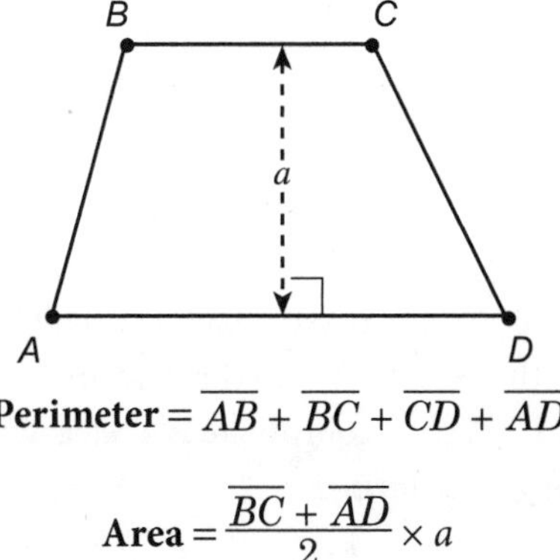

$$\textbf{Perimeter} = \overline{AB} + \overline{BC} + \overline{CD} + \overline{AD}$$

$$\textbf{Area} = \frac{\overline{BC} + \overline{AD}}{2} \times a$$

EXAMPLE:

A metal sheet in the shape of a trapezoid is to be assembled from a square piece and a triangular piece, as shown below.

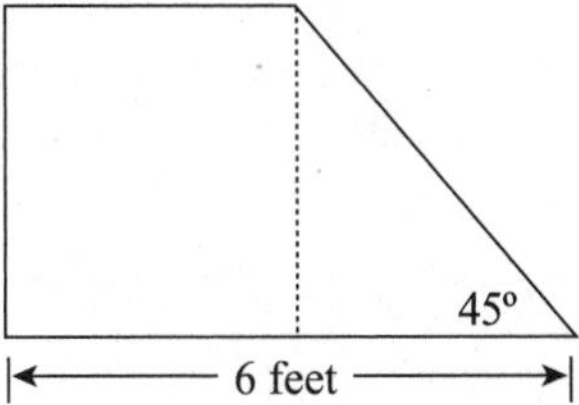

What is the area of the assembled product?

A. 12 square feet

B. $13\frac{1}{2}$ square feet

C. 15 square feet

D. $17\frac{1}{2}$ square feet

E. 18 square feet

To answer this question, you don't need to apply the area formula. The 45° angle tells you that the triangle's two legs are the same length, which is also the height of the square. Since the two pieces together run 6 feet in length, each piece is half that length. Thus, the altitude (dotted line) is 3. The area of the square = $3^2 = 9$. The area of the triangle = $\frac{1}{2} \times 3^2 = \frac{9}{2}$. The combined area is $13\frac{1}{2}$ square feet. **The correct answer is B.**

Coordinate Geometry

Finding points on a plane is the study of **coordinate geometry**. A grid is commonly used to do this. The grid is divided into four sections. Each section is called a **quadrant**. The two number lines that divide the grid into quadrants are called the ***x*-axis** (the horizontal axis) and the ***y*-axis** (the vertical axis). The center of the grid, where the two axes meet, is called the **origin**. The points that are drawn on the grid are identified by **ordered pairs**. The *x*-coordinate is always written first. Look at the grid below.

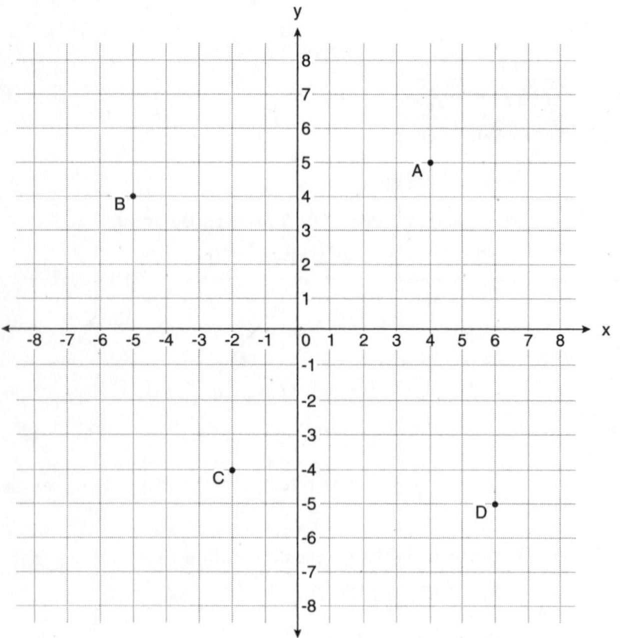

The ordered pair for the origin, in the middle of the grid, is (0, 0). To determine the ordered pair for point *A*, start at the origin, and count over four squares to the right on the *x*-axis. This gives you the coordinate for the first number of the pair. Now, count up 5 squares on the *y*-axis. The ordered pair for point *A* is (4, 5).

What ordered pair expresses point *C*'s location? Because you must count two squares to the *left* of the origin (0, 0) and four squares *below* the origin, the ordered pair for point *C* is (–2, –4). The ordered pair for point *B* is (–5, 4), and the ordered pair for point *D* is (6, –5).

Finding the Distance Between Two Points

Finding the distance between two points that are directly horizontal or vertical from each other is simply a matter of counting the number of squares that separate the points. In the next grid, for example, the distance between points *A* (2, 3) and *B* (7, 3) is 5. The distance between points *C* (2, 1) and *D* (2, –4) is also 5.

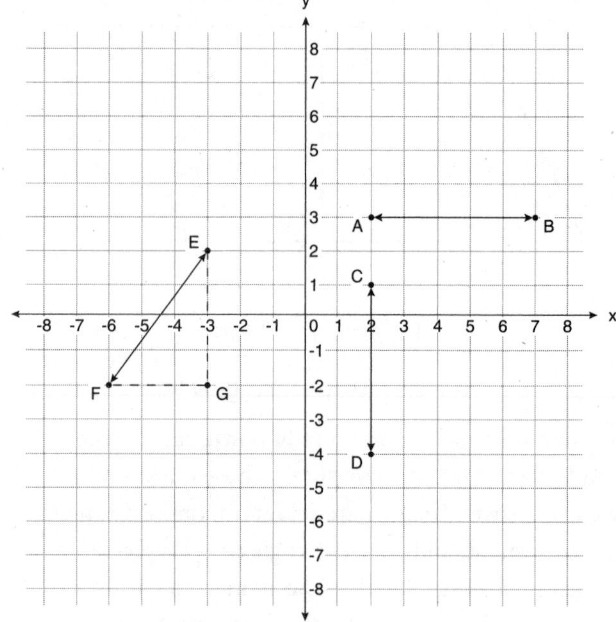

If you are asked to find the distance between two points that are not directly horizontal or vertical from each other, you can use the Pythagorean theorem. For example, to find the distance between points *E* and *F* on the preceding grid, follow these steps:

- Draw a right triangle in which $\overline{EF}$ is the hypotenuse (as shown by the broken lines on the preceding grid).
- Determine the distance between *E* and *G*. That distance is 4. This is the length of one leg of right triangle *EFG*.
- Determine the distance between *F* and *G*. That distance is 3. This is the length of the other leg of a right triangle *EFG*.

Apply the Pythagorean theorem to find the hypotenuse of ΔEFG, which is the distance between E and F:

$$4^2 + 3^2 = c^2$$
$$16 + 9 = c^2$$
$$25 = c^2$$
$$5 = c$$

In applying the Pythagorean theorem to the coordinate grid, you may want to use the formula for determining the distance between two points, which is a more specific way of expressing the theorem.

Distance between points =

$\sqrt{(x_2 - x_1)^2 + (y_2 - y_1)^2}$,where the two points are (x_1, y_1) and (x_2, y_2)

Apply this formula to the preceding example, and you obtain the same result:

$$\sqrt{(-6 - (-3))^2 + (-2 - 2)^2} = \sqrt{(-3)^2 + (-4)^2} = \sqrt{9 + 16} = \sqrt{25} = 5$$

Finding the Midpoint of a Line Segment

To find the coordinates of the midpoint (M) of a line segment, simply average the two endpoints' x-values and y-values:

$$x_M = \frac{x_1 + x_2}{2} \text{ and } y_M = \frac{y_1 + y_2}{2}$$

The **midpoint formula** is often used to find these coordinates:

$$M = \left(\frac{x_1 + x_2}{2}, \frac{y_1 + y_2}{2}\right)$$

These formulas are NOT included on the Formula Sheet provided during the test.

A question might simply ask you to find the midpoint between two given points. Or, it might provide the midpoint and one endpoint, and then ask you to determine the other endpoint.

Defining a Line on the Plane

You can define any line on the coordinate plane by the following general equation:

$$y = mx + b$$

In this equation:

- The variable m is the **slope** of the line.
- The variable b is the line's ***y*-intercept** (where the line crosses the y-axis).
- The variables x and y are the coordinates of any point on the line. Any (x, y) pair defining a point on the line can substitute for the variables x and y.

Think of the slope of a line as a fraction in which the numerator indicates the vertical change from one point to another on the line (moving left to right) corresponding to a given horizontal change, which the fraction's denominator indicates. The common term used for this fraction is **rise over run.**

You can determine the slope of a line from any two pairs of (x, y) coordinates. In general, if (x_1, y_1) and (x_2, y_2) lie on the same line, calculate the line's slope according to the following formula:

$$\textbf{slope } (m) = \frac{y_2 - y_1}{x_2 - x_1}$$

In applying the formula, be sure to subtract corresponding values. For example, a careless test taker calculating the slope might subtract y_1 from y_2 but subtract x_2 from x_1. Also be sure to calculate rise over run, and not run over rise.

A question might ask you to identify the slope of a line defined by a given equation, in which case you simply put the equation in the form $y = mx + b$, then identify the m-term. Or, it might ask you to determine the equation of a line, or just the line's slope (m) or y-intercept (b), given the coordinates of two points on the line.

For example, suppose that the following points lie on the same line.

x	2	5	−1	−3
y	1	$-\frac{7}{2}$	$\frac{11}{2}$	$\frac{17}{2}$

Since the points lie on the same line, you can use any pair of points to determine the slope. For convenience, use the first two:

$$m = \frac{y_2 - y_1}{x_2 - x_1} = \frac{-\frac{7}{2} - 1}{5-2} = \frac{-\frac{9}{2}}{3} = \frac{9}{2} \cdot \frac{1}{3} = -\frac{3}{2}$$

EXAMPLE:

On the coordinate plane, what is the slope of the line defined by the two points $P(2, 1)$ and $Q(-3, 4)$?

A. $-\frac{5}{3}$

B. −1

C. $-\frac{3}{5}$

D. $\frac{1}{3}$

E. 1

Apply the slope formula:

$$\text{slope } (m) = \frac{4-1}{-3-2} = \frac{3}{-5}, \text{ or } -\frac{3}{5}$$

The correct answer is C.

Finding the Equation of a Line on the Plane

Let's say you are asked to find the equation of the line with slope $-\frac{2}{3}$ that passes through the point (−1, −3).

The most efficient approach is to use the point-slope equation of the line. Precisely, a line with slope m passing through the point (x_1, y_1) has the equation $y - y_1 = m(x - x_1)$. Using the given information yields the equation $y-(-3) = -\frac{2}{3}(x-(-1))$. This can be simplified in different ways.

Slope-intercept form:

$$y + 3 = -\frac{2}{3}(x+1)$$

$$y = -\frac{2}{3}x - \frac{11}{3}$$

Standard form:

$$2x + 3y = -11$$

You can also write the equation of a line when given 2 points on that line. For example, if you know the line passes through the points (2, −5) and (4, −1), first, determine the slope of the line:

$$m = \frac{-1-(-5)}{4-2} = \frac{-1+5}{2} = \frac{4}{2} = 2$$

Now, use the point-slope formula of a line to write the equation. You can use either of the two points—the equation will be the same. Using (2, −5) yields $y - (-5) = 2(x - 2)$ or equivalently, $y = 2x - 9$.

Two lines are parallel if they have the same slope, while they are perpendicular if the product of their slopes is −1. For instance, the line $y = 3x - 1$ is parallel to $y = 3x + 4$ because they both have slope 3. Similarly, the line $y = -2x + 3$ is perpendicular to $y = \frac{1}{2}x - 1$ because the product of their slopes is $(-2)\left(\frac{1}{2}\right) = -1$.

- Say you are given the line $2x - 4y = 1$ and you know it passes through the origin. How do you find a line parallel to this given line?
- First, find the slope of the given line by putting the equation into slope-intercept form; doing so yields $y = \frac{1}{2}x - \frac{1}{4}$. So the slope is $\frac{1}{2}$. Since parallel lines have the same slope, this is the slope of the line whose equation we seek. Using the point-slope formula for the equation of a line with this slope and the point (0, 0) yields $y = \frac{1}{2}x$.

Graphing a Line on the Plane

You can graph a line on the coordinate plane if you know the coordinates of any two points on the line. Just plot the two points, and then draw a line connecting them. You can also graph a line from one point on the line if you also know either the line's slope or its y-intercept.

A question might ask you to recognize the value of a line's slope (m) based on a graph of the line. If the graph identifies the precise coordinates of two points, you can determine the line's precise slope (and the entire equation of the line). Even without any precise coordinates, you can still estimate the line's slope based on its appearance.

Lines that slope upward from left to right:

- A line sloping *upward* from left to right has a positive slope (m).
- A line with a slope of 1 slopes upward from left to right at a 45° angle in relation to the x-axis.
- A line with a fractional slope between 0 and 1 slopes upward from left to right but at less than a 45° angle in relation to the x-axis.
- A line with a slope greater than 1 slopes upward from left to right at more than a 45° angle in relation to the x-axis.

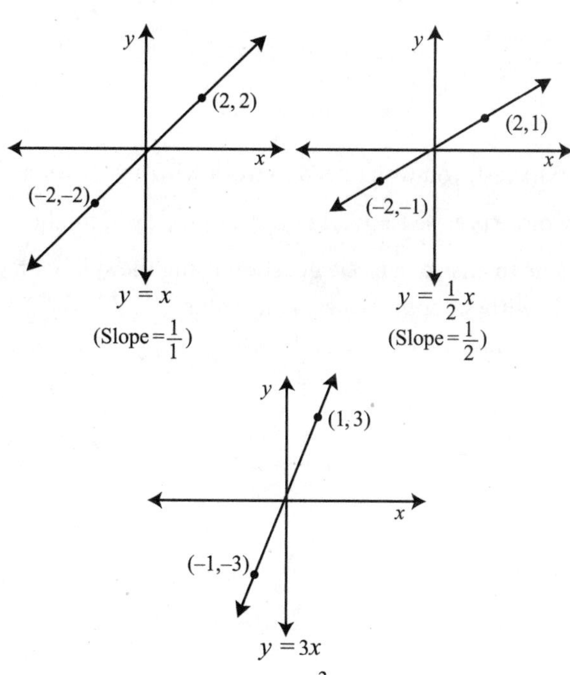

Lines that slope downward from left to right:

- A line sloping *downward* from left to right has a negative slope (m).
- A line with a slope of –1 slopes downward from left to right at a 45° angle in relation to the x-axis.
- A line with a fractional slope between 0 and –1 slopes downward from left to right but at less than a 45° angle in relation to the x-axis.
- A line with a slope less than –1 (for example, –2) slopes downward from left to right at more than a 45° angle in relation to the x-axis.

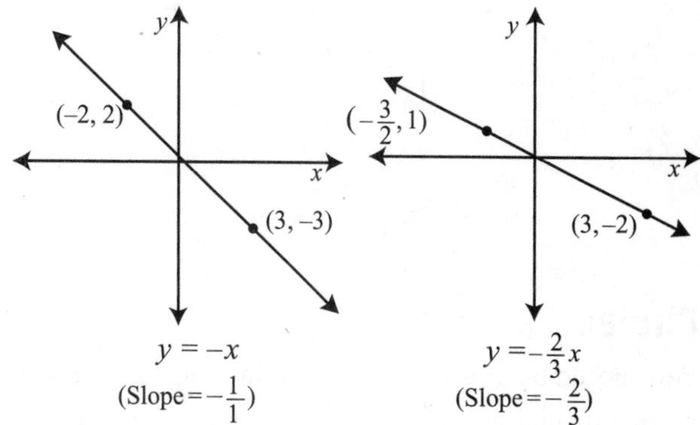

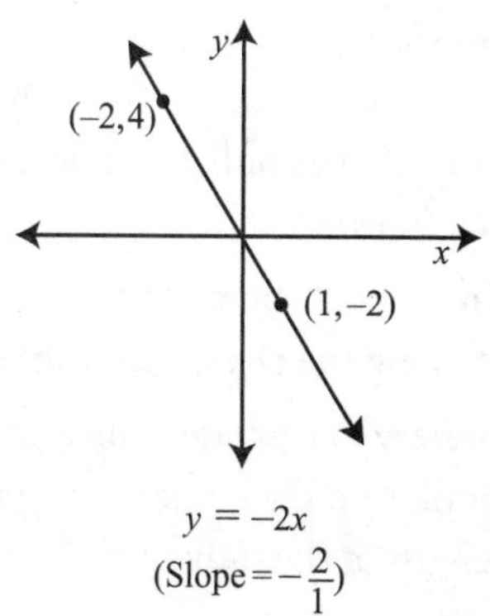

Horizontal and vertical lines:

- A horizontal line has a slope of **zero** ($m = 0$, and $mx = 0$).
- A vertical line has either an **undefined** or an **indeterminate** slope (the fraction's denominator is 0), so the m-term in the equation is ignored.

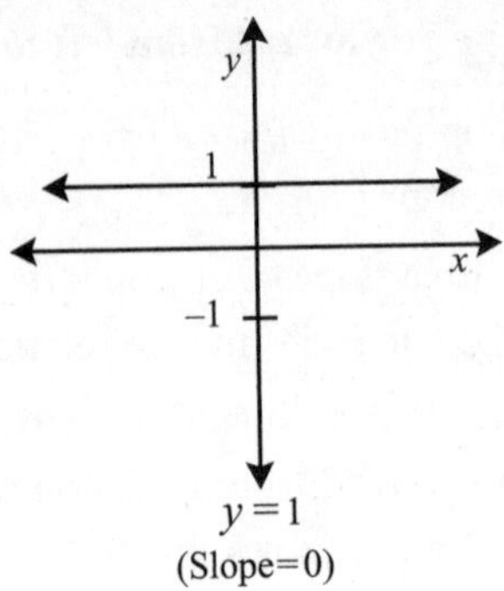

$y = 1$
(Slope=0)

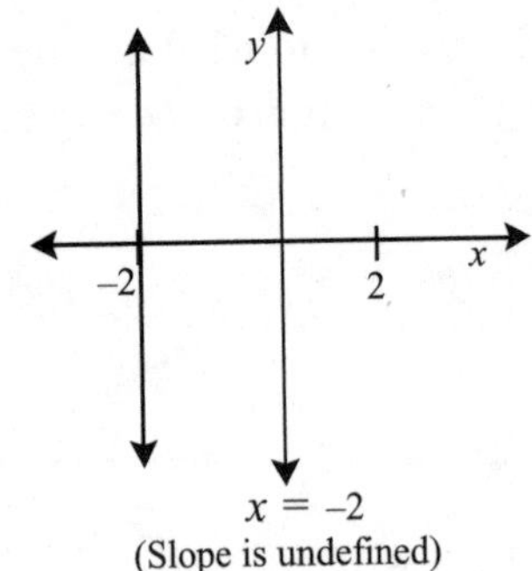

$x = -2$
(Slope is undefined)

Circles

You should be familiar with the following basic terminology involving circles:

- **Circumference:** The distance around the circle (the same as "perimeter," but the word "circumference" applies only to circles, ovals, and other curved figures)
- **Radius:** The distance from a circle's center to any point along the circle's circumference
- **Diameter:** The greatest distance from one point to another on the circle's circumference (twice the length of the radius)
- **Chord:** A line segment connecting two points on the circle's circumference (a circle's longest possible chord is its diameter, passing through the circle's center)

As noted previously, a circle's diameter is twice the length of its radius. The next figure shows a circle with radius 6 and diameter 12.

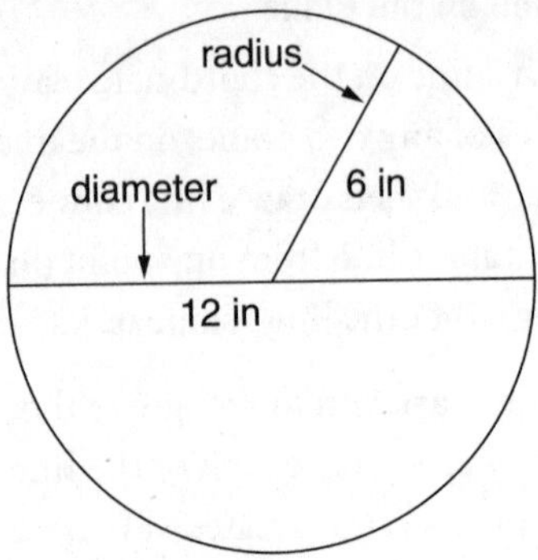

During the test, you'll apply one, or possibly both, of two basic formulas involving circles (r = radius, d = diameter):

Circumference $= 2\pi r$, or πd

Area $= \pi r^2$

The value of π is approximately 3.14. A close fractional approximation of π is $\frac{22}{7}$.

With the circumference and area formulas, all you need is one value—area, circumference, diameter, or radius—and you can determine all the others. Referring to the circle shown above:

Given a circle with a diameter of 12:

radius $= 6$

circumference $= 12\pi$

area $= \pi(6)^2 = 36\pi$

For the test, you won't need to work with a value of π any more precise than 3.14 or $\frac{22}{7}$. In fact, you might be able to answer a circle question using the symbol π itself, without approximating its value.

EXAMPLES:

If a circle with radius r has an area of 4 square feet, what is the area of a circle whose radius is $3r$?

A. 6π square feet

B. 36 square feet

C. 12π square feet

D. 48 square feet

E. 60 square feet

The area of a circle with radius $r = \pi r^2$, which is given as 4. The area of a circle with radius $3r = \pi(3r)^2 = 9\pi r^2$. Since $\pi r^2 = 4$, the area of a circle with radius $3r = (9)(4) = 36$. **The correct answer is B.**

If a circle's circumference is 10 centimeters, what is the area of the circle?

A. $\frac{25}{\pi}$ cm^2

B. 5π cm^2

C. 22.5 cm^2

D. 25 cm^2

E. 28 cm^2

First, determine the circle's radius. Applying the circumference formula $C = 2\pi r$, solve for r:

$$10 = 2\pi r$$
$$\frac{5}{\pi} = r$$

Then, apply the area formula, with $\frac{5}{\pi}$ as the value of r:

$$\begin{aligned} A &= \pi\left(\frac{5}{\pi}\right)^2 \\ &= \pi\left(\frac{25}{\pi^2}\right) \\ &= \frac{25}{\pi^2} \cdot \frac{\pi}{1} \\ &= \frac{25}{\pi} \end{aligned}$$

The correct answer is A.

Arcs and Degree Measures of a Circle

An **arc** is a segment of a circle's circumference. A **minor arc** is the shortest arc connecting two points on a circle's circumference. For example, in the figure shown, minor arc $\overparen{AB}$ is the one formed by the 60° angle from the circle's center (O).

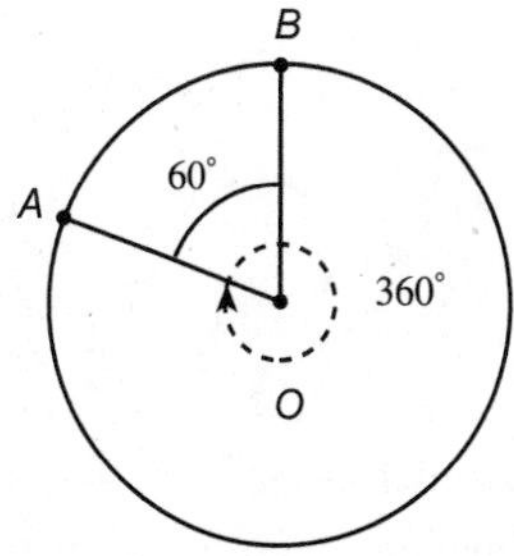

A circle, by definition, contains a total of 360°. The length of an arc relative to the circle's circumference is directly proportionate to the arc's degree measure as a fraction of the circle's total degree measure of 360°. For example, in the preceding figure, minor arc $\overparen{AB}$ accounts for $\frac{60}{360}$, or $\frac{1}{6}$, of the circle's circumference. An arc of a circle can be defined either as a length (a portion of the circle's circumference) or as a degree measure. In the preceding figure, $\overparen{AB} = 60°$. If the circumference is 12π, then the length of minor arc $\overparen{AB}$ is $\frac{1}{6}$ of 12π, or 2π.

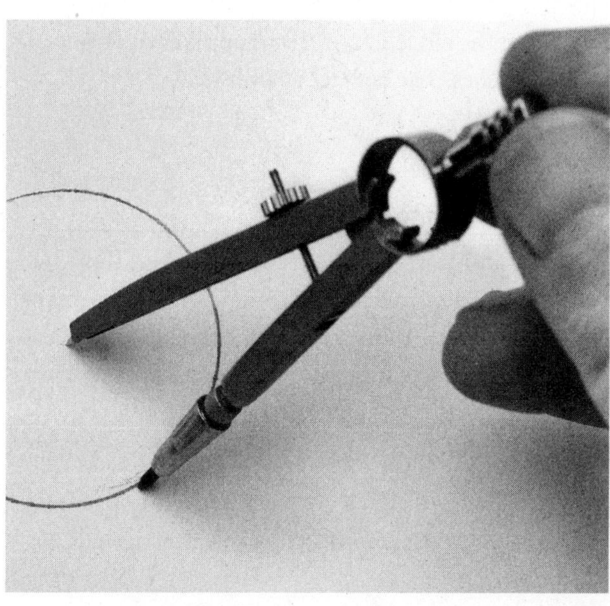

EXAMPLE:

Circle O has diameters $\overline{DB}$ and $\overline{AC}$, as shown in the figure below.

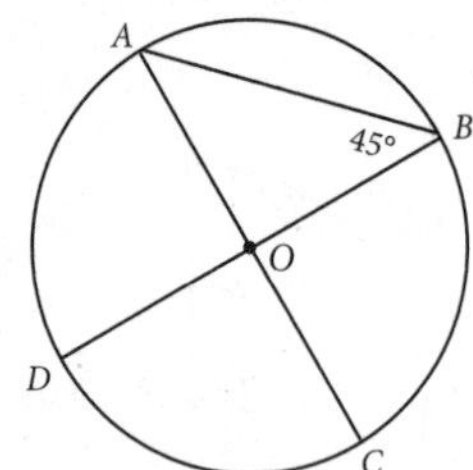

If the circumference of circle O is 12 inches, what is the length of minor arc $\overset{\frown}{BC}$?

A. 3 inches

B. $\frac{13}{4}$ inches

C. $\frac{11}{3}$ inches

D. 4 inches

E. 5 inches

Since $\overline{AO}$ and $\overline{BO}$ are both radii, ΔAOB is isosceles, and therefore $m\angle BAO = 45°$. It follows that $m\angle AOB = 90°$. That 90° angle accounts for $\frac{1}{4}$ of the circle's 360°. Accordingly, minor arc $\overset{\frown}{BC}$ must account for $\frac{1}{4}$ of the circle's 12-inch circumference, or 3 inches. **The correct answer is A.**

Circles and Tangent Lines

A circle is **tangent** to a line (or line segment) if the two intersect at one and only one point (called the **point of tangency**). Here's the key rule to remember about tangents: A line that is tangent to a circle is *always* perpendicular to the line passing through the circle's center and the point of tangency.

The figure shows a circle with center O inscribed in a square. Point P is one of four points of tangency. By definition, $\overline{OP} \perp \overline{AB}$.

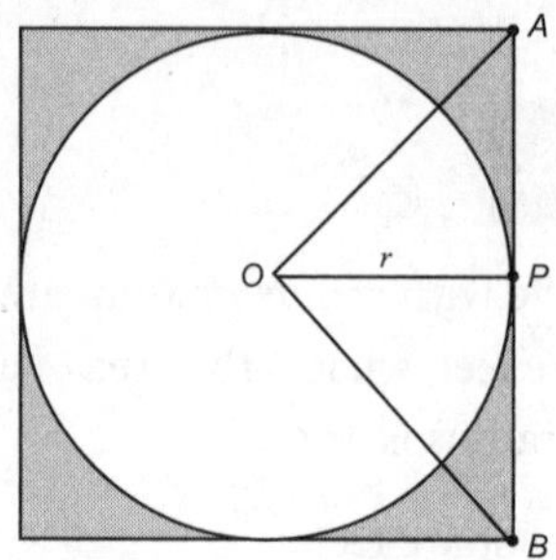

Also, notice the following relationships between the circle in the preceding figure and the inscribing square (r = radius):

Each side of the square is $2r$ in length.

The square's area is $(2r)^2$, or $4r^2$.

EXAMPLE:

Two parallel lines are tangent to the same circle. What is the shortest distance between the two lines?

A. The circle's radius

B. The circle's diameter

C. The circle's circumference

D. The product of the circle's radius and π

E. The product of the circle's diameter and π

The two lines are both perpendicular to a chord that is the circle's diameter. Thus, the shortest distance between them is that diameter. **The correct answer is B.**

3-D Figures

You may encounter three-dimensional (3-D) figures on the subtests, including cubes and other rectangular prisms (box-shaped objects), cylinders, cones, and so-called "square" pyramids (pyramids that have a square base).

Rectangular Prisms

Rectangular prisms are box-shaped figures in which all corners are right angles. Any box-shaped figure has a total of six sides, or *faces*. The length of a side is generally referred to as an *edge*. A test question about a rectangular prism will involve one or both of two basic formulas (p = perimeter of base, B = area of base ($l \times w$), h = height):

Volume = Bh, or lwh

Surface Area = $ph + 2B$

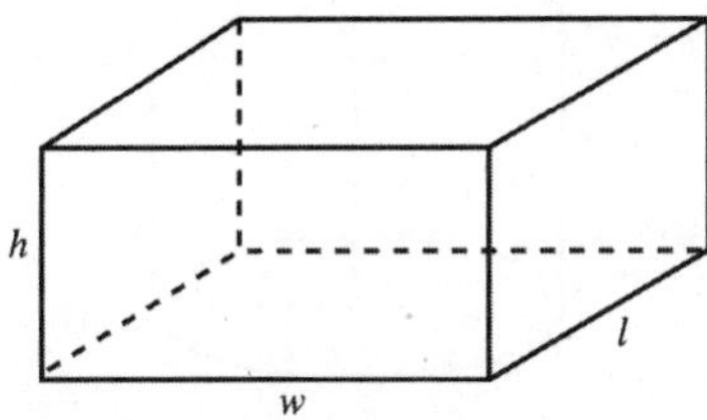

To answer a question involving a rectangular prism, plug what you know into the appropriate formula—surface area or volume—and then solve for the missing term. Depending on the question, you might need to apply both formulas.

For example, when given the surface area of a cube, you can then find the length of one of its edges. Say you are given that a cube has surface area of 294 square inches. Since this is a cube, you know that all the edges are the same length. Let's call that length e:

$$SA = ph + 2B$$
$$SA = 4e(e) + 2(e^2)$$
$$SA = 4e^2 + 2e^2$$

So the formula for the surface area of a cube is $6e^2$. To find the length of an edge, solve the equation $6e^2 = 294$ for e, as follows:

$$6e^2 = 294$$
$$e^2 = 49$$
$$e = 7$$

The edges of this cube each measure 7 inches in length.

EXAMPLE:

A closed rectangular box with a square base is 5 inches in height. If the volume of the box is 45 square inches, what is the box's surface area?

A. 66 square inches
B. 78 square inches
C. 81 square inches
D. 90 square inches
E. 94 square inches

First, determine the dimensions of the square base. The box's height is given as 5. Accordingly, the box's volume (45) = $5lw$, and $lw = 9$. Since the base is square, the base is 3 inches long on each side. Now you can calculate the total surface area:

$$2lw + 2wh + 2lh = (2)(9) + (2)(15) + (2)(15) = 78$$

The correct answer is B.

Cubes

A **cube** is a rectangular prism whose length, width, and height are all the same—in other words, all six faces are squares. The volume and surface area formulas are similar to but simpler than other rectangular prisms (let s = any edge):

volume = s^3, or $s = \sqrt[3]{\text{Volume}}$

surface area = $6s^2$

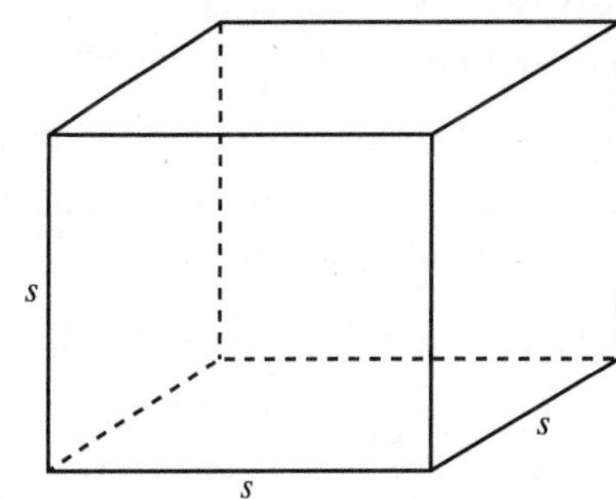

Some questions involving cubes (or other box shapes) are sometimes presented as "packing" problems. In this type of problem, your task is to determine how many small boxes fit into a larger box. Another type of cube question could focus on the *ratios* among the cube's linear, square, and cubic measurements.

EXAMPLE:

How many cube-shaped boxes, each box 18 inches on a side, can be packed into a storage unit measuring 6 feet long, 6 feet wide, and 5 feet high?

A. 36

B. 42

C. 48

D. 64

E. 72

First, convert inches to feet: 18 inches = $1\frac{1}{2}$ feet. You can pack 3 levels of 16 cube-shaped boxes, with a half-foot space left at the top of the storage unit. $3 \times 16 = 48$. **The correct answer is C.**

Cylinders

A **cylinder** is a three-dimensional figure with a circular base. Questions might involve a **right cylinder**, in which the height and base are at 90° angles. The surface area of a right cylinder is the sum of three areas:

- The circular base
- The circular top
- The rectangular surface around the cylinder's vertical face (visualize a rectangular label wrapped around a soup can)

The area of the vertical face is the product of the circular base's circumference (i.e., the rectangle's width) and the cylinder's height. The volume of a right cylinder is the product of the circular base's area and the cylinder's height. Given a radius r and height h of a cylinder:

Surface Area (SA) $= 2\pi rh^2 + 2\pi r^2$

Volume $= \pi r^2 h$

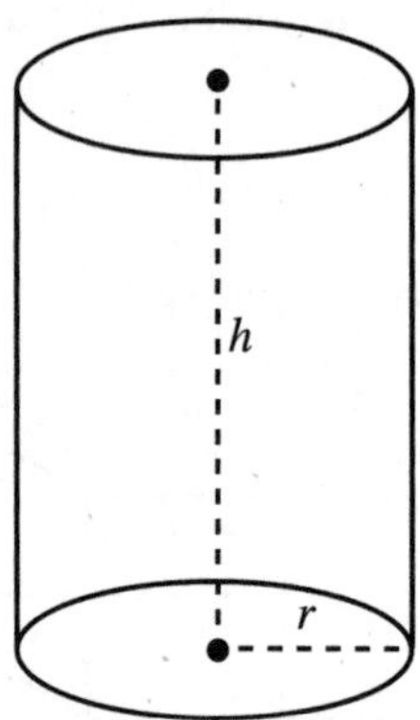

A cylinder problem might require little more than a straightforward application of either the surface-area or the volume formula. As with rectangular-solid questions, just plug what you know into the formula, then solve for what the question asks. A more complex cylinder problem might require you to apply other math concepts or to convert one unit of measurement to another.

EXAMPLE:

What is the volume of a cylinder whose circular base has a radius of 3 centimeters and whose height is 7 centimeters?

A. 21π cm^3

B. 42π cm^3

C. 63π cm^3

D. 81 cm^3

E. 126 cm^3

The cylinder's volume $= \pi(3)^2(7) = 63\pi$ cm^3. **The correct answer is C.**

Cones and Pyramids

Two other three-dimensional figures you might encounter: the **cone** and the **square pyramid** (a four-sided pyramid with a square base). Both are shown below, along with their volume formulas:

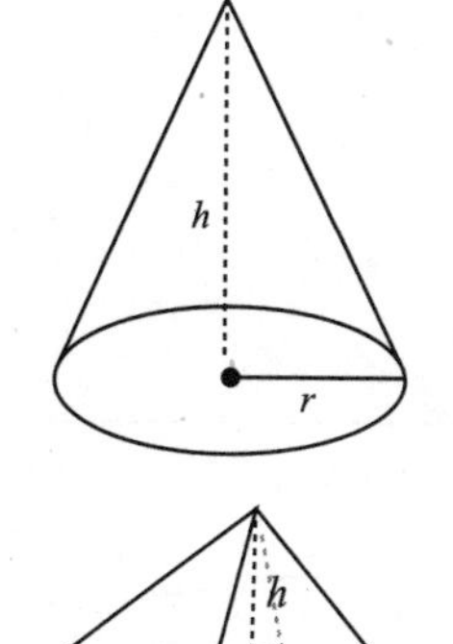

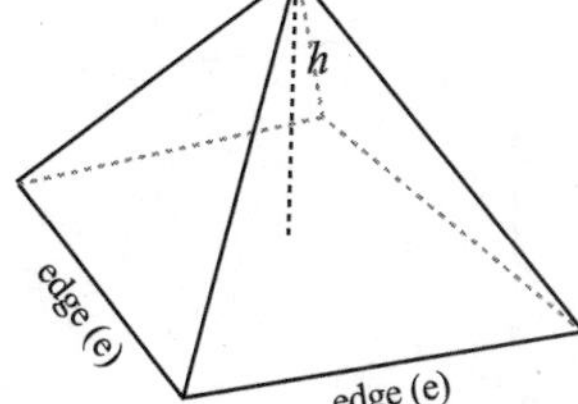

Volume of a cone: $\frac{1}{3}\pi \times \text{radius}^2 \times \text{height}$ ($\pi \approx 3.14$)

Volume of a square pyramid: $\frac{1}{3} \times (\text{base edge})^2 \times \text{height}$

Notice that the volume of a cone is simply one-third that of a right cylinder, and that the volume of a square pyramid is simply one-third that of a rectangular prism.

EXAMPLE:

What is the volume of a pyramid with a height of 24 feet and a square base that measures 10 feet on each side?

A. 240 cubic feet

B. 480 cubic feet

C. 760 cubic feet

D. 800 cubic feet

E. 840 cubic feet

The volume of the pyramid $= \frac{1}{3} \times \text{edge}^2 \times \text{height} = \frac{1}{3} \times 100 \times 24 = 800$ cubic feet. **The correct answer is D.**

Spheres

The **sphere** is the final three-dimensional figure you could encounter.

The volume and surface area of a sphere with radius r are given by the following formulas:

Volume $= \frac{4}{3}\pi r^3$

Surface Area $= 4\pi r^2$

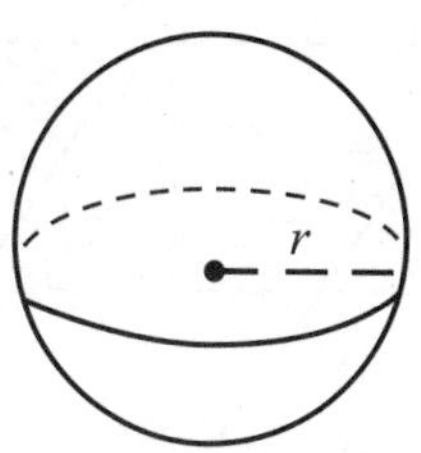

EXAMPLE:

What is the volume of a sphere with a surface area of 100π square meters?

A. $\frac{100}{3}\pi$ cubic meters

B. 166π cubic meters

C. $\frac{500}{3}\pi$ cubic meters

D. 250π cubic meters

E. 500π cubic meters

We must determine the radius to compute the volume. Using the formula for the surface area enables us to do this:

$$4\pi r^2 = 100\pi$$
$$r^2 = 25$$
$$r = 5$$

So the volume of the sphere is $\frac{4}{3}\pi \times 5^3 = \frac{4}{3}\pi \times 125 = \frac{500}{3}\pi$ cubic meters.

The correct answer is C.

Test Yourself: Geometry

1. Assume that l is parallel to m. Find the value of y.

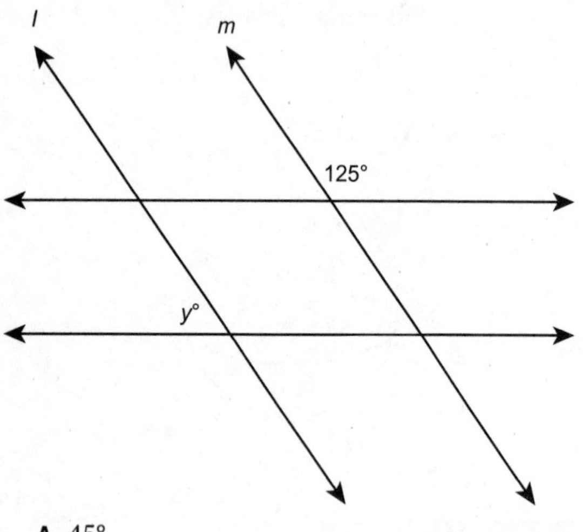

A. 45°

B. 55°

C. 90°

D. 125°

E. 135°

2. Find z:

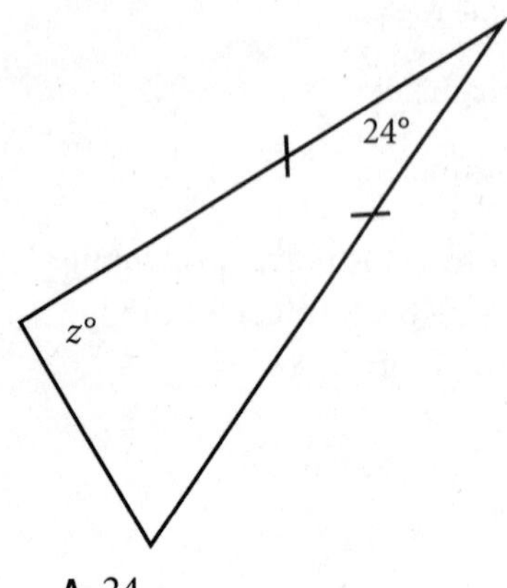

A. 24

B. 78

C. 90

D. 156

E. 180

3. What is the equation of the graphed line?

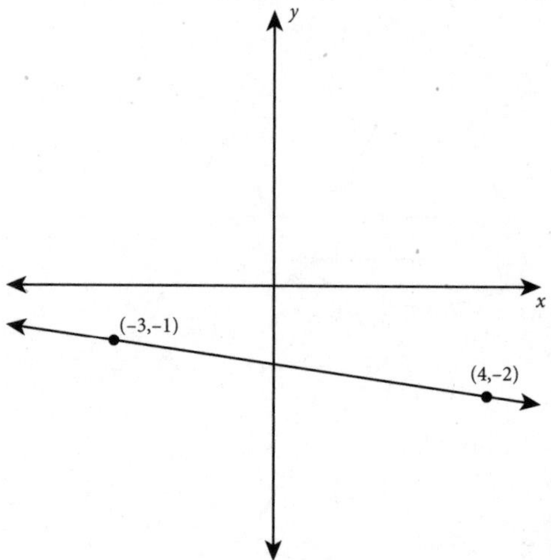

A. $x + 7y = -10$

B. $2x + 47 = -21$

C. $y + 7x = -22$

D. $y + 3x = -10$

E. $-x + 3y = 10$

4. What is the area of the following parallelogram?

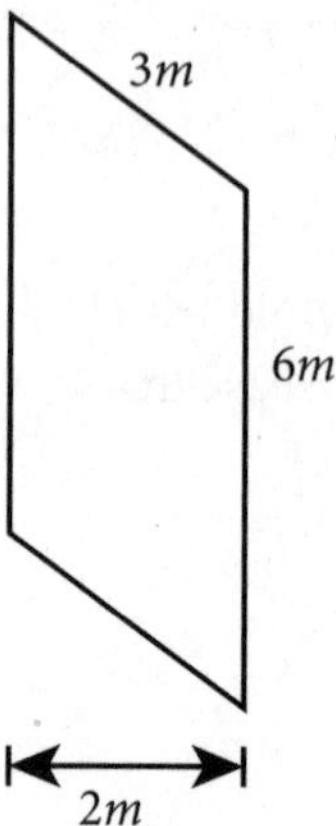

A. 6 square meters

B. 11 square meters

C. 12 square meters

D. 18 square meters

E. 24 square meters

5. Which of the following expressions is equivalent to y?

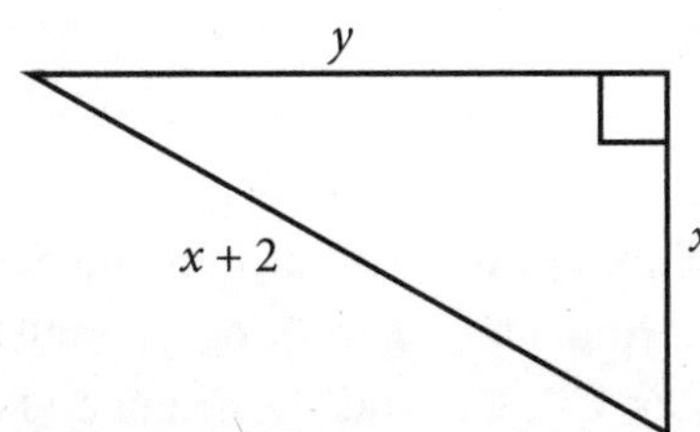

A. $2\sqrt{x+1}$

B. $4x+4$

C. 2

D. $\sqrt{2x^2+4x+4}$

E. $2x$

6. The surface area of a cube is 13.5 square inches. What is its volume?

A. 4.5 cubic inches

B. 1.5 cubic inches

C. 3.375 cubic inches

D. 2.25 cubic inches

E. 1 cubic inch

7. What is the measure of the largest angle in the following triangle?

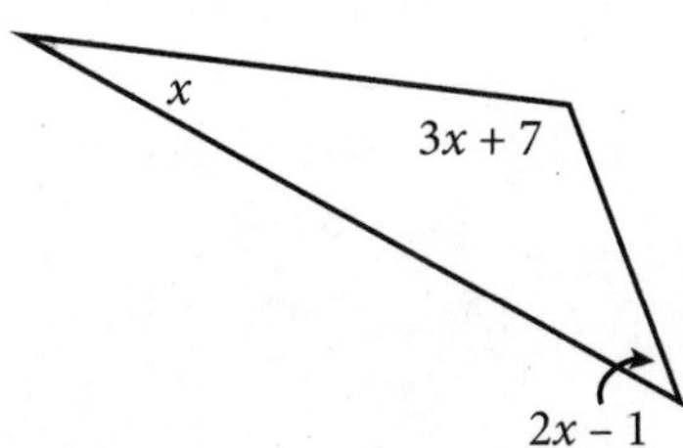

A. 29

B. 57

C. 94

D. 117

E. 123

8. What is the equation of the line passing through the points (0,-3) and (-6, 0)?

A. $y=-\frac{1}{2}x-3$

B. $y=-\frac{1}{2}x-6$

C. $y=-2x-6$

D. $y=-2x-3$

E. $x=-2y-3$

9. The sides of a square have a length of x inches. If they are decreased by 30%, what is the perimeter of the resulting square?

A. $0.49x$ inches

B. $0.70x$ inches

C. $1.20x$ inches

D. $2.80x$ inches

E. $3.00x$ inches

10. What is the circumference of a circle with an area of $\sqrt{\pi}$ square centimeters?

A. $\frac{1}{\pi^{\frac{1}{4}}}$ centimeters

B. $2\pi^{\frac{1}{2}}$ centimeters

C. $2\pi^{\frac{5}{4}}$ centimeters

D. $2\pi^{\frac{1}{4}}$ centimeters

E. $2\pi^{\frac{3}{4}}$ centimeters

Answer Key and Explanations

1. B	3. A	5. A	7. C	9. D
2. B	4. C	6. C	8. A	10. E

1. **The correct answer is B.** The angles adjacent to the one labeled as 125° each measure 55° because they are supplementary angles. Because *l* is parallel to *y*, the angle labeled as *m* is the corresponding angle to one whose measure is 55°, so it also measures 55°.

2. **The correct answer is B.** Angles opposite the congruent sides of an isosceles triangle are congruent. Using this fact, together with the fact that the sum of the three angles in a triangle is 180°, yields the equation $z + z + 24 = 180$. Solve for *z*, as follows:

$$\begin{aligned} z + z + 24 &= 180 \\ 2z + 24 &= 180 \\ 2z &= 156 \\ z &= 78 \end{aligned}$$

3. **The correct answer is A.** The slope of the line is:

$$\begin{aligned} m &= \frac{-1-(-2)}{-3-4} \\ &= \frac{-1+2}{-7} \\ &= -\frac{1}{7} \end{aligned}$$

Using the point-slope form of the equation of a line, namely $y - y_1 = m(x - x_1)$ with the point $(x_1, y_1) = (-3,-1)$ yields

$$\begin{aligned} y-(-1) &= -\frac{1}{7}(x-(-3)) \\ y+1 &= -\frac{1}{7}(x+3) \\ -7(y+1) &= x+3 \\ -7y-7 &= x+3 \\ x+7y &= -10 \end{aligned}$$

4. **The correct answer is C.** The height and base used in the area formula for a parallelogram must be perpendicular. Using 2*m* for the height and 6*m* for the base, we conclude the area is (2*m*)(6*m*) = 12 square meters.

5. **The correct answer is A.** Use the Pythagorean theorem:

$$\begin{aligned} y^2 + x^2 &= (x+2)^2 \\ y^2 + x^2 &= x^2 + 4x + 4 \\ y^2 &= 4x + 4 \\ y &= \sqrt{4x+4} \end{aligned}$$

6. **The correct answer is C.** Let *e* be the edge of the cube. The surface area is $6e^2 = 13.5$. Solve for *e*:

$$\begin{aligned} 6e^2 &= 13.5 \\ e^2 &= 2.25 \\ e &= \sqrt{2.25} = 1.5 \end{aligned}$$

So the volume is $e^3 = (1.5)^3 = 3.375$ cubic inches.

7. **The correct answer is C.** The sum of the three angles in a triangle is 180°. Using this fact yields the following:

$$\begin{aligned} x + (2x-1) + (3x+7) &= 180 \\ 6x + 6 &= 180 \\ 6x &= 174 \\ x &= 29 \end{aligned}$$

So the three angles are 29°, 57°, and 94°.

8. **The correct answer is A.** The slope of the line is $m = \frac{-3-0}{0-(-6)} = -\frac{1}{2}$. Since the *y*-intercept is (0, –3), we know that *b* in the slope-intercept form for the equation of a line, which is $y = mx + b$, is –3. So the equation is $y = -\frac{1}{2}x - 3$.

9. **The correct answer is D.** The new side (after the reduction) has length $x - 0.30x = 0.70x$. So the perimeter of the new square is $4(0.70x) = 2.8x$ inches.

10. **The correct answer is D.** Using the area formula for a circle yields the equation $\pi r^2 = \sqrt{\pi}$, where r is the radius. Solve for r:

$$\pi r^2 = \sqrt{\pi}$$

$$r^2 = \frac{\sqrt{\pi}}{\pi} = \frac{1}{\sqrt{\pi}}$$

$$r = \sqrt{\frac{1}{\sqrt{\pi}}} = \left(\frac{1}{\pi^{1/2}}\right)^{1/2}$$

$$r = \frac{1}{\pi^{1/4}}$$

So the circumference is $2\pi\left(\frac{1}{\pi^{1/4}}\right) = 2\pi^{3/4}$ centimeters.

NOTES

MINI-QUIZ: MATH FOR THE AFOQT AND OAR

Directions: This part of the test measures your ability to use arithmetic to solve problems. Each problem is followed by five possible answers. You are to decide which one of the five choices is correct.

1. $4.83 + 7.18 + 2.31 =$

A. 13.54

B. 14.25

C. 14.32

D. 15.34

E. 15.45

2. 0.1667 is equivalent to

A. $\frac{1}{6}$

B. $\frac{1}{4}$

C. $\frac{1}{3}$

D. $\frac{1}{2}$

E. $\frac{2}{3}$

3. π is equivalent to

A. $2\frac{2}{7}$

B. $2\frac{4}{7}$

C. $3\frac{1}{7}$

D. $4\frac{3}{7}$

E. $22\frac{1}{7}$

4. In the expression, $166 \div 42 + (17 \times 2) - 7^2$, what operation will you perform first to simplify?

A. $166 \div 42$

B. $42 + (17 \times 2)$

C. -7^2

D. 17×2

E. $(17 \times 2) - 7^2$

5. A right triangle's legs measure 3 inches and 4 inches. How long is the hypotenuse?

A. 5 inches

B. 9 inches

C. $\sqrt{23}$ inches

D. 78 inches

E. 81 inches

6. The circumference of a circle with a radius of 9 inches is

A. 9π

B. 18π

C. 81π

D. $40\pi h$

E. 324π

7. The volume of a rectangular solid measuring 6 inches long, 7 inches wide, and 3 inches high is

A. 16 cu. in.

B. 21 sq. in.

C. 42 cu. in.

D. 126 sq. in.

E. 126 cu. in.

8. The area of a triangle measuring 17 cm at its base and 8 cm high is

A. 25 cu. cm

B. 52 sq. cm

C. 58 cm

D. 68 sq. cm

E. 86 cu. cm

9. There are ______ mm in 7 km.

A. 700

B. 7,000

C. 70,000

D. 700,000

E. 7,000,000

10. The internal angles of a triangle add up to

A. 90°

B. 180°

C. 270°

D. 360°

E. 365°

ANSWER KEY AND EXPLANATIONS

1. C	3. C	5. A	7. E	9. E
2. A	4. D	6. B	8. D	10. B

1. **The correct answer is C.**

$$\begin{array}{r} 4.83 \\ 7.18 \\ \underline{+2.31} \\ 14.32 \end{array}$$

2. **The correct answer is A.** $1 \div 6 = 0.1667$
3. **The correct answer is C.** $\pi = \frac{22}{7} = 3\frac{1}{7}$
4. **The correct answer is D.** Remember PEMDAS, and you will know that the first step is to solve what is inside the parentheses. 17×2 is the expression inside the parentheses, so it is the first thing you should solve.
5. **The correct answer is A.** Remember to use the Pythagorean Theorem, $a^2 + b^2 = c^2$:

$$3^2 + 4^2 =$$
$$9 + 16 = 25$$
$$25 = c^2$$
$$\sqrt{25} = 5$$

6. **The correct answer is B.** The equation for the circumference of a circle is $2\pi r$:

$$\pi\, 2\, (9) = 18\pi$$

7. **The correct answer is E.** Volume is always expressed in cubic units. For a rectangular solid, the equation is $l \times w \times h$:

$$V = 6 \times 7 \times 3$$
$$42 \times 3 = 126 \text{ cu. in.}$$

8. **The correct answer is D.** Area is always expressed in square units. The formula for the area of a triangle is $\frac{1}{2}bh$:

$$A = \frac{1}{2}(17 \times 8)$$
$$\frac{1}{2}(136) = 68 \text{ sq. cm}$$

9. **The correct answer is E.** There are 10 mm in 1 cm, 100 cm in 1 m, and 1,000 m in 1 km.

$$\begin{aligned} 7(10 \times 100 \times 1{,}000) &= 7(1{,}000 \times 1{,}000) \\ &= 7(1{,}000{,}000) \\ &= 7{,}000{,}000 \end{aligned}$$

10. **The correct answer is B.** The internal angles of a triangle add up to 180°.

NOTES

SUMMING IT UP

- The AFOQT has an Arithmetic Reasoning and a Math Knowledge subtest while the OAR has a Math Skills subtest. For these subtests, it is important to know how to factor, solve, and simplify algebraic expressions and understand exponents, absolute values, and systems of equations.
- Know the different types of numbers: whole numbers, integers, rational numbers, irrational numbers, and mixed numbers.
- When solving complex or simplifying expressions, use the mnemonic device "Please excuse my dear Aunt Sally" to remember the order of operations: Parentheses, Exponents, Multiplication, Division, Addition, and Subtraction.
- Decimals and fractions are used to indicate portions of numbers, which can also be expressed as percentages.
- Questions centered on probability may ask you to calculate the odds of performing a certain task by dividing the number of ways it could happen by the total number of possible outcomes. Similar questions might require you to identify patterns and determine relationships to anticipate the next item in a series. Factors are whole numbers that can be divided into other whole numbers without leaving a remainder.
- Exponents are used to express products involving multiple identical numbers (for example, 2^5 instead of $2 \times 2 \times 2 \times 2 \times 2$) and are used to more efficiently express very small and very large numbers in scientific notation, like 2.3×10^3, which equals 2,300.

7

- Remember the three basic rules for exponents:
  - To multiply powers of the same base, add the exponents.
  - To divide powers of the same base, subtract the exponent of the divisor from the exponent of the dividend.
  - To raise a product to a power, apply the power to each term and multiply the results.
- The square root of a number x is a number that you "square," meaning that you multiply the number by itself.
- Simplify radicals by moving what's under the radical sign to the outside of the sign. Check inside square-root radicals for perfect squares. The same advice applies to perfect cubes, and so on.
- Polynomials are expressions comprising terms with non-negative exponents and are usually written in a standard form: $Ax^2 + Bx + C$.
- When multiplying binomials, remember the mnemonic device FOIL (First, Outer, Inner, and Last) to determine which terms to multiply first.
- When asked to solve for one or both variables in two linear equations, combine the two equations or use the substitution method to solve for each variable.
- To calculate the slope of a line on a graph, use the slope-intercept equation: $y = mx + b$, where m is the slope and b is the point where the line crosses the y-axis.
- To solve for the hypotenuse of a right triangle, use the Pythagorean theorem ($a^2 + b^2 = c^2$).
- Pi (π) is the ratio of a circle's circumference and diameter and is used to find the area of a circle.
- Calculating the area of a shape requires multiplying the dimensions of length, width, sides, etc., while calculating the volume of a shape requires you to know the height as well.

READING COMPREHENSION

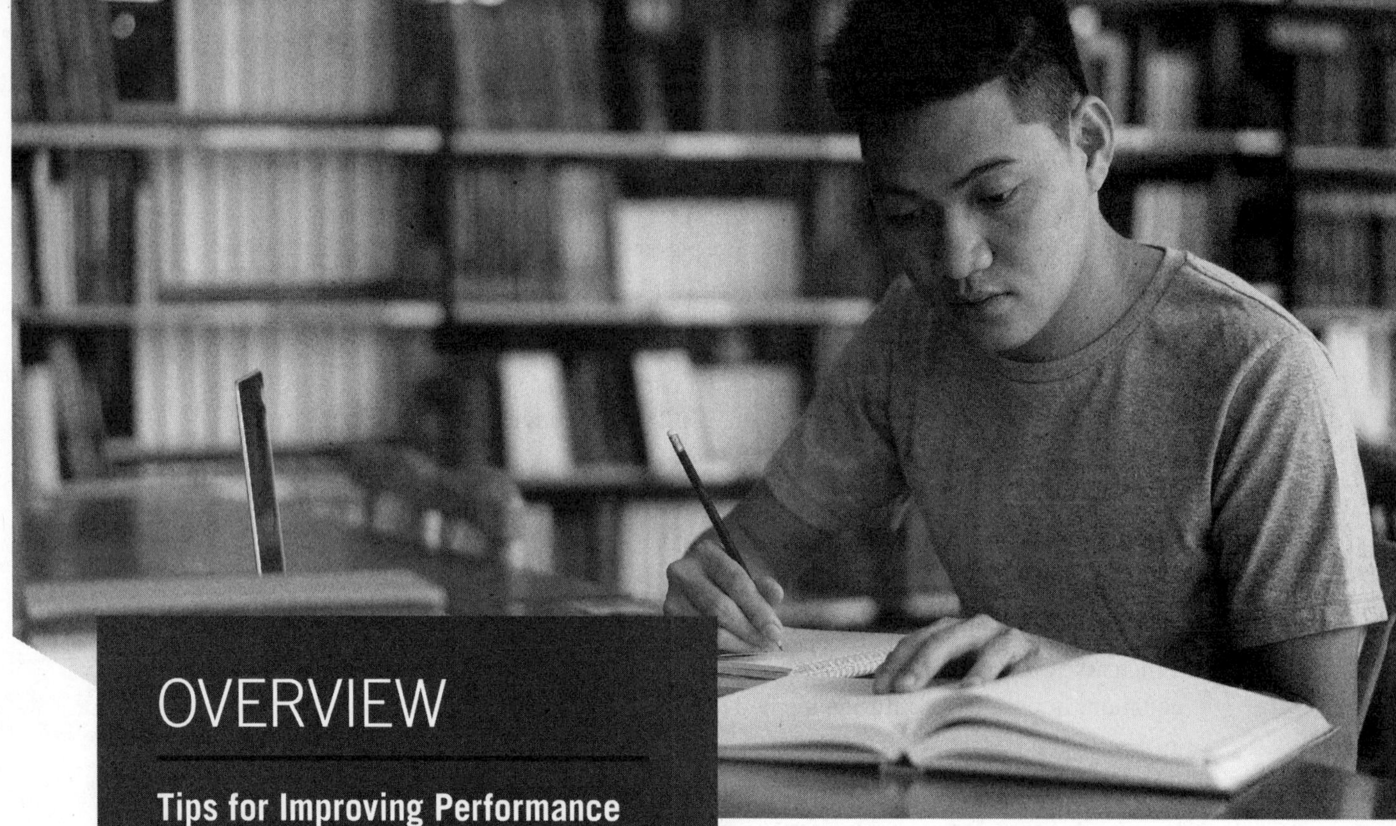

OVERVIEW

The Reading Comprehension subtest assesses your reading level and ability to retain and evaluate information provided in a technical writing passage. The AFOQT and OAR subtests are set up in a similar fashion wherein you will be given passages to read and a set of questions to answer based on the passage you just read. Questions will ask you to comprehend vocabulary terms and also assess the purpose of passages, the author's viewpoint, and other inferences.

For the AFOQT, you will have 22 minutes to answer 25 multiple-choice questions. The subtest will have five passages, each with 4-6 questions. For the paper format of the OAR, you will have 30 minutes to answer 20 multiple-choice questions. For the computer-adapted format, you have a limit of 30 minutes to answer as many multiple-choice questions as the program needs to assess your ability. As such, time is the primary limitation on your ability to thoroughly read and understand the passages and answer the question sets. However, by understanding the types of questions you will be asked, you can practice *how* you read each passage so that you can note critical information.

This chapter details five types of questions you will encounter on the exam: primary purpose, applied meaning, statement agreement and inferences, lists, and supportive statements. The following questions demonstrate the kinds of tasks you will be asked to perform on this subtest:

- What is the primary purpose of the passage?
- What is the applied meaning of a term or phrase?
- Would the author agree with a statement about the passage or topic at large?
- What can you infer from the passage?
- Does an item belong to a list of items or concepts from the passage?
- Is a statement supported by the passage?

While the question presentation may vary between the AFOQT and OAR, the skills applied are equivalent.

TIPS FOR IMPROVING PERFORMANCE

The following tips can improve performance on most reading comprehension passages. Experiment with how you approach passages and questions to discover what can compensate for your challenges on the subtest.

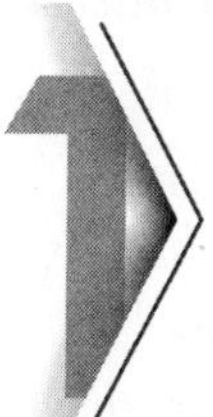

Read actively: Active reading means that you're summarizing what you're reading while you read, even asking questions, taking notes, or marking the text, if possible. After reading a paragraph, you should be able to recall the topic and purpose of the paragraph. Being able to do so will allow you to not only quickly return to relevant paragraphs based on the needs of a question but also remember and understand the passage better. Active reading also means activating what you know about reading and writing to get what you need from a text. For example, a well-written paragraph follows a particular structure. The first and last sentences of a paragraph (and a passage as a whole) often provide clear insight into topic and purpose.

Strategically work through questions: To perform well, nearly every reading comprehension test demands that you be thorough but efficient when reading passages and answering questions. You can avoid many of the typical time traps for test takers by following a set series of steps, as follows:

- Read the full question
- Make a prediction of the answer
- Read all answer choices
- Eliminate unsupported answers
- Find evidence for your choice

Be certain in your answers: There's an excellent reason why the right answer is right and why each wrong answer is wrong. Sometimes this will come down to the details of the passage, and other times it will come down to the specific wording of the answer. For instance, an answer choice may use the word *inform* when the purpose of the passage is to persuade, making the answer choice incorrect. Sometimes an answer can be true in the universal sense (known beyond the passage) but is not supported by the passage itself—in which case, it is incorrect. Regardless, you can be absolutely certain that your choice is correct if you have evidence to support it and evidence to eliminate other choices. If you can't be certain, then be aware that you're guessing. And you should return to any questions you guessed on, time and test format permitting.

PRIMARY PURPOSE

Understanding the primary purpose of a passage is about answering an essential question: "What is it about?" The purpose of a passage is often revealed in its first and last sentences with the author's thesis or conclusion. However, it's not just about what the author is saying but how they say it. When identifying the primary purpose, answer choices often rely on a series of key verbs that best summarize the purpose and form of the passage. For example, words such as *advocate, discuss,* or *inform* will typically begin the sentences for each option and summarize the author's intentions behind the passage. A solid understanding of what these words mean can aid you on the test:

- *Advocate* means "to support or argue for something." In other words, what is the passage recommending or supporting?
- *Discuss* means to "talk about" or "investigate by reasoning or argument." What is the passage talking about or investigating?
- *Inform* means to "give information." Is the passage providing factual information and context around a topic?

EXAMPLE:

John Patrick Rose began his career in 2014 with the launch of his introductory appliance repair program. When sales skyrocketed in less than two weeks, his instruction was in high demand. He began a weekly mentoring group for newly certified technicians, which only solidified his status as a vocational guru.

What is the primary purpose of this passage?

A. To advocate for appliance repair certification programs as a national standard

B. To discuss the life of John Patrick Rose and explore the perceived value behind his contributions to vocational education

C. To inform the reader about John Patrick Rose and his success in the field of appliance repair education

D. To encourage appliance repair persons to follow a mentor

E. To give readers a reason to start their own training programs

This example illustrates the importance of understanding the key words. This passage does not advocate or discuss. It clearly informs. The passage also does not suggest that the reader should start their own training course. The passage does provide solid facts about John Patrick Rose and his career as an appliance repair education guru. **Therefore, choice C is the correct answer.**

The key to understanding primary purpose questions is understanding what words such as *provide, highlight, discuss, inform*, etc., mean and how they are used.

APPLIED MEANING

Applied meaning questions ask a reader to determine the meaning of a word or phrase in the context of the passage. These questions take advantage of how words may shift in definition depending on the situation in which they are used. Take for instance the word *restrained.* A combatant may be restrained (bound) when captured during the course of an operation. Alternatively, an individual may be restrained (measured or controlled) in how they communicate dissatisfaction. Context can make all the difference.

Applied meaning questions will often take the following forms:

"In the first paragraph, the word ______________ most likely means"

"The author most likely uses the phrase ______________ in order to convey"

The best way to assess applied meaning questions is to return to the placement of the phrase in the passage and read the entire sentence and the sentences before and after it. The word or phrase itself can oftentimes mean multiple things if read alone, but in the context of the passage, it will have a specific meaning.

EXAMPLE:

Hippos and humans have a long history, with some of the earliest depictions of our interactions dating to around 4400 BCE in Egypt. At best, our relationship could be characterized as strained. Hippos have long had a reputation as one of the most dangerous animals in the world. They've been known to attack people near waterways and boats at random, sometimes resulting in the injury or death of passengers. Some sources estimate at least 500 deaths per year can be attributed to the aquatic mammal. However, despite their penchant for fierceness, hippos are also the victims of human aggression. To compensate for dwindling elephant populations, ivory poachers have turned to harvesting hippo teeth for income. Subsistence hunting and shrinking habitats have also impacted the hippo population with a 2017 assessment labeling the animal as vulnerable to extinction. For centuries, both humans and hippos have threatened one another. And it's safe to say that we'd both be best served by maintaining a safe and respectful distance.

The author uses the phrase "our relationship could be characterized as strained" to convey

A. the history of the species' interactions is filled with mutual tension.

B. humans have struggled to understand how hippos live.

C. both humans and hippos have injured one another.

D. humans have been plagued by hippos for thousands of years.

E. hippos are victims of human aggression.

Essentially, the question asks for the meaning of the paragraph's second sentence. To understand the meaning, you need to understand not only the words used but also the supporting sentences to establish context. The strained relationship between humans and hippos, as described by the author, is elaborated in the paragraph as the result of the acts of aggression that have come from both sides. According to the passage, human poachers have hunted hippos for their ivory, and hippos have been known to attack boats filled with people. However, as this helps us understand the reason for the "strained relationship" between hippos and humans, it does not answer the question. Our understanding of the passage could lead us to select choice C, but the question wants us to assess the meaning of the phrase, not its cause.

With the exception of choice A, each answer option describes specific ways in which humans and hippos have interacted—some supported by the passage and some not. While some of these choices use words that could be synonyms for *strained*, the keywords of the original phrase are not represented. "Relationship," "characterized," and "strained" direct us to look for a general description of the species' tense history without offering information that goes beyond the words used. Choice A states, "the history of the species' interactions is filled with mutual tension." While the "tension" in question is the result of injuries caused by the two sides (choice C), no word in the original phrase can be defined in context as meaning injury or aggression. **The correct answer is A.**

STATEMENT AGREEMENTS AND INFERENCES

Statement Agreement questions will ask you to determine how the author or speaker of the passage would respond to a certain statement. The question may reference exact quotes from the passage or make an inference based on phrases found within the passage. The author or speaker will either agree with one of the answer options, or they will not. An Inference question requires similar thinking in that you must use the explicit information in the passage to come to a well-supported conclusion that aligns with the author's purpose.

Statement Agreement and Inference questions rely on your understanding of the primary purpose of the passage as well as your ability to understand relationships between details. Let's look at a passage and a statement agreement and inference question.

EXAMPLE:

America stands today at the opening of a second Space Age. Innovative NASA programs and American entrepreneurs together are transforming the space industry. These initiatives—both at NASA and in the private sector—are expanding the nation's opportunities for exploration and for the economic development of the solar system.

Today's space economy extends some 36,000 kilometers (22,369 miles) from the surface of the Earth and includes an array of evidence-based technologies—satellite communications, global positioning satellites, and imaging satellites—on which our economy depends. These technologies are now an integral part of our economy, and they would not exist if not for the over 50 years of research, development, and investment in the enabling technologies by NASA and other government agencies that seeded these efforts and allowed them to bloom. As we expand our activities in the solar system over the next decades, NASA programs and investments will provide the seed and soil that encourage economic development increasingly farther from Earth. The first signs of this are already visible.

The next era of space exploration will see governments pushing technological development and the American private sector using these technologies as they expand their economic activities to new worlds. NASA's next objectives for exploration—visits to asteroids and Mars— are more complex than any previous space mission attempted. They will happen in the context of relatively smaller NASA budgets and an expanding commercial space economy. Teaming with private-sector partners to develop keystone markets like low Earth orbit (LEO) transportation and technological capabilities like asteroid mining will help NASA achieve its mission goals, help the space economy evolve to embrace new ambitions, and provide large economic returns to the taxpayer through the stimulation and growth of new businesses and 21st-century American jobs.

Excerpt from "Emerging Space: The Evolving Landscape of 21st Century American Spaceflight" as produced by the Office of the Chief Technologist at NASA

How might the author respond to news of a partnership between NASA and a private space exploration company for a future Mars mission?

A. Criticize the private company for siphoning funds away from NASA's own research and exploration activities

B. Express support for the partnership only if NASA has full control of any resulting technology

C. Celebrate the partnership as a step toward achieving NASA's mission goals

D. Contend that such partnerships distract from attempts to expand NASA's budget

E. Argue that government agencies and their regulations will likely only hamper the endeavors of the private sector toward space exploration

This question requires your understanding of the purpose of the passage, best summarized by the final sentence of the first paragraph, "These initiatives—both at NASA and in the private sector—are expanding the nation's opportunities for exploration and for the economic development of the solar system." Relevant to this question in particular are the positive framing around the phrase "expanding the nation's opportunities" and the mention of both NASA and the private sector. This can lead us to infer positive reception of any announcement that melds those groups together. Choices A, D, and E all offer verbiage and ideas that run counter to the message of collaboration and partnership present throughout the passage. While choice B expresses support for the partnership, it creates a condition for the support that misconstrues statements from the second paragraph regarding "enabling technologies by NASA." Choice C also expresses support and aligns with a statement from the final paragraph of the passage, stating "Teaming with private-sector partners [. . .] will help NASA achieve its mission goals." **Choice C is the correct answer.**

EXAMPLE:

As inferred from the passage, which of the following factors will likely support the future exploration of space?

A. Dwindling funding for governmental space agencies

B. Economic incentives from governments to encourage visits to asteroids and Mars

C. An economy built on the technologies developed by NASA in the 20th century

D. Government-supported technological development

E. The ability to provide larger taxpayer returns and new jobs

The question asks that you use the details provided in the passage to infer what activities will impact future space exploration. Choice A misrepresents a detail from the last paragraph of the passage ("in the context of relatively smaller NASA budgets"). It infers a shrinking budget instead of a "smaller" budget, assumes that this applies to all governmental space agencies, and, in terms of the question, offers this as a supporting factor for space exploration, rather than it more likely having the opposite effect. Choices B and C offer similar misrepresentations of passage details and misalignment with the question's goal. No mention is made in the passage of direct incentives for exploration or similar measures, only that the technological development pursued by NASA can "provide the seed and soil that encourage economic development increasingly farther from Earth." For choice C, the technologies already developed by NASA are mentioned as having laid the groundwork for much of our modern economy; the emphasis on further development allows you to infer that such technology is insufficient for future needs. Choice E describes a potential effect of investment in expanded space travel, not a supporting factor. Only choice D presents a supporting factor for the future exploration of space. With "governments pushing technological development and the American private sector using these technologies," the expansion of "economic activities to new worlds" implies continued and future space exploration. **The correct answer is D.**

LISTS

Lists are infrequent within passages but may be drawn upon by test makers to assess a reader's ability to determine whether an item belongs to a group or set of items or terms. You will be asked to determine if an item or concept listed among the answer choices belongs to a list of items or concepts from the passage.

EXAMPLE:

When you are planning a birthday party, one of the first questions that may enter your mind is, "What type of cake would the person enjoy?" Cakes often symbolize a celebration of some type. Many types of parties beyond the quintessential birthday party incorporate cakes. Wedding receptions, baby showers, anniversaries, and graduations all frequently include a cake in some capacity. The cake has been and will continue to be a cornerstone of many celebrations for years to come.

What is a type of party that may include a cake?

A. Bar Mitzvah

B. Promotion

C. Anniversary

D. Block party

E. Family reunion

The easiest way to answer this type of question is to locate any lists that appear in the passage. In this case, a quick scan of the passage leads you to the fourth sentence. It lists "Wedding receptions, baby showers, anniversaries, and graduations" as parties that frequently include a cake. Although a cake is likely to be included in a Bar Mitzvah (choice A), a promotion (choice B), a block party (choice D) and a family reunion (choice E), none of those are mentioned in the list and **thus anniversary (choice C) is the correct choice.**

All the information you need is provided within a list. There's no need to scour the passage for hidden information. You just need to find the list and determine what belongs or what does not.

SUPPORTIVE STATEMENTS

You will encounter questions on the exam that will ask you to determine if a statement is supported or not supported by the passage. Supportive Statement questions require that you retain or can locate key information provided in the passage and understand the passage's primary purpose. In that regard, they are similar to Statement Agreement and Inference questions. However, these questions will likely present in one or two specific formats:

"Which of the following statements is supported by the passage?"

"Which of the following statements is NOT supported by the passage?"

EXAMPLE:

"The Party said that Oceania had never been in alliance with Eurasia. He, Winston Smith, knew that Oceania had been in alliance with Eurasia as short a time as four years ago. But where did that knowledge exist? Only in his own consciousness, which in any case must soon be annihilated. And if all others accepted the lie which the Party imposed — if all records told the same tale — then the lie passed into history and became truth. 'Who controls the past,' ran the Party slogan, 'controls the future: who controls the present controls the past.' And yet the past, though of its nature alterable, never had been altered. Whatever was true now was true from everlasting to everlasting. It was quite simple. All that was needed was an unending series of victories over your own memory. 'Reality control', they called it: in Newspeak, 'doublethink.'"

Excerpt from *1984* by George Orwell

Which of the following statements is supported by the passage?

A. Winston Smith had imagined the alliance between Oceania and Eurasia.

B. The past is insignificant to the present.

C. The Party created its own version of history.

D. Ruling effectively requires brainwashing your constituents.

E. Memories are often wrong.

In this passage, the speaker is describing the tension between Winston Smith's memory about the past, specifically an alliance between Oceania and Eurasia, and how the Party has rewritten the past (choice C). Winston Smith knows that there was an alliance between Oceania and Eurasia; the passage does not suggest that he imagined it (choice A). It is clear that Winston Smith's memory contradicts the version of reality presented by the Party, but the passage does not imply that Winston's memories, or memories generally, are incorrect (choice E). The passage discusses how the past is used to shape the present and future, so choice B is incorrect. There is no discussion of ruling effectively in this passage, so choice D is also incorrect. **Choice C is the correct answer.**

PUTTING IT ALL TOGETHER

Now that we have explored how to best approach each reading passage and effectively answer the most common types of questions, let's put it all together with one full example. Immediately after this example is a mini-quiz, giving you further practice for this subtest.

EXAMPLE:

The Globe Theater's production of *As You Like It* relies on base, minimalistic storytelling and production wherein the empathy of the actors with the characters and the empathy of the audience with the actors takes center stage. Each week, the performers at Shakespeare's home theater use the entire performance space to embody the famous dictum from the play's second act that "all the world's a stage, and all the men and women merely players." The production enfolds the audience into the show without the confusion of multi-layer props, costumes, and set pieces. Instead of set changes and moving pieces, the only cue of a scenery change is the entrance and exit patterns of the actors and the removal of the black tarp over the columns used to indicate trees. At times, the actors venture into the audience when the confines of the stage are unable to convey properly the meaning of their spacing. And it's these movement patterns that define their personas; the fool struts the stage, but the shepherds toil in the wings tending their fields and flocks. You see Jacques, the play's perpetual melancholiac, use the audience as a scene partner as he seeks solace within its masses. But not all would cross that theatrical line. As he likes it, the Duke Frederick, a stuffy and arrogant aristocrat, is a man apart from the people and associates little with them.

While any Shakespearean play may seem daunting to most modern audiences, in this production, the Globe's actors lean into exaggerated character actions and speech to emphasize the humor of the pastoral comedy. You see Touchstone, the fool, summon ad-libbed lines, exaggerated speech, songs, and mimed humor. In the third act, the repartee between the shepherd Corin and Touchstone has the latter at the top of his absurdist comical ability as well as his wordplay. Even if the audience may miss the meaning, the fool's delivery sows the seed of the joke. As the Globe's production proves, Shakespeare's plays speak best when the story can speak for itself—when all the pomp and show is stripped away and the storytelling rests on the backs of the players who truly play their parts.

1. The primary purpose of this passage is to

   A. advocate for the use of Shakespearean text in modern-day theater.

   B. explain the premise of *As You Like It.*

   C. discuss minimalistic storytelling through the Globe production of *As You Like It.*

   D. describe the Globe Theater's modern performances of Shakespearean plays.

   E. dissuade theatergoers from watching Shakespeare at the Globe.

EXPLANATION The correct answer is C. The primary verbs used to possibly convey the purpose of the passage among the five choices are *advocate, explain, discuss, describe,* and *dissuade.* Certainly, the language does not advocate (choice A), but neither does it dissuade (choice E). The passage does not explain the premise of *As You Like It* (choice B) or discuss how the Globe Theater performs Shakespeare nowadays (choice D). The first sentence expresses that the Globe Theater's production of *As You Like It* relies on "base, minimalistic storytelling and production" to convey the story of the play and then goes on to discuss why. The only option that mentions minimalistic storytelling is choice C.

2. In the second paragraph, the word *pomp* most likely means

   A. ceremony.

   B. fluff.

   C. occasion.

   D. pageantry.

   E. ritual.

EXPLANATION The correct answer is D. The passage distinguishes between storytelling and "pomp and show." In the context of the passage, it's clear that the minimalist presentation of Shakespeare's plays relies on the actors' skilled storytelling, as opposed to elaborate costumes, props, and sets. Thus, *pomp* best means "pageantry."

3. Which of the following statements would the author most likely agree with?

   A. Minimalistic theater is best when done in Shakespeare's Globe Theater.

   B. Shakespearean plays must be performed in the Globe Theater.

   C. All Shakespeare shows must be performed with big costumes and even bigger sets.

   D. The actors in *As You Like It* used the entire performance space—not just the stage.

   E. All the characters in *As You Like It* ventured into the audience.

EXPLANATION The correct answer is D. The primary purpose of the passage is to discuss minimalistic storytelling though the Globe production of *As You Like It.* Besides discussing the concept, the author has no perspective on the theater or art form itself, and thus the best answer would be that the actors in *As You Like It* used the entire performance space—not just the stage.

4. Which of the following exaggerated character choices was NOT used by the fool in *As You Like It*?

   A. Song choice

   B. Exuberant costume

   C. Mimed humor

   D. Exaggerated speech

   E. Ad lib

EXPLANATION The correct answer is B. In the second paragraph, the author lists the ways in which the fool exaggerates his character choices. The only option not listed is exuberant costume.

5. Which of the following statements is NOT supported by the passage?

   A. The Globe Theater only produces plays that use minimalist storytelling.

   B. Duke Frederick's character does not walk among the audience because he would not walk among the people.

   C. Minimalist storytelling makes use of staging and acting choices as opposed to elaborate set design and costume.

   D. The fool is a perfect example of exaggerated character choices used in order to convey humor.

   E. The removal of a black tarp over the columns signifies trees.

EXPLANATION The correct answer is A. The passage makes no indication that the Globe Theater only produces plays that use minimalist storytelling, only that this particular play did.

Now that you have an idea what questions in the Reading Comprehension subtest look like, test yourself to gauge your understanding with the following mini-quiz.

MINI-QUIZ: READING COMPREHENSION

Directions: This part of the test measures your ability to read and comprehend longer passages. Each passage is followed by a series of multiple-choice questions, which relate in some fashion to the passage itself. You must choose the best option based on the passage. No additional knowledge is needed as the goal is to use only the passage.

Questions 1–5 are based on the following passage.

In the early 1800s, a phenomenon known as "interventionism" became very popular among some of the stronger countries. The premise centered around the idea that the more powerful nations could control everyone else in order to keep peace. The Quadruple Alliance—a treaty signed by Austria, Prussia, Russia, and Great Britain—formed under this philosophy of interventionism, as they were the most powerful contemporaries at the time. They believed in borders, traditions, organized religion, strong central power, and order in Europe. They thought they should be the ones who kept the peace. This concept worked quite well at first, but soon nationalism and romanticism began assuming greater public support. The Ottoman Empire was particularly opposed to such new philosophies as they inspired revolt in the people, who no longer felt tied to the country so much as the culture. Romanticism was a whole new way of life. People started to believe that humans could be perfected if they were properly taught and guided in a certain way of life. This would eventually evolve into nationalism, and the narrative became one of individual rights and freedoms, specifically from government. They would go on to say that people with similar emotions and thoughts should be identified as a singular culture. This philosophy effectively damaged the reputation and political prowess of the Quadruple Alliance as the borders between the leading countries became blurred and thus irrelevant. People began picking fights, and in the Crimean War, the alliance was ended, and nationalism took hold just in time for World War I.

1. The primary purpose of this passage is to
   - A. provide insight into a philosophical debate that leads to a key historical event.
   - B. highlight the flawed government philosophies that existed before World War I.
   - C. mourn the loss of a powerful philosophy.
   - D. point out the advantages of nationalism as a political philosophy.
   - E. identify the philosophy behind the Quadruple Alliance.

2. According to the passage, interventionism is best defined as a philosophy
   - A. centered around survival of the fittest.
   - B. predicated on the belief that the most powerful countries should control the rest.
   - C. advocating for one great race to rule them all.
   - D. centralizing power on one continent.
   - E. dependent upon the people's approval of those in power.

3. It can be inferred from the passage that
   - A. World War I was the result of a rise in nationalism in Europe.
   - B. World War I would not have happened had the Quadruple Alliance not disbanded.
   - C. the disbandment of the Quadruple Alliance was the direct result of World War I.
   - D. romanticism and nationalism evolved on a parallel timeline.
   - E. the Crimean War was the reason for World War I.

4. Based on the passage, the concept of nationalism included

A. strict borders.

B. patriotism to the country.

C. organized religion.

D. traditions.

E. individual freedoms.

5. Which of the following statements would the countries included in the Quadruple Alliance most likely agree with?

A. Tradition promotes individual rights and freedoms.

B. National culture is what makes a country powerful.

C. A lack of borders between countries lessens the power of each individual nation.

D. There is one superior nation to rule them all.

E. Nationalism is a philosophy that supports the ideals of the Quadruple Alliance.

Questions 6–10 are based on the following passage.

The early life of steamboat and railroad mogul Cornelius Vanderbilt was a long and hard-fought one. Born on Staten Island in 1794, Cornelius Vanderbilt was a hardworking child from the beginning. He was raised with an abundance of siblings, most of whom died before reaching adulthood. At the age of eleven, he stopped going to school and instead began working on his father's ferry boat in New York Harbor. This eventually led to him starting his very own ferry boat service by the time he was 16, for which he acquired a periauger that he named *The Swiftsure.* He ran this boat from Staten Island to Manhattan and back all day long and, because he was such an eager sailor, it didn't take long for his fellow captains to nickname him "The Commodore" in jest. When the War of 1812 arose, Cornelius was fortunate enough to receive a government contract to provide supplies to forts along the Hudson River. The war kick-started the expansion of his business, and Cornelius was soon able to acquire boats for freight and passenger services. He could now sail in Long Island and in the coastal trade from New England to Charleston, South Carolina. This was the turning point in his life, a life in which he would always be known as a hard worker, but perhaps not such a poor one.

6. The primary purpose of this passage is to

A. explain the success of Cornelius Vanderbilt.

B. inform about a famous historical figure.

C. inspire readers to work hard like Cornelius Vanderbilt.

D. describe the early life of the famous American success story, Cornelius Vanderbilt.

E. clear up common misconceptions about the life of Cornelius Vanderbilt.

7. Which of the following statements is best supported by this passage?

A. Cornelius Vanderbilt was handed success from a young age.

B. Cornelius Vanderbilt was a sailor.

C. Cornelius Vanderbilt had aspirations to become a mogul.

D. Cornelius Vanderbilt was born poor.

E. Cornelius Vanderbilt was contracted into the military.

8. According to this passage, Cornelius Vanderbilt was

A. born rich.

B. an orphan.

C. an entrepreneur at 16.

D. denied the ability to work on a ferry.

E. a Commodore.

9. Which of the following is an accurate and descriptive title for the passage?
   A. The Early Life of Cornelius Vanderbilt
   B. Cornelius Vanderbilt: The Man Behind the Mogul
   C. Rags to Riches: The Story of Cornelius Vanderbilt
   D. The Ferry Story
   E. The Dawn of Ferry Travel

10. Based on the text, a *periauger* refers to a
   A. type of passenger boat.
   B. sailboat.
   C. tugboat.
   D. freight boat.
   E. steamship.

NOTES

ANSWER KEY AND EXPLANATIONS

1. A	3. A	5. C	7. B	9. A
2. B	4. E	6. D	8. C	10. A

1. **The correct answer is A.** The primary purpose of the passage is to discuss three different political philosophies that each, in and of themselves, led to the beginning of World War I. Choice B is incorrect because it is only a facet of the primary purpose of the passage. The passage does not mourn the loss of any of the philosophies listed (choice C). It also does not highlight any advantages to nationalism (choice D). The passage does not only highlight the philosophy behind the Quadruple Alliance but two other philosophies as well (choice E).

2. **The correct answer is B.** The exact definition of *interventionism* given is "the idea that the more powerful nations could control everyone else in order to keep peace." The other choices are incorrect because they were not the given definition of *interventionism.*

3. **The correct answer is A.** The only given piece of information is that the rise of nationalism in Europe, as derived from the other two philosophies, was what led to World War I. Choices B and C are incorrect because the Quadruple Alliance disbanded before World War I. Romanticism evolved before nationalism, so choice D is also incorrect. The reason for World War I was the rise in nationalism, not the Crimean War (choice E).

4. **The correct answer is E.** Individual freedoms are specifically defined as a narrative stemming from nationalism. Choices A, B, C, and D are all components of interventionism.

5. **The correct answer is C.** The Quadruple Alliance subscribed to interventionism, which stands for a firm border, and so they would be likely to agree with the statement that weaker borders decrease the power of each individual nation. All of the other choices are incorrect because they do not follow the philosophy of interventionism.

6. **The correct answer is D.** The passage is a purely historical account of a famous American success story. The passage only details the early life of Vanderbilt and not his later successes (choice A). Vanderbilt being a famous figure (choice B) is only one facet of the passage. Choice C is incorrect because it is not meant to inspire as much as inform. There are no common misconceptions about the life of Cornelius Vanderbilt given in the passage (choice E).

7. **The correct answer is B.** Cornelius Vanderbilt, as a sailor of ferry boats, was a sailor at his core. Vanderbilt worked hard for any success he achieved at a young age (choice A). The passage never stated that Cornelius had aspirations to become a mogul (choice C). Choice D is incorrect because the passage never states that Cornelius was impoverished and that his father owned a ferry company. Cornelius was not contracted into the military, just given a contract by the military (choice E).

8. **The correct answer is C.** Cornelius Vanderbilt started his own business at 16. The other choices are incorrect because they do not describe Cornelius Vanderbilt.

9. **The correct answer is A.** The passage chiefly describes the early life of Cornelius Vanderbilt with very little bias or intention. The passage did not describe Cornelius Vanderbilt as a person (choices B and C), just his early life. The passage is not about ferries (choices D and E).

10. **The correct answer is A.** The text states that he started his own ferry service, which would require a passenger boat. Sailboats (choice B) were not conducive for a ferry service. Tugboats (choice C) and freight boats (choice D) are both boats used for alternate transport, such as waste or supplies. There is not enough information in the passage to clearly define a periauger as a steamship (choice E), only as a type of passenger boat.

SUMMING IT UP

- The Reading Comprehension subtest of the AFOQT and OAR assesses your ability to read and retain information.
- The AFOQT gives you 22 minutes to answer 25 questions with five passages and 4-6 questions per passage.
- The OAR gives you 30 minutes for 20 questions on the paper format or a variable number of questions in the CAT format.
- To improve performance, remember to actively read, strategically work through questions, and be certain about your answers.
- There are five types of questions typically found in a reading comprehension exam:

1. Primary Purpose
    - What is the primary purpose of the passage? What is it about?
    - Look for terms like *advocate, discuss*, or *inform* at the beginning of the answer choices.
    - Pay attention to syntax in both the question and the answer choices.
2. Applied Meaning
    - What is the applied meaning of a term or phrase? What does the word or phrase mean?

- Look for terms like *most likely means* and *most likely uses the word/phrase.*
- Read the sentence(s) around the word or phrase in question to help understand the context.

3. Statement Agreements and Inferences
   - Would the author (or character, if a work of fiction) agree with a statement about the passage?
   - Understanding the purpose of the passage is key in answering Statement Agreement questions correctly.
4. Lists
   - Does an item belong to a list of items or concepts from the passage?
   - Look for groups of objects, events, names, ideas, etc.
5. Supportive Statements
   - Is a given statement supported by the passage?
   - Look for questions like "Which of the following statements is/is NOT supported?"
   - Answers to Supportive Statement questions rely on syntax, or how the words are used in the question.

SITUATIONAL JUDGMENT

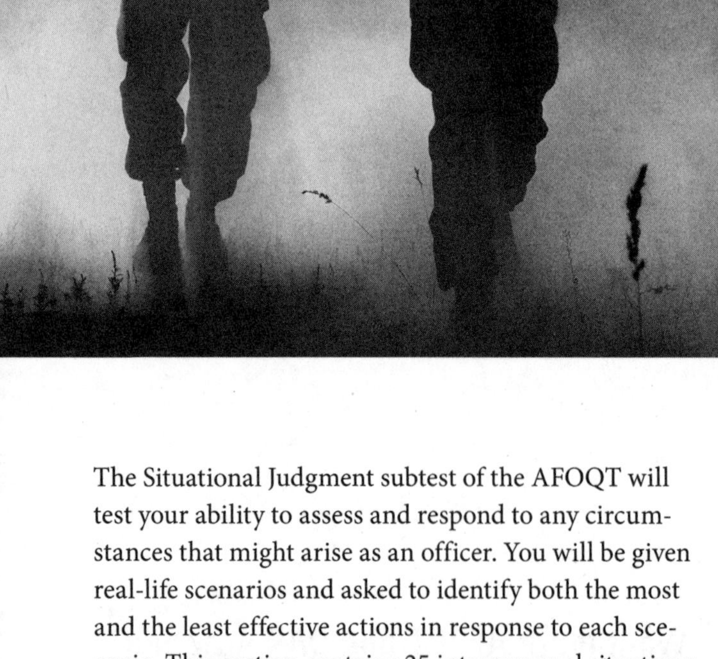

OVERVIEW

- **What Are the Core Competencies?**
- **Response Analysis**
- **Sample Situation**
- **Mini-Quiz: Situational Judgment**
- **Answer Key and Explanations**
- **Summing It Up**

The Situational Judgment subtest of the AFOQT will test your ability to assess and respond to any circumstances that might arise as an officer. You will be given real-life scenarios and asked to identify both the most and the least effective actions in response to each scenario. This section contains 25 interpersonal situations with two questions per situation, giving you a total of 50 questions to answer within 35 minutes.

In this chapter, you'll learn more about the core competencies expected of an officer. Your main objective is to understand what the application of those traits will look like in different situations and anticipate similar scenarios you might encounter on the subtest.

9

WHAT ARE THE CORE COMPETENCIES?

The six core competencies represent the concepts and ideals to which all officers should aspire as part of their professional development. They represent the professional ethics every officer should develop as a means of guiding the process of effective leadership and decision-making. In many of the situations that officers may face in their careers, several of these core competencies may apply. For this subtest of the AFOQT, each scenario will fall under a primary core competency. To answer appropriately, you will need to understand the core competency addressed in each situation and then select the action that best represents that core competency.

Integrity and Professionalism

Integrity is adherence to a code of morals and ethics. For members of the military, the ethics of honor, honesty, responsibility, and morality form the backbone of what it means to serve with integrity. These ethics help guide your decision-making process. Does the action taken in response to this situation represent the moral code upheld by an officer? Honesty—widely considered to be the best policy—is probably the most dominant ethic.

Professionalism goes beyond getting to work on time. Professionalism is acting with the proper code of conduct, attitude, or behavior expected within a professional work environment. This could range from wearing your uniform properly to how you conduct yourself when placed in stressful situations. Professionalism is most often reflected in how an officer goes through their workday—for example, being on time and prepared for scheduled activities and acting in a selfless manner. This behavior is directly associated with integrity, as both include being mindful of how any actions taken might be rooted in bias or a conflict of interest.

Leadership

Leadership is the ability to lead others by example rather than by rank or position. Even among peers, be it team leaders or team members, leadership means being cognizant of the core competencies and applying them to the best of your ability in such a way that benefits the team as a whole. It is being able to identify a problem and then take the necessary steps to solve it.

When analyzing situations, assume that leadership is responding in a way that benefits the greatest number of people possible. Do not make the mistake of assuming that leadership is taking control of your peers in the best way that you see fit. Leadership will often present itself in the form of taking responsibility for your actions, overcoming peer pressure, guiding lower-ranked officers, and setting an example for those in your same rank.

Resource Management

Resource management is the allocation of money, materials, personnel, and other assets that must be applied to a team or job in a way that maximizes the efficiency of work being done. Oftentimes, this skill will present itself in the form of a team that must be assembled or a job that must be completed. When analyzing such situations, be conscious of the individuals associated with the task and what job is required of them. The best way to go about managing resources is to consider the job first and foremost, then the person. Consider whether this person is going to effectively complete the job given to them, when it is given to them, and whether they will need guidance.

Resource management also applies to personal organization. Timetables, work schedules, and the general organization of your own personal resources will allow you to maximize your own efficiency. Use the resources at your disposal, whether that is your own skill or the expertise of others. Resource management also means knowing when to tap into available resources in order to maximize efficiency and avoid waste. This includes when to ask others for assistance or advice; don't hesitate to reach out to others when you need help.

Communication

Arguably one of the most important of the core competencies, communication is a necessary tool when working in any professional environment. It plays a key role in conflict resolution between yourself and fellow officers, between yourself and your superiors, and between yourself and those under your command. Communication skills can be applied in a number of different scenarios, but sometimes miscommunication can still result.

Miscommunication happens when there is a disconnect between what one person believes was communicated and what was truly communicated. This will often occur between a number of different parties:

- Officers of different backgrounds
- Superior officers and their junior officers
- Different teams

When there is a perceived miscommunication between officers, integrity and professionalism must once again be applied to ensure that further communication remains congenial and honest without heightening conflicts. Without exercising proper communication skills, misunderstandings can quickly turn into disagreements. In order to communicate effectively and resolve any brewing hostilities, it is best to acknowledge the differences as strengths instead of weaknesses and actively listen to the other person first before assuming their position or point of view is wrong. Active listening means paying attention to what is being communicated, asking clarifying questions, recapping to ensure the message is clear, and most importantly *not formulating your response* until after the other person is done making their statement. This goes back to the competency of integrity and professionalism and acting without bias or conflict of interest.

Another common way in which communication skills can be best applied is within situations of perceived conflict that do not involve you. Perception is not always truth, and when perceiving conflict from the outside, it is best to first ask a participating party whether or not your intervention is needed. Communication is only necessary when you are involved in the conflict. If you are not a participating party, then be respectful of other people's affairs.

Innovation

Innovation does not necessarily mean invention. It simply means taking action, applying a new idea or method, and taking responsibility for it. Being innovative involves taking initiative and bringing new ideas to whatever task you are given. It involves thinking outside the box when problem-solving and completing any given task. This particular core competency is tricky because it is difficult to discern whether or not innovation is necessary in a given situation. Some procedures have been fine-tuned over years. If there is a method that works, there may not be an opportunity for innovation. However, if circumstances change, such as when a new piece of equipment is introduced, take the initiative and formulate new ideas for how to complete the mission.

Mentoring

As an officer, you will have many opportunities to serve as a mentor to less experienced officers, enlisted, and members of your own team. This is a significant responsibility that requires use of all core competencies. Mentorship requires:

- honesty and integrity while maintaining professionalism.
- leadership and setting a good example for those you are mentoring.
- strong communication skills and the ability to pass on knowledge effectively.
- time management and organization of your schedule.
- taking initiative and being innovative with teaching methods.

Do not assume that mentorship involves leaving the mentee to learn on their own, as they aren't going to learn as effectively or efficiently without another officer's guidance. However, mentorship does include knowing when to step away.

Mentorship also describes your role as the mentee to a mentor, whether that's an officer, senior enlisted, or a member of your team. Being open to learning how tasks are completed can make the difference between a mediocre performance review and a stellar one.

RESPONSE ANALYSIS

On the AFOQT, you must be familiar with the core competencies in order to identify both the most and least effective responses. The most effective response will apply the core competencies in a way that is appropriate to the given scenario. In order to discern what the least effective response might be, you must consider one question:

What course of action will make the problem worse?

The least effective course of action can take a number of different forms, including the following:

- Ignoring the problem
- Escalating conflict
- Getting involved where you are not welcome
- Acting without integrity
- Making the same mistake again

Depending upon the situation that presents itself, any one of the listed actions could be the least effective action taken. For example, if it's a matter of miscommunication that has resulted in conflict, the least effective action would be to ignore the problem entirely and not take the steps to resolve the conflict. Another example would be a situation in which you have been reprimanded for making a mistake. The least effective response would be to make that same mistake again.

SAMPLE SITUATION

Let's look at how a sample question would appear on the actual exam:

EXAMPLE:

One of your subordinates has been noticeably aggressive and rude to members of your own team lately. When you first ask him about it and discuss the situation, he apologizes and assures you that he will try to remedy this behavior. Quite some time later, another team leader comes to you and expresses concerns regarding that same officer and his behavior toward members of his own team.

Possible Actions:

A. Ask for the names of the officers that reported this, have them discuss the situation with you personally, and then bring in the offending officer.

B. Write up the offending officer yet again and let him know that this is the last time you should hear about this.

C. Ignore these concerns as you have already discussed the situation with the offending officer, and he has assured you that he will change his behavior.

D. Ask the offending officer first if he knows anything about this and then go from there.

E. Tell the team leader that he's wrong as you have already had this discussion with your officer and you trust him.

1. Select the MOST EFFECTIVE action (A–E) in response to the situation.
2. Select the LEAST EFFECTIVE action (A–E) in response to the situation.

REMINDER: Each scenario will ask the same two questions.

Let's analyze how to approach each question using the information found in this chapter.

Select the MOST EFFECTIVE action (A–E) in response to the situation.

Step 1: Identify the problem.

In this particular scenario, there are four parties involved: you, your aggressive subordinate, the team leader, and the members of the team that reported the behavior. It is a question of communication, integrity, and leadership. The most effective response ensures that all information is known before deciding on a course of action.

Step 2: Use the core competencies.

EXPLANATION: The correct answer is A.

Communication is the core competency most applicable in this case. There are three other parties involved and yet you have only heard from one. The only choice that involves speaking with the other two parties is choice A.

Select the LEAST EFFECTIVE action (A–E) in response to the situation.

Step 1: Identify the problem.

The problem is the same. There are reports of aggressive behavior, and you have only heard from one of the parties involved.

Step 2: Determine how the problem can be made worse.

EXPLANATION: The correct answer is E.

The least effective action is no action. Both options C and E involve ignoring the problem, but only one involves offending a fellow team leader. This not only disregards the problem but also makes it worse.

Now that we have reviewed the layout and the core competencies, test yourself to assess your understanding.

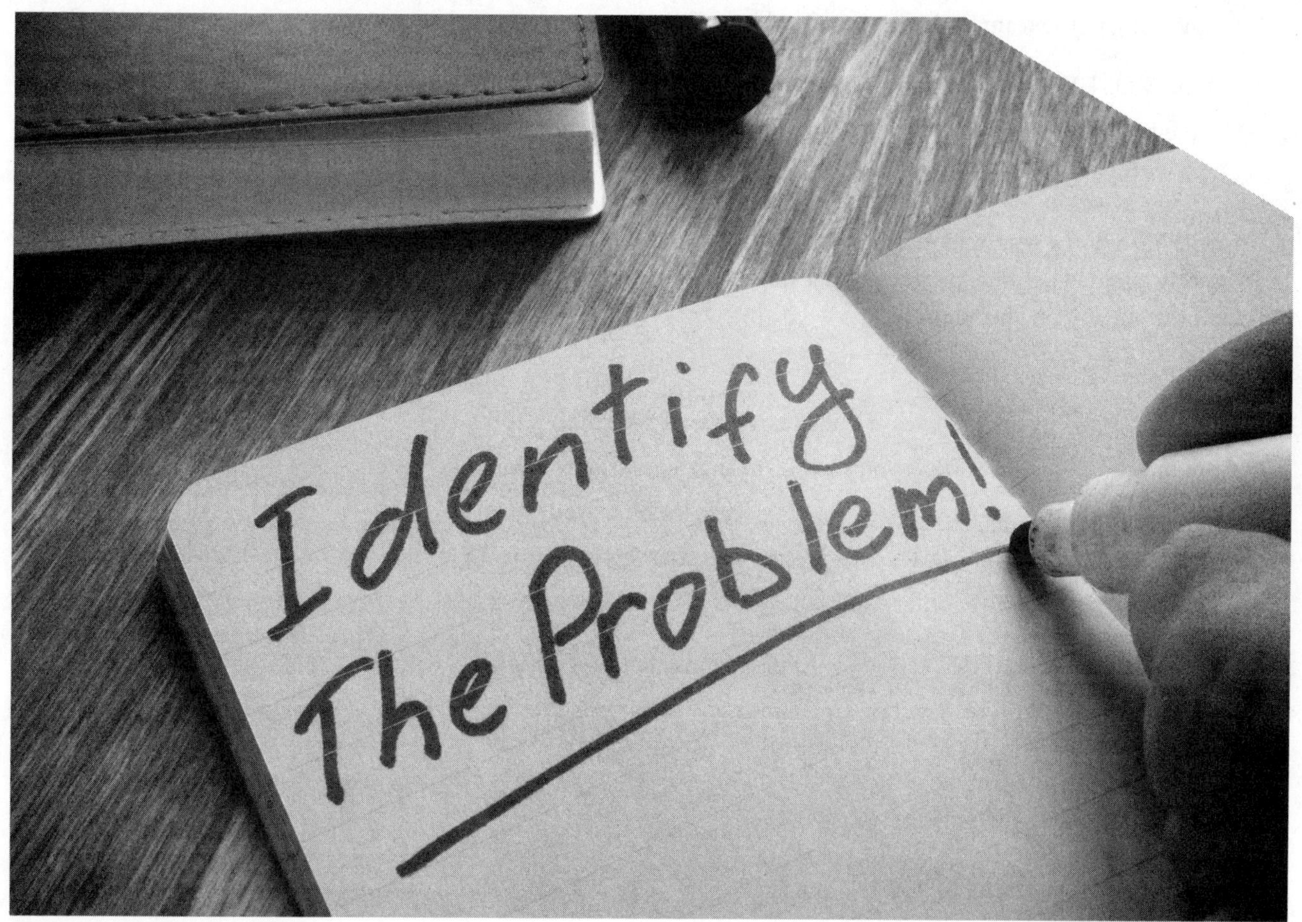

MINI-QUIZ: SITUATIONAL JUDGMENT

Directions: This part of the test measures your ability to clearly and efficiently judge interpersonal situations similar to those you may experience as an officer. For each situation, you must respond to two questions. First, select which one of the five actions listed is the MOST EFFECTIVE action in response to the situation. Second, choose which one of the five actions listed is the LEAST EFFECTIVE action in response to the situation.

Other officers on your team have been making derogatory comments about your team leader. They never make these comments in front of the team leader, but they speak about it openly in front of the other members of your team. No one else has come forward to tell the team leader about the behavior of the other officers or the derogatory comments.

Possible Actions:

A. Defend the team leader when the comments happen but do nothing to tell him.

B. Write an anonymous letter to the team leader explaining the situation and asking that he act immediately.

C. Tell the officers that their comments are unappreciated and will be reported if they don't stop.

D. Immediately report the comments to the team leader so that the officers responsible will be punished.

E. Say nothing to the team leader or the offending officers.

1. Select the MOST EFFECTIVE action (A–E) in response to the situation.
2. Select the LEAST EFFECTIVE action (A–E) in response to the situation.

You've been doing research on a new strategy for your team to approach their projects. Your team leader has recently adopted a different strategy that works just fine. You don't know if your strategy would be better than the current one being used.

Possible Actions:

A. Offer your strategy up to the team leader as a possible alternative.

B. Convince the rest of the officers on your team that your strategy would be better.

C. Say nothing about your new strategy to your team leader or your team.

D. Ask another member of your team to present this strategy to your team leader.

E. Offer the strategy up to another team.

3. Select the MOST EFFECTIVE action (A–E) in response to the situation.
4. Select the LEAST EFFECTIVE action (A–E) in response to the situation.

You are responsible for organizing a team to work on a new project that you will be leading. There are only a certain number of officers allowed on your team to stretch between multiple positions. These officers are not specialized but neither are the positions. However, the amount of work that needs to be done is not proportionate with the number of officers on the team.

Possible Actions:

A. Request for more people to be placed on your team.
B. Assume most of the work for yourself and give the rest of your team an equal amount of work.
C. Have each officer complete only one task at a time and disregard the leftover tasks.
D. Assign team members multiple positions so that the work itself is evenly dispersed.
E. Give most of the work to your officers and supervise their work as needed.

5. Select the MOST EFFECTIVE action (A–E) in response to the situation.
6. Select the LEAST EFFECTIVE action (A–E) in response to the situation.

A fellow officer has been cutting corners during preflight safety checks, reviewing the checklist briefly without ensuring every box is checked and accounted for. During your last flight together, there was a problem with the landing gear, but it resolved itself before the landing gear was needed. You are hesitant about flying with that pilot again.

Possible Actions:

A. Be more diligent in your observations to see if this behavior continues.
B. Discuss your concerns with your commanding officer.
C. Bring your safety concerns to the fellow officer and refuse to fly with them if safety checks are not done properly moving forward.
D. Ensure that you do all of the preflight safety checks moving forward.
E. Report the safety concern to the authorities, highlighting the landing gear incident as an example.

7. Select the MOST EFFECTIVE action (A–E) in response to the situation.
8. Select the LEAST EFFECTIVE action (A–E) in response to the situation.

You overhear a conversation between two commanding officers in which they are discussing their disdain for the current government leadership. They express great regret in remaining in the Air Force under the new administration. They are even making suggestions to refuse to fight should orders come down.

Possible Actions:

A. Ask a fellow officer for advice.

B. Report the conversation and your concerns to your own commanding officer.

C. Ask the commanding officers about their military background to see if they will repeat their conversation.

D. Brush the conversation off as gossip and ignore it.

E. Confront the commanding officers and share your concerns.

9. Select the MOST EFFECTIVE action (A–E) in response to the situation.

10. Select the LEAST EFFECTIVE action (A–E) in response to the situation.

Your commanding officer has just assigned you an independent project to work on for the next month. This project requires an extraordinary amount of organization and improvement upon skills you have yet to exercise. There are no other people working on this project with you, and you have never been well-versed in organization and time management.

Possible Actions:

A. Ask your commanding officer to assign the project to someone else.

B. Make a schedule and have a fellow officer hold you accountable to it.

C. Ask a fellow officer to do some of the work with you.

D. Do a little every day without a concrete plan but with work hours carved out each day.

E. Ask for some clarity and guidance from your commanding officer.

11. Select the MOST EFFECTIVE action (A–E) in response to the situation.

12. Select the LEAST EFFECTIVE action (A–E) in response to the situation.

Your commanding officer has been assigning you additional tasks that are not morally or ethically objectionable but are nonetheless outside of your normal assignments. No one else in your squadron has been required to do such tasks, and it seems as if this commanding officer is specifically targeting you. As a junior officer, you are not of the authority to refuse such tasks, but the commanding officer has made his disdain for you quite clear.

Possible Actions:

A. Blatantly refuse to follow any more orders from this commanding officer.

B. Privately discuss any miscommunication and continue to follow orders.

C. Ask another member of your squadron to confront the commanding officer for you.

D. Discuss your frustration about the commanding officer with other members of your squadron.

E. Go to a superior officer and report the commanding officer's behavior toward you.

13. Select the MOST EFFECTIVE action (A–E) in response to the situation.

14. Select the LEAST EFFECTIVE action (A–E) in response to the situation.

As a new lieutenant, you are given authority over a number of enlisted soldiers that have been in the military for years. These enlisted are more knowledgeable on procedures, everyday tasks, and the flight exercises required of them than you are. You are in a position of authority and have been ranked above them, but their experience is more extensive than your own. They are willing to give you advice.

Possible Actions:

A. Immediately assert your authority over the enlisted soldiers by disregarding their advice.

B. Let the enlisted give you guidance before you make any decisions.

C. Try not to spend as much time with the enlisted so they respect you as an authority figure.

D. Converse with the enlisted on your willingness to take advice and ask for their respect.

E. Ask a superior officer to give orders before you are ready to take over an authority position.

15. Select the MOST EFFECTIVE action (A–E) in response to the situation.

16. Select the LEAST EFFECTIVE action (A–E) in response to the situation.

You have been assigned to work with another officer in your flight on an important project. You have not had the opportunity to work together or be around each other in social circumstances. After the first day on the project, you realize that you and the other officer have vastly different personalities that contradict each other. You also have trouble effectively communicating with each other.

Possible Actions:

A. Ask for a different partner to work with or opt out of the project.

B. Work on the project together and expect communication to develop from there.

C. Discuss your differences beforehand and express a shared desire to do well on the project.

D. Ask a mutual friend to work on the project with you as a liaison.

E. Let the other officer finish the project as you will be of no help with a lack of communication.

17. Select the MOST EFFECTIVE action (A–E) in response to the situation.

18. Select the LEAST EFFECTIVE action (A–E) in response to the situation.

Another officer in your flight has been making lewd and derogatory comments toward you and others around you. These comments are suggestive and make you feel unsafe in the presence of this officer. Some other officers in your flight write these comments off as offhand jokes or sarcasm.

Possible Actions:

A. Confront the officer and ask him to cease making such comments.

B. Let the comments continue as long as they are not intended with malice.

C. Ask another member of your flight to confront the offending officer and ask him to cease his comments.

D. Report the behavior to a superior officer as sexual harassment.

E. Ask to be transferred to another flight in the event that these comments continue.

19. Select the MOST EFFECTIVE action (A–E) in response to the situation.

20. Select the LEAST EFFECTIVE action (A–E) in response to the situation.

ANSWER KEY AND EXPLANATIONS

1. C	5. D	9. B	13. B	17. C
2. E	6. C	10. D	14. A	18. E
3. A	7. C	11. B	15. D	19. D
4. B	8. A	12. C	16. A	20. B

1. **The correct answer is C.** The core competency in this situation is Integrity and Professionalism. Warn the offending officers before taking any immediate action. If they have not been warned against their actions yet, then it is your responsibility. Lead by example.
2. **The correct answer is E.** It is your professional responsibility to speak up. Saying nothing condones the behavior. The officers in question will continue to make derogatory comments. Take a stand for what you know is right.
3. **The correct answer is A.** The core competency in this situation is Innovation. Take initiative and offer up new ideas. If your ideas are used, great; if not, then you advocated for yourself.
4. **The correct answer is B.** Being in the military means you are required to follow the legal orders of your commanding officer, even if you think your idea presents a better way to complete the assigned tasks.
5. **The correct answer is D.** The core competency in this situation is Resource Management. You are called on to effectively manage your team members. If the tasks aren't specialized, then more than one person can do them at a time. Efficiently organize your team.
6. **The correct answer is C.** Disregarding tasks given to you defeats the point of the team. The work is not going to be efficiently completed if only one person is assigned to each task. Use your resources wisely.
7. **The correct answer is C.** The core competency in this situation is Integrity and Professionalism. It is unprofessional to allow lax work to continue. Safety is paramount. However, the officer may not be aware that they have become lax. It is important to bring your concerns directly to this officer. In addition, refusing to fly until the lax behavior is changed sends a clear signal that you value safety as a top priority.
8. **The correct answer is A.** Safety should never be overlooked. It is your duty as a copilot to ensure that every flight is safe. If you sit back and say nothing, lives may be in jeopardy.
9. **The correct answer is B.** The core competency in this situation is Integrity and Professionalism. Such acts violate military code and should be reported immediately. The officers' threatened actions could jeopardize the safety and security of other officers and the country.
10. **The correct answer is D.** Ignoring such conversation and a potential refusal to fight could put both those officers and those under their command in an unsafe position.
11. **The correct answer is B.** The core competency in this situation is Resource Management. By creating and adhering to a schedule, you are effectively managing your most valuable resource: your time. By having another officer hold you accountable, you are giving yourself additional resources in the form of advice and suggestions on how to effectively complete the project.
12. **The correct answer is C.** Never pass off someone else's work as your own. If you are assigned an independent task, it is your job to finish it independently and to the best of your own ability. An integrity-driven officer is reflective of an integrity-driven team.

13. **The correct answer is B.** The core competency in this situation is Communication. If you believe you are being singled out, you need to privately discuss your concerns with your commanding officer. Your commander might have reasons for assigning these additional tasks to you and effectively communicating with them is the best way to learn why you are being given the extra work.
14. **The correct answer is A.** The worst response that you could have toward a commanding officer is to blatantly disobey orders and disrespect their authority. Never disregard the orders given by superiors, regardless of whether or not you agree with them (barring any moral or ethical objections).
15. **The correct answer is D.** The core competency in this situation is Mentoring. A leader is willing to take advice from those with more expertise than themselves. Be open about your newness and willingness to learn, and you will earn the respect of those under your command.
16. **The correct answer is A.** A good leader looks to those with more experience. Be willing to listen and to take advice, but more importantly, make sure that those to whom you are giving orders trust your decisions and your judgment. Those under your command won't listen to or trust you if you don't listen to or trust them.
17. **The correct answer is C.** The core competency in this situation is Communication. Acknowledge any miscommunications or personal differences between you and your peers. No professional relationship is ever established with a lack of communication, so in order to combat that, communicate.
18. **The correct answer is E.** If you are responsible for part of a project, do your part. Running away from uncomfortable situations only hurts both parties more. As a leader and teammate, be willing to work through disagreements or miscommunication, and never pass off another's work as your own.
19. **The correct answer is D.** If another officer is making suggestive or lewd comments to you or about you that make you feel unsafe, that is textbook sexual harassment. Report it immediately, as such behavior is not tolerated in the military under any circumstances.
20. **The correct answer is B.** Never let sexual harassment continue, especially if you feel unsafe. If this behavior is directed toward other members of your flight, it is your responsibility to report it if they do not. Always be willing to speak up.

SUMMING IT UP

- The Situational Judgment section of the AFOQT is designed to test your ability to act appropriately in a given situation.
- You will be given 25 interpersonal situations with two questions each.
- You will have 35 minutes to answer 50 questions.
- You will use the six core competencies to guide your answers:
    - Integrity and Professionalism
    - Leadership
    - Resource Management
    - Communication
    - Innovation
    - Mentoring
- Questions will center on your understanding of these core competencies and your ability to apply them as you interpret each given situation and identify the most and least effective responses.

SELF-DESCRIPTION INVENTORY

OVERVIEW

The Self-Description Inventory subtest of the AFOQT measures your personal attitudes and styles—that is, your behavioral patterns and preferences across situations—to help find the "best fit" training and career path for each officer. You will have 45 minutes to answer 240 questions. To complete all of the questions within the time limit, you must answer approximately 6 questions every minute. Fortunately, there are no right or wrong answers.

The subtest is a personality assessment known as **the NEO Personality Inventory—Revised (NEO PI-R)**. It is similar to the Situational Judgment subtest in that it is a separately assessed category. However, unlike other subtests and categories, the output generates an array of information, none of which is shared with you as a test taker. The Air Force conducted tests of the NEO PI-R between 1994 and 2011, which resulted in the inclusion of the personality measure in the 2014 AFOQT revision. Results from Air Force research trials indicated personality trait differences between military officers and military aviators relative to the general population.

While standard scoring metrics are used in officer candidacy and rated career selection, the NEO PI-R can be used as an additional consideration for both. Because you are providing information that may be used in your selection, it is important for you to understand the assessment. In addition, exploratory studies have been conducted relative to personality differences between a general population of junior officers and senior command track officers. The future potential use of information you provide may have long-term implications not currently incorporated in career progression considerations.

THE NEO PI-R

The NEO PI-R is a psychological assessment that measures the five major personality domains: **Neuroticism**, **Extraversion**, **Openness to Experience**, **Agreeableness**, and **Conscientiousness**. Each domain is further defined by six subgroups. Each subgroup is measured from an assortment of questions using a 5-point Likert scale ranging from "Strongly Disagree" to "Strongly Agree."

1.	Easily makes friends	Strongly Disagree	Disagree	Neither Agree nor Disagree	Agree	Strongly Agree
		❍	❍	❍	❍	❍

Likert scale example. Figure depicts the type of question used in personality assessments.

The USAF study results indicated that pilots have dramatically higher Extraversion, Openness to Experience, and Conscientiousness, and lower Neuroticism and Agreeableness than the general population. Female pilots scored even higher on Extraversion and Openness to Experience relative to women in the general population. Additionally, differences were found between fighter and bomber pilots, and airlift and tanker pilots, all of which could also be used for additional track selection considerations. The following table details the personality differences the USAF found between pilots and the general population.

USAF FINDINGS OF PILOTS VS. THE GENERAL US POPULATION

Neuroticism (-)	Extraversion (+)	Openness to Experience (+)	Agreeableness (-)	Conscientiousness (+)
Anxiety (-)	Warmth (+)	Fantasy (+)	Trust (0)	Competence (+)
Angry Hostility (-)	Gregariousness (+)	Aesthetics (-)	Straightforwardness (-)	Order (0)
Depression (-)	Assertiveness (+)	Feelings (0)	Altruism (0)	Dutifulness (+)
Self-Consciousness (-)	Activity (+)	Action (0)	Compliance (+)	Achievement Striving (+)
Impulsiveness (-)	Excitement Seeking (+)	Ideas (+)	Modesty (-)	Self-Discipline (+)
Vulnerability (-)	Positive Emotions (-)	Values (-)	Tender-mindedness (-)	Deliberation (0)

Note: The symbols indicate USAF pilots scored (-) less than, (+) more than, and (0) about the same as the general US population.

PERSONALITY DOMAINS AND SUBGROUPS

The following pages describe each of the personality domains and subgroup categories of the NEO PI-R.

NEUROTICISM

Neuroticism is the degree to which a person wants to experience emotionally unstable behavior such as anger, sorrow, and fear. It has the following subgroups:

- **Anxiety:** The propensity to not control nervousness, apprehension, and dread.
- **Angry Hostility:** The inclination to project frustration, hatred, and bitterness.
- **Depression:** The predisposition to feelings of gloominess, misery, and desolation.
- **Self-Consciousness:** The degree of unassertiveness, timidness, reluctance, and group avoidance.
- **Impulsiveness:** A tendency for reckless behavior, carelessness, and thoughtlessness.
- **Vulnerability:** The degree of susceptibility to the effects of stress.

EXTRAVERSION

Extraversion is the extent of social situational enjoyment, excitement, and self-stimulation. It has the following subgroups:

- **Warmth:** Cordiality and kindness toward others.
- **Gregariousness:** The acceptability of companionship, fellowship, and comradeship.
- **Assertiveness:** The extent of resoluteness, decisiveness, and desire for purpose of action.
- **Activity:** The degree to which a person pursues liveliness and hustle in their life.
- **Excitement Seeking:** The extent a person is motivated by a sense of adventure and environmental engagement.
- **Positive Emotions:** A propensity for hopefulness, liveliness, cheerfulness, and joy.

OPENNESS TO EXPERIENCE

Openness to Experience is the degree of willingness to explore new innovative ideas or differing values. It has the following subgroups:

- **Fantasy:** The extent of broad-mindedness towards inventiveness, creativity, and ingenuity.
- **Aesthesis:** The appreciation of beauty, art, and detail.
- **Feelings:** The degree of emotional intelligence, or receptiveness, in recognizing feelings and emotions.
- **Actions:** A willingness for new experiences and responsibility.
- **Ideas:** The degree of creative, rational, and scholarly interest.
- **Values:** An ability to synthesize and formulate constructive criticism.

AGREEABLENESS

Agreeableness is a measure of the degree of sympathy toward others. It has the following subgroups:

- **Trust:** The extent of confidence in the sincere intentions of others.
- **Straightforwardness:** To what extent a person is outspoken and impartial.
- **Altruism:** The propensity to selflessness and benevolence for the welfare of others.
- **Compliance:** A behavior associated with an ability to conform to communal order.
- **Modesty:** A humility and unpretentiousness of achievement.
- **Tendermindedness:** The degree of compassion and empathy for others.

CONSCIENTIOUSNESS

Conscientiousness is the degree of behavioral tendency to plan and organize; it is also associated with self-discipline. It is divided into the following subgroups:

- **Competence:** The extent a person facilitates their own aptitude and effectiveness.
- **Order:** A behavior associated with a need to organize and plan outcomes.
- **Dutifulness:** The extent of self-accountability of obligations.
- **Achievement Striving:** The degree that a person exhibits a drive for personal accomplishment.
- **Self-Discipline:** The tendency to self-organize and complete a responsibility despite environmental distractions or boredom.
- **Deliberation:** A behavior of desiring planned outcomes.

NEO PI-R PRACTICE

The Pennsylvania State University (PSU) Department of Psychology has a free online test that is similar to the NEO PI-R and includes an informed consent form and an option to provide an unofficial name to promote privacy. The questions are not the same copyrighted material used in the NEO PI-R; however, they are close and are used to assess the same personality domains and subgroups within the five domains. Instead of 240 questions, the long test uses 300 questions, and the short version has 60 questions. The actual NEO PI-R test is copyrighted and controlled, inclusive of a USAF contract for use and application.

If you want practice taking a personality survey, take the PSU test to familiarize yourself with the types of questions you will see in the Self-Description Inventory subtest of the AFOQT and how your responses score.

WHY IT MATTERS

To understand the importance of the NEO PI-R and how this assessment can affect you, consider the following statement. It approximates the kinds of statements you'll see in the Self-Description Inventory subtest.

1. I prefer to fix mistakes right away rather than later on.

   A. Strongly Disagree

   B. Disagree

   C. Neither Agree nor Disagree

   D. Agree

   E. Strongly Agree

The use of the Myers-Briggs test to assess your personality in preparation for NEO PI-R is NOT recommended, as it is geared more toward civilian careers rather than military officer placement.

To learn more about the free PSU online test, visit the following website: **http://www.personal.psu.edu/~j5j/IPIP/.**

> Although a career as a military pilot of any sort can be desirable, both job satisfaction and job performance can suffer when someone does not have the right personality for the job.

When writing a report, if you fix typos immediately rather than later on, you'd likely agree with the statement and choose choice D or E as your answer. On the other hand, if you prefer to heavily revise, you would likely disagree with the statement and choose either choice A or B. If you think the choice is job dependent, you might answer with choice C. But why pick C? When you read the statement, you might have thought of some jobs that should be done correctly the first time, such as changing the oil in your car, while some tasks allow you to fix your mistakes later, like when writing an email.

While there are no right or wrong answers, it is important that you are honest with your answers. And while the strict time limit for the section encourages honest responses, you need to fully understand the potential consequences of misleading choices. Why? Here's a hypothetical situation to help explain:

> Dan Reynolds has wanted to be a fighter pilot since he was a child. Once he graduates from high school, he enrolls into the AFROTC program in college, where he has to take the AFOQT. After talking to his instructors, he senses that pilots, especially fighter pilots, are self-assured, aggressive, and a little rebellious. Dan realizes he doesn't have those character traits, at least not as much as he thinks he should. However, he's sure he can develop those traits in flight school. When Dan takes the AFOQT, he completes the Self-Description Inventory subtest with responses that indicate he's more aggressive, rebellious, and self-assured than he truly is.
>
> Dan learns that when he graduates from college, he'll go to flight school. After finishing at the top of his class in the initial flight training, he learns he has been selected to train on the F-22 Raptor. But when he arrives at the program, he discovers that the answers he gave for the subtest have placed him in a program with people he does not relate to. Ultimately, this impacts his performance, and Dan drops out of the program, dramatically altering his career in the Air Force.

This scenario is unlikely but still possible. Although a career as a military pilot of any sort can be desirable, both job satisfaction and job performance can suffer when someone does not have the right personality for the job. Had Dan been honest with his answers, he might have been placed into a program that better suited his temperament rather than wasting time, energy, and resources on a path better traveled by someone else.

SUMMING IT UP

- The Self-Description Inventory subtest is an assessment of your personality traits.
- You will have 45 minutes to answer 240 questions.
- The inventory measures five personality domains: neuroticism, extraversion, openness to experience, agreeableness, and conscientiousness.
- Unlike a normal multiple-choice test, there are no wrong answers; there are only inaccurate answers that do not reflect your personality traits.
- Be honest with your answers. The point of this assessment is to determine your personality traits and attitude according to the domains and subgroups to find the best fit career path. Remember, the Self-Description Inventory can affect consideration of your position.

FOUNDATIONS OF PHYSICAL SCIENCE

OVERVIEW

- **Measurements**
- **Physical Characteristics and Properties of Matter**
- **Force and Motion**
- **Energy**
- **Mini-Quiz: Foundations of Physical Science**
- **Answer Key and Explanations**
- **Summing It Up**

The Physical Science subtest is a relatively new addition to the AFOQT, replacing the general science subtest in 2015. It covers basic physical science often learned at the high school level. You will have 10 minutes to answer 20 questions. This chapter cover the basics of standard scientific measurements, matter, chemistry, energy, and physics to prepare you not only for the AFOQT's subtest but also for the application of these concepts in Chapter 12: Mechanical Comprehension. Prior to moving on to Chapter 12, be sure that you fully understand the concepts presented here. Because there are many areas of physical science that we are unable to cover, consider consulting additional resources in order to further your understanding of specific content areas as needed.

MEASUREMENTS

Measurements in physical science are completed using the International System of Units (SI), a globally accepted system of measurement. The International System of Units, also called the SI system, is simplistic in its design, using powers of 10 for all conversions. A *power of 10* is also referred to as an *order of magnitude*. You should strive to memorize the prefixes associated with each unit. To convert units, you multiply or divide by the correct multiple of ten to convert the unit. The following is a quick reference for the most used metric system prefixes in the physical sciences:

INTERNATIONAL SYSTEM OF UNITS

Prefix	Abbreviation	Power	Meaning
kilo	k	10^3	1,000
hecto	h	10^2	100
deca	da	10^1	10
Base Unit		10^0	1
deci	d	10^{-1}	0.1
centi	c	10^{-2}	0.01
milli	m	10^{-3}	0.001
micro	μ	10^{-6}	0.000001
nano	n	10^{-9}	0.000000001

Within the study of physical science, the SI system uses certain fundamental units of measurement called the physical standards. They are as follows:

BASE UNITS OF MEASUREMENT

Base Quantity	Name	Symbol
Time	Second	s
Mass	Kilogram	kg
Amount of Substance	Mole	mol
Length	Meter	m
Fluid	Liter	L
Temperature	Kelvin	K
Electricity	Ampere	amp

While most US-based systems have transitioned to the SI system, we may occasionally reference standard measurements, such as inches or feet, since these are still used in certain contexts. However, this guide will focus on the SI measurements.

Converting Units

To convert units, move the decimal point. If there is no decimal point, add one to the end of the number. When converting from a larger number prefix to a smaller prefix, move the decimal place to the RIGHT. When converting from a smaller prefix to a larger one, move the decimal place to the LEFT. The following are examples of each:

Convert 513 meters into decimeters.

A decimeter is one order of magnitude SMALLER than a meter, the base unit of measurement for distance. We will move the decimal place one spot to the right. Any empty spaces will be filled in with zeros.

513.0 m = 5,130 dm

Convert 57.3 milligrams into hectograms.

A hectogram is 5 orders of magnitude LARGER than a milligram. We will move the decimal place five spots to the left. Any empty spaces will be filled in with zeros.

57.3 mg = 0.000573 hg

PHYSICAL CHARACTERISTICS AND PROPERTIES OF MATTER

This section covers the physical characteristics and properties of matter, including states of matter, the building blocks of matter, and the chemical composition and properties of substances.

States of Matter

The three constant states of matter on earth are solid, liquid, and gas, though more exist but only under extreme conditions. Each of these states of matter consists of atoms formed by particles. The arrangement and movement of atoms arranged in molecules give each state of matter its unique properties. These properties allow us to predict how different states of matter interact with each other. The following list is an overview of the different types of matter and their properties.

- **Solids:** Of the three main states of matter, solids have the highest density of particles, meaning a large number of particles occupies a relatively small amount of space. This gives solids a definite volume and shape. The particles that constitute solids do not move about, though they do vibrate. Solids keep a consistent shape regardless of the container they are placed into.
- **Liquids:** Liquids have a consistent volume, but no specific shape. Instead, a liquid takes on the shape of the container containing it. For example, water in a glass takes on the shape of the glass, while water in a balloon takes on the shape of the balloon. Liquids have a high density of particles but are not as dense as solids. This lower density means there is more space between atoms, which allows liquids to flow. Compressing liquids requires a significant amount of pressure because the particles in a liquid are so close together and liquids keep the same volume.
- **Gases:** Gases have no consistent shape or volume. The density of atoms that make up a gas is low, so a gas can move freely unless it is in a container. The low density of atoms makes gases easier to compress. For example, a scuba tank contains air, or other gases, at pressure as high as 3,500 pounds per square inch (psi).

Changing States

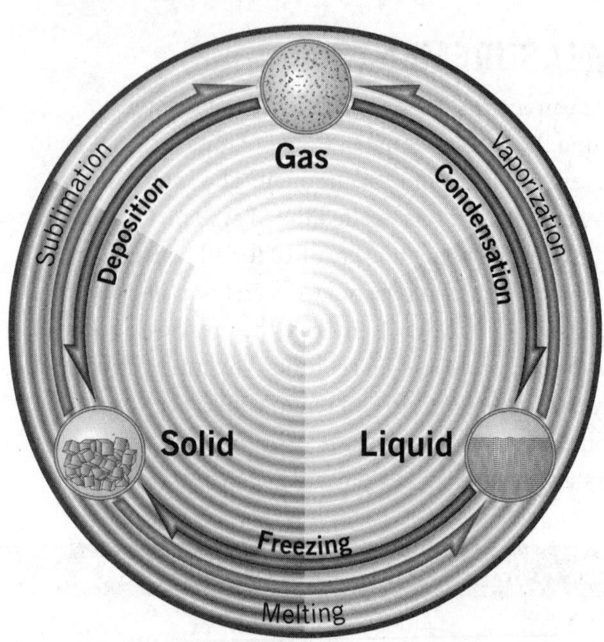

Matter can change from one state to another, even from solid to gas. This diagram highlights the terms used to identify shifts in matter from one state to another. The process by which each of these states of matter changes from one to the other is important to remember for both exams. The following is a simple chart to help you:

CHANGES IN MATTER		
Starting Matter	**Ending Matter**	**Term**
Liquid	Gas	Evaporation
Gas	Liquid	Condensation
Liquid	Solid	Freezing/Solidification
Solid	Liquid	Melting/Fusion
Gas	Solid	Deposition
Solid	Gas	Sublimation

Temperature

The process of changing from one state to the next is often dictated by temperature. Solids tend to exist in colder temperatures with an increase in energy causing a change in state from solid to liquid. As the temperature continues to rise, the liquid will turn into a gas. The freezing point, melting point, and boiling point all provide valuable information on what will cause matter of a pure substance to change state.

- **Freezing point:** the temperature at which a liquid changes into a solid.
- **Melting point:** the temperature at which a solid changes into a liquid.
- **Boiling point:** the temperature at which a liquid changes into gas.

It is important to note that these rules are specific to pure substances. When dealing with compounds and solutions, the chemical makeup of the substance may affect the way it changes states.

Atoms and Atomic Charges

All matter is made up of atoms, and atoms are made up of fundamental particles: electrons, neutrons, and protons.

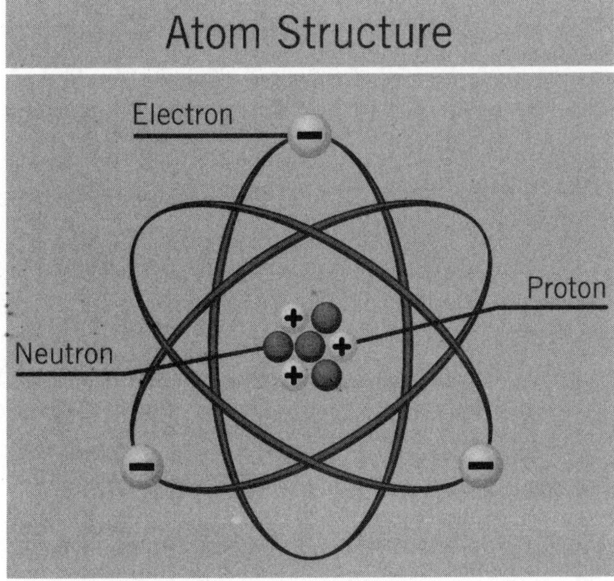

- **Electrons:** Electrons orbit around the nucleus, which is the center of an atom, in what is referred to as the electron cloud. They are negatively charged particles and can move from one atom to another. When an atom has more electrons than protons, the atom is negatively charged.
- **Neutrons:** Neutrons are found in the nucleus. They do not carry a charge and only affect the atom in terms of its mass.
- **Protons:** Protons are also found in the nucleus. They are positively charged particles, and when there are more protons than electrons, the atom is positively charged.

Elements and The Periodic Table

Atoms are the building blocks of the elements that make up every substance on earth. The Periodic Table organizes the elements and gives insight into their structure and composition. It functions as a reference tool that provides essential information about each known element, including its symbol, name, mass, atomic number, and more. Knowing how to read the periodic table and locate key information is necessary for understanding the properties of various elements and how elements interact under certain conditions and with other elements. The next page shows the periodic table in its complete format.

The table is set up very specifically, using atomic number and elemental state as a method of organization. First, the order of the elements is structured based on the atomic number of each element, starting from the top left corner and working both across and down, in order of increasing atomic number. There are a total of seven rows on the periodic table; the rows are called periods, which indicate the highest energy level that an element in that group occupies. As you proceed down the table, the energy level of the atom in an element increases. The vertical columns group elements according to similar properties. Elements can generally be categorized as metals and nonmetals, but several elements are considered transition metals, meaning they possess properties that fall between metals and nonmetals. Some versions of the periodic table will use color-coding to indicate other properties, such as an element's state of matter or whether an element is a metal, metalloid, or non-metal.

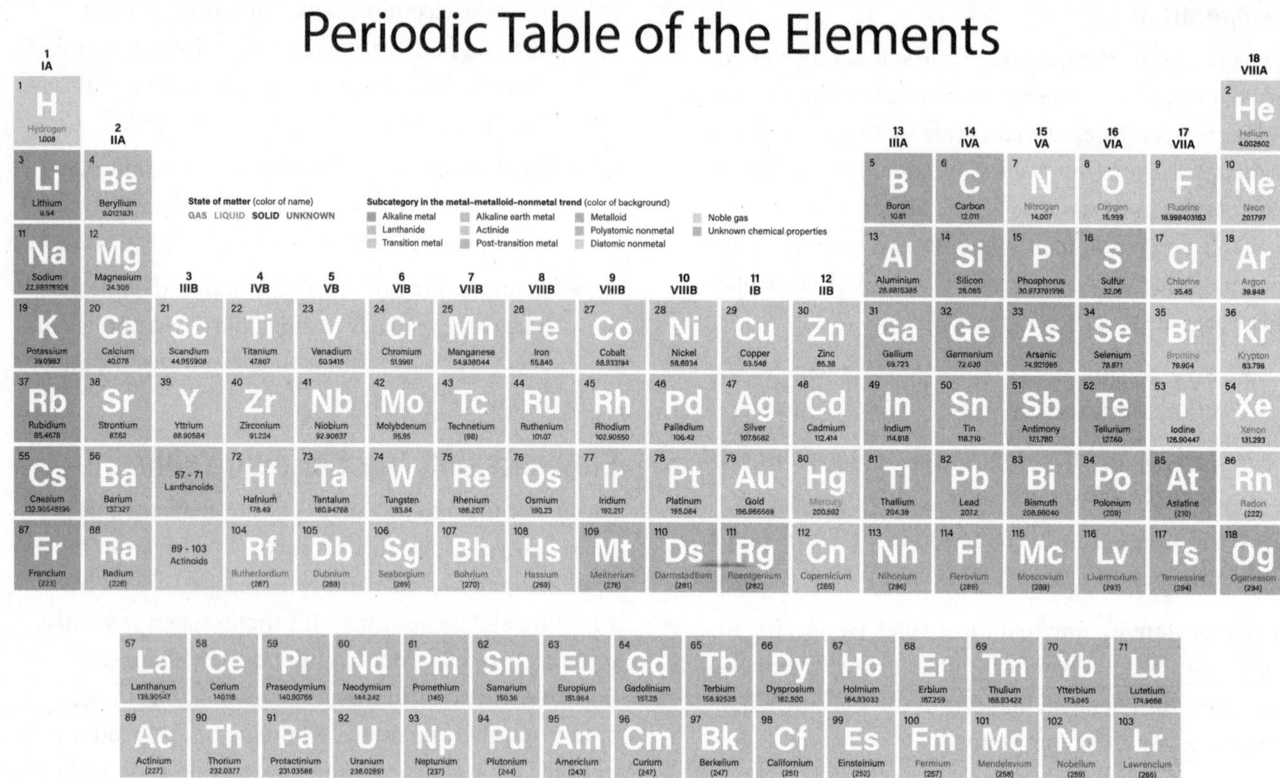

How to Read the Periodic Table

Each element has vital information about it housed within its block on the table. Below is an explanation using Hydrogen, the first element.

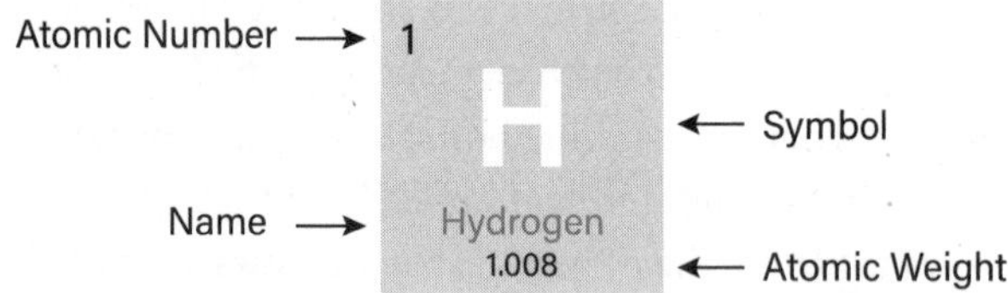

Using the illustration, let's discuss each component and what it means.

- **Atomic Number:** The atomic number is the number of protons in the nucleus of an atom. It is also the number of electrons in a neutral atom. (Note: Most atoms are neutral in their natural state.) The atomic number for hydrogen is 1. It has one proton and one electron.
- **Symbol:** This is a simple abbreviation of the element. The first letter is always capitalized, followed by one or two lowercase letters as needed. The symbol for hydrogen is H.
- **Name:** The name of the element is written directly below the symbol. In some versions of the periodic table, names of elements are color-coded to indicate the element's state of matter in its pure form.
- **Atomic Weight:** The atomic weight is another way to express the relative atomic mass of the element. This number is an average of atomic masses (approximately the number of protons plus neutrons in the atomic nucleus) for different isotopes of the element in question in a ratio to the atomic mass constant, a unit also called a dalton (one twelfth the mass of isotope carbon-12 at rest). The atomic weight of hydrogen is 1.008.

Additional information on electrons, protons, neutrons, and atoms are outside the scope of this chapter. As such, consider reviewing additional resources for more information to supplement your knowledge of these topics.

Ions and Isotopes

The periodic table displays elements and the makeup and property of each of them. However, we can take these elements and manipulate them by adding or removing electrons and neutrons. These adjustments alter the element beyond its pure form, thus creating either an ion or an isotope.

Ion

An ion results when an element either loses or gains electrons, thus creating a net electrical charge (this can be either positive or negative). Each element has a specific number of electrons. The one exception to this rule is hydrogen with an atomic number of 1, meaning it only has one electron. The loss of its electron automatically creates an ion.

The standard scientific notation for ions is $\textit{Element}^{\text{Charge}}$. Using this notation, a positively charged hydrogen ion would be written H^{1+}.

Isotope

An isotope is an atom of a chemical element that has a different number of neutrons than the standard number for that element. Isotopes of an element have different atomic masses but possess the same chemical properties.

The standard scientific notation for isotopes is $^{\text{Atomic mass}}\textbf{Element}$. Using this notation, a helium isotope with 2 protons and 1 neutron has an atomic mass of 3 and is written $^{3}\textbf{He}$.

It is possible to have an isotope that is also an ion. Let's use our original isotope to illustrate this.

If the original helium isotope $^{3}\textbf{He}$ lost 1 electron, it would be rewritten $^{3}\textbf{He}^{1+}$.

Reading from left to right, we have the new atomic mass (3), the element (helium), and the net electrical charge (positive 1).

Mixtures and Solutions

Now that we have a basic understanding of the elements and the periodic table, we can discuss all the different possibilities related to matter. The following image is a standard flow chart illustrating the various ways in which matter can be expressed.

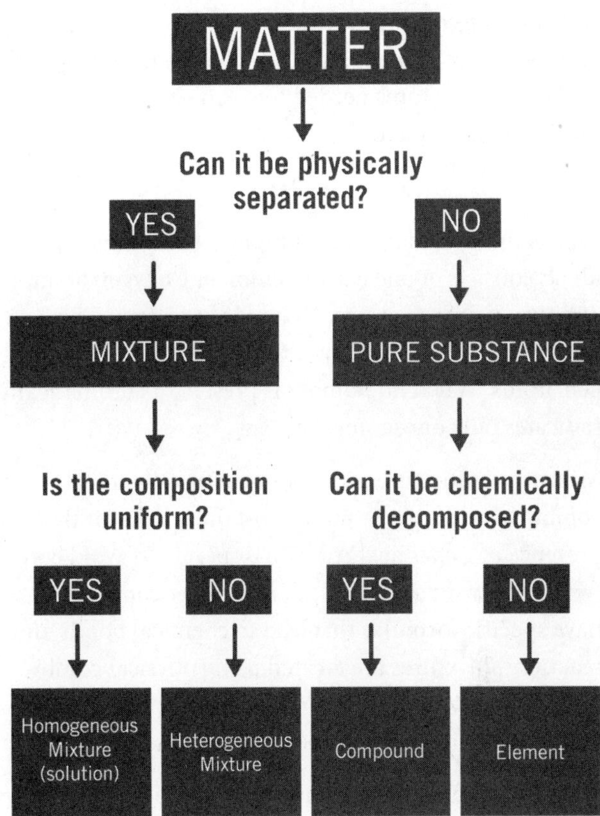

Pure Substance: This is the purest form of matter. It cannot be physically separated as it is only one substance.

Element: An element is made up of only one type of atom, unique in atomic number and mass. It cannot be broken down into any smaller units and still retain its chemical properties. Example:

$$Fe$$

This is the symbol for iron, a chemical element.

Compound: When two or more pure substances combine through chemical bonds, they form a compound. A compound can be chemically decomposed (i.e., broken down) into the elements that it is composed of. The following is an example of a chemical compound:

$$NaCl$$

This is the formula for the compound sodium chloride, more commonly known as salt. It is made up of sodium (Na) and chloride (Cl).

Note on compound formulas: Many formulas contain numbers after element symbols. These numbers specify the number of atoms needed for each element. The following is an example:

$$BaOH_2$$

This is the formula for the compound barium hydroxide. It consists of one barium atom, one oxygen atom, and two hydrogen atoms, all bonded together. The 2 after the H symbol indicates the presence of two hydrogen atoms. When no number is present, it automatically indicates only one atom is present.

Mixture: A mixture is the physical (not chemical) combination of two or more substances without the presence of a chemical reaction or bond. To avoid confusing this with a compound, remember compounds have specific formulas that lead to chemical bonds and reactions. Mixtures are created using physical combinations (i.e., pouring water onto sand or mixing smoke and fog), but no chemical bonds are formed.

Homogeneous mixture: Also known as a solution, this type of mixture has equal parts of the substances throughout the entire mixture. To create a solution, add a solute (the substance being dissolved) to a solvent, which is the dissolving medium. For example, add salt to water in a pot to create a saltwater solution. In this scenario, the salt is the solute, and the water is the solvent. Saltwater in a pot is a solution because salt and water are evenly distributed throughout the mixture.

Heterogeneous mixture: This type of mixture has varying parts of each substance depending on where the measurement is taken. One standard example of this is oil and vinegar. When shaken, a mixture of oil and vinegar appears to be evenly mixed. However, the parts will separate and become apparent with time. In addition, the vinegar may be more heavily concentrated in one part of the mixture and almost completely absent in the other part. The most important thing to remember with heterogeneous mixtures is that they can be separated and are often visually observed as multiple substances.

FORCE AND MOTION

Now that we have established the building blocks of matter, we will focus on the forces that act upon matter. Forces are vector quantities with size and direction, causing objects at rest or in motion to undergo certain changes. Motion is a change in position during a specific period, relative to a frame of reference, such as a fixed object. Motion describes how fast an object moves, how and where it moves, and at what rate the object speeds up or slows down. To understand forces and the measurement of motion, review the following terms and explanations:

- **Force** is a push or pull exerted on an object, causing it to change speed, direction, or shape. In mathematical form, force = mass × acceleration. The formula is represented as $F = ma$.
- **Mass** is the quantity of matter in an object. It is measured in kilograms (kg).
    - While mass and weight are often confused, weight is a force. **Weight** is a measure of the force of gravity acting on the mass of an object.
- **Velocity** is the rate of change of position. It is similar to speed in that it measures the distance traveled in a given time. However, velocity always includes direction. It is calculated using the formula $V = d/t$ which is read velocity equals distance divided by time. Velocity is usually expressed in units of meters per second (m/s).
- **Momentum** is defined as the product of the mass of an object and its velocity. Momentum = mass × velocity. The formula used is $p = mv$. Momentum is measured in kilogram-meter/seconds (kg·m/s).
- **Acceleration** is the rate of change of velocity. Keep in mind that objects that are slowing down are also changing velocity. Therefore, they are accelerating, but it is negative acceleration, also called deceleration. Because acceleration involves a change in velocity, an object accelerates if either its speed or its direction changes.

$$\text{Acceleration} = \frac{\text{Final velocity} - \text{initial velocity}}{\text{change in time}}.$$

If the pressure is known, but force or area is not, then the equation can be rearranged with simple algebra to solve for the missing value: force = pressure × area, or area = pressure × force.

The formula used is $a = \frac{\upsilon_f - \upsilon_i}{\Delta t}$. Acceleration is usually expressed in meters/second/second (m/s^2).

- **Gravity** is the force that draws all objects towards Earth's center. The force of gravity is a constant, as all objects accelerate towards Earth at the same rate. Acceleration due to gravity is denoted as g and is equal to 9.8 meters per second per second (m/s^2).
- **Inertia** is an object's propensity to oppose forces that attempt to put it in motion or change the magnitude or direction of its velocity.
- **Work** is the energy gained or lost by an object when an external force is applied to it, changing its motion through a distance. The force must act in the same direction or opposite to the direction that the object moves. The unit of work is joule (J). A joule is equivalent to the force of one newton (N) times a distance of 1 meter (m). 1 joule (J) = 1 newton-meter (N·m).
- **Power** is the energy lost or gained per unit of time. It is also the rate at which work is done. The unit of power is the watt. A watt is one joule of work per second (J/s).

Newton's laws of motion help to lay the foundation for all subsequent conversations in physics moving forward. When we keep in mind how and why motion occurs, we can better understand forces and motion.

- **Newton's First Law:** An object will remain in motion or at rest unless something influences it and changes its course. This property is referred to as inertia.
- **Newton's Second Law:** The force acting on an object is equal to the mass of that object times its acceleration. The greater the applied force, the greater the change in motion.
- **Newton's Third Law:** For every action (or applied force) there is an equal and opposite reaction.

Pressure

Solids, liquids, and gases are all susceptible to the influence of pressure. Pressure is the application of force to an object's unit area. When force is applied, it is distributed throughout the area of the object. Pressure is measured in two different units: Pascals and atm (standard atmosphere).

In mathematical form, $pressure = \frac{force}{area}$. The force is measured in Newtons, so if it is said that Newton units were applied to an object, then that is referencing the force applied, not the pressure.

Pascals measure pressure in Newtons per square meter.

Pressure (Pascals) =
force (Newtons) ÷ area (square meters)

Atm measures pressure relative to the standard atmospheric pressure, which is 101,325 Pascals at sea level.

Area

The area of an object can be found by multiplying the length by the width: area = length × width. It is important to consider how area impacts both the force being applied to an object and the object itself. For example, if force remains constant, increasing the surface area of an object will decrease the total pressure applied to it. This is because the more area there is on the object, the more the object can distribute the pressure applied to it.

Consider the following example:

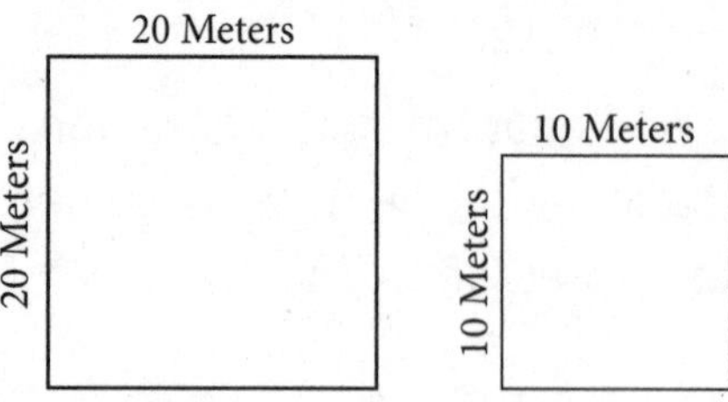

To find how force affects each square:

First square: pressure (Pascals) = 200 Newtons ÷ 400 square meters = 0.5 Newtons per square meter.

Second square: pressure (Pascals) = 200 Newtons ÷ 100 square meters = 2 Newtons per square meter.

The larger solid square can better distribute the force that is applied to it than the smaller square because it is experiencing 0.5 Newtons per square meter. The smaller square is experiencing 2 Newtons per square meter, meaning that it experiences more pressure.

Laws of Pressure

Once the basics of pressure are understood, the next step is to fully understand the laws of pressure based on the state the matter is in. The behavior and movement of fluids, which include gases and liquids, is known as fluid dynamics. We will explore both gas and pressure laws here. There are three main laws for gases regarding pressure: Boyle's Law, Charles' Law, and Avogadro's Law. Together, they make up the Ideal Gas Law.

Boyle's Law

When a gas is at a constant temperature, pressure is inversely proportional to the volume.

$$P_1V_1 = P_2V_2$$

P_1 is the starting pressure and P_2 is the ending pressure, and V_1 is the starting volume and V_2 is the ending volume. This means that if volume increases, pressure decreases and vice versa. The following graph represents this law:

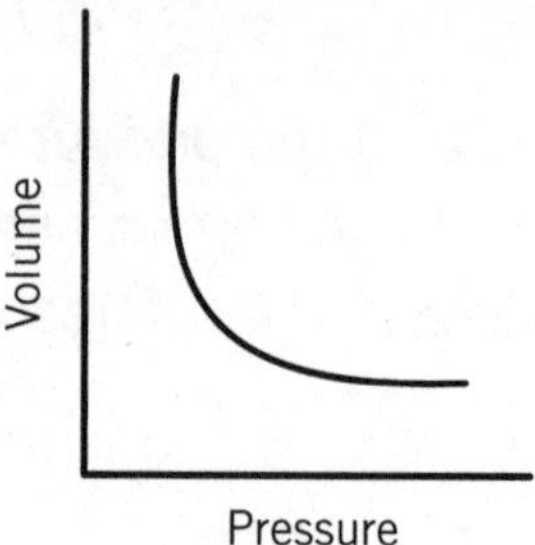

Stated simply, Boyle's Law says as you increase pressure, you decrease the volume. Same goes the other way: decrease pressure, increase volume.

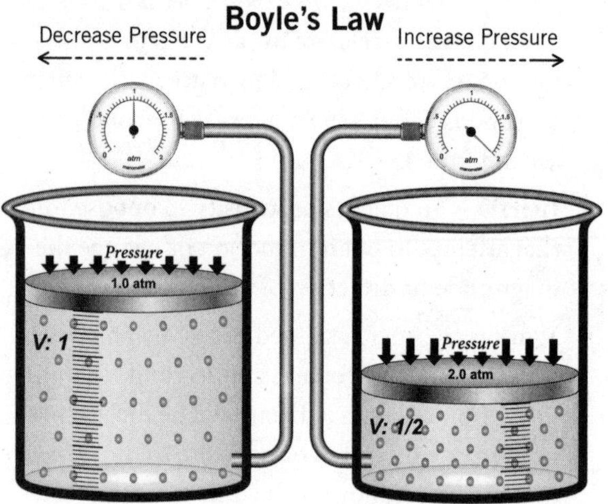

Suppose you have a balloon that holds 1L of air at sea level, which is 101,325 Pascals of pressure. What would happen if you took that balloon to the top of Mt. Everest? Boyle's law states that the decreased air pressure outside of the balloon would cause the balloon to expand, increasing the volume. Why? We are decreasing the pressure exerted on the balloon (101,325 Pascals vs. 33,775 Pascals), and Boyle's law states that volume and pressure are inversely proportional. If one decreases, the other increases.

Take that same balloon and dive 10 meters under water. At that depth, you have doubled the amount of pressure exerted on the balloon (101,325 Pascals vs. 202,650 Pascals). What happens to the balloon? It shrinks. We have increased the pressure, and that means a corresponding decrease in volume. If you took a picture of the balloon at 10 meters down and compared it to a picture of the balloon on the surface, you would see that the balloon is half the size (and half the volume). Keep going down, and the balloon's volume keeps shrinking.

Charles' Law

This law deals with the relationship between volume and temperature. When an ideal gas is at a constant pressure, volume is linearly and directly proportional to temperature.

$$\frac{V_1}{T_1} = \frac{V_2}{T_2}$$

V_1 is the starting volume, and V_2 is the ending volume. T_1 is the starting temperature, and T_2 is the ending temperature. This means that as a container's temperature increases, the volume also increases and vice versa. The following graph represents this law:

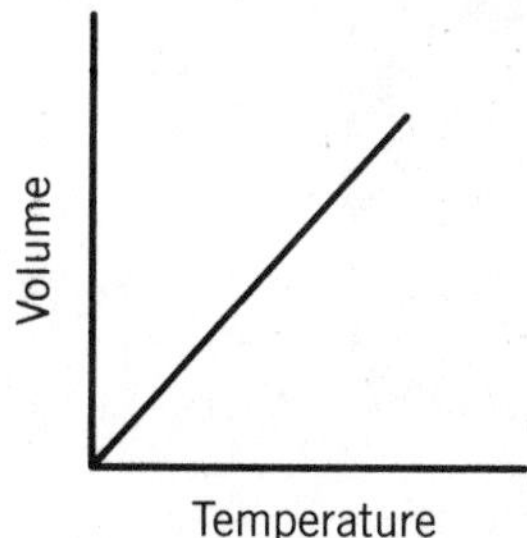

Charles' law explains how gases expand when heated. The temperature and volume of a gas are directly proportional when pressure is constant. When pressure is constant, an increase in temperature will result in an increase in the volume of a gas. This is because the increase in temperature causes gas molecules to move farther apart from each other, thus increasing the volume. When the pressure is constant, a decrease in temperature will result in a decrease in the volume of a gas. The decrease in temperature causes gas molecules to move closer together, thereby decreasing the volume of a gas.

Charles' Law

Cool

Heat

Avogadro's Law

With constant temperature and pressure, the volume is linearly and directly proportional to the amount of gas in a container.

$$\frac{V_1}{n_1} = \frac{V_2}{n_2}$$

V_1 is the starting volume and V_2 is the ending volume, while n_1 is the starting number of moles of the gas and n_2 is the ending number of moles. This means that if the amount of gas in a container is increased, the volume will increase as well and vice versa. The following graph represents this law:

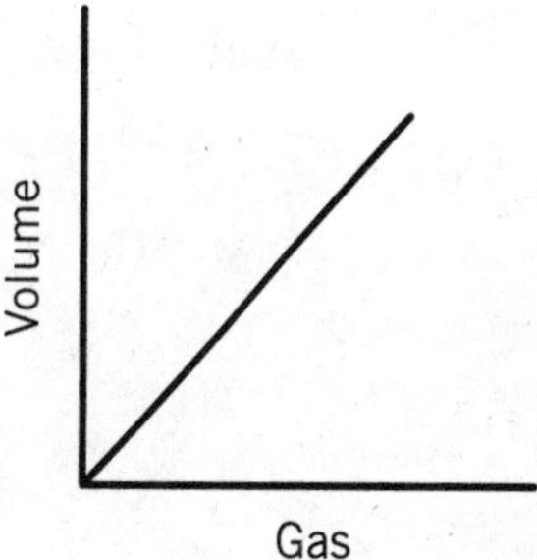

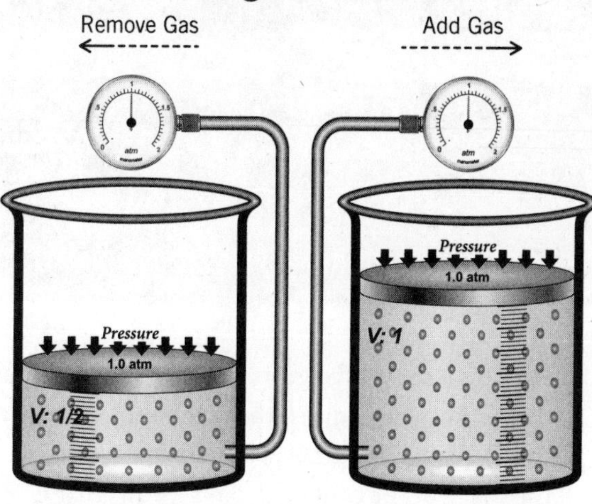

It is important to understand that the increase in pressure on a liquid is directly proportional to the depth, regardless of the shape. For example, a narrowing glass with a wide-mouth rim does not have a greater pressure at the base in comparison with a traditional cylindrical glass if the depth remains constant.

A basketball that is only partially deflated has a lower volume and thus a lower number of moles of gas versus a completely inflated basketball.

Laws of Pressure for Liquids

There are five main laws for liquids and pressure. Each of these laws helps to form a better understanding of liquids, pressure, and expected outcomes based on their relationship.

Pascal's Law

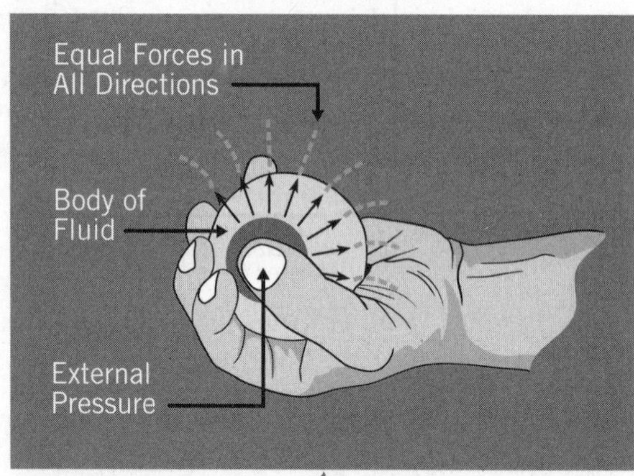

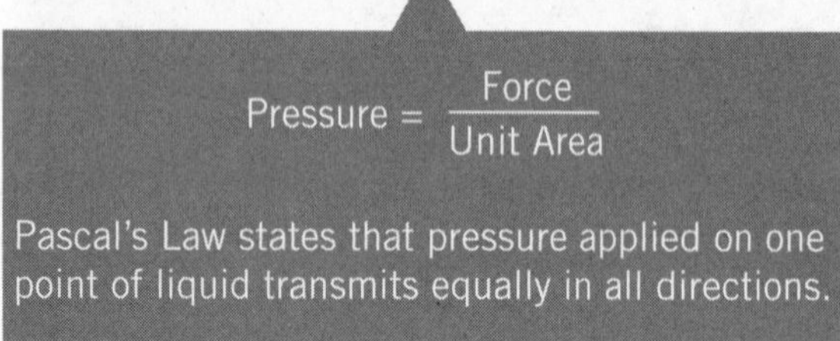

Pressure = Force / Unit Area
Pascal's Law states that pressure applied on one point of liquid transmits equally in all directions.

1. **Pascal's Law:** A change in pressure at any point in a fluid is transmitted throughout the fluid, so the change occurs everywhere, regardless of the shape of the container. This means that if pressure is applied at one spot, all the fluid will experience the pressure change.

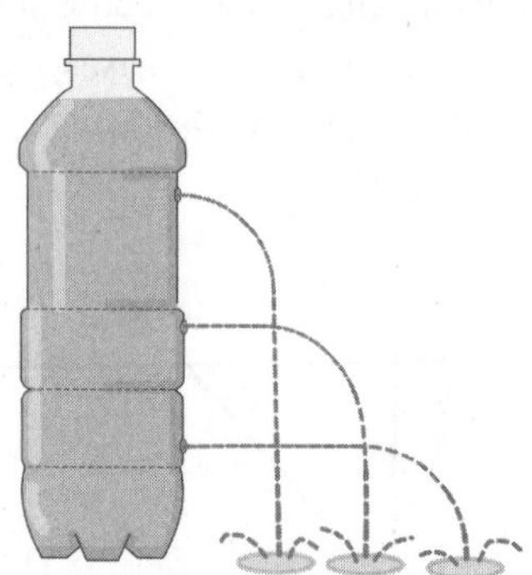

2. Pressure inside a liquid will increase as the depth of the liquid increases. This means that the water at the bottom of a container has more pressure put on it due to all the water above it. The water at the top of a glass will have much less pressure since it has little to no water above it.
3. In the case of a stationary liquid, pressure is the same at all points in the liquid along a horizontal plane. This means that the pressure is the same all across the top of the liquid, as well as at every point along the bottom. The difference in pressure is linear and not horizontal.
4. The pressure at the same depth between two different liquids may not be the same since pressure increases with the density of liquids. A liquid with a lower density will have a lower amount of pressure.
5. Liquids will always seek their own "level." This means that when placed on a horizontal plane, a liquid will flow until pressure is evenly distributed and the liquid is level.

Additional Laws of Fluid Dynamics

In addition to gas and pressure laws, fluid dynamics covers principles related to the viscosity and buoyancy of fluids. This section provides a brief overview of Newton's law of viscosity, Bernoulli's principle, and Archimedes' law.

- **Newton's Law of Viscosity:** The viscosity of a fluid, meaning its resistance to flow, will remain constant regardless of shear rate, meaning the rate of change of velocity at which a layer of fluid moves over an adjacent layer of fluid. For example, the viscosity of water will remain unchanged, regardless of how quickly it is forced through a pipe.
- **Bernoulli's Principle:** If the speed of a fluid increases, the pressure decreases (gases and liquids are both fluids). Because Bernoulli's principle is integral to understanding the mechanics of flight, this concept is discussed more in depth in Chapter 16, which focuses on the Aviation Information subtest of the AFOQT.
- **Archimedes' Law:** Any object that is completely, or partially, submerged in a fluid is buoyed by an upward force equal to the weight of the fluid displaced by the object itself.
    - **Negative Buoyancy:** If the density displaced is less than the density of the object, the object will sink.
    - **Neutral Buoyancy:** If the density displaced is equal to the object, it will be submerged, but remain suspended in the fluid.
    - **Positive Buoyancy:** If the density displaced is more than the density of the object, it will float.

ENERGY

Now that we have discussed matter and how forces influence motion, we will provide an overview of energy, which is possessed by both objects at rest and objects in motion. Together, matter and energy constitute the observable universe and its phenomena. Energy is the ability to perform work, meaning the capacity to exert force that causes change. It can be divided into sources and forms. Finally, we will provide an overview of the different types and sources of energy, with an emphasis on electromagnetic radiation; waves, sound, and light; and electricity.

Types and Sources of Energy

Energy is generally categorized into two main types: **kinetic energy**, that which bodies in motion possess, or

SOURCES OF ENERGY		
Type of Energy	**Source Examples**	**How it's produced**
Electromagnetic Radiation	Light, microwaves, radio waves	Energy transported through waves
Chemical Potential Energy	Chemical bonds, such as fuels or foods	Chemical composition existing in a local equilibrium above lowest possible state
Gravitational Potential Energy	Dams, apple in a tree	Natural gravitational pull resisted by some other force
Nuclear Energy	The sun, uranium	Fusion (combining of nuclei) or Fission (division of a nucleus) creates a chain reaction
Thermal Energy	A heated substance, such as water	Any time energy causes molecules to vibrate
Electrical Energy	Earth's electric field	The movement of electrons from one atom to another

One easy way to remember not only the name of each type of electromagnetic wave but also the order in which they appear in size and wavelength is this mnemonic:

Radio **M**an **I**nterviews **V**ery **U**nusual **X**-Ray **G**uards

R: Radio waves

M: Microwaves

I: Infrared

V: Visible Light

U: Ultraviolet

X: X-rays

G: Gamma Rays

potential energy, or that which is possible. An object at rest stores or conserves some amount of potential energy—its capacity to perform work—depending on its weight, position in relation to other objects, and other factors. Kinetic energy is the work required to put a body at rest into motion. Once the object has reached a constant speed, the object maintains that kinetic energy until its speed changes. For example, the kinetic energy to compress a spring is stored as potential energy until it can be released. When the spring is released, the potential energy then becomes kinetic energy.

The following table below illustrates the six main types of energy and the sources behind them.

Kinetic energy, or the energy of motion, comprises the energy forms we encounter most often: electromagnetic radiation; waves, sound, and light; and electrical energy. Let's take a closer look at these forms in the following sections.

Electromagnetic Radiation

A wave is a disturbance in space and time that transfers energy as it moves. Waves of the electromagnetic field carry radiant energy, known as electromagnetic radiation. Though electromagnetic radiation is

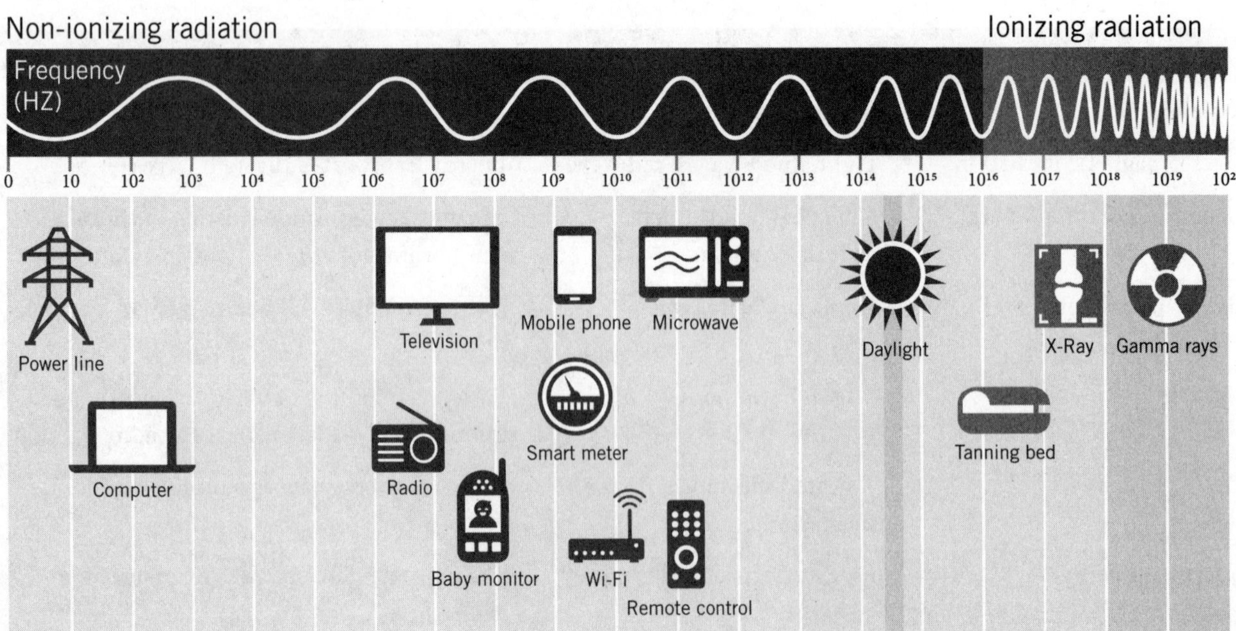

frequently thought of as light waves, light represents only a small section of the electromagnetic spectrum. Light waves constitute the visible spectrum, and white light contains a combination of the entire color spectrum; however, there are numerous types of waves, as demonstrated in the illustration of the electromagnetic spectrum.

Electromagnetic radiation has a wide range of applications, depending on the wavelength, frequency, and energy of the wave. Radio waves, which have the longest wavelength but lowest energy and frequency, mostly assist with communication. Because radio waves are easily transmitted through air, their uses go beyond AM and FM radio to military communications and wireless networks. Infrared waves exist beyond the visible light spectrum. For example, while people encounter infrared waves everyday as heat, thermal imaging makes it possible to see the infrared waves generated by body heat. X-rays are high in energy with a shorter wavelength, so they can pass through the human body. In medical imaging, x-rays can provide a high-contrast image of bones and soft tissue. Because gamma rays are produced by nuclear reactions and because they have the highest energy, the applications and uses of gamma rays are more limited. However, they can be used as a targeted method of killing cancer cells.

Waves, Sound, and Light

Wave properties can be used to measure any type of wave. There are four principal properties of all waves:

- **Wavelength:** This is the distance from the crest (top) of one wave to the crest of the next wave.
- **Amplitude:** This is the distance from the middle of the wave to either the crest or trough (bottom) of the wave.
- **Frequency:** This is measured by calculating the number of waves that pass through a specific point within a prescribed timeframe. The shorter the wavelength, the higher the frequency.
- **Velocity:** Velocity is the rate of change of position. It measures the distance traveled in a given time and always includes the direction of motion.

How it Works	Example	Type of Wave
The wave produced oscillates in a perpendicular motion to the source of the wave.	**Music System** Sound Waves	**Type of Wave:** Longitudinal Wave (Source, Amplitude, Expansion, Direction, Compression, Wavelength)
The wave produced oscillates parallel to the source of the wave.	**Television** Visible Light	**Type of Wave:** Transverse Wave (Source, Crest, Amplitude, Direction, Trough, Trough, Wavelength)

Note: Although these are the top two types, some waves are a combination of these two—such as ocean waves, which combine longitudinal and transverse to create circular-type waves.

The Law of Conservation of Energy

This is also referred to as the first law of thermodynamics. It states that energy can neither be created nor destroyed, but rather it can only be transferred or transformed. One example is the conversion of the gravitational potential energy of a waterfall to create electricity using a dam. The electricity was not created, but rather the energy to produce it was transformed through the energy of the water.

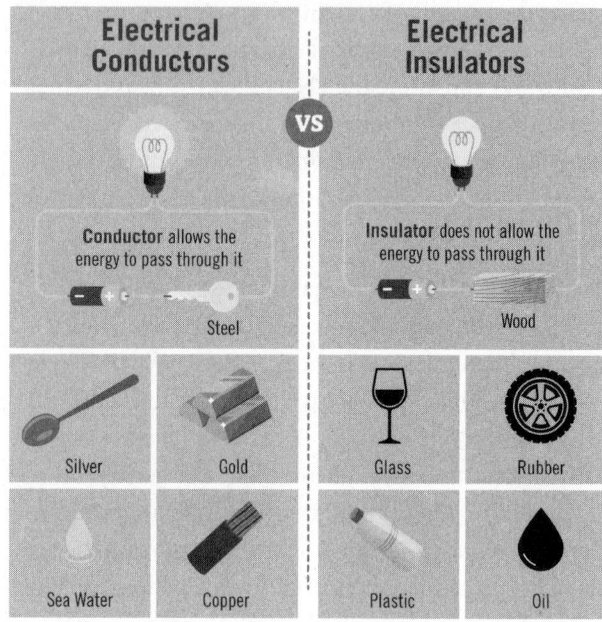

Electricity

Electrical charges (as we have encountered with ions) create electrical fields. When we harness these electrical charges into concentrated areas, we can use them as a form of energy called electricity. Electricity can be **static**, bundled together in one concentrated location, or moved through **electrical currents.**

Electron Flow

Electron flow is the movement of electrons from one atom to another. It is the movement of electrons across atoms that creates an electrical current. Electrons pass through conductors such as a metal wire, a silver connector, graphite, and water. Electrons cannot pass through insulators, such as plastic, rubber, glass, and dry wood. Because of this, insulators are used to protect conductors. Examples of insulators include the plastic covering on a piece of electrical wire or a piece of dry wood between a car battery and the concrete.

Types of Electricity

Electricity is housed in a number of ways but is typically broken down into two types: static and current.

Static Electricity

Static electricity occurs when the accumulation of electrical charges remains stagnant in one concentrated area and electricity is stored on the surface of an insulator. There are two ways this can occur:

- **Friction:** Rubbing, or resistance against another object, can supply the object with an excess of electrons, thus creating static electricity. One common example is when a person slides down a plastic slide. The electrons are transferred to the person by the friction on the slide.
- **Conduction:** The addition of a good conductor, such as metal, can cause electrons to move quickly and freely into an uncharged object. The free electrons present in metal allow it to easily assist in the transfer of electrons and the conduction of electricity.

A common example of this is a balloon that sticks to the wall after being rubbed against some fabric, carpet, or your hair. The balloon is made of rubber, so it insulates any positive or negative charge inside the balloon from the electrons transferred to the outside when it gets rubbed with a piece of cloth. This negative charge on the outside of the balloon is attracted to the more positively charged surface of the wall. An imbalance of electrical charges can result in static electricity. Static electricity builds up under dry conditions with low to no humidity. This is because humidity adds a layer of water that prevents the static electricity from building up.

Current Electricity

Current electricity happens when electrons are moving through a conductor from one location to another. Electricity moves through a circuit, which consists of a power source, conductor, and a load, which work

Static Electricity

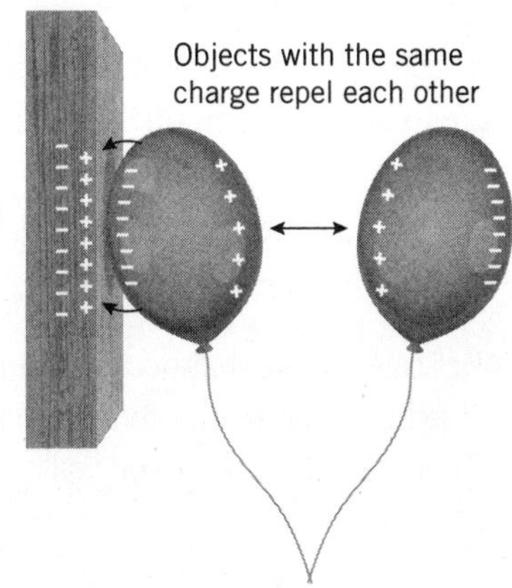
Objects with the same charge repel each other
Negative charges on the balloon attract the positive charges on the wall

together to supply electrical energy and convert it into other forms of energy, like heat and light. The most common type of electrical current is one that flows through wires; copper wire is often used as a conductor. If there is a short or fault in the wiring system, grounding—the process of removing extra electrons—can safely return electrical current to the ground through a conductor. Electric circuits are explained in more depth in the following chapter.

Measuring Electricity

Now that you have a basic understanding of the types of electricity and how you can make them work, let's take a look at how you measure electricity.

There are three key components when measuring electricity: voltage, resistance, and current. Voltage measures the force needed to send electrons between two points in an electric unit. Current is the rate of flow of electricity through a conductor. Resistance refers to the friction that limits the flow of electrons within an electric circuit.

Electric Energy

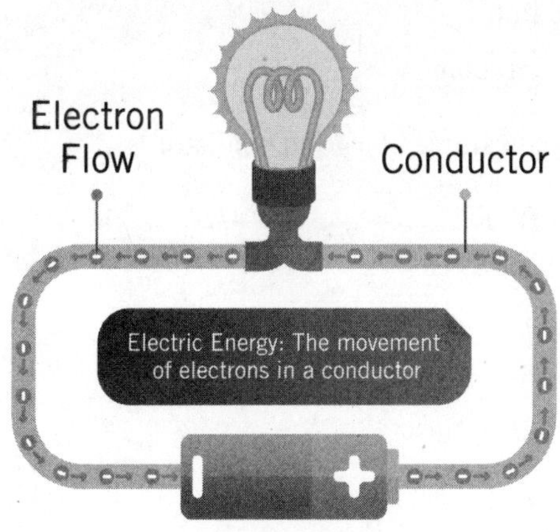
Electron Flow
Conductor
Electric Energy: The movement of electrons in a conductor
Electrical Cell

The relationships between voltage (V), current (I), and resistance (R) are described by Ohm's law. Ohm's law states that the current between two points in a circuit is directly proportional to the voltage across those two points. The equation for Ohm's law is as follows:

$$I = \frac{V}{R}$$

In the equation, current is measured in amperes, or amps. Voltage is measured in volts. Resistance is measured in ohms (Ω).

If the values for two of the components are known, the equation can be converted to solve for the variable. For example, this equation can be converted if you already know the amps and one other value:

$$R = \frac{V}{I}$$
$$V = I(R)$$

EXAMPLE:

A circuit has a resistance of 18 Ω and a current of 15 amps. What is the voltage?

(Remember, V = voltage in volts, I = current in amps, R = resistance in ohms)

$V = I(R)$

$V = 15(18)$

$V = 270$

The voltage of the circuit is 270 volts.

MINI-QUIZ: FOUNDATIONS OF PHYSICAL SCIENCE

Directions: This part of the test focuses on your knowledge base connected to physical science. Each of the questions or incomplete statements is followed by five choices. You are to decide which one of the choices best answers the question or completes the statement.

1. Convert 64.3 milliliters into liters.

   A. 6,430 L

   B. 0.643 L

   C. 6.43 L

   D. 0.00643 L

   E. 0.0643 L

2. What is the SI measurement for mass?

   A. Pounds

   B. Ounces

   C. Liters

   D. Volts

   E. Kilograms

3. What does the atomic number measure?

   A. Number of neutrons

   B. The mass of an element

   C. Number of protons

   D. Number of protons and electrons combined

   E. Number of nuclei

4. The conversion of a solid directly into a gas is called

   A. sublimation.

   B. condensation.

   C. evaporation.

   D. boiling.

   E. deposition.

5. What is the wave that occurs just before visible light as it relates to size on the electromagnetic spectrum?

   A. Microwaves

   B. Gamma rays

   C. X-rays

   D. Infrared

   E. Ultraviolet light

6. A dam is an example of which type of energy?

   A. Nuclear energy

   B. Electrical energy

   C. Chemical potential energy

   D. Gravitational potential energy

   E. Thermal energy

7. Transverse waves run __________ to the wave producer.

   A. parallel

   B. perpendicular

   C. diagonal

   D. into

   E. circular

8. An example of a good insulator is

   A. copper.

   B. gold.

   C. dry wood.

   D. steel wool.

   E. graphite.

9. Ten meters is equivalent to how many kilometers?

A. 0.01 km

B. 0.1 km

C. 1 km

D. 10 km

E. 100 km

10. A decrease in the wavelength results in

A. an increased amplitude.

B. an increased rate of frequency.

C. a decreased rate of frequency.

D. a larger wave.

E. no changes in frequency.

11. A solvent is

A. the substance that dissolves something.

B. the substance that is dissolved.

C. the result of two substances combined.

D. the result of two substances successfully mixed.

E. a substance in its purest form.

12. Which of the following is an example of a solute when combined with water?

A. Oil

B. Salt

C. Ice

D. Sand

E. Milk

13. How many total atoms are in one molecule of sulfuric acid written H_2CO_4?

A. 2

B. 3

C. 4

D. 6

E. 7

14. The temperature at which a solid changes into a liquid is called the

A. boiling point.

B. heat transfer.

C. melting point.

D. thermal shift.

E. point of transition.

15. Friction against an insulator produces

A. alternating current.

B. direct current.

C. static electricity.

D. electrical resistance.

E. solar power.

16. A disturbance in space and time that carries energy from one place to another is called

A. a wave.

B. a volt.

C. kinetic energy.

D. potential energy.

E. an ohm.

17. Of the following, which is the smallest unit of matter?

A. Molecule

B. Nucleus

C. Cell

D. Atom

E. Neutron

18. Which of the following is NOT affected by gravitational force?

A. Mass

B. Volume

C. Weight

D. Light

E. Density

19. What SI unit of measurement is used for temperature?

A. Fahrenheit

B. Kelvin

C. Celsius

D. Absolute zero

E. Moles

20. A state of matter in which the matter takes on the shape of an open container is called a

A. solid.

B. liquid.

C. gas.

D. vapor.

E. semi-solid.

ANSWER KEY AND EXPLANATIONS

1. E	5. D	9. A	13. E	17. D
2. E	6. D	10. B	14. C	18. A
3. C	7. B	11. A	15. C	19. B
4. A	8. C	12. B	16. A	20. B

1. **The correct answer is E.** When converting from a smaller unit to a larger unit, we move the decimal point to the left. Since a milliliter is 1/1000 of a liter, we need to move the decimal point to the left three spaces. The other answers are the result of erroneous calculations.
2. **The correct answer is E.** Kilogram is the universally accepted unit of measurement for mass. Pounds (choice A) and ounces (choice B) are both primarily used in the United States. Liters (choice C) is a unit for liquids. Volts (choice D) is a unit for electricity.
3. **The correct answer is C.** The atomic number is the number of protons in the nucleus of an atom. The number of neutrons (choice A), protons and electrons combined (choice D), and nuclei (choice E) are not represented by the atomic number. The mass of an element (choice B) is represented by the atomic mass not the atomic number.
4. **The correct answer is A.** Sublimation is the process in which a solid changes directly into a gas without first becoming a liquid. Condensation (choice B) is the process of a gas changing into a liquid. Evaporation (choice C) is the process of a liquid turning into a gas. Boiling (choice D) occurs when a liquid reaches a specific temperature and begins to turn into a gas. Deposition (choice E) is the process of a gas turning into a solid without first turning into a liquid.
5. **The correct answer is D.** Infrared waves occur just before visible light on the electromagnetic spectrum. If you recall the mnemonic **R**adio **M**an **I**nterviews **V**ery **U**nusual **X**-ray **G**uards, it will help you remember the order of electromagnetic waves. The I stands for Infrared, which occurs just before V, which stands for Visible Light. Microwaves (choice A) are the largest waves on this list, while gamma rays (choice B) are the smallest. X-rays (choice C) are much smaller than visible light waves, and ultraviolet light waves (choice E) occur just after visible light.
6. **The correct answer is D.** A dam works because of the gravitational pull of the Earth. The water naturally falls because of the gravitational pull. This energy is then used to turn turbines, thus creating energy. Choices A, B, C, and E are not connected to dams.
7. **The correct answer is B.** Transverse waves run perpendicular to the wave producer. Longitudinal waves run parallel (choice A) while circular waves run circular (choice E). Choices C and D do not represent the direction of any waves.
8. **The correct answer is C.** Dry wood is the only suitable insulator on this list as it does not promote the transferring of electrons. However, wood with high moisture content in the presence of high voltage can easily conduct electricity. Copper (choice A), gold (choice B), and steel wool (choice D) are all metal-based materials that are poor insulators because they promote rather than prevent the transferring of electrons. Graphite (choice E) is one of the only non-metal conductors currently in use; thus, it would be a poor insulator.
9. **The correct answer is A.** The root of kilometer is *kilo*, which means 1,000. Thus, there are 1,000 meters for every 1 kilometer. Since we are going the opposite direction, one meter equals one thousandth (0.001) of a kilometer. To convert meters to

kilometers, we multiply the number of meters (10) by 0.001 (one thousandth): $10 \times 0.001 = 0.01\text{km}$. The other choices are the result of incorrect calculations.

10. **The correct answer is B.** The rate of frequency increases as the wavelength (distance between two wave crests) decreases, as this indicates that the waves are coming more quickly. Based on this, choices C and E are incorrect. The size of the wave lessens with a decreased wavelength (choice D), and the amplitude would decrease (choice A) with a decreased wavelength.
11. **The correct answer is A.** The solvent does the dissolving, while the solute is the substance that is dissolved (choice B). The combination of two substances (choice C) is a compound. The combination of two substances mixed together (choice D) is a solution. A substance in its purest form (choice E) is an element.
12. **The correct answer is B.** A solute is what is dissolved to make a solution. Water dissolves the salt, thus making saltwater. Oil (choice A) and sand (choice D) both retain their properties and do not actually dissolve. Ice (choice C) is also water and does not dissolve itself. Milk (choice E) is not a pure substance but is a mixture. It does not dissolve when mixed with water.
13. **The correct answer is E.** There are 7 total atoms in sulfuric acid: 2 hydrogen atoms, 1 carbon atom, and 4 oxygen atoms. Two (choice A) represents only the hydrogen atoms. Three (choice B) is the total number of different types of atoms, not the total number of atoms. Four (choice C) represents only the oxygen atoms. Six (choice D) doesn't account for the carbon atom.
14. **The correct answer is C.** The melting point is the precise temperature at which a solid changes into a liquid. After the melting point is reached, additional heat will no longer increase the temperature. The boiling point (choice A) refers to the temperature in which a liquid changes to a gas. Heat transfer (choice B), thermal shift (choice D), and point of transition (choice E) are not directly connected to temperature.
15. **The correct answer is C.** Friction occurs when an object is rubbed and results in an accumulation of charges, which is also called static electricity. Alternating current (choice A) and direct current (choice B) are both the result of charges being moved and not stored up. Resistance (choice D) is related to the restriction of electrical current. Solar power (choice E) is unrelated.
16. **The correct answer is A.** A wave is a disturbance in space and time that carries energy from one place to another. A volt (choice B) is the SI unit of measurement for voltage. Kinetic energy (choice C) is the force connected to an object in motion while potential energy (choice D) is the energy the object possesses while at rest. An ohm (choice E) is the SI unit of measurement for resistance.
17. **The correct answer is D.** The smallest unit of matter is an atom. Molecules (choice A) are made up of many atoms. A cell (choice C) is a small building block for living things only. A nucleus and neutron (choices B and E) are both found within an atom and are not units of matter.
18. **The correct answer is A.** Mass is the measure of how much matter there is in something, which remains constant regardless of gravity. Weight (choice C) is directly related to the gravity of a given location. For example, the weight of an object is lighter on the moon versus on Earth. Volume and density (choices B and E) both increase or decrease depending on the strength of the gravitational pull. Gravity can both bend and change the energy of light (choice D).
19. **The correct answer is B.** Kelvin is the official SI unit of measurement for temperature. Although you may see both Fahrenheit (choice A) and Celsius (choice C) referenced at times, for equations and research purposes, temperature will always be converted to Kelvin. Absolute zero (choice D) refers to a specific temperature and is not a unit of

measurement. Moles (choice E) are the SI unit for amount of substance and not temperature.

20. **The correct answer is B.** A liquid will take on the shape of whatever space it fills. For example, if it is transferred from a bowl to a cup, it will simply take the shape of the new container. A solid (choice A) will retain its shape independent from the space it occupies. Neither a gas (choice C) nor a vapor (choice D) has a specific shape and will move freely unless actively contained on all sides, as in an airtight container. A semi-solid (choice E) may start to conform to a new space over time, but it will not completely fill it as it will retain at least some of its original shape.

NOTES

SUMMING IT UP

- The Physical Science subtest is designed to test your knowledge of basic, high school-level science. You will have 10 minutes to answer 20 questions.
- Physical science utilizes the International System of Units, also called the SI system, which uses powers of 10 for all conversions. Be sure to learn the prefixes and their corresponding abbreviations, powers, and meanings. Using the appropriate units is critical when performing calculations on the exam.
- The states of matter—solids, liquids, and gases—constitute the foundation of physics. Changes in matter from one state to another are influenced by temperature. Matter is made up of atoms, and the periodic table organizes all the known elements in the world by atomic number and elemental state. Each block provides information about a specific element, like its name, atomic number, symbol, and atomic weight. Knowing how to read and reference the periodic table is essential for predicting the properties of certain elements and how they react to or form bonds with other elements.
- Forces act upon matter, causing objects at rest or in motion to undergo change. Motion is a change in position over a specific period of time. Be sure to review the definitions of key concepts—force, mass, weight, velocity, momentum, acceleration, gravity, inertia, work, and power—and related formulas. Pressure is the application of force to an object's unit area. It is important to remember gas laws, pressure laws, and laws pertaining to fluid dynamics so that you can apply these principles to anticipate the behaviors of liquids and gases.

- Energy is the ability to do work and generally manifests in six ways: electromagnetic radiation, chemical potential energy, gravitational potential energy, nuclear energy, thermal energy, and electrical energy. Waves are disturbances in space and time that transfer energy from one position to another. Remember that energy can neither be created nor destroyed, only transferred or transformed.
- Some materials, like water and metals, are conductors of electricity, meaning electricity (specifically current electricity) can pass through them. Other materials—including plastics, rubber, and dry wood—are insulators, so electricity cannot pass through them. Insulators can store static electricity and can be used to protect conductors.
- Electricity can be measured in ohms, which measure resistance; volts, which measure potential difference; and amperes, which measure the rate of current flowing through a conductor. If you have at least two of these values, you can solve for the remaining variable by using Ohm's law, which states that the electric current passing through a conductor (amps) is directly proportional to the voltage across a conductor ($I = \frac{V}{R}$).

MECHANICAL COMPREHENSION

OVERVIEW

The Mechanical Comprehension subtest of the Officer Aptitude Rating (OAR) examines the test-taker's knowledge of machines, both simple and complex. For that subtest, you will have 15 minutes to answer 30 questions. Some of this material will also be helpful in preparing for the AFOQT Physical Science subtest. Much of this material will be familiar to you if you have already taken the ASVAB, but some areas may be a bit more in-depth. This chapter focuses on the practical application of the concepts covered in the previous chapter.

12

SIMPLE MACHINES

The term *simple machine* refers to any basic mechanical device that changes motion or force to simplify or amplify work while having little to no moving parts. This is accomplished using leverage, which is more commonly referred to as mechanical advantage, where the simple machine provides an advantage to the user in the form of increased force without increased input. Mechanical advantage (MA) is the ratio of output force to input force. To calculate mechanical advantage, divide the output force, or the force generated by the machine, by the input force, or the force put into the machine. Because simple machines amplify force in different ways, the equation for calculating the force needed varies depending on which simple machine is used.

The seven basic simple machines are as follows: levers, pulleys, inclined planes, wedges, screws, wheels and axles (gears), and springs.

Simple Machines

Levers

Pulleys

Screws

Inclined planes

Wedges

Wheels and axles

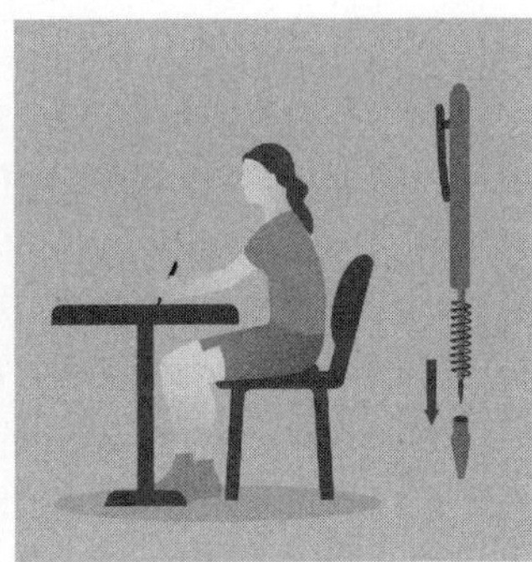

Springs

Levers

Levers are simple machines that utilize leverage to reduce the effort needed to lift an object. Levers are rigid in design and utilize a fulcrum to amplify the force applied. Fulcrums are essentially the pivoting point of a lever, and levers come in three different classes:

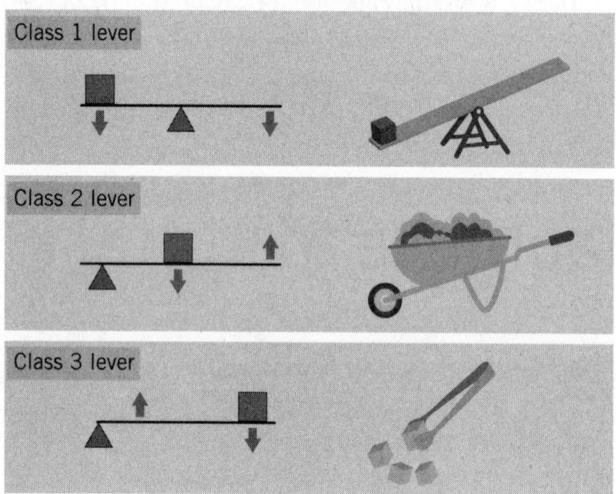

- **Class 1 lever:** This type of lever has the fulcrum in the middle, a load on one end, and the point to apply effort on the other end. The effort is applied on one end, thus affecting the load on the other. Examples of a class 1 lever are a seesaw and crowbar.
- **Class 2 lever:** A Class 2 lever has the fulcrum on one end, the effort on the other end, and the load in the middle. For this class lever, the load is specifically in the middle. A good real-world example of a class 2 lever is a wheelbarrow.
- **Class 3 lever:** This lever has the fulcrum on one end, the load on the other end, and the point to apply effort in the middle. With this class lever, the effort is situated between the load and the fulcrum, which are on opposite ends of the lever. Real-world examples of this include a shovel, a pair of tongs, or a pair of tweezers.
- **Compound Levers:** Different classes of levers can both be in the same system and work together to improve the efficiency of the system. When this is done, it is called a compound lever, and a real-world example of this would be a pair of nail clippers, which uses both a class 2 and class 3 lever.

Archimedes' Law of the Lever

The law of the lever states that the distance between the point of applied force and the fulcrum should be greater than the distance between the fulcrum and the load. Using a class 1 lever as an example to explain this law, the longer the side of the lever where the effort is applied, the easier it is to lift the load on the other side. With this in mind, it is best to keep the fulcrum closest to the load in order to get the maximum length possible for the effort side of the lever. In class 3 levers, the mechanical advantage is lower, compared to class 1 and class 2 levers, because the effort is applied between the fulcrum and the load, which are on opposite ends of the lever. Class 3 levers require more work but allow for a more precise application of force, like when using a pair of tongs to remove food from a hot grill.

Pulleys

Pulleys are simple machines that help redirect and reduce the effort of lifting an object. Pulleys consist of a turning wheel connected to a harness with a length of rope or cable running over the wheel. Sometimes, the wheel in a pulley will have an indent to accommodate the rope or cable to help keep it in place, and

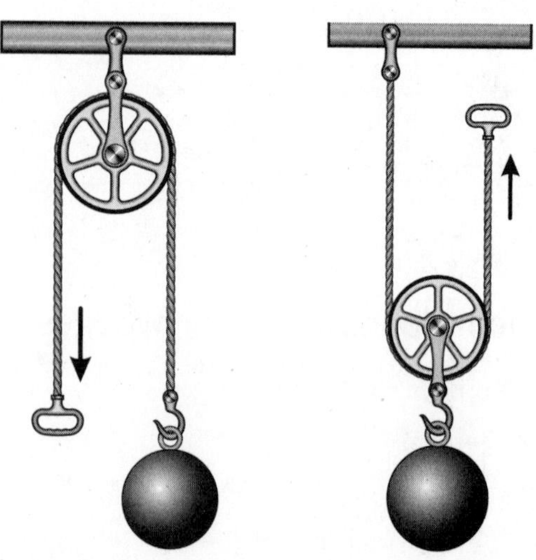

other times, the harness itself will keep the rope/cable in place. There are two main types of pulleys: fixed and movable. There are also pulley systems that use a combination of both.

A fixed pulley is attached to the ceiling (or other higher elevation) and remains fixed in one place. In a fixed pulley, the load and the effort are equal. This is often used to lift something to a higher elevation. Consider a flagpole. It does not provide any mechanical advantage, but it does redirect the effort needed to raise the flag.

A movable pulley is free to move up and down and attaches to both the object and the stationary area (ceiling, fixed pulley, etc.) by ropes. Unlike the fixed pulley, the movable pulley has free reign to move as needed. This increases the mechanical advantage to two, which reduces the effort needed to move an object by half.

Pulley Systems

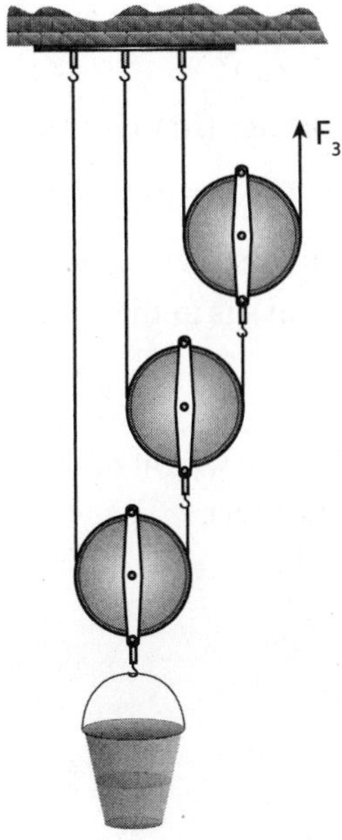

The number of pulleys used to lift an object directly relates to the mechanical advantage gained. For the effort needed to raise the object to be reduced, at least half of the pulleys used should be attached to the object itself if possible. The others can be a mix of fixed and movable pulleys or all movable.

When there is a pulley in a fixed point and a pulley in a moving position (usually attached to the object being lifted), it is called a block and tackle.

The mechanical advantage is gained from the number of ropes pulling the object up, as each one helps in lifting the object. The mechanical advantage can also be referred to simply as "efficiency." For a pulley system to be able to lift heavier loads, extra pulleys are required to maximize the mechanical advantage of the pulley system. The increased number of pulleys makes it easier for the user to lift heavier loads, but the law of conservation of energy explains how the user must still perform the same amount of work. The pulley system reduces the amount of force required from the user. However, with the addition of more pulleys and more ropes, which support the weight of the object and assist in pulling the object up, the user must pull the rope farther to lift the load. The amount of force required to lift the load is not reduced but rather redirected. To find the number of ropes required, count all sections of rope excluding the rope that will be pulled by the user. Each rope used amplifies the mechanical advantage that many times. The following illustration demonstrates this concept:

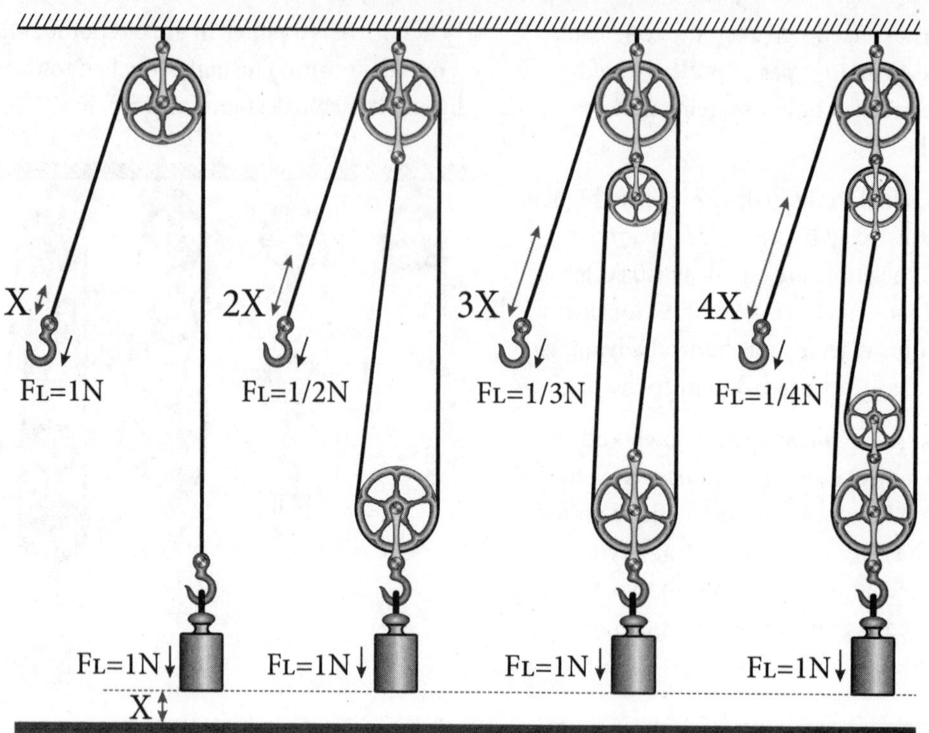

The mechanical advantage of a 2-rope pulley is 2, which equates to only $\frac{1}{2}$ the effort needed to lift the object. A 3-rope pulley system increases the MA to 3, thus requiring $\frac{1}{3}$ the effort and so on. The number of ropes will likely vary depending on the user and the size of the load. It is important to note that pulley systems cannot reach 100% efficiency/MA, as some effort will always be required to overcome the friction that exists in the system.

Calculating Force Needed

The force needed to lift an object with a system of pulleys can be found by dividing the weight of the object by the number of ropes supporting/pulling the object up (excluding the rope pulled by the user).

$$\text{Force needed} = \frac{\textit{weight of load}}{\textit{number of ropes}}$$

Pulleys are used in many different systems for many different things. Some pulleys are as simple as a belt that is driven by gears, and others are as advanced as a block and tackle found in an industrial crane. Though pulleys are not used by hand as commonly as they once were, they can be found in engines and heavy lifting systems everywhere. Knowing the basics of pulleys will help to explain how these more complex systems operate.

Let's look at an example to see how this works:

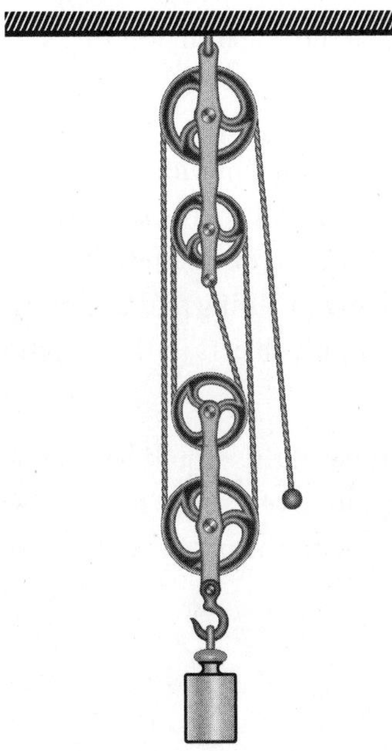

50 lbs.

The figure above has a 50-pound dumbbell attached to the end of a pulley system. How much force is needed to lift this weight?

We can see from this image that there are four ropes supporting the weight. Using the following equation, we can calculate the needed force:

$$\text{Force needed} = \text{weight of load} \div \text{number of ropes}$$

$$\text{Force needed} = \frac{50 \text{ lb.}}{4}$$

$$\text{Force needed} = 12.5 \text{ lb. of force}$$

Inclined Planes

Inclined planes are common the world over. From wheelchair ramps to moving trucks and loading docks, the inclined plane proves to be a vital simple machine with benefits for lifting or lowering an object from one level to another. This is because the effort to lift an object is greater than the effort needed to push that same object up an inclined plane.

Slope

The slope of an inclined plane affects the mechanical advantage. A steep slope will decrease the mechanical advantage but will also require less horizontal space. The flatter the inclined plane, the higher the mechanical advantage. A common problem with this option is the lack of space available for the longer length necessary for a flatter incline.

Wedges

Wedges are very similar to inclined planes in design as they are two inclined planes placed back-to-back. However, their function as a simple machine is completely different. Wedges are triangles with a thin end and a thick end, which gives them an advantage mechanically and makes it easier to push things apart or separate them. Force is applied on the thicker end, which distributes it throughout the wedge, maximizing the mechanical advantage of the user. The longer and thinner the wedge, the greater its mechanical advantage.

There are three common uses for wedges:

1. To Split/Cut: The inclined plane of a wedge can be used to split objects or sections of an object apart. Blades utilize this function after the thinnest point of the edge makes the first cut. As the blade continues through the material, the blade itself widens, which then spreads the material apart, making the cut wider than just the edge of the blade's width.
2. To Lift: Wedges can be used as ramps to lift objects up. If an extremely heavy object cannot be lifted up onto a cart or dolly to move it, a wedge can be placed on the ground by the edge of it and forced underneath. Since the edge of a wedge comes to a point, it has the advantage of working its way underneath the object. As it is worked further and further under the object, it will start to raise the object up as the incline increases. Once the object is raised enough, the cart or dolly can be placed underneath and the wedge can be removed.
3. To Hold: Wedges can stop an object and keep it in place. An example of this would be a door stopper. Door stoppers are jammed underneath a door, which creates a stopping point that will keep the door in place until the wedge is removed.

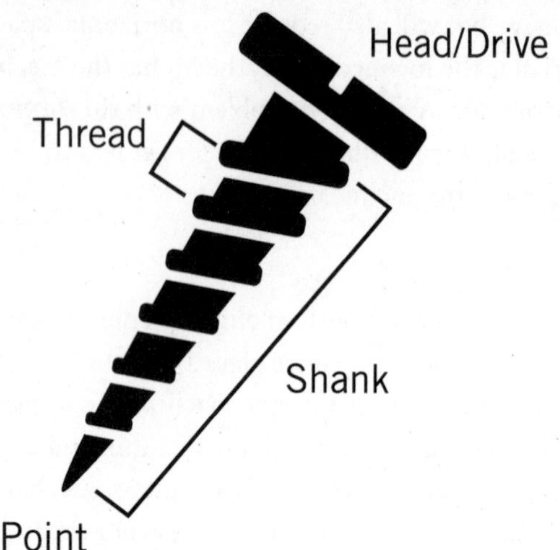

Screws

Screws are not frequently thought of as machines, but they are in fact one of the seven simple machines. They hold buildings, furniture, and vehicles together and make it possible to contain things in an enclosed atmosphere.

Screws, in their purest form, are just inclined planes that have been twisted to have helical ridges (we will call these threads, but they can also be called ribs) that wrap around a shank. Screws modify force and motion using these helical threads.

Anatomy of a Screw

The four main components that make up a screw are as follows: head, shank, thread, and point.

- **Head:** This is the top of the screw and incorporates the drive as well. It can be flat or domed and is usually wider than the shank and thread.
- **Shank:** This is the body of the screw, where the thread is located. Most shanks are fully threaded with helical ridges, although partially threaded shanks are possible as well.
- **Thread:** This is the spiraled inclined plane. Threads come in a variety of angles and pitches (distance between threads), which ultimately depend on the use of the screw. For example, drywall screws have a much steeper pitch, which helps prevent dislodging.
- **Point:** The bottom end of the screw is the point, which works like a wedge in that the screw is separating the material as it turns.

Uses for Screws

Screws utilize rotational motion to lift objects and materials upwards, while at the same time moving them in circles. As a screw rotates, the threads act as constantly moving inclining and declining planes that can push or pull objects in the direction they are moving.

One good example of this would be a screw pump. This tool uses the rotation of a screw to scoop water and push it upwards with the incline of the threads.

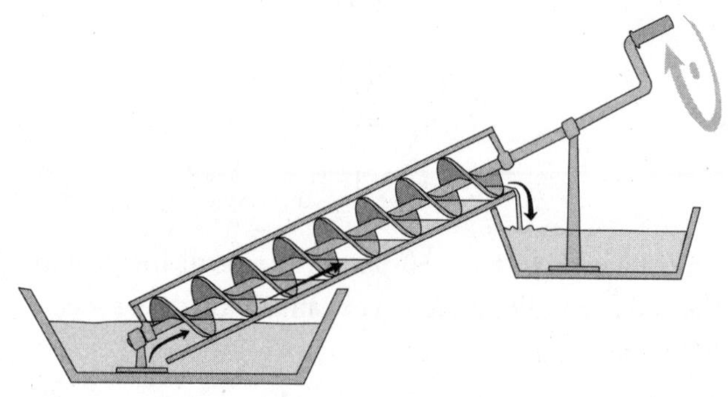

Screws can also be used to hold and secure objects together. Types of screws that can do this are self-tapping screws and setscrews. Similar to how a screw can scoop and move something upwards, a self-tapping screw's threads allow it to dig into a solid material. The material displaced by the threads is not removed but rather made to flow around the threads of the screw. This allows the screw to create pressure around itself to anchor in place. Screws are used in many places to connect two objects and hold them together. Examples of materials held together with screws, especially self-tapping screws and setscrews, would be the framing of a house or any other connection between pieces of wood that need more strength than adhesives can provide.

Setscrews are headless screws fully threaded from end to end that are used in pre-threaded holes. The threads of the screw will flow with the threads of the hole to create a connection between the two objects. The goal of a setscrew is to avoid any inefficiencies in function if a screw head were to protrude.

Examples of setscrews can be found in a gear and shaft assembly. A protrusion from the head of a screw could interfere with operations. A setscrew provides a streamlined alternative. Setscrews are attached using either an Allen wrench or internal wrenching drive.

Wheel and Axle (Gears)

The wheel and axle includes a wheel with a hole in the middle placed onto a rigid cylinder that is used to move an object. This design is used in all types of modern-day machines, including wells, bicycles, and even tractor trailers. This section focuses on gears, as the exam incorporates this specific subtype of wheel and axle combination in its test questions.

Gears are essentially wheels with teeth that are made to mesh with other teeth. Meshing refers to two sets of teeth being interlocked at some point. This meshing allows for one turning gear to directly turn another gear. Gears are major components of engines and heavy machinery and can be made in many shapes and sizes. Though they are used in some very advanced machines and systems, they are still a simple machine at their core.

Rotational energy is the main kinetic energy that gears transfer. This energy is used to turn items like belts, wheels, and the arms on a clock. When gears mesh, meaning the teeth of one gear make contact with another, gears can transfer motion. Each consecutive gear moves in the opposite direction of the previous gear. For example, if a gear is meshed with another gear and that first gear is turning clockwise, then the other gear it is meshed with will turn counterclockwise. This fact would be true all the way down a path of gears. If four gears were meshed together forming a path, and the first gear in the path is turning clockwise, then the direction of gears after the first would be counterclockwise, clockwise, and counterclockwise.

Systems of three or more meshed gears (in which all gears are in contact with each other) result in no rotation. From the first gear that turns, the others will turn in the opposite direction. However, since each gear is meshed with the others, each gear will attempt to turn its neighbors in the opposite direction of its own rotation as well. This will lock up all the gears and result in no rotation across the system.

Nuts and bolts fall under the heading of screws but function together and cannot function separately; thus, they are not individually a simple machine. However, when combined, they function much like a screw and serve the same purpose.

Another instance where gears do not turn in opposite directions when meshed is the meshing of a standard gear with an internal cogwheel. Internal cogwheels are just gears with teeth on the inside instead of the outside. They could be called internal gears, but for the sake of avoiding confusion, we will call them internal cogwheels. Internal cogwheels will move in the same rotational direction as the standard gear that they are meshed with. Therefore, if a gear was turning counterclockwise, then so would the internal cogwheel it is meshed with.

Gear size and the number of teeth on the gear affect the speed at which it rotates. The larger the gear, the slower it rotates. In addition, the more teeth it has, the slower it rotates. If a large gear is meshed with a smaller gear, then the smaller gear will turn faster. This means that it would take less effort to turn the larger gear, and the smaller gear would turn at a faster rate, causing a more efficient use of power.

Gears and Pulleys

Gears work in tandem with pulleys in some systems, and oftentimes, the pulleys are in the form of a belt with teeth. At times though, the pulleys can also be a smooth belt attached to a shaft that comes from the center of a gear. Gears use pulleys for several reasons, but one of the most common is that they make a connection between two gears that cannot be close enough to be meshed.

When two gears are connected using a belt, the rotational energy is delivered in the same direction. This means that the opposite of meshed gears will happen, and if one gear is turning clockwise, then so will the other. At times, belts can be replaced with a toothed bar. These bars will also turn gears in the same directions when moving across them.

Gear with belt

Gear with toothed bar

A good real-world example of this would be the serpentine belt in a car's engine. The serpentine belt drives multiple components in a car's engine including the alternator and water pump. If there is a twist in the belt between two gears, then the gears will turn in opposite directions as if they were meshed.

Gear Shapes

Gears can come in many shapes. Each shape of a gear serves its own purpose to provide rotational power to where it is needed. Along with these shapes, gears can also come in different orientations. The following is a brief overview of gear shapes and orientations.

Parallel gears have their shafts in parallel with one another. Examples of parallel gears include the following: spur gears, single helical gears, and double helical gears.

Intersecting gears have an angle between their driving and driven shafts. Examples of these gears include bevel gears and miter gears. Bevel gears and miter gears are essentially the same gear; the only difference is that miter gears are two beveled gears with the same size and number of teeth.

Non-intersecting and non-parallel gears have the shaft of two gears on two separate planes. This means that the shafts are at some angle between each other, but one is also above or below the other. Examples of these gears would be hypoid and worm gears. Hypoid gears are essentially spiral bevel gears; however, their shafts do not intersect and are not parallel.

Spur Gear

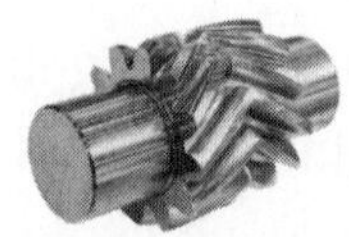

Single Helical Gear

Double Helical Gear

Bevel Gear

Miter Gear

Hypoid Gear

Worm Gear

Torsion spring

Compression spring

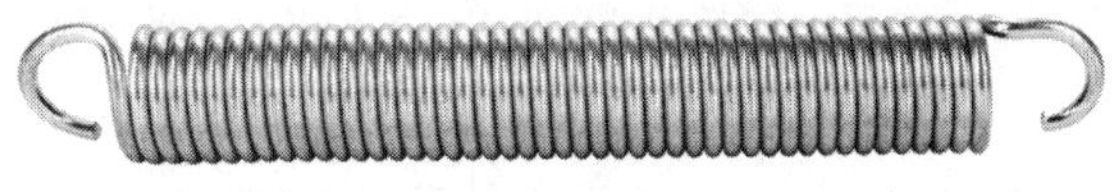
Tension spring

Springs

Springs are objects with elasticity that can store mechanical energy. They come in many different shapes and orientations, but the most common form they come in is a length of coiled wire. Coiled wire springs can be made to resist extension, compression, or rotation. Through their resistance, they can store mechanical energy, and they will exhibit a force where the magnitude increases linearly as the spring is pushed, pulled, or twisted. Though most springs that are referenced are made of metal, many other materials can make a spring as long as they have the properties of a spring. This includes materials such as rubber and wood, to name a few, which can be manipulated into the form of a spring.

Tension coil springs, also known as extension coil springs, take the shape of a coiled wire. In this type of spring, each coil is touching the coils above and below them. Oftentimes, tension coil springs come equipped with a hook or eye made from the same wire at each end.

Tension springs are meant to resist the motion of extension. They are always trying to pull back into their original shape whenever they are extended. They are commonly found in garage doors, trampolines, and older screen doors. Both garage doors and screen doors provide a returning force when opened and always attempt to return to a closed state. They also have what is called an elastic limit, which is the point at which the spring cannot stretch anymore without breaking or becoming deformed.

Compression coil springs resist the motion of compression. Their form is a coiled wire with spacing in between each coil, which gives them the ability to store mechanical power in the form of compression.

Since they resist compression, they are always pushing back to try and return to their original shape. You will find these springs in retractable pens, older mattresses, and as a suspension system in some vehicles. The best representation of the function of a compression spring is retractable pens. When the clicker is pushed down, the end of the ink cartridge is pushed out of the barrel of the pen, and when this is done, a spring connected to the ink cartridge is compressed. When the clicker is pushed again, the locking mechanism disengages, and the compression stored in the spring is released and pushes the ink cartridge back up into the barrel. If a compression spring is compressed to the point that it cannot compress anymore, and the coils are all touching, then it has reached what is called its solid length.

Torsion springs are mainly used to resist rotational motion and store it as mechanical energy. Their form is similar to tension springs, where each coil of wire is touching the ones above and below; however, they generally have far fewer coils and the ends of the wire go straight out to the side of the spring. These straight wires can form any degree of angle between themselves. Sometimes, they are custom bent to form a hook or other shape if needed by the user.

These springs are often found in clothespins or in the clip mechanism of a clipboard.

Spring Strength

Springs come in varying strengths that are dependent on their geometry, their size, and the material used in their construction. Aside from the difference between shapes, changing the geometry between two coil springs is enough to have a considerable variation in strength. For example, if a coil spring is the right size to fit the application that is needed but is not strong enough to withstand the force, then another coil of the same size can be made with a thicker gauged wire to give it more rigidity.

Laws and Principles

Springs, like other simple machines, follow laws and principles that help to define their capabilities.

- **Hooke's Law:** The force that compresses or extends a spring by a distance will increase the force linearly based on the distance. This means that springs are not able to amplify force, as what is put in is put out.

- **Springs in a Series:** When springs are in a series, they are connected end to end and essentially become one large spring with the same amount of resistance. This means that if a singular spring were to be given a specific load, and a series of two springs were given an equally sized load, the series of springs would not resist the push/pull of the load any better than the singular spring would.

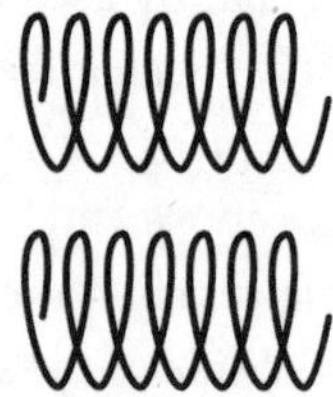

- **Parallel Springs:** If springs are put in parallel with one another (side by side), they will be able to bear a load better than a singular spring would. This is because the springs in parallel with one another evenly split the load's force, making them more difficult to compress.

Weight Distribution

Many of the simple machines work towards moving or redistributing weight more efficiently. That being said, understanding weight distribution can also assist in performing work in a maximized capacity.

Distributing weight is essential when moving heavy loads in order to move them efficiently and safely. There is a common misconception that weight should simply be evenly distributed regardless of load and

situation. This is not true. In some cases, weight should be evenly distributed across the individuals or object carrying them, and at other times, it should be distributed with a 60:40 ratio. To help improve weight distribution, some devices are designed specifically to shift weight into the direction that it is needed.

Even Distribution

When two individuals are lifting a heavy object, it is best for weight to be distributed evenly. If one person were carrying more of the weight, they would be under more stress and would be more at risk. This is an easy thing to accomplish when lifting a uniform object such as a box. However, if something with a handle, such as a bucket, is lifted using a carrying pole, the object should be equidistant between the people to have the weight distributed evenly. The same can be said when loading a four-wheeled cart because if more weight is on one side, there is a chance that the cart could tip or become more difficult to control.

60:40 Rule

The even distribution rule, however, does not apply to trailers. When a trailer is loaded, the load should be split into a 60:40 ratio. Sixty percent of the load should be at the front section of the trailer, which is ahead of the wheels and closer to the vehicle itself. The remaining 40% should be put in the rear of the trailer behind the wheels.

ENGINES

Engines are found in many types of machines. They serve to harness and utilize energy for a specific purpose. The examination of engines can encompass a wide variety of topics, but for the purposes of this section, we will focus on internal combustion engines and their associated systems.

Basic Engine Anatomy

Engine anatomy can be divided into two major types of engines: four-stroke and two-stroke. The term *stroke* refers to the motion of the piston moving to the very top or bottom of the cylinder. When the piston moves from the very bottom to the very top, or vice versa, that is one stroke.

ENGINE ANATOMY		
Engine Type	**2-Stroke Engine**	**4-Stroke Engine**
Design	Simple	Complex
Fuel Consumption	Consumes fuel quickly	Fuel-efficient
Performance	High torque at lower RPM	Lower torque at higher RPM
Sound	Louder	Quieter
Fuel Preparation	Premix oil and fuel	No premixing needed
Repairs	Inexpensive—fewer parts, simple design	Complex—more parts, complex design
Examples	Lawnmower, chainsaw	Auto, diesel truck

Two-Stroke Engine

Two-stroke engines are light and portable and have a high power-to-weight ratio. Their simple design makes them inexpensive and easier to fix, so two-stroke engines have a wide range of applications. However, because two-stroke engines are so powerful, they often wear out quickly, so they are primarily used in smaller applications, such as chainsaws, weed whackers, and dirt bikes. The following list provides an overview of the parts of a two-stroke engine:

- **Spark Plug:** This component provides a spark to ignite fuel.
- **Intake Port:** This component provides passage for fuel and air into the crankcase, where the mixture will ultimately continue to the combustion chamber.

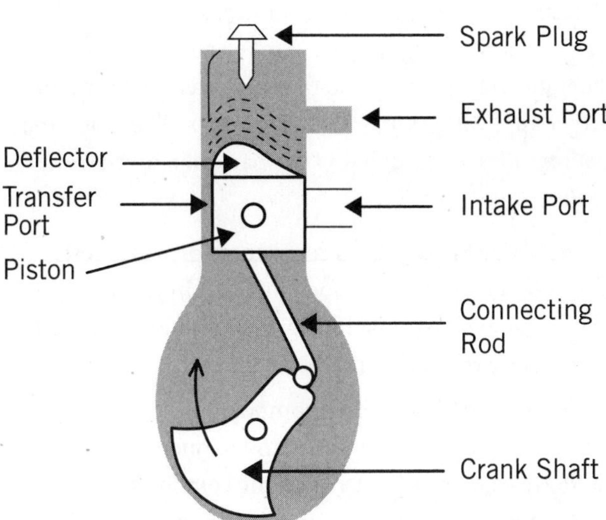

- **Exhaust Port:** This component provides passage for combusted fuel and air (exhaust) to exit the combustion chamber.
- **Transfer Port:** This component provides passage from the crankcase to the combustion chamber for the fuel and air mixture.
- **Connecting Rod:** This component, also known as the piston rod, is used to connect the piston to the crankshaft.
- **Crankshaft:** This component is the main shaft that the entire engine is meant to turn. It takes the movement of reciprocation from the pistons and turns it into a movement of rotation to power the vehicle or machine that comprises the engine.
- **Piston:** This component resides in the cylinder and is a part of the internal combustion process to create reciprocating power and motion.
- **Deflector:** This component is found on top of the pistons in some two-stroke engines to direct fuel and exhaust where they are needed.

Four-Stroke Engine

Four-stroke engines are designed to reduce exhaust, making them more fuel-efficient. However, this requires more moving parts, so four-stroke engines are heavier, more complex, and more expensive to repair. Because their power-to-weight ratio is lower than that of a two-stroke engine, four-stroke engines are considerably more durable, so they are often preferred in larger applications, like cars and trucks. The following list provides an overview of the parts of a four-stroke engine:

- **Valve Spring:** This component provides resistance to the valve opening to let in fuel or let out exhaust. The resistance it provides is used to close the valve and keep a good seal.
- **Exhaust Valve:** This component is used both to seal the exhaust port and to open in order to release the exhaust from the combustion chamber. Note that this component is not found in two-stroke engines.

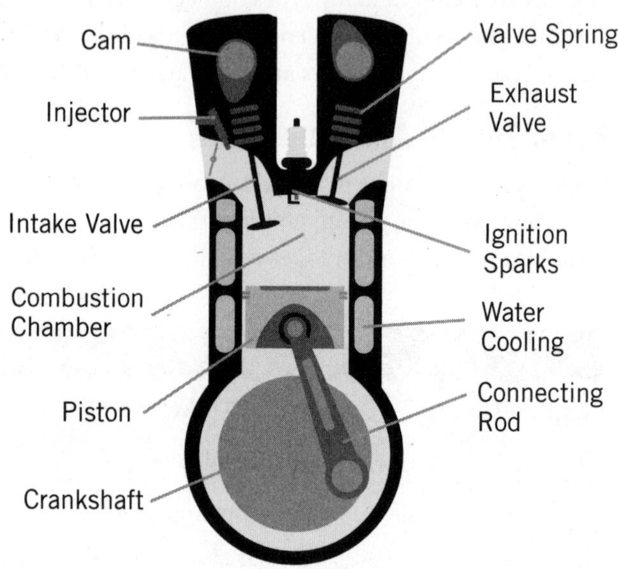

- **Spark Plug:** This component provides a spark to ignite fuel.
- **Water Cooling:** These are channels that run through the engine delivering water that absorbs the heat from the engine and carries it away.
- **Connecting Rod:** This component helps to connect the piston to the crankshaft.
- **Crankshaft:** This component is the main driving shaft that the entire engine is working to turn. It takes the movement of reciprocation from the pistons and turns it into a movement of rotation to power the vehicle or machine that comprises the engine.
- **Piston:** This component resides in the cylinder and is a part of the internal combustion process to create reciprocating power and motion.
- **Combustion Chamber:** This is the area within the cylinder in which the combustion of fuel takes place.
- **Intake Valve:** This component is used both to seal the intake port and to open to let fuel into the combustion chamber. Note that this component is not found in two-stroke engines.

- **Injector:** This component injects fuel into the combustion chamber. It has replaced the carburetor on most modern cars.
- **Cam:** This component is attached to the camshaft. When the camshaft rotates, the elongated end of the cam pushes the valves down in order to intake or release fuel or exhaust from the combustion chamber. Since this component is for controlling the valves, it is not found in two-stroke engines.

Internal Combustion Process

Internal combustion engines are systems that can be found in many different places in our daily lives. They can be found in vehicles, lawn mowers, and generators, to name a few things. The combustion process is made up of four phases: intake, compression, power, and exhaust.

Intake

Fuel and air intake is necessary for the combustion of fuel, which powers the engine. This can be done through a carburetor or direct fuel injection. A carburetor mixes the fuel with air before it goes into the combustion chamber. With direct fuel injection, the fuel and air do not mix until they are inside the combustion chamber.

There are three types of air intake:

- **Naturally aspirated air intake:** This component utilizes the vacuum and surrounding pressure created by the exhaust to draw air into the engine.
- **Turbochargers:** These utilize compressors driven by exhaust gases to draw more air into the engine than naturally aspirated engines.
- **Superchargers:** These utilize a compressor driven directly by the engine to draw more air into the engine than both naturally aspirated and turbocharged engines.

Compression

Compression takes place when the piston moves upwards in the cylinder. As the piston moves upwards, it creates a smaller area for the fuel and air mixture to dwell in, which increases the pressure in the combustion chamber. The increased pressure creates a more powerful combustion that forces the piston downwards.

Power

After the fuel ignites, the resulting power is transferred into the piston. This transfer of power happens because the piston is a moving component of the engine, and as it goes downwards, it turns the crankshaft with more power. The crankshaft is the main shaft of the engine that takes the movement from the pistons and turns it into a movement of rotation. The crankshaft is connected to the pistons through the connecting rod/piston rod and is in the crankcase.

Exhaust

After the fuel and air mixture is combusted and spent, it becomes exhaust. This exhaust is no longer needed and is then removed from the combustion chamber so that it makes room for the new fuel and air mixture that will come into the chamber. After this, the internal combustion process starts all over.

This process is the same for both four-stroke and two-stroke engines, but how it occurs and by what mechanism differ.

In civilian vehicles, direct fuel injection is standard on newer vehicles. However, it is important to understand the function and mechanism behind carburetors as some military vehicles and older models of common vehicles may still use them.

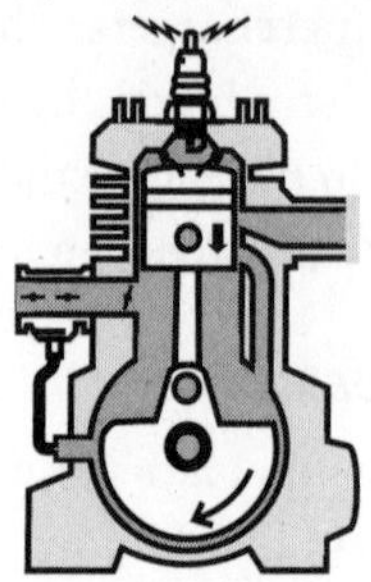

Intake + Compression

Stroke 1: Compression

Combustion + Exhaust

Stroke 2: Power

Two-Stroke Internal Combustion Process

Two-stroke engines only need two strokes of the piston to turn the crankshaft once and accomplish all four phases of the internal combustion process. The first stroke accomplishes both the intake (where the fuel and air are brought into the chamber) and the compression (where the fuel and air mixture is compressed for combustion). The second stroke accomplishes both the power (the fuel and air mixture ignites and sends the piston downwards) and the exhaust phase (where the exhaust is expelled). The two-stroke cycle is often labeled with only the compression and power phases to simplify the process. However, it is important to understand that all four phases occur within the two strokes.

Because two-stroke engines have no valves or strokes dedicated to intaking fuel and expelling exhaust, they are less fuel-efficient than four-stroke engines. However, because they fire once every revolution, they have higher torque than four-stroke engines, which only fire once every other revolution.

Four-Stroke Internal Combustion Process

Four-stroke engines require four strokes of a piston to turn the crankshaft twice. The intake stroke is the first stroke of the cycle, and it involves the piston moving down to bring a mixture of fuel and air into the combustion chamber. Next is the compression stroke, during which the piston moves upwards and compresses the fuel and air mixture prior to combustion. Third is the power stroke, in which the fuel and air mixture combusts, and the piston is driven downwards. Finally, there is the exhaust stroke, which is when the piston moves upwards and expels the spent air and fuel mixture (exhaust).

Because four-stroke engines use valves to regulate fuel and exhaust, as well as having strokes dedicated to intaking fuel and expelling exhaust, they are more fuel-efficient than two-stroke engines. However, because they only fire once every other revolution, they have less torque than two-stroke engines that fire once every revolution.

Cylinders

The combustion cylinders in an engine can vary in number anywhere from one cylinder to eight or more, depending on the engine's use. There are engines that will run on only one cylinder, but the combustion cycle will take longer compared to the multiple, smaller combustions of an engine with more cylinders and the same overall volume. The cylinder itself is the entire structure that the piston moves in, not just the combustion chamber.

The combustion chamber is the specific spot in which the ignition of the fuel and air mixture takes place. The fuel and air mixture that is brought into the combustion chamber is done so through the intake valves in four-stroke engines. Two-stroke engines do not have valves, and the fuel and air mixture is brought in through ports to the chamber. The exhaust left over after combustion is released through the exhaust valve in four-stroke engines, and for two-stroke engines, it is released through the exhaust port.

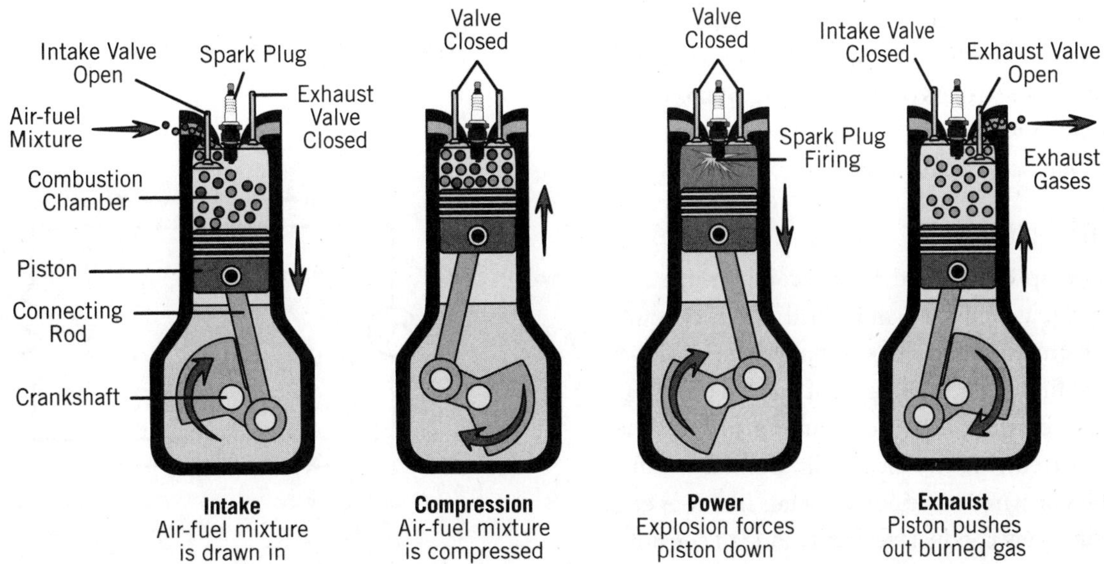

Fuel

There are two types of fuel used in combustion engines: gas (also called petrol) and diesel. Each type of fuel works in a specific way, and an engine is meant to run on one or the other. In fact, using the wrong fuel type not only damages the engine but will also cause it to fail over time. Both four-stroke and two-stroke engines can use one or the other of these fuels.

Gas/Petrol

Gasoline, also called gas or petrol, is a flammable mixture of hydrocarbons that come from the processing of crude petroleum (also known as crude oil). Gas has a lower viscosity and combustion temperature than diesel. To ignite gas at the right temperature, a spark plug is triggered when the fuel and air mixture is fully compressed in the cylinder. Gasoline has a lower efficiency in fuel consumption compared to other fuels because it does not convert heat into energy.

If an engine meant to run on gas was instead given diesel, it might run for a short time but would inevitably fail. This would happen because the spark plug's spark ignition would not adequately combust the diesel, and the diesel's viscosity is too difficult for the fuel pump to move through the engine.

Diesel

Diesel fuel is also derived from crude petroleum (crude oil) and has the small additions of oxygen, nitrogen, and sulfur. These additional substances that are present make molecular structures with the hydrocarbons from the petroleum, and the result is new structures that are no longer hydrocarbons. Diesel has a higher viscosity and combustion temperature than gasoline, so it does not use a spark plug to aid in combustion. The combustion instead is a product of the heat and compression generated by the piston moving up the cylinder. Diesel provides better fuel efficiency and delivers more torque to the crankshaft, which makes it ideal for both heavy-duty work vehicles and commuter cars alike. Diesel provides this fuel efficiency and torque because it converts heat into energy. The downsides, however, are that it is not the best choice for high-speed performance, and it is not as fuel-efficient for short trips or city driving.

If an engine meant to run on diesel was instead given gas/petrol, it would run for a short while before the engine would start sustaining damage. This happens because the gasoline does not combust in the same manner as diesel within an engine using compression ignition. This incorrect combustion will lead to inadequate engine performance and will result in engine damage.

CIRCUITS

An electric circuit is a pathway that conducts the flow of electric current. Circuits are how electricity is used to power a device, whether it's a light bulb or an advanced radar system. Regardless of what the circuit does, there are standard symbols used to diagram the components used to assemble a circuit.

Types of Circuits

Electric circuits consist of three key components: a power source, a conductor, and a load. A power source, such as a battery or power line, supplies electrical energy that drives electrical current around the circuit. A conductor carries the flow of charge, also known as electrical current, around the circuit. Conductors are often cables or wires made out of metals like copper or iron because they conduct electricity. A load consumes power and converts it into another form of energy, such as light or heat. In order to conduct electricity, circuits must be closed so that electrons can continuously flow. Depending on the type of current flowing, a circuit is classified as either direct current (DC) or alternating current (AC).

Direct Current (DC)

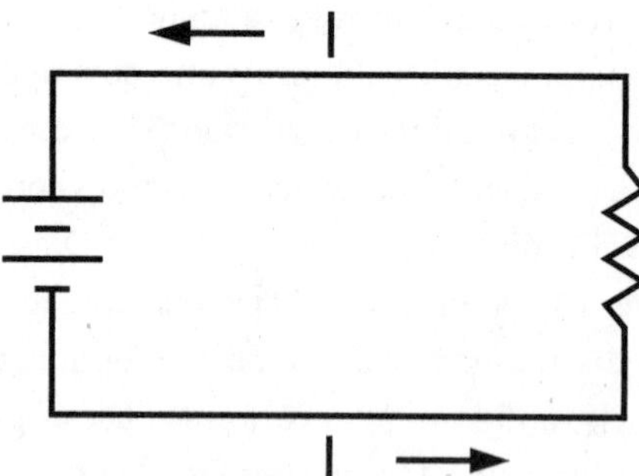

- DC Circuits
    - Electrons flow from negative to positive.
    - DC currents are usually powered by a battery circuit but can also be produced by fuel cells and solar panels.
    - DC electricity is more easily stored than AC electricity.

In the direct current image, the symbol on the left indicates the DC power supply, and the symbol on the right indicates a resistor. The arrows show that the flow of charge is moving in one direction.

Alternating Current (AC)

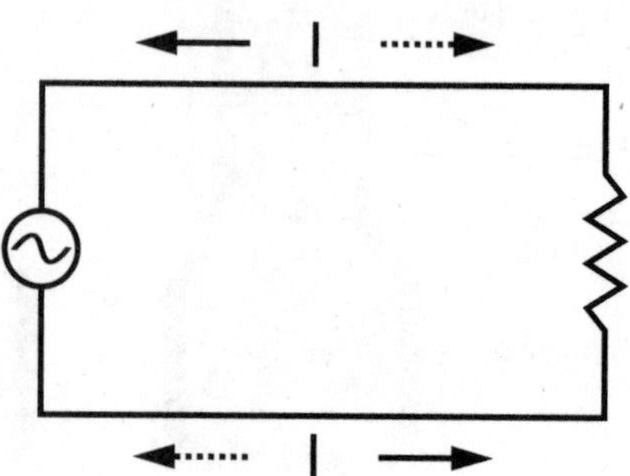

- AC Circuits
    - Electrons change their direction of flow, meaning they can flow from negative to positive and vice versa.
    - Voltage levels can be adjusted to high or low, depending on what is needed.
    - AC electricity is not as easily stored as DC electricity, but it can travel farther since it can be converted to a higher voltage with the use of a transformer. As such, AC electricity is typically used in power grids.

In the alternating current image, the symbol on the left indicates the AC power supply, and the symbol on the right indicates a resistor. The arrows indicate that the flow of charge is alternating directions.

Resistors

Resistors can be found in almost every electrical circuit because they regulate the flow of electrons and resist the movement of electric current. This prevents damage to delicate components and overloading of the circuit, which results in a complete loss of power. A circuit often has more than one resistor to ensure a consistent stream of current. Resistors can also be put in series or in parallel.

CIRCUIT COMPONENTS		
Component	**Definition**	**Symbol**
DC voltage source	This component, usually a battery, provides direct current to power a DC circuit. It is represented in a circuit diagram as four parallel lines perpendicular to a wire.	
AC voltage source	This component, such as a wall socket or generator, provides a voltage source for AC circuits. It is represented by a circle with a wavy line inside.	
Conductor	A conductor carries the flow of electricity. It is represented by a single straight line.	
Switch	A switch is used to break the connection in a circuit. It is represented by an angled break in the wire and can appear with or without circles demarcating the switch. If the circuit is closed, the line will be touching both circles.	
Resistor	Resistors reduce the current flow. They are represented by a wire with a zigzag.	
Light bulb	This component is used to represent the part of a circuit that needs the current to function, such as a light bulb. It is represented in three main ways: by a circle with a loop inside and wires coming out; by a circle with an X inside it and wires coming out; and by a circle with wires coming out and a line inside that curves upward in the middle.	
Diode	Diodes limit the current flow to only one direction. They are represented as a wire with a triangular arrow with a vertical line at the tip.	
Transistor	Transistors are used to amplify the current in a circuit. They are represented by three wires, one with an arrow depicting the current flow connecting to a line that is perpendicular to them all within a circle.	
Capacitor	Capacitors are used to absorb unwanted electrical pulses or to store and release power. There are several diagrams to represent a capacitor, but the most basic is a wire broken by two perpendicular lines, which are parallel to each other.	
Ground	This component allows the safe dispersal of leftover current. It is represented by a wire terminating with three perpendicular lines, which are parallel to each other, of decreasing length forming an arrow, or a wire ending in a perpendicular line and three angled lines (like a rake).	

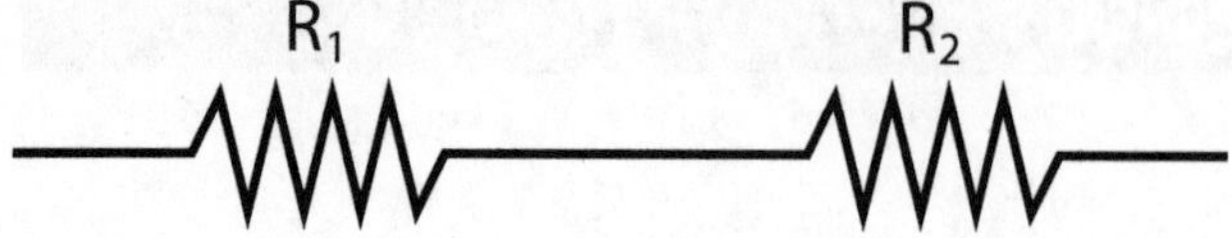

Resistors in Series

Components that are in series are connected end to end and are often treated as a single component. When placed in series, the resistance for that path increases.

When resistors are in a series, their ohms of resistance can be added together to find the total resistance of that path. If a 500-ohm resistor was in a series with a 600-ohm resistor, then the total resistance would be 500 ohms + 600 ohms = 1,100 ohms.

Resistors in Parallel

When resistor components are parallel, as shown in the following image, it means they are on separate but parallel paths. Because of this, they need to be thought of as two separate components.

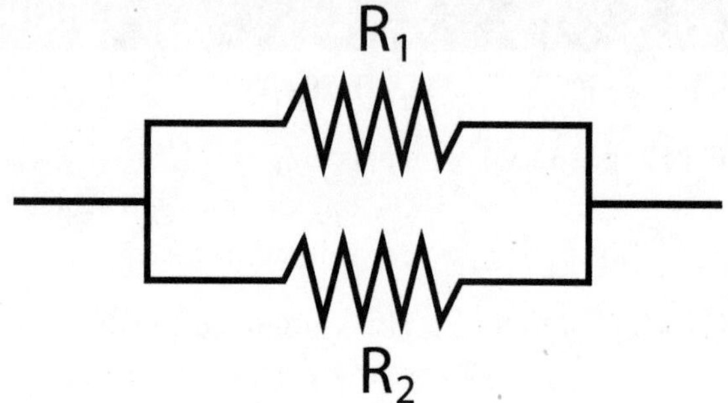

Unlike resistors in a series, parallel resistors result in a reduction of the total resistance. Since they are on separate paths, the electrons have more than one way to travel. In addition, the resistance is reduced because it is not combined. Unlike the simple addition method for resistors in a series, the formula for calculating ohms for parallel resistors is more complicated. Use the following formula for this process, where R_1 equals the first resistor, R_2 the second, and so forth:

$$R_{TOTAL} = \frac{1}{\frac{1}{R_1} + \frac{1}{R_2} + \frac{1}{R_3} + \frac{1}{...R_n}}$$

MINI-QUIZ: MECHANICAL COMPREHENSION

Directions: This part of the exam will test your mechanical comprehension abilities. Each question has 3 choices. Choose the best option based on the information provided.

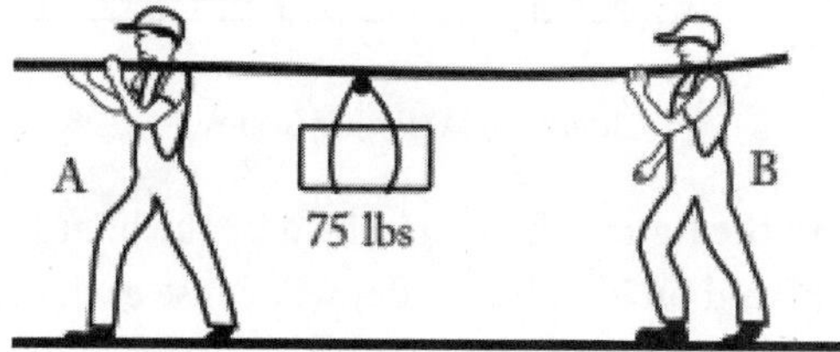

1. The weight is being carried entirely on the shoulders of the two people shown in the image. Which person bears more weight on the shoulder?

   A. A

   B. B

   C. Both are carrying the same weight.

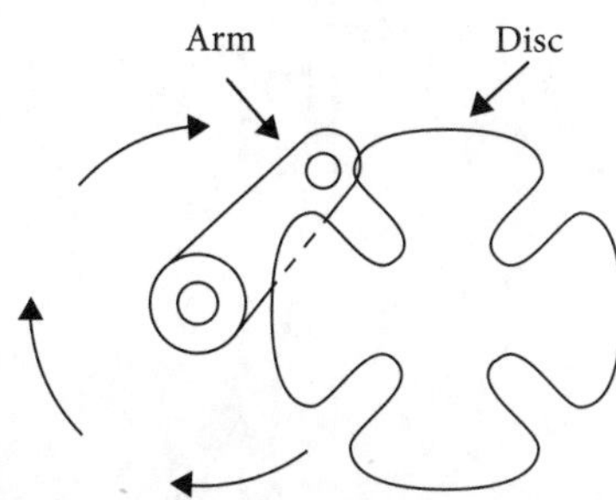

2. The figure shows a slotted disc turned by a pin on a rotating arm. One complete revolution of the arm will turn the disc

   A. ¼ turn.

   B. one complete turn.

   C. ½ turn.

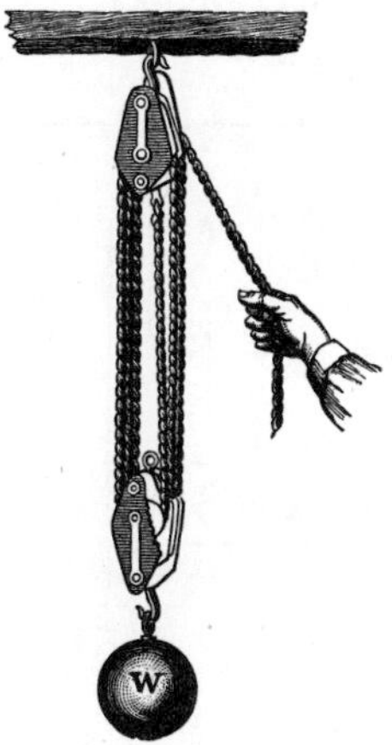

3. What is the mechanical advantage of using block and tackle?

   A. It will amplify the force of the pulling.

   B. It will use less rope than a single pulley.

   C. The load can be pulled up faster than with a single rope.

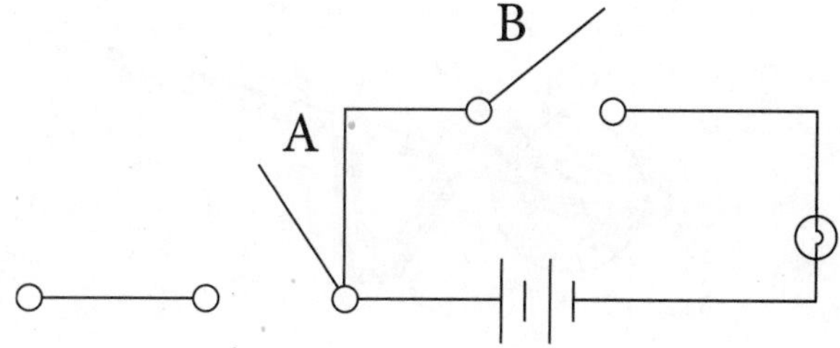

4. Which switches need to be closed for the bulb to turn on?

   A. Switch A

   B. Switch B

   C. They both need to be closed.

5. What is a spring's elastic limit?

   A. The length of a spring completely stretched out

   B. The length where, if a spring were to stretch more, it would not return to its original shape

   C. The maximum length it can be stretched before the metal breaks

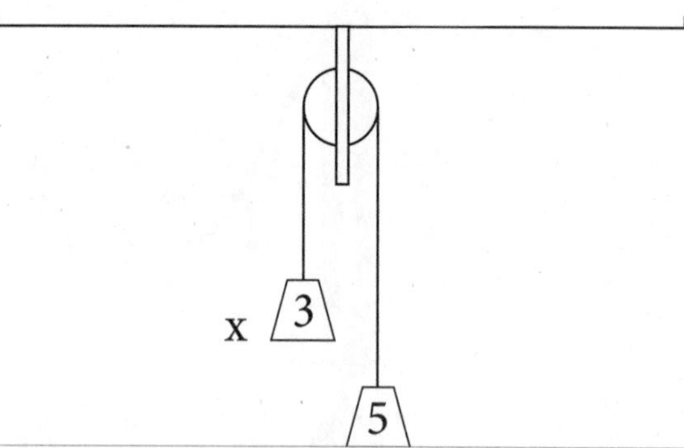

6. What is the minimum amount of weight needed to add to the 3-pound weight on the left side for it to touch the ground?

   A. 1 pound

   B. 2 pounds

   C. 3 pounds

7. What class lever is exhibited in the image?

   A. Class 1 lever

   B. Class 2 lever

   C. Class 3 lever

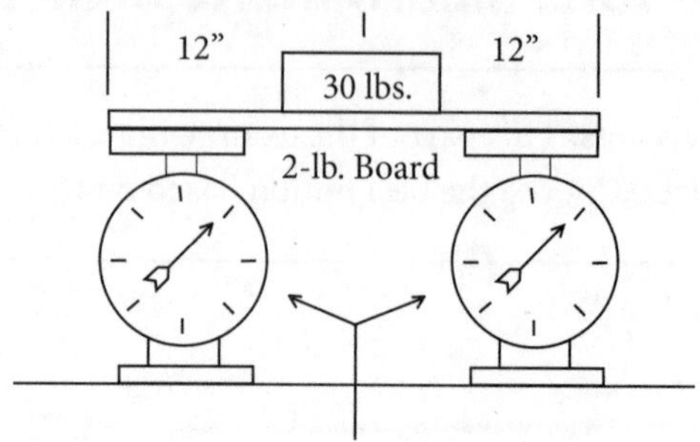

Identical Weighing Scales

8. In the figure, the weight held by the board and placed on identical scales will cause each scale to read

   A. 8 pounds.

   B. 16 pounds.

   C. 32 pounds.

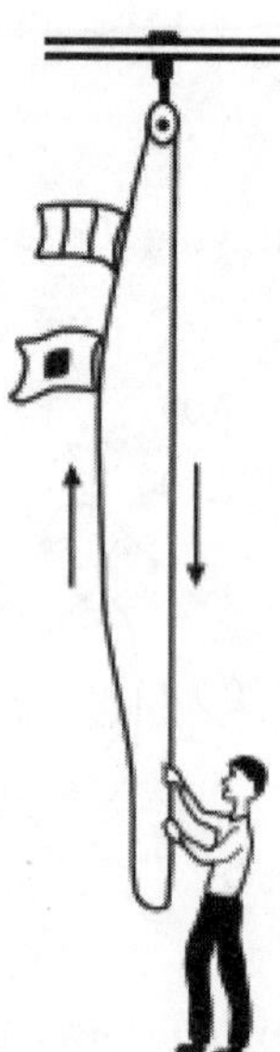

9. Neglecting friction, what is the mechanical advantage in using a single fixed pulley, as shown in the image?

   A. 1

   B. 2

   C. 3

10. Which direction do electrons flow in an electric circuit?

A. From positive to negative

B. From negative to positive

C. It depends on the circuit's current type.

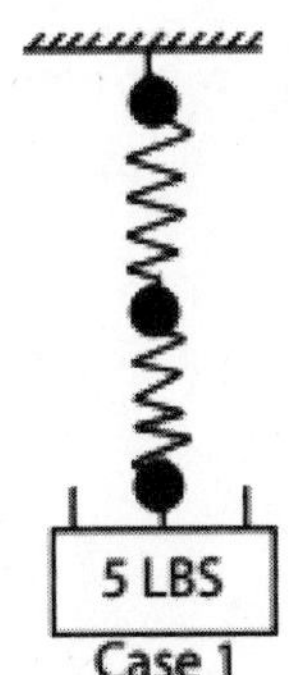

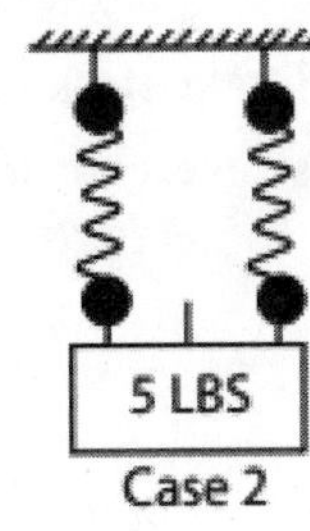

11. In the figure, all four springs are identical. In Case 1, with the springs end to end, the stretch of each spring due to the 5-pound weight is

A. $\frac{1}{2}$ as much as in Case 2.

B. the same as in Case 2.

C. twice as much as in Case 2.

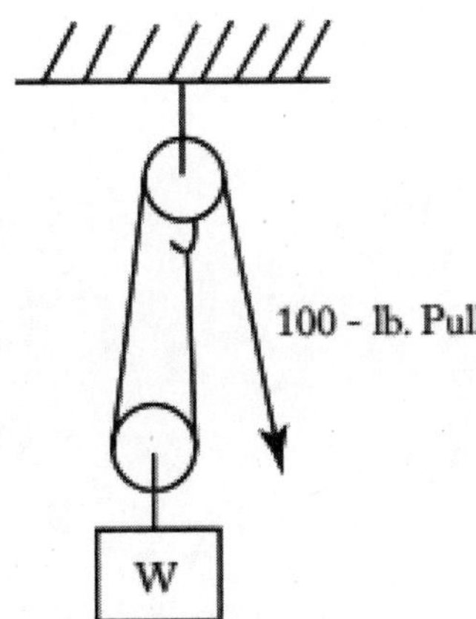

12. The maximum weight, *W*, that can be lifted as shown with a pull of 100 pounds is

A. 100 pounds.

B. 200 pounds.

C. 300 pounds.

13. If two resistors are placed in series, the final resistance is

A. lower.

B. higher.

C. unable to be determined.

14. You are a member of the road crew for a musician. You need to get a grand piano up on a stage that is about 14 feet off the ground. Which of the following simple machines would be the best choice to move the piano?

A. Lever

B. Fixed pulley

C. Movable pulley

15. The wedge and the screw are both special types of

A. inclined plane.

B. lever.

C. wheel and axle.

16. Four resistors are hooked together in parallel. The resistors have values of 20Ω, 40Ω, 60Ω, and 80Ω respectively. What is the total resistance of the resistors?

A. 4.4Ω

B. 9.6Ω

C. 14.8Ω

17. Which of the following engine components is NOT part of a two-stroke gasoline engine?

A. Piston

B. Exhaust valve

C. Crankshaft

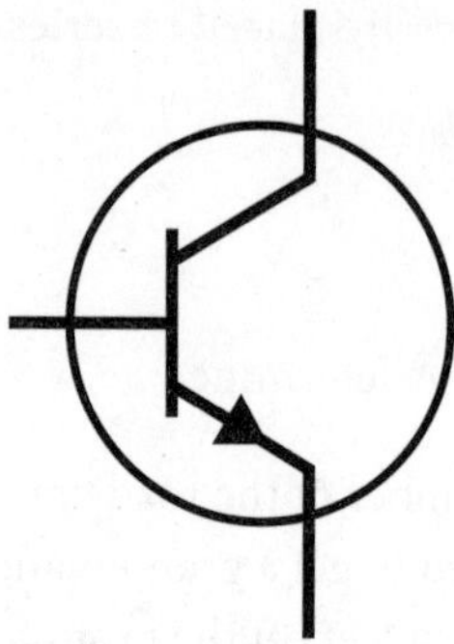

18. In a circuit, this symbol represents a

A. transistor.

B. diode.

C. capacitor.

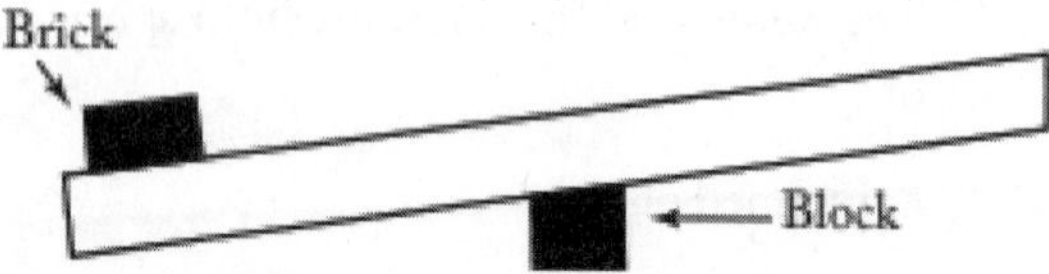

19. In this diagram, if the block on which the lever is resting is moved closer to the brick, the brick will be

A. easier to lift but will not be lifted as high.

B. easier to lift and will be lifted higher.

C. harder to lift and will not be lifted as high.

20. In the four-stroke cycle gasoline engine, the sequence of the steps in each cylinder to complete a cycle is which one of the following?

A. Intake stroke, power stroke, compression stroke, exhaust stroke

B. Intake stroke, compression stroke, exhaust stroke, power stroke

C. Intake stroke, compression stroke, power stroke, exhaust stroke

ANSWER KEY AND EXPLANATION

1. A	5. B	9. A	13. B	17. B
2. A	6. C	10. C	14. C	18. A
3. A	7. B	11. C	15. A	19. A
4. B	8. B	12. B	16. C	20. C

1. **The correct answer is A.** The weight is not centered but is closer to A. The distance from the center of the load to A is less than the distance from the center of the load to B. Therefore, A would support the greater part of the load.
2. **The correct answer is A.** Each rotation of the arm turns the slotted disc ¼ turn. It would need to complete two full revolutions for the disc to complete a ½ turn (choice C) and four revolutions for one complete turn (choice B).
3. **The correct answer is A.** The block and tackle is a system of movable pulleys that amplify the force. The disadvantages are that it uses more rope to do so (choice B) and will take more time to pull up (choice C).
4. **The correct answer is B.** Only switch B needs to be closed for the circuit to be complete and the light to turn on. Closing switch A doesn't have any effect on whether the bulb will be on or not (choices A and C).
5. **The correct answer is B.** The elastic limit is the length where if the spring were to stretch more it would not be able to return to its original shape. The length of a spring completely stretched out (choice A) and the maximum stretched length before the metal breaks (choice C) do not refer to the elastic limit as it will no longer retain its elasticity at either point.
6. **The correct choice is C.** You would need more weight than the other load for the left side of the system to touch the ground. Less weight (choice A) would be insufficient, and an equal amount of weight (choice B) would allow the system to go into balance but not tip in favor of the left side of the system.
7. **The correct answer is B.** Class 2 levers have the load in the middle with the fulcrum on one end and the effort on the other. If the fulcrum had been in the middle with the effort on one end and the load on the other, it would be a class 1 lever (choice A). If the effort was in the middle with the load and fulcrum on either ends, it would be a class 3 lever (choice C).
8. **The correct answer is B.** The total weight is 32 pounds, which is balanced equally between the two scales; thus, the answer is 16 pounds. Eight pounds (choice A) is too low, and 32 pounds (choice C) does not account for the equal distribution between two scales.
9. **The correct answer is A.** A single fixed pulley is a first-class lever with equal arms. The mechanical advantage, neglecting friction, is 1.
10. **The correct answer is C.** Electron flow depends on the circuit's current type, which are respectively alternating current (AC) and direct current (DC). Alternating currents can be found in household outlets, and they alternate the flow of electrons (choice A and B). Direct currents are used in battery-operated circuits, and they only allow electrons to move in one direction (choice B).
11. **The correct answer is C.** In Case 2, each spring is supporting $2\frac{1}{2}$ pounds $\left(\frac{1}{2}\text{ of 5 pounds}\right)$ and would extend a certain distance. In Case 1, each spring is supporting 5 pounds (the full weight) and would extend twice the distance of that for Case 2.
12. **The correct answer is B.** The number of parts of rope going to and from the movable block indicates a mechanical advantage of 2. Accordingly, a 100-lb. pull can lift, theoretically, a 200-lb. weight.

13. **The correct answer is B.** Total resistance is found by simply adding up the resistance values of the individual resistors. With multiple resistors in series, the resistance will be higher.

14. **The correct answer is C.** Choice A would not be the appropriate tool, nor would it be effective at lifting a heavy piano to the height of 14 feet. Choice B is the correct principle but wrong model, as it is meant for objects of lesser weight; the force required to use a single pulley to lift a piano would be inefficient. Movable pulleys are needed to lift a load of this size.

15. **The correct answer is A.** The screw presents a spiral inclined plane, and the wedge illustrates a two-sided incline plane.

16. **The correct answer is C.** The total resistance for a set of resistors in parallel is found by using the sum of the reciprocals. That is to do the following:

$$R_{TOTAL} = \frac{1}{\frac{1}{R_1}+\frac{1}{R_2}+\frac{1}{R_3}+\frac{1}{R_4}}$$ yielding the decimal solution $\frac{1}{R_{TOTAL}} = .05 + .025 + .0167 + .0124$, which equals $\frac{1}{R_{TOTAL}} = .1041 = 9.6\Omega$.

17. **The correct answer is B.** Two-stroke engines manage intake and exhaust gases through the use of intake and exhaust ports along the cylinder walls. Thus, no valves are required for separate intake and exhaust strokes, as in a four-stroke engine.

18. **The correct answer is A.** The symbol for a transistor is represented by three wires, one with an arrow depicting the current flow, connecting to a line that is perpendicular to them all within a circle.

19. **The correct answer is A.** If the block is moved toward the brick, the movement for a given force exerted will increase (being further from the force), making it easier to lift; the height will be made smaller, hardly raising the brick when moved to the limit (directly underneath it).

20. **The correct answer is C.** The four strokes of an internal combustion engine are the intake stroke, the compression stroke, the power stroke, and the exhaust stroke.

SUMMING IT UP

- The Mechanical Comprehension subtest of the OAR tests your knowledge of simple machines, two- and four-stroke engines, and circuits. You will have 15 minutes to answer 30 questions.
- Simple machines maximize the efficiency of work by providing a mechanical advantage, meaning they increase the amount of force applied without increasing input. The seven simple machines include levers, pulleys, inclined planes, wedges, screws, wheels and axles (gears), and springs. Remember that depending on which simple machine you're using, the equation for calculating the force required to perform a task will change.
    - Levers utilize a fulcrum to amplify force applied to lift an object.
    - Pulleys can redirect and reduce the force required to move an object.
    - Inclined planes provide a slope that makes it easier to move an object upwards.
    - When force is applied to the thick end of a wedge, it is evenly distributed throughout the wedge, making it easier to separate, hold, or push apart materials.
    - Screws can move and secure objects through their use of helical threads.
    - Gears, a sub-type of wheels and axles, use rotational energy to turn belts, wheels, and more.
    - Springs are objects with elasticity that can store mechanical energy and will exhibit a force where the magnitude increases linearly as the spring is pushed, pulled, or twisted.
- When recalling engine anatomy, remember that there are two primary types of engines: the two-stroke engine and the four-stroke engine. The number of strokes refers to how many strokes of the piston each engine requires to complete the internal combustion process. The two-stroke engine fires once every revolution and therefore has more torque. In contrast, the four-stroke engine is more fuel-efficient because it fires every other revolution and has valves and strokes dedicated to fuel intake and the expulsion of exhaust.
- To maximize work capacity, consider how weight distribution can help you move heavy loads safely and efficiently. In some situations, an even distribution of weight is critical, such as when two individuals are carrying a heavy box. In other situations, you might consider using a 60:40 ratio.
- Circuits are pathways that conduct the flow of electric current and convert it into another form of energy, such as light or heat. Direct currents are usually powered by batteries, and the electrons flow from negative to positive. In alternating currents, electrons can change their direction of flow and voltage levels can be adjusted to high or low.

TABLE READING

OVERVIEW

The Table Reading subtest of the AFOQT assesses your ability to locate information in table form quickly and efficiently. You will need to answer 40 questions in 7 minutes, so the turnaround time for each question is mere seconds.

TABLE DESIGN

Tables are designed to help both summarize a large set of data and to assist the reader in quickly and efficiently locating information. Efficient use depends on clear understanding of a table's key elements and the table's axes.

Key Elements

There are three key points connected to table design:

A

COLUMN AND ROW HEADINGS

The column and row headings are there to streamline and clarify the table, allowing you to understand the components of the table quickly.

B

TABLE BODY

The table body is where the data is located, whether numerical or textual. Values in the table body are placed at the intersection of column and row headings to indicate relationships between the different categories in the data.

C

VARIABLES

All data tables have at least one independent variable (that which is purposefully changed) and usually one dependent variable (that which is measured). Dependent variables can also be identified by the title of the table, as seen in the following example.

AVERAGE ANNUAL PILOT FLIGHT HOURS BY YEAR AND STATE

	2016	2017	2018	2019	2020
Massachusetts	2,310	2,360	2,340	2,370	2,320
Maryland	2,205	2,256	2,269	2,316	2,328
Delaware	2,387	2,213	1,980	2,344	2,115

In the preceding table, the column and row headings indicate that data from different states are being tracked over time. The table body, in conjunction with the title of the table, indicates that the values correspond to the average number of annual pilot flight hours. Additionally, the table title and column and row headings further reinforce that year and state are acting as variables that lead to the output data in the table body (e.g., 2,256 pilot flight hours on average for Maryland in 2017, 2,320 flight hours for Massachusetts in 2020, and so on).

The X and Y Axes

Every table consists of two main components—the x-axis and the y-axis.

X-AXIS					
	−4	−3	−2	−1	0
+4	1	3	5	7	9
+3	2	4	6	8	10
+2	19	21	23	25	27
+1	30	32	34	36	38
0	45	47	49	51	53
−1	64	66	68	70	72
−2	63	65	67	69	71

The x-axis always runs LEFT to RIGHT. The labels run horizontally across the top of the columns. X-values always represent the columns. Just as in algebra and coordinate geometry, if given an ordered pair (e.g., (−2, 0)), the first value is the x-value.

The y-axis always runs TOP to BOTTOM. The labels run vertically down the rows. Y-values always represent the rows. If given a coordinate pair, the second value is the y-value.

To locate information, first scan the x-axis, locate the column heading (an independent variable), then go down vertically until you find the intersecting y-axis variable (also independent). The point of intersection represents the dependent variable.

Y-AXIS					
	−4	−3	−2	−1	0
+4	1	3	5	7	9
+3	2	4	6	8	10
+2	19	21	23	25	27
+1	30	32	34	36	38
0	45	47	49	51	53
−1	64	66	68	70	72
−2	63	65	67	69	71

USING TABLES

The ability to navigate tables quickly and accurately depends not only on an understanding of table design but also an understanding of table reading conventions, specifically those related to the use of ordered pairs.

Ordered Pairs

Questions related to the previous table will rely on ordered pairs. See the following example:

What value is located at (−2, −1)?

	−4	−3	−2	−1	0
+4	1	3	5	7	9
+3	2	4	6	8	10
+2	19	21	23	25	27
+1	30	32	34	36	38
0	45	47	49	51	53
−1	64	66	68	70	72
−2	63	65	67	69	71

The question tells you the ordered pair (−2, −1). First, follow the x-axis to locate −2. Next, go down the rows until you find the appropriate y-value, −1; the point of intersection is 68. Thus, **the correct answer is 68.**

Tables with Word Labels

You can expect many of the questions on the AFOQT to come in the form of ordered pairs. But let's look at an example using word labels to vary your practice:

On average, how many hours did pilots from Maryland fly in 2018?

AVERAGE ANNUAL PILOT FLIGHT HOURS BY YEAR AND STATE					
	2016	**2017**	**2018**	**2019**	**2020**
Massachusetts	2,310	2,360	2,340	2,370	2,320
Maryland	2,205	2,256	2,269	2,316	2,328
Delaware	2,387	2,213	1,980	2,344	2,115

While this is not an ordered pair, you still have a value for the x-axis (year) and for the y-axis (state). When reading the question, identify the key elements that correspond with the table. In this case, you see the state name and the year. With that in mind, locate the value for the x-axis referenced in the question, the year 2018. Next, identify the y-axis variable, Maryland. Follow the column and row until their point of intersection, 2,269 hours. Thus, **the correct answer is 2,269.**

Let's look at another example.

STATES AND ZIP CODES		
State Name and Abbreviation	**City**	**Zip Code Range**
Colorado (CO)	Denver	80201 thru 80239
Connecticut (CT)	Hartford	06101 thru 06112
Delaware (DE)	Dover	19901 thru 19905
District of Columbia (DC)	Washington	20001 thru 20020
Georgia (GA)	Atlanta	30301 thru 30381
Hawaii (HI)	Honolulu	96801 thru 96830
Idaho (ID)	Montpelier	83254
Rhode Island (RI)	Newport	02840 thru 02841
South Carolina (SC)	Camden	29020
South Dakota (SD)	Aberdeen	57401 thru 57402
Tennessee (TN)	Nashville	37201 thru 37222
Texas (TX)	Austin	78701 thru 78705
Utah (UT)	Logan	84321 thru 84323
Wisconsin (WI)	Milwaukee	53201 thru 53228
Wyoming (WY)	Pinedale	82941

Which city has a zip code of 83254?

A. Austin

B. Denver

C. Hartford

D. Montpelier

E. Pinedale

This table is a little different in that you must find the zip code first. It is located in the body of the table, and not along the column or row headings. However, you still need the column heading to identify where you need to look. The information you need is in the column labels along the x-axis; in this case, it's the column labeled **Zip Code Range**. Slide your finger down the column until you find the value you're looking for, 83254. Once you find the appropriate zip code, move across until you find the matching city, the objective of the question. The city with zip code 83254 is Montpelier, ID.

13

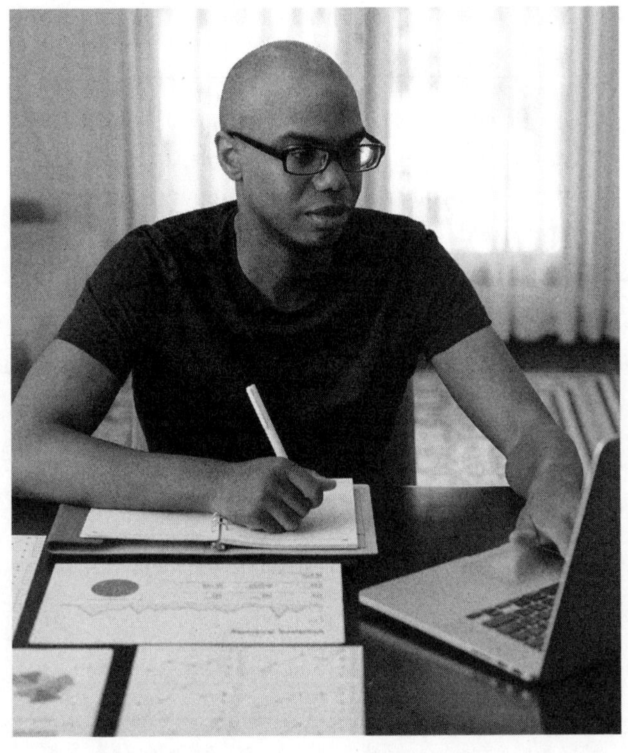

Tips and Practice

The following table and the accompanying questions can offer further practice. Remember that the test demands both speed and accuracy. To reach those goals, use the information indicated by the question, scan the table in the appropriate order (x-axis then y-axis), and don't be afraid to use your finger or a straight edge to navigate the columns and rows. Pointing can help prevent mistakes your eyes might make.

	-4	-3	-2	-1	0
+4	1	3	5	7	9
+3	2	4	6	8	10
+2	19	21	23	25	27
+1	30	32	34	36	38
0	45	47	49	51	53
-1	64	66	68	70	72
-2	63	65	67	69	71

1. What number is located at (-4, 2)?

   A. 63
   B. 19
   C. 5
   D. 64
   E. 6

   EXPLANATION: **The correct answer is B.** Go along the x-axis and locate -4. Then, go down the rows until you locate 2. The point of intersection is 19. The coordinates for 63 (choice A) are (-4, -2). The coordinates for 5 (choice C) are (-2, 4). The coordinates for 64 (choice D) are (-4, -1). The coordinates for 6 (choice E) are (-2, 3).

2. What number is located at (-3, -2)?

   A. 66
   B. 21
   C. 65
   D. 23
   E. 6

   EXPLANATION: **The correct answer is C.** Go along the x-axis and locate -3. Then, go down the rows until you locate -2. The point of intersection is 65. The coordinates for 66 (choice A) are (-3, -1). The coordinates for 21 (choice B) are (-3, 2). The coordinates for 23 (choice D) are (-2, 2). The coordinates for 6 (choice E) are (-2, 3).

MINI-QUIZ: TABLE READING

Directions: This part of the test measures your ability to read a table efficiently and accurately. Each table will require you to use the x-values along the top of the table and the y-values along the left side of the table. The x-values are column values, and the y-values are row values. Each question will ask you to find information by locating the block using the correct x- and y-values based on the information provided.

X

Y	-12	-11	-10	-9	-8	-7	-6	-5	-4	-3	-2	-1	0	1	2	3	4	5	6	7	8	9	10	11	12
12	45	46	47	48	49	50	51	52	53	54	55	56	57	58	59	60	61	62	63	64	65	66	67	68	69
11	46	47	48	49	50	51	52	53	54	55	56	57	58	59	60	61	62	63	64	65	66	67	68	69	70
10	47	48	49	50	51	52	53	54	55	56	57	58	59	60	61	62	63	64	65	66	67	68	69	70	71
9	48	49	50	51	52	53	54	55	56	57	58	59	60	61	62	63	64	65	66	67	68	69	70	71	72
8	49	50	51	52	53	54	55	56	57	58	59	60	61	62	63	64	65	66	67	68	69	70	71	72	73
7	50	51	52	53	54	55	56	57	58	59	60	61	62	63	64	65	66	67	68	69	70	71	72	73	74
6	51	52	53	54	55	56	57	58	59	60	61	62	63	64	65	66	67	68	69	70	71	72	73	74	75
5	52	53	54	55	56	57	58	59	60	61	62	63	64	65	66	67	68	69	70	71	72	73	74	75	76
4	53	54	55	56	57	58	59	60	61	62	63	64	65	66	67	68	69	70	71	72	73	74	75	76	77
3	54	55	56	57	58	59	60	61	62	63	64	65	66	67	68	69	70	71	72	73	74	75	76	77	78
2	55	56	57	58	59	60	61	62	63	64	65	66	67	68	69	70	71	72	73	74	75	76	77	78	79
1	56	57	58	59	60	61	62	63	64	65	66	67	68	69	70	71	72	73	74	75	76	77	78	79	80
0	57	58	59	60	61	62	63	64	65	66	67	68	69	70	71	72	73	74	75	76	77	78	79	80	81
-1	58	59	60	61	62	63	64	65	66	67	68	69	70	71	72	73	74	75	76	77	78	79	80	81	82
-2	59	60	61	62	63	64	65	66	67	68	69	70	71	72	73	74	75	76	77	78	79	80	81	82	83
-3	60	61	62	63	64	65	66	67	68	69	70	71	72	73	74	75	76	77	78	79	80	81	82	83	84
-4	61	62	63	64	65	66	67	68	69	70	71	72	73	74	75	76	77	78	79	80	81	82	83	84	85
-5	62	63	64	65	66	67	68	69	70	71	72	73	74	75	76	77	78	79	80	81	82	83	84	85	86
-6	63	64	65	66	67	68	69	70	71	72	73	74	75	76	77	78	79	80	81	82	83	84	85	86	87
-7	64	65	66	67	68	69	70	71	72	73	74	75	76	77	78	79	80	81	82	83	84	85	86	87	88
-8	65	66	67	68	69	70	71	72	73	74	75	76	77	78	79	80	81	82	83	84	85	86	87	88	89
-9	66	67	68	69	70	71	72	73	74	75	76	77	78	79	80	81	82	83	84	85	86	87	88	89	90
-10	67	68	69	70	71	72	73	74	75	76	77	78	79	80	81	82	83	84	85	86	87	88	89	90	91
-11	68	69	70	71	72	73	74	75	76	77	78	79	80	81	82	83	84	85	86	87	88	89	90	91	92
-12	69	70	71	72	73	74	75	76	77	78	79	80	81	82	83	84	85	86	87	88	89	90	91	92	93

	X	Y
1	-3	3
2	-6	+5
3	-11	+8
4	+6	-5
5	+8	+11
6	+3	-5
7	-9	0
8	+11	-10
9	-4	-5
10	-7	+7
11	-10	+7
12	+4	-4
13	-1	-7
14	-9	+5
15	-2	+1
16	-9	-11
17	+4	+5
18	+10	0
19	-10	-6
20	-1	-6

A	B	C	D	E
65	63	64	59	57
60	57	62	70	58
49	50	51	48	53
80	78	81	82	79
64	67	66	65	71
75	74	78	77	72
60	64	66	58	59
90	93	88	89	91
73	65	66	69	70
53	58	55	56	57
54	52	49	48	50
76	61	78	72	77
74	76	75	73	78
55	54	50	51	65
67	65	61	66	63
70	72	69	71	68
64	68	66	67	69
81	76	78	79	80
64	62	65	63	67
72	68	71	69	74

STOP.

If you finish before time is up, you may check your work on this section only. Do not turn to any other section in the test.

ANSWER KEY AND EXPLANATIONS

1. B	5. C	9. E	13. C	17. B
2. E	6. D	10. C	14. A	18. D
3. B	7. A	11. B	15. D	19. C
4. A	8. A	12. E	16. D	20. E

1. **The correct answer is B.** The coordinates (-3, +3) intersect at 63.
2. **The correct answer is E.** The coordinates (-6, +5) intersect at 58.
3. **The correct answer is B.** The coordinates (-11, +8) intersect at 50.
4. **The correct answer is A.** The coordinates (+6, -5) intersect at 80.
5. **The correct answer is C.** The coordinates (+8, +11) intersect at 66.
6. **The correct answer is D.** The coordinates (+3, -5) intersect at 77.
7. **The correct answer is A.** The coordinates (-9, 0) intersect at 60.
8. **The correct answer is A.** The coordinates (+11, -10) intersect at 90.
9. **The correct answer is E.** The coordinates (-4, -5) intersect at 70.
10. **The correct answer is C.** The coordinates (-7, +7) intersect at 55.
11. **The correct answer is B.** The coordinates (-10, +7) intersect at 52.
12. **The correct answer is E.** The coordinates (+4, -4) intersect at 77.
13. **The correct answer is C.** The coordinates (-1, -7) intersect at 75.
14. **The correct answer is A.** The coordinates (-9, +5) intersect at 55.
15. **The correct answer is D.** The coordinates (-2, +1) intersect at 66.
16. **The correct answer is D.** The coordinates (-9, -11) intersect at 71.
17. **The correct answer is B.** The coordinates (+4, +5) intersect at 68.
18. **The correct answer is D.** The coordinates (+10, 0) intersect at 79.
19. **The correct answer is C.** The coordinates (-10, -6) intersect at 65.
20. **The correct answer is E.** The coordinates (-1, -6) intersect at 74.

SUMMING IT UP

- The Table Reading subtest will assess your ability to find information on a table.
- You will have 7 minutes to answer 40 questions.
- Tables consist of an x-axis across the top, a y-axis along the side, and a table body.
- Questions may come in the form of an ordered pair, two independent variables, or a dependent and independent variable. You will have to use the information provided to find the correct answer to the question.
- Each question will have five answer choices.
- Understand the goal of the question, use proper table reading conventions, and try using a straight edge or finger to guide your eyes when scanning the columns and rows.

INSTRUMENT COMPREHENSION

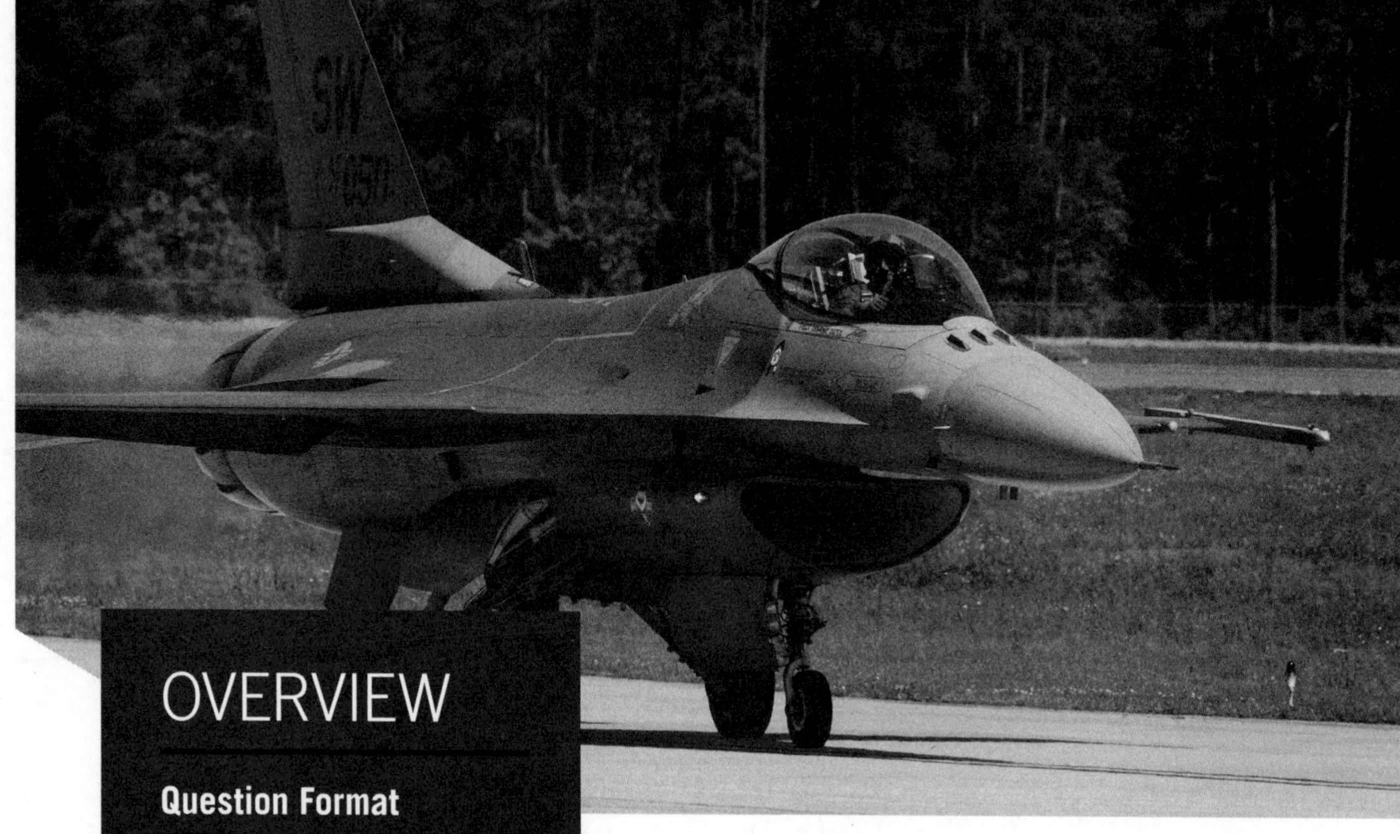

OVERVIEW

The Instrument Comprehension subtest of the AFOQT will assess your ability to determine the position of an airplane in flight by reading and comprehending instruments that show compass heading, plane pitch, and degree of banking. Unlike other subtests, there are only 4 answer choices per question to select from. You will be expected to answer quickly and accurately as you have only 5 minutes to answer 25 questions. Anyone aspiring to a Pilot or Air Battle Manager specialization should aim to score as high as possible, as this subtest is necessary for those fields.

QUESTION FORMAT

Let's take a look at what an Instrument Comprehension question will resemble on the test:

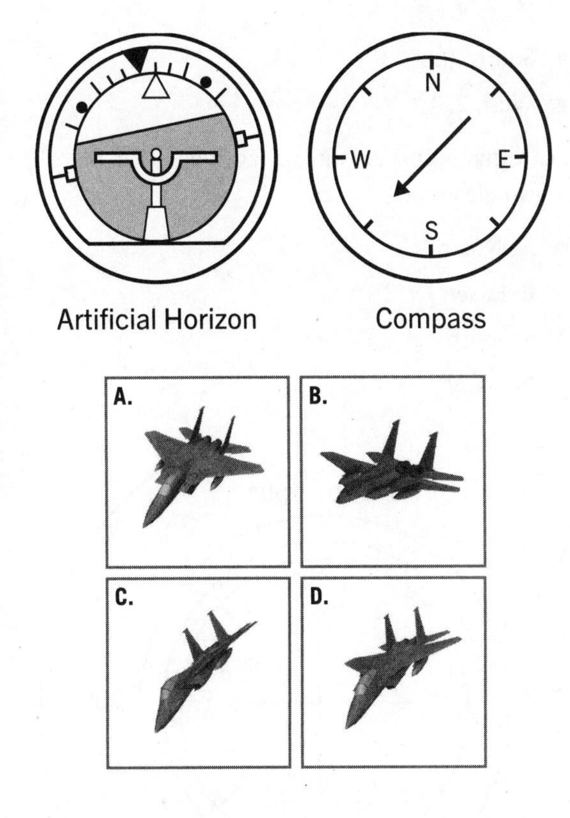

There are two elements visible in the question. From left to right, you have an artificial horizon and a compass. For the answer choices, you are given four images of an airplane. You need to look at the artificial horizon and compass and determine which of the four answer choices most closely represents what the instruments are showing. In the case of the above question, the correct answer is choice D. We'll discuss why that is later in the chapter. Before we pull it all together, let's explore a bit about the plane models and each of the instruments to learn how to read the dials and answer the questions.

THE PLANE

Before dissecting the dials attached to the questions, let's explore the plane model itself. As alluded to with the question earlier, every plane image represents the combination of three different variables: heading (the direction of the plane's travel), pitch (the climb or dive of the plane), and bank (the tilt of the wings). The following images represent aircraft with changes to these different variables, similar to what you will see in practice and on test day.

For plane heading, you will always be looking NORTH at the same altitude as each of the planes. That has the following effects on the appearance of the plane:

- A plane flying north will look like it's flying away.
- A plane flying south will look like it's heading toward you.
- A plane heading east will be flying to the right.
- A plane heading west will be flying to the left.

Here are some examples of the different headings:

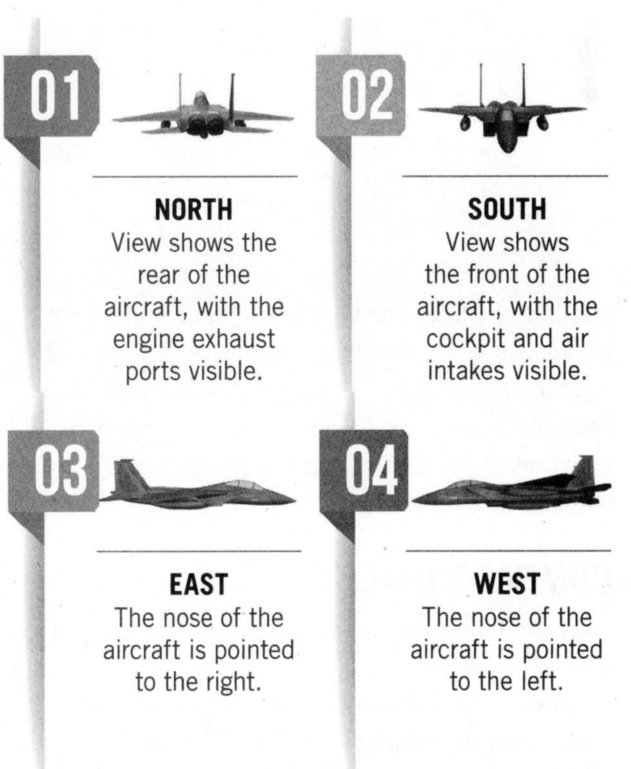

01
NORTH
View shows the rear of the aircraft, with the engine exhaust ports visible.
02
SOUTH
View shows the front of the aircraft, with the cockpit and air intakes visible.
03
EAST
The nose of the aircraft is pointed to the right.
04
WEST
The nose of the aircraft is pointed to the left.

Meanwhile, changes to pitch and banking will affect the visibility of the top and bottom of the plane model, as well as the appearance of the wings. As seen in the following images, pitching downward or upward reveals more of the aircraft.

Planes with banking can appear with one wing being more prominent than the other, the bottom of the aircraft being more visible, and so on. See the following for examples of aircraft banking:

01

Banking slightly to the RIGHT. Note that the left wing is not as fully visible when compared to the right wing.

02

Banking slightly to the LEFT. Note that the right wing is not as fully visible when compared to the left wing.

03

The top of the aircraft will show some detail for a cockpit as well as the vertical and horizontal stabilizers.

04

The bottom of the plane may give glimpses into landing gear, fuel tanks, and weaponry.

Heading, pitch, and banking can significantly affect the appearance of the plane model, with hundreds of combinations possible. To prepare for the possibilities, you need to see what the different instrument dials represent and how the different readings determine a plane's positioning.

COMPASS DIAL

Each question includes a dial labeled COMPASS. This dial will show the compass direction of the airplane in question. Note that this compass is rudimentary without any degree labels. The cardinal points of north, south, east, and west are abbreviated, and tick marks indicate the intercardinal points of northeast, northwest, southeast, and southwest.

Compasses are graduated in degrees CLOCKWISE from north. The cardinal (or main) points are as follows:

- North, 0° or 360°
- East, 90°
- South, 180°
- West, 270°

The cardinal points are always labeled with a coordinating single letter.

- **N:** North
- **E:** East
- **S:** South
- **W:** West

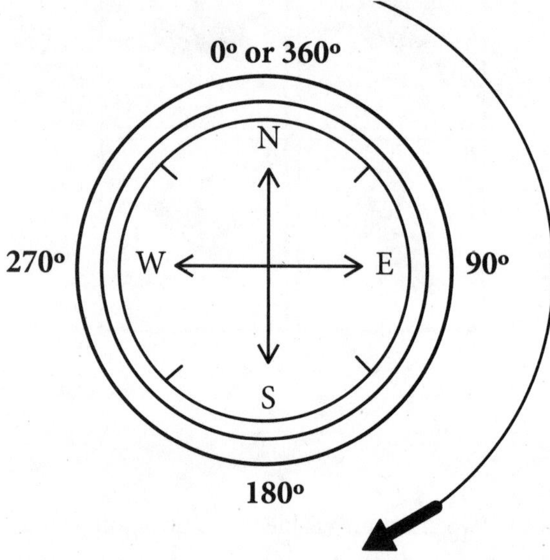

In addition, there are intercardinal points between each set of cardinal points. These represent the distance halfway between the two cardinal points referenced. The intercardinal points are as follows:

- Northeast, which equals 45°
- Southeast, which equals 135°
- Southwest, which equals 225°
- Northwest, which equals 315°

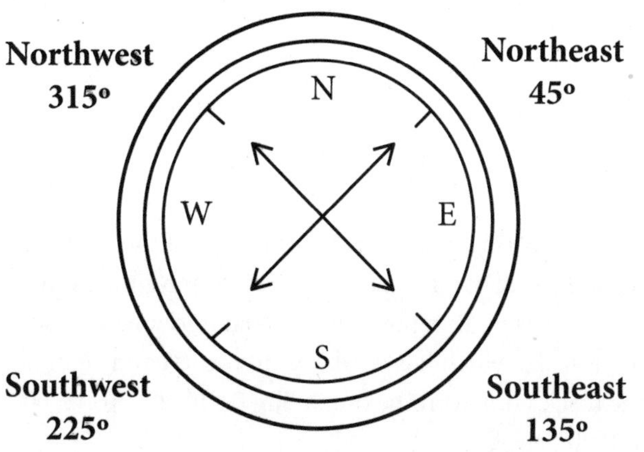

As noted in this illustration, the intercardinal points are always labeled with a tick mark only. You will need to memorize these if you have not yet done this.

Examples of test versions of the compass dial are as shown:

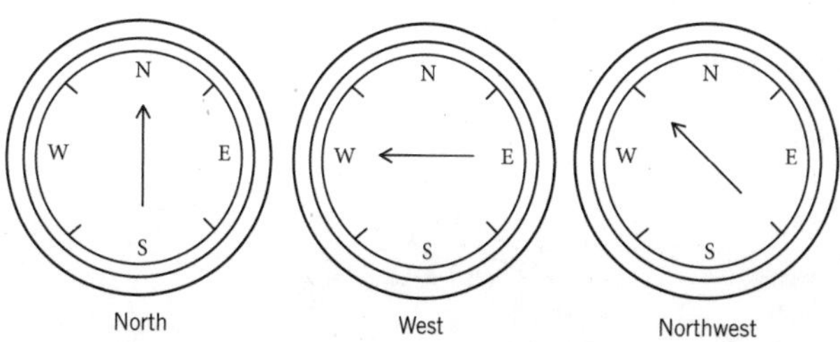

When interpreting the image of the plane, remember that you are always looking north at the same altitude as each of the planes. East is always to your right as you look at the page, west to your left, and south towards you.

Once you understand the direction of the plane, you are ready to interpret all eight possible headings. The following can act as a quick reference:

COMPASS AND PLANE STATES

Direction	Compass	Plane Behavior	Plane Example	Direction	Compass	Plane Behavior	Plane Example
North		Faces AWAY		South		Faces TOWARD YOU	
Northeast		Faces AWAY and to the RIGHT		Southwest		Faces TOWARD YOU and to the LEFT	
East		Faces to the RIGHT		West		Faces to the LEFT	
Southeast		Faces TOWARD YOU and to the RIGHT		Northwest		Faces AWAY and to the LEFT	

ARTIFICIAL HORIZON

In addition to the compass, each question will present an artificial horizon dial that incorporates two main areas requiring analysis: the plane's pitch and bank.

Here's an example of an artificial horizon:

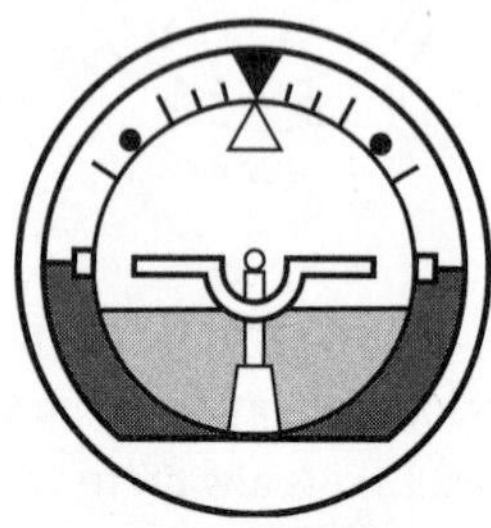

Understanding both pitch and bank is necessary to answer the question accurately. The following sections will break down both concepts to help you better understand how they are presented and how they affect plane positioning.

Pitch

Pitch describes the degree of upward or downward tilt resulting in a climb or dive in which the plane ascends or descends, respectively. The nose of the plane is illustrated using a round circle in the middle of the dial:

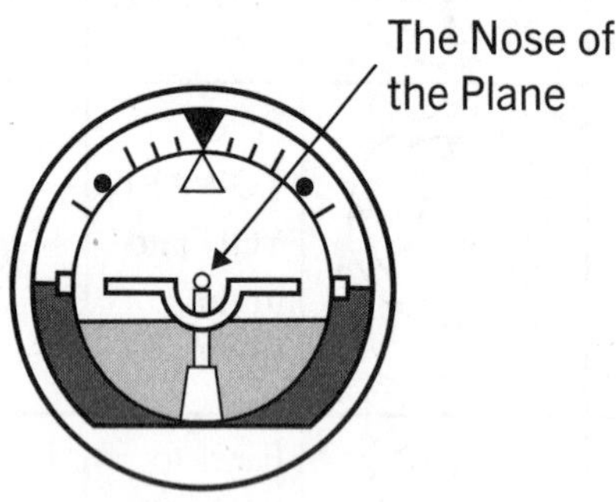

The location of the nose of the plane relative to the white space (the sky) and the gray space (the ground) indicates the plane's pitch. The plane will be level with the horizon (where the two colors meet in the middle) or have some degree of climb or dive.

Banking

The term banking refers to the lowering or raising of a plane's ailerons, thus changing the angle between the wings and the horizon. A plane can bank to the left or right. This leads to changes in the direction of the plane.

In essence, this results in the "turning" of the plane or the adjusting of its heading. To determine which way the plane is banking on the artificial horizon, use the bank scale, which has markings to the left and right of the black pointer in the outer ring (at 10, 20, 30, 45, 60, and 90 degrees of bank).

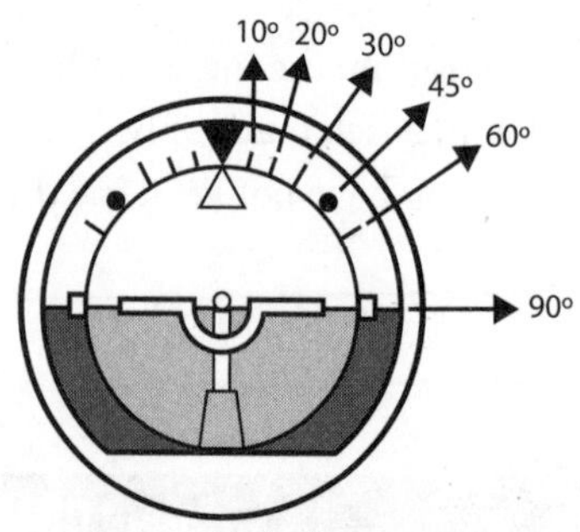

The white triangle on the artificial horizon will point to the degree of bank on the right or left. To discern whether it is a right or left bank, note the position of the black triangle. It is your zero-degree marker, or "pointer." If the white arrow is pointing to the right of the black pointer, you are banking right and vice versa for the left.

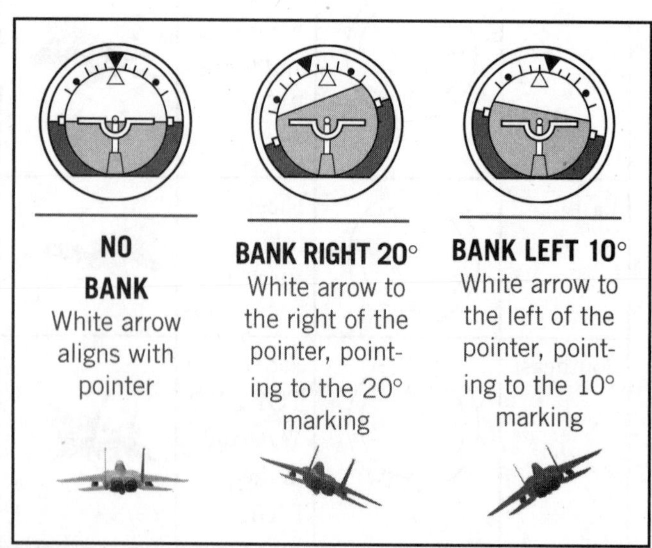

The following is a quick reference to help you identify the pitch of the plane:

ARTIFICIAL HORIZON - PITCH AND PLANE STATES							
Pitch Degree	**Artificial Horizon Behavior**	**Artificial Horizon**	**Plane State**	**Pitch Degree**	**Artificial Horizon Behavior**	**Artificial Horizon**	**Plane State**
No Climb or Dive	Nose on the Horizon			Slight Dive	Nose slightly in the GRAY region		
Slight Climb	Nose slightly in the WHITE region			Moderate Dive	Nose fully in the GRAY region		
Moderate Climb	Nose fully in the WHITE region			Steep Dive	Nose completely in the GRAY region, with minimal, if any, white showing		
Steep Climb	Nose completely in the WHITE region, with minimal, if any, gray showing			Inverted	The WHITE and GRAY regions are inverted.		

PUTTING IT ALL TOGETHER

Now that we have examined the plane states and different instrument elements, we can combine all of this information to quickly and accurately interpret the dials. The following are three basic steps to employ when answering questions:

- Step 1: Identify plane DIRECTION
  - Using the COMPASS DIAL, identify the relative direction. Is it traveling away from you to the north? Southeast, toward you and to your right?
- Step 2: Identify plane PITCH
  - Using the nose of the plane, analyze if it is level, climbing, diving, and at what rate. Is it a steep climb? Is it a slight dive?

- Step 3: Identify plane BANK
    - Using the white triangle, identify whether the plane is aligned to the pointer or banking to the right or left and to what degree. Is it banking to the right 20 degrees? Banking past 90 degrees to the left?

Using the combination of DIRECTION, PITCH, and BANK, discern what the plane would look like. Work through each of the variables to eliminate answer choices and find the appropriate plane state. Each element must match to be the correct answer.

Practice on the following question to check your comprehension:

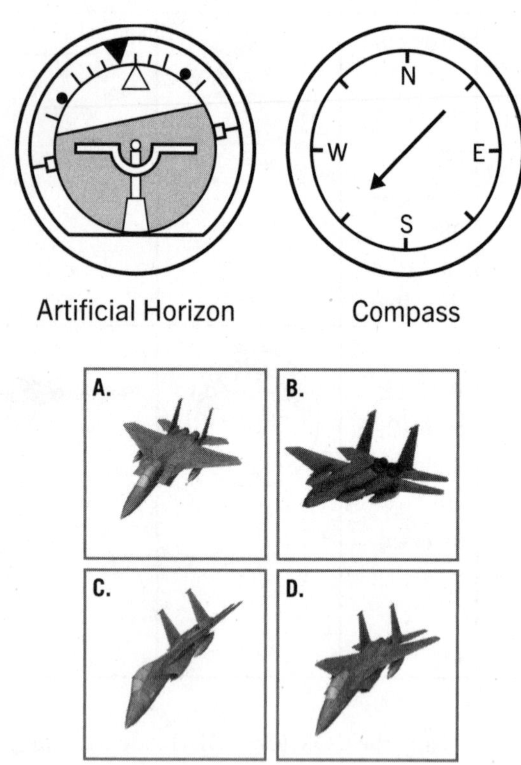

Remember, start with heading. The compass states that the plane has a heading of southwest. The plane should be traveling toward you and to the left. You can now eliminate choice B, which is traveling northwest, away from you and to the left. Next, examine pitch. The plane will have a slight dive. Unfortunately, this still leaves choices A, C, and D. Although choice C may have a steeper dive than the artificial horizon depicts, we should check it against our last instrument reading: banking. The artificial horizon shows a right bank of 10 degrees. Eliminate choice A as it is banking left. To decide between choices C and D, consider the steepness of their banks. Choice C is banking harder, likely closer to 30 degrees, well over the milder bank of choice D. Thus, choice C does not represent the instruments as well as choice D. **The correct answer is choice D.**

Try one more:

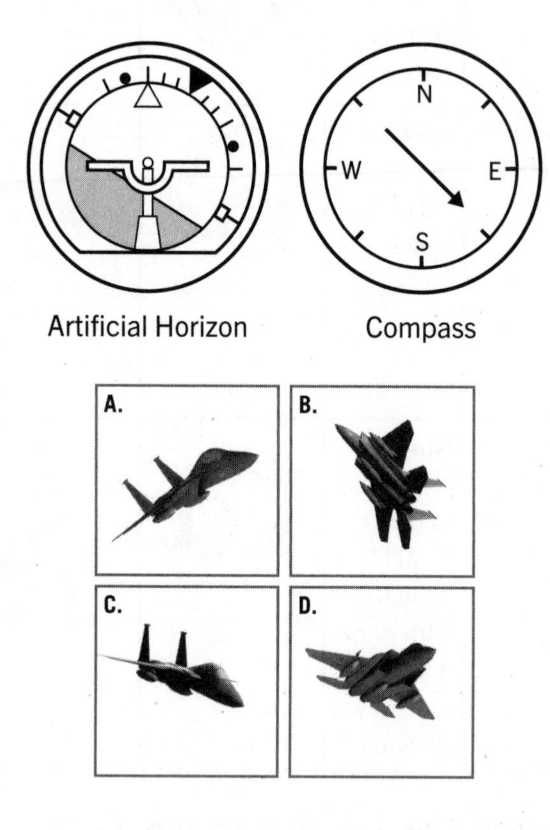

The compass reads southeast, and the artificial horizon shows a left bank of 30 degrees and a slight climb. **The correct answer is choice D.**

You now know what you need to in order to conquer the Instrument Comprehension subtest. It's time to practice. Try your hand at the following mini-quiz to test your skills.

MINI-QUIZ: INSTRUMENT COMPREHENSION

Directions: In each problem, the left-hand dial is labeled ARTIFICIAL HORIZON and the right-hand dial is labeled COMPASS. Each problem consists of two dials and four airplanes in flight. Your task is to determine which one of the four airplanes is MOST NEARLY in the position indicated by the two dials.

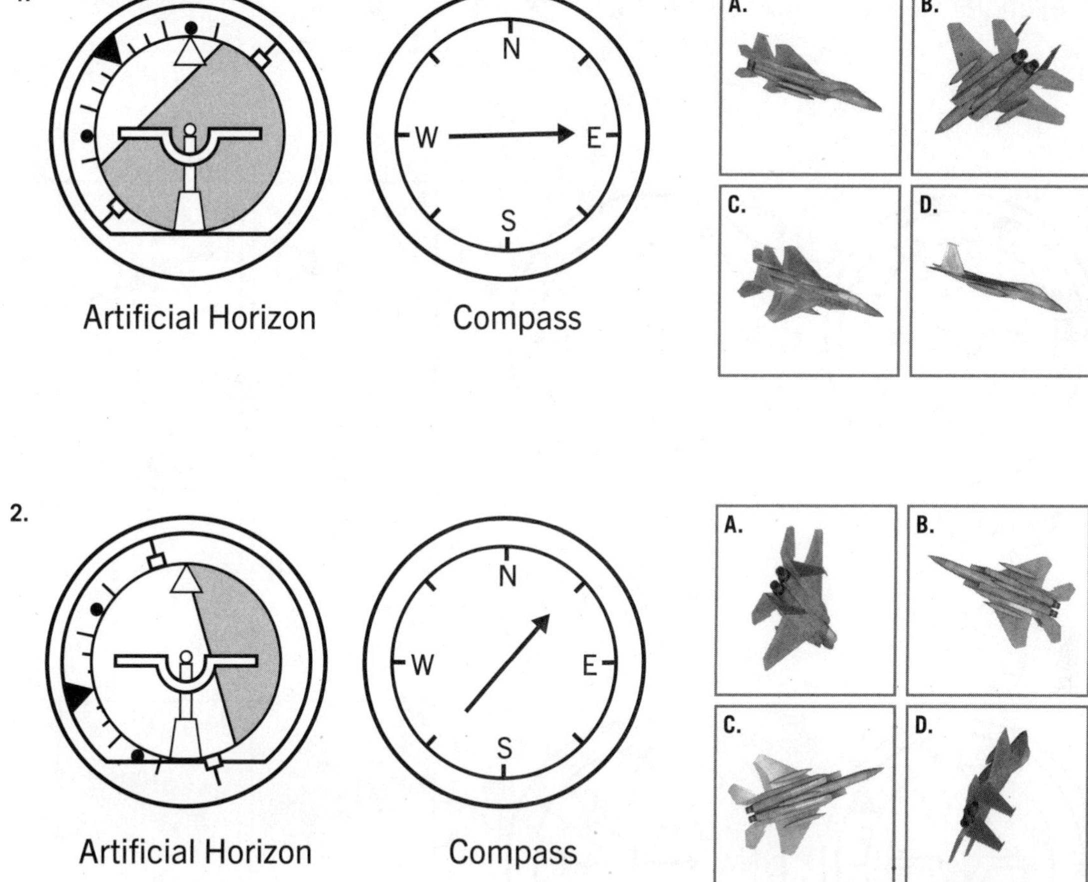

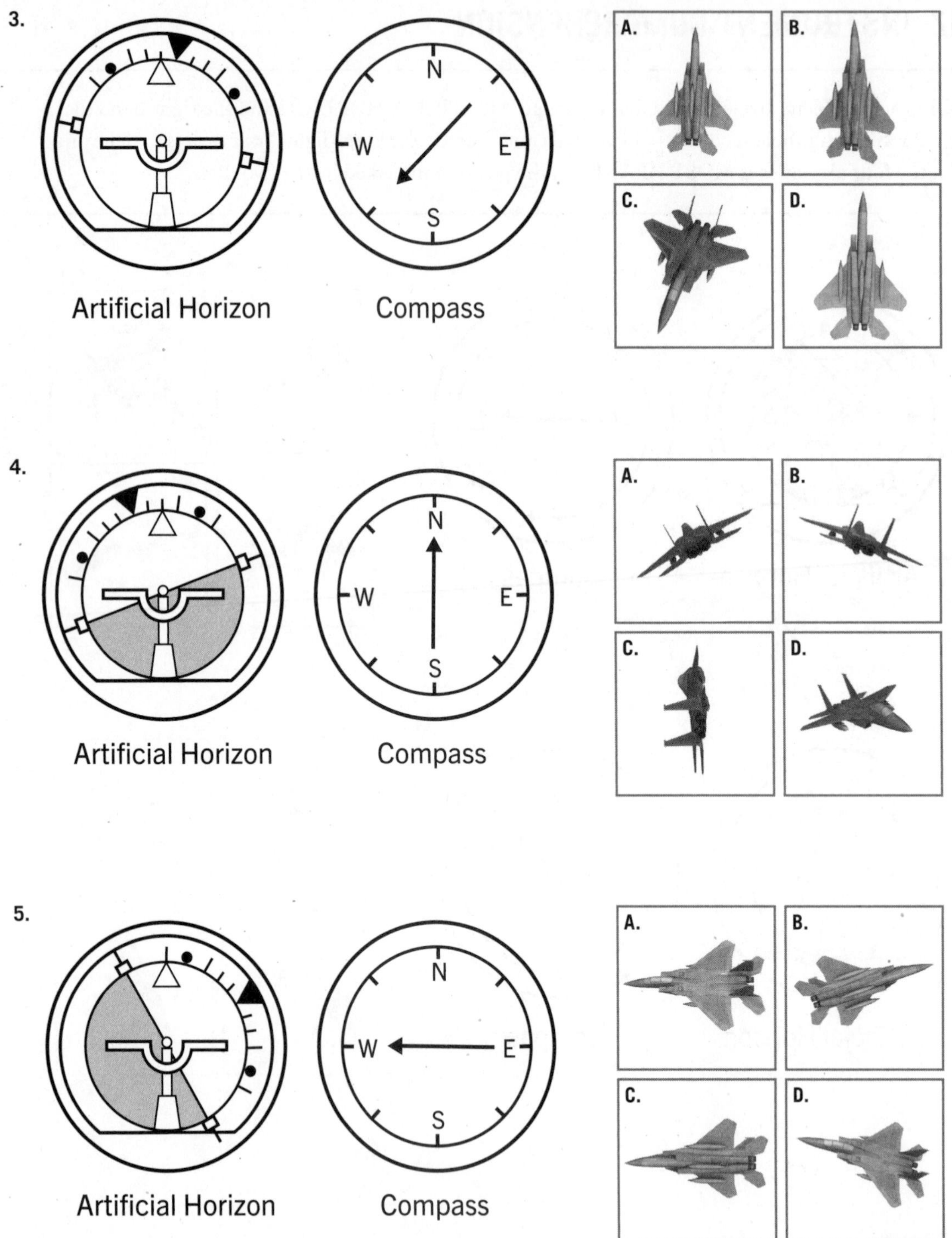
3.
N
W
E
S
Artificial Horizon
Compass
A.
B.
C.
D.
4.
N
W
E
S
Artificial Horizon
Compass
A.
B.
C.
D.
5.
N
W
E
S
Artificial Horizon
Compass
A.
B.
C.
D.

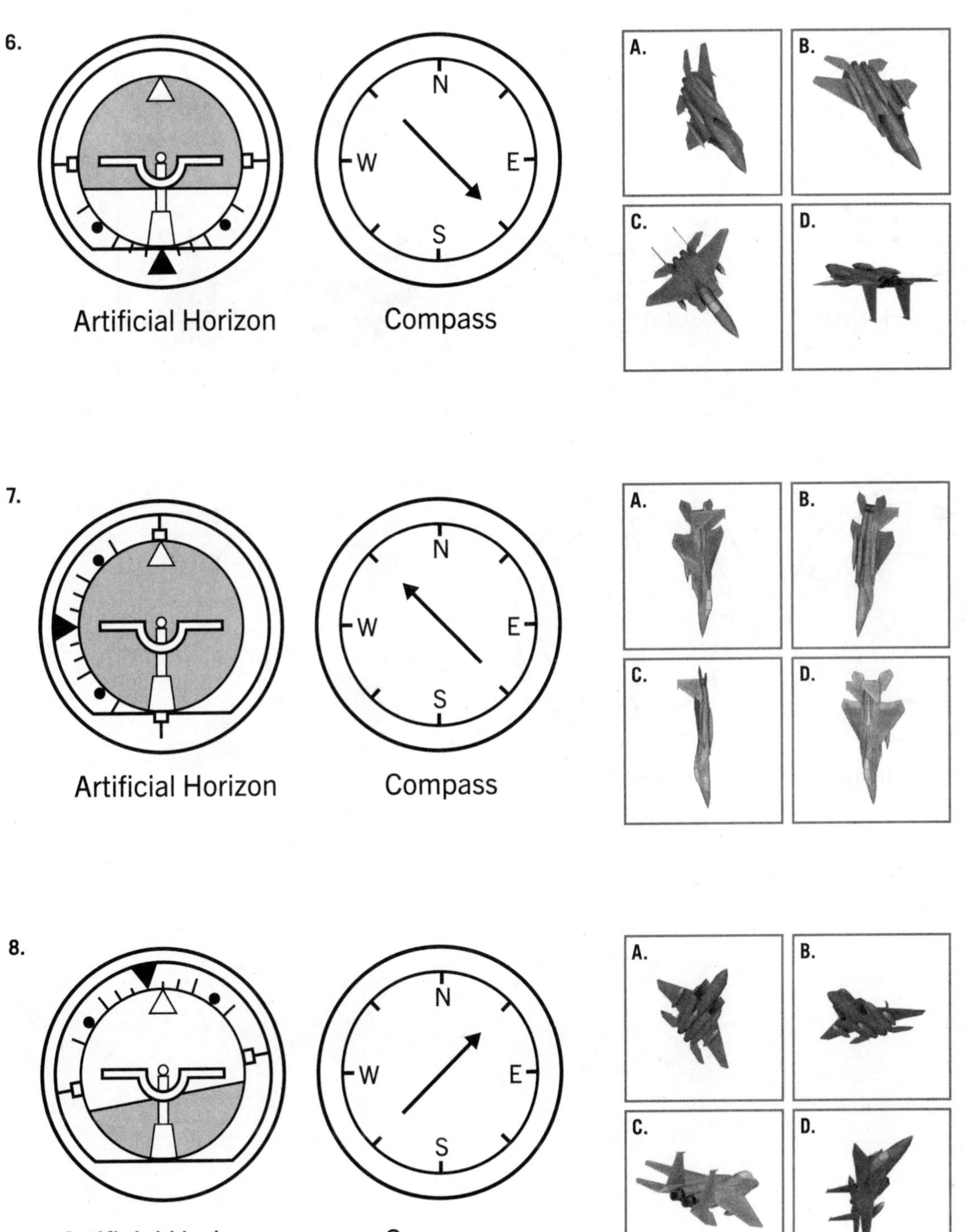
6.
Artificial Horizon
N
W
E
S
Compass
A.
B.
C.
D.
7.
Artificial Horizon
N
W
E
S
Compass
A.
B.
C.
D.
8.
Artificial Horizon
N
W
E
S
Compass
A.
B.
C.
D.

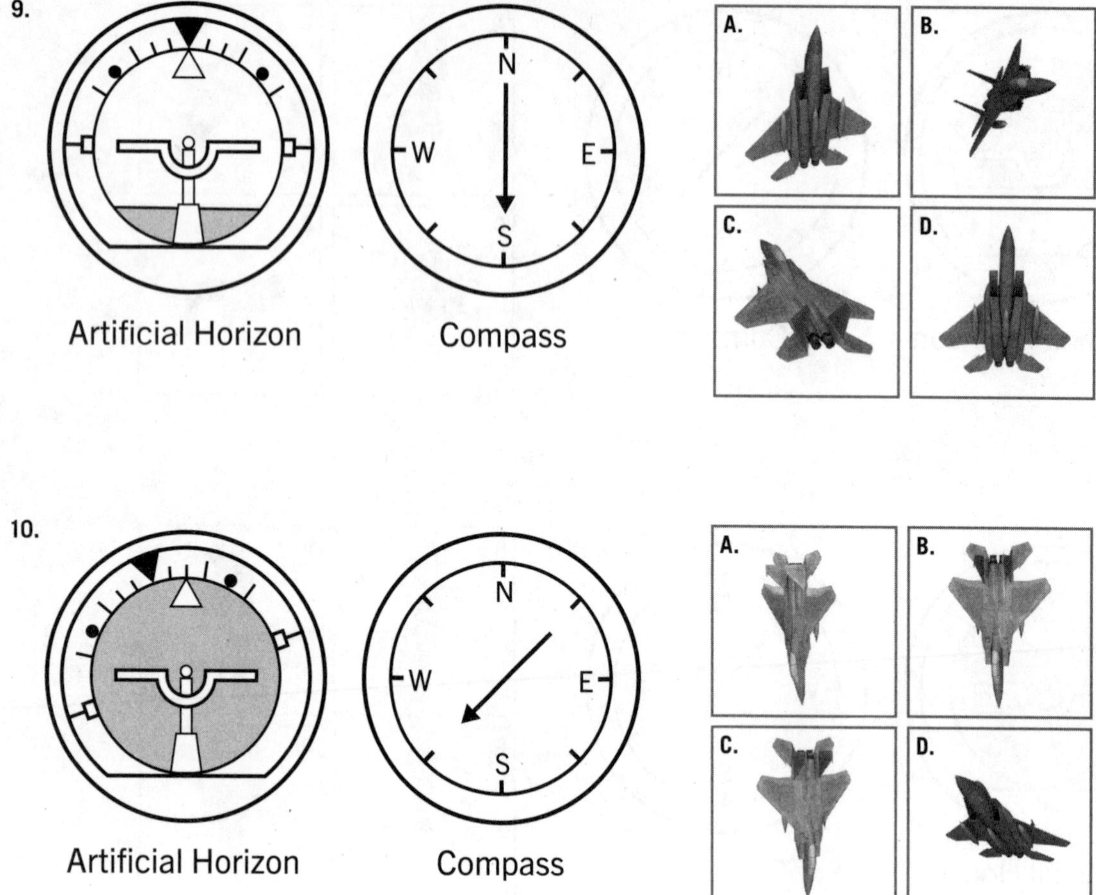
9.
N
W
E
S
Artificial Horizon
Compass
A.
B.
C.
D.
10.
N
W
E
S
Artificial Horizon
Compass
A.
B.
C.
D.

ANSWER KEY AND EXPLANATIONS

1. C	3. B	5. A	7. B	9. D
2. D	4. B	6. B	8. C	10. A

1. **The correct answer is C.** The plane is slightly descending and banking 45 degrees to the right. Choice A is banking to the left. Choice B is heading northwest. Choice D is not banking.
2. **The correct answer is D.** The plane is slightly ascending and banking more than 90 degrees to the right. Choice A is slightly descending. Choice B is heading west. Choice C is heading east and banking left 90 degrees.
3. **The correct answer is B.** The plane is ascending straight up, banking 10 degrees to the left. Choice A has no bank. Choice C is slightly descending and banking 20 degrees to the left. Choice D is heading southeast and banking 20 degrees to the left.
4. **The correct answer is B.** The plane is level with the horizon, banking 20 degrees to the right. Choice A is banking 30 degrees to the left. Choice C is slightly ascending, banking 90 degrees to the left. Choice D is heading southeast.
5. **The correct answer is A.** The plane is level with the horizon, banking 60 degrees to the left. Choice B is slightly ascending and heading east. Choice C is banking 60 degrees to the right. Choice D is slightly ascending.
6. **The correct answer is B.** The plane is heading southeast, slightly descending, and inverted. Choice A is banking 90 degrees to the left. Choice C is banking 45 degrees to the right. Choice D is heading northwest and is level with the horizon.
7. **The correct answer is B.** The plane is descending, banking 90 degrees to the right. Choice A is heading northeast. Choice C is banking 60 degrees to the left. Choice D is heading south and banking right 45 degrees.
8. **The correct answer is C.** The plane is heading northeast, slightly ascending, and banking 10 degrees to the right. Choice A is heading south and banking 60 degrees to the left. Choice B is heading southwest. Choice D is banking 90 degrees to the right.
9. **The correct answer is D.** The plane is heading south, ascending with no bank. Choice A is banking 10 degrees to the right. Choice B is heading southeast and banking 60 degrees to the right. Choice C is heading northwest.
10. **The correct answer is A.** The plane is heading southwest, descending, and banking 20 degrees to the right. Choice B is banking 20 degrees to the left. Choice C is heading south and is banking 45 degrees to the left. Choice D is slightly ascending and has no bank.

SUMMING IT UP

- The Instrument Comprehension subtest assesses your ability to determine the position of an airplane in flight based on readings from a compass and an artificial horizon.
- You will have 5 minutes to answer 25 questions.
- A high score on this subtest is required for the Pilot and Air Battle Manager career fields.
- Questions will come in the form of an artificial horizon showing pitch and bank and a compass showing direction. With that information, you must select one of the four aircraft images that best represents what the instruments show.
- A basic three-step approach can help you pick the correct aircraft:
    - Identify the DIRECTION
        - The compass will indicate what direction the plane is heading.
    - Identify the PITCH
        - The artificial horizon will show pitch: Nose in the white portion means climb, gray portion means dive. From there, it is a matter of determining whether the climb or dive is slight, moderate, steep, or inverted.
    - Identify the BANK
        - Along the outer edge of the artificial horizon are markings indicating the angle of bank: 10°, 20°, 30°, 45°, 60°, and 90°. Pointer placement to the left of the 0° mark (the inverted black triangle) indicates a left bank and vice versa.
- As you look at each aircraft, remember that you are always facing north and you are level with the aircraft; if the nose is pointed toward you, the aircraft is heading south. If all you see are engine exhaust ports, the plane is headed north.

NOTES

BLOCK COUNTING

OVERVIEW

Block Counting, like Instrument Comprehension, is designed to test your spatial orientation, visual processing, and ability to think in three dimensions. Those skills are necessary for memorizing battlespace environments and creating a mental map of how various avionics systems interact. The subtest presents 30 questions to be answered in 4.5 minutes. As with other AFOQT subtests, the time constraints require a quick working pace and, in this case, task you with answering almost seven questions every minute.

THINKING IN THREE DIMENSIONS

The Block Counting subtest requires that you "see" into a three-dimensional pile of blocks. In a given set, any block may be touching another block on the side, top, bottom, front, or back. To help you visualize this, think of the game Jenga. Layers of blocks are stacked on top of each other, each layer turned 90° from the previous. Block

Counting is similar, just with more blocks and some additional block rotations.

The question sets will present an elevated view from the corner of a stack of blocks, giving you a view of the top of the pile as well as two sides. From this vantage point, you should be able to see a face (a flat surface) of each of the blocks in the pile. Remember that the blocks are all the same lengths and go all the way through, so you know the blocks in the second row are the same as the ones in the first row, even though you cannot see them. Some of the blocks will be numbered, and your task is to count how many adjacent blocks are touching one of the numbered blocks. **Corners don't count,** only the faces that contact the top, bottom, front, back, or either side of the numbered block.

For each question, you will be shown a pile of blocks with a table next to it. Some of the blocks will be numbered but most will not. On the table, the left column has a number that corresponds to a block in the pile. Across the top are five answer options. Count the number of blocks that touch the numbered block, then go across the row for that block in the table until you find the same number. Take a look at the following example:

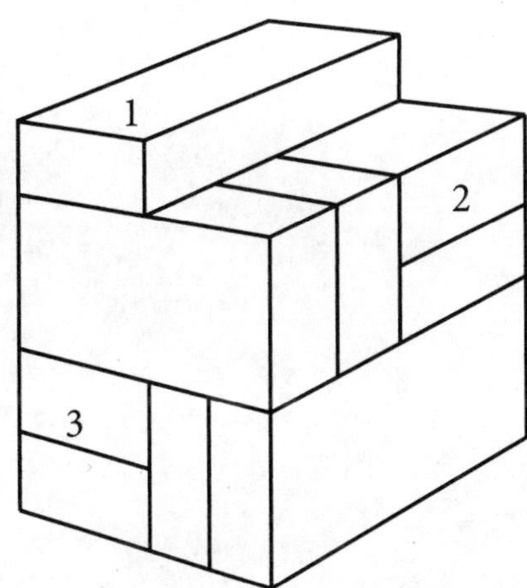

Block	A	B	C	D	E
1	2	3	4	5	6
2	1	2	3	4	5
3	2	3	4	5	6

Looking at the diagram, you can see that block 1 contacts three blocks, and all three are below block 1. In the following image, all the blocks touching block 1 are shaded in:

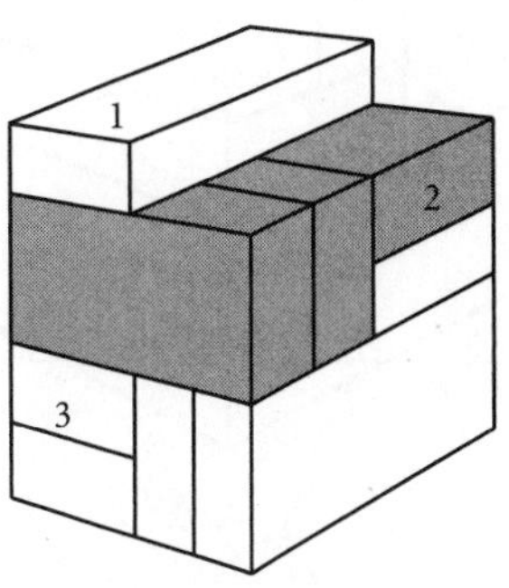

For block 2, there is contact with one below, one to the side, and one above:

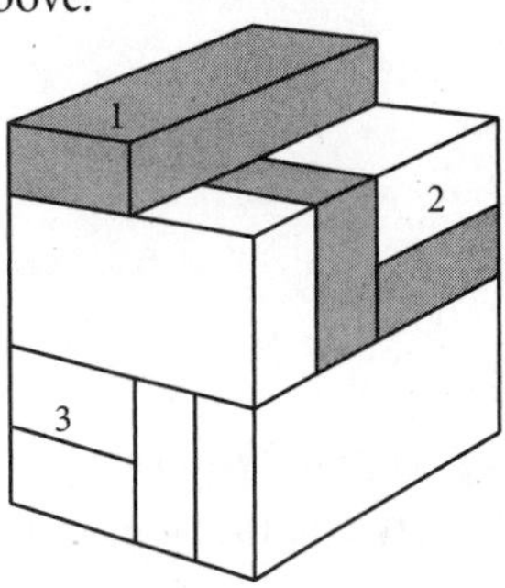

For block 3, there is one below, one to the side, and three above.

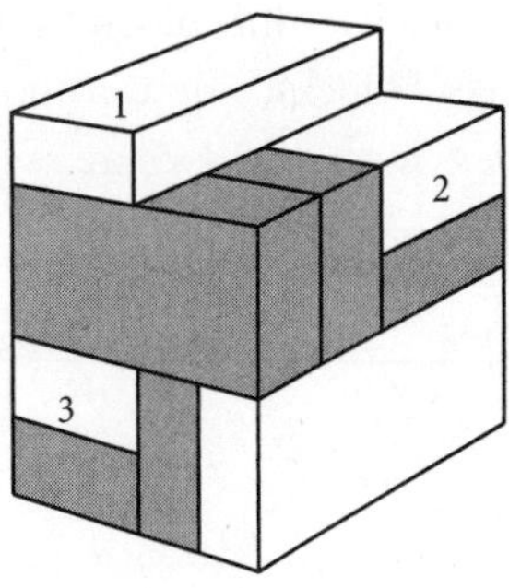

The correct answers for blocks 1, 2, and 3 are as follows:

1. B
2. C
3. D

Now try a diagram with five blocks:

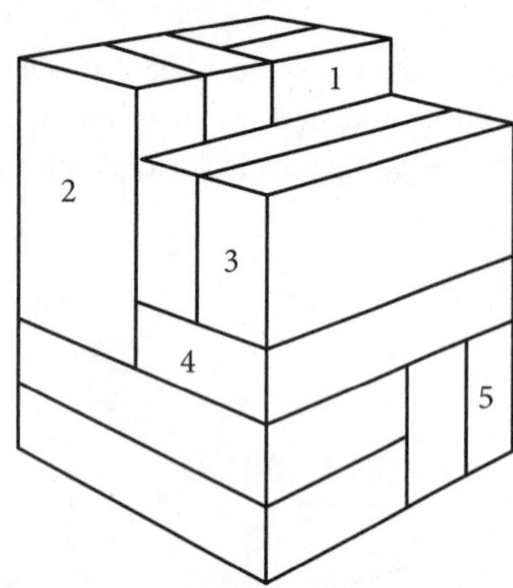

Block	A	B	C	D	E
1	2	3	4	5	6
2	1	2	3	4	5
3	2	3	4	5	6
4	5	6	7	8	9
5	4	5	6	7	8

For block 1, there is contact with two blocks along the bottom, one behind, one to the side, and two in front, for a total of 6. Block 2 has two sides empty along with the top, but two blocks touch in the front, one behind, and one underneath for a total of 4. Block 3 only touches two other blocks, while block 4 touches 8 others. Block 5 touches 4 blocks, 3 on top and 1 to the side. The correct answers for blocks 1–5 are as follows:

1. E
2. D
3. A
4. D
5. A

BUILDING YOUR BLOCK COUNTING SKILLS

To build your skills before test day, try using wooden or 3-D printed blocks to build your own piles. Use blocks that are half as tall as they are wide and four times as long as they are wide, so they can all fit together evenly. Get 10–15 of them, number the short faces of 3–5 blocks, and pile them up in rows. Don't forget to rotate some blocks. Now, practice counting how many other blocks that block #1 is touching. Remember, corners and edges do not count, just faces. If you are unsure or just want to confirm your answers, take the pile apart so you can see how each block is touching the others. Then, shuffle the blocks up and practice again. You will see in some of the diagrams in this chapter that blocks can be positioned so there can be gaps, or so that some blocks seemingly float above others. Try building some piles this way and notice how every block is touching *at least* one other. If you have extra blocks, paint or color them so you know they are not really there but rather are acting as negative space and holding other blocks in position.

Now that you have an idea of how Block Counting questions work and ideas about how to prepare, test yourself to gauge your current abilities.

MINI-QUIZ: BLOCK COUNTING

Directions: This part of the test measures your ability to "see into" a 3-dimensional pile of blocks. Given a certain numbered block, your task is to determine how many other blocks the numbered block touches. Blocks are considered touching only if all or part of their faces touch. Blocks that only touch corners do not count. All of the blocks in each pile are the same size and shape.

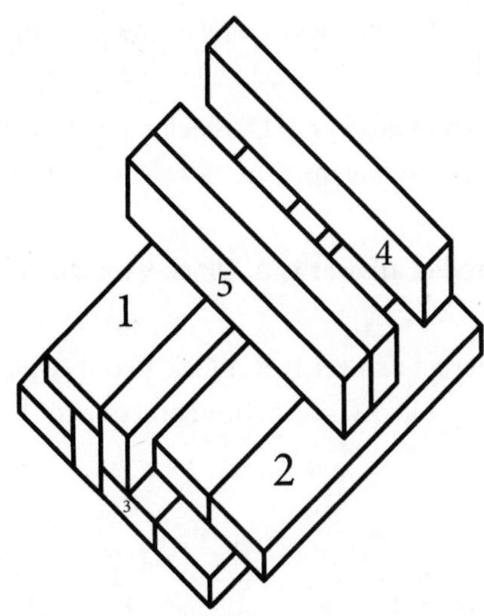

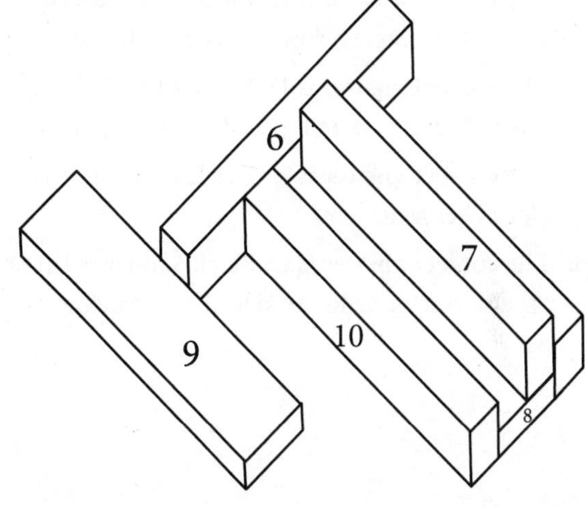

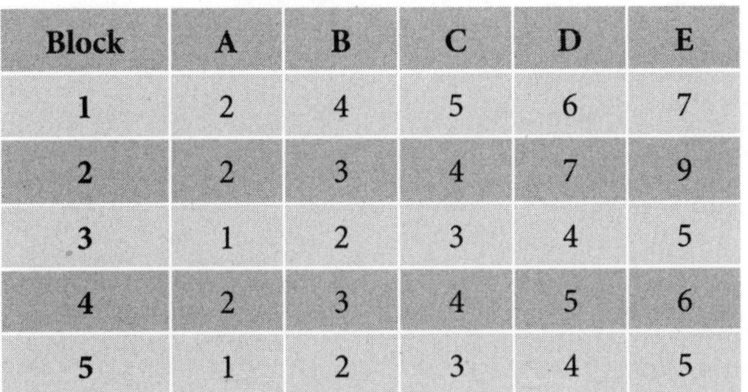

Block	A	B	C	D	E
1	2	4	5	6	7
2	2	3	4	7	9
3	1	2	3	4	5
4	2	3	4	5	6
5	1	2	3	4	5

Block	A	B	C	D	E
6	1	2	3	5	6
7	1	2	3	5	7
8	1	2	3	4	5
9	1	2	4	5	6
10	1	2	3	4	7

ANSWER KEY AND EXPLANATIONS

1. C	3. D	5. C	7. C	9. A
2. A	4. A	6. D	8. D	10. B

1. **The correct answer is C.** Block 1 touches five other blocks: one below, one to the side, and three that are on top.
2. **The correct answer is A.** Block 2 touches two other blocks: one below and one to the side.
3. **The correct answer is D.** Block 3 touches four other blocks: two on top and one to either side.
4. **The correct answer is A.** Block 4 touches two blocks below it.
5. **The correct answer is C.** Block 5 touches three other blocks: one to the side and two below.
6. **The correct answer is D.** Block 6 touches five other blocks: four in front and one to the side.
7. **The correct answer is C.** Block 7 touches three other blocks: one below, one to the side, and one behind.
8. **The correct answer is D.** Block 8 touches four other blocks: one on either side, one on top, and one behind.
9. **The correct answer is A.** Block 9 touches only one block.
10. **The correct answer is B.** Block 10 only touches two other blocks, one behind and one to the side.

SUMMING IT UP

- The Block Counting section of the AFOQT requires you to demonstrate spatial recognition and the ability to think in three dimensions.
- Consider practicing on your own by using wooden or 3-D printed blocks to help you visualize different configurations of blocks.
- You will have four and a half minutes to answer 30 questions, so you need to work quickly.
- Unless you see evidence to the contrary, always assume the blocks are all the same size and shape.

AVIATION INFORMATION

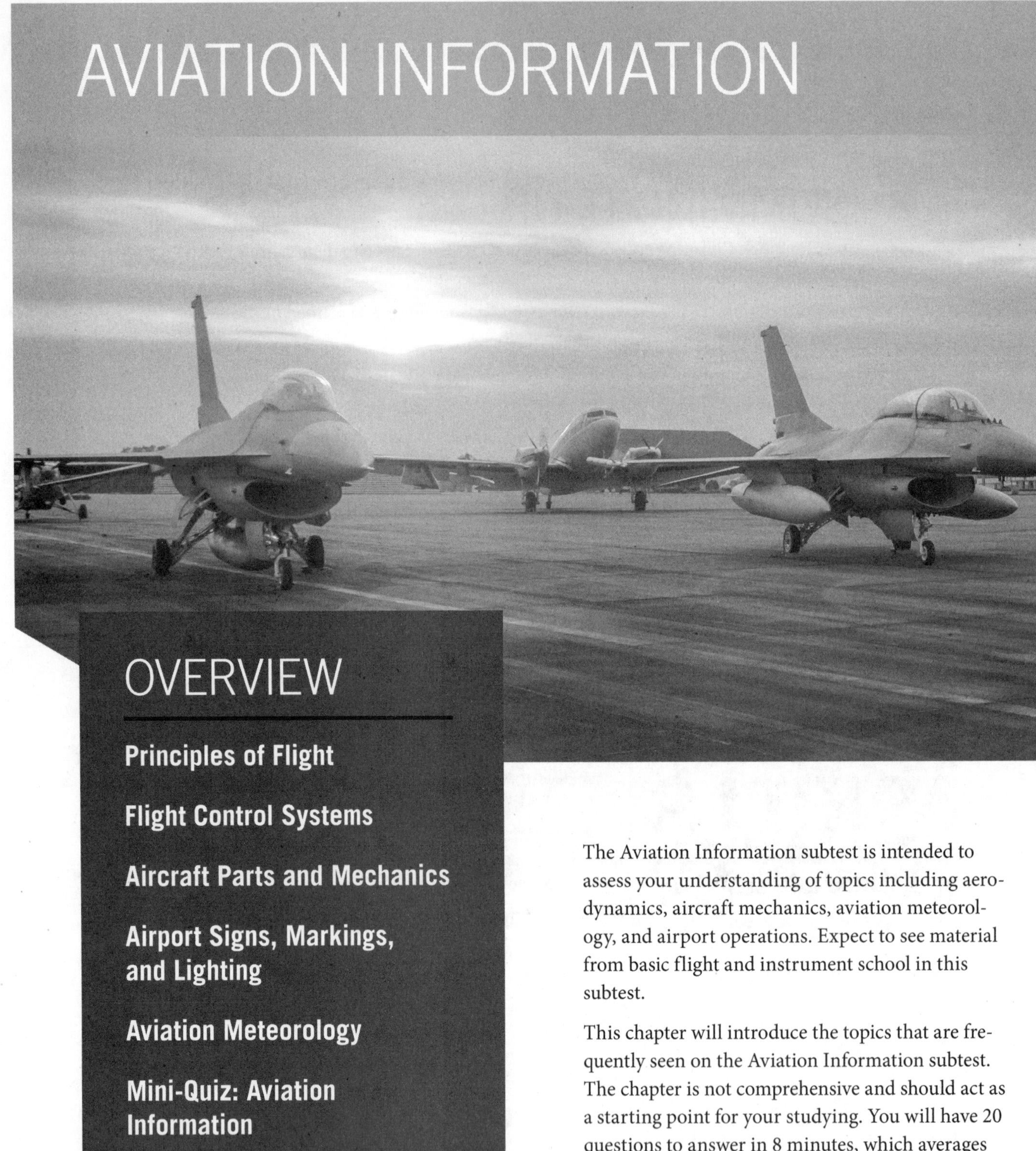

OVERVIEW

The Aviation Information subtest is intended to assess your understanding of topics including aerodynamics, aircraft mechanics, aviation meteorology, and airport operations. Expect to see material from basic flight and instrument school in this subtest.

This chapter will introduce the topics that are frequently seen on the Aviation Information subtest. The chapter is not comprehensive and should act as a starting point for your studying. You will have 20 questions to answer in 8 minutes, which averages out to 24 seconds per question. Each of the questions or incomplete statements on the test is followed by five choices. You will need to decide which option best answers the question or completes the statement.

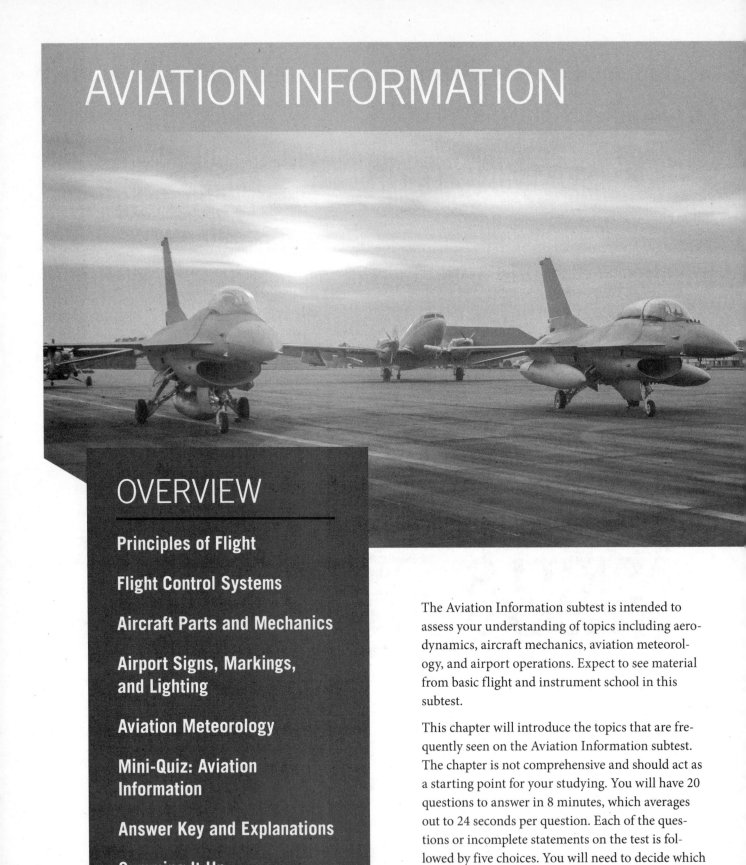

16

Here are some online resources to help you study:

- FAA Aeronautical Information Manual (AIM)
  https://www.faa.gov/air_traffic/publications/atpubs/aim_html/
- FAA Federal Aviation Regulations (FARs)
  https://www.faa.gov/regulations_policies/faa_regulations/
- FAA Pilot's Handbook of Aeronautical Knowledge
  https://www.faa.gov/regulations_policies/handbooks_manuals/aviation/phak/

PRINCIPLES OF FLIGHT

For future Air Force officers, knowing the principles of flight is fundamental. This section will help you prepare for the exam by providing an overview of aerodynamics. Aerodynamics is the study of how gases (air) interact with moving bodies, which is integral for understanding how flight is possible.

All aircraft are subject to the following forces: *lift, weight, thrust*, and *drag*. Aerodynamics considers how aircraft must work with these forces in order to take off, climb, cruise, descend, and land safely.

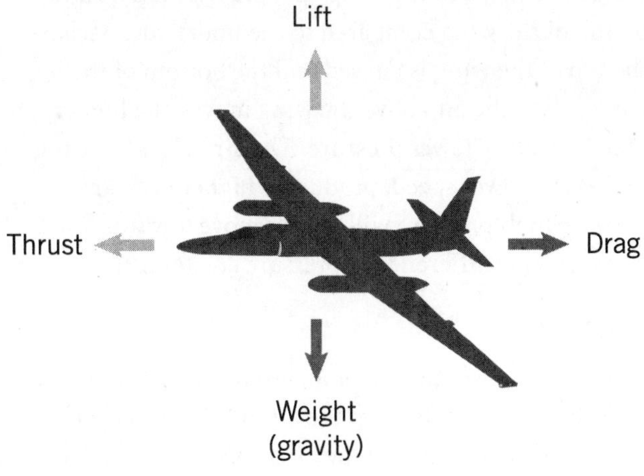

LIFT
The aerodynamic force that holds an airplane up in the air, primarily through the design of its wings.

WEIGHT
The combined load of the aircraft itself, the crew, the fuel, and the cargo or baggage. Weight pulls the aircraft downward because of the force of gravity.

THRUST
The force generated by an airplane's engine that propels it forward by air that is pulled in and then pushed out in the opposite direction.

DRAG
The force that acts opposite (or backwards) to the direction of motion and tends to slow an airplane because of friction and differences in air pressure.

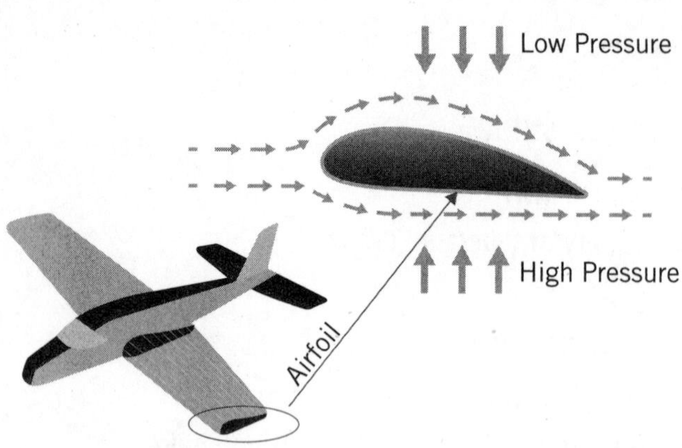

Newton's Laws of Motion

To understand how flight is possible, recall Newton's laws of motion:

Newton's First Law: An object will remain in motion or at rest unless something influences it and changes its course. This property is referred to as inertia.

Newton's Second Law: The force acting on an object is equal to the mass of that object times its acceleration. The greater the applied force, the greater the change in motion.

Newton's Third Law: For every action (or applied force) there is an equal and opposite reaction.

Newton's laws of motion help to explain how the relationships between these forces make it possible for an aircraft to achieve and sustain flight. According to Newton's third law, the four forces of flight—lift, weight, thrust, and drag—have equal and opposite reactions to each other. As thrust propels the aircraft forward, drag also creates resistance for the aircraft. As gravity pulls down on the aircraft, lift acts in the opposite direction to keep the aircraft in flight. While gravity is a constant, the pilot can control thrust and attitude, which affect lift and drag.

To take off, the force of an aircraft's thrust must overcome the force of drag and at the same time produce enough lift to overcome gravity and fly. In order for the object in motion—in this case, the aircraft—to stay in motion in level flight, the forces must be balanced: thrust vs. drag and lift vs. gravity. The force required for an aircraft to accelerate is equal to the mass of the aircraft times the desired acceleration. When the force of thrust is greater than the force of drag, the aircraft will accelerate, but drag increases as well in an effort to balance out the thrust. When the force of drag is greater than the force of thrust, the aircraft will decelerate. Acceleration from increased thrust also creates more lift. Likewise, deceleration, caused by reducing thrust, reduces lift.

Bernoulli's Principle

While some scientists explain lift using Newton's third law of motion, other scientists see the Bernoulli principle as a more fitting explanation. Bernoulli's principle establishes an inverse relationship between the speed of a moving fluid (meaning a liquid or gas) and pressure.

An airfoil is a shaped object, like a wing, propellor blade, or tail, designed to produce an aerodynamic reaction perpendicular to the airstream. Airfoils are designed and customized to create the most effective balance of lift and drag for the flight conditions in which an aircraft is expected to perform. A wing's shape and **angle of attack**, the angle between the chord of an airfoil and the relative motion of the aircraft, will affect how much lift is produced.

When an airfoil passes through the air, the air is split; some goes under the wing, and some goes over the wing. The shape of the wing changes the air pressure on top of the wing compared to the underside. Because the top of the wing is curved and the bottom of the wing is flat, the air above the wing moves at a higher speed, creating lower pressure. The air below the wing moves at a lower speed, producing higher pressure. Because high pressure will always move towards low pressure, this difference in pressure creates lift.

Attitude

While thrust is required for an aircraft to achieve flight and lift is required to keep the aircraft in level flight, the pilot can also control the aircraft's attitude. **Attitude** refers to the orientation or position of an aircraft relative to the natural horizon along its three axes of

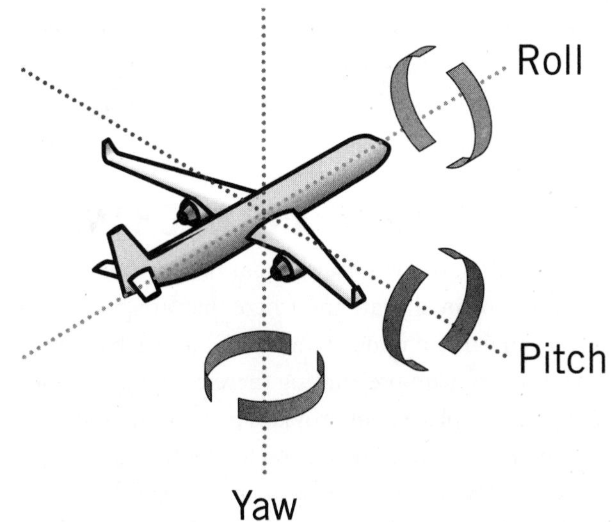

rotation. These three axes describe the plane's lateral, longitudinal, and vertical movement. Pitch is the movement of an aircraft's nose up or down. Yaw is the movement of an aircraft's nose right or left. Roll is the movement of an aircraft's wing up or down.

FLIGHT CONTROL SYSTEMS

Aircraft flight control systems consist of both primary and secondary systems and are used by pilots to control the direction and altitude of an aircraft in flight. The primary control system consists of an elevator, ailerons, and a rudder, and each component is critical to controlling an aircraft safely during flight. Pilots can maneuver an aircraft around each of its three axes, generating the motions of pitch, roll, and yaw. Pilots steer the aircraft's path as needed with a control wheel (or stick) and foot pedals located in the cockpit. These cockpit controls are then connected to movable sections, called flight control surfaces, that are attached to the airplane's structure. The secondary control system can refine these movements and improve performance while also easing the burden on the pilot.

Primary Flight Controls

Each component of the primary flight control system controls movement of the aircraft along each of its three axes of rotation: yaw, pitch, and roll. By changing the airflow and distribution of pressure around the airfoil, the pilot can affect how much lift or drag is produced by the flight control surfaces and modify as needed. By controlling the movement of the elevator, ailerons, and rudder, a pilot can, in effect, modify the shape of the airfoil. The primary surfaces are named the elevator, ailerons, and rudder. Their functions are as follows:

- **Elevator:** This generates pitch up or down when the pilot moves the control stick or yoke backward or forward. An elevator is movable and can be raised upward or downward to control the position of the aircraft and its lift. When a pilot tilts an elevator up, the nose of the aircraft will move upward and the tail will move downward, causing the plane to climb. When a pilot tilts an elevator down, the nose of the aircraft will move downward and the tail will move upward, causing the plane to dive.
- **Ailerons:** These cause the airplane to roll right or left corresponding to right or left movement of the control stick or yoke. When one aileron is moved upward, lift is decreased, and the other aileron is moved downward, which increases lift. As a result, this differential lift allows the aircraft to bank, or roll, in one direction. If a pilot raises the aileron on the right wing, the right wing will experience reduced lift, causing it to move downward and bank the aircraft to the right.
- **Rudder:** This generates right or left yaw corresponding to right or left rudder pedal movement. In controlling the rudder, the pilot can create sideward lift, which effectively changes the

Primary Control Surface	Airplane Movement	Axes of Rotation	Type of Stability
Aileron	Roll	Longitudinal	Lateral
Elevator/Stabilator	Pitch	Lateral	Longitudinal
Rudder	Yaw	Vertical	Directional

direction of the aircraft. Deflecting the rudder left will yaw the nose to the left and move the tail to the right. Deflecting the rudder right will yaw the nose to the right and move the tail to the left.

Secondary Flight Controls

Secondary flight controls complement the primary flight controls by helping to improve the performance characteristics of the aircraft or relieve the pilot of the need to use extreme control force. The secondary surfaces may consist of slats, wing flaps, spoilers, and trim systems. Their functions are as follows:

- **Slats:** These increase the critical angle of attack of the aircraft and prevent the aircraft from stalling too early.
- **Flaps:** These are used to give the aircraft extra lift and decrease the landing speed, thus reducing the length of the landing.
- **Spoilers:** These are used to decrease wing lift and can also generate a rolling motion if installed on only one wing.
- **Trim Systems:** These allow the pilot to achieve perfect balance without exerting any pressure on the control stick or rudder pedals while in cruising altitude.

AIRCRAFT PARTS AND MECHANICS

In this section, you will learn about the parts and mechanics of an aircraft and where they are positioned so you can gain an understanding of how each component works. Comprehending these components and their strategic placement provides insight into their functionality while allowing you to identify them. This overall review will give you an opportunity to see how they systematically work together to create an operational aircraft. Listed below are key components that make an aircraft function; however, this is not an exhaustive list.

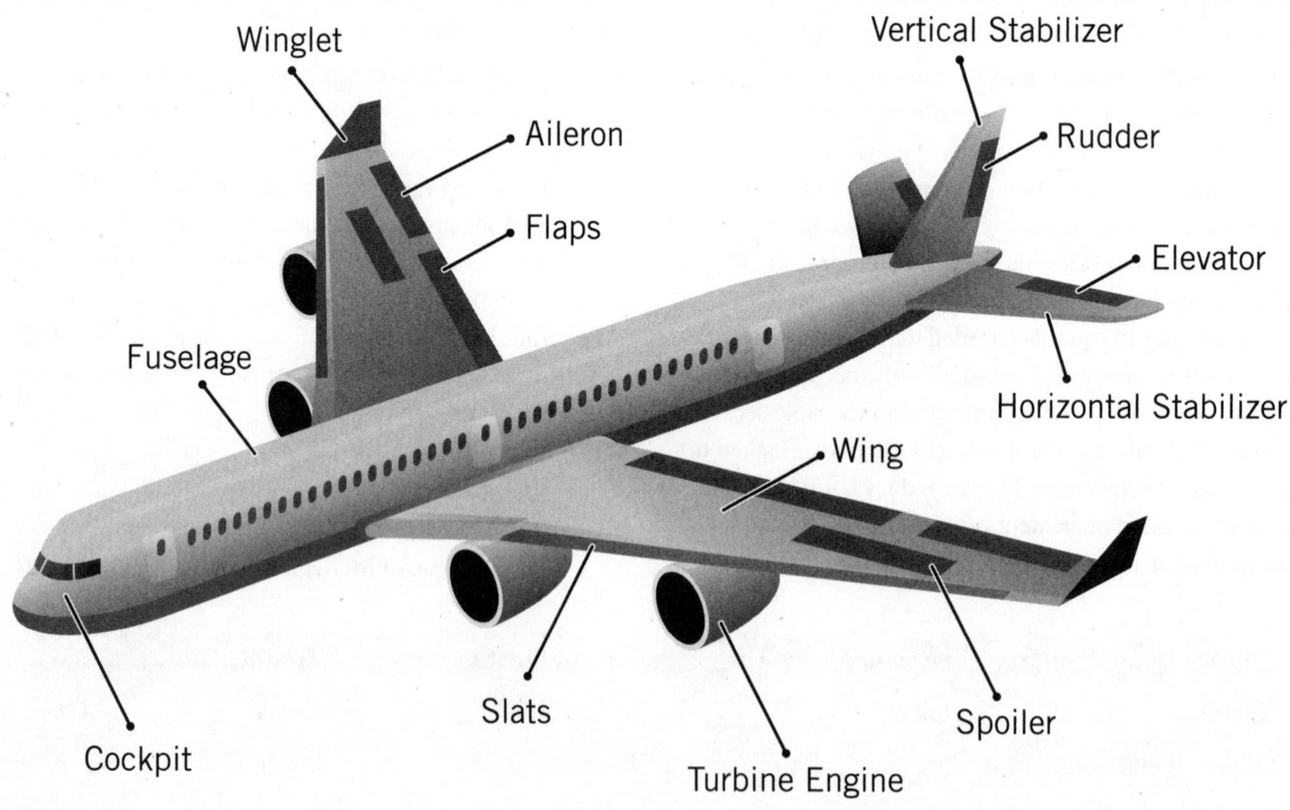

Airplane Parts and Functions

- **Turbine Engines:** An aircraft has at least one engine—and as many as eight engines—that drive an aircraft propeller to generate the thrust needed to fly. Their basic function is to take the air that is in front of the aircraft, accelerate it, and then push it out behind the aircraft.
- **Cockpit/Flight Deck:** This is where the pilot and the co-pilots manage the aircraft. The cockpit has two main functions—to provide the pilot with a strategic angle and to make all control systems accessible to the pilots.
- **Fuselage:** This is the body of the aircraft that holds the crew members, passengers, and cargo safely inside.
- **Slats:** These are flaps mounted on the leading edge of the wing that assist in changing the camber, or curvature, of the wing to improve lifting capability at slower speeds.
- **Spoilers:** These are on the wings of larger aircrafts and can have two types mounted.
    - The in-flight spoilers are small and intended to reduce the lifting capability of the wing just enough to permit the aircraft to descend faster without gaining airspeed.
    - The ground spoilers release automatically on landing. They terminate the lifting ability of the wing upon landing, ensuring that the weight of the aircraft sits firmly on the wheels and the brakes are more effective while also reducing the length of runway required to stop the aircraft.
- **Ailerons:** The ailerons are located at the rear of the wing, typically one on each side, and work to increase the lift on one wing while reducing the lift on the other. In doing this, they are rolling the aircraft sideways, causing it to turn. This is the main technique used to steer a fixed-wing aircraft.
- **Flaps:** They are located on the wing and improve lifting ability at slower speeds by changing the camber, or curvature, of the wing, but when they are completely extended, they create more drag. This means an aircraft can descend quicker, without gaining airspeed in the process.
- **Elevator:** It is located on the tail and guides the nose either upwards or downwards (pitch) in order to have the airplane climb and descend along the lateral axis of the aircraft.
- **Rudder:** It is connected to the vertical stabilizer and located on the tail of the aircraft. Although it helps to steer the nose of the aircraft left and right (yaw), this is not its main job. Its primary responsibility is to counteract certain types of drag, or friction, making certain that the aircraft's tail follows the nose, rather than gliding out to the side.
- **Vertical Stabilizer:** It is located at the tail and stabilizes the left-right motion (yaw) of the aircraft.
- **Horizontal Stabilizer:** It is located at the tail and is like an upside-down wing that provides a downward force (pitch) to keep the nose level with the rest of the aircraft.
- **Aft:** This is a directional term meaning at, near, or toward the rear of an aircraft.
- **Empennage:** This is the entire tail section of the aircraft, including the horizontal and vertical stabilizers, the rudder, and the elevator. As a collective unit, it works to guide the aircraft to its destination, much like a feather on an arrow.
- **Wings:** They deliver most of the lift for an aircraft's flight. Their shape is precisely designed for the aircraft to which it is connected and, on most, is the location where the fuel is stored.
- **Winglet:** On some aircraft wings, there is an additional part called a winglet, located at the end of each wing. It reduces the drag the wing yields as it pushes through the air. It allows the aircraft to fly faster and burn less fuel in the process.

Helicopter Parts and Functions

The Aviation Information subtest focuses on fixed-wing aircraft, which are powered by propellers or engines and, as the name implies, have wings that do not move. However, on the exam, you might also encounter questions about rotary-wing aircraft. Rotary-wing aircraft, such as helicopters, are powered by rotary blades that generate vertical propulsion in order to achieve flight. To help you prepare for the exam, this section will provide a basic overview of helicopter parts and their functions.

- **Cockpit/fuselage:** The main cabin of the aircraft, where the pilot manages the aircraft; houses the pilot, crew, and passengers, as well as a limited amount of cargo.
- **Engine:** Generates the power required to rotate the blades and lift the aircraft.
- **Landing skid:** Fixed landing gear that enables the helicopter to land safely.
- **Mast:** A metal shaft that extends upward from the fuselage and attaches to the main rotor system.
- **Main rotor:** A rotor system that operates as an airfoil, which generates lift using blades that spin horizontally around the rotor mast.
- **Blade:** An airfoil that rotates to produce lift and sustain the weight of the helicopter in flight.
- **Tail cone/tail boom:** A structure that connects the tail rotor to the fuselage; also functions as an exhaust pipe that regulates the airflow of exhaust gases.
- **Tail rotor:** Complements the main rotor and controls yaw by compensating for torque.
- **Tail fin:** A vertical stabilizer designed to help control the yaw of the aircraft.

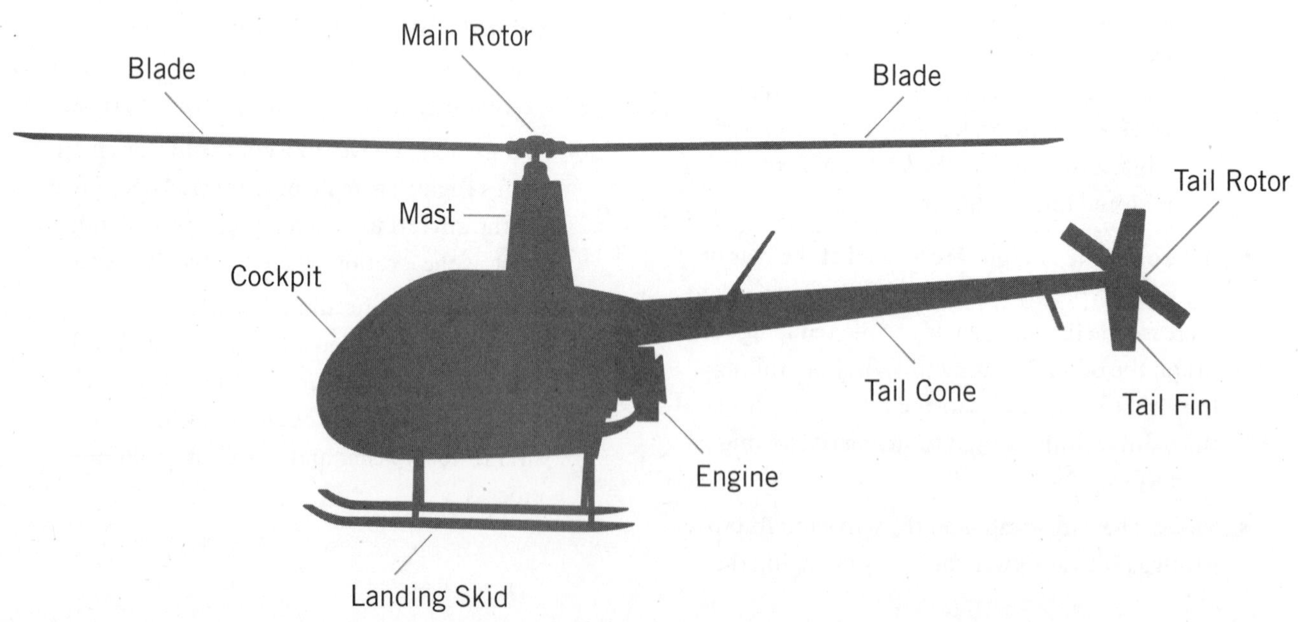

This section is a brief overview of what to know about airport signs, markings, and lighting in preparation for the Aviation Information subtest of the AFOQT. For more information on this subject, refer to the FAA's Airfield Standards: https://www.faa.gov/airports/southern/airport_safety/part139_cert/media/airfield-standards-quikref-aso.pdf

AIRPORT SIGNS, MARKINGS, AND LIGHTING

The signs, markings, and lights used at airports provide pilots with visual cues, directions, and support in all airfield operations. This allows safe and efficient movement within and around the airfield as to avoid risk and complications of runway collisions, damage, or fatalities. The identification and interpretations of these common airport features can be recognized through distinctive signs, markings, and lighting both in the United States and internationally. The signs, markings, and lighting have been standardized by the International Civil Aviation Organization (ICAO) to improve safety and enhance efficiency. This section is not an exhaustive list of airport signs, markings, and lighting, so consult additional resources as needed to strengthen your understanding of this topic.

Airport Signs

Airport signs direct the pilot and provide useful information about the airport itself. For example, signs can identify areas that are off limits, provide directions to specific locations, or assist pilots during takeoff or landing.

Mandatory Instruction Signs: White letters on a red surface.

These signs specify the point or location beyond which the aircraft or vehicle is not allowed to enter or cross. Examples are Runway Holding Position Signs, Runway Approach Area Holding Position Signs, ILS Critical Area Holding Position Signs, and No Entry Signs.

Location Signs: Yellow inscription on a black background or black inscription on a yellow background.

These signs identify the taxiway or runway locations, the runway boundaries, or the instrument landing system (ILS) critical areas.

Direction Signs: Black inscription on a yellow background.

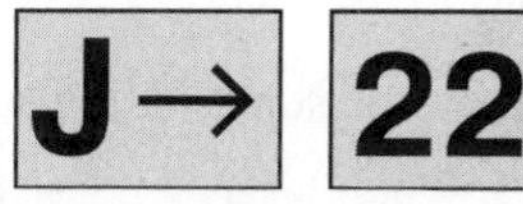

These signs provide directions and designations. Each designation is accompanied by an arrow indicating direction of the turn.

Destination Signs: Black inscription on a yellow background.

Indicates the general direction to a remote location with arrow pointing to common places like runways, terminals, and cargo areas.

Information Signs: Black inscription on a yellow background.

NOISE ABATEMENT
PROCEDURES IN EFFECT
2300 - 0500

Information signs are used to provide the pilot with information on such things as areas that cannot be seen from the control tower, applicable radio frequencies, crossing vehicle roadways, and noise abatement procedures.

Runway Distance Remaining Signs: White numeral inscription on a black background.

The number on Runway Distance Remaining signs indicate the distance (in thousands of feet) of landing runway remaining.

Runway Types and Markings

There are three types of runways depending on the size, location, and uses of an airport. Generally, runways can be categorized according to how much approach guidance they offer to pilots.

Visual: Visual runway markings are used at small airstrips and typically have no markings; pilots must be able to see the runway to use them.

Nonprecision Instrument: Nonprecision runway markings are used at small to mid-sized airports; they may be marked with threshold markings, designator markings, centerlines, and aiming point. These runways often provide lateral guidance but not vertical guidance to pilots.

Precision Instrument: Precision runway markings are used at mid-sized and large airports; they consist of side stripes, threshold markings, designator marking, centerline, aiming point, and touchdown zone marks at intervals of 500 feet, from 500 feet to 3,000 feet. These runways have an existing instrument approach procedure that utilizes either an instrument landing system or precision approach radar.

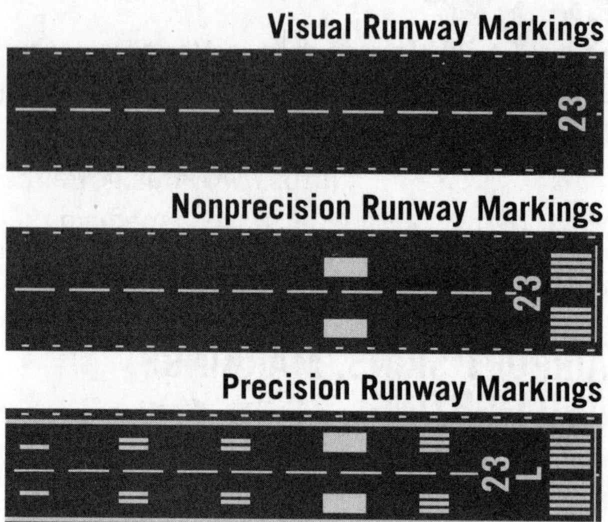

Other Airport and Runway Markings

Additional airport and runway markings may be used to indicate or designate unique features of an airport. Taxiway markings in particular are used to safely guide pilots to and from the runway. Both nonprecision and precision instrument runways may utilize some combination of these markings to provide assistance to pilots.

Taxiway Centerline: A single continuous yellow line; provides a visual cue to permit taxiing along a designated path.

Demarcation Line: A single, unbroken yellow line across the runway; identifies a runway with a displaced threshold from a blast pad, stopway, or taxiway that precedes the runway.

Runway Aiming Point Marker: Two broad white stripes located on each side of the runway; serve as visual targets for landing the aircraft.

Runway Threshold Markings: Either eight longitudinal stripes of equal dimensions about the runway centerline or the number of stripes connected to the width of the runway.

Touchdown Zone Markings: Groups of one, two, and three rectangular bars symmetrically arranged in pairs about the runway centerline; coded to provide distance information in increments of 500 feet (150 meters).

Closed Runway and Taxiway Marking: consists of a yellow X symbol; located at both ends of permanently closed runways.

Airport Lighting

Airport lighting is designed to provide precise guidance to pilots regarding where to taxi, take off, and land. Nonprecision instrument runways rely on signs, markings, and a basic approach light system. Precision instrument runways utilize more informative approach aids in combination with other signs and markings.

Approach Light System (ALS): Presents the basic method to transition from instrument flight to visual flight for landing; it consists of a configuration of signal lights starting at the landing threshold and extending into the approach area up to a distance of 2,400–3,000 feet for precision instrument runways and 1,400–1,500 feet for non-precision instrument runways.

Visual Approach Slope Indicator (VASI): An airport lighting system that provides visual descent guidance to pilots during approach to facilitate a safe landing. This system consists of a series of red and white lights that signal when modifications to the vertical approach path of the aircraft are required before landing. This guidance is especially useful when approaching upsloping or downsloping runways, which may disorient a pilot. When the plane is "on path," the pilot will see red/white. When the plane is too high, the "above path" lights appear as white/white. When the plane is too low, the pilot will see "below path" lights, which are red/red.

Precision Approach Path Indicator (PAPI): An airport lighting system similar to VASI, providing visual descent guidance to aircraft during approach to landing. PAPIs use a single row of either two or four lights, typically installed on the left side of the runway. When the plane is "on path," the pilot will see an equal number of white lights and red lights. When the plane is "above path," the pilot will see more white than red lights. When the plane is "below path," the pilot sees more red than white lights.

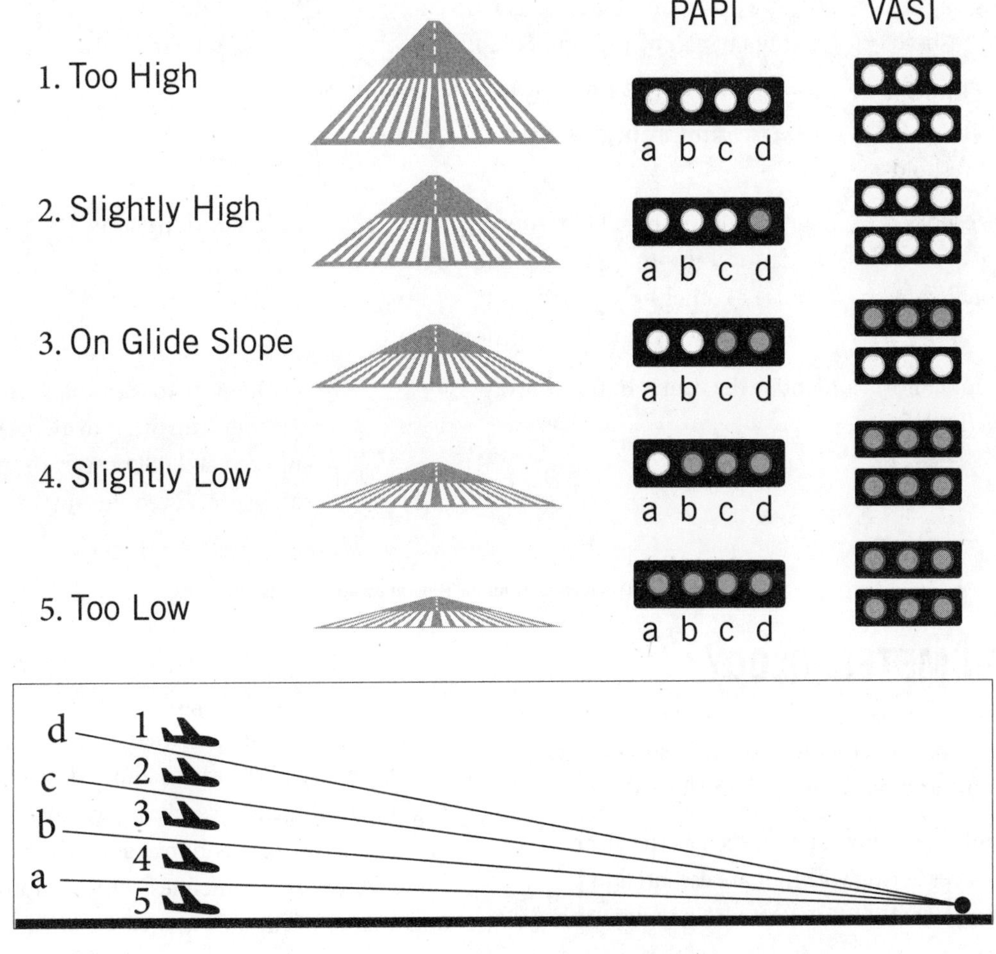

AIRPORT LIGHTING COLORS		
Type of Light	**Function**	**Description**
Runway threshold / end lights	Mark the end of a runway to departing aircraft and identifies the threshold to landing aircraft	Green / Red (bidirectional); departing aircraft see red and landing aircraft see green
Runway edge light (instrument runways)	Outline the edge of runways at night or during poor visibility conditions	White, but yellow replaces white for the last 2,000 feet of the runway to indicate a caution zone
Runway edge light	Outline the edge of runways at night or during poor visibility conditions	White
Runway edge light (in-pavement)	Enhance runway visibility at large airports; often used in combination with precision instrument runways	White
Runway threshold / End light	Designate the end of a usable runway	Red
Taxiway edge light	Outline the edges of taxiways at night or during poor visibility conditions	Blue
Runway edge light at displaced threshold	Indicate pavement that is unavailable for landing but can be used for takeoff	Yellow / Red; departing aircraft see yellow and landing aircraft see red
Threshold / Runway edge lights at displaced threshold	Designate the start of the landing threshold where the runway begins	Green
Runway threshold light with a unidirectional	Identify approach end of a runway; useful for identifying runways that are hard to see because of other lighting, the surrounding terrain, or poor visibility conditions	Green (unidirectional)
Land and Hold Short Operations (LAHSO)	Identify the center of the runway	White near the approach end of the runway but transition to alternating white and red at 3,000 feet from the end of the runway and red for the final 1,000 feet of the runway

Note: This material is adapted from the Federal Aviation Administration.

AVIATION METEOROLOGY

Weather elements, theory, and patterns, along with other factors, work together to assist pilots in perceiving, processing, and performing their flight duties.

Here, you will review how factors such as the atmosphere and forces acting within it are essential to understanding how flight is affected. The relationship between pilots and aviation weather services is designed to be supportive during the flight planning process. Weather theory and knowledge of weather principles affect the way pilots make sound decisions during flight planning after receiving weather briefings. These coordinated efforts enhance a pilot's understanding of these factors and principles, which improve the safety and quality of flight.

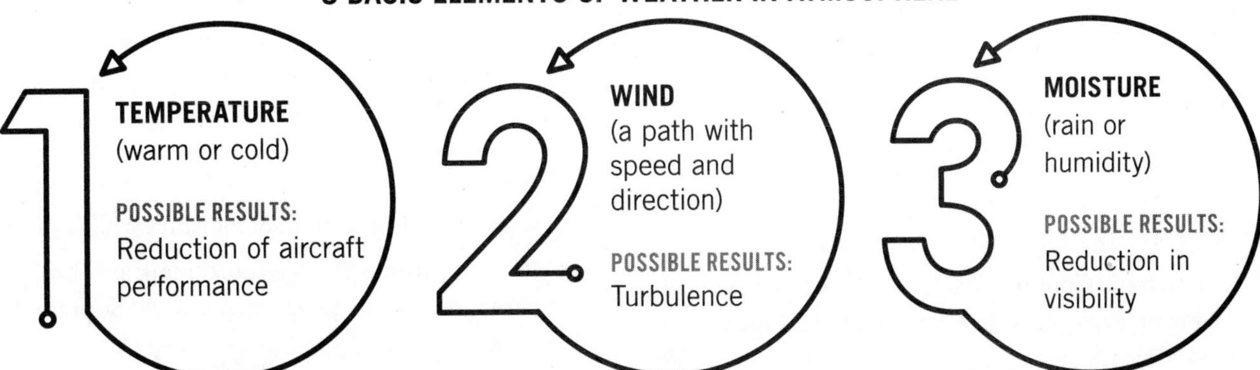

3 BASIC ELEMENTS OF WEATHER IN ATMOSPHERE
1
TEMPERATURE
(warm or cold)
POSSIBLE RESULTS:
Reduction of aircraft performance
2
WIND
(a path with speed and direction)
POSSIBLE RESULTS:
Turbulence
3
MOISTURE
(rain or humidity)
POSSIBLE RESULTS:
Reduction in visibility

The basic steps of preflight weather planning and in-flight weather decision-making are presented here:

- Perceive the weather possibilities that could adversely affect the flight.
- Obtain this information through Flight Station Service briefing.
- Process the data to establish whether the prospects create risk.
- Study and assess the data to realize what it means for your situation.
- Perform by taking action to eliminate the possibility or diminish the risk.
- Evaluate and update the in-flight situation consistently.

Pressure Altitude: Sea Level

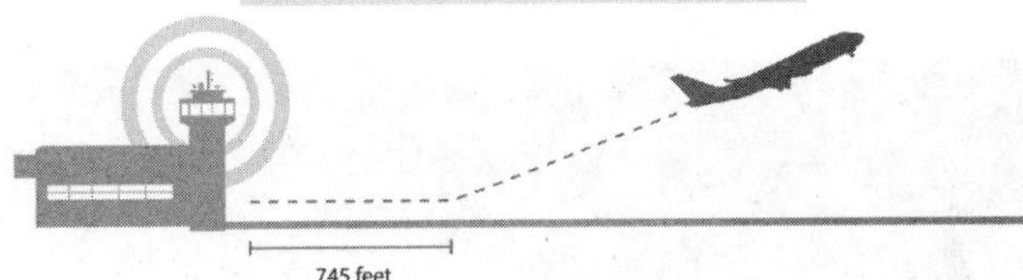

Pressure Altitude: 8,000 feet

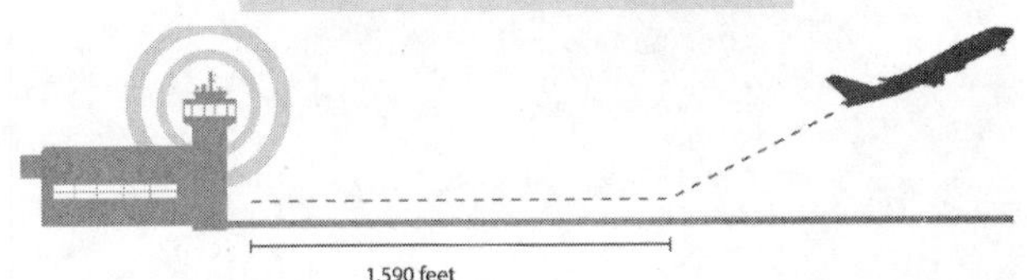

Pressure

One of the most important components of weather theory as it relates to flying is that of air pressure.

Types of Pressure

- **High:** An area of higher pressure bordered by an area of lower pressure. An extended area of high pressure is called a ridge.
- **Low:** An area of lower pressure surrounded by an area of high pressure. An extended area of low pressure is called a trough.

Altitude, Pressure, and Takeoff Distance

An aircraft requires more ground run at higher pressure altitudes. The following table outlines the specific changes in ground roll at different pressure altitudes for a small aircraft. Notice the direct relationship between pressure altitude and ground roll.

TAKEOFF DISTANCE MAXIMUM WEIGHT 2,400 LB

Pressure altitude (feet)	0 °C	
	Ground roll (feet)	Total feet to clear 50-foot obstacle
Sea Level (S.L.)	745	1,320
1,000	815	1,445
2,000	895	1,585
3,000	980	1,740
4,000	1,075	1,920
5,000	1,185	2,125
6,000	1,305	2,360
7,000	1,440	2,635
8,000	1,590	2,960

Stability

The stability of the atmosphere depends on its ability to withstand vertical movement. It is determined by the Adiabatic lapse rate, which consists of three factors:

- **Adiabatic Heating:** As atmospheric pressure increases, the temperature of descending air increases as it is condensed.
- **Adiabatic Cooling:** Rising air expands and cools due to the decrease in air pressure as altitude increases.
- **Inversion Layers:** Shallow layers of smooth, stable air that are close to the ground.

Weather Patterns

Weather patterns consist of a combination of moisture, clouds, and fronts. The following is an explanation of important points to consider with each weather factor.

Moisture

- **Humidity:** The amount of moisture in air.
- **Relative Humidity:** The actual moisture compared to the total moisture that could be present in the air.
- **Fog:** When moist, warm air passes over cooler surface air and water vapor condenses.

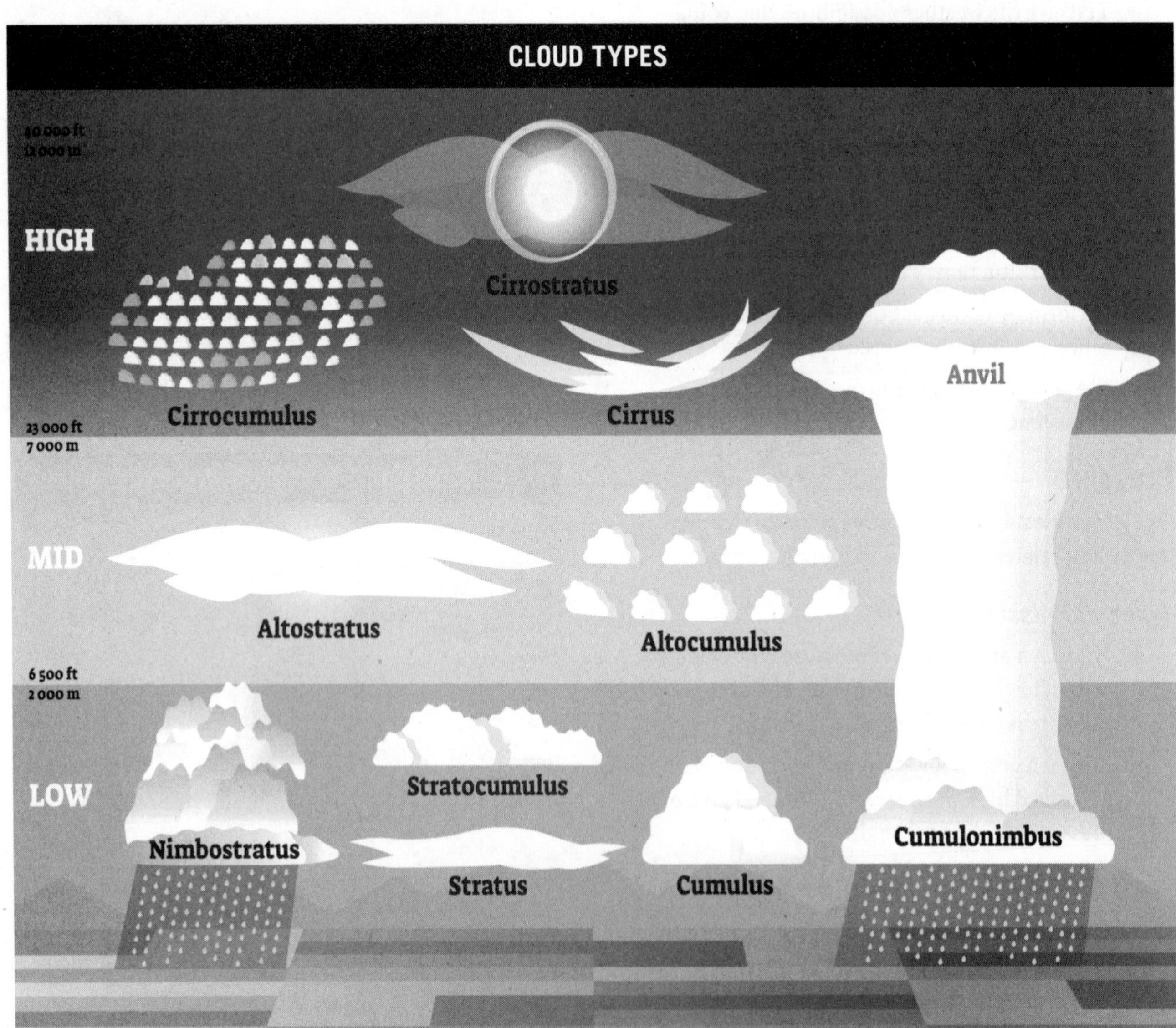

Clouds

The types of clouds can be divided into three levels in the troposphere, the lowest layer of the Earth's atmosphere, and consist of the following:

- **Low Level Clouds:** Sea level to 6,500 feet (cumulus, stratus, stratocumulus).
- **Middle Level Clouds:** 6,500 to 20,000 feet (usually prefixed [alto]; altocumulus, altostratus, nimbostratus).
- **High Level Clouds:** Above 20,000 feet (always prefixed [cirr]; cirrus, cirrocumulus, cirrostratus).

Depending on climate and altitude, pilots will encounter different types of clouds. Higher clouds, like those above 20,000 feet, are less likely to cause turbulence. Pilots can expect some turbulence when encountering low or middle level clouds. Clouds with significant vertical development, especially cumulonimbus clouds, are often associated with hazardous weather, including heavy rain, thunderstorms, and tornadoes. Lenticular clouds are stationary clouds that form in standing waves over mountains and generate severe turbulence. Low level stratus clouds are blanket clouds that form in thick layers and create overcast conditions, which significantly reduce visibility.

Fronts

A front is a boundary between air masses having different temperatures and moisture matter. It is often considered a line of confrontation and has serious flying hazards. Types include the following:

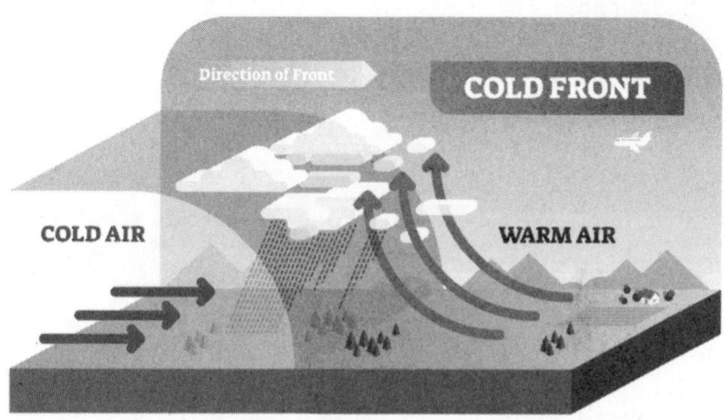

Cold Front: Colder air slides beneath and overtakes warmer air.

Warm Front: Warmer air travels above and overtakes cooler air.

Stationary Front: Cool and warm air exist in the same region and there is no movement.

Occluded Front: Quick-moving cool air mass catches up and blends with the warm front often causing a low-pressure area to form.

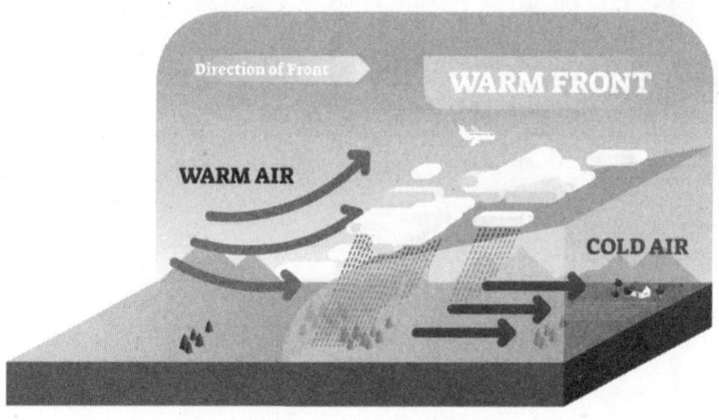

MINI-QUIZ: AVIATION INFORMATION

Directions: This section of the exam measures your aviation knowledge. Each question or incomplete statement has five choices. You need to decide which of the choices best answers the question or statement.

1. A front where cool and warm air exists with no movement is called

   A. stationary.
   B. cold.
   C. occluded.
   D. warm.
   E. fog.

2. The body of the plane is also known as the

   A. yaw.
   B. pitch.
   C. fuselage.
   D. camber.
   E. cargo.

3. During takeoff and landing, an aircraft is steered by

   A. moving the stick or turning the yoke.
   B. an engine thrust.
   C. the rudder pedals.
   D. turning the trim.
   E. moving the ailerons.

4. The cloud type that is frequently associated with turbulence is

   A. altocumulus.
   B. lenticularis.
   C. nimbostratus.
   D. cirrus.
   E. noctilucent.

5. A term referring to the rear of the aircraft is

   A. the angle of bank.
   B. aft.
   C. speed brakes.
   D. the tail rotor.
   E. the swash plate.

6. A 3-foot yellow bar that runs across the runway is called the

   A. runway side stripe marking.
   B. normal taxi centerline marking.
   C. runway designation marking.
   D. information sign.
   E. demarcation bar.

7. What type of airfield sign has yellow lettering on a black background?

   A. Mandatory instruction sign
   B. Destination sign
   C. Location sign
   D. Information sign
   E. Temporarily closed runway and taxi signs

8. Identify the part of the plane that changes yaw.

   A. Flaps
   B. Spoiler
   C. Elevator
   D. Rudder
   E. Slat

9. Crosswinds occur when

   A. there is a sudden change of wind velocity and/or direction.

   B. an angle forms between the wind and the runway centerline.

   C. there are severe variations in wind speeds and/or directions.

   D. ultraviolet solar radiation is heating up lower regions of hills and mountains.

   E. there is a cold flow of air traveling down a hill or mountain.

10. Which aerodynamic force is responsible for holding an aircraft up in the air?

    A. Torque

    B. Thrust

    C. Lift

    D. Gravity

    E. Drag

ANSWER KEY AND EXPLANATIONS

1. A	3. C	5. B	7. C	9. B
2. C	4. B	6. E	8. D	10. C

1. **The correct answer is A.** A stationary front does not have any movement of cool and warm air. A cold (choice B) front is when colder air slides beneath and overtakes warmer air. An occluded (choice C) front is a quick-moving cool air mass that catches up and blends with the warm front causing a low-pressure area to form. A warm (choice D) front is warmer air that travels above and overtakes cooler air. Fog (choice E) is when moist, warm air passes over cooler surface air and water vapor condenses.
2. **The correct answer is C.** The fuselage is the aircraft's main body section and holds the crew, passengers, and cargo. Yaw (choice A) is the rotation around the vertical (right to left movement) axis of the aircraft's nose. Pitch (choice B) is the rotation around the lateral (side-to-side) axis of the aircraft. Camber (choice D) is the curvature of the top surface of an airfoil. Cargo (choice E) are goods or products carried on a plane instead of passengers.
3. **The correct answer is C.** Pilots use a tiller to steer a plane when it is on the ground and moving slowly, but during takeoff and landing, the most efficient way to steer a plane is by utilizing the rudder pedals. A pilot using the stick or yoke (choice A) instrument is controlling the altitude of an aircraft. An engine thrust (choice B) or differential throttling can only be used in conjunction with differential braking. Turning the trim (choice D) is used to establish the desired altitude with the primary flight controls. Although they do not steer the aircraft, moving the ailerons (choice E) causes one wing tip to move up and the other wing tip to move down.
4. **The correct answer is B.** Lenticularis clouds form in standing waves over mountains and are frequently associated with severe turbulence. Altocumulus (choice A) is a thin layer of lumps or cotton-like heaps of clouds. Nimbostratus (choice C) clouds are low, shapeless layers of dark gray clouds nearly uniform in appearance. Cirrus (choice D) are thin fibrous clouds. Noctilucent (choice E) are thin clouds of ice crystals that occur at great heights in the mesosphere.
5. **The correct answer is B.** Aft means near, at, or toward the tail of the aircraft. The angle of bank (choice A) occurs between the wings and the horizon, as viewed from the rear of the airplane. The speed brakes (choice C) are hinged or movable control surfaces used for reducing the velocity of an aircraft. The tail rotor (choice D) is a smaller rotor mounted so that it rotates vertically or near-vertically at the end of the tail of a traditional single-rotor helicopter. The swash plate (choice E) is a helicopter flight control that converts stationary control inputs from the pilot into rotating inputs, which can be connected to the rotor blades.
6. **The correct answer is E.** The demarcation bar is a 3-foot yellow bar that runs across the runway and outlines a runway with a displaced threshold from a blast pad, stopway, or taxiway. The runway side stripe markings (choice A) consist of continuous white stripes located on each side of the runway and provide a visual contrast between runway pavement and the ground. The normal taxi center-line marking (choice B) is a continuous yellow line located along the center of the taxiway. Runway designation markings (choice C) are numbers and letters that identify a runway. Information signs

(choice D) have a yellow background with black inscription and provide procedural or other specialized information.

7. **The correct answer is C.** Location signs are used to identify the taxiway or runway locations, the runway boundaries, or the instrument landing system (ILS) critical areas. Mandatory instruction signs (choice A) are white inscriptions on a red background and are used to signify an entrance to a runway, a critical area, or a prohibited area. Destination signs (choice B) have a yellow background with black inscription and define directions for planes to take off or arrive. Information signs (choice D) have a yellow background with black inscription and are used to convey information like radio frequencies, noise abatement procedures, crossing vehicle roadways, and areas not evident from the control tower. Temporarily closed runway and taxi signs (choice E) are yellow crosses placed at the end of each runway or taxiway notifying the pilots of this situation.

8. **The correct answer is D.** The rudder is a primary flight control surface that regulates yaw on an aircraft's tail. Flaps (choice A) are installed on the trailing edge on the inboard section of each wing and bend downward to increase the effective curving of the wing. Spoilers (choice B) are used to interrupt airflow over the wing to significantly reduce lift. Elevators (choice C) are a primary flight control, which regulate the pitch movement, the lateral axis of the aircraft. Slats (choice E) are meant to reduce the stalling speed by shifting the airflow over the wing.

9. **The correct answer is B.** Crosswinds pose a hazard to aircrafts during takeoff and landing because they blow across the runway as opposed to straight down the runway. The sudden change of wind velocity and/or direction (choice A) is wind shear and occurs close to the ground. The severe variations in wind speeds and/or directions (choice C) cause severe turbulence. Since ultraviolet solar radiation heats up the lower regions of hills and mountains (choice D), the air becomes fairly buoyant and rises up the orographic slope, causing anabatic winds. Since there is a cold flow of air traveling down a hill or mountain (choice E), the air cools and becomes denser, causing katabatic winds.

10. **The correct answer is C.** Lift is created by a difference in pressure, generated by the movement of air over the wings, and keeps an aircraft up in the air. Torque (choice A) is the twisting force that tends to cause rotation. Thrust (choice B) is the force generated by the engine and propels the aircraft forward. Gravity (choice D) is the force that pulls objects toward Earth and counteracts lift. Drag (choice E) slows an airplane down and acts opposite to thrust.

SUMMING IT UP

- The Aviation Information subtest consists of 20 questions. You will have 8 minutes to complete this test, providing an average of 24 seconds per question.
- Knowing the basics of aerodynamics, the study of how gases (air) interact with moving bodies, will be critical to demonstrating your knowledge of aircraft functions and mechanics. Be sure to know the four forces of flight—lift, weight, thrust, and drag—and how they each impact the motion of an aircraft. Additionally, review how a pilot can control the orientation of an aircraft along its three axes of rotation (yaw, pitch, and roll).
- Know the differences between primary and secondary flight control systems, as well as their key components and functions. Remember that primary flight control systems are important for controlling and maneuvering the aircraft safely, while secondary flight control systems allow the pilot to refine specific movements and controls as needed.
- Review the images that illustrate the key components of an aircraft. Each part is placed strategically on the aircraft, so make sure that you understand the placement and function of key components and how they work together to create an operational aircraft. Be sure to know how different components of an airplane allow the pilot to control the aircraft along its three axes of motion: pitch, roll, and yaw.
- Pilots must be familiar with a variety of signs, markings, and lighting systems used to facilitate safe and efficient movement around the airfield. Signs identify important locations and provide instructions. Airport and runway markings help pilots know where to land and taxi. Lighting can assist pilots with landing the aircraft safely, especially under unique conditions.
- Knowledge of weather theory and principles is critical to making sound decisions during flight. Temperature can reduce an aircraft's performance, wind can cause turbulence, and moisture can reduce visibility. Be sure to review how pressure, weather patterns, clouds, and fronts can impact flight duties.

NOTES

PART IV

PRACTICE TESTS

AFOQT PRACTICE TEST

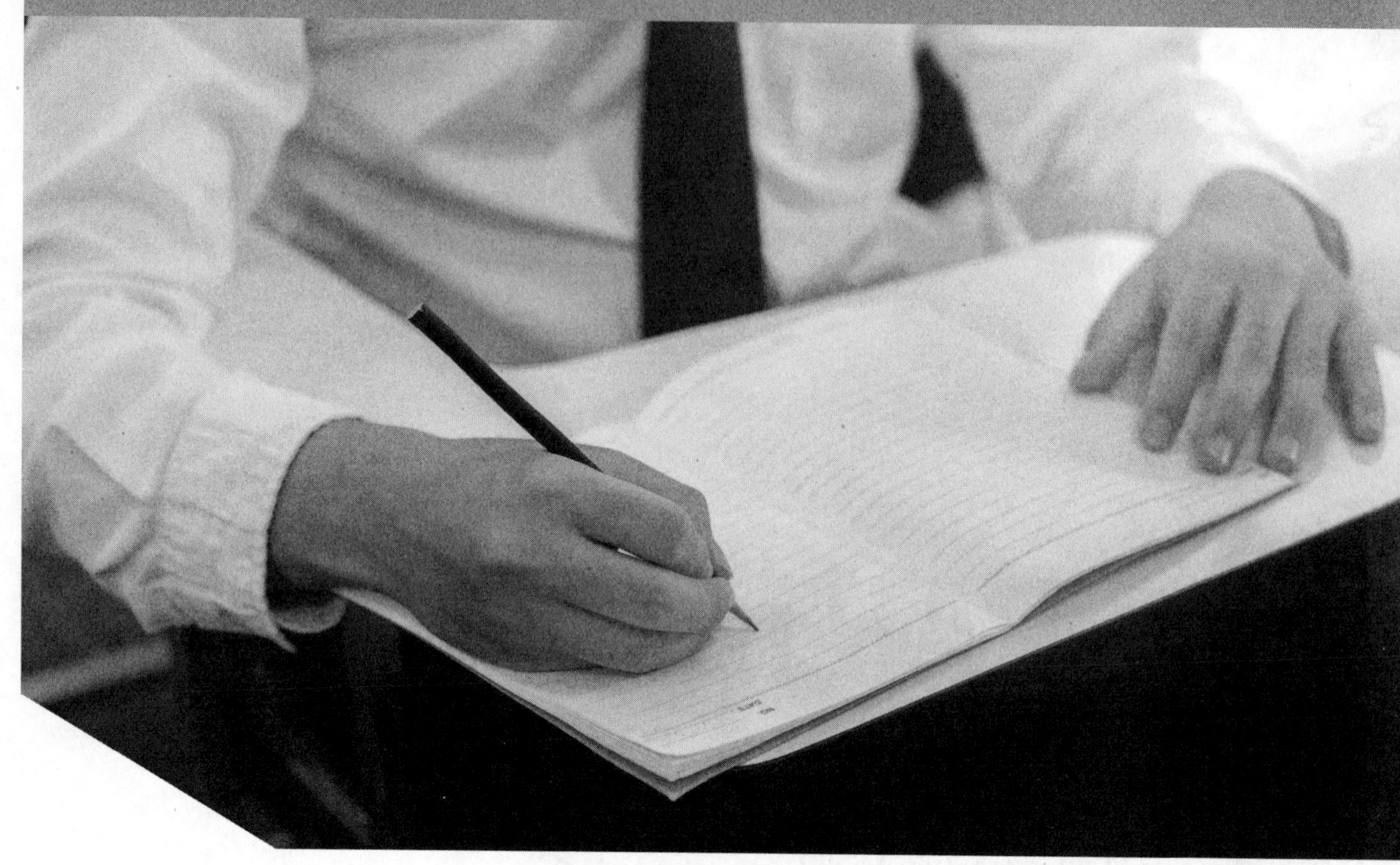

AFOQT PRACTICE TEST

This practice test is designed to help you recognize your strengths and weaknesses. You'll find practice versions of each subtest of the AFOQT, with the exception of the Self-Description Inventory.

ANSWER SHEET: AFOQT PRACTICE TEST

Verbal Analogies

1. Ⓐ Ⓑ Ⓒ Ⓓ Ⓔ
2. Ⓐ Ⓑ Ⓒ Ⓓ Ⓔ
3. Ⓐ Ⓑ Ⓒ Ⓓ Ⓔ
4. Ⓐ Ⓑ Ⓒ Ⓓ Ⓔ
5. Ⓐ Ⓑ Ⓒ Ⓓ Ⓔ
6. Ⓐ Ⓑ Ⓒ Ⓓ Ⓔ
7. Ⓐ Ⓑ Ⓒ Ⓓ Ⓔ
8. Ⓐ Ⓑ Ⓒ Ⓓ Ⓔ
9. Ⓐ Ⓑ Ⓒ Ⓓ Ⓔ
10. Ⓐ Ⓑ Ⓒ Ⓓ Ⓔ
11. Ⓐ Ⓑ Ⓒ Ⓓ Ⓔ
12. Ⓐ Ⓑ Ⓒ Ⓓ Ⓔ
13. Ⓐ Ⓑ Ⓒ Ⓓ Ⓔ
14. Ⓐ Ⓑ Ⓒ Ⓓ Ⓔ
15. Ⓐ Ⓑ Ⓒ Ⓓ Ⓔ
16. Ⓐ Ⓑ Ⓒ Ⓓ Ⓔ
17. Ⓐ Ⓑ Ⓒ Ⓓ Ⓔ
18. Ⓐ Ⓑ Ⓒ Ⓓ Ⓔ
19. Ⓐ Ⓑ Ⓒ Ⓓ Ⓔ
20. Ⓐ Ⓑ Ⓒ Ⓓ Ⓔ
21. Ⓐ Ⓑ Ⓒ Ⓓ Ⓔ
22. Ⓐ Ⓑ Ⓒ Ⓓ Ⓔ
23. Ⓐ Ⓑ Ⓒ Ⓓ Ⓔ
24. Ⓐ Ⓑ Ⓒ Ⓓ Ⓔ
25. Ⓐ Ⓑ Ⓒ Ⓓ Ⓔ

Arithmetic Reasoning

1. Ⓐ Ⓑ Ⓒ Ⓓ Ⓔ
2. Ⓐ Ⓑ Ⓒ Ⓓ Ⓔ
3. Ⓐ Ⓑ Ⓒ Ⓓ Ⓔ
4. Ⓐ Ⓑ Ⓒ Ⓓ Ⓔ
5. Ⓐ Ⓑ Ⓒ Ⓓ Ⓔ
6. Ⓐ Ⓑ Ⓒ Ⓓ Ⓔ
7. Ⓐ Ⓑ Ⓒ Ⓓ Ⓔ
8. Ⓐ Ⓑ Ⓒ Ⓓ Ⓔ
9. Ⓐ Ⓑ Ⓒ Ⓓ Ⓔ
10. Ⓐ Ⓑ Ⓒ Ⓓ Ⓔ
11. Ⓐ Ⓑ Ⓒ Ⓓ Ⓔ
12. Ⓐ Ⓑ Ⓒ Ⓓ Ⓔ
13. Ⓐ Ⓑ Ⓒ Ⓓ Ⓔ
14. Ⓐ Ⓑ Ⓒ Ⓓ Ⓔ
15. Ⓐ Ⓑ Ⓒ Ⓓ Ⓔ
16. Ⓐ Ⓑ Ⓒ Ⓓ Ⓔ
17. Ⓐ Ⓑ Ⓒ Ⓓ Ⓔ
18. Ⓐ Ⓑ Ⓒ Ⓓ Ⓔ
19. Ⓐ Ⓑ Ⓒ Ⓓ Ⓔ
20. Ⓐ Ⓑ Ⓒ Ⓓ Ⓔ
21. Ⓐ Ⓑ Ⓒ Ⓓ Ⓔ
22. Ⓐ Ⓑ Ⓒ Ⓓ Ⓔ
23. Ⓐ Ⓑ Ⓒ Ⓓ Ⓔ
24. Ⓐ Ⓑ Ⓒ Ⓓ Ⓔ
25. Ⓐ Ⓑ Ⓒ Ⓓ Ⓔ

Word Knowledge

1. Ⓐ Ⓑ Ⓒ Ⓓ Ⓔ
2. Ⓐ Ⓑ Ⓒ Ⓓ Ⓔ
3. Ⓐ Ⓑ Ⓒ Ⓓ Ⓔ
4. Ⓐ Ⓑ Ⓒ Ⓓ Ⓔ
5. Ⓐ Ⓑ Ⓒ Ⓓ Ⓔ
6. Ⓐ Ⓑ Ⓒ Ⓓ Ⓔ
7. Ⓐ Ⓑ Ⓒ Ⓓ Ⓔ
8. Ⓐ Ⓑ Ⓒ Ⓓ Ⓔ
9. Ⓐ Ⓑ Ⓒ Ⓓ Ⓔ
10. Ⓐ Ⓑ Ⓒ Ⓓ Ⓔ
11. Ⓐ Ⓑ Ⓒ Ⓓ Ⓔ
12. Ⓐ Ⓑ Ⓒ Ⓓ Ⓔ
13. Ⓐ Ⓑ Ⓒ Ⓓ Ⓔ
14. Ⓐ Ⓑ Ⓒ Ⓓ Ⓔ
15. Ⓐ Ⓑ Ⓒ Ⓓ Ⓔ
16. Ⓐ Ⓑ Ⓒ Ⓓ Ⓔ
17. Ⓐ Ⓑ Ⓒ Ⓓ Ⓔ
18. Ⓐ Ⓑ Ⓒ Ⓓ Ⓔ
19. Ⓐ Ⓑ Ⓒ Ⓓ Ⓔ
20. Ⓐ Ⓑ Ⓒ Ⓓ Ⓔ
21. Ⓐ Ⓑ Ⓒ Ⓓ Ⓔ
22. Ⓐ Ⓑ Ⓒ Ⓓ Ⓔ
23. Ⓐ Ⓑ Ⓒ Ⓓ Ⓔ
24. Ⓐ Ⓑ Ⓒ Ⓓ Ⓔ
25. Ⓐ Ⓑ Ⓒ Ⓓ Ⓔ

Math Knowledge

1. Ⓐ Ⓑ Ⓒ Ⓓ Ⓔ
2. Ⓐ Ⓑ Ⓒ Ⓓ Ⓔ
3. Ⓐ Ⓑ Ⓒ Ⓓ Ⓔ
4. Ⓐ Ⓑ Ⓒ Ⓓ Ⓔ
5. Ⓐ Ⓑ Ⓒ Ⓓ Ⓔ
6. Ⓐ Ⓑ Ⓒ Ⓓ Ⓔ
7. Ⓐ Ⓑ Ⓒ Ⓓ Ⓔ
8. Ⓐ Ⓑ Ⓒ Ⓓ Ⓔ
9. Ⓐ Ⓑ Ⓒ Ⓓ Ⓔ
10. Ⓐ Ⓑ Ⓒ Ⓓ Ⓔ
11. Ⓐ Ⓑ Ⓒ Ⓓ Ⓔ
12. Ⓐ Ⓑ Ⓒ Ⓓ Ⓔ
13. Ⓐ Ⓑ Ⓒ Ⓓ Ⓔ
14. Ⓐ Ⓑ Ⓒ Ⓓ Ⓔ
15. Ⓐ Ⓑ Ⓒ Ⓓ Ⓔ
16. Ⓐ Ⓑ Ⓒ Ⓓ Ⓔ
17. Ⓐ Ⓑ Ⓒ Ⓓ Ⓔ
18. Ⓐ Ⓑ Ⓒ Ⓓ Ⓔ
19. Ⓐ Ⓑ Ⓒ Ⓓ Ⓔ
20. Ⓐ Ⓑ Ⓒ Ⓓ Ⓔ
21. Ⓐ Ⓑ Ⓒ Ⓓ Ⓔ
22. Ⓐ Ⓑ Ⓒ Ⓓ Ⓔ
23. Ⓐ Ⓑ Ⓒ Ⓓ Ⓔ
24. Ⓐ Ⓑ Ⓒ Ⓓ Ⓔ
25. Ⓐ Ⓑ Ⓒ Ⓓ Ⓔ

Reading Comprehension

1. Ⓐ Ⓑ Ⓒ Ⓓ Ⓔ	6. Ⓐ Ⓑ Ⓒ Ⓓ Ⓔ	11. Ⓐ Ⓑ Ⓒ Ⓓ Ⓔ	16. Ⓐ Ⓑ Ⓒ Ⓓ Ⓔ	21. Ⓐ Ⓑ Ⓒ Ⓓ Ⓔ
2. Ⓐ Ⓑ Ⓒ Ⓓ Ⓔ	7. Ⓐ Ⓑ Ⓒ Ⓓ Ⓔ	12. Ⓐ Ⓑ Ⓒ Ⓓ Ⓔ	17. Ⓐ Ⓑ Ⓒ Ⓓ Ⓔ	22. Ⓐ Ⓑ Ⓒ Ⓓ Ⓔ
3. Ⓐ Ⓑ Ⓒ Ⓓ Ⓔ	8. Ⓐ Ⓑ Ⓒ Ⓓ Ⓔ	13. Ⓐ Ⓑ Ⓒ Ⓓ Ⓔ	18. Ⓐ Ⓑ Ⓒ Ⓓ Ⓔ	23. Ⓐ Ⓑ Ⓒ Ⓓ Ⓔ
4. Ⓐ Ⓑ Ⓒ Ⓓ Ⓔ	9. Ⓐ Ⓑ Ⓒ Ⓓ Ⓔ	14. Ⓐ Ⓑ Ⓒ Ⓓ Ⓔ	19. Ⓐ Ⓑ Ⓒ Ⓓ Ⓔ	24. Ⓐ Ⓑ Ⓒ Ⓓ Ⓔ
5. Ⓐ Ⓑ Ⓒ Ⓓ Ⓔ	10. Ⓐ Ⓑ Ⓒ Ⓓ Ⓔ	15. Ⓐ Ⓑ Ⓒ Ⓓ Ⓔ	20. Ⓐ Ⓑ Ⓒ Ⓓ Ⓔ	25. Ⓐ Ⓑ Ⓒ Ⓓ Ⓔ

Situational Judgment

1. Ⓐ Ⓑ Ⓒ Ⓓ Ⓔ	11. Ⓐ Ⓑ Ⓒ Ⓓ Ⓔ	21. Ⓐ Ⓑ Ⓒ Ⓓ Ⓔ	31. Ⓐ Ⓑ Ⓒ Ⓓ Ⓔ	41. Ⓐ Ⓑ Ⓒ Ⓓ Ⓔ
2. Ⓐ Ⓑ Ⓒ Ⓓ Ⓔ	12. Ⓐ Ⓑ Ⓒ Ⓓ Ⓔ	22. Ⓐ Ⓑ Ⓒ Ⓓ Ⓔ	32. Ⓐ Ⓑ Ⓒ Ⓓ Ⓔ	42. Ⓐ Ⓑ Ⓒ Ⓓ Ⓔ
3. Ⓐ Ⓑ Ⓒ Ⓓ Ⓔ	13. Ⓐ Ⓑ Ⓒ Ⓓ Ⓔ	23. Ⓐ Ⓑ Ⓒ Ⓓ Ⓔ	33. Ⓐ Ⓑ Ⓒ Ⓓ Ⓔ	43. Ⓐ Ⓑ Ⓒ Ⓓ Ⓔ
4. Ⓐ Ⓑ Ⓒ Ⓓ Ⓔ	14. Ⓐ Ⓑ Ⓒ Ⓓ Ⓔ	24. Ⓐ Ⓑ Ⓒ Ⓓ Ⓔ	34. Ⓐ Ⓑ Ⓒ Ⓓ Ⓔ	44. Ⓐ Ⓑ Ⓒ Ⓓ Ⓔ
5. Ⓐ Ⓑ Ⓒ Ⓓ Ⓔ	15. Ⓐ Ⓑ Ⓒ Ⓓ Ⓔ	25. Ⓐ Ⓑ Ⓒ Ⓓ Ⓔ	35. Ⓐ Ⓑ Ⓒ Ⓓ Ⓔ	45. Ⓐ Ⓑ Ⓒ Ⓓ Ⓔ
6. Ⓐ Ⓑ Ⓒ Ⓓ Ⓔ	16. Ⓐ Ⓑ Ⓒ Ⓓ Ⓔ	26. Ⓐ Ⓑ Ⓒ Ⓓ Ⓔ	36. Ⓐ Ⓑ Ⓒ Ⓓ Ⓔ	46. Ⓐ Ⓑ Ⓒ Ⓓ Ⓔ
7. Ⓐ Ⓑ Ⓒ Ⓓ Ⓔ	17. Ⓐ Ⓑ Ⓒ Ⓓ Ⓔ	27. Ⓐ Ⓑ Ⓒ Ⓓ Ⓔ	37. Ⓐ Ⓑ Ⓒ Ⓓ Ⓔ	47. Ⓐ Ⓑ Ⓒ Ⓓ Ⓔ
8. Ⓐ Ⓑ Ⓒ Ⓓ Ⓔ	18. Ⓐ Ⓑ Ⓒ Ⓓ Ⓔ	28. Ⓐ Ⓑ Ⓒ Ⓓ Ⓔ	38. Ⓐ Ⓑ Ⓒ Ⓓ Ⓔ	48. Ⓐ Ⓑ Ⓒ Ⓓ Ⓔ
9. Ⓐ Ⓑ Ⓒ Ⓓ Ⓔ	19. Ⓐ Ⓑ Ⓒ Ⓓ Ⓔ	29. Ⓐ Ⓑ Ⓒ Ⓓ Ⓔ	39. Ⓐ Ⓑ Ⓒ Ⓓ Ⓔ	49. Ⓐ Ⓑ Ⓒ Ⓓ Ⓔ
10. Ⓐ Ⓑ Ⓒ Ⓓ Ⓔ	20. Ⓐ Ⓑ Ⓒ Ⓓ Ⓔ	30. Ⓐ Ⓑ Ⓒ Ⓓ Ⓔ	40. Ⓐ Ⓑ Ⓒ Ⓓ Ⓔ	50. Ⓐ Ⓑ Ⓒ Ⓓ Ⓔ

Physical Science

1. Ⓐ Ⓑ Ⓒ Ⓓ Ⓔ	5. Ⓐ Ⓑ Ⓒ Ⓓ Ⓔ	9. Ⓐ Ⓑ Ⓒ Ⓓ Ⓔ	13. Ⓐ Ⓑ Ⓒ Ⓓ Ⓔ	17. Ⓐ Ⓑ Ⓒ Ⓓ Ⓔ
2. Ⓐ Ⓑ Ⓒ Ⓓ Ⓔ	6. Ⓐ Ⓑ Ⓒ Ⓓ Ⓔ	10. Ⓐ Ⓑ Ⓒ Ⓓ Ⓔ	14. Ⓐ Ⓑ Ⓒ Ⓓ Ⓔ	18. Ⓐ Ⓑ Ⓒ Ⓓ Ⓔ
3. Ⓐ Ⓑ Ⓒ Ⓓ Ⓔ	7. Ⓐ Ⓑ Ⓒ Ⓓ Ⓔ	11. Ⓐ Ⓑ Ⓒ Ⓓ Ⓔ	15. Ⓐ Ⓑ Ⓒ Ⓓ Ⓔ	19. Ⓐ Ⓑ Ⓒ Ⓓ Ⓔ
4. Ⓐ Ⓑ Ⓒ Ⓓ Ⓔ	8. Ⓐ Ⓑ Ⓒ Ⓓ Ⓔ	12. Ⓐ Ⓑ Ⓒ Ⓓ Ⓔ	16. Ⓐ Ⓑ Ⓒ Ⓓ Ⓔ	20. Ⓐ Ⓑ Ⓒ Ⓓ Ⓔ

Table Reading

1. Ⓐ Ⓑ Ⓒ Ⓓ Ⓔ	9. Ⓐ Ⓑ Ⓒ Ⓓ Ⓔ	17. Ⓐ Ⓑ Ⓒ Ⓓ Ⓔ	25. Ⓐ Ⓑ Ⓒ Ⓓ Ⓔ	33. Ⓐ Ⓑ Ⓒ Ⓓ Ⓔ
2. Ⓐ Ⓑ Ⓒ Ⓓ Ⓔ	10. Ⓐ Ⓑ Ⓒ Ⓓ Ⓔ	18. Ⓐ Ⓑ Ⓒ Ⓓ Ⓔ	26. Ⓐ Ⓑ Ⓒ Ⓓ Ⓔ	34. Ⓐ Ⓑ Ⓒ Ⓓ Ⓔ
3. Ⓐ Ⓑ Ⓒ Ⓓ Ⓔ	11. Ⓐ Ⓑ Ⓒ Ⓓ Ⓔ	19. Ⓐ Ⓑ Ⓒ Ⓓ Ⓔ	27. Ⓐ Ⓑ Ⓒ Ⓓ Ⓔ	35. Ⓐ Ⓑ Ⓒ Ⓓ Ⓔ
4. Ⓐ Ⓑ Ⓒ Ⓓ Ⓔ	12. Ⓐ Ⓑ Ⓒ Ⓓ Ⓔ	20. Ⓐ Ⓑ Ⓒ Ⓓ Ⓔ	28. Ⓐ Ⓑ Ⓒ Ⓓ Ⓔ	36. Ⓐ Ⓑ Ⓒ Ⓓ Ⓔ
5. Ⓐ Ⓑ Ⓒ Ⓓ Ⓔ	13. Ⓐ Ⓑ Ⓒ Ⓓ Ⓔ	21. Ⓐ Ⓑ Ⓒ Ⓓ Ⓔ	29. Ⓐ Ⓑ Ⓒ Ⓓ Ⓔ	37. Ⓐ Ⓑ Ⓒ Ⓓ Ⓔ
6. Ⓐ Ⓑ Ⓒ Ⓓ Ⓔ	14. Ⓐ Ⓑ Ⓒ Ⓓ Ⓔ	22. Ⓐ Ⓑ Ⓒ Ⓓ Ⓔ	30. Ⓐ Ⓑ Ⓒ Ⓓ Ⓔ	38. Ⓐ Ⓑ Ⓒ Ⓓ Ⓔ
7. Ⓐ Ⓑ Ⓒ Ⓓ Ⓔ	15. Ⓐ Ⓑ Ⓒ Ⓓ Ⓔ	23. Ⓐ Ⓑ Ⓒ Ⓓ Ⓔ	31. Ⓐ Ⓑ Ⓒ Ⓓ Ⓔ	39. Ⓐ Ⓑ Ⓒ Ⓓ Ⓔ
8. Ⓐ Ⓑ Ⓒ Ⓓ Ⓔ	16. Ⓐ Ⓑ Ⓒ Ⓓ Ⓔ	24. Ⓐ Ⓑ Ⓒ Ⓓ Ⓔ	32. Ⓐ Ⓑ Ⓒ Ⓓ Ⓔ	40. Ⓐ Ⓑ Ⓒ Ⓓ Ⓔ

Instrument Comprehension

1. Ⓐ Ⓑ Ⓒ Ⓓ	6. Ⓐ Ⓑ Ⓒ Ⓓ	11. Ⓐ Ⓑ Ⓒ Ⓓ	16. Ⓐ Ⓑ Ⓒ Ⓓ	21. Ⓐ Ⓑ Ⓒ Ⓓ
2. Ⓐ Ⓑ Ⓒ Ⓓ	7. Ⓐ Ⓑ Ⓒ Ⓓ	12. Ⓐ Ⓑ Ⓒ Ⓓ	17. Ⓐ Ⓑ Ⓒ Ⓓ	22. Ⓐ Ⓑ Ⓒ Ⓓ
3. Ⓐ Ⓑ Ⓒ Ⓓ	8. Ⓐ Ⓑ Ⓒ Ⓓ	13. Ⓐ Ⓑ Ⓒ Ⓓ	18. Ⓐ Ⓑ Ⓒ Ⓓ	23. Ⓐ Ⓑ Ⓒ Ⓓ
4. Ⓐ Ⓑ Ⓒ Ⓓ	9. Ⓐ Ⓑ Ⓒ Ⓓ	14. Ⓐ Ⓑ Ⓒ Ⓓ	19. Ⓐ Ⓑ Ⓒ Ⓓ	24. Ⓐ Ⓑ Ⓒ Ⓓ
5. Ⓐ Ⓑ Ⓒ Ⓓ	10. Ⓐ Ⓑ Ⓒ Ⓓ	15. Ⓐ Ⓑ Ⓒ Ⓓ	20. Ⓐ Ⓑ Ⓒ Ⓓ	25. Ⓐ Ⓑ Ⓒ Ⓓ

Block Counting

1. Ⓐ Ⓑ Ⓒ Ⓓ Ⓔ	7. Ⓐ Ⓑ Ⓒ Ⓓ Ⓔ	13. Ⓐ Ⓑ Ⓒ Ⓓ Ⓔ	19. Ⓐ Ⓑ Ⓒ Ⓓ Ⓔ	25. Ⓐ Ⓑ Ⓒ Ⓓ Ⓔ
2. Ⓐ Ⓑ Ⓒ Ⓓ Ⓔ	8. Ⓐ Ⓑ Ⓒ Ⓓ Ⓔ	14. Ⓐ Ⓑ Ⓒ Ⓓ Ⓔ	20. Ⓐ Ⓑ Ⓒ Ⓓ Ⓔ	26. Ⓐ Ⓑ Ⓒ Ⓓ Ⓔ
3. Ⓐ Ⓑ Ⓒ Ⓓ Ⓔ	9. Ⓐ Ⓑ Ⓒ Ⓓ Ⓔ	15. Ⓐ Ⓑ Ⓒ Ⓓ Ⓔ	21. Ⓐ Ⓑ Ⓒ Ⓓ Ⓔ	27. Ⓐ Ⓑ Ⓒ Ⓓ Ⓔ
4. Ⓐ Ⓑ Ⓒ Ⓓ Ⓔ	10. Ⓐ Ⓑ Ⓒ Ⓓ Ⓔ	16. Ⓐ Ⓑ Ⓒ Ⓓ Ⓔ	22. Ⓐ Ⓑ Ⓒ Ⓓ Ⓔ	28. Ⓐ Ⓑ Ⓒ Ⓓ Ⓔ
5. Ⓐ Ⓑ Ⓒ Ⓓ Ⓔ	11. Ⓐ Ⓑ Ⓒ Ⓓ Ⓔ	17. Ⓐ Ⓑ Ⓒ Ⓓ Ⓔ	23. Ⓐ Ⓑ Ⓒ Ⓓ Ⓔ	29. Ⓐ Ⓑ Ⓒ Ⓓ Ⓔ
6. Ⓐ Ⓑ Ⓒ Ⓓ Ⓔ	12. Ⓐ Ⓑ Ⓒ Ⓓ Ⓔ	18. Ⓐ Ⓑ Ⓒ Ⓓ Ⓔ	24. Ⓐ Ⓑ Ⓒ Ⓓ Ⓔ	30. Ⓐ Ⓑ Ⓒ Ⓓ Ⓔ

Aviation Information

1. Ⓐ Ⓑ Ⓒ Ⓓ Ⓔ	5. Ⓐ Ⓑ Ⓒ Ⓓ Ⓔ	9. Ⓐ Ⓑ Ⓒ Ⓓ Ⓔ	13. Ⓐ Ⓑ Ⓒ Ⓓ Ⓔ	17. Ⓐ Ⓑ Ⓒ Ⓓ Ⓔ
2. Ⓐ Ⓑ Ⓒ Ⓓ Ⓔ	6. Ⓐ Ⓑ Ⓒ Ⓓ Ⓔ	10. Ⓐ Ⓑ Ⓒ Ⓓ Ⓔ	14. Ⓐ Ⓑ Ⓒ Ⓓ Ⓔ	18. Ⓐ Ⓑ Ⓒ Ⓓ Ⓔ
3. Ⓐ Ⓑ Ⓒ Ⓓ Ⓔ	7. Ⓐ Ⓑ Ⓒ Ⓓ Ⓔ	11. Ⓐ Ⓑ Ⓒ Ⓓ Ⓔ	15. Ⓐ Ⓑ Ⓒ Ⓓ Ⓔ	19. Ⓐ Ⓑ Ⓒ Ⓓ Ⓔ
4. Ⓐ Ⓑ Ⓒ Ⓓ Ⓔ	8. Ⓐ Ⓑ Ⓒ Ⓓ Ⓔ	12. Ⓐ Ⓑ Ⓒ Ⓓ Ⓔ	16. Ⓐ Ⓑ Ⓒ Ⓓ Ⓔ	20. Ⓐ Ⓑ Ⓒ Ⓓ Ⓔ

VERBAL ANALOGIES

25 Questions (8 Minutes)

Directions: This part of the test measures your ability to reason and see relationships among words. You are to choose the option that best completes the analogy developed at the beginning of each statement.

1. POT is to SOUP as OVEN is to

   A. PHONE
   B. BAKING
   C. GRILL
   D. BREAD
   E. DRINK

2. WET is to ARID as HOT is to

   A. BREEZY
   B. DAMP
   C. COLD
   D. RAINY
   E. SWELTERING

3. LOBSTER is to OCEAN as SCORPION is to

   A. ZOO
   B. DESERT
   C. STING
   D. ANIMAL
   E. CLAW

4. TEA is to LEAVES as COFFEE is to

   A. CAFFEINE
   B. HOT
   C. DRINK
   D. BEANS
   E. ESPRESSO

5. DOZEN is to GROSS as INCH is to

   A. FOOT
   B. METER
   C. MEASUREMENT
   D. RULER
   E. YARD STICK

6. SLICE is to PIE as PIECE is to

   A. WATER
   B. AIR
   C. PUDDING
   D. PUZZLE
   E. APPLESAUCE

7. SNAIL is to SLIMY as RABBIT is to

   A. CARROT
   B. HOP
   C. FURRY
   D. SMART
   E. EARS

8. ELECTRICITY is to WIRE as WATER is to

   A. SOCKET
   B. CLOUD
   C. HOSE
   D. POWER
   E. BUCKET

9. SPICE is to SALT as DRAWING is to
   A. CLIPBOARD
   B. PANEL
   C. CANVAS
   D. DOODLE
   E. PENCIL

10. ANATOMY is to BODY as ANALYSIS is to
    A. GRAPH
    B. DATA
    C. PRESENTATION
    D. DECISION
    E. UNDERSTANDING

11. RADAR is to BLIP as DOORBELL is to
    A. KNOCK
    B. CHIME
    C. RETURN
    D. DOOR
    E. PEEPHOLE

12. RADIATOR is to COOLANT as FUEL TANK is to
    A. NOZZLE
    B. AIR
    C. GASOLINE
    D. OIL
    E. HEAT

13. FLOWER is to BEE as HAY is to
    A. WASP
    B. DOG
    C. GUINEA PIG
    D. BIRD
    E. HORSE

14. AROUSE is to PACIFY as AGITATE is to
    A. SMOOTH
    B. RUFFLE
    C. UNDERSTAND
    D. IGNORE
    E. MAGNIFY

15. QUERY is to ANSWER as TASK is to
    A. CHORE
    B. PERFORM
    C. JOB
    D. DEMONSTRATE
    E. RESOLVE

16. SEAL is to FISH as BIRD is to
    A. WING
    B. MINNOW
    C. WORM
    D. SNAIL
    E. SNAKE

17. SHOE is to LEATHER as HIGHWAY is to
    A. PASSAGE
    B. ROAD
    C. TRAIL
    D. ASPHALT
    E. TUNNEL

18. SECURE is to SAFE as DISTANT is to
    A. CONVENIENT
    B. FAR
    C. SECRET
    D. DULL
    E. CLOSED

19. HORSE is to FOAL as MOTHER is to

A. MARE
B. SON
C. STALLION
D. FATHER
E. BROTHER

20. FINDER is to REWARD as REPENTER is to

A. RELIGION
B. SIN
C. ABSOLUTION
D. CONTRITION
E. WORSHIP

21. TELEGRAPH is to PHONE as WAGON is to

A. WIRE
B. HORSE
C. CALL
D. WHEEL
E. CAR

22. ALL CAPS is to LOWER CASE as

A. LOTION is to SMOOTH
B. SHOUT is to WHISPER
C. COLA is to DRINK
D. FIRE is to FLAME
E. PHONE is to EMAIL

23. RED is to PINK as BLACK is to

A. BEIGE
B. WHITE
C. DARK
D. GRAY
E. PURPLE

24. YOUTH is to YOUNG as AGE is to

A. PEOPLE
B. PARENTS
C. GRANDMOTHER
D. OLD
E. UNCLE

25. SAND is to BEACH as SOIL is to

A. EARTH
B. PLANTS
C. WATER
D. FARM
E. FOREST

STOP.

If you finish before time is up, you may check your work on this section only. Do not turn to any other section in the test.

ARITHMETIC REASONING

25 Questions (8 Minutes)

Directions: This part of the test measures your ability to use arithmetic to solve problems. Each problem is followed by five possible answers. You are to decide which of the five choices is correct.

1. Which of these equations represents a line that will pass though the point (0, –2) with a slope of $-\frac{3}{2}$?

   A. $y+2=\frac{3}{2}x$

   B. $y-2=\frac{3}{2}x$

   C. $y+2=-\frac{3}{2}x$

   D. $y-2=-\frac{3}{2}x$

   E. $y+-\frac{3}{2}=2x$

2. A line is represented by the equation $y=\frac{5}{4}x-2.5$. If the slope is divided by 2 to form a new line with the same y-intercept, at which point will the new line cross the x-axis?

   A. (–4, 0)

   B. (–1.25, 0)

   C. (0, 0)

   D. (4, 0)

   E. (4, 1)

3. Nutrition guidelines suggest 65 total grams of fat per day for a 2,000-calorie diet. How many grams of fat would be recommended for a 2,500-calorie diet?

   A. $16\frac{1}{4}$

   B. 52

   C. $65\frac{1}{4}$

   D. $81\frac{1}{4}$

   E. 80

4. What is the solution to the equation $3(4m - 3m) = -m(-1 - 2) + 4$?

   A. $m = 3$

   B. $m = 5$

   C. $m = 4$

   D. There are infinitely many solutions.

   E. There is no solution.

5. Which term best describes the relationship between x and y represented in the table shown?

x	y
1	135
3	267.642
5	400.284
7	532.926

   A. Exponential growth

   B. Exponential decay

   C. Increasing linear

   D. Decreasing linear

   E. There is no way to tell from the information provided.

6. An exit poll of randomly selected voters asked which candidate they voted for in a state election. The results are shown in the table. What percent of those who voted for Candidate Y were age 47 or older? Round your answer to the nearest tenth of a percent.

	Candidate X	Candidate Y	Total
Age 46 or younger	76	60	136
Age 47 or older	92	72	164
Total	168	132	300

A. 24.00%

B. 43.90%

C. 54.50%

D. 78.30%

E. 30.50%

7. The results of a poll indicated that 46% of the respondents are in favor of an education bill. The margin of error for the poll was 3%. Which of the following statements is best supported by the data?

A. The actual percentage of people who are in favor of a new education bill is likely less than 43%.

B. The actual percentage of people who are in favor of a new education bill is likely between 43% and 49%.

C. The actual percentage of people who are in favor of a new education bill is likely between 46% and 49%.

D. The actual percentage of people who are in favor of a new education bill is likely between than 49% and 52%.

E. The actual percentage of people who are in favor of a new education bill is likely greater than 52%.

8. The pesticide DDT was widely used in the United States until its ban in 1972. The half-life of DDT is about 15 years. A half-life is the amount of time it takes for half of the amount of a substance to decay. If there are 100 grams of DDT, how much will be remaining after 45 years?

A. 50 grams

B. 25 grams

C. 12.5 grams

D. 6.25 grams

E. 10 grams

9. Which shows the sum of $\frac{2x+5}{x-3}+\frac{4x+1}{x+1}$?

A. $\frac{6x+4}{x^2-2x-3}$

B. $\frac{6x^2+10x+4}{x^2-2x-3}$

C. $\frac{6x^2+18x+2}{x^2-2x-3}$

D. $\frac{6x^2-6x+8}{x^2-2x-3}$

E. $\frac{6x^2+6x+4}{x^2-2x-3}$

10. If $6 + x + y = 20$ and $x + y = k$, then $20 - k =$

A. 0

B. 4

C. 2

D. 8

E. 6

11. If there are 4 boys and 2 girls in a family, what is the ratio of boys in the family to children in the family?

A. 1:2

B. 2:1

C. 4:1

D. 2:3

E. 1:3

12. If a cyclist takes 4 hours to travel 72 miles, what is the cyclist's average speed in miles per hour?

    A. $\frac{1}{18}$

    B. 9

    C. 18

    D. 28

    E. 288

13. A bag contains 3 blue marbles, 7 red marbles, and 5 yellow marbles. If Joe picks 1 marble from the bag at random, what is the probability that it will be blue?

    A. $\frac{1}{5}$

    B. $\frac{1}{4}$

    C. $\frac{1}{2}$

    D. $\frac{3}{4}$

    E. $\frac{4}{5}$

14. If $6y - 8 = 28$, what is the value of y?

    A. 4

    B. 5

    C. 6

    D. 7

    E. 8

15. In the triangle, what is the value of x?

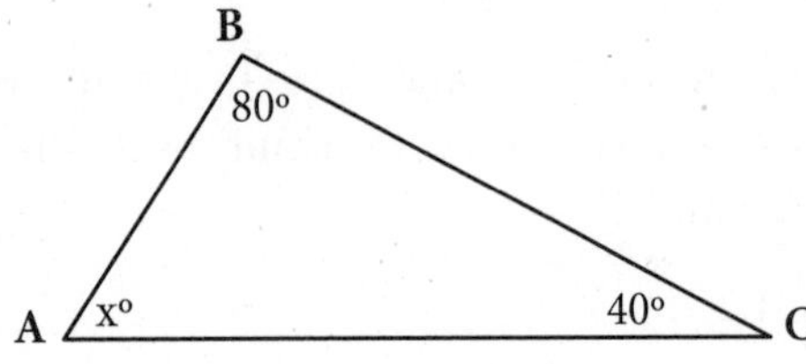

    A. 30

    B. 60

    C. 70

    D. 80

    E. 90

16. A plumber charges $45 for a service call plus $25 for each hour that he is working at a customer's house. If he conducts a service call that takes 3 hours, what will the customer's bill be?

    A. $45

    B. $75

    C. $105

    D. $110

    E. $120

17. Joey's height and Keith's height combined is one half of Steve's height. Which equation represents this statement?

    A. $J + K = \frac{1}{2}S$

    B. $J + K = 2S$

    C. $J + K = S + \frac{1}{2}$

    D. $J - K = 2S$

    E. $J - K = \frac{1}{2}S$

18. Al has 50 pictures. If he gives half of these pictures to his friend Joe and $\frac{2}{5}$ of the remaining pictures to his mother, how many pictures does he still have?

    A. 10

    B. 15

    C. 20

    D. 25

    E. 30

19. What is the value of x in the figure?

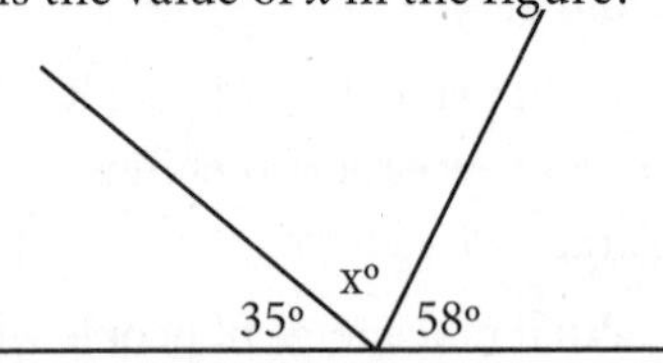

    A. 32

    B. 55

    C. 87

    D. 90

    E. 112

20. Michael delivers y papers on Wednesdays. He delivers two times that number on Sundays and half that number on Mondays. How many papers does Michael deliver in one week?

A. $y^2 + \frac{3y}{2}$

B. $\frac{7y}{2}$

C. $\frac{5y}{2}$

D. $y^2 + 3y$

E. $y^2 + 7y$

21. Sawyer owns a bicycle shop. During one week, he sells b bicycles for \$125 each. He also sells 3 helmets, which cost \$14 each. If Sawyer's total revenue for the week was \$917, how many bicycles did he sell?

A. 4

B. 7

C. 8

D. 9

E. 11

22. If $2x + y = 4$ and $3x - 2y = 13$, then $x = ?$

A. 2

B. 3

C. 4

D. 7

E. 13

23. Which of the following is equivalent to $(a - b)(a + b)$?

A. $a^2 - b^2$

B. $a^2 + ab - b^2$

C. $a^2 - ab - b^2$

D. $a^2 + b^2$

E. $a^2 + ab + b^2$

24. Paul recently purchased some new clothing for work. He has 4 ties, 7 dress shirts, and 5 pairs of dress pants. How many different outfits can he make?

A. 16

B. 45

C. 97

D. 110

E. 140

25. If $\frac{7a}{2} = 5a - 3$, what is the value of a?

A. –2

B. –1

C. 1

D. 2

E. 3

STOP.

If you finish before time is up, you may check your work on this section only. Do not turn to any other section in the test.

WORD KNOWLEDGE

25 Questions (5 Minutes)

Directions: This part of the test measures your knowledge of words and their meanings. For each question, you are to choose the word below that is closest in meaning to the capitalized word above.

1. ANIMATE
   - A. Color
   - B. Alive
   - C. Breathe
   - D. Grow
   - E. Damp

2. BRAZEN
   - A. Unrestrained
   - B. Shiny
   - C. Hot
   - D. Masked
   - E. Fast

3. CALLOUS
   - A. Communicate
   - B. Depth
   - C. Planner
   - D. Hardened
   - E. Grip

4. COHERENT
   - A. Temperate
   - B. Present
   - C. Orderly
   - D. Humid
   - E. Tight

5. DEBASE
   - A. Corrupt
   - B. Foundation
   - C. Unnerving
   - D. Organic
   - E. Airtight

6. EXTOL
   - A. Free
   - B. Former
   - C. Hidden
   - D. Waterproof
   - E. Praise

7. FURTIVE
   - A. Sound
   - B. Secret
   - C. Porous
   - D. Video
   - E. Doorway

8. HAUGHTY
   - A. Stuffed
   - B. Temperate
   - C. Painful
   - D. Arrogant
   - E. Intelligent

9. IMPECCABLE

A. Eaten

B. Electrical

C. Gooey

D. Closed

E. Faultless

10. KILN

A. Ceramic

B. Oven

C. Skirt

D. Untapped

E. Normal

11. LUCRATIVE

A. Profitable

B. Anatomical

C. Cooling

D. Dividing

E. Helpful

12. MANGLE

A. Staircase

B. Unnatural

C. Male

D. Taut

E. Injure

13. NEPOTISM

A. Sacred

B. Favoritism

C. Fear

D. Slick

E. Electric

14. OBVERSE

A. Front

B. Clear

C. Visible

D. Predominant

E. Vacuum

15. PUGILIST

A. Catalog

B. Artist

C. Erase

D. Fighter

E. Canine

16. RESCIND

A. Cancel

B. Manual

C. Bottle

D. Agreement

E. Bandaged

17. SHILL

A. Loud

B. Hollow

C. Grate

D. Promote

E. Request

18. SNIVEL

A. Aground

B. Insect

C. Journal

D. Request

E. Whine

19. TRANSPARENT
    - A. Clear
    - B. Sticky
    - C. International
    - D. Adoptive
    - E. Sliding

20. TYRO
    - A. Hyper
    - B. Novice
    - C. Round
    - D. Frame
    - E. Wind

21. ULTERIOR
    - A. Angry
    - B. Literate
    - C. Hidden
    - D. Pinnacle
    - E. Growing

22. VENAL
    - A. Corruptible
    - B. Blood
    - C. Meat
    - D. Fresh
    - E. Smooth

23. VICTUAL
    - A. Empty
    - B. Supply
    - C. Amulet
    - D. Food
    - E. Strainer

24. WRAITH
    - A. Cover
    - B. Vine
    - C. Ghost
    - D. Banner
    - E. Vase

25. PUMMEL
    - A. Unpleasant
    - B. Waste
    - C. Acid
    - D. Beat
    - E. Stick

STOP.

If you finish before time is up, you may check your work on this section only. Do not turn to any other section in the test.

MATH KNOWLEDGE

25 Questions (38 Minutes)

Directions: This part of the test measures your knowledge of mathematical terms and principles. Each problem is followed by five possible answers. You are to decide which of the five choices is correct.

1. 1,000,000 may be represented as

   A. 10^3
   B. 10^4
   C. 10^5
   D. 10^6
   E. 10^7

2. If x is less than 0 and y is greater than 0, then

   A. x is greater than y.
   B. $x + y$ is greater than 0.
   C. xy is less than 0.
   D. xy is greater than 0.
   E. xy equals 0.

3. If $3^{n-2} = 27$, then n equals

   A. 5
   B. 7
   C. 8
   D. 9
   E. 12

4. What is the square root of 4 raised to the fifth power?

   A. 8
   B. 16
   C. 32
   D. 64
   E. 100

5. The third root of 64 is

   A. 2
   B. 3
   C. 4
   D. 7
   E. 8

6. Angle E is 40° smaller than its complement. What is the number of degrees in angle E?

   A. 25°
   B. 45°
   C. 60°
   D. 75°
   E. 90°

7. What is the perimeter of a right triangle whose legs are 3 and 4 feet?

   A. 10 feet
   B. 12 feet
   C. 14 feet
   D. 16 feet
   E. 20 feet

8. Sabrina received grades of 96, 88, and 82 on three tests. What grade must she receive on the next test so that her average for these tests is 90?

   A. 80
   B. 90
   C. 91
   D. 92
   E. 94

9. If the sum of the edges of a cube is 24 inches, what is the volume of the cube?

A. 4 cubic inches

B. 8 cubic inches

C. 12 cubic inches

D. 16 cubic inches

E. 64 cubic inches

10. If $a = 4b$ and $8b = 30c$, then $a =$

A. $6c$

B. $9c$

C. $10c$

D. $12c$

E. $15c$

11. A surround sound entertainment system originally priced at $1,000 is first discounted by 20 percent, then later by 10 percent. If a 5 percent sales tax is added to the purchase price, how much would a customer buying the system at the lowest discounted price pay for the system to the nearest dollar?

A. $720

B. $750

C. $756

D. $800

E. $820

12. In the figure shown, what is the measure of angle x?

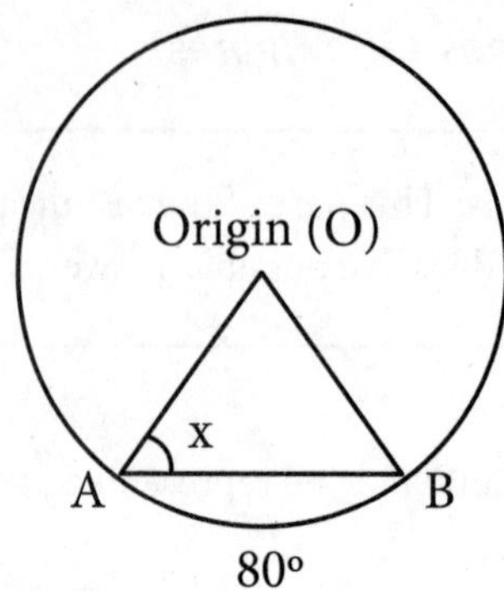

A. 35°

B. 45°

C. 50°

D. 70°

E. 80°

13. In a 4-hour examination of 420 questions, there are 60 mathematics problems. If twice the amount of time should be allowed for each mathematics problem than for each of the other questions, how many minutes should be spent on the mathematics problems?

A. 60 minutes

B. 65 minutes

C. 70 minutes

D. 75 minutes

E. 80 minutes

14. A farmer, Cole, who is 6 feet tall, wants to determine the height of his barn. Cole notices that his shadow is 14 feet long. The shadow cast by his barn is 70 feet long. How tall is the barn?

A. 35 feet

B. 30 feet

C. 40 feet

D. 45 feet

E. 50 feet

15. If $(x - y)^2 = 60$ and $x^2 + y^2 = 40$, then $xy =$

A. –40

B. –20

C. –12

D. –15

E. –10

16. A closed rectangular box with a square base has a height of 3 inches. If the volume of the box is 48 cubic inches, what is the box's surface area in square inches?

A. 66

B. 80

C. 81

D. 90

E. 84

17. Two ships are 2,000 miles apart and sailing toward each other. One sails at the rate of 80 miles per day and the other at the rate of 100 miles per day. How far apart will they be at the end of 9 days?

A. 380 miles

B. 420 miles

C. 440 miles

D. 460 miles

E. 500 miles

18. The Moellers drove from New York to San Francisco, a distance of 3,000 miles. The first day, they drove $\frac{1}{8}$ of the distance and $\frac{1}{7}$ of the remaining distance on the second day. How many miles did they have remaining to reach their destination?

A. 2,200 miles

B. 2,250 miles

C. 2,300 miles

D. 2,400 miles

E. 2,450 miles

19. A class of 216 recruits consists of three racial and ethnic groups. If $\frac{1}{3}$ are African American, $\frac{1}{4}$ are Hispanic, and the remaining are Caucasian, how many of the recruits are Caucasian?

A. 94

B. 90

C. 82

D. 75

E. 68

20. If x^2 varies directly to y, and when $x = 2$, then $y = 10$; what is the value of y when $x = 8$?

A. 32

B. 130

C. 160

D. 138

E. 142

21. A Naval detachment has enough rations to feed 15 people for 8 days. If 5 more people join the detachment, for how many fewer days will the rations last?

A. 1

B. 2

C. 3

D. 4

E. 5

22. Two trains running on the same track travel at the rates of 40 and 45 mph, respectively. If the slower train starts an hour earlier, how long will it take the faster train to catch up to the slower train?

A. 4 hours

B. 5 hours

C. 6 hours

D. 7 hours

E. 8 hours

23. A field can be plowed by 12 machines in 7 hours. If four machines are in need of repair and cannot be used, how many hours will it take to plow the field?

A. 7.5 hours

B. 8.5 hours

C. 9.5 hours

D. 10 hours

E. 10.5 hours

24. A cash box contains a certain number of coins, of which 63 are dimes, 33 are nickels, and the rest are quarters. If the probability of selecting a quarter from this bank is $\frac{1}{5}$, how many quarters does the cash box contain?

A. 24

B. 27

C. 30

D. 32

E. 35

25. If Jonah completes a trip of 240 miles at the rate of 30 mph, at what rate would he have to travel on the return trip in order to average 40 mph for the round trip?

A. 50 mph

B. 55 mph

C. 60 mph

D. 62 mph

E. 65 mph

STOP.

If you finish before time is up, you may check your work on this section only. Do not turn to any other section in the test.

READING COMPREHENSION

25 Questions (22 Minutes)

Directions: This part of the test measures your ability to read and understand written material. Each passage is followed by a series of multiple-choice questions. You are to choose the option that best answers the question based on the passage. No additional information or specific knowledge is needed.

Questions 1-4 are based on the following passage.

Many people can recall a time when they were told that they were either left-brained or right-brained by a parent or teacher. It is an integral part of how we view ourselves, and how others view us. Think about this: a woman's old, worn out car has finally broken down and she is hoping for a new model. How should she make her decision? There are three common approaches to this question. The first choice is to do some research on the model she wants and consider whether the price is reasonable. The second approach is to sit in the car and get a "feel" for it. If it feels right, then she will know it is the right choice. The third and most common approach is to do a little research on the one she likes and then take it for a test drive. She then makes the decision based on how she feels in it. Depending on how she picks the car, she would be organized into either completely right-brained, completely left-brained, or a mixture of the two.

This analysis of personality and mentality is an example of the widely recognized right-brain/left-brain theory. This rudimentary view of the human brain excludes scientific fact and assumes that humans are born using only one side of their brain for every activity. In actuality, humans cannot consciously choose to use one side of their brain over the other, and typically use their whole brain in even the most mundane activities. This is clearly illustrated in the example of the woman and car choices.

1. What is the primary purpose of this passage?

A. To defend a controversial psychological theory

B. To contradict a widely accepted theory on human mentality

C. To inform on the importance of right-brain/left-brain theory in human psychology

D. To inspire people to subscribe to the right-brain/left-brain theory

E. To explain a complicated theory not fully grasped by most people

2. Why did the author choose to use the example of the woman buying the car?

A. To better exemplify the basic premise of the right-brain/left-brain theory

B. To list the various ways one can go about buying a car

C. To highlight the differences between right-brained and left-brained people

D. To mock a simplistic form of psychological analysis

E. To describe the intricacies of what it means to be right-brained

3. In the second paragraph, the word *rudimentary* most likely means

A. immature.

B. elementary.

C. complicated.

D. undeveloped.

E. rough.

4. Which of the following claims would the author most likely agree with?

   A. People who buy cars based on the "feeling" they get while sitting in them are right-brained.

   B. The right-brain/left-brain theory is the most accurate representation of the human psyche.

   C. Those who subscribe to the right-brain/left-brain theory are left-brained.

   D. Humans use both sides of their brain for all activities.

   E. Humans can choose to use one side of their brain or the other.

Questions 5-8 are based on the following passage.

The downfall of the Confederate army began at the Appomattox River in northern Virginia. General Robert E. Lee, blocked by federal troops from reaching confederate soldiers in North Carolina, cut west across the Appomattox River. His objective was to reach food supplies at the Appomattox County railroad station before forging ahead to the north. These plans were thrown askew when Brigadier General George A. Custer reached the station first and burned three full supply trains, rendering Lee's troops vulnerable and susceptible to capture.

In a final attempt to aid Lee's army and reach further supplies in Lynchburg, Confederate Major General John B. Gordon attacked Union cavalry near the county courthouse. However, upon realizing that the Union cavalry was supported by thousands of Union troops separating him from his own Confederate soldiers nearby, the General stopped, and Lee was trapped. On April 9th, Lee and Grant exchanged messages agreeing to meet at the Wilmer Mclean home in Appomattox County, where a formal surrender would be signed by Lee, effectively ending the war in Virginia. The events at Appomattox inspired similar events across the country, instigating the end to the Civil War.

5. The primary purpose of this passage is to

   A. give a historical account of the monumental shift in the war.

   B. describe Robert E. Lee's failure as a general.

   C. explain the significance of the Appomattox River.

   D. disprove a popular belief about the end of the Civil War.

   E. celebrate the Union victory in the Appomattox County.

6. Which of the following statements is supported by the passage?

   A. The Confederate army was intending to head south before being cut off by Gen. Custer.

   B. The Union army was planning an attack on Lee before he surrendered.

   C. Lee was pressured to surrender due to the lack of supplies for his starving troops.

   D. The Civil War ended on April 9th, when Lee surrendered to Grant.

   E. The Union soldiers were short on food supplies as well.

7. What is the primary purpose of the second paragraph?

   A. Explain the significance of the Wilmer Mclean house in Appomattox County.

   B. Highlight the attempted Confederate rescue of Lee's troops.

   C. Retell the events directly leading up to the final surrender.

   D. Explain the importance of Appomattox County as a historical landmark.

   E. Analyze the strategy utilized by Union soldiers against Lee's armies.

8. Which of the following is an accurate and descriptive title of the passage?

A. The Strategies of the Union Army

B. Appomattox County: The End of the War in Virginia

C. The Battle of Appomattox County

D. Appomattox River: The End of the Civil War

E. The Surrender of General Lee

Questions 9-12 are based on the following passage.

The term apartheid in the Afrikaans language means "apartness" and the word itself inspired just that in South Africa for the better part of 50 years. Apartheid was a piece of segregationist legislation that enforced the separation of white and non-white South African people in every aspect of their public and private lives. The 1913 Land Act forced blacks to live on reserves and barred them from becoming sharecroppers. By 1950, apartheid had forbidden marriage and sexual relations between whites and non-whites, the latter of which were legally classified based on race and denied participation in national government.

Opposition to apartheid existed in parallel to its birth. The African National Congress (ANC), in league with the South Indian National Congress, organized all manner of opposition strategies, ranging from peaceful protests to political action to armed resistance. It was the government sanctioned 1960 massacre in Sharpeville, a black township, that solidified the anger of anti-apartheid leaders and assured them that non-violence was an ineffective method. With the support of the UN General Assembly and the leadership of Nelson Mandela, who later won a peace prize for his efforts aiding the resistance, apartheid was legally abolished in 1994. A new constitution was written, and new leadership instated that ensured equality in the legal sense. However, the scars left by apartheid would affect South Africa for decades in its wake.

9. What does the author mention in the second paragraph was the reason for riotous anti-apartheid protests?

A. The enactment of the Land Act of 1913

B. The disbandment of the African National Congress

C. The arrest of Nelson Mandela

D. The United Nations' lack of support

E. The massacre in Sharpeville

10. Why does the author define the word *apartheid* in the first sentence?

A. To highlight the use of the Afrikaans language in legislation

B. To introduce the nature of the legislation itself before describing it in literal terms

C. To imply that segregation did not only exist in the United States

D. To explain the origins of the controversial term

E. To describe the depth of the racism that permeated the South African government

11. The primary purpose of the second paragraph is to

A. describe the opposition to apartheid and its eventual demise.

B. introduce the key players in the resistance to apartheid.

C. criticize the actions taken by rioters in their fight against apartheid.

D. explain the role of Nelson Mandela in the anti-apartheid activism.

E. illustrate the actions taken by protesters in order to overthrow apartheid.

12. Which of the following is an accurate and descriptive title of the passage?

A. Apartheid: South African Apartness

B. The Land Act of 1913: A Historical Account of Apartheid

C. Segregation Across the World

D. Controversial South African Legislation

E. Nelson Mandela and Living with Apartheid

Questions 13-16 are based on the following passage.

Faux fur is the absence of furry creatures in your fluffy sweaters. In recent years, animal rights activists have successfully made real fur in clothing stores a taboo fabric, and faux fur labeling has become the norm. This reality was challenged, however, when it became public that British labels were marketing their supposedly synthetic clothing as "faux" when in fact it originated on the backs of woodland creatures. With no laws in place banning this marketing strategy, it is left to consumers to discern faux from fur.

There are ways to tell, though. Faux fur, while certainly similar in appearance and texture, is not shaped the same way as real fur. Real fur will taper at the end to a sharp point, while faux fur is blunt and uniform—much like a manufactured, unsharpened pencil. The bases of the fur also differ, as real fur takes hold in the hide of the animal from which it was skinned, and thus the lining is leathery. Fake fur was born of machine weaving, and thus takes root in similar cloth-like fabric that never touched the back end of an animal. The final way to tell if fur is fake or not is likely not appropriate for browsing a shop but never fails to identify a fur from a fraud: burning it. Real fur will singe in response to fire; fake fur will melt and return to the plastic state it was cut from.

13. The primary purpose of the passage is to

A. persuade labels to properly label the usage of faux fur in lieu of real fur.

B. raise awareness for a flaw in the fashion industry.

C. advocate for the usage of real fur as opposed to faux fur.

D. inform consumers about the differences between faux fur and real fur.

E. dissuade consumers from buying real fur.

14. What does the word *taboo* most likely mean in this passage?

A. Controversial

B. Nonexistent

C. Useful

D. Popular

E. Difficult

15. Which of the following statements would the author most likely agree with?

A. Labels will never be forthcoming about the origins of their fabrics, so it is necessary for consumers to identify the materials themselves.

B. Consumers should be made aware of the differences between fake fur and real fur as labels will not always make that information available.

C. Real fur has better texture than fake fur as it isn't made of plastic.

D. The price difference between real and fake fur is another way to identify the material's origins.

E. Manufacturers that use real fur without informing the consumer should be held legally responsible for the misinformation provided.

16. The author uses the phrase "manufactured, unsharpened pencils" to illustrate the

A. inferiority of the faux fur in comparison with the real fur.

B. process by which faux fur is produced.

C. texture of the faux fur to be easily identified.

D. man-made nature of the faux fur vs the real fur.

E. contrast between texture and nature of the real fur and the faux fur.

Questions 17-20 are based on the following passage.

In September of 2007, a group of private security contractors (PSCs) employed by the United States opened fire on a crowd in Baghdad, killing 17 people. Controversy surrounding this incident triggered international dispute and raised questions pertaining to the legal ramifications of such acts. While it is often assumed that PSCs operate within a legal void, both international and domestic law outline a certain legal structure meant to ensure that those in such a line of work are held accountable for any illicit activity or abuses on the job. However, the use of PSCs in and of itself is not illegal.

Certainly, under international humanitarian law, there are criminal acts that are considered criminal acts whether they were committed by PSCs or not. PSCs that are employed during times of armed conflict are subject to the same rules that apply to state actors; they are subject to the rules established by the four Geneva Conventions of 1949 and the two Additional Protocols of 1977. This is outlined in Common Article 3 to the Geneva Convention which lists numerous acts and prohibits "all parties to the conflict" to commit such acts.

International human rights laws are trickier. While international humanitarian laws blanketly prohibit various crimes no matter the perpetrator, international human rights laws provide a necessity for state involvement in order to be considered a violation. Individual PSCs can be found liable for human rights violations under theories of state conspiracy. PSC companies can be found liable for human rights violations if employed by a state. It is unclear, however, if a corporation or individual that employs PSCs can be found liable for human rights violations.

In terms of domestic accountability, PSCs are ordinarily subject to the laws of the country within which they are operating. Thus, any war crimes or gross abuses of human rights must be deemed illegal. This is also true of instances in which PSCs are granted immunity. In the instance of Baghdad, the PSCs involved had been granted immunity under the US Coalition Provisional Authority (CPA). This immunity, though legal, is not absolute. Any violation of the state contract employing PSCs severs their immunity and results in their being subject to domestic accountability laws.

In 2014, the five PSCs employed by the US government in Baghdad were found guilty of murder in the first degree and various charges of manslaughter. Though the state was not found to be in violation of international humanitarian or human rights laws, the PSCs were found to be in breach of contract with the US government and thus their immunity was severed. While assuredly tragic, the actions committed by PSCs in Baghdad allowed the US and the world to see the ostensible international and domestic PSC laws at work.

17. The primary purpose of the passage is to

A. advocate for the use of PSCs in times of war.

B. raise awareness of the 2007 incident in Baghdad.

C. dissuade others from entering the employ of or becoming PSCs.

D. discuss the legality of PSCs as questioned in the incident in Baghdad.

E. inform the reader about the profession and use of PSCs on a global scale.

18. The word *blanketly* in the third paragraph most likely means

    A. mostly.

    B. softly.

    C. comprehensively.

    D. intentionally.

    E. unrestrictedly.

19. The author would agree with the statement that

    A. laws pertaining to PSCs, while occasionally convoluted, are effective.

    B. PSCs operate within a void that protects them from legal ramifications.

    C. the actions committed by PSCs in Baghdad are a perfect example of humanitarian law violations.

    D. international human rights laws are ineffective in holding PSCs accountable as there must be substantial proof of state involvement.

    E. PSCs are legally responsible for any and all actions committed overseas, even in times of war.

20. Which of the following is an accurate and descriptive title of the passage?

    A. PSCs: A Discussion of International Humanitarian Law

    B. What are Private Security Contractors?

    C. The Art of Private Warfare: A Study of PSCs

    D. The Truth About the Baghdad Massacre

    E. The Baghdad Massacre: An Analysis of the Legality of PSCs

Questions 21-25 are based on the following passage.

One of the most commonly made assumptions about those with color blindness is that the world appears black and white. Certainly, that may sound like the correct definition given the implication that those afflicted are blind to color; however, color blindness operates on a categorical basis. There are three different forms of color blindness, and seven subcategories, only one of which is complete color blindness. The other six subcategories operate under either red-green color blindness or blue-yellow color blindness; both of which confuse their titular colors and are less common than the infamous monochrome option known as true color blindness.

Most people with color blindness have difficulty perceiving the differences between certain colors, shades, and tones. For instance, deuteranomaly is a form of red-green color blindness that makes green tones look more red, but otherwise does not interrupt normal activities. Protanopia and deuteranopia make it almost impossible to tell the difference between the two. On the more extreme side of the spectrum, you have tritanopia, which renders those afflicted unable to perceive the differences between blue and green, purple and red, and yellow and pink. It is only in the most extreme cases, however, that those affected are entirely unable to perceive color, and thus true color blindness is a rarity.

21. According to the passage, there are

A. three types of colorblindness.

B. seven types of colorblindness.

C. six types of colorblindness that confuse titular colors.

D. seven subcategories of colorblindness that stem from shades of gray.

E. both red-green and blue-yellow types of true colorblindness.

22. According to the passage, people with color blindness

A. have various degrees of color blindness depending on the day.

B. confuse red with purple.

C. are always capable of seeing color.

D. are not necessarily incapable of seeing color.

E. cannot perceive any color tone, as opposed to any color at all.

23. In the first paragraph, *titular* most likely means

A. title.

B. brighter.

C. favorite.

D. symbolic.

E. token.

24. The primary purpose of the second paragraph is to

A. examine the differences between the various subcategories of color blindness.

B. define all the various types of color blindness.

C. disprove the assumption that color blindness means blind to color.

D. provide insight into the more extreme side of color blindness.

E. inspire sympathy for those with color blindness.

25. Which of the following statements would the author most likely agree with?

A. Color blindness operates on a spectrum, ranging from vaguely tone blind to completely blind to color.

B. Color blindness affects the tone of all colors perceived by the eyes.

C. Some people with color blindness are incapable of perceiving color.

D. Deuteranopia makes red tones look more green.

E. Color blindness in and of itself is a rarity.

STOP.

If you finish before time is up, you may check your work on this section only. Do not turn to any other section in the test.

SITUATIONAL JUDGMENT

50 Questions (35 Minutes)

Directions: This part of the test measures your judgment in responding to interpersonal situations similar to those you may encounter as an officer. Your responses will be scored relative to the consensus judgment across experienced U.S. Air Force officers. For each situation, you must respond to two questions. First, select which one of the five actions listed you judge the MOST EFFECTIVE action in response to the situation. Then, select which one of the five actions listed you judge the LEAST EFFECTIVE action in response to the situation. [NOTE: Although some actions may have been judged equally effective or equally ineffective by experienced officers, select only one action (A-E) for each question.]

You are a brand-new junior officer with numerous enlisted under your command. A seasoned enlisted that has been in the military for much longer than you refuses to follow your orders. He claims that due to his years of service he knows better than you do and thus should not be subject to your orders.

Possible Actions:

- **A.** Publicly reprimand and write him up as an example to the other enlisted.
- **B.** Go to your commanding officer with the problem and ask for his intervention.
- **C.** Do nothing because he has every right to ignore your orders if he has been in the military for longer.
- **D.** Confront him on your own to discuss the problem privately and if he continues to disobey your orders, write him up.
- **E.** Ask one of his friends to discuss the problem with him and see if they can get him to obey orders.

1. Select the MOST EFFECTIVE action (A-E) in response to the situation.
2. Select the LEAST EFFECTIVE action (A-E) in response to the situation.

You perceive favoritism being displayed towards one of your fellow junior officers by your commanding officer. This other junior officer is often late, makes significant mistakes, and is never reprimanded. You and other junior officers are often reprimanded by your commanding officer when making these mistakes.

Possible Actions:

- **A.** Ignore the favoritism as it is not your place to question a commanding officer.
- **B.** Reprimand your fellow junior officer yourself if your commanding officer won't.
- **C.** Privately discuss the perceived favoritism with your fellow junior officer before going to the commanding officer.
- **D.** Call out the commanding officer publicly for the favoritism.
- **E.** Go directly to the commanding officer's superior so that they can deal with the perceived favoritism as they see fit.

3. Select the MOST EFFECTIVE action (A-E) in response to the situation.
4. Select the LEAST EFFECTIVE action (A-E) in response to the situation.

While off duty with other members of your squadron, you catch another officer smoking marijuana by himself. The other members of your squadron claim that this is normal and that he will be sober by morning. However, the Air Force strictly forbids any use of cannabis products, recreationally or otherwise.

Possible Actions:

A. Report offending officer immediately.

B. Wait and see if it happens again before deciding to do anything about it.

C. Go and discuss the situation with the offending officer.

D. Ask one of the members in your squadron to write the officer up for you.

E. Accept that the marijuana is harmless and try it yourself.

5. Select the MOST EFFECTIVE action (A-E) in response to the situation.
6. Select the LEAST EFFECTIVE action (A-E) in response to the situation.

You and another officer in your squadron are consistently trying to outdo each other in exercises and flight tests. Both of you want to be a leader and have a positive influence on your fellow officers and enlisted, but neither one of you is willing to let another person outdo you. The competition escalates to the point where you cannot trust one another on missions.

Possible Actions:

A. Continue to try and outdo your fellow officer until one of you wins.

B. Confront the other officer outright.

C. One of you must request to change squadrons.

D. Discuss the competition with your fellow officer.

E. Bring concerns over competition to your superior officer.

7. Select the MOST EFFECTIVE action (A-E) in response to the situation.
8. Select the LEAST EFFECTIVE action (A-E) in response to the situation.

Various items and pieces of property begin to disappear around the base. Something of value has been stolen from you, and it is imperative that you find it. You and your peers have a suspicion as to who might have been stealing from you, but there is no proof.

Possible Actions:

A. Accuse the suspect in front of his peers.

B. Bring your concerns to superior officers.

C. Attempt to investigate the suspect's property yourself.

D. Wait for the proper authorities to investigate.

E. Voice your concerns to other members of the squadron.

9. Select the MOST EFFECTIVE action (A-E) in response to the situation.
10. Select the LEAST EFFECTIVE action (A-E) in response to the situation.

The captain of your squadron gives you an order that you disagree with and refuse to obey. The other members of your squadron have no problems completing the tasks given to them and obeying orders, but you have no intention of doing so as a result of pride. Your captain reprimands you in front of your fellow officers for this show of disrespect and punishes you for disobeying orders.

Possible Actions:

- **A.** Rely on your instincts to disobey and refuse to apologize.
- **B.** Admit fault, move forward, and obey future orders.
- **C.** Tell your captain that you are not willing to obey certain orders and ask that he respect this.
- **D.** Convince your fellow officers to speak on your behalf with the captain and ask for clemency.
- **E.** Follow further orders but refuse to apologize or discuss the disobedience with the captain.

11. Select the MOST EFFECTIVE action (A-E) in response to the situation.

12. Select the LEAST EFFECTIVE action (A-E) in response to the situation.

Another member of your squadron has been making derogatory comments regarding the race of your fellow officers. You are of a different race than these other officers, but they have made it clear to both you and the other officer that they find the comments offensive and wish them to cease. The offending officer has yet to cease making these comments, thinking them to be in good humor and inoffensive.

Possible Actions:

- **A.** Convince the officers subject to these comments that they are in good humor and mean no harm.
- **B.** Politely suggest to the offending officer that perhaps the comments are in bad taste.
- **C.** Report the behavior immediately as it is considered racially based harassment.
- **D.** Ignore the behavior as it is none of your business and it would be rude to get involved.
- **E.** Convince other members of the squadron to discuss the behavior with the offending officer.

13. Select the MOST EFFECTIVE action (A-E) in response to the situation.

14. Select the LEAST EFFECTIVE action (A-E) in response to the situation.

There's a misunderstanding between you and another member of your flight. You are new to the specialty and learned certain procedures a different way than she did. She sees this difference in procedure as a lack of skill on your part, and you see her unwillingness to cooperate as bull-headed. There are now personal issues between the two of you as a result of this misunderstanding.

Possible Actions:

- **A.** Prove to her that you are correct in your procedural process and that she is wrong.
- **B.** Let the misunderstanding stand as you are unlikely to change her mind.
- **C.** Do the procedure her way as she has more experience than you in the field.
- **D.** Express concern over this misunderstanding and tell her that you were taught the procedure a different way than she was.
- **E.** Go to a superior officer and ask him to convince her of your capability.

15. Select the MOST EFFECTIVE action (A-E) in response to the situation.

16. Select the LEAST EFFECTIVE action (A-E) in response to the situation.

As a high-ranking officer, you are responsible for a number of people in your flight. One of these people has just been given a rank equal to your own, and you no longer have authority over him. He wants to be included in decisions and procedures but continues to make multiple mistakes that you would not make if you were in his position.

Possible Actions:

A. Reprimand the officer for his behavior and reassert your authority.

B. Try to separate yourself from the officer as you have no business commenting on his work now that you are of the same rank.

C. Offer him guidance in his new job and allow him leeway to make mistakes.

D. Explain to him how you would perform the responsibilities and make decisions.

E. Let another person guide him in his new rank because you are too close to the situation to be of any use.

17. Select the MOST EFFECTIVE action (A-E) in response to the situation.

18. Select the LEAST EFFECTIVE action (A-E) in response to the situation.

Your sector of the Air Force has a certain policy that you do not agree with. It's not harmful to anyone, but you find that it makes your job more difficult to do. You would like it changed, but after discussing the subject with a higher-ranking officer, you've found that there is unwillingness to change it.

Possible Actions:

A. Blatantly disregard the policy as you have made your feelings on the subject clear and it makes your job all that more difficult to do.

B. Convince other officers in your sector that this policy affects them as well and that they should campaign with you to have it changed.

C. Be aggressive in your campaign against this policy—if it makes your job difficult, it must be changed.

D. Adapt to the policy and attempt to understand where it derives purpose from, as it cannot be intended specifically to make your job harder.

E. Ask another member of your sector to campaign against the policy instead as you have already exhausted all your efforts.

19. Select the MOST EFFECTIVE action (A-E) in response to the situation.

20. Select the LEAST EFFECTIVE action (A-E) in response to the situation.

On a night out with some friends, you see a fellow officer using an illegal substance with a number of other officers around him. Upon approaching the group, they offer you a chance to use it as well. According to them, this is a normal occurrence and none of them have ever been reprimanded for it, although you suspect that none of their commanding officers have ever found out.

Possible Actions:

A. Report the use immediately as it could be a danger to both themselves and those around them.

B. Politely convince them that this is perhaps not the best pastime and that they should quit using it.

C. Take it away from them immediately as you could potentially be saving both their life and career.

D. Refrain from taking part in the substance use, but don't let any other higher-ranking officers know about it.

E. Take part in using the substance offered to you, as they don't seem to be in any danger and won't be getting in any trouble.

21. Select the MOST EFFECTIVE action (A-E) in response to the situation.

22. Select the LEAST EFFECTIVE action (A-E) in response to the situation.

You notice that another officer in your squadron has been targeted as the subject of subtle harassment. This isn't bigoted harassment, but a few other officers have identified him as weak and frequently verbally abuse him and laugh at his expense. They attempt to involve you in this behavior, saying that it's all fun and games and none of it is meant to offend.

Possible Actions:

A. Suggest that the behavior is unbecoming of coworkers and that they should quit for the sake of peace.

B. Convince the officer that the behavior is not meant to offend and that he should perhaps laugh along with them.

C. Offer your support to the targeted officer and offer to speak on their behalf with the offending officers.

D. Take part in the antics and laugh along with the offenders as it is humorous and not meant to offend.

E. Do not become involved in the situation, as no physical harm is being done, and they mean no offense.

23. Select the MOST EFFECTIVE action (A-E) in response to the situation.

24. Select the LEAST EFFECTIVE action (A-E) in response to the situation.

You have recently made public your sexual orientation, and another officer has taken to making comments about this in your workplace environment. Numerous other officers, including yourself, have tried to explain to this officer that his comments are in bad taste, but he insists that they are meant to be taken lightheartedly. You do not feel unsafe around this officer, but his comments are occasionally derogatory and deeply offend you.

Possible Actions:

A. You do not feel threatened, so ignore the behavior and let him tire of his fun.

B. Report the behavior to a senior officer as it is sexual harassment and cannot be tolerated.

C. Continue to insist that the behavior is degrading and dehumanizing and that he should cease it.

D. Do not take his comments lying down and make your own comments about his sexual orientation, whatever that may be.

E. Discuss the behavior with him and attempt to reason that it is not the lighthearted humor that he thinks it is.

25. Select the MOST EFFECTIVE action (A-E) in response to the situation.

26. Select the LEAST EFFECTIVE action (A-E) in response to the situation.

Another member of your flight is very vocal about his faith and his beliefs, and another friend of yours in your flight took offense to these beliefs and told him that he was wrong. You share the same religious beliefs as your friend, but you wish to keep them private. The animosity between the two officers continues to escalate, until they both ask you for your opinion on the matter.

Possible Actions:

A. Go to a higher-ranking officer for their opinion and ask for guidance on the situation.

B. Reprimand the officer that shares the same beliefs as you for entering into this conflict as it was none of his business.

C. Stay out of the conflict as it has nothing to do with you and your involvement will only escalate the situation.

D. Politely ask not to be included in the discussion but suggest that they be open to discussion instead of debate or that they drop the subject altogether.

E. Try to convince the person with different beliefs than your own that their faith is wrong and that your own faith is correct.

27. Select the MOST EFFECTIVE action (A-E) in response to the situation.

28. Select the LEAST EFFECTIVE action (A-E) in response to the situation.

There is a very important election happening in your state, and you have very strong opinions pertaining to this election. While you are voicing your opinions on this election, a friend of yours in your flight voices a different opinion that is just about the opposite of your own. You feel very strongly that she is wrong, and she feels very strongly that you are wrong.

Possible Actions:

A. Debate the subject until one of you is convinced that the other's assertions are correct.

B. Resolve to never bring up the subject again, as it is a point of discord and could lead to hostility.

C. Discuss your differences in opinion and agree to disagree if no common ground can be found.

D. Insist that she is wrong and refuse to listen to her opinions on the matter as it will only incite conflict.

E. Pretend that you agree with her, as it will ease tensions and you will be able to work in peace.

29. Select the MOST EFFECTIVE action (A-E) in response to the situation.

30. Select the LEAST EFFECTIVE action (A-E) in response to the situation.

You were given explicit orders from your flight commander to complete a task. However, upon attempting to complete that task, your squadron leader told you that he had given the job to another officer, and that you were no longer needed. Your flight commander was unaware of this and reprimanded you for failing to complete the task as it was given to you.

Possible Actions:

A. Explain the situation and politely direct him to the squadron leader who will verify your story.

B. Apologize for failing to complete the task and receive whatever punishment he intends to give you.

C. Approach the squadron leader first and ask him to verify your story to the flight commander.

D. Reprimand him for falsely accusing you of failing to do your job and insist that he apologize.

E. Be respectful and ask that a friend of yours instead approach the flight commander with your story.

31. Select the MOST EFFECTIVE action (A-E) in response to the situation.

32. Select the LEAST EFFECTIVE action (A-E) in response to the situation.

You are working more hours in a week than any other members of your flight and you haven't been sleeping well lately. A higher-ranking officer offers you another task that would take more time out of your schedule. This other task is a great opportunity for you to advance your career but is not particularly well suited to your skill set.

Possible Actions:

A. Take the job and attempt to hone your skills towards this particular task while continuing with your other work.

B. Take this job and cut back on your other tasks so that you can focus on this more frequently.

C. Decline the job and cut back on the hours you are working so that you can rest.

D. Create a schedule that encompasses your new responsibilities as well as your current ones and compartmentalize, prioritizing rest.

E. Suggest that they offer the task to another member of your flight who is more suited to it and compartmentalize your other tasks, prioritizing rest.

33. Select the MOST EFFECTIVE action (A-E) in response to the situation.

34. Select the LEAST EFFECTIVE action (A-E) in response to the situation.

An enlisted soldier in your flight has given you advice on a decision you made recently with the intention of giving you insight into the effects of it. She has been in the Air Force far longer than you have and has seen these decisions be made in different and potentially better ways. You are not sure if you did, in fact, make the wrong decision.

Possible Actions:

A. Reprimand the enlisted for questioning your decision as it is not her decision to make.

B. Stand by your decision and ask that she not give you any more advice on the subject.

C. Retract your decision immediately as you are sure that she has more experience with the matter than you do.

D. Express your willingness to receive her advice and consider her options but make the decision you think is best.

E. Ask for her opinion on all future decisions, as she is more experienced with these matters than you are.

35. Select the MOST EFFECTIVE action (A-E) in response to the situation.

36. Select the LEAST EFFECTIVE action (A-E) in response to the situation.

You are continually late to a number of exercises and meetings throughout the week. Your flight commander oftentimes does not reprimand you for this tardiness, but a number of other officers in the flight are disconcerted by the lack of initiative on your part. They are even more frustrated with your flight commander for allowing you to get away with this behavior that they themselves get reprimanded for.

Possible Actions:

A. Take it upon yourself to ask your flight commander why he hasn't reprimanded you for this behavior and ask that he do so in the future.

B. Take the initiative to apologize to both your fellow officer and flight commander and make an effort to show up early.

C. Continue to show up late until your flight commander finally reprimands you for the behavior because, until that happens, you aren't doing anything wrong.

D. Ask that your fellow officers take up their concerns with the flight commander, as it is he who is displaying favoritism.

E. Attempt to show up on time to future exercises and meetings so that your fellow officers feel better about the favoritism.

37. Select the MOST EFFECTIVE action (A-E) in response to the situation.

38. Select the LEAST EFFECTIVE action (A-E) in response to the situation.

New enlisted soldiers under your command are unaware of certain exercises and procedures that occur within your flight. They are unsure of how to complete tasks assigned to them and oftentimes find themselves creating more problems than solving them. These mistakes reflect badly on you.

Possible Actions:

A. Ask that they be transferred to a new flight so that their mistakes no longer reflect badly on you and your flight.

B. Take the time to guide them and give them advice on how to properly complete the tasks given to them.

C. Ask other members of your flight to watch them and give them advice when necessary.

D. Give them time to learn from their peers and from experience before stepping in.

E. Reprimand them for their ignorance and behavior so that they know not to make the same mistakes again.

39. Select the MOST EFFECTIVE action (A-E) in response to the situation.

40. Select the LEAST EFFECTIVE action (A-E) in response to the situation.

A new team project is assigned to you and a few other officers in your flight. You are all unfamiliar with the subject matter in this project and with the people working on it with you, but you are all eager to do a good job. This project requires the use of skills that you do not possess but that other officers working on it do.

Possible Actions:

A. Take charge of the group and assign tasks to each individual member randomly so as to increase efficiency.

B. Work on all aspects of the project together; this will allow you to correct each other on shortcomings that one of you doesn't see.

C. Discuss which aspects of the project are suited to each officer's skill set and divide the work accordingly.

D. Have a hand in every aspect of the project so that you can correct your peers when necessary.

E. Allow your peers to direct what you do before taking any immediate action.

41. Select the MOST EFFECTIVE action (A-E) in response to the situation.

42. Select the LEAST EFFECTIVE action (A-E) in response to the situation.

Every month, each officer in your flight contributes to the officer's fund: a sum of money collected and saved for the use of all the officers in your flight. Sometimes it's used to buy drinks and food for all the officers in the flight, and sometimes it's used to pay for activities that the entire group participates in. One of the officers in your flight does not contribute to the officer's fund.

Possible Actions:

- **A.** Get some of the other officers to chip in more money to make up for a minor shortage in funds.
- **B.** Forget about it and hope that he contributes next time.
- **C.** Ask the officer why he didn't contribute his share for the fund and decide what to do from there.
- **D.** Ask another officer to convince the offending officer to contribute to the fund.
- **E.** Refuse to allow the officer to share in the spoils bought with the officer's fund.

43. Select the MOST EFFECTIVE action (A-E) in response to the situation.

44. Select the LEAST EFFECTIVE action (A-E) in response to the situation.

Your new specialty requires a lot of training and schooling on your part. You have never had experience with anything like this specialty, and the job itself is high risk. You fail the first test given to you and begin to doubt whether this was a good decision.

Possible Actions:

- **A.** Drop this specialty and try a new one that will be more suited to your skill set.
- **B.** Begin looking for a new specialty before deciding to drop this one so that you have a plan.
- **C.** Ask a friend of yours for their opinions on your training in this specialty and whether or not they think you should quit.
- **D.** Remind yourself of the reasons you chose this specialty in the first place and attack the training from a new angle.
- **E.** Train and study the same way that you have been so that you can get accustomed to the workload of this new specialty.

45. Select the MOST EFFECTIVE action (A-E) in response to the situation.

46. Select the LEAST EFFECTIVE action (A-E) in response to the situation.

Another junior officer that works for you has expressed concerns regarding his ability to complete a particular task that you have given him. You know that he can meet the physical and mental demands needed to complete the task. However, he has expressed a reluctance regarding the moral implications of the task. You are sure that there is no moral conflict associated with this task that he should be wary of.

Possible Actions:

- **A.** Discuss the matter with him and hear his concerns before making a decision.
- **B.** Send him off immediately with the assurance that he would be tasked with nothing of moral consequence.
- **C.** Reprimand him for failure to follow orders and complete the task given to him.
- **D.** Give the task to another officer with absolutely no moral qualms regarding the work.
- **E.** Allow him the leeway to do as he will with the task in order to make it less morally taxing for him.

47. Select the MOST EFFECTIVE action (A-E) in response to the situation.

48. Select the LEAST EFFECTIVE action (A-E) in response to the situation.

A poor flight training exercise leaves you with a low grade and a step behind the rest of the officers in your flight. You have been practicing a specific way for these training exercises and this is the first time that practice has failed you. None of the other officers practice in this manner, but it has worked for you in the past on various other training exercises.

Possible Actions:

A. Try this method of practice again just to be sure of whether it works or not.

B. Tweak various aspects of your practice method to weed out what works and what doesn't.

C. Ask a fellow officer who has done exceedingly well in these training exercises how he practices and take his advice.

D. Copy another officer's actions on the next flight training exercise and attempt to learn on the job.

E. Try not studying and work off of your instincts from the past training exercises.

49. Select the MOST EFFECTIVE action (A-E) in response to the situation.

50. Select the LEAST EFFECTIVE action (A-E) in response to the situation.

STOP.

If you finish before time is up, you may check your work on this section only. Do not turn to any other section in the test.

PHYSICAL SCIENCE

20 Questions (10 Minutes)

Directions: This part of the test measures your knowledge in the area of science. Each of the questions or incomplete statements is followed by five choices. You are to decide which one of the choices best answers the question or completes the statement.

1. How many total atoms are present in the following formula for alcohol: C_2H_6O?

   A. 6
   B. 2
   C. 8
   D. 9
   E. 4

2. The number directly below the symbol of every element on the periodic table represents

   A. the atomic number.
   B. the atomic weight.
   C. the number of electrons.
   D. the number of neutrons.
   E. the number of protons.

3. Which of the following is NOT affected by gravitational force?

   A. Mass
   B. Volume
   C. Weight
   D. Light
   E. Density

4. Which component related to light is unaffected by gravity?

   A. Direction
   B. Energy
   C. Speed in a vacuum
   D. Curves
   E. Frequency

5. Which type of electromagnetic wave is the shortest?

   A. AM radio wave
   B. Microwaves
   C. Gamma rays
   D. X-rays
   E. Ultraviolet light

6. Convert 10,000 meters into decimeters.

   A. 1,000 decimeters
   B. 10 decimeters
   C. 1,000,000 decimeters
   D. 100 decimeters
   E. 100,000 decimeters

7. Which is an example of radioactivity?

   A. Magnetism
   B. Heat
   C. Nuclear decay
   D. Electric fields
   E. Radiation

8. Absolute zero is measured at what approximate temperature?

   A. 0°F
   B. 32°F
   C. 0°C
   D. –1,000°C
   E. –273.15°C

9. Which would make the best insulator with regards to electricity?

A. Copper

B. Aluminum

C. Gold

D. PVC

E. Steel

10. What does AC stand for as it relates to electricity?

A. Air conditioning

B. Alternative current

C. Alternating current

D. Affected current

E. Artificial conduction

11. A compound is defined as

A. two or more different elements chemically bonded into a bulk substance.

B. two or more atoms of the same element.

C. a variety of atoms in an element with different neutron counts.

D. a solid, liquid, or gas that is dissolved into a fluid.

E. the chemical bond between nonmetal elements.

12. The following are all SI units of measurement EXCEPT:

A. Ampere

B. Kilogram

C. Inch

D. Second

E. Mole

13. Which of the following is an example of a solution?

A. Sand and water

B. Tea

C. Oil and vinegar

D. Lightning

E. Aluminum

14. When a rock goes from standing still to rolling on the ground, it is demonstrating what type of energy?

A. Thermal energy

B. Potential energy

C. Kinetic energy

D. Nuclear energy

E. Heat energy

15. Earthquakes are classified as which type of wave?

A. Transverse

B. Circular

C. Longitudinal

D. Electromagnetic

E. Transverse and longitudinal

16. Shock waves occur when the sound produced by an object is faster than the

A. speed of light.

B. speed of sound.

C. speed of transverse waves.

D. object.

E. processing speed of the person hearing the sound.

17. Which of the following is the correct equation for measuring density?

A. Density = mass × volume

B. Density = mass / volume

C. Density = mass + volume

D. Density = 2 (mass + volume)

E. Density = (mass × volume) / 2

18. The temperature at which water changes from a liquid to gas at sea level is

A. 100°F.

B. 100°C.

C. 212°C.

D. 220°F.

E. 98.6°F.

19. All types of waves must be formed by a medium being disturbed by force EXCEPT:

A. Light

B. Sound

C. Wind

D. Transverse

E. Circular

20. The conversion from gas to liquid is called

A. evaporation.

B. condensation.

C. conduction.

D. precipitation.

E. melting point.

STOP.

If you finish before time is up, you may check your work on this section only. Do not turn to any other section in the test.

TABLE READING

40 Questions (7 Minutes)

Directions: This part of the test measures your ability to read and interpret a table quickly and accurately. Use the table on the next page. Notice that the X values appear at the top of the table and Y values are shown on the left side of the table. The X values are the column values. The Y values are the row values. For each question, you are given an X and Y value. Your task is to find the block where the column and row intersect, note the number that appears there, and then find this number among the five answer options.

		X																								
		-12	-11	-10	-9	-8	-7	-6	-5	-4	-3	-2	-1	0	1	2	3	4	5	6	7	8	9	10	11	12
	12	35	36	37	38	39	40	41	42	43	44	45	46	47	48	49	50	51	52	53	54	55	56	57	58	59
	11	36	37	38	39	40	41	42	43	44	45	46	47	48	49	50	51	52	53	54	55	56	57	58	59	60
	10	37	38	39	40	41	42	43	44	45	46	47	48	49	50	51	52	53	54	55	56	57	58	59	60	61
	9	38	39	40	41	42	43	44	45	46	47	48	49	50	51	52	53	54	55	56	57	58	59	60	61	62
	8	39	40	41	42	43	44	45	46	47	48	49	50	51	52	53	54	55	56	57	58	59	60	61	62	63
	7	40	41	42	43	44	45	46	47	48	49	50	51	52	53	54	55	56	57	58	59	60	61	62	63	64
	6	41	42	43	44	45	46	47	48	49	50	51	52	53	54	55	56	57	58	59	60	61	62	63	64	65
	5	42	43	44	45	46	47	48	49	50	51	52	53	54	55	56	57	58	59	60	61	62	63	64	65	66
	4	43	44	45	46	47	48	49	50	51	52	53	54	55	56	57	58	59	60	61	62	63	64	65	66	67
	3	44	45	46	47	48	49	50	51	52	53	54	55	56	57	58	59	60	61	62	63	64	65	66	67	68
	2	45	46	47	48	49	50	51	52	53	54	55	56	57	58	59	60	61	62	63	64	65	66	67	68	69
	1	46	47	48	49	50	51	52	53	54	55	56	57	58	59	60	61	62	63	64	65	66	67	68	69	70
Y	0	47	48	49	50	51	52	53	54	55	56	57	58	59	60	61	62	63	64	65	66	67	68	69	70	71
	-1	48	49	50	51	52	53	54	55	56	57	58	59	60	61	62	63	64	65	66	67	68	69	70	71	72
	-2	49	50	51	52	53	54	55	56	57	58	59	60	61	62	63	64	65	66	67	68	69	70	71	72	73
	-3	50	51	52	53	54	55	56	57	58	59	60	61	62	63	64	65	66	67	68	69	70	71	72	73	74
	-4	51	52	53	54	55	56	57	58	59	60	61	62	63	64	65	66	67	68	69	70	71	72	73	74	75
	-5	52	53	54	55	56	57	58	59	60	61	62	63	64	65	66	67	68	69	70	71	72	73	74	75	76
	-6	53	54	55	56	57	58	59	60	61	62	63	64	65	66	67	68	69	70	71	72	73	74	75	76	77
	-7	54	55	56	57	58	59	60	61	62	63	64	65	66	67	68	69	70	71	72	73	74	75	76	77	78
	-8	55	56	57	58	59	60	61	62	63	64	65	66	67	68	69	70	71	72	73	74	75	76	77	78	79
	-9	56	57	58	59	60	61	62	63	64	65	66	67	68	69	70	71	72	73	74	75	76	77	78	79	80
	-10	57	58	59	60	61	62	63	64	65	66	67	68	69	70	71	72	73	74	75	76	77	78	79	80	81
	-11	58	59	60	61	62	63	64	65	66	67	68	69	70	71	72	73	74	75	76	77	78	79	80	81	82
	-12	59	60	61	62	63	64	65	66	67	68	69	70	71	72	73	74	75	76	77	78	79	80	81	82	83

	X	Y	A	B	C	D	E
1	+3	-3	63	59	65	67	60
2	+6	+3	62	61	58	66	56
3	+11	-8	78	79	74	69	77
4	-4	+5	53	48	50	51	60
5	-8	-11	64	62	59	57	56
6	-3	-11	66	54	60	61	67
7	+9	0	70	64	59	68	71
8	-11	+10	35	42	38	59	58
9	+4	+5	60	61	58	55	49
10	+7	-11	76	75	78	79	77
11	+10	-5	73	74	75	68	71
12	-4	-10	65	63	67	61	53
13	+1	+7	52	51	50	49	53
14	+9	-4	72	71	68	66	69
15	+2	-1	61	64	55	62	56
16	+9	-9	78	77	76	68	71
17	-4	-7	77	81	62	65	76
18	-10	0	50	48	46	49	70
19	+10	-9	62	77	38	47	78
20	+1	-6	66	60	39	59	69
21	+11	-3	57	75	67	73	71
22	+8	-10	82	79	59	77	73
23	+6	+2	62	63	56	47	53
24	-3	+5	57	55	51	50	48
25	+2	-8	66	65	73	70	69
26	-2	-3	65	73	64	60	79
27	-9	-2	46	52	45	38	55
28	-3	-7	61	71	58	63	64
29	+4	-5	66	78	76	68	56
30	0	+10	45	53	49	50	47
31	-3	-8	64	74	58	65	66
32	+9	-11	81	83	67	79	78
33	+4	-4	68	80	67	74	71
34	-8	0	54	51	59	61	40
35	-11	-6	60	54	69	42	57
36	+10	-1	70	71	75	76	68
37	+3	+3	61	59	47	58	64
38	+8	+8	76	77	64	65	59
39	-3	+2	53	48	47	52	54
40	-9	-8	42	37	38	41	40

STOP.

If you finish before time is up, you may check your work on this section only.

Do not turn to any other section in the test.

INSTRUMENT COMPREHENSION

25 Questions (5 Minutes)

Directions: This part of the test measures your ability to determine the position of an airplane in flight from reading instruments showing its compass direction heading, amount of climb or dive, and degree of bank to right or left. Each problem consists of two dials and four answer options. In each problem, the left-hand dial is labeled ARTIFICIAL HORIZON. On the face of the dial a stationary indicator in the center represents the airplane, while the positions of the heavy black line, black pointer, and markings along the outer edge vary with changes in the position of the airplane in which the instrument is located.

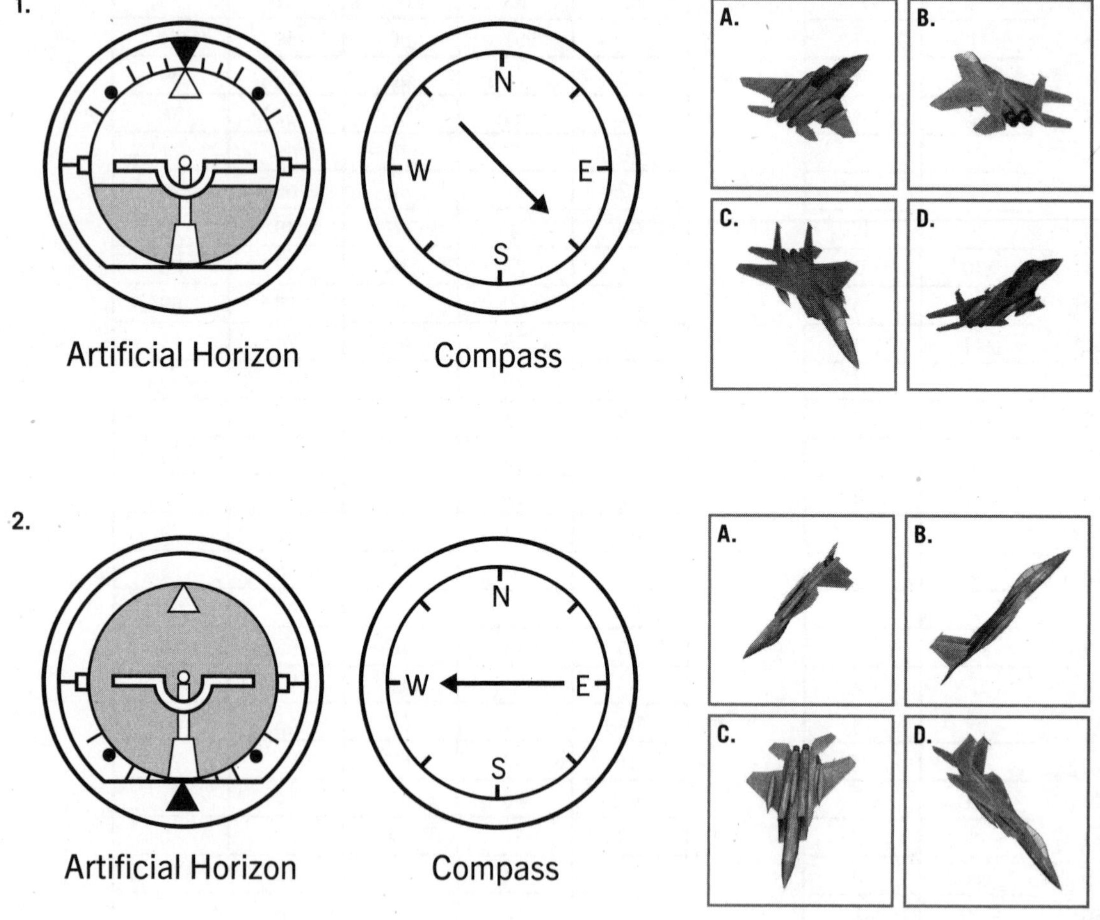

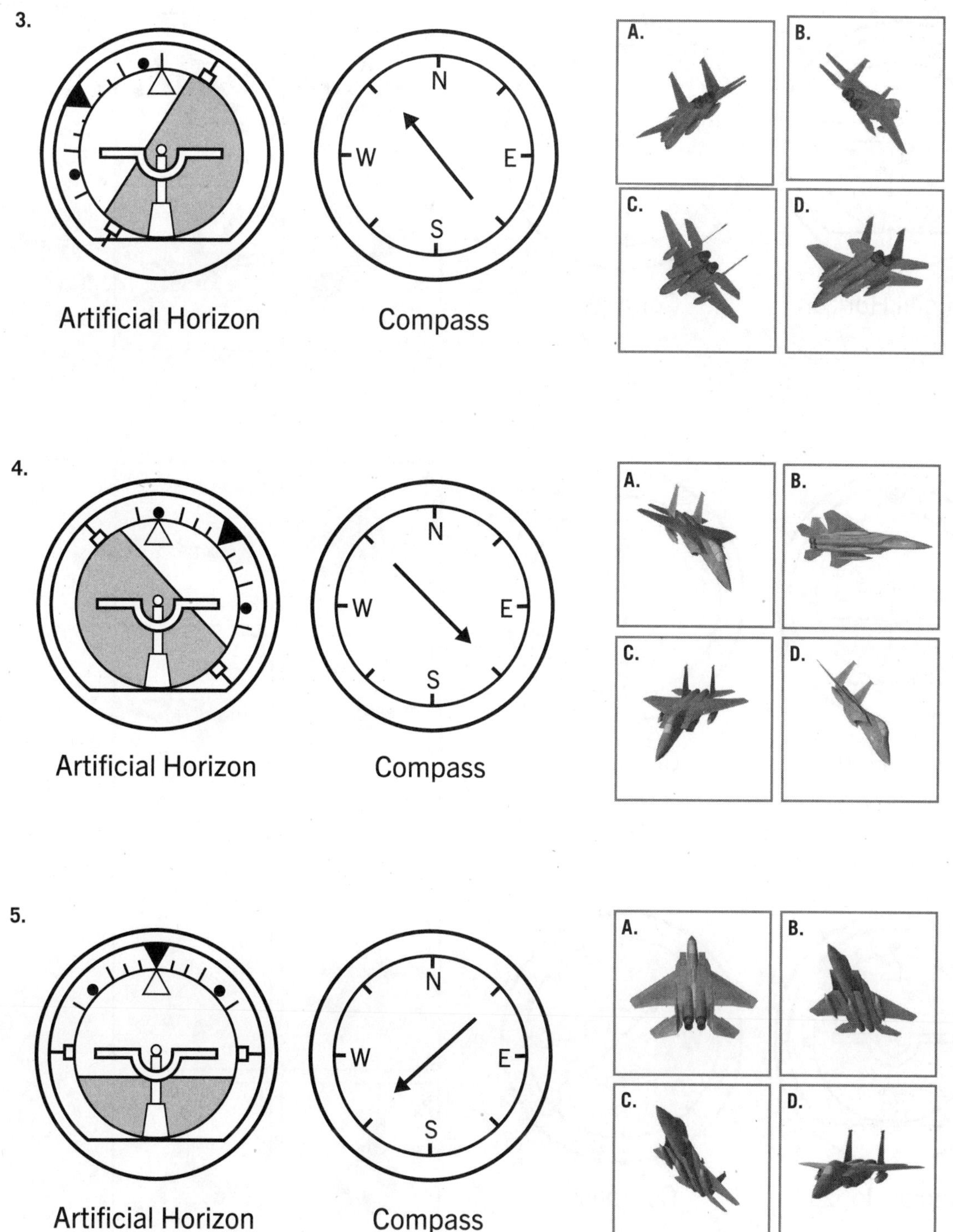
3.
Artificial Horizon
N
W
E
S
Compass
A.
B.
C.
D.
4.
Artificial Horizon
N
W
E
S
Compass
A.
B.
C.
D.
5.
Artificial Horizon
N
W
E
S
Compass
A.
B.
C.
D.

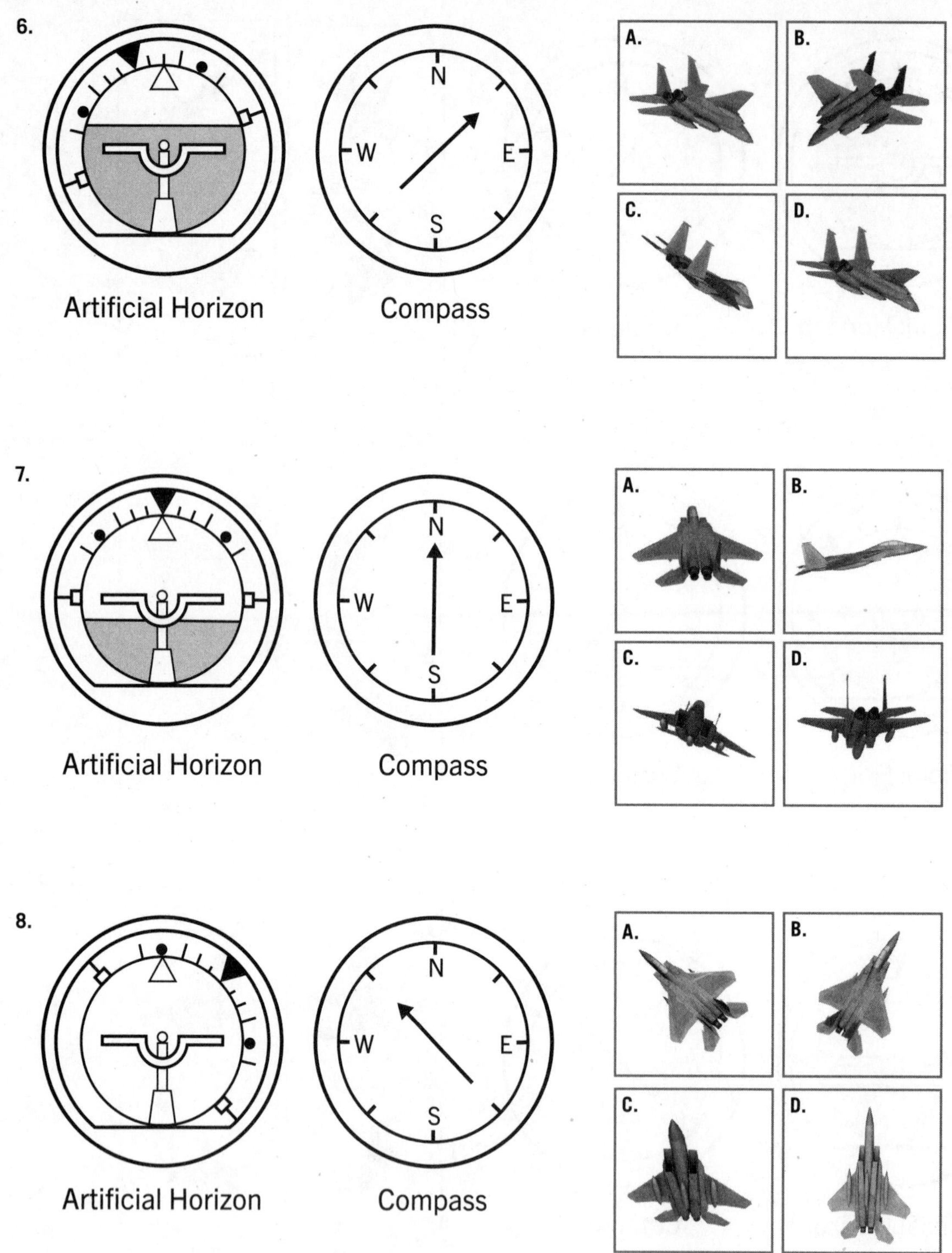
6.
N
W
E
S
A.
B.
C.
D.
Artificial Horizon
Compass
7.
N
W
E
S
A.
B.
C.
D.
Artificial Horizon
Compass
8.
N
W
E
S
A.
B.
C.
D.
Artificial Horizon
Compass

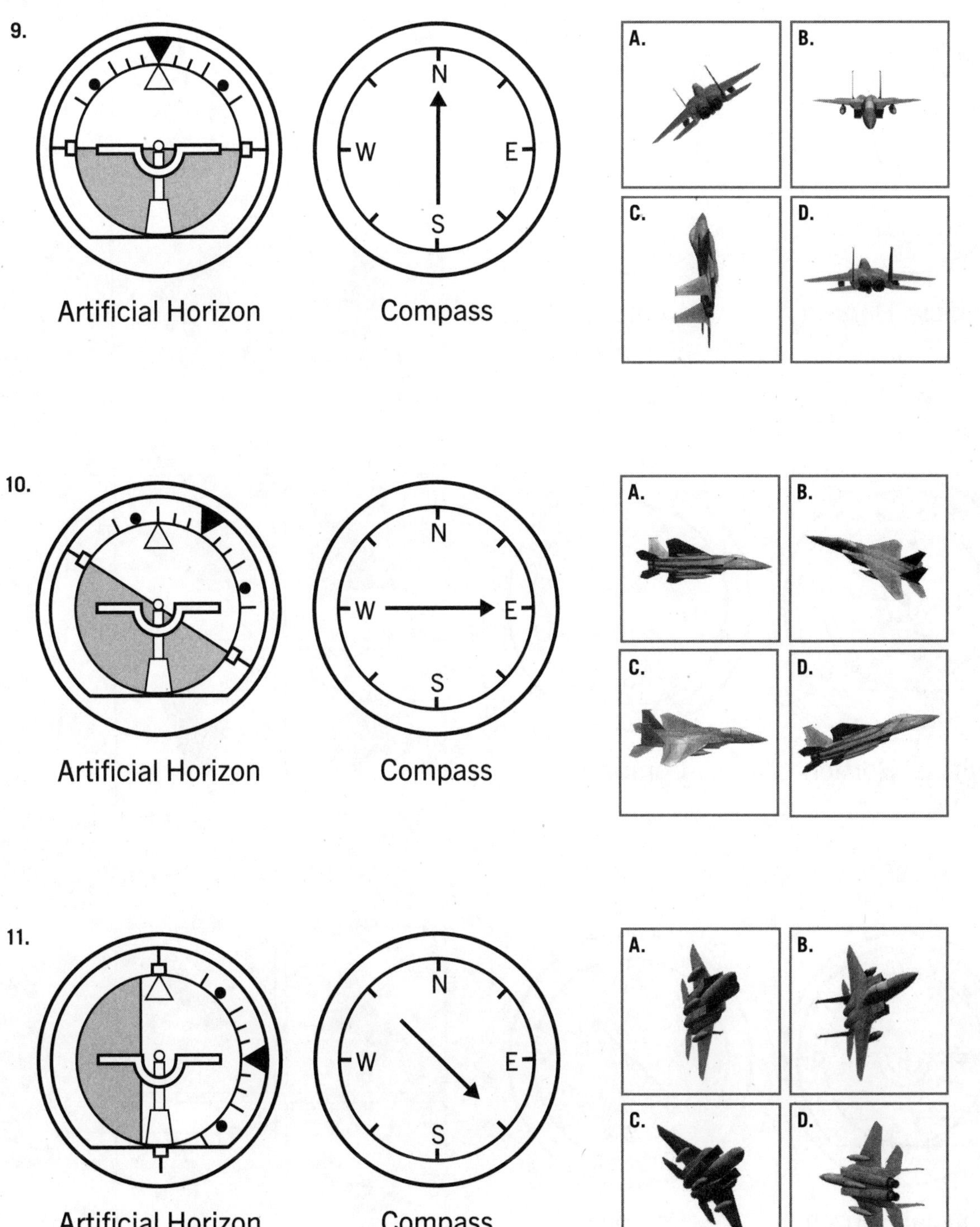
9.
N
W
E
S
Artificial Horizon
Compass
A.
B.
C.
D.
10.
N
W
E
S
Artificial Horizon
Compass
A.
B.
C.
D.
11.
N
W
E
S
Artificial Horizon
Compass
A.
B.
C.
D.

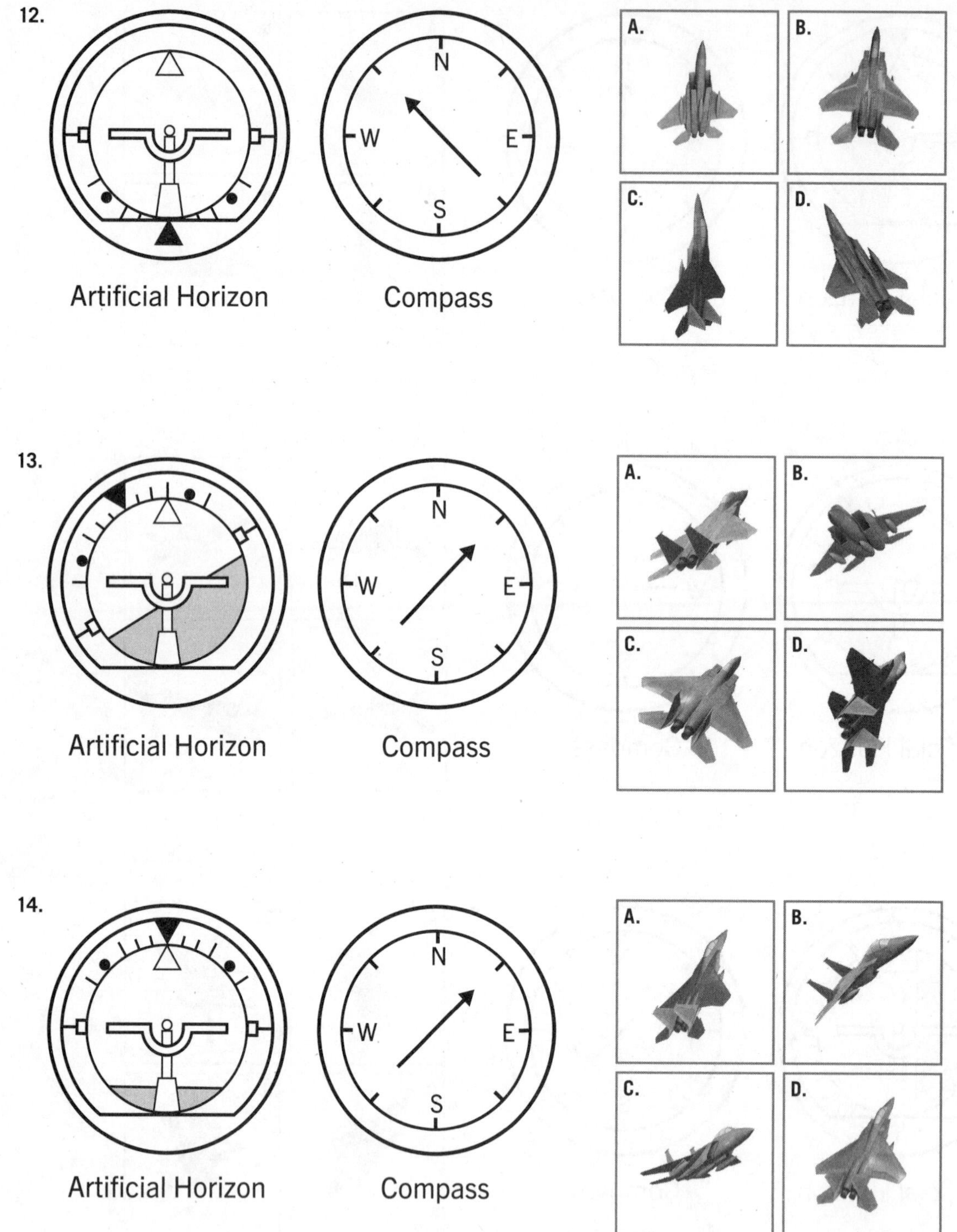
12.
N
W
E
S
Artificial Horizon
Compass
A.
B.
C.
D.
13.
N
W
E
S
Artificial Horizon
Compass
A.
B.
C.
D.
14.
N
W
E
S
Artificial Horizon
Compass
A.
B.
C.
D.

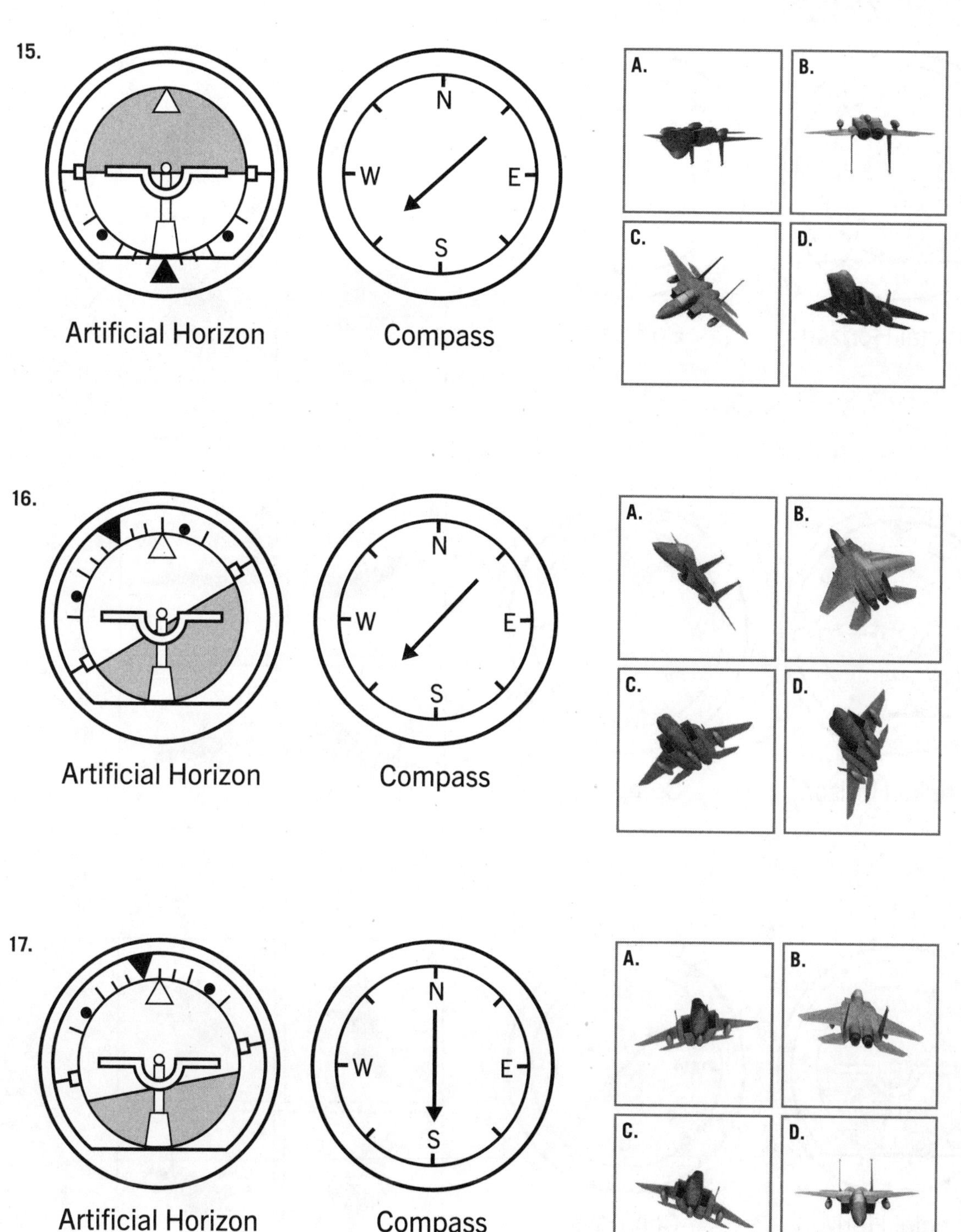

AFOQT PRACTICE TEST

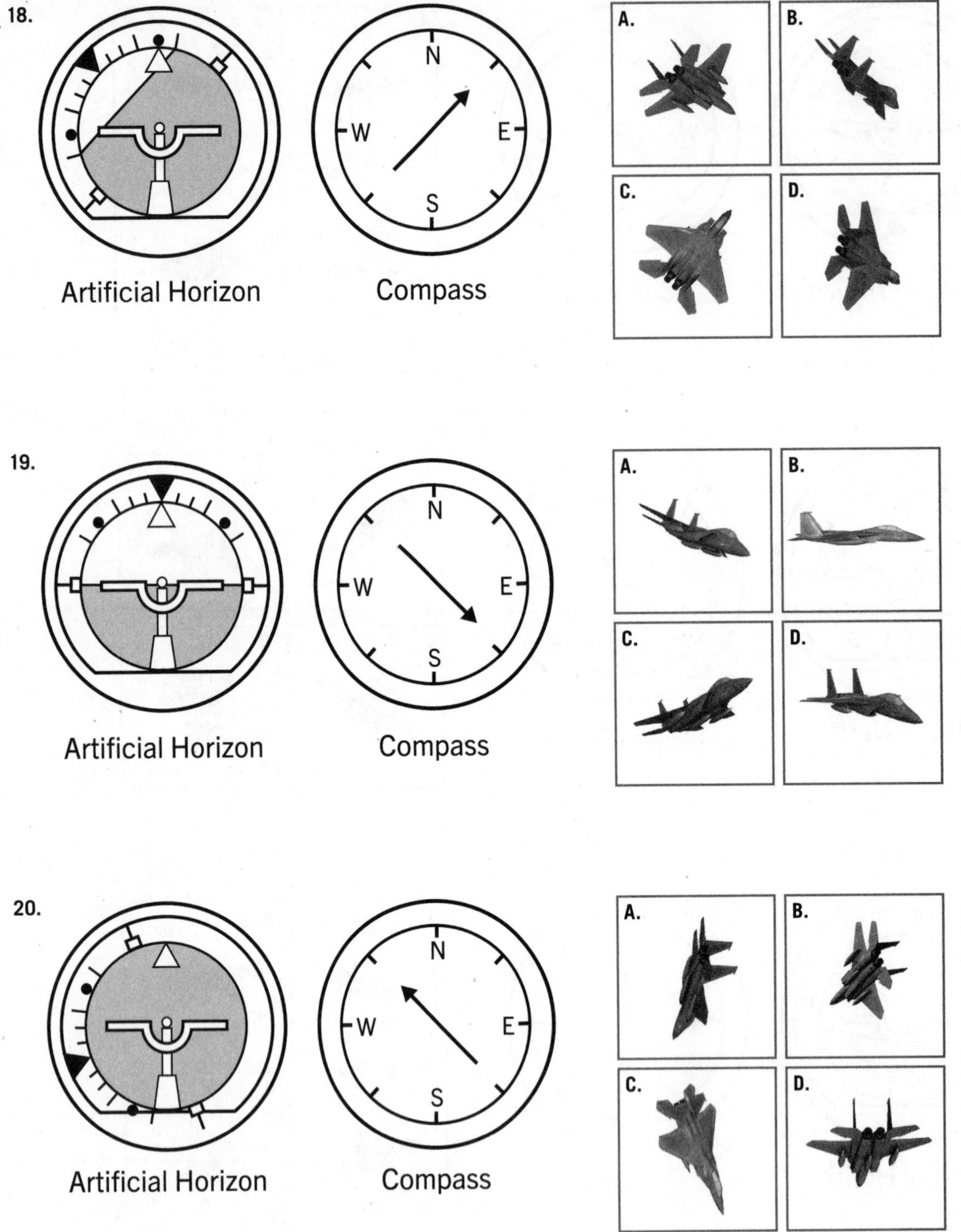
18.
Artificial Horizon
N
W
E
S
Compass
A.
B.
C.
D.
19.
Artificial Horizon
N
W
E
S
Compass
A.
B.
C.
D.
20.
Artificial Horizon
N
W
E
S
Compass
A.
B.
C.
D.

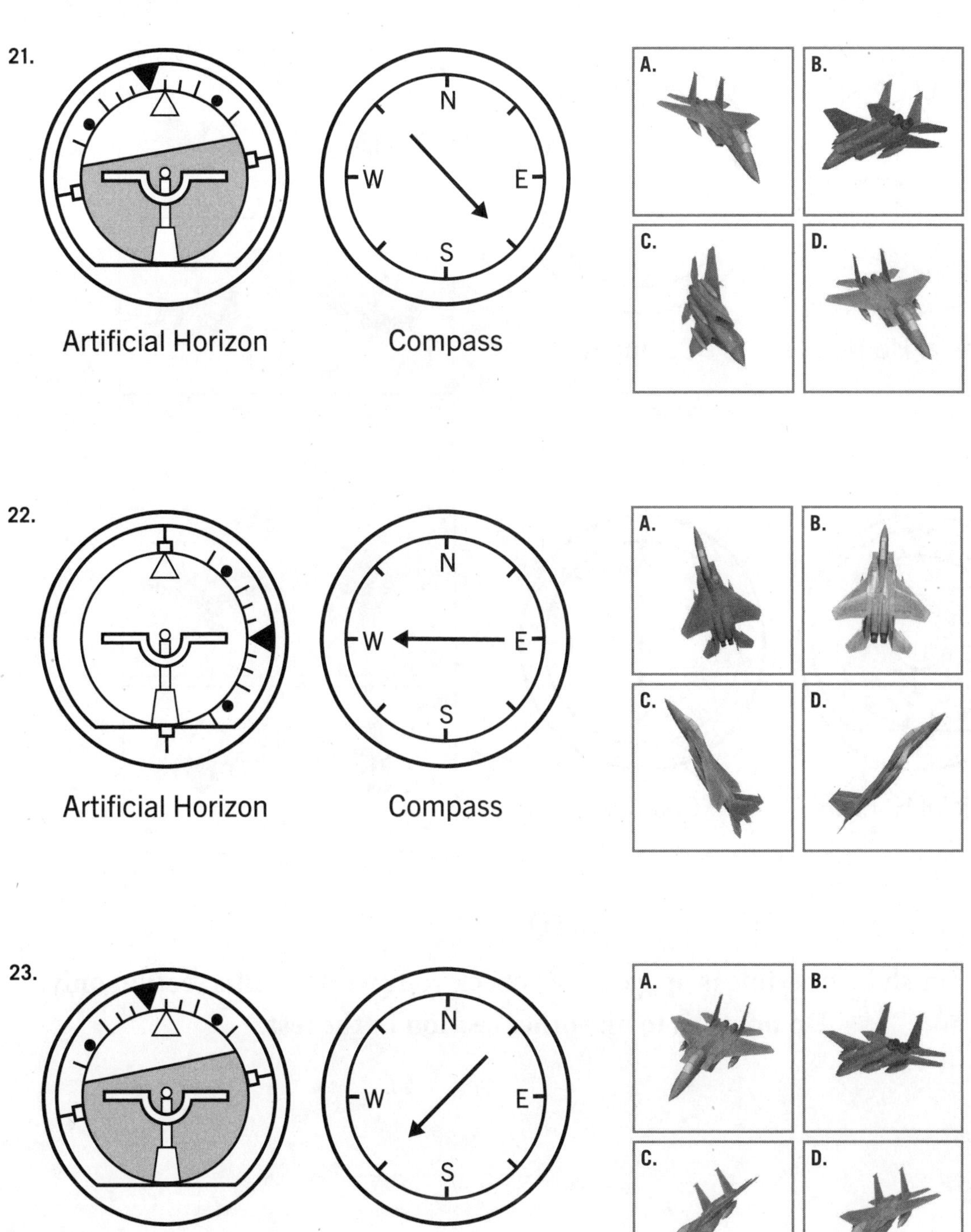
21.
N
W
E
S
Artificial Horizon
Compass
A.
B.
C.
D.
22.
N
W
E
S
Artificial Horizon
Compass
A.
B.
C.
D.
23.
N
W
E
S
Artificial Horizon
Compass
A.
B.
C.
D.

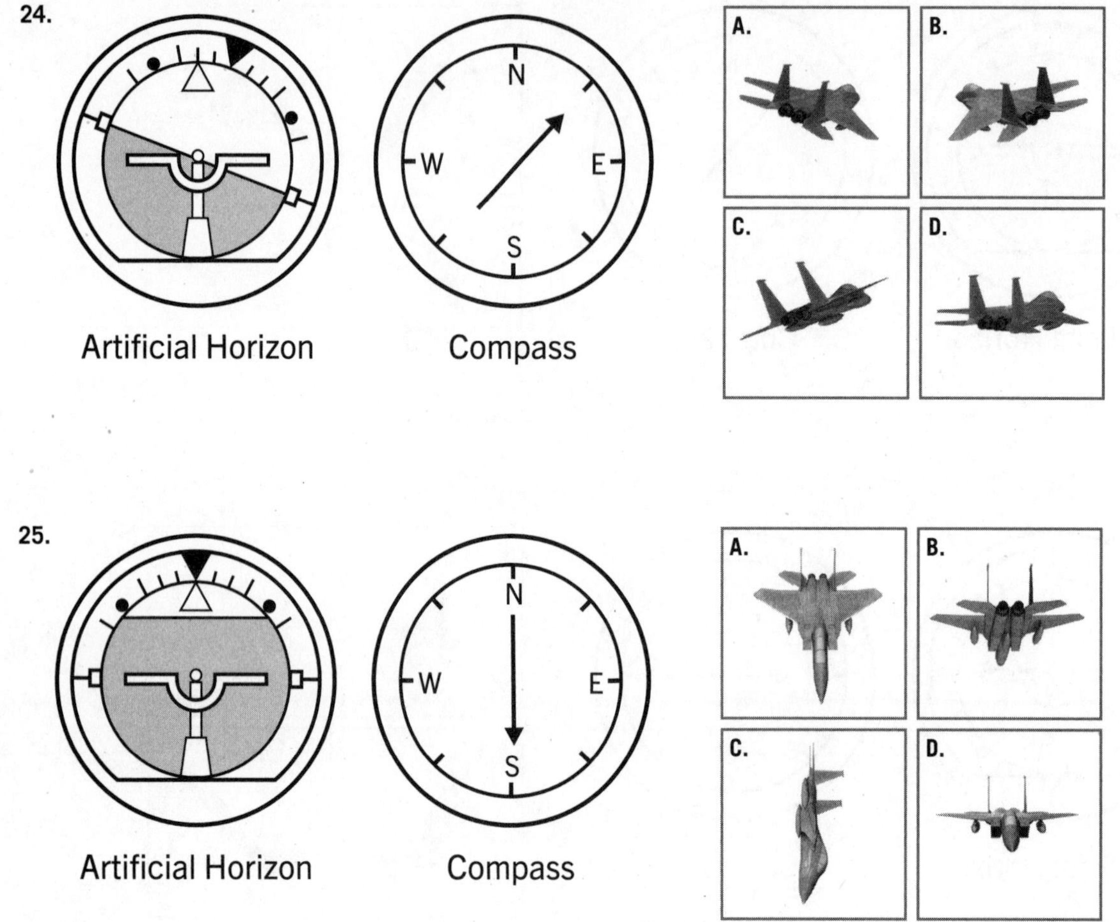

STOP.

If you finish before time is up, you may check your work on this section only. Do not turn to any other section in the test.

BLOCK COUNTING

30 Questions (4.5 Minutes)

Directions: This part of the test measures your ability to "see into" a 3-dimensional pile of blocks. Given a certain numbered block, your task is to determine how many other blocks the numbered block touches. Blocks are considered touching only if all or part of their faces touch. Blocks that only touch corners do not count. All of the blocks in each pile are the same size and shape.

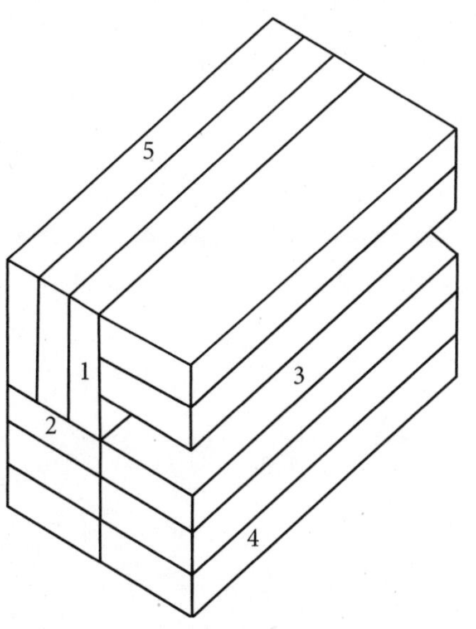

Block	A	B	C	D	E
1	1	2	3	4	5
2	6	2	4	1	5
3	4	2	3	5	6
4	3	4	5	6	2
5	5	3	2	6	4

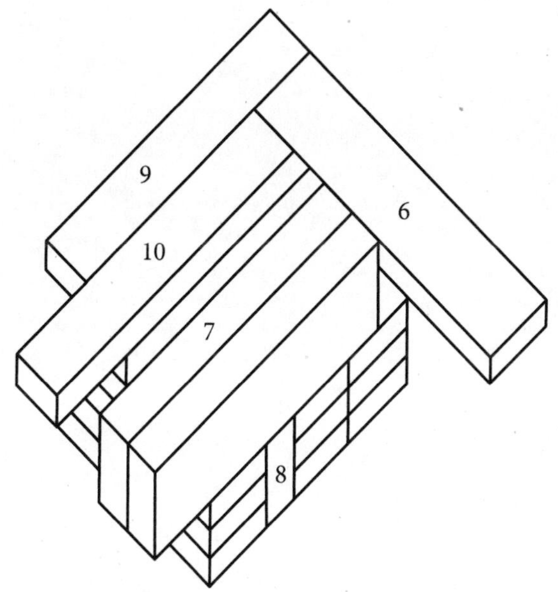

Block	A	B	C	D	E
6	2	7	4	5	3
7	5	4	6	7	2
8	8	7	10	4	9
9	1	7	5	3	2
10	5	3	2	6	4

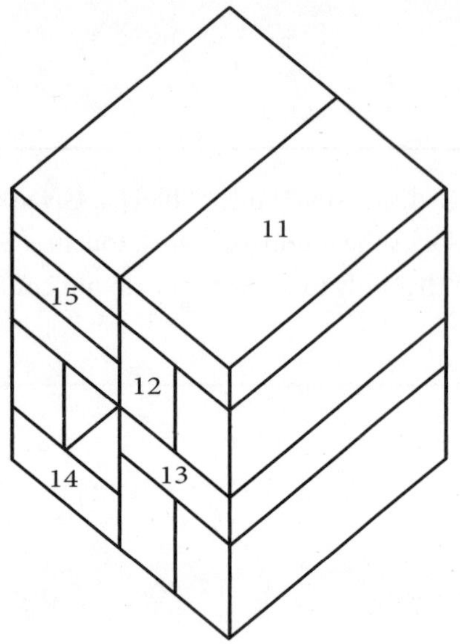

Block	A	B	C	D	E
11	3	4	2	1	5
12	6	2	4	1	5
13	4	2	3	5	6
14	3	4	5	6	2
15	5	3	2	6	4

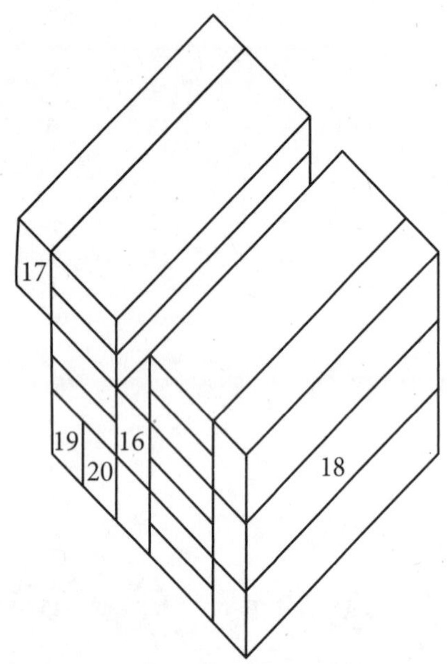

Block	A	B	C	D	E
16	8	4	6	2	5
17	6	2	4	3	5
18	4	2	3	5	6
19	3	4	5	6	2
20	5	3	2	6	4

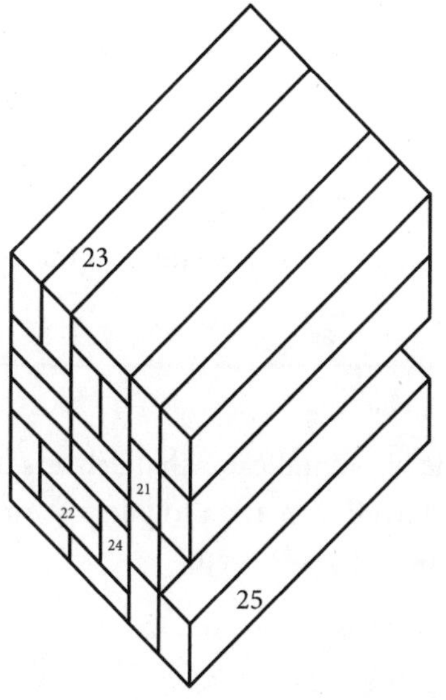

Block	A	B	C	D	E
21	1	2	3	4	5
22	6	2	4	1	5
23	4	2	3	5	6
24	3	4	5	6	2
25	5	3	1	6	4

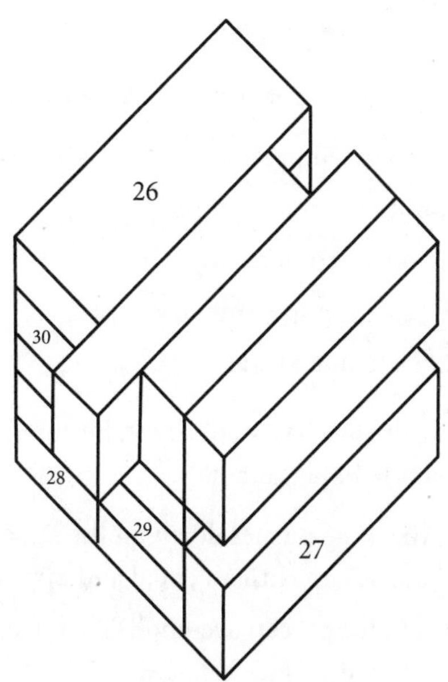

Block	A	B	C	D	E
26	1	2	3	4	5
27	6	2	4	1	5
28	4	1	3	2	6
29	3	4	5	6	2
30	5	3	2	6	4

STOP.

If you finish before time is up, you may check your work on this section only. Do not turn to any other section in the test.

AVIATION INFORMATION

20 Questions (8 Minutes)

Directions: This part of the test measures your knowledge of aviation. Each of the questions or incomplete statements is followed by five choices. You are to decide which one of the choices best answers the question or completes the statement.

1. The study of air and how it moves around objects is

   A. aerodynamics.
   B. aerodonetics.
   C. aerolithology.
   D. aerology.
   E. aeronautics.

2. The force that has to be stronger than the drag and comes from an aircraft's engines is termed

   A. lift.
   B. weight.
   C. acceleration.
   D. thrust.
   E. velocity.

3. An aircraft's balance or desired position is called

   A. a boundary layer.
   B. stratosphere.
   C. a roll.
   D. the flight envelope.
   E. trim.

4. Any surface, such as a wing, an aileron, or stabilizer, that is designed to aid in lifting or controlling an aircraft is called a(n)

   A. angle of attack.
   B. chord.
   C. airfoil.
   D. camber.
   E. pitch.

5. The visual indicator that delivers traffic pattern information to pilots at airports without a control tower is a(n)

   A. compass deviation.
   B. threshold line.
   C. segmented circle.
   D. heading.
   E. air traffic controller.

6. All aircrafts perform most efficiently in

   A. warm temperatures.
   B. hotter temperatures.
   C. cooler temperatures.
   D. colder temperatures.
   E. icy temperatures.

7. For the mechanics of flight, Bernoulli's Principle helps to explain that

   A. the wing pushes down on the air, and the air pushes up with an equal and opposite force.
   B. an aircraft can accomplish lift because of the structure of its wings.
   C. there is a correlation between the force of the air on the plane, the mass of the plane, and the acceleration of a plane.
   D. the total energy of an isolated system remains constant.
   E. there is a reduction in pressure of a fluid resulting from speed increases.

8. A course flown parallel to the landing runway in the direction of landing is called
   A. a crosswind leg.
   B. an upwind leg.
   C. a downwind leg.
   D. a base leg.
   E. a final approach.

9. A positive pitching motion of the aircraft does what to the plane?
   A. It lowers the right wing and raises the left wing.
   B. It raises the nose and lowers the tail.
   C. It causes a blade pitch angle that has a negative value.
   D. It causes left-to-right movement of the aircraft's nose.
   E. It ensures motion that keeps the nose stable.

10. The force that resists movement of an aircraft through the air is called
   A. thrust.
   B. lift.
   C. gravity.
   D. viscosity.
   E. drag.

11. Controlled, uncontrolled, special use, and other are four types of
   A. visual flight rules (VFR).
   B. instrument flight rules (IFR).
   C. airspace.
   D. satellite communications (SATCOM).
   E. runway centerline light system (RCLS).

12. Which force results in two sections going in the opposite direction?
   A. Compression
   B. Shearing
   C. Torsion
   D. Tension
   E. Bending

13. National Transportation and Safety Board (NTSB) Part 830 does NOT require being notified as a result of which event?
   A. Damage to a gear door after the hot brakes were applied and the left main tire blew
   B. Inflight fire
   C. Any essential flight crew member unable to perform flight duties
   D. A person on board suffers serious injury or illness
   E. Aircraft collision in flight

14. To avoid collision, which way should the pilot fly the aircraft when encountering a flock of birds?
   A. Descend
   B. Ascend
   C. Fly to the right
   D. Fly to the left
   E. Continue straight

15. Any unruly person is held to Federal Aviation Administration (FAA) rules when the roles and responsibilities of any crew member are violated EXCEPT when they demonstrate which one of these behaviors?
   A. Assault on a member
   B. Threaten a member
   C. Intimidate a member
   D. Interfere with the responsibilities of a member
   E. Security protocol violations

16. FAA approved projects, which improve or develop safety, security, or capacity, are funded through which of these airport-imposed fees?

A. Passenger Ticket Tax

B. Passenger Facility Charge (PFC)

C. Customs User Fee

D. Overflight Fee

E. September 11 Fee

17. Unless otherwise authorized, the maximum indicated airspeed allowed for a person operating an aircraft below 10,000 feet mean sea level (MSL) is

A. 175 knots.

B. 100 knots.

C. 250 knots.

D. 275 knots.

E. 200 knots.

18. Which is a minimum eligibility requirement for student pilots who want to complete a solo flight?

A. Must have completed a solo flight at the end of the training program

B. Be fluent in a language other than English

C. Have applied for pilot certificate to meet guidelines

D. Have one endorsement for all the solo flights a student attempts

E. Be at least 16 years old

19. A lighted heliport may be identified by

A. blue omnidirectional lights.

B. a green, yellow, and white rotating beacon.

C. dual peaked (two quick) white flashes between green flashes.

D. a blue hashed line.

E. broken magenta dash lines.

20. An Air Traffic Controller (ATC) is primarily responsible for

A. coordinating with flight service personnel.

B. the management of the aircraft crew schedules.

C. coordinating maintenance control.

D. the separation of air transportation operating to and from airports.

E. the organization of the various company ground stations.

STOP.

If you finish before time is up, you may check your work on this section only. Do not turn to any other section in the test.

ANSWER KEYS AND EXPLANATIONS

Verbal Analogies

1. D	6. D	11. B	16. C	21. E
2. C	7. C	12. C	17. D	22. B
3. B	8. C	13. E	18. B	23. D
4. D	9. D	14. A	19. B	24. D
5. A	10. B	15. B	20. C	25. D

1. **The correct answer is D.** One is made in the other; just as *soup* is made in a *pot*, so is *bread* made in an *oven*.
2. **The correct answer is C.** *Wet* is the opposite of *arid* as *hot* is opposite to *cold*.
3. **The correct answer is B.** A *lobster* lives in an ocean, just as a *scorpion* lives in the *desert*.
4. **The correct answer is D.** *Coffee* is made from *beans*, just as *tea* is made from *leaves*.
5. **The correct answer is A.** There are twelve *dozens* in a *gross*, just as there are twelve *inches* in a *foot*.
6. **The correct answer is D.** You have a *slice* of *pie* just as you have a *piece* to a *puzzle*.
7. **The correct answer is C.** A *snail* is *slimy* just as a *rabbit* is *furry*.
8. **The correct answer is C.** *Electricity* travels through a *wire*, just as *water* travels through a *hose*.
9. **The correct answer is D.** *Salt* is a type of *spice*, just as a *doodle* is a kind of *drawing*.
10. **The correct answer is B.** *Anatomy* is the study of the *body*, just as *analysis* is the study of *data*.
11. **The correct answer is B.** *Radar* generates a *blip*, just as a *doorbell* generates a *chime*.
12. **The correct answer is C.** A *radiator* is filled with *coolant*, just as a *fuel tank* is filled with *gasoline*.
13. **The correct answer is E.** *Flowers* are food for *bees*, just as *hay* is food for *horses*.
14. **The correct answer is A.** *Arouse* and *pacify* are opposites. *Smooth* is the opposite of *agitate*.
15. **The correct answer is B.** You *answer* a *query*, just as you *perform* a *task*.
16. **The correct answer is C.** A *seal* eats a *fish*, just as a *bird* eats a *worm*.
17. **The correct answer is D.** A *shoe* is made of *leather*, just as a *highway* is made of *asphalt*.
18. **The correct answer is B.** *Secure* means the same as *safe*. *Distant* means the same as *far*.
19. **The correct answer is B.** A *horse* gives birth to a *foal*, just as a *mother* gives birth to a *son*.
20. **The correct answer is C.** A *finder* gets a *reward*, just as a *repenter* gets *absolution*.
21. **The correct answer is E.** The *telegraph* preceded the *phone*, just as the *wagon* preceded the *car*.
22. **The correct answer is B.** *All caps* is the opposite of *lower case*, just as a *whisper* is opposite of a *shout*.
23. **The correct answer is D.** *Pink* is a light shade of *red*, just as *gray* is a light shade of *black*.
24. **The correct answer is D.** *Youth* is an adjective for *young*, just as *age* is an adjective for *old*.
25. **The correct answer is D.** *Sand* is found at the *beach*, just as *soil* is found on a *farm*.

Arithmetic Reasoning

1. C	6. C	11. D	16. E	21. B
2. D	7. B	12. C	17. A	22. B
3. D	8. C	13. A	18. B	23. A
4. E	9. D	14. C	19. C	24. E
5. C	10. E	15. B	20. B	25. D

1. **The correct answer is C.** Using the point-slope form of the equation of a line, $y-(-2)=-\frac{3}{2}(x-0)$ gives you $y+2=-\frac{3}{2}x$

2. **The correct answer is D.** The slope of the original equation is $\frac{5}{4}$. Dividing the slope by 2 gives a new slope of $\frac{5}{4}\div 2=\frac{5}{8}$. Using this slope results in an equation of the new line $y=\frac{5}{8}x-2.5$. Set $y=0$ and solve to find x:

$$0=\frac{5}{8}x-2.5$$
$$2.5=\frac{5}{8}x$$
$$x=2.5\left(\frac{8}{5}\right)=4$$

The line will cross the x-axis at (4, 0).

3. **The correct answer is D.** This is a proportion of the number of grams of fat over the number of calories. To solve this problem, start by setting up a proportion:

$$\frac{65}{2,000}=\frac{x}{2,500}$$

Next, solve for x:

$$\frac{162,500}{2,000}=x$$
$$81\frac{1}{4}=x$$

4. **The correct answer is E.**

$$3(4m-3m)=-m(-1-2)+4$$
$$3(m)=-m(-3)+4$$
$$3m=3m+4$$
$$0=4$$

Since the last step is not possible, the equation has no solution.

5. **The correct answer is C.** There is a common difference of 132.642 for every other x-value, or 66.321 for every x-value. Because the difference is constant, the relationship is linear. Because the y-values increase as the x-values increase, the relationship is increasing linearly.

6. **The correct answer is C.** The probability is the number of people who are age 47 and older and voted for Candidate Y, 72, divided by the total number of who voted for Candidate Y, 132. $72 \div 132 = 0.545 = 54.5\%$.

7. **The correct answer is B.** The margin of error of 3% means that the actual percent of people who approve of the education bill is likely within the interval (46% - 3%, 46% + 3%), or between 43% and 49%.

8. **The correct answer is C.** Let a equal the initial amount before the decay begins, which is 100, r is the decay rate, which is 0.5, and x = the number of intervals. Divide 45 by 15 to get the half-life interval: $45 \div 15 = 3$.

$$y=a(1-r)^x$$
$$y=100(1-0.5)^3$$
$$y=12.5$$

9. **The correct answer is D.** Write both terms using a common denominator, and then simplify expressions and combine like terms. To get a common denominator, multiply the first fraction by (x + 1) and the second fraction by (x - 3):

$$\frac{2x+5}{x-3}+\frac{4x-1}{x+1}=\frac{(2x+5)(x+1)}{(x-3)(x+1)}+\frac{(4x-1)(x-3)}{(x+1)(x-3)}$$
$$=\frac{(2x^2+7x+5)+(4x^2-13x+3)}{(x^2-2x-3)}$$
$$=\frac{6x^2-6x+8}{x^2-2x-3}$$

10. **The correct answer is E.**

$6 + x + y = 20$

$x + y = 14 = k$; now substitute

$20 - 14 = 6$

11. **The correct answer is D.** There are 4 boys in the family and 6 total children (4 boys + 2 girls) in the family, so the ratio of boys in the family to children in the family is 4:6. Both numbers can be divided by 2: $4 \div 2 = 2$ and $6 \div 2 = 3$. Therefore, the ratio in its simplest form is 2:3.

12. **The correct answer is C.** This question is asking for the average speed, or rate, of the cyclist. Here is the rate formula:

Rate = Distance / Time

Plug in the proper values from the question to find the rate:

$$\text{Rate} = \frac{72}{4}$$
$$= 18$$

13. **The correct answer is A.** Use the probability formula:

Probability = Favorable Events / Possible Events

There are 15 marbles (3 blue + 7 red + 5 yellow) in the bag, so there are 15 possible events. The favorable event is selecting a blue marble. There are 3 chances for this because there are 3 blue marbles in the bag.

Plug these numbers into the probability formula, and reduce the fraction:

$$\text{Probability} = \frac{3}{15}$$
$$= \frac{3 \div 3}{15 \div 3}$$
$$= \frac{1}{5}$$

14. **The correct answer is C.** When solving equations, get the variable by itself on one side of the equation. Do this by undoing what has been done to the variable. First, add 8 to both sides of the equation.

$$6y - 8 + 8 = 28 + 8$$
$$6y = 36$$
$$\frac{6y}{6} = \frac{36}{6}$$
$$y = 6$$

15. **The correct answer is B.** The measures of a triangle's three angles always add up to 180°. If you know the measures of two of the angles, you can subtract those measures from 180° to find the measure of the third angle.

In this triangle, two of the measures are 80° and 40°. Therefore:

$$180° - (80° + 40°) = 180° - 120°$$
$$= 60°$$

16. **The correct answer is E.** The total bill will be the charge for the service call plus the charge for the number of hours worked. The charge for the service call is \$45. The charge for the number of hours worked is the fee per hour multiplied by the number of hours worked: \$25 per hour × 3 hours = \$75. Add these values together to find the total amount of the bill: \$45 + \$75 = \$120.

17. **The correct answer is A.** When setting up an equation from a word problem, move from left to right and translate the English into math:

Joey's height and Keith's height combined → $J + K$

is → =

one half of Steve's height → $\frac{1}{2} \times S$

Therefore, the correct translated equation is

$J + K = \frac{1}{2}S$

ANSWERS >> AFOQT PRACTICE TEST

18. The correct answer is B. Al "gives half of" his 50 pictures to his friend. Multiply one half by 50 to find out how many pictures he gives to his friend:

$$\frac{1}{2} \times 50 = \frac{1}{2} \times \frac{50}{1}$$
$$= \frac{50}{2}$$
$$= 25$$

Al gives 25 pictures away, so he now has $50 - 25 = 25$ pictures. Then, Al gives away two fifths of what he has left. Multiply two fifths by 25 to find out how many pictures he gives to his mother.

$$\frac{2}{5} \times 25 = \frac{2}{5} \times \frac{25}{1}$$
$$= \frac{50}{5}$$
$$= 10$$

Al gives 10 pictures to his mother, so he is left with $25 - 10 = 15$ pictures.

19. The correct answer is C. When multiple angles connect to form a straight line, the angle measures must add up to 180°. The question provides the measures of two of the angles. Subtract their measures from 180° to find the value of x (the measure of the third angle):

$$180° - (35° + 58°) = 180° - 93° = 87°$$

20. The correct answer is B. Michael delivers papers on Wednesdays, Sundays, and Mondays, so the number of papers he delivers in one week is equal to the sum of the number of papers he delivers on those 3 days.

Wednesday: y papers

Sunday: $2y$ papers

Monday: $\frac{1}{2}y$ papers

Now add the values together:

$$y + 2y + \frac{1}{2}y = 3y + \frac{1}{2}y$$
$$= 3\frac{1}{2}y$$

That value is not one of the answer choices, so you must convert the mixed number to an improper fraction. To do so, multiply the denominator of the fraction by the whole number ($2 \times 3 = 6$) and then add the numerator of the fraction to that total ($6 + 1 = 7$). That value (7) will be the numerator of the improper fraction and the denominator will be the original denominator (2). The result is:

$$3\frac{1}{2}y = \frac{7}{2}y$$
$$= \frac{7y}{2}$$

21. The correct answer is B. Use the information about the revenue, the cost of the items, and the number of items sold to determine how many bicycles Sawyer sold. Sawyer's total revenue is equal to the sum of the amount of bicycle revenue and the amount of helmet revenue.

His total revenue is stated as $917. The amount of bicycle revenue is $125*b* since he sells *b* number of bicycles for $125 each. The amount of helmet revenue is $14(3) since he sells 3 helmets at $14 each.

Set up the equation, put in the known values, and solve for *b* (the number of bicycles sold) by getting the variable alone on one side of the equation. Do this by undoing what has been done to the variable:

Total revenue = Bicycle revenue + Helmet revenue

$$917 = 125b + 14(3)$$
$$917 = 125b + 42$$
$$917 - 42 = 125b + 42 - 42$$
$$875 = 125b$$
$$\frac{875}{125} = \frac{125b}{125}$$
$$7 = b$$

22. The correct answer is B. Solve the first equation for y:

$$2x + y = 4$$
$$2x + y - 2x = 4 - 2x$$
$$y = 4 - 2x$$

Now replace y in the second equation with this result, and solve the second equation for x:

$$3x - 2y = 13$$
$$3x - 2(4 - 2x) = 13$$
$$3x - 8 + 4x = 13$$
$$7x - 8 = 13$$
$$7x - 8 + 8 = 13 + 8$$
$$7x = 21$$
$$7x \div 7 = 21 \div 7$$
$$x = 3$$

23. **The correct answer is A.** Use FOIL to multiply the terms:

First: $a \times a = a^2$

Outer: $a \times b = ab$

Inner: $-b \times a = -ab$

Last: $-b \times b = -b^2$

Put the terms together: $a^2 + ab - ab - b^2 = a^2 - b^2$

24. **The correct answer is E.** This is a combination question, so order does not matter. Multiply the number of each type of clothing together to find the number of possible outfits Paul can make:

$$4 \times 7 \times 5 = 140$$

25. **The correct answer is D.** When solving equations, get the variable by itself on one side of the equation. To do this, undo what has been done to the variable. First, undo the fraction by multiplying both sides by 2:

$$\frac{7a}{2} \times 2 = (5a - 3) \times 2$$
$$7a = 2(5a - 3)$$
$$7a = 10a - 6$$

Next, combine the terms with the variable in them on one side of the equation. Subtract $10a$ from each side:

$$7a - 10a = 10a - 6 - 10a$$
$$-3a = -6$$

Finally, undo the multiplication by dividing both sides by -3:

$$\frac{-3a}{-3} = \frac{-6}{-3}$$
$$a = 2$$

NOTES

Word Knowledge

1. B	6. E	11. A	16. A	21. C
2. A	7. B	12. E	17. D	22. A
3. D	8. D	13. B	18. E	23. D
4. C	9. E	14. A	19. A	24. C
5. A	10. B	15. D	20. B	25. D

1. **The correct answer is B.** *Animate* means "full of life."
2. **The correct answer is A.** *Brazen* means "unrestrained by convention."
3. **The correct answer is D.** *Callous* means "to be emotionally hardened."
4. **The correct answer is C.** *Coherent* means "orderly or consistent."
5. **The correct answer is A.** *Debase* means "to corrupt."
6. **The correct answer is E.** *Extol* means "to praise or glorify."
7. **The correct answer is B.** *Furtive* means "secret."
8. **The correct answer is D.** *Haughty* means "arrogant."
9. **The correct answer is E.** *Impeccable* means "faultless."
10. **The correct answer is B.** A kiln is an oven.
11. **The correct answer is A.** *Lucrative* means "profitable."
12. **The correct answer is E.** *Mangle* means "to injure or damage."
13. **The correct answer is B.** *Nepotism* means "favoritism, particularly of a family member."
14. **The correct answer is A.** *Obverse* means "the front or principal side."
15. **The correct answer is D.** A pugilist is a fighter or boxer.
16. **The correct answer is A.** *To rescind* means "to cancel, remove, or take back."
17. **The correct answer is D.** *To shill* means "to promote or sell."
18. **The correct answer is E.** *To snivel* means "to whine."
19. **The correct answer is A.** *Transparent* means "clear."
20. **The correct answer is B.** *Tyro* means "novice or a beginner, particularly in learning."
21. **The correct answer is C.** *Ulterior* means "intentionally hidden."
22. **The correct answer is A.** *Venal* means "corruptible."
23. **The correct answer is D.** *Victual* means "food."
24. **The correct answer is C.** A wraith is a ghost.
25. **The correct answer is D.** *Pummel* means "to pound or beat."

Math Knowledge

1. D	6. A	11. C	16. B	21. B
2. C	7. B	12. C	17. A	22. E
3. A	8. E	13. A	18. B	23. E
4. C	9. B	14. B	19. B	24. A
5. C	10. E	15. E	20. C	25. C

1. **The correct answer is D.** The value of the exponent is equal to the number of zeros in the product. In this case, $10 \times 10 \times 10 \times 10 \times 10 \times 10 =$ 1,000,000 or 10 to the sixth power.

2. **The correct answer is C.** In this case, x is a negative number and y is a positive number, and, as such, the product is a negative value. Choice B is incorrect as you cannot know if the sum of x and y is greater than 0.

3. **The correct answer is A.** For 3 to some exponential value to equal 27, the exponent must equal 3. Therefore, n must equal 5 or $3^{n-2} = 27$

$$3^3 = 27$$

$$n - 2 = 5$$

4. **The correct answer is C.** $(\sqrt{4})^5 = 2 \times 2 \times 2 \times 2 \times 2$

5. **The correct answer is C.** $\sqrt[3]{64} = 4 \times 4 \times 4$

6. **The correct answer is A.** Complementary angles are two angles that add up to 90 degrees total. As such, one angle is 40 degrees smaller than its complement. The equation is then $x + (x + 40) =$ 90 degrees; $2x + 40 = 90$; $2x = 50$; $x = 25$.

7. **The correct answer is B.** First, solve for the hypotenuse of the right triangle using the Pythagorean theorem, $3^2 + 4^2 = z^2$; $z^2 = 9 + 16 = 25$; $z = \sqrt{25}$; $z = 5$. Solve for the perimeter by adding all of the sides, $3 + 4 + 5 = 12$.

8. **The correct answer is E.** Solve for the missing examination score by setting up the equation for the examination mean (average):

$$\frac{(96+88+82+x)}{4} = 90$$

Solve for the x:

$$\frac{(266+x)}{4} = 90$$

$$266 + x = 360$$

$$x = 94$$

9. **The correct answer is B.** A cube has equal side dimensions and 12 total edges. As such, divide the sum of the edges by the number of edges and then cube the result.

$$\frac{24}{12} = 2$$

$$2^3 = 8 \text{ cubic inches}$$

10. **The correct answer is E.** Use basic substitution to solve for c.

$$a = 4b \text{ and } 8b = 30c$$

If $b = \frac{a}{4}$, substitute in the next equation:

$$8\left(\frac{a}{4}\right) = 30c$$

$$2a = 30c$$

$$a = 15c$$

11. **The correct answer is C.** The initial 20% discount of the surround sound system brings the price down to \$800. The second discount reduces the price by another 10% or \$80 to \$720. The 5% sales tax is based on the final discounted price of \$720 and adds \$36 for a total of \$756.

12. **The correct answer is C.** Angle AOB is the same as the arc, 80 degrees. All triangles have 180 degrees total, so subtract 80 degrees to obtain the remaining angle measures, which equals 100

degrees. The two sides of the triangle, AO and OB are the same length because they are also the radii of the circle. Therefore, the angles OAB (x) and OBA must be equal and are calculated by dividing the remaining 100 degrees by 2 to obtain 50 degrees.

13. **The correct answer is A.** The total examination time equals 240 minutes (4 hours × 60 minutes). There are 60 mathematics questions and 360 other questions. The variable x represents the time to solve the mathematics problems, and $\frac{x}{2}$ represents the time to solve the remaining problems on the examination. To solve for x,
$60x + 360\left(\frac{x}{2}\right) = 240$ minutes; $60x + 180x = 240$; $240x = 240$; $x = 1$ minute or a total of 60 minutes for all of the mathematics problems.

14. **The correct answer is B.** The key to solving this problem is to recognize that the ratio between Cole and his shadow will be proportionate to the height of the barn and its shadow. Set up a proportion, simplify, cross-multiply, and solve for the unknown height of the barn.

$$\frac{6}{14} = \frac{x}{70}$$
$$\frac{3}{7} = \frac{x}{70}$$
$$7x = 210$$
$$x = 30$$

The barn is 30 ft. tall.

15. **The correct answer is E.** Use substitution to determine the value of xy. Expand:

$$(x - y)^2 = 60$$
$$x^2 - xy - xy + y^2 = 60$$
$$x^2 - 2xy + y^2 = 60$$

Substitute 40 for $x^2 + y^2$ in the expanded equation:

$$40 - 2xy = 60$$

Solve:

$$-2xy = 60 - 40$$
$$xy = \frac{20}{-2}$$
$$xy = -10$$

16. **The correct answer is B.** The rectangular box has a base that is square and the height is 3 inches in length. So the equation for the volume would be $3x^2 = 48$ or 3 × length × width, which are equal.

Solve for x:
$$x^2 = \frac{48}{3}$$
$$x = 4$$

To solve for the surface area, there are two square sizes with an area of 4 × 4 = 16 each and four connecting sides with dimensions 4 × 3 = 12 each. The total surface area is 2(16) + 4(12) = 80.

17. **The correct answer is A.** Two ships are traveling directly toward each other over a 9-day period. The first ship travels 80 miles per day for a total of 80 miles/day × 9 days = 720 miles. The other ship travels 100 miles per day for a total of 100 miles/day × 9 days = 900 miles. The ships started 2,000 miles apart and are headed toward each other. Subtract both travelled distances from the 2,000 mile total for 2,000 – 720 – 900 = 380.

18. **The correct answer is B.** Use the following equation to solve the problem:
$$3{,}000 - 3{,}000\left(\frac{1}{8}\right) - \left(\frac{1}{7}\right)(3{,}000 \times \frac{7}{8}) = 2{,}250$$

19. **The correct answer is B.** The group of 216 recruits are classified into three groups. As such, the equation $216\left(\frac{1}{3}\right) + 216\left(\frac{1}{4}\right) + x = 216$ can be used to determine the specific ratios. Solving for x, $72 + 54 + x = 216$; $x = 216 - 126$; $x = 90$.

20. **The correct answer is C.** Use a proportion ratio to solve for y. The relationship as stated is $\frac{x^2}{y}$. Solve for y: $\frac{x^2}{y}$ where $x = 2$ and $y = 10$ is $\frac{4}{10}$ and $x = 8$ and y is unknown is $\frac{64}{y}$:

$$\frac{4}{10} = \frac{64}{y}$$
$$4y = 640$$
$$y = 160$$

21. **The correct answer is B.** Use x to depict the number of ration days for 20 personnel. Solve for x: $15(8) = 20x$; $120 = 20x$; $x = 6$ ration days for 20 people. Subtract the 6 days from the initial 8 to determine how many fewer days the rations will last.

22. **The correct answer is E.** The slower train will gain a 40-mile lead in the first hour. To determine how long the other train needs to catch up, divide the distance by the speed difference of 5 mph: 40 miles ÷ 5 mph = 8 hours.

23. **The correct answer is E.** Use x to depict the number of hours to plow with only 8 operational machines. Originally there were 12 machines that did the job in 7 hours or 12 × 7 hours. Compare (12 machines) (7 hours) = (8 machines) x; $8x = 84$; $x = \frac{84}{8}$; $x = 10.5$ hours.

24. **The correct answer is A.** Use x to depict the number of quarters in the cash box. There is a 1 in 5 chance that the coin pulled is a quarter. The number of quarters is equal to $\frac{1}{5}$ or x in the numerator of the equation. The value $x + 63 + 33$ represents the total number of coins in the bank and is placed in the denominator as the equivalent to the total of the ratio. Use the following ratio to solve for the number of quarters:

$$\frac{1}{5} = \frac{x}{(x+63+33)}$$

$$\frac{1}{5} = \frac{x}{(x+96)}$$

$$x+96 = 5x$$

$$4x = 96$$

$$x = 24$$

25. **The correct answer is C.** If Jonah drives 30 mph for 240 miles, his travel time is 8 hours for that proportion of the trip. If Jonah wants to improve his overall travel time and achieve a round trip average of 40 mph, he only has 240 miles in which to make up the time. To average 40 mph for 480 miles in which he has already traveled 240 miles in 8 hours, the remaining travel time would take 4 hours based on the following equation: 40 mph = 480 ÷ x hours; $40x = 480$; $x = 12$ hours, 8 of which have been used. So to calculate the speed needed to meet the average, 240 ÷ 4 hours = 60 miles per hour.

Reading Comprehension

1. B	6. C	11. A	16. D	21. C
2. A	7. C	12. A	17. D	22. D
3. D	8. B	13. D	18. C	23. A
4. D	9. E	14. A	19. A	24. A
5. A	10. B	15. B	20. E	25. C

1. **The correct answer is B.** The example used and the purpose of the second theory was meant to contradict the assumptions made by the right-brain/left-brain theory. The passage provides no defense or support for the right-brain/left-brain theory (choices A and D). The passage also spends very little time explaining the premise of the right-brain/left-brain theory (choices C and E).

2. **The correct answer is A.** The example is purely meant to explain the basic idea behind the right-brain/left brain theory. The passage is not about buying a car (choice B), but the thought processes around it. Choice C is incorrect because there is nothing to exemplify a contrast. Choice D is incorrect because the passage doesn't show support for the right-brain/left brain theory. The passage also does not only mention right-brained people (choice E).

3. **The correct answer is D.** *Rudimentary* implies that something is in its most basic form, or otherwise underdeveloped and incomplete. *Immature* (choice A) implies youth. *Elementary* (choice B) implies ease. *Complicated* (choice C) does not imply simplicity. *Rough* could mean tough, hard, or textured (choice E).

4. **The correct answer is D.** The second paragraph makes clear that humans use both sides of their brain for most activities. Choice A is incorrect because the passage never specifies which choices are right-brained oriented. Choice C is also incorrect because the idea that people are left-brained was never implied, and the definition of left-brained was never stated. The passage specifically contradicts the right-brain/left-brain theory (choice B). The passage also specifically states that humans cannot choose which side of their brain is dominant (choice E).

5. **The correct answer is A.** The passage begins by saying, "The downfall of the Confederate army began . . ." and therefore implies a historical account of a certain shift towards events. Choice B is incorrect because the passage is not only about Robert E. Lee. Choice C is incorrect because the Appomattox River is not the focal point of the passage. Choice D is incorrect because the passage does not disprove any theory or commonly accepted belief. Choice E is incorrect because the Union victory at Appomattox is not the central theme of the passage.

6. **The correct answer is C.** Lee's surrender was dependent upon his lack of resources, both fiscally, nutritionally, and militarily, but his starving troops were what kept him from fighting the Union cavalry himself. Choice A is incorrect because the passage never states which direction the Confederate army was intending to travel. Choice B is incorrect because the passage never states the Union strategy before Lee's surrender. Choice D is incorrect because the Civil War didn't end on the day fighting stopped in Virginia. Choice E is incorrect because the Union soldiers burned the supplies instead of using them.

7. **The correct answer is C.** The second paragraph details only the final events of the Confederate surrender in Virginia and what led to it. Choice A is incorrect because the Wilmer Mclean house is not the primary focus of the information provided in the second paragraph. Choice B is incorrect because the failed Confederate rescue of Lee's troops was only a facet of the second paragraph's

purpose. Choice D is incorrect because Appomattox County itself was not the primary focal point of the second paragraph. Choice E is incorrect because the strategy used by Union soldiers was not stated in the second paragraph.

8. **The correct answer is B.** This title acknowledges the events of Appomattox County and their significance in the big picture. The passage was not about either army's strategy (choice A). More than one battle took place in Appomattox County during the Civil War (choice C), and neither battle was the primary purpose of the passage. The events at Appomattox County did not end the Civil War (choice D). General Lee's surrender was only a facet of the events that took place in this passage (choice E).

9. **The correct answer is E.** In the second paragraph, it states that it was the government sanctioned massacre in Sharpeville that inspired them to abandon peaceful protest in favor of anti-apartheid riots. The Land Act of 1913 (choice A) was only the beginning of apartheid. The African National Congress was never disbanded (choice B). The arrest of Nelson Mandela was never acknowledged in this passage (choice C). The United Nations did support the abolition of apartheid (choice D).

10. **The correct answer is B.** The word *apartheid* was both the name of the legislation and a perfect description of its nature. The use of Afrikaans language in legislation (choice A) is irrelevant. Segregation in the United States (choice C) was never mentioned by the passage. Some readers might not know what the controversial term meant before reading (choice D). The word itself does not convey the depth of the racism that permeated the South African government (choice E).

11. **The correct answer is A.** The entirety of the second paragraph details the opposition to apartheid and ends in its abolishment. The key players in the resistance to apartheid (choice B) were not the focal point of the paragraph. The actions of the rioters were never criticized in the passage (choice C). Nelson Mandela was only mentioned once (choice D). The actions taken by protesters were only a facet of the opposition to and eventual demise of apartheid (choice E).

12. **The correct answer is A.** The passage is about apartheid and begins by defining the word. The passage is not about the Land Act of 1913 (choice B). No other countries are mentioned when referencing segregation (choice C). The passage mentions no other South African legislation (choice D). Nelson Mandela is only mentioned once (choice E).

13. **The correct answer is D.** The passage makes consumers aware of the various ways in which they can tell faux and real fur apart. Choices A, C, and E are incorrect because the passage shows no preference towards real fur or faux fur. Choice B is incorrect because the passage is not meant to raise awareness, and no fabric preference is ever stated as being a flaw in the fashion industry.

14. **The correct answer is A.** *Taboo* implies that a thing is distasteful or not preferred, and therefore controversial. Choice B is incorrect because real fur does exist, but it is not implied to be useful (choice C). Choice D is incorrect because the passage implies that real fur is, in fact, unpopular. Choice E is incorrect because neither real nor faux fur is difficult to use or work with.

15. **The correct answer is B.** The purpose of the passage is to give consumers the tools to determine for themselves the difference between faux fur and real fur as it has been recently discovered that some British labels, and potentially others, will not provide that information for them. Labels might occasionally be forthcoming about the origins of their fabric (choice A), beyond faux fur versus real fur. The passage shows no preference towards the texture of real fur as opposed to fake fur (choice C). The price difference between real fur and fake fur is never a point made by the passage (choice D).The legality of labeling real fur as faux fur, and vice versa, is never mentioned (choice E).

16. **The correct answer is D.** The phrase "manufactured and unsharpened" implies that the product is man-made. Choice A is incorrect because the

phrase does not imply inferiority. Neither does the phrase imply the form of production process that was used (choice B). Choices C and E are incorrect because the words do not denote texture.

17. **The correct answer is D.** The majority of the passage focuses on the laws surrounding PSCs, with special consideration for the incident in Baghdad and how such laws applied. The passage does not advocate for the use of PSCs (choice A). The 2007 incident in Baghdad (choice B) is only a catalyst for the true discussion of PSC legality. The passage shows no preference for or against the use of PSCs (choice C). The profession of the PSC (choice E) is not the primary focus of the passage.

18. **The correct answer is C.** *Blanketly* implies fully and completely, and thus comprehensively. *Mostly* (choice A) connotes incompletion. *Softly* (choice B) does not describe thoroughly developed laws. *Intentionally* (choice D) is not a synonym of blanketly. Choice E is incorrect because laws have restrictions.

19. **The correct answer is A.** The author is cognizant of the complicated nature of PSC laws but states at the end of the passage that they are effective when put to good use. The passage specifically states that PSCs do not operate within a legal void (choice B). The actions committed by PSCs in Baghdad were not in violation of the given humanitarian laws (choice C). International laws, while complicated, are not ineffective (choice D). PSCs are excused for some actions during times of war (choice E), just as soldiers are.

20. **The correct answer is E.** The Baghdad Massacre was a catalyst for the discussion of PSC legality. The passage was not merely about international humanitarian law (choice A). The passage does not give an in-depth description of the PSC profession (choice B). The passage is not a study of PSCs or private warfare (choice C). The passage is not solely about the Baghdad massacre (choice D).

21. **The correct answer is C.** The passage specifically states that there are six types of colorblindness that confuse titular colors. Choice A and B are incorrect because there are not three types, but rather three forms of colorblindness with seven subcategories. Choice D is incorrect because the seven subcategories do not stem from the monochromatic shades of gray. Choice E is incorrect because the only true colorblindness is the ability to only see black and white.

22. **The correct answer is D.** Some people with color blindness are incapable of seeing color, and some people with color blindness are not. Choice A is incorrect because color blindness diagnosis is not ever evolving. Choice B is incorrect because not all people with color blindness confuse red with purple. Choice C is incorrect because not all people with color blindness are capable of seeing color. Choice E is incorrect because some people with color blindness can perceive some color tones.

23. **The correct answer is A.** *Titular* means being of the title. Those with red and green color blindness confuse those colors. Brightness (choice B) is an element of color blindness categories. Those with color blindness do not choose their favorite colors to perceive (choice C). The symbolism of colors (choice D) is not relevant. Color names are not token names (choice E).

24. **The correct answer is A.** The second paragraph focuses primarily on the various types of color blindness. The paragraph does not define every kind of color blindness (choice B). The passage also does not disprove any more assumptions about color blindness (choice C). The paragraph does not provide insight into the extreme side of color blindness so much as the various kinds of color blindness (choice D). The paragraph is not meant to inspire sympathy (choice E) so much as to inform and discuss.

25. **The correct answer is C.** There are people diagnosed with true color blindness, in which the world appears black and white. There are not color blindness spectrums (choice A) as much as there are categories. Not all color tones are affected by color blindness (choice B). Deuteranopia makes green tones look more red, not the other way around (choice D). Some forms of color blindness are not described as rare (choice E).

Situational Judgment

1. D	11. B	21. A	31. A	41. C
2. C	12. A	22. E	32. D	42. E
3. C	13. C	23. C	33. E	43. C
4. B	14. D	24. D	34. B	44. E
5. A	15. D	25. B	35. D	45. D
6. E	16. B	26. D	36. A	46. A
7. D	17. C	27. D	37. B	47. A
8. C	18. A	28. E	38. C	48. C
9. D	19. D	29. C	39. B	49. C
10. C	20. A	30. D	40. A	50. D

1. **The correct answer is D.** As a leader, you are responsible for the enlisted under your command, and if they refuse to follow orders, then it is your responsibility to discipline them. However, have enough respect for those that have been serving for longer than yourself and try to save the relationship.

2. **The correct answer is C.** A leader strives for unity. Doing nothing will only allow him to think that he has every right to disobey you, which could lead to far more dangerous disagreements in far more dangerous circumstances. A leader must be able to trust their team.

3. **The correct answer is C.** Good communication fosters a positive and open work environment. Make sure your peer knows how you feel and see if they perceive the same differences in treatment. Remember that perceptions are not truth and can be misguided. However, if you both feel strongly about the situation, you can discuss it with your commanding officer.

4. **The correct answer is B.** The least effective way to address the problem is by involving yourself. Do not attempt to remedy a situation that does not involve you, especially when you are not the superior. It will only make the situation worse.

5. **The correct answer is A.** Air Force restrictions on cannabis are meant to protect the officers and those around them. Recreational use of marijuana while in service is strictly prohibited, and as an officer, you are required to uphold the rules.

6. **The correct answer is E.** Never become a part of the problem or take part in an action that you know is against the rules. Approving the behavior will only cause it to continue, which in the case of substances can be dangerous for those in the military.

7. **The correct answer is D.** Establish trust with your comrades. When competition begins to arise, discuss it and attempt to find the source of the problem before allowing hate to fester.

8. **The correct answer is C.** Running away from confrontation or disagreement is never the answer, especially when both of you are an asset to the squadron. Learn to peacefully coexist and trust, even if you might not be each other's best friend.

9. **The correct answer is D.** Don't create a problem where there might not be one. Trust your peers. The proper authorities will investigate, and in the meantime, keep a tight lock on your property and give your fellow officer the benefit of the doubt.

10. **The correct answer is C.** Responding to one wrongdoing with another is never the answer, especially when it involves invading another person's privacy. If you are wrong in your assumptions, you could be the one in trouble instead.

11. **The correct answer is B.** Be willing to admit fault. Otherwise, move forward and respect the authority that higher ranking officers have over you. Trust their judgment and be willing to follow orders whether you agree with them or not.

12. **The correct answer is A.** Disobedience and disrespect will only foster frustration and animosity between individuals, and you want to be able to trust the people you are working with and under.

13. **The correct answer is C.** Harassment is never tolerated under any circumstances and must be reported immediately to be dealt with. Any derogatory comments pertaining to another's race are considered racial harassment and cannot be allowed to continue.

14. **The correct answer is D.** Never ignore injustice. Racism within the military cannot be tolerated, and the worst thing you can do is to do nothing at all.

15. **The correct answer is D.** Misunderstandings can foster agitation and distrust in any workplace environment. Get ahead of the misunderstanding before it can impede the relationship and your ability to do your job.

16. **The correct answer is B.** Letting the misunderstanding fester will only lead to more strife between the two of you and affect the ability of those around you to do their jobs. Do your best to remedy any personal issues between the two of you as well.

17. **The correct answer is C.** As a leader, it is your responsibility to offer guidance to those struggling and asking for help. Be willing to help your fellow officers no matter their rank and be forgiving.

18. **The correct answer is A.** Never allow ego to poison your workplace attitude and your ability to do your job. Ego is dangerous when it comes to ranks and positions, and you shouldn't let it affect your ability to work with your fellow officers or their ability to do their jobs.

19. **The correct answer is D.** Policies are in place for certain reasons. If they have yet to be changed after you have made it clear that they are difficult to abide by, then trust the people who created them.

20. **The correct answer is A.** A key part of working on a team is working within the rules of that team. You might not like the rules, but it's better to unhappily follow them than to happily break them.

21. **The correct answer is A.** The Air Force has a zero-tolerance drug policy. If these officers are using and using consistently, it could affect not only their health but also their ability to do their job. That, in turn, could lead to them endangering the lives of those around them.

22. **The correct answer is E.** Never take part in using controlled substances offered to you if you know it's wrong. Becoming a part of the problem is never a solution and listening to your peers can sometimes lead to more trouble than good. Be willing to say no and to report them.

23. **The correct answer is C.** While harassment is not tolerated, this is not your fight. Perceptions are not always based in reality, so don't act on someone's behalf before they want you to—but be sure to voice your support and encourage them in whatever way you can.

24. **The correct answer is D.** Do not be persuaded to take part in any form of harassment, no matter the intention. If it hurts another officer, it is not humorous. Be empathetic and willing to defend your fellow officers.

25. **The correct answer is B.** If asking politely and continually has failed, report the behavior as harassment. Harassment is not tolerated in the workplace. Discussion of the problem is courteous, but as that approach has not worked, reporting it must be the next step.

26. **The correct answer is D.** Never respond to harassment with more harassment. Two wrongs do not make a right, and a good leader and teammate is able to rise above it.

27. **The correct answer is D.** Religious discussions are normal, as long as they don't escalate to the point of aggression or animosity between the two

parties. If you do not wish to be a part of these discussions, then do not be a part of these discussions, but suggest to coworkers that they should be open to accepting others despite their beliefs.

28. **The correct answer is E.** Imposing your beliefs on someone else or telling them that they are wrong is never a good way to foster inclusion. Be open to discussion, or do not discuss at all.

29. **The correct answer is C.** Resolving conflicts takes compromise and respect. Respect your fellow teammates and their opinions even if you do not share those opinions. The best way to show that respect is to listen and share. Communication is key to a healthy work environment.

30. **The correct answer is D.** Failing to listen to each other leads to a lack of trust. You must be able to trust your fellow officers above all else, so communication is key. Be respectful and willing to listen.

31. **The correct answer is A.** Be respectful of your superior officers and be honest about any misunderstandings that might occur. Explain the situation beforehand and direct him to a person who can verify if necessary. Don't allow a misunderstanding to breach any trust between the two of you.

32. **The correct answer is D.** Don't escalate the situation by being disrespectful and temperamental. It is not your place to reprimand those in positions above your own, especially when the situation is the result of a misunderstanding and not a true disagreement. Be understanding and explain the miscommunication.

33. **The correct answer is E.** If you are not well suited to a task or cannot undertake the task without detriment to yourself and the task itself, do not take it. Acknowledge that the best person for the job is not always you and be willing to step aside for the sake of your mental and physical health.

34. **The correct answer is B.** Taking a job that you are not well-suited for is detrimental to both you and the job itself. Your other responsibilities will suffer for it, as will your mental health.

35. **The correct answer is D.** Be willing to consider advice from those with more experience than you, but don't let your opinion be easily swayed by the opinions of others. If the decision is considered from all angles, and you think that you made the right choice, then stay true to your decision.

36. **The correct answer is A.** Don't dismiss or criticize others for their opinions, especially those with more experience than you. Escalating the situation by creating conflict is no way to interact with your enlisted or fellow officers.

37. **The correct answer is B.** Be willing to admit fault when you are at fault and take the initiative to change your behavior. Even if you are being shown favoritism, it's important not to take advantage of it. Be organized with your time and respectful of your teammates' time.

38. **The correct answer is C.** Failure to accept fault and take responsibility for your actions is not respectful of yourself or your teammates. Just because you have not been made aware by a superior that your behavior is wrong does not mean that it is not. Practice self-awareness and take initiative with your time and organization.

39. **The correct answer is B.** As a junior officer, it is your responsibility to be a leader among new enlisted and to lead by example. Guide them and show them what they are doing wrong so that they will not make the same mistakes again. Sometimes, a little bit of encouragement goes a long way.

40. **The correct answer is A.** Do not avoid action and responsibility for those under your command. They need leadership, so be a leader and don't hand the job off to someone else.

41. **The correct answer is C.** Working on a team means being a leader among leaders. Do your part and work as one of the whole. Everyone on the team has a certain skill unique to a certain task, so you should use that to your advantage.

42. **The correct answer is E.** Don't wait for someone else to hand you a task or a way to contribute. Contribute intentionally and immediately. Offer

your skills to a certain task or aspect of the project, or simply contribute to the distribution of tasks and be a leader among your peers.

43. **The correct answer is C.** Never assume the intentions of your fellow officers before acting. Listen to them and be willing to compromise. This displays communication and a sense of professionalism.
44. **The correct answer is E.** Exclusion could incite mutual agitation and hostility. Make him aware of the situation first. Make sure that there was no miscommunication.
45. **The correct answer is D.** Signing up for difficult tasks means getting frustrated, but you have to remind yourself why you chose this path in the first place. Changing your strategy is the best way to change the outcome. It takes a strong sense of professionalism and innovation to confront situations such as these.
46. **The correct answer is A.** Running away from a problem never solved any of them. Confront your struggles head-on. If your strategy isn't working, get a new strategy.
47. **The correct answer is A.** Good communication goes hand in hand with mentorship. If he believes the task to have immoral implications, and you are sure that it does not, then you must be willing to express your view of the situation and allow him to express his. This will foster trust between the two of you.
48. **The correct answer is C.** Failure to communicate or listen to genuine concern from your subordinates is the mark of a poor leader. Though you might be sure you are correct, it is possible he might think he is as well. Be willing to communicate.
49. **The correct answer is C.** Communicate your shortcomings and accept the help of those who are doing better than you. If your method does not work, change the method. Your fellow officers are there to support you as you are there to support them.
50. **The correct answer is D.** Use integrity to drive your decision-making. The least effective action you could take would be to copy the work of another officer and fail to learn how to complete the training exercise on your own.

NOTES

Physical Science

1. D	5. C	9. D	13. B	17. B
2. B	6. E	10. C	14. C	18. B
3. A	7. C	11. A	15. E	19. A
4. C	8. E	12. C	16. B	20. B

1. **The correct answer is D.** Each element has 1 atom, unless another number is specified immediately after the elemental symbol. The formula is written $C_2\ H_6\ O$. If we break it apart like this, we can easily see that there are 2 carbon atoms, 6 hydrogen atoms, and 1 oxygen atom. $2 + 6 + 1 = 9$. Only paying attention to one of the numbers in the formula (choices A and B) or adding/subtracting the visible numbers in some fashion (choices C and E) is incorrect.

2. **The correct answer is B.** The atomic weight is the number located directly below the elemental symbol on the periodic table. The atomic number is located directly above the symbol (choice A). The number of electrons (choice C) and the number of protons (choice E) are both connected to the atomic number. The number of neutrons is not readily available on the periodic table for all elements (choice D).

3. **The correct answer is A.** Mass is the measure of how much matter there is in something, which remains constant regardless of gravity. Weight (choice C) is directly related to the gravity of a given location. For example, the weight of an object is lighter on the moon versus on Earth. Volume and density (choices B and E) both increase or decrease depending on the strength of the gravitational pull. Gravity can both bend and change the energy of light (choice D).

4. **The correct answer is C.** Speed (in a vacuum) is the only component related to light that is unaffected by gravity. This is because of Einstein's Theory of General Relativity, which states that light travels at the same speed independent of its surroundings or location. Thus, gravity has no effect on it. Direction (choice A) and curves (choice D), synonyms for the same component, are specifically connected to the gravitational pull. The frequency of light (choice E) shifts to longer wavelengths as a result of gravity, thus sapping some of its energy (choice B).

5. **The correct answer is C.** Gamma rays are the shortest with a wavelength of 0.001 nanometers. The easiest way to remember the length of electromagnetic waves is to cluster them by types. From longest to shortest they are radio waves (choice A), microwaves (choice B), ultraviolet light (choice E), x-rays (choice D), and gamma rays.

6. **The correct answer is E.** The ratio from meter to decimeter is 1:10; to find the answer, simply multiply the original number (10,000) by 10, which equals 100,000. To remember this unit, focus on the root "deci," which means a unit of 1/10. Choice A is the result of dividing by 10. Choice D is the result of dividing by 100. Choice B is merely the ratio without taking the given number into consideration. Choice C is the result of multiplying by 100.

7. **The correct answer is C.** Nuclear decay occurs when an atom of a radioactive element spontaneously changes the composition of its nucleus. Magnetism (choice A) and heat (choice B) are both unrelated physical concepts. Electric fields (choice D) are not connected to radioactivity. Radiation (choice E) is the energy given off when a nucleus decays. Radioactivity is the measure of this radiation.

8. **The correct answer is E.** Absolute zero is the lowest temperature that is theoretically possible and is also measured as zero on the Kelvin scale. 0°F (choice A) is cold but bearable with proper clothing. 32°F and 0°C (choices B and C) are both

the temperature at which water freezes. -1,000°C (choice D) is not possible.

9. **The correct answer is D.** PVC is a type of plastic that is an excellent insulator. It does NOT transfer electrons easily and thus it works well to keep the electrical current contained within the wire and safe from starting any fires or sparks outside of the designated area. All the other options are poor insulators because they readily transfer electrons and would actually conduct electricity instead of insulating it.
10. **The correct answer is C.** There are two types of current in electricity: alternating current (AC) and direct current (DC). The term AC can relate to air conditioning (choice A), but only when discussing heating and air, not solely electricity. Alternative (choice B), affected (choice D), and artificial (choice E) currents are not related to electricity.
11. **The correct answer is A.** A compound is formed when two or more different elements are chemically bonded. A chemical bond between nonmental elements (choice E) specifically is called a covalent bond. An isotope is an element that has atoms with varying numbers of neutrons (choice C). A solid, liquid, or gas dissolved into a fluid (choice D) is called a solvent. Two or more atoms of the same element (choice B) are referred to as a pure substance.
12. **The correct answer is C.** Although the inch is a unit of measurement, it is not an SI (system international) unit of measurement that is accepted worldwide. Inches are specific for use within the United States only. Amperes (choice A) are the SI unit for electric current. Kilograms (choice B) are the SI unit for mass. Seconds (choice D) are the SI unit for time. Moles (choice E) are the SI unit for the amount of substance.
13. **The correct answer is B.** Tea is the only example of a solution and is created by straining water through tea leaves to create a new substance. Sand and water (choice A) both retain their original properties when mixed. Oil and vinegar (choice C) do not mix at all and easily separate when combined. Lightning (choice D) is the light given off from massive electrical discharge. Aluminum (choice E) is an element.
14. **The correct answer is C.** Kinetic energy is present when an object is in motion. Thermal energy (choice A) is related to heat. Potential energy (choice B) is what an object possesses whether or not it is in motion. Nuclear energy (choice D) is connected to fusion and fission. Heat energy (choice E) is a synonym for thermal energy.
15. **The correct answer is E.** Earthquakes can be labeled as both transverse and longitudinal as the movement travels both parallel and perpendicular to the source at the same time. This is why the movement from the epicenter decreases in intensity in a circular pattern.
16. **The correct answer is B.** Shock waves occur when the sound produced by an object is faster than the speed of sound. The speed of light (choice A) is not affected by sound. Shock waves are a type of sound wave which are longitudinal and not transverse (choice C). The object (choice D) has no relation to the speed at which the sound travels. The processing speed of the person hearing the sound (choice E) does not produce the shock wave and is relative to the individual.
17. **The correct answer is B.** Density is the mass of an object divided by its volume. In simple terms, density measures the "compactness" of an object. The other equations are incorrect when calculating the density of an object.
18. **The correct answer is B.** 100°C is equivalent to 212°F, which is the boiling point for water and the temperature at which it turns into a gas, also called water vapor. Although 100°F (choice A) is hot, it is not hot enough to change the state from liquid to gas. At 212°C (choice C), the water is already in a gaseous state as it is a full 120 degrees hotter than needed for a change in state. 220°F (choice D) is also hotter than needed to convert water to gas. 98.6°F (choice E) is the average body temperature of a human and is nowhere near hot enough for a change to a gaseous state.

19. The correct answer is A. Light waves are electromagnetic waves, the only type of waves that do not require a "medium" or host. Light waves are produced when atoms emit quanta, which is a type of energy. Since every other choice is NOT a type of electromagnetic wave, they are incorrect.

20. The correct answer is B. Condensation (choice A) is the conversion of a gas to a liquid. Evaporation is the opposite when a liquid becomes a gas. Conduction (choice C) is related to electricity. Precipitation (choice D) is the release of a liquid or substance. The melting point (choice E) is when a solid turns into a liquid.

NOTES

Table Reading

1. C	9. C	17. C	25. E	33. C
2. A	10. E	18. D	26. D	34. B
3. A	11. B	19. E	27. B	35. B
4. C	12. A	20. A	28. E	36. A
5. B	13. E	21. D	29. D	37. B
6. E	14. A	22. D	30. C	38. E
7. D	15. D	23. B	31. A	39. E
8. C	16. B	24. C	32. D	40. A

1. **The correct answer is C.** The coordinates (+3, –3) intersect at 65.
2. **The correct answer is A.** The coordinates (+6, +3) intersect at 62.
3. **The correct answer is A.** The coordinates (+11, –8) intersect at 78.
4. **The correct answer is C.** The coordinates (–4, +5) intersect at 50.
5. **The correct answer is B.** The coordinates (–8, –11) intersect at 62.
6. **The correct answer is E.** The coordinates (–3, –11) intersect at 67.
7. **The correct answer is D.** The coordinates (+9, 0) intersect at 68.
8. **The correct answer is C.** The coordinates (–11, +10) intersect at 38.
9. **The correct answer is C.** The coordinates (+4, +5) intersect at 58.
10. **The correct answer is E.** The coordinates (+7, –11) intersect at 77.
11. **The correct answer is B.** The coordinates (+10, –5) intersect at 74.
12. **The correct answer is A.** The coordinates (–4, –10) intersect at 65.
13. **The correct answer is E.** The coordinates (+1, +7) intersect at 53.
14. **The correct answer is A.** The coordinates (+9, –4) intersect at 72.
15. **The correct answer is D.** The coordinates (+2, –1) intersect at 62.
16. **The correct answer is B.** The coordinates (+9, –9) intersect at 77.
17. **The correct answer is C.** The coordinates (–4, –7) intersect at 62.
18. **The correct answer is D.** The coordinates (–10, 0) intersect at 49.
19. **The correct answer is E.** The coordinates (+10, –9) intersect at 78.
20. **The correct answer is A.** The coordinates (+1, –6) intersect at 66.
21. **The correct answer is D.** The coordinates (+11, –3) intersect at 73.
22. **The correct answer is D.** The coordinates (+8, –10) intersect at 77.
23. **The correct answer is B.** The coordinates (+6, +2) intersect at 63.
24. **The correct answer is C.** The coordinates (–3, +5) intersect at 51.
25. **The correct answer is E.** The coordinates (+2, –8) intersect at 69.
26. **The correct answer is D.** The coordinates (–2, –3) intersect at 60.

27. **The correct answer is B.** The coordinates (–9, –2) intersect at 52.

28. **The correct answer is E.** The coordinates (–3, –7) intersect at 63.

29. **The correct answer is D.** The coordinates (+4, –5) intersect at 68.

30. **The correct answer is C.** The coordinates (0, +10) intersect at 49.

31. **The correct answer is A.** The coordinates (–3, –8) intersect at 64.

32. **The correct answer is D.** The coordinates (+9, –11) intersect at 79.

33. **The correct answer is C.** The coordinates (+4, –4) intersect at 67.

34. **The correct answer is B.** The coordinates (–8, 0) intersect at 51.

35. **The correct answer is B.** The coordinates (–11, –6) intersect at 54.

36. **The correct answer is A.** The coordinates (+10, –1) intersect at 70.

37. **The correct answer is B.** The coordinates (+3, +3) intersect at 59.

38. **The correct answer is E.** The coordinates (+8, +8) intersect at 59.

39. **The correct answer is E.** The coordinates (–3, +2) intersect at 54.

40. **The correct answer is A.** The coordinates (–9, –8) intersect at 42.

NOTES

Instrument Comprehension

1. D	6. C	11. A	16. C	21. D
2. A	7. A	12. D	17. A	22. A
3. C	8. A	13. C	18. B	23. D
4. D	9. D	14. D	19. D	24. C
5. B	10. A	15. A	20. A	25. A

1. **The correct answer is D.** The plane is heading southeast, slightly ascending with no bank. Choice A is banking 20 degrees left. Choice B is heading northwest. Choice C is descending.
2. **The correct answer is A.** The plane is heading west, inverted, and descending. Choice B is not inverted and is heading east. Choice C is heading south. Choice D is banking 20 degrees right and is heading east.
3. **The correct answer is C.** The plane is heading northwest, slightly descending and banking 60 degrees to the right. Choice A is banking 20 degrees to the left. Choice B is heading northeast and banking 45 degrees right. Choice D is only banking 20 degrees to the right.
4. **The correct answer D.** The plane is heading southeast, slightly descending, and banking 45 degrees left. Choice A is banking 20 degrees left. Choice B is heading east. Choice C is heading southwest with no bank.
5. **The correct answer is B.** The plane is heading southwest, ascending with no bank. Choice A is heading north. Choice C is banking left 20 degrees. Choice D is level with the horizon.
6. **The correct answer is C.** The plane is heading northeast, slightly decending, and banking 20 degrees to the right. Choice A is banking 20 degrees left. Choice B is heading northwest. Choice D is not banking.
7. **The correct answer is A.** The plane is heading north, slightly ascending with no bank. Choice B is heading east. Choice C is heading south and banking 20 degrees left. Choice D is slightly descending.
8. **The correct answer is A.** The plane is heading northwest, ascending sharply and banking 45 degrees left. Choice B is banking but heading northeast. Choice C is heading south and has a minor left bank. Choice D is heading southeast and banking 20 degrees left.
9. **The correct answer is D.** The plane is heading north, level with the horizon, and not banking. Choice A is banking 30 degrees left. Choice B is heading south. Choice C is slightly ascending and banking 90 degrees left.
10. **The correct answer is A.** The plane is heading east, level with the horizon, and banking 30 degrees left. Choice B is heading west and is slightly ascending. Choice C is banking 20 degrees right. Choice D is slightly ascending.
11. **The correct answer is A.** The plane is heading southeast, slightly ascending, and banking 90 degrees to the left. Choice B is banking 90 degrees right. Choice C is banking 45 degrees left. Choice D is heading northwest, level with the horizon, and banking 90 degrees to the right.
12. **The correct answer is D.** The plane is heading northwest, ascending, and inverted. Choice A is heading south. Choice B is heading northeast and is not inverted. Choice C is heading southeast.
13. **The correct answer is C.** The plane is heading northeast, slightly ascending, and banking 30 degrees right. Choice A is banking 20 degrees left. Choice B is heading southwest. Choice D is banking 90 degrees right.
14. **The correct answer is D.** The plane is heading northeast, ascending with no bank. Choice A is banking 20 degrees left. Choice B is heading

southeast and banking 45 degrees right. Choice C is heading southeast with no bank.

15. **The correct answer is A.** The plane is heading southwest, level with the horizon, and inverted. Choice B is heading north. Choice C is banking 45 degrees left. Choice D is slightly ascending and not inverted.

16. **The correct answer is C.** The plane is heading southwest, slightly ascending, and banking 30 degrees right. Choice A is banking left. Choice B is heading northwest. Choice D is banking about 90 degrees.

17. **The correct answer is A.** The plane is heading south, slightly ascending, and banking 10 degrees to the right. Choice B is heading north. Choice C is banking 20 degrees left. Choice D is level with the horizon.

18. **The correct answer is B.** The plane is heading northeast, descending and banking 45 degrees right. Choice A is banking 45 degrees left. Choice C is ascending. Choice D is overbanking 90 degrees.

19. **The correct answer is D.** The plane is heading southeast, level with the horizon, and not banking. Choice A is banking left 30 degrees. Choice B is heading east. Choice C is slightly ascending.

20. **The correct answer is A.** The plane is heading northwest, descending, and banking greater than 90 degrees to the right. Choice B is slightly descending. Choice C is heading southeast and banking 90 degrees right. Choice D has no bank.

21. **The correct answer is D.** The plane is heading southeast, slightly descending, and banking 10 degrees right. Choice A is banking left. Choice B is heading northwest. Choice C is banking greater than 90 degrees left.

22. **The correct answer is A.** The plane is heading west, ascending, and banking 90 degrees left. Choice B is heading north. Choice C is banking left 20 degrees. Choice D is heading east.

23. **The correct answer is D.** The plane is heading southwest, slightly descending, and banking 10 degrees right. Choice A is banking left. Choice B is heading northwest. Choice C is banking 45 degrees right.

24. **The correct answer is C.** The plane is heading northeast, level with the horizon, and banking 20 degrees left. Choice A is banking 20 degrees right. Choice B is heading northwest. Choice D has no bank.

25. **The correct answer is A.** The plane is heading south and descending with no bank. Choice B is heading north. Choice C is banking 90 degrees left. Choice D is level with the horizon.

Block Counting

1. D	7. C	13. A	19. E	25. C
2. E	8. C	14. E	20. B	26. B
3. B	9. E	15. B	21. E	27. B
4. E	10. B	16. E	22. E	28. D
5. C	11. A	17. B	23. A	29. B
6. D	12. E	18. A	24. D	30. B

1. **The correct answer is D.** Block 1 is touching four blocks: two on one side, one to the other side, and one below.
2. **The correct answer is E.** Block 2 is touching five blocks: one to the side, one below, and three across the top.
3. **The correct answer is B.** Block 3 is touching two blocks: one to the side, and one below.
4. **The correct answer is E.** Block 4 is touching two blocks: one to the side, and one above.
5. **The correct answer is C.** Block 5 is touching two blocks: one to the side, and one below.
6. **The correct answer is D.** Block 6 is touching five blocks: three to the side, one behind, and one below.
7. **The correct answer is C.** Block 7 is touching six blocks: one to the side, one behind, and four below.
8. **The correct answer is C.** Block 8 is touching nine blocks: three on either side, and three above.
9. **The correct answer is E.** Block 9 is touching two blocks: two to the side.
10. **The correct answer is B.** Block 10 is touching three blocks: one to the side, one behind, and one below.
11. **The correct answer is A.** Block 11 is touching three blocks: one to the side and two below.
12. **The correct answer is E.** Block 12 is touching five blocks: two to one side, one to the other side, one above, and one below.
13. **The correct answer is A.** Block 13 is touching four blocks: two above and two below.
14. **The correct answer is E.** Block 14 is touching two blocks: one to the side and one above.
15. **The correct answer is B.** Block 15 is touching three blocks: one to the side, one above, and one below.
16. **The correct answer is E.** Block 16 is touching five blocks: two to either side and one below.
17. **The correct answer is B.** Block 17 is touching two blocks: two to the side.
18. **The correct answer is A.** Block 18 is touching four blocks: two to the side, one above, and one below.
19. **The correct answer is E.** Block 19 is touching two blocks: one to the side and one above.
20. **The correct answer is B.** Block 20 is touching three blocks: one to either side and one above.
21. **The correct answer is E.** Block 21 is touching five blocks: two to one side, one to the other side, one above, and one below.
22. **The correct answer is E.** Block 22 is touching five blocks: one to either side, one above, and two below.
23. **The correct answer is A.** Block 23 is touching four blocks: two to one side, one to the other side, and one below.
24. **The correct answer is D.** Block 24 is touching six blocks: two to either side, one above, and one below.
25. **The correct answer is C.** Block 25 is touching one block to the side.

26. **The correct answer is B.** Block 26 is touching two blocks: one to the side and one below.

27. **The correct answer is B.** Block 27 is touching two blocks to the side.

28. **The correct answer is D.** Block 28 is touching two blocks: one to the side and one above.

29. **The correct answer is B.** Block 29 is touching four blocks: one above, one below, and one on either side.

30. **The correct answer is B.** Block 30 is touching three blocks: one above, one below, and one to the side.

NOTES

Aviation Information

1. A	5. C	9. B	13. A	17. C
2. D	6. D	10. E	14. B	18. E
3. E	7. B	11. C	15. E	19. B
4. C	8. B	12. B	16. B	20. D

1. **The correct answer is A.** Aerodynamics is the dynamics of gases and the movement of air or gas around the object. Aerodonetics (choice B) is the science or study of gliding. Aerolithology (choice C) is the study of aerolites or meteorites. Aerology (choice D) is study of the atmosphere. Aeronautics (choice E) is the study of navigation through air or space.

2. **The correct answer is D.** Thrust helps to move the aircraft through the air. Lift (choice A) happens at the wings as air passes over them. The weight (choice B) of the aircraft determines how much lift and thrust it takes to get it off the ground. Acceleration (choice C) is the increase in the rate or speed of the aircraft. Velocity (choice E) is the speed of something in a given direction.

3. **The correct answer is E.** The trim is what controls the axes of the aircraft and is needed to keep the aircraft in balance or in its desired position. The boundary layer (choice A) is the thin layer of a flowing gas or liquid that contacts a surface like that of an airplane wing or the inside of a pipe. Commercial airline aircrafts typically fly in the stratosphere (choice B) layer of the atmosphere. An adjustment of the ailerons (edge of the wings) controls the aircraft's longitudinal axis, also known as roll (choice C). The flight envelope (choice D) comprises the Mach number, altitude, and the angle of attack of an airplane.

4. **The correct answer is C.** An airfoil does this by making use of the air currents through which it moves. An angle of attack (choice A) is the downward slant, from front to back of an airfoil. A chord (choice B) is the distance between the leading edge to the trailing edge of the wing and measures parallel to the normal airflow over the wing. A camber (choice D) is the curvature of the top surface of an airfoil. A pitch (choice E) is the upward or downward motion of the nose of the airplane.

5. **The correct answer is C.** Pilots will be able to look at the segmented circle on the ground as they fly over the airport and establish the correct runway to land on and determine the proper traffic pattern. The compass deviation (choice A) is the miscalculation of the magnetic compass due to local magnetism and relies on the headings and the aircraft's geographical location. The threshold line (choice B) is the start of the usable section for landing an aircraft on the runway. The heading (choice D) is the direction in which the aircraft's longitudinal axis is pointed. Since the airport is without a control tower in the scenario, there would not be an air traffic controller (choice E) to provide any visuals.

6. **The correct answer is D.** The colder air allows the engine to work more efficiently because colder air is more dense. Although it requires using more mass of air/fuel mixture in the same intake volume, it does allow more power for the most efficient performance. In warmer (choice A) and hotter (choice B) temperatures, the air is less dense, and the aircraft produces less lift, so it has to travel faster and farther to take off and fly. Cooler temperatures (choice C) are better but not most efficient. Icy temperatures (choice E) on the ground require de-icing of the wings during preflight procedures and are not the most efficient use of time and resources.

7. **The correct answer is B.** Wings are shaped to allow quicker air flow over the top of the wing

and slower air flow underneath. Newton's Third Law of Motion (choice A) states that there is a pair of forces (air pushing down and up) acting on the two interacting objects (the wings). Newton's Second Law of Motion (choice C) states that the acceleration of an object (the plane) as produced by net force (airspeed) is directly proportional to the magnitude of the net force, in the same direction as the net force, and inversely proportional to the mass of the object. The Conservation of Energy principle (choice D) states that the total energy of an isolated system remains steady; it is said to be preserved over time. The Venturi effect (choice E) occurs as fluids are forced to flow faster through narrow spaces.

8. **The correct answer is B.** An upwind leg is a course flown at controlled airports in a path parallel to the landing runway in the same direction as landing traffic. A crosswind leg (choice A) is a short climbing course flown at right angles to the landing runway off its takeoff end. A downwind leg (choice C) is a long level course flown parallel to the landing runway in the opposite direction of landing. A base leg (choice D) is a short descending course flown at right angles to the landing runway off its approach end and extending from the downwind leg to the intersection of the extended runway centerline. A final approach (choice E) is a descending course flown in the direction of landing along the extended runway centerline from the base leg to the runway.

9. **The correct answer is B.** Positive pitch motion is a rotation about a lateral axis that allows the nose of the plane to raise and the tail of the plane to lower. The ailerons (choice A) raise and lower the wings. Blade pitch (choice C) has to do with the angle between the propeller blade chord line and the plane of rotation of the propeller. Yaw (choice D) is the left and right movement of the aircraft's nose. The vertical stabilizer (choice E) prevents the nose of the plane from swaying left to right while the horizontal stabilizer keeps the nose from going up and down.

10. **The correct answer is E.** A drag force functions to slow an aircraft's movement through the air. Thrust (choice A) is a forward force that moves an aircraft through the air. Lift (choice B) is the upward force on the aircraft that causes an aircraft to rise in altitude. Gravity (choice C) is a force that attracts any two objects with mass. Viscosity (choice D) measures oil's resistance to flow; it thins with increasing temperature or thickens with decreasing temperature.

11. **The correct answer is C.** There are two categories of airspace, regulatory and non-regulatory, but within these categories controlled, uncontrolled, special use, and other are the four types of airspace. VFR (choice A) are a set of rules created by the FAA under which a pilot operates an aircraft during generally good weather conditions. IFR (choice B) are required to be used by pilots when the meteorological conditions are compromised according to the visual meteorological conditions. SATCOM (choice D) is used when airborne radio telephone communication via a satellite is used. RCLS (choice E) is used to offer a quick and positive identification for aircrafts on the approach end of a particular runway.

12. **The correct answer is B.** Shearing is a cutting force when a shear stress is applied to an object. Compression (choice A) is a force that presses together. Torsion (choice C) is a force that results in a twisting motion. Tension (choice D) is a force that pulls apart. Bending (choice E) is a combination of compression and tension forces on a single piece.

13. **The correct answer is A.** After reviewing what is deemed significant damage and what is a reportable event, damage to a gear door is not required to be reported. However, being a responsible and proactive pilot, reporting this event is always a good plan. An inflight fire (choices B), any essential crew member's inability to perform their duties (choice C), any person suffering serious injury or illness while on an aircraft (choice D), and an aircraft collision while in flight (choice E) are all required to be reported to the NTSB.

14. **The correct answer is B.** Pilots should ascend to avoid collision because birds in flocks spread in a downward pattern. Since birds in flocks commonly distribute themselves downward, descending (choice A) is not recommended. The lead birds are at the highest altitude and the remaining birds expand in V formation, so flying to the right (choice C) and flying to the left (choice D) would not be the best options. Flying straight (choice E) would most likely result in a collision with the flock of birds.

15. **The correct answer is E.** Security protocol violations, such as walking through the airport security area without a boarding pass, are excluded because they are handled by the Transportation Safety Administration (TSA). When an unruly person assaults (choice A), threatens (choice B), intimidates (choice C), or interferes (choice D) with the roles and responsibilities of a crew member, they violate the law and are handled by the FAA.

16. **The correct answer is B.** Airports use the PFC program fees to fund FAA-approved projects that enhance safety, security, or capacity; reduce noise; or increase air carrier competition. The Passenger Ticket Tax (choice A) is an amount paid by consumers for commercial air transportation and in turn is submitted to the Internal Revenue Service (IRS). The Customs User Fee (choice C) is given to the US Border and Customs Protection to fund inspections. The Overflight Fee (choice D) is used by the FAA to recover the cost of providing air traffic control and other safety services to aircraft that are navigating through U.S. airspace but do not take-off or land in the U.S. The September 11 Fee (choice E) is given to the Transportation Safety Administration (TSA) and has also been redirected by Congress to fill unrelated budget gaps.

17. **The correct answer is C.** When factoring in weather, altitude, airspace class, and many other components, the FAA determined 250 knots to be the maximum velocity for better speed control at lower, more congested altitudes. Speeds of 175 knots (choice A) or 100 knots (choice B) can be utilized as the speed for an aircraft holding pattern, but these are not the ideal maximum indicated airspeeds. Unless otherwise authorized by an Air Traffic Control (ATC) service, the speed of 275 knots (choice D) is over the maximum indicated airspeed below 10,000 MSL. Unless otherwise authorized, flying in the airspace underlying Class B OR when at or below 2,500 feet above ground level (AGL) and within 4 nautical miles of the primary airport of Class C airspace, the maximum indicated airspeed is 200 knots (choice E).

18. **The correct answer is E.** The student must be at least 16 years old except if the student is operating a glider or a balloon, in which case the student must be at least 14 years of age. Although this is the goal, the student pilot does not have to complete a solo flight at the end of the training program (choice A). The student must be able to read, speak, write, and understand the English language (choice B) without problems, nothing more. The student must apply for the pilot AND medical certifications (choice C) as outlined by the FAA guidelines. The flight instructor must make an endorsement for each make or model of aircraft that a student pilots solo (choice D).

19. **The correct answer is B.** The heliport beacons have a vertical light from 1 to 10 degrees above the horizon, so they are most helpful to the pilots at night or during inclement weather throughout the day. The blue omnidirectional lights (choice A) identify the airport's taxiway edge lights at night. The military airport is identified at night by the dual peaked (two quick) white flashes between green flashes (choice C). A blue hashed line (choice D) signifies a prohibited area such as the White House. Broken magenta dash lines (choice E) represent the class E controlled airspace, which extends from 1,200 feet above ground level (AGL) to 17,999 feet mean sea level (MSL).

20. **The correct answer is D.** The ATC principally directs aircrafts on the ground and through regulated airspace. An Aircraft Dispatcher is responsible for coordinating with flight service personnel (choice A) for the management of the aircraft crew schedules (choice B), for coordinating maintenance control (choice C), and for the organization of the various company ground stations (choice E).

SCORE SHEET

Although your actual exam scores will not be reported as percentages, it might be helpful to convert them so you can better visualize your strengths and weaknesses.

AFOQT SCORE SHEET		
Subject	**# Correct ÷ # of questions**	**× 100 = ______ %**
Verbal Analogies	______ ÷ 25 = ______	× 100 = ______ %
Arithmetic Reasoning	______ ÷ 25 = ______	× 100 = ______ %
Word Knowledge	______ ÷ 25 = ______	× 100 = ______ %
Math Knowledge	______ ÷ 25 = ______	× 100 = ______ %
Reading Comprehension	______ ÷ 25 = ______	× 100 = ______ %
Situational Judgment	______ ÷ 50 = ______	× 100 = ______ %
Physical Science	______ ÷ 20 = ______	× 100 = ______ %
Table Reading	______ ÷ 40 = ______	× 100 = ______ %
Instrument Comprehension	______ ÷ 25 = ______	× 100 = ______ %
Block Counting	______ ÷ 30 = ______	× 100 = ______ %
Aviation Information	______ ÷ 20 = ______	× 100 = ______ %

STUDY REFERENCE GUIDE		
Subject	**Chapter**	**Page**
Verbal Analogies	Chapter 5	130
Arithmetic Reasoning	Chapter 7	154
Word Knowledge	Chapter 6	144
Math Knowledge	Chapter 7	154
Reading Comprehension	Chapter 8	220
Situational Judgment	Chapter 9	236
Physical Science	Chapter 11	256
Table Reading	Chapter 13	306
Instrument Comprehension	Chapter 14	316
Block Counting	Chapter 15	330
Aviation Information	Chapter 16	336

OAR PRACTICE TEST

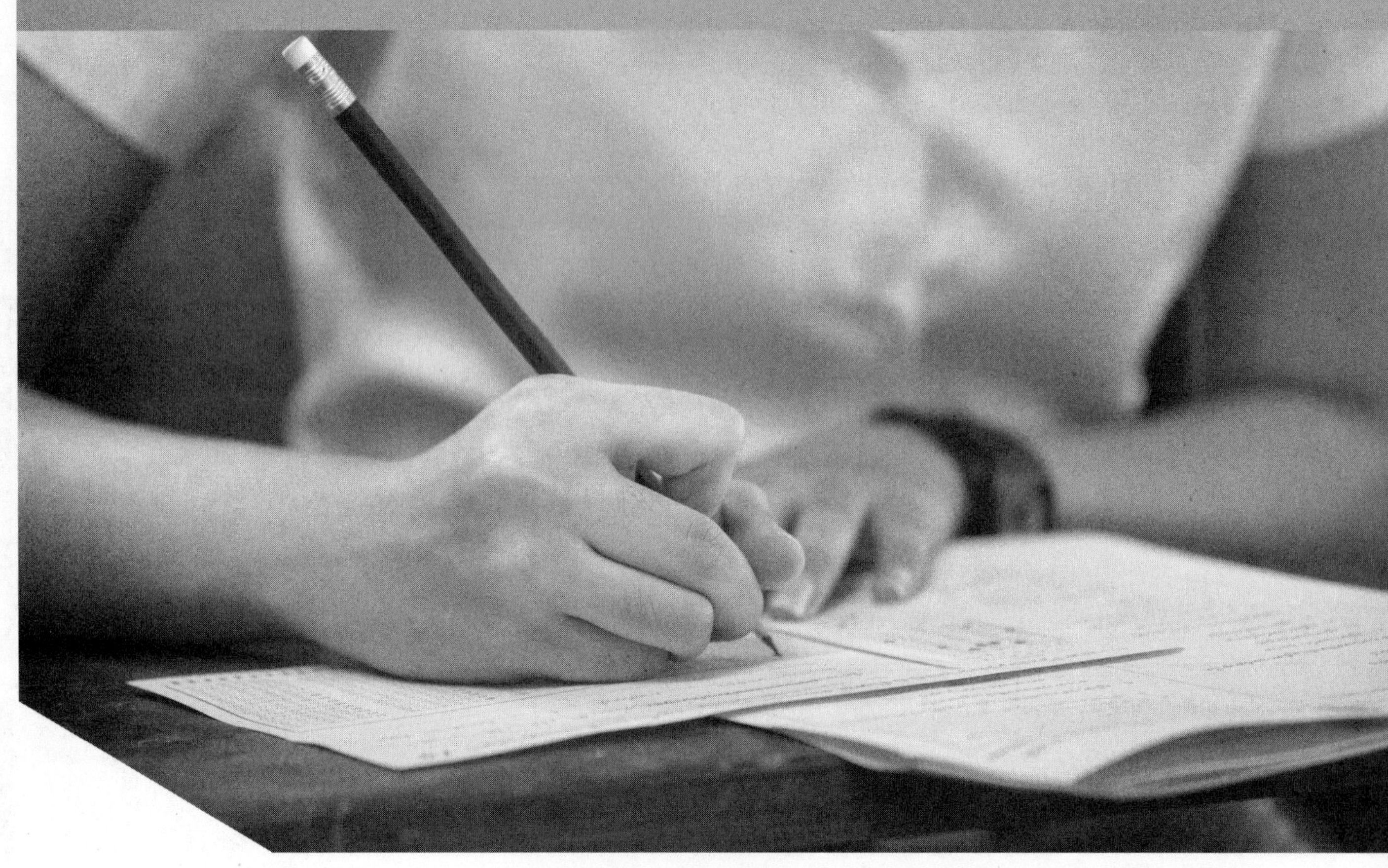

OAR PRACTICE TEST

This practice test is designed to help you recognize your strengths and weaknesses. The questions cover information from all of the subtests of the OAR exam.

ANSWER SHEET: OAR PRACTICE TEST

Math Skills

1. Ⓐ Ⓑ Ⓒ Ⓓ	7. Ⓐ Ⓑ Ⓒ Ⓓ	13. Ⓐ Ⓑ Ⓒ Ⓓ	19. Ⓐ Ⓑ Ⓒ Ⓓ	25. Ⓐ Ⓑ Ⓒ Ⓓ
2. Ⓐ Ⓑ Ⓒ Ⓓ	8. Ⓐ Ⓑ Ⓒ Ⓓ	14. Ⓐ Ⓑ Ⓒ Ⓓ	20. Ⓐ Ⓑ Ⓒ Ⓓ	26. Ⓐ Ⓑ Ⓒ Ⓓ
3. Ⓐ Ⓑ Ⓒ Ⓓ	9. Ⓐ Ⓑ Ⓒ Ⓓ	15. Ⓐ Ⓑ Ⓒ Ⓓ	21. Ⓐ Ⓑ Ⓒ Ⓓ	27. Ⓐ Ⓑ Ⓒ Ⓓ
4. Ⓐ Ⓑ Ⓒ Ⓓ	10. Ⓐ Ⓑ Ⓒ Ⓓ	16. Ⓐ Ⓑ Ⓒ Ⓓ	22. Ⓐ Ⓑ Ⓒ Ⓓ	28. Ⓐ Ⓑ Ⓒ Ⓓ
5. Ⓐ Ⓑ Ⓒ Ⓓ	11. Ⓐ Ⓑ Ⓒ Ⓓ	17. Ⓐ Ⓑ Ⓒ Ⓓ	23. Ⓐ Ⓑ Ⓒ Ⓓ	29. Ⓐ Ⓑ Ⓒ Ⓓ
6. Ⓐ Ⓑ Ⓒ Ⓓ	12. Ⓐ Ⓑ Ⓒ Ⓓ	18. Ⓐ Ⓑ Ⓒ Ⓓ	24. Ⓐ Ⓑ Ⓒ Ⓓ	30. Ⓐ Ⓑ Ⓒ Ⓓ

Reading Comprehension

1. Ⓐ Ⓑ Ⓒ Ⓓ	5. Ⓐ Ⓑ Ⓒ Ⓓ	9. Ⓐ Ⓑ Ⓒ Ⓓ	13. Ⓐ Ⓑ Ⓒ Ⓓ	17. Ⓐ Ⓑ Ⓒ Ⓓ
2. Ⓐ Ⓑ Ⓒ Ⓓ	6. Ⓐ Ⓑ Ⓒ Ⓓ	10. Ⓐ Ⓑ Ⓒ Ⓓ	14. Ⓐ Ⓑ Ⓒ Ⓓ	18. Ⓐ Ⓑ Ⓒ Ⓓ
3. Ⓐ Ⓑ Ⓒ Ⓓ	7. Ⓐ Ⓑ Ⓒ Ⓓ	11. Ⓐ Ⓑ Ⓒ Ⓓ	15. Ⓐ Ⓑ Ⓒ Ⓓ	19. Ⓐ Ⓑ Ⓒ Ⓓ
4. Ⓐ Ⓑ Ⓒ Ⓓ	8. Ⓐ Ⓑ Ⓒ Ⓓ	12. Ⓐ Ⓑ Ⓒ Ⓓ	16. Ⓐ Ⓑ Ⓒ Ⓓ	20. Ⓐ Ⓑ Ⓒ Ⓓ

Mechanical Comprehension

1. Ⓐ Ⓑ Ⓒ	7. Ⓐ Ⓑ Ⓒ	13. Ⓐ Ⓑ Ⓒ	19. Ⓐ Ⓑ Ⓒ	25. Ⓐ Ⓑ Ⓒ
2. Ⓐ Ⓑ Ⓒ	8. Ⓐ Ⓑ Ⓒ	14. Ⓐ Ⓑ Ⓒ	20. Ⓐ Ⓑ Ⓒ	26. Ⓐ Ⓑ Ⓒ
3. Ⓐ Ⓑ Ⓒ	9. Ⓐ Ⓑ Ⓒ	15. Ⓐ Ⓑ Ⓒ	21. Ⓐ Ⓑ Ⓒ	27. Ⓐ Ⓑ Ⓒ
4. Ⓐ Ⓑ Ⓒ	10. Ⓐ Ⓑ Ⓒ	16. Ⓐ Ⓑ Ⓒ	22. Ⓐ Ⓑ Ⓒ	28. Ⓐ Ⓑ Ⓒ
5. Ⓐ Ⓑ Ⓒ	11. Ⓐ Ⓑ Ⓒ	17. Ⓐ Ⓑ Ⓒ	23. Ⓐ Ⓑ Ⓒ	29. Ⓐ Ⓑ Ⓒ
6. Ⓐ Ⓑ Ⓒ	12. Ⓐ Ⓑ Ⓒ	18. Ⓐ Ⓑ Ⓒ	24. Ⓐ Ⓑ Ⓒ	30. Ⓐ Ⓑ Ⓒ

MATH SKILLS

30 Questions (40 Minutes)

Directions: This part of the test measures your knowledge of mathematical terms and principles. Each problem is followed by four possible answers. You are to decide which of the four choices is correct.

1. If $x^2 + 3y - 1 = 15$ and $y = -3$, then what is x?

   A. 2
   B. 3
   C. 4
   D. 5

2. What is the product of $(5x - 3)$ and $(x + 4)$?

   A. $5x^2 + 17x - 1$
   B. $5x^2 - 12$
   C. $5x^2 - 3x - 1$
   D. $5x^2 - x - 1$

3. The Halls are moving to a new home and want to fence in a space for their dog, Molly. Previously, Molly had a fenced-in area of 2,100 square feet to play. One side of the new lawn is 42 feet long. If the Halls want the same space for Molly and use 42 feet for one side of a rectangular space, how much fencing will they need to purchase?

   A. 168 ft.
   B. 180 ft.
   C. 184 ft.
   D. 192 ft.

4. Jonah and Sabrina have an outdoor swing set and a 20-foot square tarp. They want to build a "lean-to" using the swing set as one side and the tarp along the top to provide them a shaded play area when it is hot. If they attach the tarp to the top of the swing set and secure the other side directly to the ground, how much shaded area will they have underneath the tarp?

   A. 240 $ft.^2$
   B. 320 $ft.^2$
   C. 360 $ft.^2$
   D. 400 $ft.^2$

5. Aaron drove 4 hours to see his sister, Allison. His average speed due to traffic was 45 mph for the first hour, 62 mph for the second hour, 59 mph for the third hour, and 64 mph for the fourth hour. His Honda gets 22 miles per gallon. How many gallons of gas did Aaron use, one way?

   A. 9 gallons
   B. 9.5 gallons
   C. 10 gallons
   D. 10.5 gallons

6. On the return trip, Allison drove Aaron back and was able to drive a bit faster because there was no traffic. She drove 63 miles the first hour, 68 miles the second hour, 64 miles the third hour, and 35 miles during the last 30 minutes of the trip. What was Allison's average speed during the duration of the trip?

   A. 63 mph
   B. 65.7 mph
   C. 64 mph
   D. 62.5 mph

7. A Navy and Marine F/A-18E Super Hornet each leave Miramar Air Station at the same time. The Marine Super Hornet is flying due east at 775 mph and the Navy Super Hornet is flying due west at 625 mph. How long will it take for the two aircraft to be separated by 3,500 miles?

   A. 2.00 hours
   B. 2.30 hours
   C. 2.50 hours
   D. 3.00 hours

8. If $x^2 + 5x - 10 = 14$, what is x?

   A. 3
   B. 4
   C. 5
   D. 6

9. The measure of one of the angles of a complementary angle is 50 degrees. What is the measure of the other complementary angle?

   A. 10 degrees
   B. 30 degrees
   C. 40 degrees
   D. 50 degrees

10. Allison wants to paint her new room. The room measures 12 feet (length) by 10 feet (width) by 9 feet (height) and has two 8-foot by 3-foot doors that will not be painted and a 3-foot by 4-foot window. If she is not painting the ceiling, how much area will she need paint to cover?

    A. 516 ft.^{2}
    B. 456 ft.^{2}
    C. 396 ft.^{2}
    D. 336 ft.^{2}

11. $(\sqrt{5}-\sqrt{3})^2$

    A. $2 - 2 - 2\sqrt{3}$
    B. $-2 - - 2 - 2\sqrt{3}$
    C. $8 + 8 + 2\sqrt{15}$
    D. $8 - 8 - 2\sqrt{15}$

12. In a class of 375 students, 28% are taking shop, 36% are taking home economics, and 12% are taking both courses. How many students are not taking either course?

    A. 82
    B. 90
    C. 93
    D. 104

13. A surveillance radar can detect moving objects up to 15 km away. If the radar is able to cover a 40-degree segment of a circle around the radar, how many square miles is the detection field? (Use 3.14 for π.)

    A. 10 km.^{2}
    B. 78.5 km.^{2}
    C. 96.5 km.^{2}
    D. 157 km.^{2}

14. Dave wants to purchase a new telescope, but he can only afford to spend \$1,000 total. If the current price of the telescope he wants is \$1,300 and sales tax is 5%, how much will the telescope have to be discounted for him not to exceed his budget?

A. 20%

B. 23%

C. 25%

D. 27%

15. A patrol aircraft has a maximum range of 600 miles without refueling. If the aircraft departs the airfield and is tasked to make a maximum range circular orbit around the field and return, what is the maximum radius of that orbit? (Use 3.14 for π.)

A. 72 miles

B. 75 miles

C. 80 miles

D. 82 miles

16. If you were to roll a 10-sided die once, what is the probability that it will land on an odd number?

A. 1 out of 2

B. 1 out of 5

C. 3 out of 10

D. 6 out of 10

17. Solve the following for x: $\frac{4}{x+5} = \frac{5}{x+7}$

A. –1

B. 0

C. 3

D. 4

18. Simplify the following expression, assuming all variables represent nonzero real numbers: $(-3x)^7(-3x)^4$

A. $(-3x)^{11}$

B. $(-3x)^{28}$

C. $9x^{11}$

D. $9x^{28}$

19. Perform the indicated operation: $(5x^3 + 3x - 2x^2) + (4x^2 - 2x^3 + 7x)$

A. $9x^3 + x + 5x^2$

B. $9x^3 + 5x + 5x^2$

C. $3x^3 + 2x^2 + 10x^2$

D. $3x^3 + x + 9x^2$

20. Successive discounts of 20% and 10% are equivalent to a single discount of

A. 28%.

B. 29%.

C. 30%.

D. 31%.

21. Which of the following is equivalent to $(k - 6)(k + 2)$?

A. $k^2 - 8k - 12$

B. $k^2 + 4k - 12$

C. $k^2 - 4k + 3$

D. $k^2 - 4k - 12$

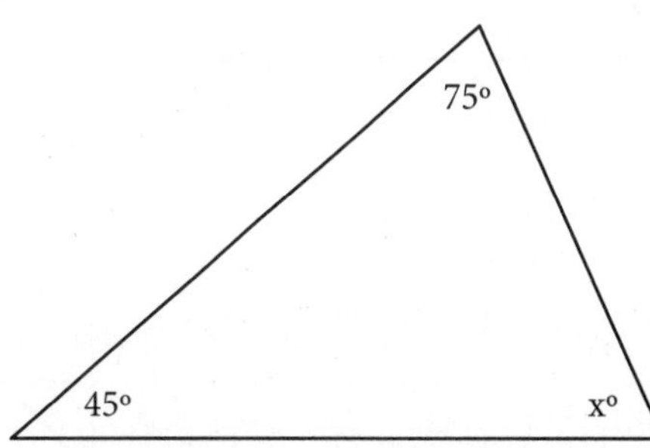

22. In the triangle, what is the value of x?

A. 30

B. 60

C. 90

D. 100

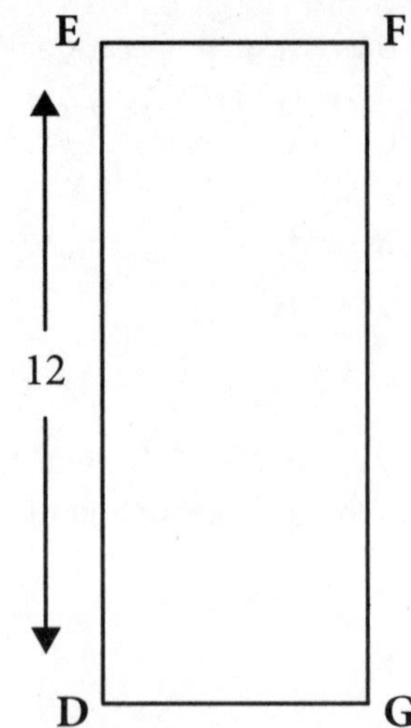

23. If the rectangle has an area of 60, what is the length of side DG?

A. 3

B. 5

C. 6

D. 8

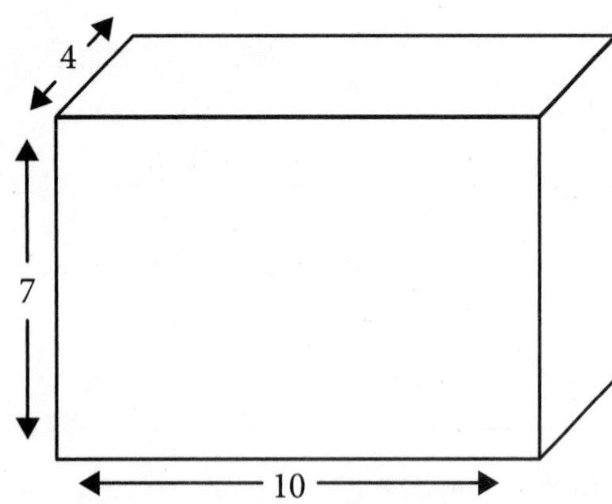

24. What is the volume of the rectangular solid?

A. 21

B. 47

C. 74

D. 280

25. A rental car agency charges an initial fee of $65 per day to rent a car. The agency charges an additional $0.30 for each mile that the car is driven. If a customer rents a car for two days and drives for 149 miles, how much will the customer's bill be?

A. $130

B. $150.70

C. $174.70

D. $181.50

26. $6! =$

A. 6

B. 36

C. 600

D. 720

27. What is 3.79×10^{-6} in standard form?

A. 0.00000379

B. 3,790,000

C. 379,000

D. 0.000379

28. Ty jogs on Mondays, Wednesdays, and Fridays. He covers 20 miles over the course of a week. He jogs for y miles on Mondays, and half that amount on Wednesdays. How many miles does Ty jog on Fridays?

A. $20 - 3y$

B. $20 - \frac{3y}{2}$

C. $20 - 2y$

D. $20 - \frac{3y}{2}$

29. Kayla loves to read books. She owns x memoirs, 3 books of poetry, and 10 historical biographies. The number of novels she owns is twice the number of all her other books combined. How many total books does Kayla own?

A. $2x + 13$

B. $\frac{5+26}{2} = \frac{31}{2}$

C. $3x + 39$

D. $2x + 26$

30. If $x - y = 5$ and $x + 3y = 21$, what is the value of y?

A. 4

B. 5

C. 8

D. 9

STOP.

If you finish before time is up, you may check your work on this section only. Do not turn to any other section in the test.

READING COMPREHENSION

20 Questions (30 Minutes)

Directions: This part of the exam will test your reading comprehension abilities. Each question has four choices. Choose the best option based on the information provided.

Since the 1950s, scientists have learned more about the intricacies of the human sleep cycle now termed the REM cycle, or "Rapid Eye Movement" cycle. People typically enter into this phase of sleep about 90 minutes after first drifting off and undergo around five to six different phases of REM before coming upon the final phase. In this final phase, the brain becomes more active and the eyes move in frantic circles around the sockets, hence the name Rapid Eye Movement. This final phase is where most dreaming occurs.

1. This passage best supports the statement that

   A. most dreaming occurs in the final phase of REM.

   B. people aren't truly sleeping until the REM cycle starts.

   C. the REM cycle occurs when you're not sleeping.

   D. REM means "Real Eye Monitoring."

There are four primary competitive swimming strokes: backstroke, butterfly, breaststroke, and freestyle. Each stroke can be swam in various races on a long course (50 meter pool) or a short course (25 meter pool). A race can be as short as one lap: swimming to the end of the pool and back. One race that includes all four is the 400 IM (individual medley) where swimmers will swim 100 meters in the order of butterfly, backstroke, breaststroke, and finally freestyle.

2. This passage best supports the statement that

   A. the 400 IM can only be swam on a long course pool.

   B. butterfly comes second in the 400 IM.

   C. one lap on a long course pool is 100 meters.

   D. a 400 IM is 4 laps.

Essential oils are a natural remedy that can be applied to the skin or diffused into the air. Each essential oil can be used for a specific purpose. For instance, tea tree oil can serve as an immunity booster and aid infection, whereas lavender can relieve stress and improve sleep. Some are used for similar purposes, like peppermint and lemon, both of which aid digestion and mood.

3. Based on the information in this passage, essential oils

   A. can be used in lieu of medicine.

   B. can be used for similar purposes.

   C. serve as immunity boosters.

   D. are as useful as medicine.

Roughly one-eighth of the officers who enter the Air Force per year become a part of special ops. Depending on the danger levels at a certain location, as many as 200 special ops officers can be placed at one base. In Texas, an air base has exactly one-fourth of the special ops officers recruited by the Air Force that year.

4. Based on the information in the passage, the airbase in Texas

A. is the largest Air Force base.

B. has 200 officers on base.

C. is in less danger.

D. has 1/32 of officers in the Air Force.

Every week, the commanders set a new distance for the officers to run before their morning workout. They also set the time in which it must be completed, and if it is not completed in that time, the officers must run an extra two miles. Lieutenant Salvatore ran five miles in 32 minutes and did not have to run an extra two miles.

5. On the day that Lieutenant Salvatore ran 5 miles in 32 minutes,

A. the distance was set to five miles.

B. the distance was set to three miles.

C. the time was set to 32 minutes.

D. Lieutenant Salvatore ran the fastest.

Lieutenants Drake and Wicklin have one class each in the morning, but one of them also has two classes in the afternoon. Drake and Wicklin both take the same course but at different times. Drake takes military management class in the afternoon.

6. Based on the information in this passage, Drake must

A. not take morning classes.

B. take three classes.

C. take two classes.

D. share no common courses with Wicklin.

The grocery store on the base receives deliveries every Tuesday. All food items that don't get sold by the next week's delivery get put on sale for 30% off. From Tuesday to Tuesday, the store only sold 150 of the 200 boxes of pasta they ordered.

7. Based on the information in this passage, the store will

A. sell 150 boxes for 30% off.

B. no longer order pasta.

C. sell 50 boxes for 30% off.

D. sell 30% of the pasta.

The orchid mantis is a favored species of domestic mantis due to its exotic coloring and floral appearance. Officially named hymenopus coronatus, this praying mantis will oftentimes sit patiently in wait for its prey before becoming hyperactive and flying away. When adopting multiple orchid mantises, owners should house the two creatures separately as cannibalism is very common among male and female mantises.

8. Based on this passage, orchid mantises are NOT

A. domestic pets.

B. cannibalistic.

C. floral in appearance.

D. active hunters.

Contrary to popular belief, Spanish moss does not in fact originate from Spain. The bromeliad flowering plant is actually native to the southernmost regions of the U.S. where it can flourish in its preferred environment of muggy swampland. Originally, it was christened "Itla-okla" by Native Americans, a name meaning "tree hair," but the French decided the moss was reminiscent of the Spanish conquistadores' thick beards and instead deemed it "Barbe Espagnole," or "Spanish Beard." Eventually, the name was shortened to Spanish moss.

9. Based on the information provided in the passage, the name Spanish Moss

A. is French.

B. was shortened from Spanish Beard.

C. means tree hair.

D. was chosen by Native Americans.

Albert Einstein once made the assertion that while a cluttered desk was indicative of a cluttered mind, an empty desk was surely the result of an empty mind. Certainly, studies show that the creative process is a messy one and thus results in quite the cluttered desk, but that isn't to say that a messy life is always the way to go. A clean desk is shown to aid healthy food choices and promote a more efficient work ethic.

10. This passage best supports the statement that

A. organization promotes positive choices.

B. a clean desk is indicative of a creative mind.

C. creativity stems from messiness.

D. Albert Einstein had an empty desk.

There's a reason that every sports team must choose its own mascot: The word itself comes from the French word "mascotte" meaning lucky charm. Originally, sports teams would use live animals, typically predators, to strike fear in the opposing team and project an image of invincibility for its fans. Eventually, these live animals were transformed into 3D characters whose chief purpose was to provide more entertainment for spectators.

11. Based on the information in this passage, mascots

A. are live animals.

B. are good luck charms and entertainment.

C. strike fear in the spectators.

D. must be predators.

In accordance with their name, sunflowers require an abundance of sunlight in order to flourish. They also require moist, nutrient-rich soil and warm weather. However, the best way to ensure that sunflowers stay in bloom is to plant a row or grouping of sunflower seeds every two weeks for around four to six weeks in the summer.

12. The passage best supports the statement that sunflowers

A. can only grow with other sunflowers.

B. produce vitamin D.

C. need sunlight, nutritious soil, and warmth.

D. do not necessarily grow tall.

The nephron is the primary functional unit of the kidney, meaning it is responsible for the filtration, reabsorption, and secretion of blood nutrients and toxins. By such means, the nephron is also able to regulate the body's blood pressure, blood volume, and plasma osmolarity. Each nephron consists of a network of tubules, one of which leads first to the glomerulus—a high-pressure capillary with the sole purpose of filtering the blood, creating a liquid called filtrate. This filtered liquid is then deposited into the glomerular (Bowman's) capsule where it will then travel through the proximal convoluted tube (PCT), the loop of Henle, and the distal convoluted tube (DCT), in that order. Throughout such a process, the nutrients contained by the filtrate will be reabsorbed by the three consecutive tubes until the filtrate exits the nephron and enters the ureter.

13. This passage best supports the statement that

A. the proximal convoluted tube and the distal convoluted tube are both responsible for the filtration of the liquid deposited from Bowman's capsule.

B. the nephron is responsible only for the filtration and reabsorption of blood toxins and nutrients alike.

C. the glomerulus produces a filtered liquid called filtrate before depositing it in Bowman's capsule where it will await being reabsorbed.

D. the kidney is responsible for regulating blood pressure and blood volume while the nephron filters and reabsorbs blood nutrients.

Modern-day critics are saying that movies are getting longer and longer. Historically, the average film runs between 90 and 120 minutes, but lately, movies are averaging over two hours. As a rule, one page equals one minute of screen time.

14. Based on the passage above, the average movie scripts are

A. getting better.

B. averaging more than 120 pages.

C. typically 45 pages.

D. maintaining the same length.

The film used in cameras uses layers of a silver compound in order to capture solid pictures. This silver compound is exposed to the light of the scene it's capturing for half a second, which forms silver atoms and creates the picture. While black and white film has just two layers of this silver compound, colored film has three, creating more depth in the photo.

15. The passage best supports the statement that

A. aluminum atoms create the picture.

B. black and white film does not require light.

C. the silver compound is only found on camera film.

D. all camera film uses a silver compound.

Mary Poppins was originally a book series written by P. L. Travers before it was adapted by Walt Disney into a film in 1964. P. L. Travers wrote 10 Mary Poppins books between 1934 and 1988, all of which achieved similar popularity and acclaim among young and old readers alike. However, while the books were undoubtedly well-known, one of the most famous Mary Poppins catchphrases ("Supercalifragilisticexpialidocious") was in fact not included in the original text.

16. Based on the information in the passage above, the Mary Poppins books

A. were written by Walt Disney.

B. included supercalifragilisticexpialidocious.

C. were written in 1964.

D. were first published in 1934.

Au pairs are a popular form of childcare for young families seeking extra help. They are typically non-citizen students looking for a work visa and experience abroad. Host families for au pairs will provide housing, food, and pay for these foreign students in exchange for childcare and occasionally housework.

17. According to the passage, au pairs are

A. not required to watch children.

B. only required to stay for 1 year.

C. typically non-citizens.

D. not from the U.S.

Makeup trends have evolved over the years in parallel with their contemporary beauty, fashion, and technological trends. At the beginning of the 21st century, beauty standards demanded thin brows, overly glossed lips, and heavy black eyeliner. Nowadays, beauty gurus will tell you to fluff and darken your eyebrows, outline a nude lip, and keep eyeliner classy and minimal.

18. The passage best supports the statement that

A. thin eyebrows are better than thick eyebrows.

B. eye makeup is less dark now than in the early 2000s.

C. beauty gurus didn't exist in the early 2000s.

D. makeup became popular in the early 2000s.

One of the central facets of Canada's national identity is its bilingual heritage. English and French are both recognized as Canada's official languages, giving a nod to the French occupancy that originally founded Canada. This is a reflection of their vast multiculturalism. Seeing as though they are few in numbers, Canadians are accepting of immigrants traveling from every continent and corner of the world.

19. Based on the information in this passage, Canadians

A. all speak French.

B. speak more than two languages.

C. are few in number.

D. are from France.

The human lungs are the site of exchange between carbon dioxide and oxygen in the blood. As blood is pumped out of the heart, it travels the body delivering oxygen to various muscles and organs that require it, before returning with carbon dioxide to the lungs, where they will exchange that carbon dioxide for oxygen and return the blood to the heart.

20. Based on the information provided in the passage, the human lung

A. exchanges oxygen for carbon dioxide.

B. creates oxygen for the blood.

C. needs carbon dioxide in order to function.

D. works in tandem with the kidneys.

STOP.

If you finish before time is up, you may check your work on this section only. Do not turn to any other section in the test.

MECHANICAL COMPREHENSION

30 Questions (15 Minutes)

Directions: This part of the exam will test your mechanical comprehension abilities. Each question has three choices. Choose the best option based on the information provided.

1. Which direction do electrons flow in an electric circuit?

   A. From positive to negative
   B. From negative to positive
   C. It depends on the circuit's current type.

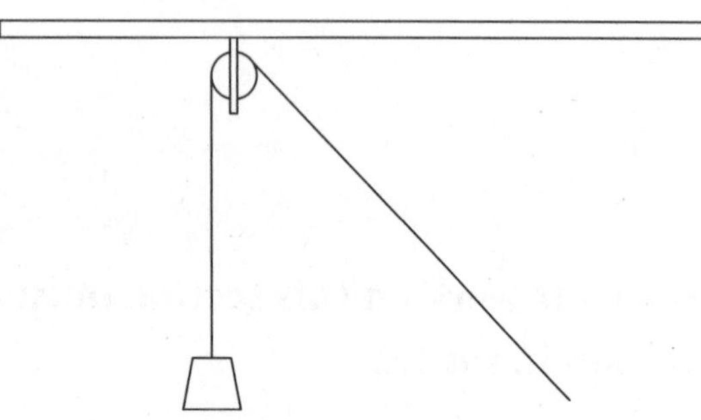

2. A man is pulling a load suspended by a fixed pulley. What will this do for his mechanical advantage?

   A. Decrease his mechanical advantage
   B. Increase his mechanical advantage
   C. The mechanical advantage remains the same.

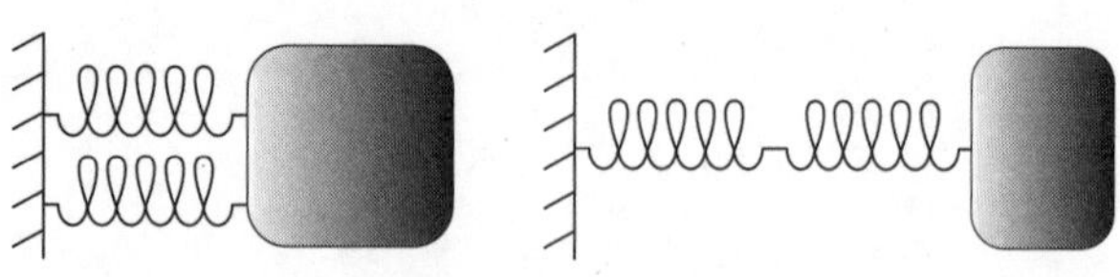

3. Which will be more difficult to compress: a series of springs or a set of springs in parallel?

   A. They require the same amount of force.
   B. The series of springs
   C. The set of springs in parallel

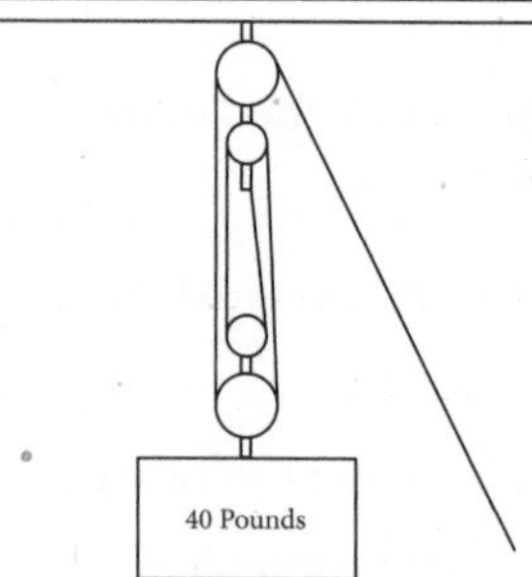

4. A 40-pound weight is being suspended by a movable pulley and fixed pulley system with two pulleys attached to the weight and two attached to the ceiling. There are 4 sections of rope supporting the weight (excluding the rope that will be pulled). How much force would be required to lift the weight?

   A. 10 pounds
   B. 160 pounds
   C. 36 pounds

5. Which gear will make the greatest number of turns in a minute?

   A. Gear A
   B. Gear B
   C. Gear C

6. What device allows current to only flow in one direction?

A. Diode

B. Transistor

C. Capacitor

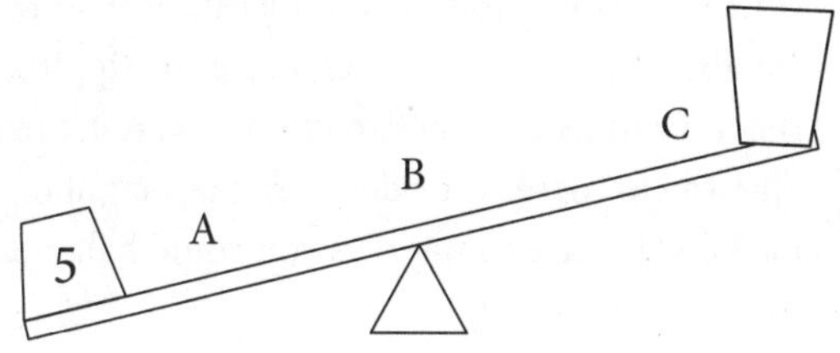

7. There is a lever with a 5-pound weight on one end and a bucket on the other with sand being poured into the bucket. As the system gradually tips in favor of the bucket, where is the plank most likely to break?

A. Point A

B. Point B

C. Point C

8. Which of the following springs have a self-limiting feature?

A. Compression springs

B. Extension springs

C. Garter springs

9. If bar X moves to the right, which way will bar Y move?

A. Left

B. Right

C. The bars will not move.

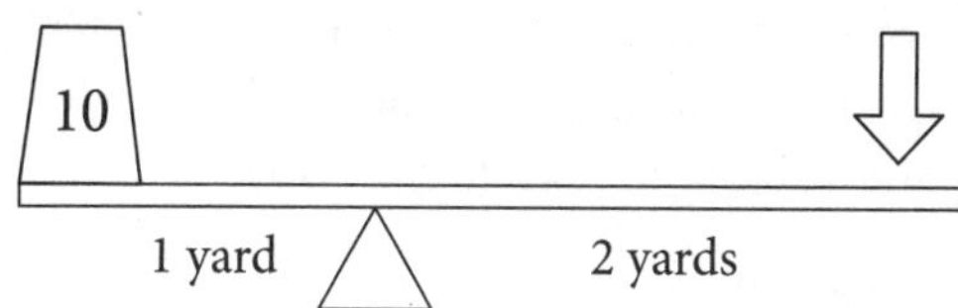

10. There is an ideal class 1 lever with the fulcrum in the middle and a load on one end. The length from the load to the fulcrum is 1 yard. The weight of the load is 10 pounds. The length from the fulcrum to the effort is 2 yards. How much force is required to lift the load?

A. 10 pounds

B. 20 pounds

C. 5 pounds

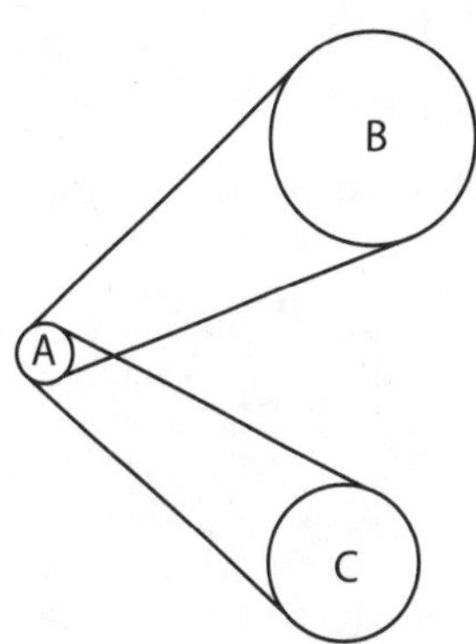

11. Pulley A is rotated one full turn. Which of the pulleys will rotate the fastest?

A. Pulley A

B. Pulley B

C. Pulley C

12. What is the purpose of a weight distribution hitch?

A. It shifts the load at the connection point upward.

B. It shifts the load at the connection point downward.

C. It is just a heavier duty hitch to allow for more weight and doesn't do anything to the load at the connection point.

13. There is an area of 1 square meter on which 3 pascals of pressure are being applied. How much force is being applied to the area?

    A. 3 Newtons

    B. 6 Newtons

    C. 12 Newtons

14. How do 2-stroke engines get their lubrication?

    A. From a sump pan

    B. Applied directly to the engine

    C. From a mixture of fuel and oil

15. Which of the following is NOT a function of a spring?

    A. Measure forces

    B. Store energy

    C. Amplify force

16. This image is an example of what type of gear?

    A. Parallel

    B. Intersecting

    C. Non-intersecting and non-parallel

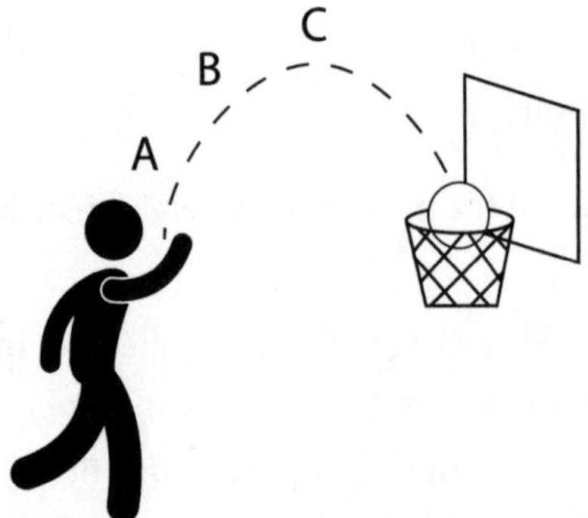

17. At which point was the ball moving the slowest?

    A. Point A

    B. Point B

    C. Point C

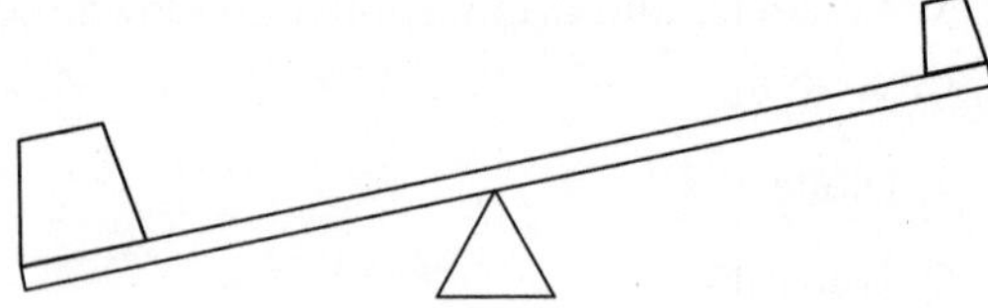

18. There is a class 1 lever that has a weight on either side, both equidistant from the fulcrum. One weighs more than the other, therefore tipping the lever in its current direction. You don't have any way to increase or decrease the weight of the loads. What are some ways you could balance the weights?

    A. Move the heavier weight closer to the fulcrum

    B. Move the lighter weight closer to the fulcrum

    C. Move the fulcrum closer to the lighter weight

19. Which of the following is NOT an important quality for the material used to create a gear?

    A. High tensile strength

    B. Low coefficient of friction

    C. Easily pliable material

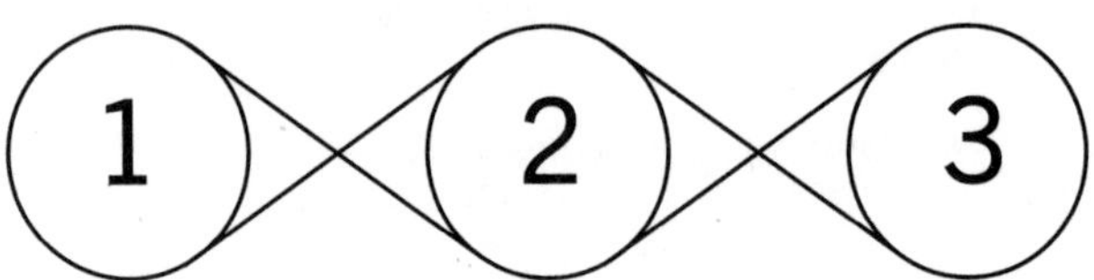

20. There are three equally sized pulleys connected by a rope. The rope is twisted in between each pair of pulleys. If the first pulley on the left is turned counterclockwise, which direction will pulley 3 turn?

    A. Clockwise

    B. Counterclockwise

    C. It won't turn at all.

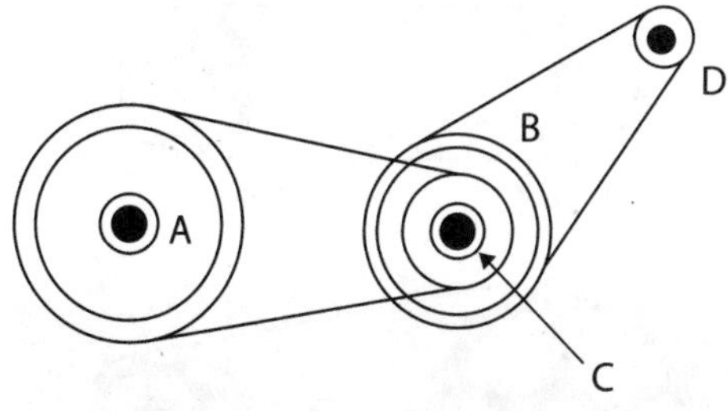

21. If pulley D is the driver in this image, which pulley will turn the slowest?

A. Pulley A

B. Pulley B

C. Pulley C

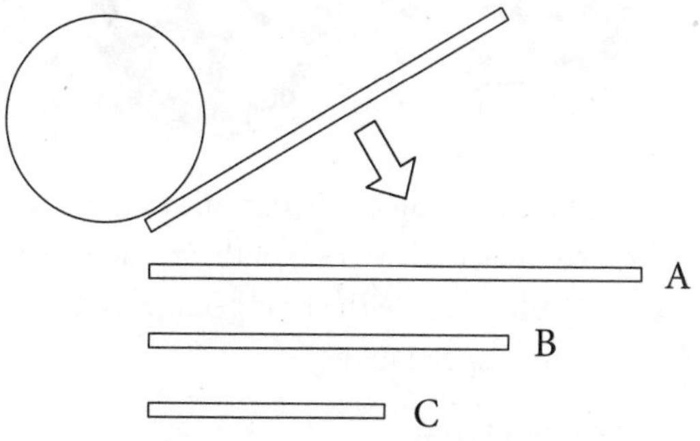

22. A man needs to roll a boulder that is too heavy for him to push himself. He devises an idea to wedge a plank underneath the boulder in order to roll it. The planks he has are of varying lengths. Which one should he use?

A. He should use the longest plank.

B. He should use the medium plank.

C. He should use the smallest plank.

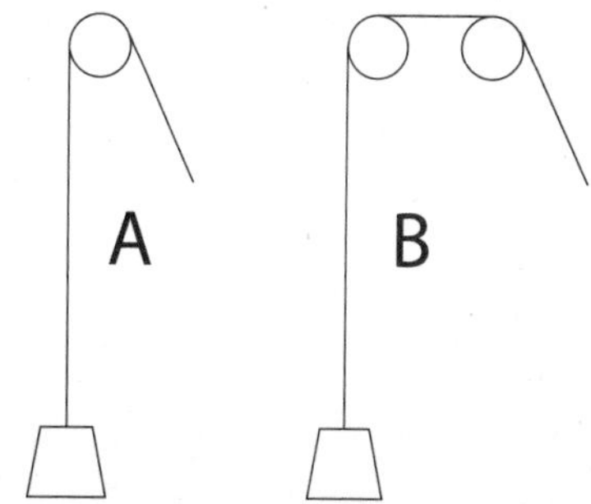

23. Which system of pulleys will take the least amount of work to lift the box?

A. System A

B. System B

C. They will require the same amount of work.

24. What is the main difference between speed and velocity?

A. They are two terms for the same concept.

B. Velocity has to do with direction.

C. Velocity has to do with how much force it takes to move an object.

25. If you decrease the number of teeth on a gear, what will happen to the speed of the gear?

A. The speed will increase.

B. The speed will decrease.

C. The speed will remain constant.

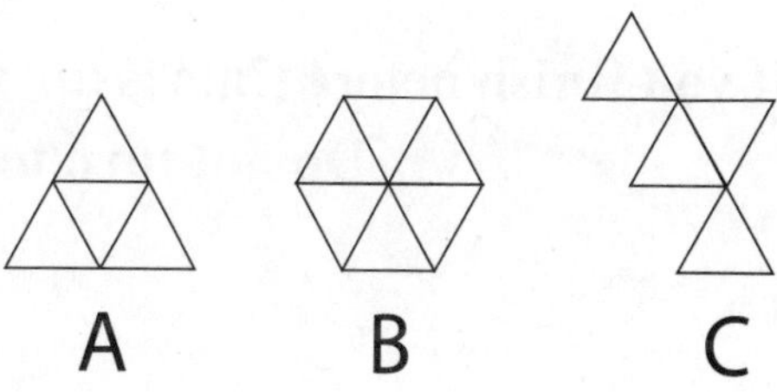

26. Which of these flattened solids would be assembled into a tetrahedron?

A. Solid A

B. Solid B

C. Solid C

27. What is the name of a substance with low electron mobility?

A. Conductor

B. Insulator

C. Inhibitor

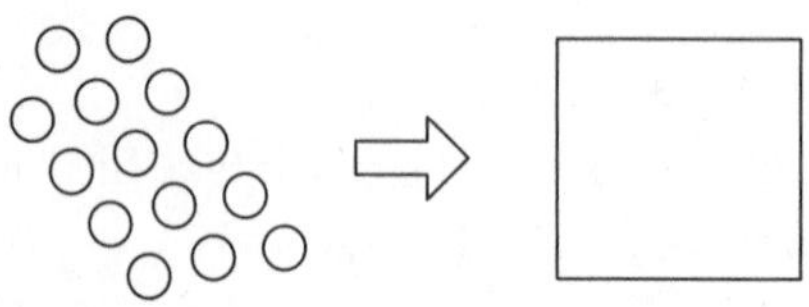

28. A substance goes directly from a gaseous to a solid state. What is this called?

A. Sublimation

B. Deposition

C. Evaporation

29. What is a spring's elastic limit?

A. The length of a spring completely stretched out

B. The length where, if a spring were to stretch more, it would not return to its original shape

C. The maximum length it can be stretched before the metal breaks

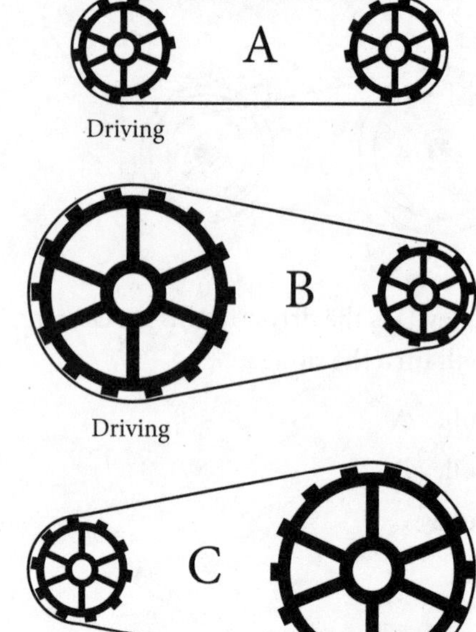

30. A cyclist is planning to retrofit one of her bikes to be a single speed. Which of the given gearing setups would provide the best pedaling efficiency for her single speed bike?

A. Gearing setup A

B. Gearing setup B

C. Gearing setup C

STOP.

If you finish before time is up, you may check your work on this section only. Do not turn to any other section in the test.

ANSWER KEYS AND EXPLANATIONS

Math Skills

1. D	6. B	11. D	16. D	21. D	26. D
2. A	7. C	12. B	17. C	22. B	27. A
3. C	8. A	13. B	18. A	23. B	28. B
4. B	9. C	14. A	19. C	24. D	29. C
5. D	10. D	15. A	20. A	25. C	30. A

1. **The correct answer is D.** Use substitution to solve for x:

$$x^2 + 3(-3) - 1 = 15$$
$$x^2 - 9 - 1 = 15$$
$$x^2 - 10 = 15$$
$$x^2 = 15 + 10$$
$$x^2 = 25x$$
$$x = \sqrt{25}$$
$$x = 5$$

2. **The correct answer is A.** The product is the result of the multiplication of $(5x - 3)$ and $(x + 4)$:

$$(5x - 3)\ (x + 4)$$
$$5x^2 + 20x - 3x - 12$$
$$5x^2 + 17x - 12$$

3. **The correct answer is C.** Use the formula for the area of a rectangle (xy = area) to determine the unknown side of the new fenced-in play space for Molly:

$$x(42) = 2{,}100$$
$$x = \frac{2{,}100}{42}$$
$$x = 50.$$

Use the formula for the perimeter of a rectangle ($2x + 2y$ = perimeter) to determine the amount of fencing required: $2(42) + 2(50) = 84 + 100 = 184$ ft.

4. **The correct answer is B.** This question is asking you to apply your knowledge of right triangles to determine the length of the side and then calculate the shaded area of the lean-to (see the following figures for a visualization of the problem). First, use the Pythagorean theorem ($x^2 + y^2 = z^2$) to solve for the length for the missing side of the triangle, x:

$$x^2 + (12)^2 = (20)^2$$
$$x^2 + 144 = 400$$
$$x^2 = 400 - 144$$
$$x^2 = 256$$
$$x = \sqrt{256}$$
$$x = 16$$

Use the formula for the area of a rectangle (xy = area) to determine the shaded area:

$16 \times 20 = 320$ ft.^{2}

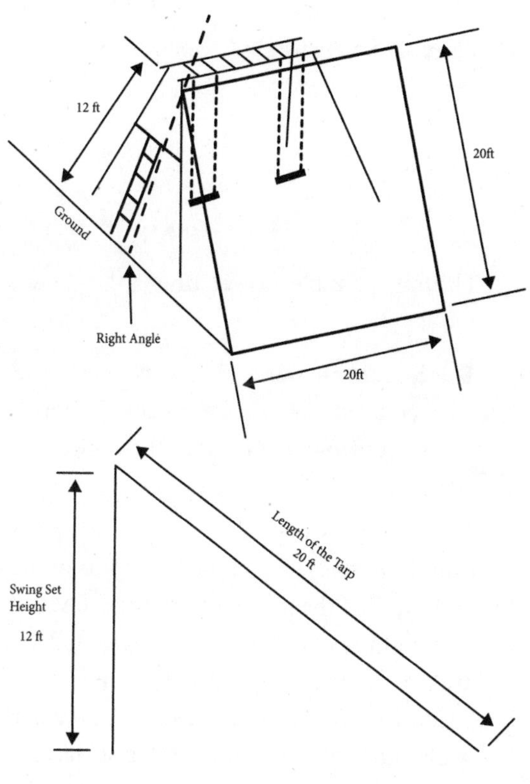

5. **The correct answer is D.** This question is a bit of a trick in that if you do not read the entire question and try to start solving the problem, you will likely do more work than required. The question is asking for the total fuel used, not the average speed over the course of the trip. Speed and time are distractors in this question. You need to focus only on the distance traveled and the miles per gallon of the vehicle. Add the distance and divide by the miles per gallon: (45 miles + 62 miles + 59 miles + 64 miles) ÷ (22 miles/gallon) = 230 miles ÷ (22 miles/gallon) = 10.5 gallons (rounded).

6. **The correct answer is B.** This problem is asking for the calculation of an average, in this case, speed. Add the four speeds and divide by the time to obtain the average:

   (63 mph + 68 mph + 64 mph + 35 mph) ÷ (3.5 hours) = 230 mph ÷ 3.5 hours = 65.7 mph.

7. **The correct answer is C.** This problem is a simple multiplication and addition exercise. The aircraft are traveling away from each other at the same time at different speeds. If t represents time to achieve the distance of 3,500 miles, then solve the following equation: $775t + 625t = 3{,}500$ miles.

8. **The correct answer is A.** Solve for x:

$$x^2 + 5x - 10 = 14$$
$$x^2 + 5x = 14 + 10$$
$$x^2 + 5x = 24$$
$$x(x + 5) = 24$$

   The only possible answer among the choices is $x = 3$.

9. **The correct answer is C.** Complementary angles must equal 90 degrees. Subtract the known 50 degrees from 90 to obtain the answer of 40 degrees.

10. **The correct answer is D.** To solve this problem, find the surface area of the four walls of the room and subtract the two doors and window.
    The room is 12 feet × 10 feet × 9 feet tall and there are two doors, each 8 feet × 3 feet, and a window, 3 feet × 4 feet. Solve for the surface area of the walls and subtract the unpainted surfaces:

$$2(12 \times 9) + 2(10 \times 9) - 2(8 \times 3) - (3 \times 4) =$$
$$2(108) + 2(90) - 2(24) - 12 =$$
$$216 + 180 - 48 - 12 = 336 \text{ ft.}^2$$

11. **The correct answer is D.** Expand to multiply:

$$(\sqrt{5}-\sqrt{3})(\sqrt{5}-\sqrt{3})$$
$$= (\sqrt{5})^2 - \sqrt{5}\sqrt{3} - \sqrt{5}\sqrt{3} - (\sqrt{3})^2$$
$$= 5 - 2\sqrt{5}\sqrt{3} + 3$$
$$= 8 - 2\sqrt{5}\sqrt{3}$$
$$= 8 - 2\sqrt{15}$$

12. **The correct answer is B.** The total class size is 375, and a number of students are taking shop, home economics, or both, and some students are taking neither. The fastest method to solve the problem is to first add the percentages of the students enrolled in one or the other course or both:

$$28\% + 36\% + 12\% = 76\%$$

    Multiply the remaining percentage of the student population by the total number of students to get the answer:

$$100\% - 76\% = 24\%$$
$$0.24(375) = 90$$

    The alternative is far more time consuming (and not recommended), but it gets the same result. Multiply each group percentage by 375 and subtract the results from the total to reach the same answer:

$$375 - 0.28(375) - 0.36(375) - 0.12(375) =$$
$$375 - 105 - 135 - 45 = 90.$$

13. **The correct answer is B.** At first glance, this problem might seem a bit complicated. It is actually a fraction of the circle area problem. Find the area of a circle with a radius of 15 km using the equation πr^2:

$$\text{total area} = 3.14(15)^2$$
$$\text{total area} = 3.14(225)$$
$$\text{total area} = 706.5 \text{ km.}^2$$

    The radius of the circle that can be viewed by the radar is 40 degrees, which is one ninth of the total 360 degrees. Divide the total area by 9 to get the area of the radar detection field:

$$706.5 \div 9 = 78.5 \text{ km.}^2$$

14. **The correct answer is D.** Dave cannot exceed his budget of \$1,000 for the telescope, so he needs the price to be discounted to a point at which the tax is also included in the final price. Set up the equation in this manner: \$1,000 = 1.05(\$1,300x). The x signifies the percentage of the total cost that Dave can afford. The 1.05 is 100 percent of the total cost of the telescope plus the 5 percent sales tax. As such:

$$\$1,000 = \$1,365x$$
$$x = \frac{1,000}{1,365}$$
$$x = 0.73 \text{ or } 73\%$$

If you multiply \$1,300 by 0.73, the sales price would be \$949. With the additional \$47.45, the total price for Dave is \$996.45, which comes in right under budget, so Dave needs the telescope to be discounted by 27%.

15. **The correct answer is A.** For this problem, you must solve for the circumference of the circle ($2\pi r$) and account for the radius twice, since the aircraft must fly out to the edge of the circle to start its orbit and return after completing the orbit once. Do not consider the angle of climb to altitude in the calculation. As such, the equation to obtain the solution should be 600 miles = $2r + 2\pi r$. Calculate and round:

$$600 \text{ miles} = 2r + 2(3.14r)$$
$$600 = 2r + 6.28r$$
$$60 = 8.28r$$
$$r = \frac{600}{8.28}$$
$$r = 72 \text{ miles}$$

16. **The correct answer is A.** For a 10-sided die, there are 10 possible outcomes for each roll. Because there are five odd numbers on the die, there is a 5-in-10 chance that the outcome will be an odd number. This simplifies to 1 out of 2.

17. **The correct answer is C.** Solve the proportion for x in the following manner:

$$5(x+5) = 4(x+7)$$
$$5x + 25 = 4x + 28$$
$$5x - 4x = 28 - 25$$
$$x = 3$$

18. **The correct answer is A.** Since the variables are all nonzero and the exponents are outside of the parentheses, indicating that it applies to all of the values within, the solution to this problem is to add the exponents together. No other operations are required.

19. **The correct answer is C.** This question is a bit tricky as you must carefully note the exponents. First, subtract $2x^3$ from $5x^3$ to get $3x^3$. Next, subtract $2x^2$ from $4x^2$ to get $2x^2$. Then, add $3x$ to $7x$ to get $10x$. The answer is then $3x^3 + 2x^2 + 10x$.

20. **The correct answer is A.** The first discount of 20% takes the price to 80% of the original. The second discount of 10% reduces the price by another 8%. The total reduction in price is 28%. For example, assume the original price of the item is \$100. A 20% discount reduces the price to \$80. The additional 10% discount reduces the price by \$8 to \$72. From the original price, the \$28 reduction divided by \$100 is a 28% discount.

21. **The correct answer is D.** Use FOIL to multiply the terms:

First: $k \times k = k^2$

Outer: $k \times 2 = 2k$

Inner: $-6 \times k = -6k$

Last: $-6 \times 2 = -12$

Then, put the terms together:
$k^2 + 2k - 6k - 12 = k^2 - 4k - 12$.

22. **The correct answer is B.** The measures of a triangle's three angles always add up to 180°. If you know the measures of two of the angles, you can subtract those measures from 180° to find the measure of the third angle. In this triangle, two of the measures are 45° and 75°. Therefore, 180° – (45° + 75°) = 180° – 120° = 60°

23. **The correct answer is B.** The area of a rectangle is its length times its width. This question gives you the area (60) and the length (DE, which equals

12) and asks for the width (DG). Plug the numbers into the area formula:

$$A = l \times w$$
$$60 = 12w$$
$$\frac{60}{12} = \frac{12w}{12}$$
$$5 = w$$

24. **The correct answer is D.** The volume of a rectangular solid is the product of its length, width, and height. All three values are given in this question, so multiply the three numbers together: $10 \times 4 \times 7 = 280$.

25. **The correct answer is C.** The total amount of the bill will be the fee per day plus the fee per mile. The initial fee is \$65 per day, and the customer rents it for 2 days: \$65 × 2 = \$130. The additional cost is \$0.30 per mile, and the customer drives 149 miles: \$0.30 × 149 = \$44.70. Add these values together to find the total amount of the bill: \$130 + \$44.70 = \$174.70.

26. **The correct answer is D.** To find the factorial of a number, multiply that number by every positive whole number below it. Therefore, the factorial of 6 is: $6 \times 5 \times 4 \times 3 \times 2 \times 1 = 720$

27. **The correct answer is A.** When converting from scientific notation to standard form, the exponent is the most important clue. This exponent is negative, so the decimal point will be moved to the left. The value of the exponent is 6, so the decimal point will be moved 6 places: $3.79 \times 10^{-6} = 0.00000379$

28. **The correct answer is B.** There are variables in the answer choices, so this is a good opportunity to plug in numbers instead of trying to write the equation. Let $y = 12$. Plug this number into the question stem and do the math. If $y = 12$, then Ty jogs 12 miles on Mondays. He jogs half that amount, or 6 miles ($12 \div 2$), on Wednesdays. The combined number of miles on Mondays and Wednesdays is $12 + 6 = 18$. If Ty covers 20 miles over the course of the week, then the amount he runs each day must add up to 20. Subtract the number of miles he jogs on Mondays and Wednesdays from the total amount for the week to find the number of miles Ty jogs on Fridays: $20 - 18 = 2$. He jogs 2 miles on Fridays. Now substitute 12 for y in the answer choices and look for the choice that gives you 2 as a result.

A. $20 - 3(12) = 20 - 36 = -16$

Eliminate choice A.

B. $20 - \frac{3(12)}{2} = 20 - \frac{36}{2} = 20 - 18 = 2$

Keep choice B.

C. $20 - 2(12) = 20 - 24 = -4$

Eliminate choice C.

D. $20 - \frac{12}{2} = 20 - 6 = 14$

Eliminate choice D.

Only choice B yields a result of 2, so it is the correct answer.

29. **The correct answer is C.** There are variables in the answer choices, so this is a good opportunity to plug in numbers instead of writing the equation. Let x equal 5. Plug this number into the question stem and do the math. If $x = 5$, then Kayla has 5 memoirs, 3 poetry books, and 10 historical biographies. To find the number of novels she owns, take the total of the other books and double it: $2(5 + 3 + 10) = 2 \times 18 = 36$. Therefore, Kayla owns a total of 18 (5 memoirs + 3 poetry + 10 biographies) + 36 (novels) = 54 books. Now substitute 5 for x in the answer choices and look for the choice that gives you 54 as a result.

A. $2(5) + 13 = 10 + 13 = 23$

Eliminate choice A.

B. $\frac{5+26}{2} = \frac{31}{2} = 15.5$

Eliminate choice B.

C. $3(5) + 39 = 15 + 39 = 54$

Keep choice C.

D. $2(5) + 26 = 10 + 26 = 36$

Eliminate choice D.

Only choice C yields a result of 54, so it is the correct answer.

30. The correct answer is A. The question asks for the value of y, so solve the first equation for x:

$$x - y = 5$$
$$x - y + y = 5 + y$$
$$x = 5 + y$$

Now replace x in the second equation with this result, and solve the second equation for y:

$$x + 3y = 21$$
$$(5 + y) + 3y = 21$$
$$5 + 4y = 21$$
$$5 + 4y - 5 = 21 - 5$$
$$4y = 16$$
$$\frac{4y}{4} = \frac{16}{4}$$
$$y = 4$$

NOTES

ANSWERS — OAR PRACTICE TEST

Reading Comprehension

1. A	5. A	9. B	13. C	17. C
2. C	6. B	10. A	14. B	18. B
3. B	7. C	11. B	15. D	19. C
4. D	8. D	12. C	16. D	20. A

1. **The correct answer is A.** The final phase of the REM cycle is the most active, which is why most dreaming occurs in this phase.
2. **The correct answer is C.** A long course pool is 50 meters long, and thus, one lap is 100 meters.
3. **The correct answer is B.** Peppermint and lemon can both be used to aid in digestion and mood.
4. **The correct answer is D.** If one-eighth of the officers who enter the Air Force each year go into special ops and one-fourth of the special ops officers recruited in a year end up at the base in Texas, then 1/32 of the officers that enter in the Air Force that year are on the air base in Texas.
5. **The correct answer is A.** Lieutenant Salvatore ran five miles in 32 minutes. He did not have to run an extra two miles, which means he completed it in the time allotted, but that does not mean that the time was set to 32 minutes. The only certainty was that he ran the set distance, which was five miles.
6. **The correct answer is B.** Only one of the two lieutenants takes afternoon classes, and that person takes two afternoon classes and one morning class. Drake takes an afternoon class, so he must take those three classes.
7. **The correct answer is C.** The store sells all leftover food for 30% off. There are 50 boxes of pasta leftover, so those pasta boxes will be sold for 30% off.
8. **The correct answer is D.** Orchid mantises will wait patiently for their prey before flying away.
9. **The correct answer is B.** The French deemed the moss Spanish Beard, later shortened to Spanish moss.
10. **The correct answer is A.** Studies show that a clean desk promotes efficiency in the workplace.
11. **The correct answer is B.** *Mascot* means good luck charm in French, and the physical characters are meant to provide extra entertainment for the audience.
12. **The correct answer is C.** The passage only provides for the fact that sunflowers need sunlight to grow and require "moist, nutrient-rich soil and warm weather."
13. **The correct answer is C.** The glomerulus is the first step on the nephron track, where all the blood is filtered and deposited into Bowman's capsule. It then travels the length of the PCT, loop of Henle, and DCT to be reabsorbed into the body.
14. **The correct answer is B.** According to the passage, one page of a movie script equals one minute of screen time. If movies are averaging more than 120 minutes, then movie scripts are averaging more than 120 pages.
15. **The correct answer is D.** Both types of camera film use the silver compound in some capacity.
16. **The correct answer is D.** Travers wrote the Mary Poppins books from 1934–1988, the first then being published in 1934.
17. **The correct answer is C.** The nature of au pairs is that they are usually non-citizen nannies.
18. **The correct answer is B.** Dark eyeliner was more popular in the early 2000s than it is now.
19. **The correct answer is C.** Canada is sparsely populated but does recognize two national languages.
20. **The correct answer is A.** The lungs are the site of exchange between oxygen and carbon dioxide for the blood.

Mechanical Comprehension

1. C	6. A	11. A	16. A	21. A	26. A
2. C	7. B	12. A	17. C	22. A	27. B
3. C	8. A	13. A	18. A	23. C	28. B
4. A	9. C	14. C	19. C	24. B	29. B
5. A	10. C	15. C	20. B	25. A	30. A

1. **The correct answer is C.** Electron flow depends on the circuit's current type, which are respectively alternating current (AC) and direct current (DC). Alternating currents can be found in household outlets and alternate the flow of electrons (choice A and B). Direct currents are used in battery operated circuits, and they only allow electrons to move in one direction (choice B).
2. **The correct answer is C.** A single pulley will not change the mechanical advantage. It will change the direction needed to lift a weight, which can be beneficial, but it does not give any mechanical advantage.
3. **The correct answer is C.** A set of springs in parallel takes more effort to compress since the springs are evenly distributing the force applied. This makes it more difficult to compress than a series of springs (choice B), which does not distribute any of the force applied and is comparable to one very long spring. A set of springs in a series and in parallel taking the same amount of force to compress (choice A) is incorrect.
4. **The correct answer is A.** Dividing the weight by the number of ropes supporting it will get you the amount of force needed to lift it: $\frac{40}{10} = 10\ pounds.$ Choices B and C are the result of incorrect calculations.
5. **The correct answer is A.** A smaller gear will take more turns than a larger gear due to the fact that it has fewer teeth. The second smallest (choice B) would be the next fastest, and the largest gear (choice C) would be the slowest of the three.
6. **The correct answer is A.** A diode allows current to flow in only one direction in an electrical circuit. Capacitors (choice C) are used to absorb unwanted electric pulses, and they can hold or release power for the circuit. Transistors (choice B) act as current amplifiers in circuits.
7. **The correct answer is B.** There is the most tension at the fulcrum point of a lever. Point A (choice A) or point C (choice C) might break if the plank is weak in those areas, but most likely the plank would break at point B due to the tension put on the plank by the fulcrum.
8. **The correct answer is A.** A compression spring cannot be pushed past its breaking point, while extension and garter springs (choices A and C) can both be extended past their elastic limit, causing the spring to break or deform.
9. **The correct answer is C.** Three gears, each meshed with the other two, will not turn. Thus, if the gears won't turn, the bars will not move either. If the gear not touching any bars was taken out, bar Y would move to the right (choice B). If the gear not touching any bars was taken out, and bar X moved left, bar Y would move to the left (choice A).
10. **The correct answer is C.** Due to Archimedes' law of levers, the weight of the load times the distance between the load and the fulcrum equals the force times the distance between the force and the fulcrum. Since we do not know the force needed for effort, we must solve for that needed force:

$$10\ pounds \times 1\ yard = force\ needed \times 2\ yards.$$

$$\frac{10\ pounds \times 1\ yard}{2\ yards} = \frac{force\ needed \times 2\ yards.}{2\ yards}$$

$$\frac{10\ pounds \times 1}{2} = force\ needed.$$

$$Force\ needed = \frac{10\ pounds}{2} = 5\ pounds.$$

11. **The correct answer is A.** The smallest pulley in the system will rotate the fastest. Larger pulleys (choices B and C) will have more torque, but the smaller the pulley, the faster it is in the system.

12. **The correct answer is A.** Weight distribution hitches shift the load at the connection point upward, which effectively distributes weight evenly over the axles.

13. **The correct answer is A.** Pressure is calculated by dividing the force by the area. Simple algebra makes it that pressure times area equals the force:

$$\frac{force}{area} = pressure$$

Multiply area on both sides:

$$\frac{force}{area} \times area = pressure \times area$$

Area cancels on the division side:

$$\frac{force}{area} \times area = pressure \times area \rightarrow force = pressure \times area$$

Thus, 3 Pascals of pressure times 1 square meter results in 3 Newtons of force. If there had been 6 Pascals of pressure, there would have been 6 Newtons of force (choice B). If there had been 12 Pascals of pressure, there would have been 12 Newtons of force (choice C).

14. **The correct answer is C.** Two-stroke engines do not have a sump pan (choice A) nor is the oil applied directly to the engine (choice B). What they do need is a mixture of fuel and oil put into the fuel tank. This allows the oil to lubricate the engine from the inside as the oil goes everywhere that the fuel goes.

15. **The correct answer is C.** A spring does not amplify force. You can use a spring to measure forces (choice A) and store energy (choice B), but not to amplify force.

16. **The correct answer is A.** These types of gears have their shafts parallel to each other, thus they are called parallel gears. Intersecting gears have some sort of angle between their driving and driven shafts. Non-intersecting and non-parallel gears have the shafts of two gears on different planes.

17. **The correct choice is C.** The vertical component of the momentum of the ball is zero only at point C. Therefore, answers A and B are incorrect.

18. **The correct answer is A.** The further away a weight is from the fulcrum, the more its force is amplified and delivered to the system. By moving the heavier weight closer you would be decreasing how much its weight is being amplified, allowing the system to go into balance. Moving the smaller weight toward the fulcrum (choice B) would be moving it in the wrong direction. Only if the smaller weight could be moved farther from the fulcrum would it help bring the system into balance. Moving the fulcrum toward the smaller weight (choice C) is moving it in the wrong direction to bring the system into balance. If the fulcrum could be moved closer to the heavier weight, it would improve the balance.

19. **The correct answer is C.** Gears should have low pliability so that they are strong. High tensile strength (choice A) is important so that the gear doesn't break. Low coefficient of friction (choice B) is important so that the gear can easily turn.

20. **The correct answer is B.** The first pulley will have been turned counterclockwise and the twisted rope will have made the second pulley turn the opposite direction, or clockwise. However, there is one more twisted rope between the second and third pulley, making the third pulley turn the other direction, or counterclockwise. If the first pulley had been turned clockwise the last pulley would have turned clockwise, (choice A). This system does work, and the pulleys will turn (choice B).

21. **The correct answer is A.** Since pulley A has the largest circumference, it will turn the slowest. Pulley C (choice C) will turn the fastest and pulley B (choice B) will turn faster than pulley A, but slower than pulley C.

22. **The correct answer is A.** The longer the plank is, the more it will amplify the man's effort. The smallest plank would amplify the force the least (choice C). The medium plank (choice B) would amplify the force more than the smaller plank, but still less than the largest plank.

23. **The correct answer is C.** No matter how many fixed pulleys you add they will not decrease the work needed to lift the object. If in either system a second pulley was attached to the box there would be less work needed to lift it (choices A and B), but since this is not the case, they both require the same amount of work.

24. **The correct answer is B.** Velocity is the speed of something in a given direction. A change in direction, even though it has the same magnitude of velocity, will result in a velocity change. Both terms (choice A) are similar in their regard for an object in motion, but they are not the same thing. Mass is what defines how much force is required to move an object (choice C), not velocity.

25. **The correct answer is A.** The fewer teeth a gear has, the faster the gear will turn. This will, however, result in the gear having less force than a larger gear with more teeth. If more teeth were added to the gear, the speed would decrease (choice B), but the force would increase. Speed will not remain constant (choice C) for a gear that gains or loses teeth.

26. **The correct answer is A.** It has four triangular sides equal to each other all with sides touching, making it a tetrahedron. There are too many triangular sides and no base to form a tetrahedron in choice B. Choice C has the correct number of triangles, but two of them are connected by corners and not by sides, thus not forming a tetrahedron.

27. **The correct answer is B.** Insulators have low electron mobility by blocking, meaning they have low conductive possibility. Conductors (choice A) are the opposite; they can easily conduct electricity along themselves, meaning they have high electron mobility. Inhibitors (choice C) are substances that inhibit transport of electrons from a donor to an acceptor.

28. **The correct answer is B.** Deposition is the term for when a substance goes directly from a gaseous state to a solid state. Sublimation (choice A) is when a substance goes directly from a solid state to a gaseous state. Evaporation (choice C) is when a substance goes from a liquid state to a gaseous state.

29. **The correct answer is B.** The elastic limit is the length where if the spring were to stretch more it would misshape and not be able to return to its original shape. The length of a spring completely stretched out (choice A) and the maximum stretched length before the metal breaks (choice C) do not refer to the elastic limit as it will no longer retain its elasticity at either point.

30. **The correct answer is A.** Gear ratios work so that a smaller gear turns faster than a larger gear when the two are connected. Less effort will be needed to turn the larger gear, and the smaller gear will turn faster, which will effectively make pedaling more efficient. Turning a larger gear with a smaller gear (choice C) is a less efficient option for a bike's gearing, as the larger gear will create greater resistance by not being able to keep up with the smaller gear's speed. Gears of the same size (choice A) will turn in a one-to-one ratio, which is more efficient than a smaller gear turning a larger gear. However, it is not as efficient as a larger gear turning a smaller gear.

SCORE SHEET

Although your actual exam scores will not be reported as percentages, it might be helpful to convert them so you can better understand your strengths and weaknesses.

OAR SCORE SHEET		
Subject	**# Correct ÷ # of questions**	**× 100 = _____ %**
Math Skills	_____ ÷ 30 = _____	× 100 = _____ %
Reading Comprehension	_____ ÷ 30 = _____	× 100 = _____ %
Mechanical Comprehension	_____ ÷ 30 = _____	× 100 = _____ %

STUDY REFERENCE GUIDE		
Subject	**Chapter**	**Page**
Math Skills	Chapter 7	154
Reading Comprehension	Chapter 8	220
Mechanical Comprehension	Chapters 11 & 12	256, 280

NOTES

ANSWERS OAR PRACTICE TEST

PART V
APPENDIXES

MATH FORMULAS AND MEASUREMENTS

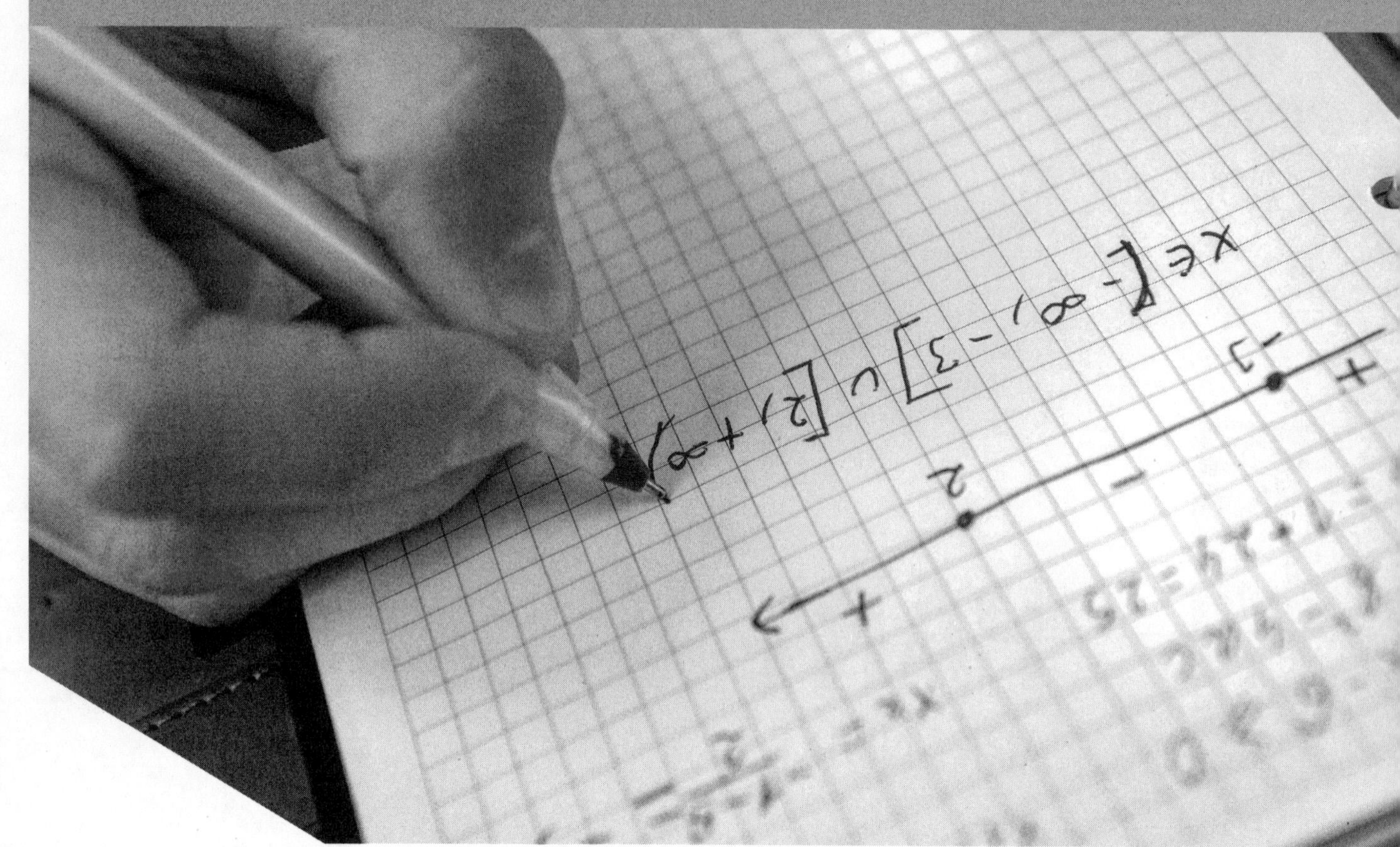

Math Formulas to Know

Perimeter

Add the lengths of the sides.

- Square: P = $4s$
- Rectangle: P = $2l + 2w$
- Triangle: P = $s_1 + s_2 + s_3$
- Circle (circumference): C = πd or $2\pi r$

Surface Area

Always express in square units.

- Square: A = s^2
- Rectangle: A = $l \times h$
- Rectangular Parallelepiped: A = $2lh + 2wh + 2lw$
- Circle: A = πr^2
- Cylinder: A = $2\pi r^2 + 2\pi rh$

Volume

Always express in cubic units.

- Cube: $V = s^3$
- Rectangular Parallelepiped: $V = lwh$
- Cylinder: $V = 2\pi r^2 h$

Angles

Always express in degrees.

- Line = 180°
- Square = 360°
- Rectangle = 360°
- Triangle = 180°
- Circle = 360°
- Polygon = $(n - 2)180°$ where n is the number of sides.

Pythagorean Theorem

$a^2 + b^2 = c^2$

The hypotenuse is always represented by c, the two sides by a and b.

Decimal to Fraction

$0.25 = \frac{25}{100} = \frac{1}{4}$

For fraction to decimal, divide the numerator by the denominator.

Percent to Decimal

$25\% = \frac{25}{100} = 0.25$

Reverse for decimal to percent.

Percent to Fraction

$25\% = \frac{25}{100} = \frac{1}{4}$

Reverse for fraction to percent.

Standard Form of a Polynomial

$Ax^2 + Bx + C$

A and B represent coefficients, C is the constant, and x represents the variable.

Slope

m = slope, b = y-intercept

$y = mx+b$

Distance/Rate/Time

Distance = rate × time

Rate = distance ÷ time

Time = distance ÷ rate

Measurements

There are two systems of measurement in common use throughout the world: metric units (officially known as the International System of units or SI), and standard units. Standard measurements are most often used in the United States, while the metric system is used throughout the rest of the world as well as in the scientific community. Metric units are based on seven constant measurements covering distance, weight, time, temperature, and even brightness.

Here is a glossary of measurement terms and abbreviations. Following the list is a table of common measurement conversions.

International System of Units

- Length = meter (m)
- Time = second (s)
- Amount of substance = mole (mole)
- Electric Current = ampere (A)
- Temperature = kelvin (K)
- Luminous intensity = candela (cd)
- Mass = kilogram (kg)

Standard (US) System

- Inch = in. or ”
- Foot = ft. or ’
- Yard = yd.
- Mile = mi.
- Ounce = oz.
- Fluid Ounce = fl. oz.
- Pound = lb. or #
- Cup = c.
- Pint = pt.
- Quart = qt.
- Gallon = gal.

Where is Celsius, you ask? While Kelvin is the official unit of measurement in the International System of Measurements, Celsius is what you see on the weather report and in cooking instructions. Celsius is based on two relative points on the temperature scale, 0° being the freezing point of water and 100° being the boiling point. Kelvin is a thermodynamic temperature, meaning it is not based on the freezing or boiling point of water. Rather, it describes the kinetic energy contained in the particles that make up matter. As temperature drops, these particles slow, until they finally stop moving altogether. This is absolute zero, the benchmark for the Kelvin scale.

It is worth noting that Kelvin and Celsius do share some commonalities. In Celsius, water freezes at 0 and boils at 100 degrees. In Kelvin, water freezes at 273.15 and boils at 373.15. Absolute zero Kelvin works out to –273.15°C, or –459.67°F. The degree symbol is not used when describing temperatures in Kelvin.

While you may not need to know how to convert from Kelvin to Fahrenheit, you will want to know a few common conversions.

- 1 km = 1,000 m = 100,000 cm = 1,000,000 mm
- 1 kg = 1,000 g = 1,000,000 mg
- 1 ft. = 12 in.
- 1 yd. = 3 ft. = 36 in.
- 1 mi. = 1,760 yds. = 5,280 ft. = 63,360 in.

You should also know that there are four quarts in a gallon, 16 ounces in a pound, 10 millimeters in a centimeter, and 1,000 milliliters in a liter. For metric measurements, remember that everything is based on factors of ten.

Metric Unit Conversions

Length and Distance

When you know:		Multiply by:		To find:
inches	×	2.5400	=	centimeters
feet	×	0.3048	=	meters
yards	×	0.9144	=	meters
miles	×	1.6093	=	kilometers
millimeters	×	0.0394	=	inches
centimeters	×	0.3937	=	inches
meters	×	3.2808	=	feet
meters	×	1.0936	=	yards
kilometers	×	0.6214	=	miles

Weight and Mass

When you know:		Multiply by:		To find:
ounces	×	28.3495	=	grams
pounds	×	0.4536	=	kilograms
short tons	×	0.9072	=	metric tons
kilograms	×	2.2046	=	pounds
metric tons	×	1.1023	=	short tons

Volume and Capacity (Liquid)

When you know:		Multiply by:		To find:
pints (U.S.)	×	0.4732	=	liters
quarts (U.S.)	×	0.9463	=	liters
gallons (U.S.)	×	3.7853	=	liters
liters	×	2.1134	=	pints (U.S.)
liters	×	1.0567	=	quarts (U.S.)
liters	×	0.2642	=	gallons (U.S.)

GLOSSARY OF MILITARY TERMS

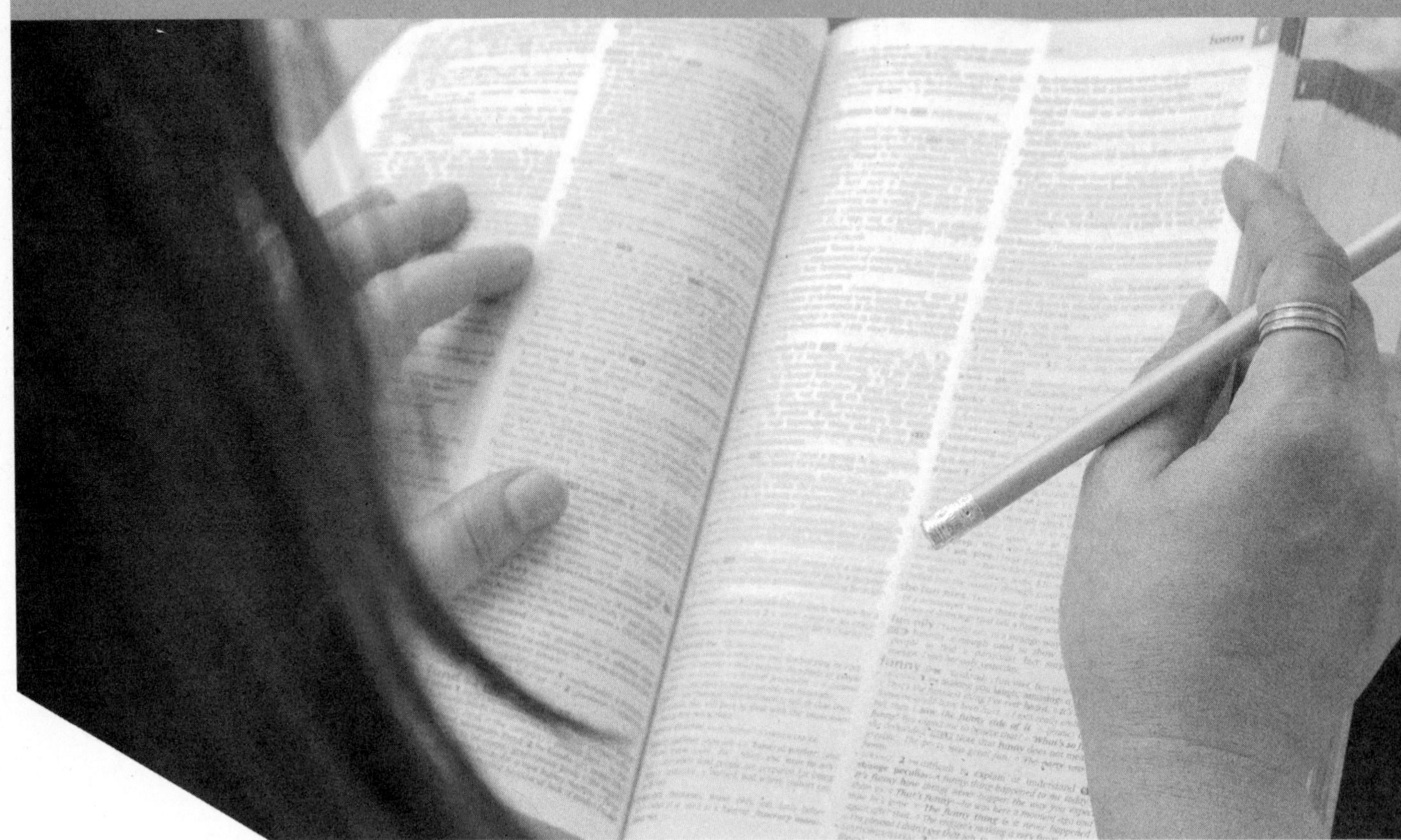

At first glance, it might seem that the military is built on acronyms and jargon meant to exclude those not wearing the uniform. They even use words to represent the letters of the alphabet! There is a reason for all of this: clarity. For example, radios—no matter how high-tech—are prone to static. Over a radio, or even over the phone, the letters B, C, D, E, G, P, T, V, and Z can all sound alike. If you have to spell something out, using the NATO phonetic alphabet (A = ALPHA, B = BRAVO, etc.) can prevent a lot of confusion.

Acronyms also save a lot of space on a page and can convey a lot of information in just a few lines of text (TS-SCI NOFORN = Top Secret, Secure Compartmented Information, Not Releasable to Foreign Nationals) or identify a location or entity (NORAD = North American Aerospace Defense Command, COMSUBPAC = Commander, Submarine Force, United States Pacific Fleet). Learning all the acronyms is almost impossible; the DoD has a dictionary of military and associated terms that runs 361 pages long. For now, we recommend sticking to the basics.

On the following pages, you'll find a basic glossary of terms and acronyms. You don't need to memorize all of them, but at least be familiar enough to know that an AO and an AOR are two different things. However, you will need to learn and memorize the phonetic alphabet. You will also find some military slang terms, but since most of them are either not suitable for print or specific to one branch, we've opted to let you learn most of the slang in the field.

A: ALPHA

Acting Rank: An individual who is temporarily placed into a senior position is said to hold an acting rank (e.g., a squad leader temporarily holding the position of platoon sergeant); see also *Frocking.*

Active Duty: Full-time duty in the armed forces

ADA: Air Defense Artillery

AFSC: Air Force Specialty Code. A code identifying a servicemember's job specialty; see also *MOC, MOS*, and *NEC.* (Air Force)

ANG: Air National Guard (Air Force)

AO: Area of Operation

AOR: Area of Responsibility

ARNG: Army National Guard (Army)

B: BRAVO

BAH: Basic Allowance for Housing

BAS: Basic Allowance for Subsistence; money provided for living expenses such as food

Belay: Secure; stop

Billet: Assigned quarters

BOQ: Basic Officer's Quarters; housing for single officers

BX: Base Exchange (Air Force), a shopping center similar to civilian big-box stores like Target and Walmart; see also *CGX*, *MCX*, *NEX*, and *PX*.

C: CHARLIE

CAC: Common Access Card

CGX: Coast Guard Exchange; see also *BX*, *MCX*, *NEX*, and *PX*.

Chem Light: A glow stick

CHU: Containerized Housing Unit; climate-controlled trailers that can house up to 8 people

CO: Commanding Officer

COB: Chief of the Boat; refers to the top enlisted person aboard a ship (Coast Guard, Navy)

COP: Combat Outpost

CONUS: Continental United States

CQ: Charge of Quarters

D: DELTA

DMZ: Demilitarized Zone

Duty Station: Geographic location where a servicemember is performing official duties

DZ: Drop Zone

E: ECHO

EOD: Explosive Ordinance Disposal

F: FOXTROT

FA: Field Artillery (Army, Marine Corps)

FOB: Forward Operating Base; larger than a COP but smaller than a base.

Frocking: Authorization to wear a rank prior to official promotion date; see also *Acting Rank.*

G: GOLF

Garrison: A military post; permanent military installation

Gun: A mortar tube or artillery piece. Never use this term to refer to a rifle or pistol.

H: HOTEL

I: INDIA

Impact Area: A designated area where ordnance will detonate or impact

Inf: Infantry (Army, Marine Corps)

J: JULIET

JAG: Judge Advocate General

K: KILO

KIA: Killed in Action

L: LIMA (LEE'-mah)

LZ: Landing Zone

M: MIKE

MCX: Marine Corps Exchange; see also *BX*, *CGX*, *MCX*, *NEX*, and *PX*.

Mess Hall: Dining facility

MI: Military Intelligence

MIA: Missing in Action

MOC: Military Occupational Code. A code identifying a servicemember's job specialty. See also *AFSC*, *MOS*, and *NEC*.

MOS: Military Occupational Specialty (Army, Marine Corps). A code identifying a servicemember's job specialty. See also *AFSC*, *MOC*, and *NEC*.

Motor Pool: Location where a unit's vehicles are parked/stored and maintenance is performed

MP: Military Police

MRE: Meals, Ready to Eat; field rations

MWR: Morale, Welfare, and Recreation

N: NOVEMBER

NBC: Nuclear, Biological, Chemical

NCO: See *Non-Commissioned Officer.*

NCOIC: Non-Commissioned Officer in Charge

NEC: Navy Enlistment Code. A code identifying a servicemember's job specialty. See also *AFSC*, *MOC*, and *MOS*. (Navy)

NEX: Navy Exchange; see also *BX*, *CGX*, *MCX*, and *PX*.

NOFORN: Not Releasable to Foreign Nationals

Non-Commissioned Officer: Enlisted personnel in leadership positions, starting at pay grade E-4 (junior NCO), up to E-9

O: OSCAR

OA: Objective Area; Operational Area

OB: Order of Battle; Overcome By; see also *ORBAT.*

OCONUS: Outside of the Continental United States

OCS: Officer Candidate School

OIC: Officer in Charge

OJT: On-the-job training

OOD: Officer on Duty

OPLAN: Operational Plan

OPSEC: Operations Security

ORBAT: Order of Battle

Ordnance: Explosives, ammunition, pyrotechnics, and similar materials

OTS: Officer Training School

P: PAPA (pah-PAH')

Pay Grade: Basic pay amount. Almost always matches rank; E = enlisted, W = warrant officer, O = officer

PCS: See *Permanent Change of Station.*

Permanent Change of Station: Reassignment to a new unit/permanent party

Permanent Party: Unit to which you are assigned

Personally Owned Vehicle: Any private vehicle owned by a servicemember

PMCS: Preventive Maintenance Checks and Services

POL: Petroleum, Oil, and Lubricant

POV: See *Personally Owned Vehicle.*

POW: Prisoner of War

PX: Post Exchange (Army); see also *BX*, *CGX*, *MCX*, and *NEX*.

Q: QUEBEC (KAY'-beck)

R: ROMEO

R&R: Rest and Recovery/Recuperation

Rack: Bed

ROTC: Reserve Officer Training Corps

S: SIERRA

Say Again: Repeat what you just said

SCI: Secure Compartmented Information

SF: Security Force (Air Force); Special Forces (Army)

SERE: Survival, Evasion, Resistance, and Escape

Smoke: To wear out, esp. as punishment (e.g., "Top's gonna smoke you for missing formation!")

SOCOM: Special Operations Command

SOF/SOG: Special operations forces or groups, such as Army Rangers, Navy Seals, Marine Recon., and others.

SOFA: Status of Forces Agreement

SOP: Standard Operating Procedure

SP: Shore Patrol

T: TANGO

TDY: See *Temporary Duty.*

Temporary Duty: Temporary assignment to another unit

TMC: Troop Medical Clinic; similar to a civilian Urgent Care office

TOA: Table of Allowance; document that prescribes basic allowances of organizational equipment

TO&E: Table of Organization and Equipment

Top: Informal name for a First Sergeant (Army, Marine Corps)

TS: Top Secret

U: UNIFORM

Unit: Any military element whose structure is prescribed by competent authority

USA: United States Army

USAF: United States Air Force

USAFR: United States Air Force Reserve

USAR: United States Army Reserve

USCG: United States Coast Guard

USCGR: United States Coast Guard Reserve

USMC: United States Marine Corps

USN: United States Navy

USNR: United States Navy Reserve

USSF: United States Space Force

V: VICTOR

VA: Department of Veterans Affairs

W: WHISKEY

WIA: Wounded in Action

X: X-RAY

XO: Executive Officer

Y: YANKEE

Z: ZULU

Zulu: Time zone indicator for Universal Coordinated Time (UCT) and Universal Time Coordinated (UTC); synonymous with the civilian term Greenwich Mean Time (GMT)

CREDITS

Excerpt from *1984* by George Orwell

Excerpt from "Emerging Space: The Evolving Landscape of 21st Century American Spaceflight" as produced by the Office of the Chief Technologist at NASA

Federal Aviation Administration's Aeronautical Information Manual

Federal Aviation Administration's Federal Aviation Regulations

Federal Aviation Administration's Pilot's Handbook of Aeronautical Knowledge

notes

notes

notes